The Cult of the Chosen Ones

They Killed JFK, Did 9/11 and Threaten to Rule the World

Makia Freeman

ISBN:
979-8-9878667-5-7 (print)

First edition: October 2025.

Visit the Author's website at
www.TheFreedomArticles.com

Other Books by Makia Freeman

- **Cancer: The Lies, The Truth and The Solutions (2020) (Controversial Truths Revealed Series Book 1)**
- **40 Incredible Real Life Alien Abductee and Contactee Experiences (2022) (Controversial Truths Revealed Series Book 2)**
- **Break Your Chains (2023)**
- **The International Satanic Network Exposed (2023)**

Made Without AI

I used no AI (Artificial Intelligence) in researching, writing or illustrating this book.

I hope that my declaration as such will become a standard for future authors.

Table Of Contents

Introduction

This is my fifth book, and with almost 900 footnotes, it is by far the most extensively researched one. It cuts to the core of who runs this world and how they have manipulated all major historical events for at least the last 150 years. It is not afraid to touch taboo and forbidden topics. In the quest for truth, absolutely no stone must be unturned. For those who know, it is our duty to speak up as loudly as possible, to make inroads into the relentless propaganda that threatens to limit the perception of every person on Earth, thus making us into docile, obedient animals. We are in a perception war. The Cult of the Chosen Ones, the Satanic cult, is doing is darnedest to hijack the perception of humanity so that its insane version of reality – which it can change at will to suit whatever its needs are at the time – becomes the only reality here on Earth. As long as I still have the ability to breathe, I will always use my energy to expand my and others' perceptions to ensure humanity doesn't get trapped by this, and instead rises up in awareness and freedom.

Since this book is focused on how this Cult arose within Judaism, this necessarily means tackling the taboo topics of Jewish identity, Judaism, Zionism, Israel, the Holocaust and much more. I am not Jewish and, to state something which will hopefully be very obvious by the end of the book, I am not antisemitic. Jewish people have been hoodwinked and manipulated just as much as non-Jews by this Cult, so it's vitally important that this message reach them, given that so much evil is being carried out in their name. The average Jewish person would be horrified or even mortified if he or she knew the scale of evil that has been perpetrated using Judaism as a cover. My hope is that good Jews can wake up to the machinations of this Cult, rise up and yell, “Not in our name!” and take back their power. The truth is that the Cult ruthlessly uses its victims, Jews and non-Jews alike, to get its way. Recent and stark examples of how the Cult tosses ordinary Jews aside like rag dolls are when Zionist misleader, war criminal and current Israeli Prime Minister, Benjamin Netanyahu, decided to make Israel a lab for Pfizer during the COVID scamdemic by allowing Pfizer to experiment with its new fake-vaccine upon the Israeli population – with severe restrictions for those who refused to take the vax. Another example (covered in chapter 17) is how the Zionist regime, after allowing Hamas to attack on October 7th 2023, then decided to invoke the Hannibal Directive, a doctrine that dictates that it’s acceptable to kill your own people in furtherance of a military objective. Around 1200 people were killed that day, two thirds of whom were not killed by Hamas but rather by the Israeli military firing on its own citizens.

So when people say “Jews run the world” that’s not the full story at all. That is intellectually lazy. To be more precise, certain ruthless people and crypto-Jews run the world by exploiting all those around them, Jew and non-Jew. And since, at the end of the day, anyone can ‘become’ a Jew, as there is no Jewish race, this Satanic Cult is a club that accepts and recruits new members who resonate with their agenda of control and evil.

However, let’s not get ahead of ourselves. This book will take you through how this Cult arose in the Middle East millennia ago, how it propagated itself down through the ages, how it gained speed again with characters such as Sabbatai Zevi and Jacob Frank, how it solidified its grip on power with the rise of the Rothschilds, and then how it proceeded to mold the world into a prison planet with an astonishing amount of greed, betrayal, manipulation and evil where virtually no single major historical event was not orchestrated by it.

Wherever possible, I will use Jewish authors and thinkers who have given their inside perspective on the issue. Humorously, such Jews are sometimes branded as ‘self-hating Jews' by the Cult (as the insult of ‘antisemitic’ doesn’t work when applied to a Jew) when their views go against Zionist propaganda or weaken the Cult narrative in some way.

With that said, let’s begin the journey of exposing this Cult, starting with its origins in the Middle East.

CHAPTER 1: THERE IS NO SUCH THING AS A JEWISH RACE NOR A HISTORICAL JEWISH HOMELAND

"The Jewish people, a thousand years ago until recent times, identified as Jews for only one reason: because of religion. The Jews were a religious community. If you did not practice the religion, it did not make any sense to call yourself a Jew."

– Rabbi Yaakov Shapiro[1]

"From what has been said, it is thus clearer than the sun at noonday that the Pentateuch was not written by Moses, but by someone who lived long after Moses."

– Baruch Spinoza, A Theologico-Political Treatise, 1670[2]

"Fishberg's ... comprehensive work ended with the conclusion that there was no basis for assuming an ethnic unity among modern Jews, nor a Jewish race, any more than one could speak of the ethnic unity of Christians or Muslims, or of a Unitarian, Presbyterian or Methodist race."

– Shlomo Sand[3]

Once upon a time there was a Satanic Cult.

Yes, I know, it's not exactly a pleasant way to start a story, but it's true nonetheless.

Image #1: a depiction of the Canaanite/Phoenician god Moloch (also Molech or Baal) accepting a child for sacrifice

This Cult has been operating a very, very long time. Who knows how long? What we do know is that it came into prominence around 4,000 BC in the area of Babylon and Sumer (and later Canaan), the so-called cradle of civilization, and that this was likely a result of the catastrophes and civilizational reset that humanity underwent around 10,000 BC. This area of the Middle East – the intersection between the three continents of Europe, Asia and Africa – is the area from which all the world's biggest religions have sprung. The traces and influence of this Satanic Cult, associated with the worship of Saturn (Saturn = Satan), can be found in all three major monotheistic Abrahamic religions of Judaism, Christianity and Islam. One example of many to illustrate this is the fact that the six-sided black cube, a prolific symbol of Saturn, crops up in Islam (the Kaaba black cube of Mecca) and Judaism (the black cube or tefillin that Jews wear strapped to their head). The Christian cross can also be drawn as an unfolded cube of six sides on a two-dimensional surface. Saturn is the sixth planet in the Solar System, Saturday (Saturn's day) is the sixth day of the week and Saturn has a permanent hexagon (a six sided shape) at its north pole. The fact that this Satanic Cult arose near Babylon is connected with that fact that one of the Jewish holy books, the

Talmud, also arose there (which is why some call it the 'Babylonian Talmud').

This book you are reading traces the development and deeds of this Satanic Cult, particularly as it multiplied itself through Judaism.

A key place to begin this tale is to clear up the massive confusion that abounds on the issue of the essence of Jewishness. Jewish identity. What makes someone a Jew? Can one become a Jew? Is one born a Jew? Is Jewishness a tripartite entity of religion, race and nationality? For both Jew and non-Jew, it be a confusing morass, a never-ending triangle that jumps from one point to the next to the next so as to evade a clear definition. Much of this, I would say, is by design.

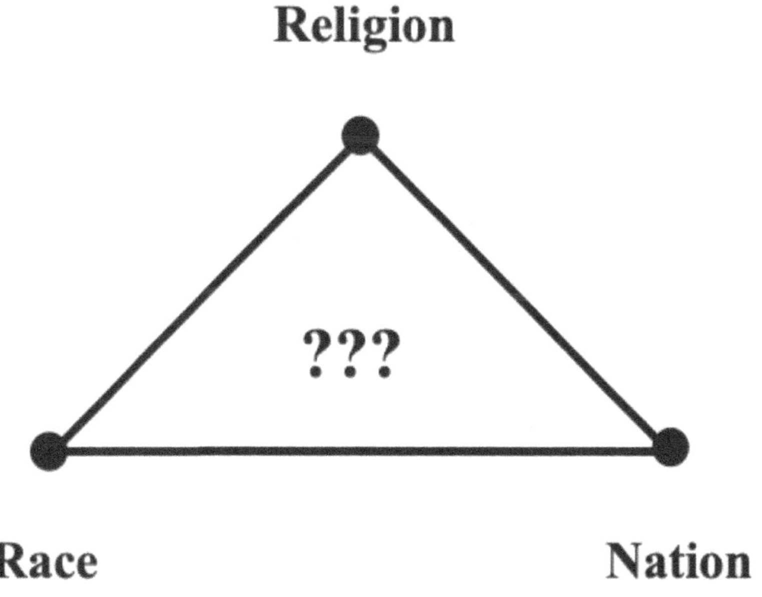

Image #2: the Jewish identity triangle of confusion

A long time ago now, certain groups, factions or what I consider to be cults, infiltrated and overtook Judaism. They not only steered Judaism in a certain way, as any leadership group will do within any organization, but they began to actually redefine Judaism for their own purposes. They stretched the definition so much that they broadened it from a belief system/religion (Judaism), or a group of people living in community together with shared values (Jews) speaking a common language (Hebrew or Yiddish), to the new magical definition which included shared genetic or ethnic characteristics, and, to go along with that shared racial ancestry, a shared common homeland or geographical area from which this 'race' supposedly sprung.

Both non-Jews and Jews alike have been suffering from this confusion, or trick if you will, which has muddled people's minds and given a fake foundation to the deflective technique of dismissing justified criticism as antisemitic. When someone calls you antisemitic, they are presupposing that all Jews are Semites, when in fact the word 'semite' refers to 'a member of any of a number of peoples of ancient southwestern Asia including the Akkadians, Phoenicians, Hebrews and Arabs.' As we shall see and expound upon, many Jews today are white-skinned and of Eastern European ancestry, having nothing to do with West Asia or the Middle East, or the people that historically lived there. One of the definitions of Semite is, indeed, 'Arab,' which is rather ironic – many people standing up for the Palestinians and against the horrific and ongoing genocide in Gaza are labelled antisemitic when they are pro-Arab or prosemitic!

This trick of confusing religion with race/nation has been deftly exploited by the Zionists. Zionism is a political philosophy whose goal is to conquer, colonize and steal Palestine from its current inhabitants due to the fabled myth that a 'racial' group of Jews supposedly lived there thousands of years ago, and that 'God' promised and gave it to them.

Jewish Mythistory

I am borrowing the term 'Jewish Mythistory' as the subheading for this section from Shlomo Sand, the great Israeli historian whose work I will discuss shortly. The term is very apt, for a close examination and analysis of Jewish history shows that, in their stories, the people they claimed to have lived and the events they claimed to have happened – including the existence of Moses, Noah, Solomon and David, the building of the first and second temples, the parting of the sea, and so on – have no factual basis. Rather, and shockingly, they appear to be characters and fables that were invented to give Jews a history and to solidify an identity.

This view is reinforced by the outstanding scholarly work done by Russell Gmirkin, author of the book *Plato and the Creation of the Hebrew Bible*. In this book, which is lined with a bibliography spanning hundreds upon hundreds of books, Gmirkin shows that Jewish 'history' as recorded in the Torah or Pentateuch (the first five books of the Bible) was given to them by Jewish scholars in around the year 270 BCE. Gmirkin reveals how Jewish scholars visited Alexandria to create a copy of Jewish 'legislation' for the Great Library, which gave them the opportunity to become well acquainted with Athenian legal institutions, with the Jewish foundation story in Hecataeus of Abdera's Aegyptiaca and with Plato's Laws. These and other Greek texts became the basis for the construction of a Jewish history. With painstaking attention to detail, he goes through the Pentateuch showing how the themes and structure are identical to those found in ancient Greek philosophy, myth, legal theory, political structure and military organization.

For example, the character of David appears to be based on Greek ideals and Greek education. In the quote below, 'ephebate' refers to Greek military training which began at age eighteen and 'hoplite' refers to an armored man or citizen-soldier:[4]

The youthful David appeared in the guise of an ephebe or youthful warrior-in-training. David was described as young, bronzed and good-looking ... in accordance with Archaic and Classical Greek aesthetic ideals. Not only was David a courageous warrior, but he was proficient with the lyre ..., an agile dancer ... and a talented songwriter ... qualities strikingly out of place for a military figure of the Ancient near East, but thoroughly consistent with a young man undergoing Greek instruction in the gymnasium ... One gains the impression that the author of the tales of military exploits in Samuel was well acquainted with the Greek gymnasium, ephebate and hoplite army; the recurrent themes taken from Homer's Iliad also suggest a basic background in Greek literature.

The evidence shows Jewish law was very closely modeled on ancient Greek law. The Letter of Aristeas reveals Jewish scholars gained access to the Great Library at Alexandria where they copied, modeled or plagiarized (however you prefer to perceive it) the Greek system of law and created Jewish law. Gmirkin writes:[5][6][7]

The Great Library of Alexandria housed an extensive section on laws that prominently included books on constitutions, laws and politics by Plato, Aristotle and other notable Athenian philosophers. Jewish access to the Great Library with its comprehensive collection of legal writings is attested in The Letter of Aristeas in connection with the Septuagint translation at Alexandria, an occasion at which the biblical authors could have conducted legal research into Athenian and later political systems as they were devising the system of constitution and laws found in the Pentateuch ... It is thus entirely legitimate to view Mosaic and Greek legal traditions, including those at Athens, as part of the same historical stream during the early Hellenistic Era, justifying a direct comparison of biblical and Greek laws ... The striking parallels between biblical and Athenian laws noted earlier remove the need to hypothesize a diffuse Eastern Mediterranean legal tradition in pre-Hellensitic times, and instead indicate a direct acquaintance with Athenian law. This does not appear conceivable prior to Alexander's conquests in the east in 332-325 BCE and even in the Hellenistic Era is best understood as reflecting Jewish access to Athenian political and legal writings, a possibility affirmed by the many parallels with Plato's Laws ... The tradition that put visiting Jewish legal experts at Alexandria in ca. 270 BCE at the invitation of Ptolemy II Philadelphus for the purpose of adding a text on Jewish laws to the holdings of the Great Library provides a historical context for the confluence of Jewish and Greek cultures that stimulated the creation of the Pentateuchal law collections.

Indeed, entire books of the Pentateuch (such as Deuteronomy) were based on Plato's Laws:[8]

Given the striking correspondence between the biblical use of paretic introductions and motive clauses and the persuasive pooimia or paramuthia first advocated in Plato's Laws, there can be little doubt regarding the influence of Plato's Laws on the text of Deuteronomy.

So much for the character called 'Moses' speaking to 'God' high up on a mountain and coming down with something original! Incidentally, the story of baby Moses being put into a papyrus basket, then hidden among the reeds at the river bank for the Pharaoh's daughter to find, is an exact narrative knock off from the birth of Sargon of Akkad, the ruler of the Akkadian Empire in the 24th to 23rd centuries BCE. So much of Judaism (and for that matter, Christianity too) is borrowed from previous religions, narratives and civilizations. The Jewish commandments are the same as the Greek commandments:[9]

The Jewish and Greek commandments possessed identical apodictic form, divine association with a famous temple, purported authorship by famous legislators of the distant past, widespread use as an educational text to instill citizen ethics and even some shared content, all pointing to their belonging to the same Greek literary genre.

Even the famous Exodus story (second book of the Bible) that many people know, Jews and non-Jews alike, where the Jews purportedly had to hurry out of Egypt, not having time for their bread to leaven, being led by Moses who parted the Red Sea, is based on Greek epic stories of the wandering hero:[10]

Comparisons with Greek literature show that the biblical account of the Israelite Exodus and Sojourn under Moses and Conquest under Joshua follow the familiar pattern of the Greek foundation story.

It was in the fictitious giving of ten commandments to Moses on Mount Sinai that the Jews were promised Canaan (part of Palestine) by 'Yahweh' (more on this Yahweh character, the idea of a 'chosen people' and a 'promised land' later). All of this is also based on ancient Greek texts, themes and motifs:[11]

The conquest and settlement of the Promised Land was portrayed as a return of the Israelites to the ancient ancestral lands after the familiar pattern of the Return of the Heraklids and other Greek charter myths ... in both biblical and Greek narratives the land was a gift from the deity, and its conquest by the colonizing forces was not only permitted, but also required. In successful colonizations, the original inhabitants of the land were typically conquered and enslaved or displaced, an action sometimes justified by some moral pretext that became part of the foundation legend.

The technique of establishing government and laws, then imbuing them with a sense of gravitas and sacredness by linking them to divine origin so as to give them more authority (and thus make citizens/people easier to control) was employed by Plato. Thus, whether we are examining a political structure or religious belief system, the idea is the same: give people a narrative, make it seem like it's come from god or has been somehow divinely ordained (throw in a couple of miracles if need be), and so make the adherents more pliable, obedient or compliant. This technique can be found both in Plato's approach and in Jewish mythistory:[12]

Plato's key strategy for persuading the colonists to adopt a new system of government he proposed and to remain loyal to them down through time was to invest these laws and institutions with an aura of antiquarianism ... Plato's Laws contained many examples of suggestive mechanisms, whereby the new laws and institutions of the polis might convincingly be portrayed as ancient and divine ... a connection between the gods and the land was to be forged by diligent inquiry into local customs ... Plato's program of creating a mythic past in which the divine laws of the nation had been established in distant antiquity faced an obvious practical difficulty, namely the living memory of the new colonists. Plato fully recognized this problem and sought to overcome it by devising strategies to erase the nation's memory of any other way of life ... One can now begin to understand the full scope of the reorganization – one might say reinvention – of Jewish national life undertaken by the legislators of ca. 270 BCE, following the ambitious program laid out in Plato's laws.

The Jewish leaders at the time copied Plato. The whole point was to make it seem like their history, commandments and laws had been around a very long time and were divinely ordained:[13]

The creation of the Pentateuch at Alexandria by Jewish and Samaritan legislators and writers appears to have been part of an initiative approved by the Jewish senate ... to refound the nation with new laws, a new literature and a new past, in line with the legislative strategies found in Plato's Laws *... which called for the legislators to use any device available to persuade the citizenry that the nation's laws and ways of life had remained unchanged for centuries since having been divinely revealed to their distant forefathers.*

In conclusion, there is virtually nothing original in Jewish mythistory that wasn't lifted or pilfered from the Greeks, whether it's the divine appointment of Moses (copied from Greek heroes who were demigods or sons/daughters of gods), places of miracles and divine power like Mount Sinai (similar to Delphi), religious festivals or annual events like Yom Kippur (similar to the Karneia which celebrated atonement), wandering heroes in exile (copied from Greek epics like *The Odyssey*) or the divine bestowing of moral commandments. The construction of Jewish myth, history and laws was an initiative approved by the Jewish rulers to mold a new character and identity. Jewish writers such as Josephus have tried to claim that Jewish mythistory influenced the Greeks because it came first, however based on the extensive evidence Gmirkin documents in his book, it is clearly the other way round: Greek ideas and writings influenced Jewish ones. Gmirkin writes:[14]

Josephus presented his second argument, that the Jewish way of life had been established 2,000 years earlier, in the time of Moses, long prior to Plato's era, and thus must necessarily have influenced Plato's writings ... although one may accept the existence of a genuine connection between the provisions in the Torah and Plato's Laws, much as Josephus and other ancient writers inferred from their knowledge of both, it now appears evident that the Mosaic writings were informed by those of Plato and not the reverse.

Abraham = Abram = Brahma = Ra

The characters from Jewish history are just that – characters. There is no reason to believe they were real people that walked upon the Earth. Many authors for hundreds of years have highlighted the Abraham/Brahma motif and how the word 'Abraham' is almost identical to 'Brahma' if you rearrange the letters. Brahma was the principal Hindu god whose wife was Saraswati; likewise, Abraham's wife was Sarah, taking the first half of the word Saraswati. As this website states,[15] both sets are derived from the older Egyptian pair of Ra/Sirius (from 3500 BC) and are based on astrotheology (a theology based on the movement of the sun and stars). Abraham is also virtually identical to 'Abram' which, when broken down, means 'Father Ram' (Ab or Abba means father). Judaism is associated with the ram in several ways. Abraham sacrifices a ram in Genesis 22:13. Researchers such as the late Jordan Maxwell, expert on symbolism, astrotheology and many other things, pointed out the astrotheological interpretation of the ram as the star sign Aries, the sign before Pisces (fish, associated with Jesus and Christianity). In the Precession of the Equinoxes, Aries comes before Pisces, just as Judaism came before Christianity. 'Father of the people of the ram' could be a description of the Jews, since in their story, the shofar or ram's horn was heard when 'God' gave the 'Torah' to ancient Hebrews as they stood at the foot of Mount Sinai.

Incidentally, Christianity is also very much a recycled religion that has taken many things from the earlier ancient Egyptian culture. Just take a look at the giant obelisk (Osiris' penis) in the courtyard of St. Peter's Basilica in Vatican City. Or don't, if that's a little too off-putting for you. You can also find another replica of Osiris' proud body part in Washington DC, where it measures exactly 666 feet – just a coincidence, of course. Christianity hijacked the cross from many indigenous cultures that used it as a form of a solar calendar, and that's also because Christianity is solar or sun worship in disguise. That, however, is another story.

Another famous character that was likely invented is Solomon. Jordan Maxwell stated in this video[16] that the word Solomon could be broken down into 3 syllables:

SOL = Sun

OM = Sacred Indian sound

ON = Heliopolis, City of the Sun, originally called ON

It is quite possible therefore that the word Solomon is more hidden symbolism which conveys a message of solar worship. Regardless, there is no reason to believe there ever was such a thing as a 'Temple of Solomon' if Solomon never existed as a man. This article on the Middle East Monitor website reports that there is no archeological evidence that such a temple ever existed:[17]

According to the Biblical passage, the temple built about 3,000 years ago stood for more than four centuries until it was destroyed in the year 587 BC by the Babylonians. It would be difficult for there to be no archaeological remains in the region, especially given the size and richness with which the work is described ... its foundations are said to have been 29 metres long and 10 metres wide. Solomon is said to have used pure gold to cover the inner sanctum of the temple, where he placed a pair of golden cherubs measuring 30 feet in width to guard the Ark of the Covenant. "He also overlaid the house with gold—the beams, the thresholds and its walls and its doors; and he carved cherubim on the walls," as described in 2 Chronicles 3:7 ... in 2015, the Director of the Institute of Archeology at Tel Aviv University, Israel Finkelstein, shattered efforts made by researchers of biblical archaeologies saying that exhaustive excavations have found no sign of major construction or Solomon's reign in Jerusalem.

As I noted in my video *Why Israel Wages War with its Archeologists,*[18] the Zionist regime and ruling class that run Israel weaponizes archeology to substantiate their claim to land – ALL of it. It's part of the game: seed biblical writing with characters and events, then manipulate events to make it all come true as a self-fulfilling prophecy. They use archeology, just as governments use science, to further their predetermined agenda. Those archeologists or scientists who 'find' evidence that bolsters the agenda get grants, funding, promotion and praise; those who produce evidence that contradicts the agenda or narrative get the opposite.

That was a whole lot of invented Jewish history. As shocking as that was, we have only just begun.

There is No Such Thing as a Jewish Race or Jewish DNA

Now that you have seen some of the substantial evidence that Jewish history was invented, it's time to turn our attention to another fictitious aspect of Jewish identity: race.

The fact that we have to deeply investigate the question of 'Jewish race' shows how much confusion there is around Jewish identity – confusion which has been deliberately sowed and stoked for centuries, not least by the Cult that hijacked Judaism. With Christianity, there is no confusion; you can easily be a Christian, white and French, for example, since they are three separate identities. With Islam, you can easily be a Muslim, Arabian and Syrian, for example. Although there is a huge overlap between Muslims and Arabs, there are non-Arab Muslims (Persians in Iran and Asians in Indonesia) and non-Muslim Arabs (the Christian communities within Lebanon and Syria). For the rest of the world outside Judaism, it seems easy to keep the identities of religion, race and nation separate, yet when it comes to the Jews, it suddenly becomes very confusing.

As I shall do for much of this book, I shall now turn to Jews themselves to offer their unique perspective on these matters. Let's start with Rabbi Yaakov Shapiro, an American and author of many books including the 2018 book *The Empty Wagon: Zionism's Journey from Identity Crisis to Identity Theft*, who has for a long time promoted the truth that Judaism is a religion, not a race or nation. He outright rejects the idea that there was ever a geographical Jewish homeland, in Palestine or anywhere else. He states that the concept of a 'Jewish homeland' is a metaphorical idea. This idea of taking things literally instead of symbolically is a problem not just within Judaism but within all religions. Fundamentalists and extremists become so rigid in their thinking that they take everything literally, as dogma, and miss the point completely. In this presentation on YouTube entitled *Has Zionism Hijacked Judaism*,[19] Shapiro explains that, historically, Jews were just part of religious Judaism. You could not be a Jew in any other way. He emphatically states that the Jews are not a race, and have never been a race; one of many compelling arguments is that you can't 'convert' to a race, but you can convert to Judaism. Therefore, Judaism cannot be a race. He believes that Zionism is the subversion of Judaism and the Jewish religious community in its attempt to change it into a nationalistic, racial and political movement. Here is a direct quote from his presentation:[20]

There were no groups of people that were nonobservant, that did not follow the religion, that still considered themselves Jews. Atheists did not consider themselves Jews.

Let's continue with Israeli Jew and professor Shlomo Sand, who has written some powerful books entitled *The Invention of the Jewish People*, *The Invention of the Land of Israel* and *How I Stopped Being a Jew*. Sand is Israeli Emeritus Professor of History at Tel Aviv University. He grew up in Israel and was friends with people of many cultures, races and religions, including many Arabs. He had Israeli Arab friends and thought of them as being just as fully Israeli as Israeli Jews. By closely studying the way that Zionist leaders had tried to forge a Jewish identity on the population, he came to realize that almost everything about 'Jewishness' had been invented, forged, revised or defined for convenience or expedience. Zionist leaders, both before the founding of Israel in 1948 and after it, needed to unite the people behind a common idea of Jewishness and 'Israel' else their Zionist national project wouldn't have had the cohesion it needed to succeed. They needed to get people to identify with, and psychologically invest in, the idea of Jewishness, so they could get them to buy into the idea of a national Jewish homeland, even though a Jew in Morocco had little in common with a Jew in Poland who had little in common with a Jew in Yemen. A big part of this meant having a shared and clearly defined history. In *The Invention of the Jewish People* (2009), Sand writes:[21]

To reinforce abstract group loyalty, the nation, like the preceding religious community, needed rituals, festivals, ceremonies and myths. To forge itself into a single, firm entity, it had to engage in continual public cultural activities and to invent a unifying collective memory.

Jewish history thus underwent many revisions in the 1800s and early 1900s before the Zionist movement gained steam in the year of 1897 which marked the first international Zionist conference in Basel, Switzerland. Sand systematically goes through and shows how key authors kept rewriting history, many of them introducing and reinforcing the idea that Jewishness was a race and a nation (not just a religion) and that there was (and should be) a national homeland in Canaan or Palestine. He shows how Heinrich Graetz, Simon Dubnow and Ben-Zion Dinur were part of this process of historical revisionism:[22]

Although he was never a complete Zionist, Graetz formed the national mold for the writing of Jewish history ... Henceforth, for many people, Judaism would no longer be a rich and diverse religious civilization that managed to survive despite all difficulties and temptations in the shadow of giants, and became an ancient people or race that was uprooted from its homeland in Canaan and arrived in its youth at the gates of Berlin.

Transforming Jewishness from a mere religion to a race gave it more gravitas. Now, the Jews were a remarkable and quasi-magical people, the seed of a mythical patriarch (Abraham) who made deals directly with God, a genetically-linked people bound by blood and a common ancestor who had endured unspeakable hardships to make it though millennia to still be flourishing all these years later:[23][24]

History now appeared clothed in a more secular, well-defined protonationalist discourse. Jewish history was the story of a nomadic people born in great antiquity, which had mysteriously and marvelously continued to exist throughout history. Graetz and Dubnow's great enterprise received, with some adjustments, the honored imprimatur of academe, and biblical truth became an unquestioned discourse – an integral part of twentieth-century historical research ... Above all, the Bible became an ethnic marker, indicating a common origin for individuals of very different backgrounds and secular cultures yet all still hated for their religion, which they barely observed. That was the meaning that underlay this image of an ancient nation, dating back almost to the Creation, that came to be imprinted in the minds of people who felt themselves dislocated in the rough-and-tumble of modernity. It became imprinted in their consciousness of the past. The welcoming bosom of the Bible, despite (or perhaps because of) its miraculous and legendary character, could provide a long, almost an eternal, sense of belonging – something that the fast-moving, freighted present could not give them. In this way, the Bible became a secular book that schoolchildren read to learn about their ancient forefathers –

children who would later march proudly as soldiers fighting wars of colonization and independence.

The narrative of constructing the Jewish 'race' was seeded with the idea of Jews as exiles, always being (unfairly) forced out of where they were living, thus having to become nomads in desperate need of a home which they deserved. As mentioned previously, this theme was a knock off from ancient Greek epic stories (like *The Odyssey*) featuring wandering heroes:[25]

[Dinur] therefore defined the Jewish identity not as belonging to a religious minority that lived for centuries among other, dominant religious cultures, sometimes repressive and at other times protective, but as the identifying profile of an alien ethnic-national body that has always been on the move and is destined to keep wandering. Only this conception of exile gave an organic sequence to the history of Jewish dispersal, and only in this way could it clarify and justify 'the return of the nation to its birthplace.'

After Graetz, Dubnow and Dinur, others came along who further cemented the fictitious narrative of the Jews being a nation-race. One such character was Haim Ze'ev Hirschberg, who served mainstream Zionist historiography very well with his devotion:[26][27]

Hirschberg had not the slightest evidence concerning the number, if any, of 'born Jews' in different classes of Himyarite society, nor about the origins of those who clung to the Jewish faith. But the ethnocentric imperative was stronger than his historical training, and demanded that he conclude his work with the 'call of the blood' ... So firm was Hirschberg's conviction that he forgot his ethnoreligious belief that the Arabs, too, had descended from the great patriarch. But this typical slip is marginal. His constant effort to prove that the Jews were a nation-race that had been torn from its ancestral homeland and gone into a wandering exile was far more significant, and, as we have seen thus far, it met the imperative of mainstream Zionist historiography. His inability to rise above the purifying essentialist ideology that guided all his research damaged his work, and it was this fault that constituted the 'scientific source' in support of the common positions in the standard history textbooks of the Israeli educational system.

That is often all it takes – a paid academic getting praised and becoming an 'authority' – for history to become standardized according to the wishes of whatever group is in power.

The Khazar Connection

At this point, it's important to introduce the concept that there are different types of Jews. The two main types are Ashkenazi Jews and Sephardic Jews. Ashkenazis or Ashkenazim are from Eastern Europe whereas Sephardics are from northern and western Africa, the Arabian peninsula and elsewhere in the Middle East. Israeli demographer and statistician Sergio Della Pergola implied that Ashkenazis comprised 65–70% of Jews worldwide in 2000[28] (since he was counting Sephardic and Mizrahi Jews and estimated them at 32%), although other sources put the percentage at more like 75% or 80%. This is an extremely important distinction as we shall see with the coming discussion of the Khazars, but first, let's look at the research of a man called Paul Wexler who was an archeologist and an expert in linguistics. His analysis revealed that the languages used by Sephardic Jews were completely different to the supposed 'Jews' from Judea. Sand writes:[29]

The sad lack of historical testimony about the early formation of Jewish groups in the Iberian Peninsula, Wexler argued, forces us to rely on the evolution of their languages and their ethnographic data. As a 'philological archaeologist,' Wexler skillfully traced linguistic vestiges found in the ethos and languages that are still in use today, and concluded that the origins of the Sephardic Jews were extremely heterogenous, and hardly Judean.

The world owes a great debt to the work of Arthur Koestler, who released an absolute bombshell of a book in 1976 called *The Thirteenth Tribe*, a clever play on the concept that there was another 'tribe' or source of Jews outside of the mythical twelve tribes of Israel in the Middle East. Koestler promoted the idea that the aforementioned Ashkenazi Jews, the sizable majority of today's Jewry, were not descended from 'historical Israelites of antiquity,' but from the Khazars, a Turkic and Caucasian people who ruled an empire between the Black Sea and Caspian Sea, north of the Caucasus mountains. The Khazarian Empire was warlike, formidable and lasted several centuries; it successfully fought off many attempted invasions from the South by Muslim armies and the West by Christian armies.

Koestler draws upon evidence in the form of historical documents and letters, one from a Khazar king himself, that show the nation underwent a mass conversion around the 8th century AD when the whole kingdom converted to Judaism and became Jewish. As the story goes, the Khazars were being pushed to adopt one of the main three monotheistic religions (Judaism, Christianity or Islam). To deal with this pressure diplomatically, the Khazar king invited an advocate from each to a discussion or debate, where they had to convince the king why their particular religion was the best. The king listened to them all, and asked each representative privately which religion was the second best; both the Christian priest and the Muslim imam said it was Judaism, so one account suggests the King chose Judaism as the national religion as a part of a calculated political move so as to cause the least upset in the region. After all, he was trying to ensure his kingdom didn't get invaded and overthrown. If the Khazars had adopted Islam, they would have become subjects to Muslim rule under the caliph. If the Khazars had adopted Christianity, they would also have become subordinate. If they had remained pagan, they would have become a target for the Muslims who did not tolerate idolatry. Hence, the transition from the ancient shamanism of the region to Jewish monotheism was a defensive ideological tactic.

Koestler presents compelling evidence that the Jewish Khazars, after the fall of Khazaria in the 12th and 13th centuries, migrated westwards into Eastern Europe (primarily Ukraine, Poland, Belarus, Lithuania, Hungary and Germany) and became the overwhelming majority constituent of today's Ashkenazis. Koestler devotes a lot of attention to notating the massive Khazar influence over the history of Russia and Hungary. He wrote:[30]

Two basic facts emerge from our survey: the disappearance of the Khazar nation from its historic habitat, and the simultaneous appearance in adjacent regions to the north-west of the greatest concentration of Jews since the beginnings of the Diaspora. Since the two are obviously connected, historians agree that immigration from Khazaria must have contributed to the growth of Polish Jewry.

Koestler was aware of the pressure exerted by modern-day Zionism for Jewish historians and academics to conform to the idea of the 'Chosen Race' when he wrote that *"the lingering influence of*

Judaism's racial and historical message, though based on illusion, acts as a powerful emotional break by appealing to tribal loyalty."[31] Sand echoes Koestler's ideas about the importance of the Khazars and how their legacy has been buried by modern Jewish historiography:[32]

Khazaria collapsed some time before the first indications of the presence of Jews in Eastern Europe, and it is difficult not to connect the two ... [but these facts] scarcely interested the scholars who were occupied in inventing the eternal history of the 'people of Israel.' They could not come to terms with the troublesome fact that there had never been a Jewish people's culture, but only a popular Yiddish culture that resembled the cultures of their neighbors much more than it did those of the Jewish communities of Western Europe or North Africa ... When we consider the tremendous effort that the memory agents in Israel have invested in commemorating their dying moments, compared with the scanty effort made to discover the rich (or wretched, depending on one's viewpoint) life lived in Yiddishland before the vision massacre, we can draw only sad conclusions about the political and ideological role of modern historiography.

The Khazarian roots of the modern Ashkenazi Jews becomes all the more significant when you consider what control they have had and still have over the modern state of Israel. Look at the following list of Prime Minister (PM) and political leader birth places of Israel since its inception in 1948. Do these Israeli leaders strike you as Middle Eastern – or Eastern European?

Chaim Weizmann:	born in Belarus
David Grün (later David Ben-Gurion):	born in Poland
Moshe Chertok (later Moshe Sharett):	born in Ukraine

Levi Yitzhak Shkolnik (later Levi Eshkol): born in Ukraine

Golda Mabovitch (later Golda Meir): born in Ukraine

Menachem Begin: born in Belarus

Szymon Perski (later Shimon Peres): born in Belarus

Yitzhak Yezernitsky (later Yitzhak Shamir): born in Belarus

Arthur Mendelowitz (later Amos Manor): born in Austria-Hungary (present-day Romania)

Benjamin Mileikowsky (later Benjamin Netanyahu): father from Poland

The last figure, the notorious war criminal and current Israeli PM Benjamin Netanyahu, had a father originally called Benzion Mileikowsky. His Polish father changed his name to Netanyahu when he came to Palestine to make it sound more Hebrew and less European. The hebraization of names is a common technique used by the Ashkenazis to make themselves sound more authentically semitic.

Consider also a letter that surfaced in 2017 that a younger British King Charles wrote in 1986, where he sympathized with the Arabs and lamented that the influx of foreign European Jews to the land of Israel had led to massive problems. He wrote the following very interesting lines, which undermine the idea of the Jews as a race and also undermine the idea that the Jews and Arabs are somehow different ethnic peoples, calling them all semitic people originally:[33]

Also begin to understand [the Arabian] point of view about Israel. Never realised they see it as a US colony. I now appreciate

that Arabs and Jews were all a Semitic people originally ... surely some US president has to have the courage to stand up and take on the Jewish lobby in the US? I must be naïve, I suppose!

Yes indeed, and we will discuss the power of the Jewish lobby later in this book.

In addition to highlighting the momentous significance of the Khazars on Jewish history, Koestler also waded deeply into the 'Jews as a race' debate, presenting potent and cogent evidence that there was no such thing as Jewish genetics or Jewish DNA. He quoted various experts in anthropology and other fields who had concluded in their research that there were no common physical Jewish characteristics that bound Jews together, despite the myth of the 'Jewish nose.' Koestler quotes Raphael Patai and Harry Shapiro:[34][35]

Summing up a very old and bitter controversy in a laconic paragraph, Raphael Patai wrote: 'The findings of physical anthropology show that, contrary to popular view, there is no Jewish race. Anthropometric measurements of Jewish groups in many parts of the world indicate that they differ greatly from one another with respect to all the important physical characteristics – stature, weight, skin colour, cephalic index, facial index, blood groups, etc. This indeed is the accepted view today among anthropologists and historians. Moreover, there is general agreement that comparisons of cranial indices, blood types, etc. show a greater similarity between Jews and their Gentile host-nation than between Jews living in different countries.'

... quotation from Harry Shapiro's contribution to the UNESCO series – 'The Jewish People: A Biological History':

'The wide range of variation between Jewish populations in their physical characteristics and the diversity of the gene frequencies of their blood groups render any unified racial classification for them a contradiction in terms. For although modern racial theory admits some degree of polymorphism or variation within a racial group, it does not permit distinctly different groups, measured by its own criteria of race, to be identified as one. To do so would make the biological purposes of racial classification futile and the whole procedure arbitrary and meaningless. Unfortunately, this subject is rarely wholly divorced from non-biological considerations, and despite the evidence efforts continue to be made to somehow segregate the Jews as a distinct racial entity.'

Koestler, like Sand, mentions the enthusiasm for proselytizing and mass conversions that happened early on the history of Judaism as reasons why the Jews have always been a racially varied and heterogenous group:[36]

In short, at the beginning of the Diaspora, the Israelites were already a thoroughly hybridized race. So, of course, were most historic nations, and the point would not need stressing if it were not for the persistent myth of the Biblical Tribe having preserved its racial purity throughout the ages. Another important source of interbreeding were the vast numbers of people of the most varied races converted to Judaism. Witness to the proselytizing zeal of the Jews of earlier times are the black-skinned Falasha of Abyssinia, the Chinese Jews of Kai-Feng who look like Chinese, the Yemenite Jews with their dark olive complexion, the Jewish Berber tribes of the Sahara who look like Tuaregs, and so on, down to our prime example, the Khazars.

Sand points out the science supporting the idea of Jewish genetics and heredity is highly dubious:[37]

Yet so far, no research had found unique and unifying characteristics of Jewish heredity based on a random sampling of genetic material whose ethnic origin is not known in advance. By and large, what little is known about the methods of selecting test subjects seems very questionable. Moreover, the hasty findings are all too often constructed and supported by historical rhetoric unconnected to the research laboratories. The bottom line is that, after all the costly 'scientific' endeavors, a Jewish individual cannot be defined by any biological criteria whosoever.

Sand mentions how even the Nazis – probably the movement most obsessed with racial ideology in the history of humanity – could not isolate a Jewish gene, even with all their Germanic scientific and technical ability:[38]

Physical anthropology and, later, imported molecular genetics also failed to come up with a scientific yardstick by which to determine the origin of an individual Jew. Let us not forget that the Nazis themselves – despite their biological race doctrine, the jewel in their ideological crown – had been unable to do this, and so they ended up having to categorize Jews on the basis of bureaucratic documentation.

Finally, in a section entitled "The Last Resort: A Jewish DNA," Sand rips apart those trying to claim there is some kind of common genetic marker of 'Jewishness':[39]

After exhausting all the historical arguments, several critics have seized on genetics. The same people who maintain the Zionists never referred to a race conclude their argument by evoking a common

Jewish gene. Their thinking can be summed up as follows: "We are not a pure race, but we are a race just the same." In the 1950s there was research in Israel on characteristic Jewish fingerprints, and from the 1970s, biologists in their laboratories (sometimes also in the USA) have sought a genetic marker common to all Jews. I reviewed in my book their lack of data, the frequent slipperiness of their conclusions, and their ethno-nationalist ardor, which is unsupported by any serious scientific findings. This attempt to justify Zionism through genetics is reminiscent of the procedures of the late nineteenth-century anthropologists who very scientifically set out to discover the specific characteristics of Europeans.

As of today, no study based on anonymous DNA samples has succeeded in identifying a genetic marker specific to Jews, and it is not likely that any study ever will. It is a bitter irony to see the descendants of Holocaust survivors set out to find a biological Jewish identity: Hitler would certainly have been very pleased! And it is all the more repulsive that this kind of research should be conducted in a state that has waged for years a declared policy of 'Judaization of the country' in which even today a Jew is not allowed to marry a non-Jew.

Zionists like to push the Rhineland Hypothesis which claims ancient Israelites were expelled from Canaan or Palestine after the Islamic invasion, and so migrated through Italy to Europe where they intermarried with Europeans. However, it's absolute nonsense. In his study *Genetic Markers Cannot Determine Jewish Descent*,[40] Raphael Falk concluded that while some detectable Middle Eastern genetic components exist in numerous Jewish communities, there is no evidence for a single Jewish prototype, and that *"any general biological definition of Jews is meaningless."* Israeli geneticist Eran

Elhaik argues that Ashkenazi Jews are not descended from the Palestine region, favoring the hypothesis that they are of mixed Irano-Turko-Slavic and southern European descent. He also reveals that the name Ashkenaz is not from the Old Testament but instead from the Iskenaz or Eskenez region in Türkiye.[41]

The evidence is indeed overpowering that a concerted effort has been made for a long time, either promoted by the Zionist ruling class or opportunistically seized by them, to forge a new Jewish identity that included a racial/genetic dimension, despite the fact that it is completely unsupported by the science. In case you think I am only cherry picking certain authors on this point, I will include a very telling quotation from a more mainstream Jewish author by the name of Kevin Alan Brook, who published a book in 2002 called *The Jews of Khazaria*. After spending almost the entire book giving the reader the impression that there was a Jewish race, he ends by using clauses such as *"considered children of Abraham"* – with "considered" here having the meaning of being adopted or being given an honorary title! He thus undid his entire book of 'science' in a single paragraph of blind religious faith and 'trust me, bro' because this idea of magically becoming the descendant of Abraham (another fictitious character, remember) has nothing to do with biology, genetics or science:[42]

After the Khazars converted to Judaism, their identity transformed from Turkic to Jewish. Jewish law requires converts to become part of the overall Jewish community and be considered children of Abraham ... As Jacob Agus wrote:

When non-Jewish groups accepted the Jewish faith, they also embraced the myth of Hebraic descent ... Even the Khazars who were converted to Judaism in the light of history regarded themselves as somehow of the 'seed' and the 'blood' of ancient Israel.

Here, the key terms are *"regarded"* and *"somehow,"* while the operative clause is *"embraced the myth of Hebraic descent." "Somehow"* implies something magical is happening, in defiance of the laws of physics, biology or everyday life as we know it. All of this is a choice people are making to identify a certain way, or a command (religious law) being given by the organization's leaders (rabbis) that converts must be identified a certain way. Again, at the risk of repeating myself, this has NOTHING to do with biology, genetics or science. It's fairy stardust – and sorry, I don't mean to offend all genuine and legitimate fairies out there. It's myth, it's faith, it's convenient religious, political or legal classification, but nothing more.

As Sand writes, *"Perhaps it was the fact that those tricky Khazars were not exactly the 'ethno-biological descendants of Israel,' and their history was alien to the Jewish metanarrative"*[43] that lead the current ruling and dominant Ashkenazis to embark on the crazy attempt to make Jewishness partially or fully race-based. Ironically, it is the European Ashkenazi Jews, who led the Zionist movement and still dominate Israeli society today, who are less related to Middle Eastern and Levantine Jews than Palestinians are.

Whatever the cause, the facts are clear: there is no such thing as a Jewish race or Jewish DNA.

There is No Such Thing as a Historical Jewish Homeland

The next sacred cow to bust – although admittedly that is the wrong metaphor to use here, since we're dealing with Judaism not Hinduism – is the idea that the Jews were a nation who had an ancient homeland that belonged exclusively to them, or that there ever was one single homeland from which they all sprung. The construction of a fake narrative that made Jews into a nation-race, descended from a mythical patriarch from a certain region of the Middle East, has given them the foundation to steal land with arrogance, viciousness and the Old Testament in hand. Sand writes:[44]

In the 1970s Israel was caught up in the momentum of territorial expansion, and without the Old Testament in its hand and the 'exile of the Jewish people' in its memory, it would have had no justification for annexing Arab Jerusalem and establishing settlements in the West Bank ... to achieve their aim, the Zionists needed to erase existing ethnographic textures, forget specific histories, and take a flying leap backward to an ancient, mythological and religious past.

As highlighted earlier, Gmirkin showed that the Jews were given their history by Jewish scholars in 270 BC, and the idea of an ancient Jewish homeland was central to this concocted history. Rabbi Yaakov Shapiro, also mentioned earlier, outright rejects the idea that there was ever a geographical Jewish homeland, in Palestine or anywhere else. He emphasizes that 'the Holy Land' of Jewish people is the Torah or the synagogue, not a geographical location or piece of dirt:[45]

The Jews had no national aspirations and no national goals ... to us it's not a homeland. Do you know where the homeland of the Jewish people is? It's the Torah, it's God.

Julian Rose also writes the following:[46]

I learned something very significant when I was working as a volunteer on an agricultural kibbutz in Northern Israel back in 1975. At that time, a retired Israeli army Colonel explained to me that, in the Hebrew language, the name 'Israel' is not a place name at all, but a description of the tribe of Israel's relationship with the God of Abraham.

Yaakov Shapiro's views stand in strong contrast to those of the Zionists who have been given lots of attention, such as the famous Austro-Hungarian Theodore Herzl (who headed the First Zionist Conference in Basel, Switzerland). In his attempt to reform Jewish identity and create support for a Jewish state, Herzl emphasized the Jews as a national group not a racial group. He wrote that *"We are a historical entity, a nation made up of different anthropological elements. That will suffice for the Jewish state. No nation has racial uniformity."*[47] The simple assertion that the Jews are a nation, however, does not make it so. As previously discussed, Sand extensively documented how key figures throughout Jewish history kept revising and reinforcing the false idea that Jews had a long continuous history which included a nation or homeland in Palestine, with all Jews coming from the seed of twelve tribes. In truth, the Jews were a diverse and heterogenous group that settled all over the Middle East, the Mediterranean (Northern Africa and Southern Europe), the Arabian Peninsula and Eastern Europe, through mass conversions and intermarriage. Sand writes:[48]

National mythology determined that the Jews – banished, deported or fugitive emigrants – were driven into a long and dolorous exile, causing them to wander over lands and seas to the far corners of the earth until the advent of Zionism prompted them to turn around and return en masse to their orphaned homeland. This homeland had never belonged to the Arab conquerors, hence the claim of the people without a land to the land without a people. This national statement, which was simplified into a useful and popular slogan for the Zionist movement, was entirely the product of an imaginary history grown around the idea of the exile.

When discussing Graetz, Dubnow and Dinur, Sand reveals how they not only promoted Jews as a race but also Jews as a nation:[49]

Dinur ... was far less inhibited by the shackles imposed by the invention of the nation – indeed, he was instrumental in forging them. If Graetz was responsible for the foundation and scaffolding of the retroactive construction of the Jewish nation, Dinur laid the bricks, hung the beams and fitted the windows and doors.

Dinur was a contemporary of David Ben-Gurion, the famous first Prime Minister of the State of Israel who will feature conspicuously later in this book, especially concerning the assassination of John Kennedy (see chapter 11). Sand describes how Ben-Gurion especially favored the idea of transforming the religious Bible into a historical document that somehow proved the Jews were a race, a nation and a people with a legal right to a piece of Middle Eastern land now occupied by Arabs:[50]

One of Dinur's many activities was participating in the regular Bible circle that in the 1950s met at the house of Israel's first prime minister, David Ben-Gurion. The charismatic leader was not only a keen reader of the ancient Hebrew book; he also made cunning political use of it. Quite early he realized that the holy book could be made into a secular national text, serve as a central repository of ancient collective imagery, help forge the hundreds of thousands of new immigrants into a unified people, and tie the younger generation to the land ... That a national leader should spend so much time being actively involved in historiographic issues is certainly unusual, and it may indicate the centrality of biblical mythistory in the construction of Zionist ideology. Reading Ben-Gurion's collection of articles, Biblical Reflections, one is struck by the easy swings between manipulative political pragmatism and a special and sincere belief in the ancient "truth." He keeps repeating that the Bible is the identity card of the Jewish people, as well as the proof of its claim to the Land of Israel.

A key psychological element of the fictitious narrative was the idea of a wandering people, in exile, without a homeland, always being unfairly expelled from places they had lived. According to Sand, this idea is just as concocted as the rest of Jewish history, but is used to bolster the assertion that they have a rightful claim to Palestine because they were unfairly driven out of it thousands of years ago:[51]

After forty years of wandering, the Children of Israel arrived in Canaan and took it by storm. Following the divine command, they annihilated most of the local population and forced the remainder to serve them as hewers of wood and drawers of water. After the conquest, the people that had been united under Moses split up into separate tribes (like the late Greek settlement in twelve city-states) and divided the territorial body among them. This ruthless myth of settlement, described in the Book of Joshua in colorful detail as one of the earliest genocides, never actually happened. The famous conquest of Canaan was the next myth to fall apart in the skirmishes of the new archeology.

Ironically, it is texts like this one (the Book of Joshua) that some Zionist religious zealots use as the basis for their erroneous claims that 'the Israelites' are the original inhabitants of the land. In the text, 'God' instructs Joshua and his warriors to commit multiple genocides to conquer the land, which clearly implies that the Jews were not the original inhabitants, since they were the ones invading and conquering it. Sand writes that later Zionist historiographers made sure to emphasize the Jews were forced off the land and did not voluntarily leave it:[52]

The exile-without-expulsion, which began in the seventh century CE – that is, some six centuries before the fall of the Second Temple – was not Yitzhak Baer's invention alone. This astonishing discovery was made by other Zionist scholars as well, notably Baer's friend and historiographical comrade-in-arms, Ben-Zion Dinur ... It is true that there was no deliberate policy of expulsion, but that does not mean that exile was undertaken voluntarily – God forbid. Dinur was worried that if it were accepted that the Jews left their country of their own volition, it would undermine their renewed claim to it in modern times.

It's a grand story, but at the end of the day, that's all it is: a story. However, the consequence for believing in nonsense can be catastrophic. To paraphrase Voltaire, those who can make you believe absurdities, can make you commit atrocities. And so, just as there is no Jewish race, there never was an ancient area of land in the Middle East that the Jews exclusively owned.

Hijacking the Meaning of the Label Jew

Historically, the label 'Jew' was used to describe people of a similar religion, custom or belief system. Sand states that before the 19th century, Jews thought of themselves as a people who shared a common religion, not a racial history. He confirms this by quoting the conception of 'Jew' by historical figures:[53]

Cassius Dio described this significant historical development, asserting: "I do not know how this title [Jews] came to be given to them, but it applies also to all the rest of mankind, although of alien race, who affect their customs." His near contemporary, the Christian theologian Origen, wrote: "The noun Ioudaios is not the name from the nation of the Jews, but of a choice [in the manner of life]. For if there be someone not from the nation of the Jews, a gentile, who accepts the ways of the Jews and becomes a proselyte, this person would properly be called a Ioudaios.

Robert Sepehr, author of *1666 Redemption Through Sin* that will be discussed in the coming chapters, claims that it was Sabbatean-Frankist and Illuminati member Moses Mendelssohn (1729-1786) who concocted the idea that the Jews could be a race not a religion, or at least that Jews could be secular (but really atheistic and opposed to historical, religious Jewry). This made possible the rise of Zionism, a nationalistic movement, and planted the seed that today has sprouted into antagonism between orthodox (religious) Jews and secular (atheistic) Jews. Ironically, these atheistic Zionist Jews don't believe in God … but they believe 'God' gave the promised land to them!

As George Orwell said, who controls the present controls the past, and who controls the past controls the future. The writing of national history by those in the present, funded and promoted by those in power in the present, is about controlling the past by inventing narratives about the past. Then, from these narratives, a control of the future springs, because the past is being used to justify future actions. In the case of Zionism, those in the present rewrite the past to justify the theft of Palestine, Lebanon, Syria and more, along the way to Greater Israel as schemed in the 1982 Oded Yinon plan:[54]

The writing of national history is not seriously meant to uncover past civilizations; its principal aim thus far has been the construction of a meta-identity and the political consolidation of the present ... a deeper exploration of the ways of life and communication in past Jewish communities might further expose a wicked little fact: that the further we move from religious norms and the more we focus our research on diverse daily practices, the more we discover that there never was a secular ethnographic common denominator between the Jewish believers in Asia, Africa and Europe. World Jewry had always been a major religious culture. Though consisting of various elements, it was not a strange, wandering nation.

Sand is very clear throughout his writings that just because there is no provable Jewish race does not mean that Israel has no right to exist. Israel exists. It's here now. I agree with him – to try to somehow undo the wrongs that were done in the past by disbanding Israel or expelling Jews would lead to chaos and insanity:[55]

If we want to organize the world as it was two thousand years ago, we will end up with a huge insane asylum. Nor does a religious link to a holy place confer any rights on it: this is true for Zionists today as it was for the Crusaders of yesterday. On this point, I must point out that this position does not lead me to deny the right of the state of Israel to exist. I have said time and again that a child born of rape has the right to live. The fact is there: refugees from Europe in the wake of the terrible Nazi genocide were forced to join the Zionist enterprise, to emigrate and settle on the land of another population. What has been done cannot be undone without creating a new series of tragedies. We can only repair the injustice as far as possible, provide compensation, and above all keep in mind in any negotiation the fundamental injustice inflicted on the inhabitants by the newcomers they had not invited.

As I will repeatedly emphasize throughout this book, there are many good Jews. Painting one group or class with the same collective paint brush is discriminatory, prejudiced and wrong on many levels. There are many good Jewish people who think of themselves as Jews but do not buy into the 'chosen ones' programming (see next chapter). This includes Israeli Jews who are not brainwashed with Zionist propaganda and simply want to live in peace with their Arab neighbors. Some Israelis realize that mixing Judaism (a religion) and the political entity of Israel (a nation) is a disaster for both.[56] However, Israel is run by a Zionist ruling class, and within that, a Satanic Cult – increasingly manifest now in the current governmental coalition of the racist, ultra rightwing Likud party and the fanatical religious messianic extremists. For these people in charge, and their many supporters, Israel is a Zionist theme park where the followers of this ideology play out their Jewish 'chosen people' and 'promised land' fantasies, with all the attendant supremacism, nationalism and expansionism, leading them to wage war and commit genocide.

Sources

[1] https://www.youtube.com/watch?v=NQ-tRrKeAfQ, 19:18 - 19:36

[2] https://sacred-texts.com/phi/spinoza/treat/tpt12.htm

[3] The Invention of the Jewish People, pg. 271

[4] Plato and the Creation of the Hebrew Bible (Gmirkin, 2017), pp. 16-17

[5] Ibid. pg. 39

[6] Ibid. pg. 74

[7] Ibid. pg. 146

[8] Ibid. pg. 203

[9] Ibid. pg. 205

[10] Ibid. pg. 225

[11] Ibid. pg. 227

[12] Ibid. pp. 254-5

[13] Ibid. pg. 270

[14] Ibid. pg. 275

[15] https://www.eoht.info/page/Abraham%20and%20Brahma

[16] https://www.youtube.com/watch?v=kRsQY-MiEO8

[17] https://www.middleeastmonitor.com/20220804-the-myth-of-the-temple-of-solomon-and-the-struggle-for-jerusalem/

[18] https://thefreedomarticles.com/why-israel-wages-war-with-its-archeologists/

[19] https://www.youtube.com/watch?v=NQ-tRrKeAfQ

[20] Ibid., minute 19:51-20:10

[21] The Invention of the Jewish People, pg. 39

[22] Ibid. pg. 73

[23] Ibid. pg. 97

[24] Ibid. pp. 127-8

[25] Ibid. pg. 141

[26] Ibid. pg. 198

[27] Ibid. pg. 206

[28] https://books.google.com/books?id=df8KrZMW09oC&pg=PA14#v=onepage&q&f=false

[29] The Invention of the Jewish People, pg. 208

[30] The Thirteenth Tribe, pg. 159

[31] Ibid. pg. 226

[32] The Invention of the Jewish People, pp. 246-7

[33] https://www.dailymail.co.uk/news/article-5073607/Letter-penned-Prince-Charles-sparks-controversy.html

[34] The Thirteenth Tribe, pg. 182

[35] Ibid. pp. 185-6

[36] Ibid. pg. 187

[37] The Invention of the Jewish People, pg. 279

[38] Ibid. pp. 280-1

[39] Ibid. pp. 318-9

[40] https://pubmed.ncbi.nlm.nih.gov/25653666

[41] https://aeon.co/ideas/how-dna-traced-the-ashkenazic-jews-to-northeastern-turkey

[42] The Jews of Khazaria, pg. 234

[43] Ibid. pg. 232

[44] Ibid. pg. 239

[45] https://www.youtube.com/watch?v=NQ-tRrKeAfQ, minute 21:11-21:42

---

[46] https://davidicke.com/2025/08/18/palestines-statehood-should-not-be-in-question-israels-statehood-should-be-julian-rose/

[47] Theodor Herzl's Diaries as a Bildungsroman, Nov. 21, 1895, *Diaries*, 1: 276, https://muse.jhu.edu/pub/3/article/18206

[48] The Invention of the Jewish People, pg. 188

[49] Ibid. pp. 104-5

[50] Ibid. pp. 107-9

[51] Ibid. pp. 118-19

[52] Ibid. pp. 139

[53] Ibid. pg. 167

[54] Ibid. pp. 246-7

[55] Ibid. pg. xv-xvi (Preface)

[56] https://x.com/loffredojeremy/status/1881735572039061515

CHAPTER 2: THE ZADDIKIM "CHOSEN ONES" - THE DELUSIONAL CORE OF JEWISH SUPREMACY

"Rather, we have a case of 'let us differentiate' between totally different species. This is what needs to be said about the body: the body of a Jewish person is of a totally different quality from the body of [members] of all nations of the world ... An even greater difference exists in regard to the soul. Two contrary types of soul exist: a non-Jewish soul comes from three satanic spheres, while the Jewish soul stems from holiness."

– Rebbe Schneerson[57]

"To what extent is Jewish Israeli society willing to discard the deeply embedded image of the 'chosen people,' and to cease isolating itself in the name of a fanciful history or dubious biology and excluding the 'other' from its midst?"

– Shlomo Sand[58]

"Every monotheism contains a potential element of mission. Unlike the tolerant polytheisms, which accept the existence of other deities, the very belief in the existence of a single god and the negation of plurality impels the believers to spread the idea of divine singularity that they have adopted. The acceptance by others of the worship of the single god proves his might and his unlimited power over the world."

– Shlomo Sand[59]

Having firmly established that there are no such things as a Jewish race and an ancient geographical Jewish homeland, and that historically Jews were so-called because they were part of a religion and neither genetically nor ethnically related, let's next examine how the Jewish religion was, early on, created or hijacked by a group of religious extremists. For this issue, we shall turn to author and Gnostic scholar John Lamb Lash, whose work *Not In His Image* contains key information about the development of Judaism and monotheistic religion in general. Lash is an unabashed lover of the Gnostics. He begins his book describing the murder of the pagan gnostic (or *gnostikoi* as Lash says is the right term) Hypatia, an incredibly well read and educated woman who ran the Great Library at Alexandria, likening it to an early form of a witch hunt. Hypatia was called a sorceress. She was beaten and killed in broad daylight by a group of Christian zealots, one of whom was linked to Cyril, the Christian bishop of Alexandria. Cyril had an axe to grind with Hypatia, because she had recently sided against him in a political dispute. The murder was symbolic of the rise of militant monotheistic Christianity, backed by the murderous might of the Roman Empire, which tolerated no religious dissent. If you did not believe in 'God,' and in the 'God' which Christianity defined and claimed as its own, then you were a nonbeliever worthy of death. The Satanic Cult had infiltrated the Roman Empire too.

In time before Jesus, when various Jewish sects lived in the Middle East, there was certain sect called the Zaddikim, plural of Zaddik, also spelt 'Tzaddikim/Tzaddik,' who lived on the Dead Sea. Zaddik translates to 'righteous one' however they were a sect of zealots and extremists, so an apt description for them would be 'conceited ones' rather than 'moral ones' or 'upstanding ones.' In his research, Lash pinpoints a highly significant – and unfortunate – occurrence that took place within this sect. In their minds, there arose the destructive idea of the 'chosen people.' They and only they were the ones whom God had exclusively chosen to receive blessings, benedictions and rewards. No one was as worthy as the chosen ones. So what could you do if you weren't a chosen one? Either stand back and allow the chosen ones to get what they wanted (more rights, more land, more money, more power) or try to convert to the sect to become a chosen one. However, if you converted, you would have to follow the leaders of that sect and do as you were told, thus granting them power. George Orwell (Eric Blair) profoundly understood the worldwide conspiracy and how society was run. The idea of the 'chosen ones' is similar if not identical to the idea Orwell revealed in his book *Animal Farm* when the pigs proclaim that some animals are more equal than others.

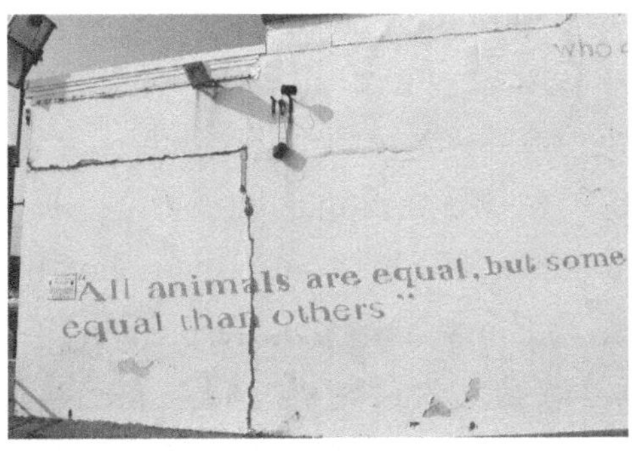

Image #3: graffiti quote from Orwell's Animal Farm

There is an important corollary you can often find alongside the idea of the 'chosen ones,' which is that if you are one of the unfortunate people who is not a chosen one, then you will not be 'saved.' What does this mean? The idea of salvation is a key element of the chosen ones narrative, because it allows for those outside of the special group to lose out and be punished. In fact, to go even deeper, Lash reveals that the concept of salvation itself is just one of four components of something he calls the 'redeemer complex':[60]

The redeemer complex has four components: creation of the world by a father god independent of a female counterpart; the trial and testing (conceived as a historical drama) of the righteous few of "Chosen People"; the mission of the creator god's son (the messiah) to save the world; and the final, apocalyptic judgment delivered by father and son upon humanity.

The Gnostics saw this repugnant complex for what it was – an aberration of thought and an abomination. Lash further reveals that the Gnostics, displaying their keen insight into the human condition and knowledge of psychology, saw what was really behind the promotion of the second component (suffering): the victim-perpetrator bond. The redeemer complex elevated suffering as an ideal (something very clearly seen in Christianity). Suffering was something to be proud of. You had to suffer to 'be saved.' In fact, suffering was so essential that 'God' sent down his only son to suffer so he could 'save' humanity, as the story goes. But what if we don't need to be saved nor need to suffer?

In sharp contrast to the idolization of suffering, another major world religion, Buddhism, teaches a way to end suffering, presupposing that suffering is not something essential or desirable. Of course, I must distinguish here between pain and suffering. Pain, especially physical pain, is an unavoidable part of life. You pull a muscle, you bang your toe, you pinch a nerve. Life happens. There will always be physical pain, but that is entirely different to suffering. Suffering is the mental anguish and resistance to what is. It is all the anxiety and fear, all the resentment and anger, all the disappointment and depression, and all the negative emotions we add on to a situation when we are not in acceptance of what is. It is this incredibly massive component which causes the bulk of human suffering, not the physical pain. The Buddha developed an eightfold path to try to help people escape suffering – not to avoid physical pain but to escape unnecessary mental suffering. Looking at this issue critically and objectively, what makes more sense – to venerate suffering or to reduce suffering?

To return now to the Gnostics' brilliant insight, they thought, according to Lash, that the attempt to lionize suffering was the attempt to cover up a very real but ugly part of the human condition: that people who are abused (victims) often go on to switch roles and later inflict abuse themselves (perpetrators). Not all victims become perpetrators, but almost all perpetrators were once victims. This principle is exploited by Satanists who conduct SRA (Satanic Ritual Abuse) on young children. They torture, rape and sacrifice some children, while designate other children as future leaders of the network. By imprinting viciousness and evil upon these young children, they hope to change them from victims to perpetrators, so that they will one day take over, and then do the same to the next generation of young victims. This is how Satanism perpetuates itself intergenerationally, often within families. For those interested in understanding more on this topic, please see my book *The International Satanic Network Exposed: Survivors Reveal Names of Presidents, Prime Ministers and Royals*, published in 2023.

Another lamentable aspect of the redeemer complex is that it requires you to look outside of yourself for salvation. It is bad enough that you are deficient, inadequate and in need of being 'saved,' but you can't even do the job yourself. You have to believe in a messiah to do your saving for you. It goes without saying that this is utterly disempowering. This does nothing to help the individual person become more awake and empowered, but it certainly does help the ruling class of that religion. The redeemer complex is not about spiritual enlightenment, but social engineering. The Gnostics, being wise and aware people, saw through this whole 'chosen people' and redeemer complex nonsense. They publicly spoke out against it, rebutting it logically and theologically. Lash writes:[616263]

The Gnostic protest against the redeemer complex aroused an enormous wave of violence in converts to the salvationist creed, as seen in the murder of Hypatia. She was a gnostikos, *a Pagan intellectual from the Mysteries, targeted by the righteous rage of people who pinned their faith on the Divine Redeemer. The mob that attacked her believed that their God had a unique way to overcome suffering, and this belief sanctioned them to inflict suffering to further His cause ... Gnostics such as Hypatia ... proposed that the unique status claimed by the Hebrews, and the entire concatenation of grandiose ideas that goes along with it, was a ruse. In the Gnostics' view, the "Divine Plan" to be realized through the Chosen People and the Messiah, culminating in an apocalyptic day of retribution, is not a calling to spiritual glory, but a grand and grievous deceit ... For the* gnostikoi, *skilled in theological debate, the element of the emergent religion that most alarmed them was the redeemer complex ... at the very moment salvationist religion first emerged, it was challenged and countered by people who were highly qualified to analyze and assess what they were seeing ... It is a monstrous error of the human mind, they argued, to make suffering into a righteous cause for those who inflict it, and a divine, redemptive calling for those on whom it is inflicted ... It is the victim-*

perpetrator bond diabolically exploited, disguised as a love connection.

Image #4: In an image from the Church of Santa Maria Novella in Florence, Melchizedek is depicted with horns on his head like the Devil. Coincidence?

So where exactly did the Zaddikim, the 'cult of righteousness,' get the idea that they were the only ones chosen to fulfill 'God's plan' on Earth? They got it from Melchizedek, whom Lash calls an eerie figure who appeared out of nowhere to anoint Abraham. The word 'Melchizedek' breaks down to mean 'prince of righteousness.' To those familiar with the Gnostic belief system, Melchizedek very much resembles what the Gnostics called an Archon. The Gnostics believed that this world was created by a cosmic accident when one of the many goddesses of creation (Sophia) from another dimension (the 'pleroma') fell in love with her created world, and, in an act never before seen, left the higher frequencies to descend to the lower ones out of passion (love for her creation), an act which upset the universal balance and caused a lot of unintended consequences. Sophia's act of descending from the pleroma accidentally caused a group of beings to be created without divine spark, intentionality or creative will. In other words, these beings (called the Archons) came to exist, but because they had no consciousness or soul in the same way that a human has, they could not create. They could only imitate. Clearly, a being that can create is naturally far more powerful, complete and whole than a being that can only copy.

However, what the Archons lack in creative power they make up for in sneakiness. Their way to survive and obtain energy is to siphon it from someone else; they live on borrowed energy. Specifically, they feed on low-vibrational dense energy, such as the human emotions we would typically call 'negative.' Since the Archons are less powerful than humans, they rely on stealth; they pretend to offer us something of value, as though we don't already have it, when actually we do. This theme is found in both Judaism and Christianity (when the Archons offer 'Abraham' and 'Jesus' things they already have by virtue of being human, or offer things like the kingship of a large city when that is not the Archons' to give away in the first place).

One of the Archons crowned himself king; the Gnostics called him the Demiurge or Yaldabaoth. He decided he was actually the one who created the world and the universe, began to get others to believe his story, and then further began to get those around him to worship him. What is worship after all? Essentially, it means giving your power away to someone else. The Archons are psychic predators, parasites who pose as gods, able to telepathically insert thoughts into people's minds, thoughts which are detrimental to the wellbeing of their 'hosts.' They are masters of deception, incredibly skilled at manipulating perception to make people think, speak and act in such a way that it benefits the Archons, not the person influenced – or, in some cases, the person possessed. Robert Monroe, who experimented with OBEs (Out of Body Experiences), picked up on the same theme when he coined the term 'loosh' to describe the energy harvested by these beings as food. The Archons deliberately set up situations designed to cause humans pain, frustration, depression, loneliness and fear, then trawl the planet to harvest these low-vibrational emotions as sustenance. It is the Archons who are behind the insidious idea of the 'chosen people.' Lash writes:[64]

... there is a select few who faithfully reflect the image of their Maker, while the rest of humanity does not. This nefarious and separatistic creed – arguably the pinnacle of racism – not only sets apart the righteous few and targets them for discrimination, it condemns the rest of humanity who do not mirror the divine image and follow the Father's plan. The Messiah comes to correct this situation, saving the select few form persecution (Jewish version) or offering divine absolution to all repentant sinners (Christian version), but the master plan is still not fulfilled on Earth, and final retribution must be imposed. Teachers in the Mysteries rejected this entire scenario as dementia, the psychotic ploy of the Archontic mind parasites.

The Archons have one main strength: they are master manipulators of perception. Since they can telepathically or psychically invade your mind and implant thoughts there (thoughts which are either untrue, half-true, distorted, based in the past not present, or based on resentment, anxiety, etc.), they can make you think and perceive things which are not real. They are promoters of fear – false evidence appearing real. They are deficient in divine creativity, but if they can pull the wool over your eyes, and pull you down to their level (or lower), they will control you. This is the meaning of the saying that in the land of the blind, the one-eyed man is king.

This concept is very important when it comes to conspiracy research, especially false flag operations (about which I have written about extensively, e.g. in my book *Break Your Chains* published in 2023), which will become very important as this book progresses. As we enter a new age of advanced AI (Artificial Intelligence) technology, machines can now simulate just about anything (e.g. Deep Fakes of people acting and talking). Any document, image or video can easily be faked, and very convincingly so. Humanity is being hit with an Archontic perceptual onslaught. For those that wish to control the entire world, the future will belong to those who can gaslight and perceptually trick the masses into believing their lies and fictitious narratives. It will be vital to remember this concept in the years and decades to come, especially if the NWO controllers attempt to pull off some kind of scenario like Operation Blue Beam (a fake alien invasion) with holographic images in the sky designed to ensnare your five senses.

Although their one main strength is considerable, the Archons cannot overcome humanity – IF humanity stands in its power. Remember, the Archons can only imitate or simulate; they cannot originate or create. They are completely stupid, illogical and insane: you can see this when Archontic think tanks and politicians push for war and tyranny on the flimsiest of pretexts, because they would lose in open debates. They have to outright lie, or at least bend and distort reality, to get their way. You can see the illogical Archontic mentality

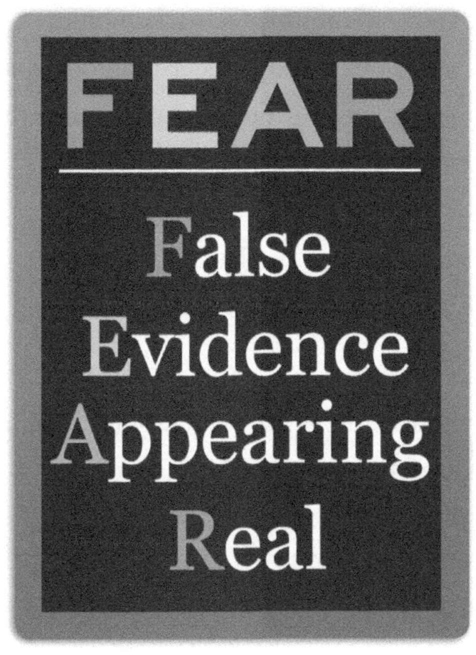

in political correctness which morphed into woke ideology, where men are women, women are men, you can just choose your gender at will, you can eliminate racism with more racism, and where job positions should be filled according to racial and gender quotas rather than with the most qualified and worthy person. You can also see the depopulation-pushing, death-promoting Archontic agenda in MSM (Mainstream Media) headlines where they proclaim absurdities that growing your own garden produces five times more carbon than buying fruits and veggies from stores,[65] that doing exercise is bad for you especially if you're a white man,[66] and that you shouldn't have kids because it's bad for the environment. The Archons reverse everything: up is down, black is white, night is day. Inversion is also the basis for Satanism: pain is pleasure. George Orwell pickup on this theme in his masterpiece *1984* when he described the motto of the ruling party ("*War is Peace. Freedom is Slavery. Ignorance is Strength.*") and when he described how the party required its citizens to perform mental gymnastics to believe in absurdities, impossibilities and lies if that was what the party required (*"2+2=5"* and "*we were always at war with Eastasia.*") Ultimately, Archontic arguments don't stand up to close scrutiny, clear thinking and activated consciousness. They can't beat scientific, logical or spiritual arguments, so they hide behind dogma or superstition, either quasi-religious or religious, and use censorship to suppress opposing views. At the end of the day, the Archons need us, but we don't need them. They also need our consent to get what they want. They can't force us or make us do anything, but only tempt, seduce and entice us. This theme of the Archons is absolutely central to understanding the Satanic Cult and its machinations.

For now, let's return to the Zaddikim. What is equally fascinating and scary is that the Zaddikim (and many Jews after them) delusionally thought themselves to be the exclusive 'chosen ones' in the exact same way that the Archon king Yaldabaoth – who seems strikingly similar to 'Yahweh' – thought himself to be the creator of the universe. Coincidence? I think not. Lash writes:[67]

Take the arrogance of the Demiurge, for instance: "It is I who am God, and there is no other apart from me." (The Reality of the Archons, NHC II, 4:94.20. The episode is repeated in several texts.) There is the primary dogma of monotheism, common to the three Abrahamic religions. The faithful take it as the supreme standard for their conception of the Creator. The Gnostic sees it as the deceit insinuated in the human mind by a monstrous alien, the demented pretender god who works against humanity and nature. Gnostics warned that the Archons are driven by envy ...

I agree wholeheartedly with Lash here. This idea and commandment has long struck me as suspicious. Why would an all-powerful being feel the need to insist it is the only god, and to further insist its subjects worship no one else? Something here smacks of envy, deceit and desperation. People usually only command and demand from a place of fear, worrying they will not get what they want, or they will get exposed. Is this Yahweh or Jehovah character the Demiurge, chief Archon, worrying he won't get his 'worship' (i.e. power and energy) from his subjects? If Yahweh, the vindictive and genocidal god of the Old Testament, were the only god in existence, of whom would he be jealous? Why is Yahweh constantly telling everyone that 'I am the One True God' and 'There is no other God but me' as though 'he' had to prove it or convince you? The Yahweh figure is highly discombobulated. As Laurent Guyénot points out, *"... even while claiming to be the Creator of the universe and humanity, Yahweh remains a national, chauvinist god; that is the basis for the dissonance between tribalism and universalism which has brought up the 'Jewish question' throughout the ages."*[68]

Lash further connects the deception of Yahweh, the nefarious and exclusionary idea of the 'chosen people' and the psychosis of the later movement which developed, Sabbatean-Frankism:[69]

For the ancient Hebrews ... the lie Yahweh tells them is that he, not Sophia, created the world. And they believed it. This inceptive Archontic deceit about the creation of the world mutated into a delusional narrative that uniquely possessed the Hebrews ... the false creator-god confers on his devotees the prevailed status of an elect, the Chosen People ... their mandate requires adherence to a hateful ideology of race supremacy that eventually morphs, after centuries, into a full-blown psychosis: the elected race does not merely serve the off-line deity, it becomes the presence of that deity in the world (the Sabbatean-Frankist heresy, 1666).

In chapter 4, I discuss the emergence of Sabbatean-Frankism and its monstrous influence on the NWO conspiracy today. For now, let's turn to modern-day Judaism to see how this foundational 'chosen people' myth is still running a significant amount of modern Jewish sects.

The Modern Day Chosen People

The chosen people program is not just some antiquated and irrelevant concept to today's Judaism. It continues to fuel current Jewish thinking. One example among many is Chabad Lubavitch, a powerful Jewish sect based in New York that is a key strand of how the Satanic Cult runs numerous governments from behind the scenes. A scandal erupted in January 2024 when police discovered a tunnel secretly dug into the side of a historic Brooklyn Chabad synagogue. Authorities arrested nine men who were trying to obstruct the police by filling the tunnel with cement.[70] Chabad Lubavitch were historically led by a "rebbe" (a word very similar to "rabbi" and with basically the same meaning). This Jewish religious website states that a "rebbe" must be a tzaddik:[71]

A Rebbe (Yiddish) is the spiritual leader in the Hasidic movement. It used to be a general honor title even before the beginning of the movement became over time almost exclusively identified with its Tzaddikim ... A rebbe is required to be a tzaddik or 'righteous man,' in the eyes of God.

Thus, we have a direct connection between a zaddik, a rebbe and a rabbi. The last Chabad leader or rebbe was an evil and influential man called Menachem Mendel Schneerson. Between 1951 and 1994, he transformed Chabad into one of the most widespread Jewish movements in the world. Schneerson was so well known that some of his followers promoted the idea he was the messiah. Since his death, there have been no more rebbes. Schneerson was a Cult agent and total supremacist. The opening quote to this chapter is his, where he clearly states that there are two types of soul, with the Jewish soul being holy and the gentile soul being Satanic. So, in his eyes, Jews were not only the ‘chosen ones’ and not only superior, but also actually possessed a different type of soul. Schneerson even took it further – he claimed non-Jews were born to serve Jews! He is quoted in the book *Jewish Fundamentalism in Israel* by Israel Shahak and Norton Mezvinsky:[72]

A Jew was not created as a means for some [other] purpose; he himself is the purpose, since the substance of all [divine] emanations was created only to serve the Jews. 'In the beginning God created the heavens and the earth' [Genesis 1:1] means that [the heavens and the earth] were created for the sake of the Jews, who are called the 'beginning.' This means everything, all developments, all discoveries, the creation, including the 'heavens and the earth' - are vanity compared to the Jews. The important things are the Jews, because they do not exist for any [other] aim; they themselves are [the divine] aim.

Many other rabbis have also promoted extremist Jewish supremacy, such as Rabbi Kook:[73]

In his book, Rachlevsky correctly claimed that Rabbi Kook, the Elder, the revered father of the messianic tendency of Jewish fundamentalism (who is featured in our book), said "The difference between a Jewish soul and souls of non-Jews – all of them in all different levels – is greater and deeper than the difference between a human soul and the souls of cattle."

There we have the reference to cattle, animals and subhumans. Do you notice something here? Think of all the destructive movements and governments in humanity’s history. A distinguishing feature has been the demonization of the 'other.' Either you're with us or against us. If you don't commit to joining our group, whatever it is (as defined by the group's leaders), then you're subhuman and not as worthy – you have to be our slave, or even worse, you have to be killed. This is, sadly, the natural corollary of such divisive thinking, and it crops up not just within Judaism but within many religions, groups, cults, nations, movements and governments. Shahak and Mezvinsky start their book by pointing out that many people can see the dangers inherent in Islamic fundamentalism and Christian fundamentalism, but fail to see the equally real dangers in Jewish fundamentalism. However, it's the same thing, the same mindset, just packaged differently.

Rabbi Kook's teachings were based upon the Lurianic Kabbalah, a school of Jewish mysticism that dominated Judaism from the late sixteenth to the early nineteenth century. Lurianic Kabbalah came from Isaac Luria, a key messianic rabbi who lived in the area of Galilee in Ottoman Syria, now Israel. One of the basic tenants of the Lurianic Kabbalah is the absolute superiority of the Jewish soul and body over the non-Jewish soul and body – the world was created solely for the sake of Jews, and the existence of non-Jews was secondary. There are still plenty of rabbis alive today, with large followings, pushing some version of this extremist and dangerous exclusivity. One example is Rabbi Michael Laitman who goes by the title of Bnei Baruch/Kabbalah Laam. He founded a Kabbalah association in the early 1990s which is estimated to have around 50,000 students in Israel and 150,000 around the world. In this presentation, he states that Israelis are like undercover commandos with a special mission. They have been sent to Earth to conquer it, and as they wake up to this supposed truth, they will also wake up to the method they need to employ to achieve their conquest. He states:[74]

We are aliens. We're coming from a different galaxy. We receive this ray of light, this awakening individually, and now we're gathering as groups, starting to prep ourselves to conquer Earth. That's the mission. How do we conquer it? We're also sent the method. We've been shown everything, gradually. We're being taught, not taught, but being trained, activated, and then that emotion and mind awakens in it. It's new to us, but it's coming from our original planet, and thanks to that original natural force we have, we will take over those living on Earth.

He receives a question from the audience:

Why are Israelis aliens? Why are they different? Doesn't everyone have to reach this purpose?[75]

He replies:[76][77][78]

I'm not talking about their external form, their body or their flesh and blood organs. I'm talking about their interior, which does not exist in other people in the world on Earth, but only in them. It's this inner software ... coming from the other world ... others don't have it ... What we're talking about now is the phase where those undercover agents have to connect together and organize themselves in order to conquer Earth.

Now we're waking up, coming from this wave from our home planet.

You have inner foundations, where this hard drive with the data is being revealed in you, and the ability to connect to that higher force, to that ray of light from the home planet, where you can feed on that, and get a feel from there. You work from the hard drive, through your external body, that operates ...

There are theories that Jews are not from this world, that they are from another planet. So I agree with that.

Laitman intersperses/covers this message with ideas of moving towards love and God as a correction, however his message is clearly rooted in the notion of Jewish supremacy. It is also very Archontic. What kind of source is feeding him the message that he and his group are special, superior and must conquer the rest of us? Messages broadcast from Saturn, perhaps? Messages from genocidal Yahweh/ Yaldabaoth or the Archons? Often the fundamentalism is hidden in Hebrew so that non-speakers cannot see it. In her article *"Why is the US Honoring a Racist Rabbi?"* activist Alison Weir writes:[79]

In Shahak's earlier book, Jewish Religion, Jewish History ... *he describes a 1962 book published in Israel in a bilingual edition. The Hebrew text was on one page, with the English translation on the facing page. Shahak describes one set of facing pages in which the Hebrew text of a major Jewish code of laws contained a command to exterminate Jewish infidels: "It is a duty to exterminate them with one's own hands." The English version on the facing page softened it to 'It is a duty to take active measures to destroy them.' The Hebrew page then went on to name which 'infidels' must be exterminated, adding 'may the name of the wicked rot.' Among them was Jesus of Nazareth. The facing page with the English translation failed to tell any of this.*

The Demiurge Chose Us!

There was a Satanic Cult existing before Judaism that appears to have seeded Judaism as a vehicle, without many good Jews even realizing. Adam Green (KnowMoreNews.org)[80] points out that the entirety of Jewish religious theology is based on the idea that there is just one god, their god, who has chosen them as his favored people above all others. This god just happened to promise them a nice piece of real estate in the Middle East. All of this is a very convenient story for the narrative originators. It should be noted that this 'chosen ones' ideology is not just part of the Talmud (the oral traditions and commentary) but is also part of the more foundational Torah (the first five books of the Hebrew Bible). These three examples are all from the Torah:

Watch out! You will have servants from all the nations. They will bow down to you. (Genesis 27:29)

If you will listen obediently to what I say and keep my covenant, and you will be my special treasure. You will be a kingdom of priests, a holy nation. (Exodus 19:5)

I and your people will be distinguished by this from all the other people on the face of the earth. (Exodus 33:16)

According to Green, the Jews invented their whole theology as a psychological operation (or theological operation) to firstly escape the Romans, whom they couldn't defeat militarily, and subsequently to conquer the world. Getting other cultures to worship your god and believe you are favored among all peoples on the earth is a pretty big accomplishment, or perhaps better put, the ultimate swindle. Later Abrahamic religions Christianity and Islam both contain some or all of the four elements of the redeemer complex, including the messianic element: a hero, prophet or 'son of god' who came (and in many versions will come again). Christianity and Islam are both Jewish spinoffs. The Torah makes up part of the Old Testament. Jesus was a Jew and so were all his apostles; in fact, Jesus' right hand man Peter was so Jewish that Paul (Saul) chastised him for being so attached to Jewish law that he wouldn't eat with gentiles.[81] The Islamic Koran, meanwhile, mentions Jesus repeatedly and stresses its respect for other 'religions of the book' (Judaism and Christianity). Christianity pushes its followers to worship the same god as the Jews, while Muhammad was written to have gone around smashing pagan idols in order to to promote monotheism – was he also following the directives of this same jealous insecure god? Lash believes that this horrific idea of exclusivity started with the Jewish Zaddikim before spreading out to infect the doctrines of the other two religions. At this point I must stress that there are many good Jews who reject the 'chosen ones' ideology, even if it is written in the Torah. Jewish extremists and fundamentalists do not represent Jewry as a whole.

The Gnostics were persecuted by Rome due to their much more complete understanding of life than standard Christianity. The Gnostics could see deeply into the nature of reality. They perceived that this world has been hijacked by a false god (Yaldabaoth) with a legion of demons (Archons) who operate via deception and perceptual manipulation. They could see that the Zaddikim had become infected with Archontic ideology that led to arrogance, exclusivity and supremacy, and would inevitably lead to theft, war and genocide. They could see that the redeemer complex was a grave imbalance which:

- Destroyed the masculine-feminine balance of the world by making 'God' solely masculine;
- Exalted suffering as a noble thing, thus covering up the victim-perpetrator bond;
- Disempowered people by promoting the idea they needed salvation (outside of themselves);
- Further disempowered people by promoting the idea that a messiah would come to save people (again, outside of themselves); and
- Introduced guilt and fear into the mix by pushing the idea that a final judgment would come for everyone.

Any kind of thinking that elevates one group above another creates an 'other' that can then be rejected and hated. History is replete with examples where the 'other' became second class citizens, deprived of rights, designated as less than fully human … and then stolen from, beaten, imprisoned and killed.

The Satanic Cult had now spread via Judaism. This was just the beginning.

Sources:

---

[57] https://muslimskeptic.com/2023/10/23/spiritual-mentor-ben-shapiro/

[58] The Invention of the Jewish People, pg. 313

[59] Ibid. pg. 151

[60] Not in His Image, pg. 16

[61] Ibid. pg. 17

[62] Ibid. pg. 67

[63] Ibid. pg. 20

[64] Not in His Image, pg. 116

[65] https://www.telegraph.co.uk/news/2024/01/22/carbon-footprint-homegrown-food-allotment-increase/

[66] https://www.dailymail.co.uk/health/article-4988992/Too-exercise-kill-white-man.html

[67] Not in His Image, pg.197

[68] https://vtforeignpolicy.com/2025/04/the-evil-of-yahweh-guyenot-is-right-alexis-isnt-even-wrong/

[69] Ibid. pg. 230-231

[70] https://abc7ny.com/chabad-headquarters-arrests-secret-tunnel-brooklyn/14301084/

[71] https://www.jewishvirtuallibrary.org/rebbe-vs-rabbi

[72] https://archive.org/stream/JewishHistoryJewishReligion_665/JewishFundamentalismInIsrael_djvu.txt

[73] Ibid.

[74] https://www.bitchute.com/video/o5ViafRLuRF0, starting at 15:36

[75] Ibid. 18:15

[76] Ibid. 21:05

[77] Ibid. 23:05

---

[78] Ibid. 25:30

[79] https://www.counterpunch.org/2014/04/07/why-is-the-us-honoring-a-racist-rabbi/

[80] https://odysee.com/@KnowMoreNews:1/Christianity-Psyop-Skrbina:d

[81] https://www.biblegateway.com/passage/?search=Galatians%202%3A11-21&version=GNT

CHAPTER 3: THE CULT CAPITALIZES ON USURY

"Yet Glafia's [the Global Mafia's] new monied merchant and banking elites wanted a world empire on a capitalist basis. One without negative interference by the Church or aristocrats, and without restrictions on usury, where they could invest and withdraw their mobile capital when and where they wanted, and bend all states to their wishes. Today, five hundred years later, we find ourselves in the End Game of that plan."

– Mees Baaijen[82]

"I am afraid the ordinary citizen will not like to be told that the banks can, and do, create money ... And they who control the credit of the nation direct the policy of Governments and hold in the hollow of their hands the destiny of the people."

– Reginald McKenna[83]

We next pick up the story around 1500 CE. During this time, the idea of private banking using a fractional reserve system became more entrenched and international than ever before in recorded human history. During this period, the Cult, via a segment of Jewish bankers and the Venetian Black Nobility, began to exploit Europe with usury. It is no exaggeration to say that the idea of fractional reserve banking is one of the most deceptive to ever have been conjured; the amount of damage and enslavement it has caused worldwide has been truly astronomical.

The NWO is ruled by the international banking cartel, especially the Rothschild and Rockefeller families. The bankers figured out they could accrue far more power by controlling the money supply (via having a monopoly over the issuance of currency and credit) than by sitting upon a nation's figurative throne, whether as a king, dictator, president or prime minister. The power to control how much money circulates in society is the same power to decide what that money is worth – and is also the very same power to create booms and busts, including recessions and depressions. By establishing government-linked and -sanctioned central banks in many countries around the world, the international bankers have deceived and ruled the rest of the population for centuries, consolidating their property, wealth and power while impoverishing everyone else.

The scam works like this. Every loan a bank makes is not backed by anything. The bank doesn't lend money it already has, as you might imagine. When a loan occurs, the money springs into existence at the moment a 'borrower' signs the document. In essence, the bank is not really 'loaning' money (since it never had it in the first place) and the borrower is not really 'borrowing' money (since you can't borrow something that someone does not have to give you). A new accounting or ledger entry is

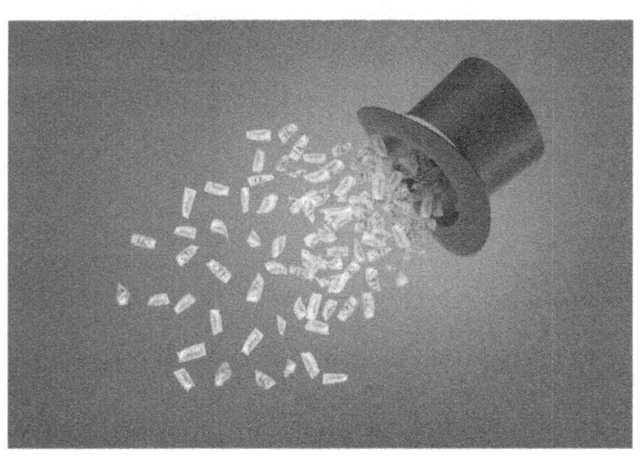

Image #6: modern banking = money out of nothing

made, signifying that the 'borrower' is to repay the amount of money that was just freshly created. Whatever amount is borrowed is actually not borrowed but rather created out of thin air and added to the existing money supply of society.

However, that is not all. Every time one of these fraudulent 'loans' occurs, the bank charges interest, so the loan must be repaid with interest. That interest has to come from the existing money supply of society, which means that for every loan cycle (loan created and repaid), already existing money is siphoned out of the rest of society and into the banks. The banks have created a system where it is a mathematical certainty that they will end up every year with more and more of the existing money supply of society – all by 'lending' out money that doesn't really exist.

Image #7: modern banking is Archontic deception. At the time of borrowing, the bank doesn't lend you anything. The money springs into existence and gets added to the money supply – but you have to pay interest on top when you repay

This is standard practice of banks around the world. They are able to get away with this trick in part because of their unholy alliance with government. The government endorses this system, declares the currency legal tender and allows this kind of 'lending' to occur. This is why in first world nations we have quasi-governmental central banks (The Federal Reserve, The Bank of England, The Reserve Bank of Australia, etc.) which have government sponsorship and protection but which nonetheless are private institutions not answerable to the head of state in the country. Their 'funny money' is not real money of intrinsic value but, separated from a gold or silver standard, is just paper money. If you read it closely, it is actually a "promise to pay" or an IOU, which shows that it is not real money, because real money would constitute payment in and of itself, and would not be a promise to pay! Guido Preparata writes:[84]

For bankers, the trick was (1) to make people accept the bank notes as if they were gold, (2) to possess the metal itself, (3) to hide it in vaults, and (4) to withdraw it gradually from circulation ... Thereafter, the name of the game was to corner the supply of gold and monopolize the circulation of money. He who controlled the money, controlled the system itself; its activity, its politics, its arts, and its sciences. Everything.

To tie back in to the previous chapter – how much more Archontic and deceptive can you get than lending out what you don't have and simultaneously making money on the deal? The American senator from Ohio and Rothschild protégé, John Sherman, was quoted by the Rothschilds in their letter to a New York banker on June 25th 1863 in support of the then proposed National Banking Act which was an early Rothschild plan to establish a central bank in America:[85]

The few who can understand the system will either be so interested in its profits, or so dependent on its favors, that there will be no opposition from that class, while on the other hand, the great body of the people, mentally incapable of comprehending the tremendous advantages that capital derives from the system, will bear its burdens without complaint, and perhaps without even suspecting that the system is inimical to their interest.

Now, to return to the 1500s … private central banking was still in its infancy, but those who knew the trick of fractional reserve lending were eager to expand their domain and bring all areas and city-states under their control. However, they had quite a few obstacles. One of the biggest ones was religion. Both Christianity and Islam forbid usury, i.e. the lending of money with interest. It is a testament to just how deeply we have been brainwashed to realize that the word 'usury' itself is so rare that the average person hasn't heard it, or if they have, doesn't know its meaning. Yet, the concept this word represents has enslaved the entire world to the bankers, or as I prefer to call them, the banksters. Although mainstream, organized religion has promulgated belief systems which have limited humanity, they also got some things right. They saw how the power to charge interest on money can be turned into the power to control and enslave. Like everything, there are many sides to this issue; it is understandable that those who have money would like to be compensated in some way for lending out their money (when they have it – not the central banking 'loans' out of thin air) since they lose the opportunity to use it during the period of repayment and they risk not getting repaid. Nonetheless, it is clear that the current 'loans out thin air' system, combined with usury, is an incredibly destructive instrument.

While Christianity and Islam forbid usury, Judaism did not, at least in the area of Jews lending to non-Jews. This is a highly significant fact, because it allowed Jews to take advantage of their religious freedom in an era when people weren't openly atheist or non-religious to move into the banking industry and charge interest on loans to non-Jews.

So, in Europe, the would-be bankers had opposition from the dominant religion, the Catholic Church. According to Mees Baaijen, author of *The Predators vs. The People*, they also had opposition from the aristocracy. What happened is that two city-states in Italy, Genoa and Venice, rose to power, and within those city-states, a new class of capitalist oligarchs rose to power. Thus, to be the most powerful class in the world's most powerful cities spelt the beginning of an international, worldwide power. Baaijen coined the term 'Glafia' as a portmanteau of 'Global Mafia' to describe the NWO international ruling class, and uses it frequently throughout his book:[86]

The 15th and 16th century marked the transition from feudalism to capitalism in Europe. In feudalism there were two, often competing, power centers: the Catholic Church and the Aristocracy. Merchants and money lenders existed but had no or little political power. By contrast, in Italian city-states like Genoa and Venice, which called themselves Republics, a new elite of capitalist oligarchs (merchants and bankers) was holding most political and economic power. During their global domination project, Glafia would gradually outsmart and incorporate both the Catholic Church and the old European aristocracy.

Baaijen details how the Venetians were descendants of the Phoenicians (Venetian = Phoenician), an old Semitic civilization (based in modern-day Lebanon) famous for its seafaring technology and its merchants. Due to their shipmaking and navigational ability, they ruled the Mediterranean and created an expansive maritime trade network that lasted over a millennium. It seems the Venetians inherited the Phoenician sailing and trading prowess. The Phoenicians, who were in turn descendants of or also known as the

Canaanites, worshipped a god called Baal or Moloch (or Molech – there are various spellings) who demanded child sacrifice and consumed babies. Hence, we have another connection here to the Satanic Cult. There are many references to Canaan in the Old Testament – in the history that was given to the Jews at Alexandria in 270 BC. Baaijen describes how many Jews ended up in Venice, became merchants and began to accumulate lots of power. They joined forces with the Genoese bankers and Venetian oligarchs, which have also been called the 'Venetian black nobility.' Edward Morgan writes:[87]

The "Black Nobility" are/were the oligarchic families of Venice and Genoa, Italy, who in the 12th century held the privileged trading rights (monopolies). The first of three crusades, from 1063 to 1123, established the power of the Venetian Black Nobility and solidified the power of the wealthy ruling class. The Black Nobility aristocracy achieved complete control over Venice in 1171, when the appointment of the Doge was transferred to what was known as the Great Council, which consisted of members of the commercial aristocracy (among them the infamous de'Medici family). Venice has remained in their hands ever since, but the power and influence of the Venetian Black Nobility extends far beyond its borders, and today it is felt in every corner of the globe. (Don't forget, our modern banking system originated in Italy.)

The Doge of Venice was the highest authority in the Republic of Venice, which lasted from 697 CE to 1797 CE. The word 'doge' is derived from the Latin 'dux' meaning leader. The Doge, elected for life, was both the head of state and head of the Venetian oligarchy. The Black Nobility was so-called apparently because of their willingness to use blackmail, kidnapping, rape, torture and assassination to quell any uprising against their monopolies or their base of power. Morgan states that the important Black Nobility families today are:

- House of Bernadotte, Sweden
- House of Bourbon, France
- House of Braganza, Portugal
- House of Grimaldi, Monaco
- House of Guelph, Britain (the most important one)
- House of Habsburg, Austria
- House of Hanover, Germany (the second most important one)
- House of Hohenzollern, Germany
- House of Karadjordjevic, Yugoslavia (former)
- House of Liechtenstein, Liechtenstein
- House of Nassau, Luxembourg
- House of Oldenburg, Denmark
- House of Orange, Netherlands
- House of Savoy, Italy
- House of Wettin, Belgium
- House of Wittelsbach, Germany
- House of Württemberg, Germany
- House of Zogu, Albania
- All the families you will find on the Windsor family tree

These are the old wealthy European families, many of which are part of European 'royal' bloodlines, and, in addition to the American families, form the large majority of the NWO cabal. Wealthy Jews began intermarrying; they married into royal European bloodlines. In the 1500s, significant merging of power occurred. The Venetian oligarchs were very familiar with the Jews due to their shared ancestry with the Phoenicians and also because the Jews, with all their capital and networks, assisted in the economic administration of the Venetian Empire, particularly after their expulsion in 1492 from Spain and later from Portugal. The trade of Venice became overwhelmingly concentrated in the hands of the Jews. Baaijen writes:[88]

With the participation of the ex-Iberian Jews, lots of capital, expertise and networks could be added to the project. The Venetians had already a longstanding working relationship with 'their' Jews, who in the 16th century were the major brokers of bills of exchange in the Venetian empire. The Venetians, while running a successful empire, controlled the flows of bullion (silver and gold) on a European level. Both had extensive international networks, not only for trade, but also for intelligence. Both were extremely ambitious, and the Jews naturally wanted to take revenge on Spain, where they had gained, and then lost, their wealthy positions through substantial control over finances, academia, the church, and government. They were now eagerly looking for new opportunities. Naturally the Venetians and Jews joined forces, although the evidence is circumstantial. The Venetian-Jewish coalition had the motive, the means and the opportunity, and with hindsight, we conclude that they did indeed ally and become uniquely successful. The early Jewish participation led to the large-scale international engagement of many elite Jews in the global domination project. In a much later stage, that also lead to the establishment of the Zionist state of Israel.

He then shares an example of a particular family, the Warburgs:[89]

Sometime after 1492, a very wealthy Sephardic family, led by Anselmo and Abraham de Palenzuela (later called Del Banco), arrived in Venice from Spain. In 1513, they were granted a charter by the Venetian Republic permitting the lending of money with interest. They soon left for Bologna and then Germany, where they adopted the name Warburg (and Kassel in another line). They established a very important German banking house, from some point in the 19th century in association with the Rothschilds. Already in 1619, the Bank of Hamburg had been established, in which more than forty Jewish families took shares. After the Thirty Years' War (which had started in 1618, and severely debilitated the Habsburg Empire, the enemy of Venice), the Warburgs moved to Altona near Hamburg. In the 20th century, the brothers Max and Paul Warburg became essential spiders in Glafia's web ...

Indeed, it was James Paul Warburg, whose family is one of the secret owners of the Federal Reserve, who said that *"We shall have World Government, whether or not we like it. The only question is whether World Government will be achieved by conquest or consent"* before a United States Senate Subcommittee on February 17th 1950.[90]

Baaijen does a great job of telling the story of how this oligarchical bankster ruling class acquired the power to mold laws in their region to their liking, to give themselves maximum ability to extract wealth through predatory lending and other exploitative capitalistic tricks. When they perceived that they couldn't control the rulers or the rules in their area, they had the vision to realize they needed to set up base in another area or country where the laws would be more favorable. They grew too big for one city or one country, so began to set their sights on continental – and world – domination. They wanted to run a world empire based on moneylending (which they called 'capitalism') without negative interference by the Church or the aristocracy, and without restrictions on usury. They wanted to invest and divest their mobile capital as they saw fit, anywhere in the world. Consequently, they migrated from Italy to Spain, making it their new base. Their moneylending and other activities became the reason why Spain rose to great heights and created an Empire. However, once Spain outlived its usefulness for them, they migrated further up the coast to Holland, making it their new base. Then, once Holland became unsuitable for

their business, they moved on to England … then to the USA. Baaijen quotes an anonymous source who said *"The rise of the Dutch can only be explained by the decline of Venice"* and also quotes Karl Marx:[91]

With the national debt arose an international credit system ... Thus the villainies of the Venetian thieving system formed one of the secret bases of the capital-wealth of Holland to whom Venice in her decadence lent large sums of money. So was it with Holland and England. By the beginning of the 18th century ... Holland had ceased to be the nation preponderant in commerce and industry. One of its main lines of business, therefore, [became] the lending out of enormous amounts of capital, especially to its great rival England ...

[And the] same thing is going on to-day [1860s] between England and the United States.

In conclusion, those who control the money control the world. This is summed up in a quote attributed to Napoleon Bonaparte: *"When a government is dependent upon bankers for money, they and not the leaders of the government control the situation."*[92]

We can scc that it was around this period of the late 15th century and early 16th century when an alliance started to coalesce that became the basis for the international NWO ruling class of today. This alliance was originally between the Jews and the rich, oligarchical banking families of Genoa and Venice, but later spread throughout Europe to include other royal bloodlines and banking families, not just Italian ones. As their center of operations moved from Italy, to Spain, to Holland, to England – and then across the ocean to America – this alliance became the Anglo-American NWO which has colonized, plundered and dominated the entire world. However, for at least 500 years, its roots have been firmly connected with a certain group Jewish bankers and Jewish oligarchs whose power over the direction of the NWO agenda has been mammoth. In the next chapter, we will see how sects of the 'chosen people' Cult that began thousands of years ago in the Middle East further developed. These sects cemented their power in Europe, the strongest and richest continent during the centuries from 1500 to 1900, and took even more concrete steps in laying the foundation for world domination.

Sources

---

[82] The Predators vs. The People, pg. 51

[83] As quoted by Carroll Quigley in *Tragedy and Hope*, pg. 325

[84] Conjuring Hitler, pp. 142-43

[85] Money! Questions and Answers (Royal Oak: The National Union for Social Justice, 1936), Rev. Charles Coughlin, pg. 171

[86] The Predators vs. The People, pg. 50

[87] https://themillenniumreport.com/2019/01/who-are-the-black-nobility/

[88] The Predators vs. The People, pg. 46

[89] Ibid. pg. 49

[90] https://en.wikisource.org/wiki/James_Warburg_before_the_Subcommittee_on_Revision_of_the_United_Nations_Charter

[91] Karl Marx (1818-1883), Das Kapital, https://www.marxists.org/archive/marx/works/1867-c1/ch31.htm

[92] https://quotepark.com/quotes/1743745-napoleon-i-of-france-money-has-no-motherland-financiers-are-without-pa/

CHAPTER 4: SALVATION THROUGH SIN: THE CULT OF THE SABBATEAN-FRANKISTS

"The anomaly of Jewish theocracy triggered a shockwave that escalated for centuries, destined to inflict deleterious effects upon the entire world. The wave finally broke in the seventeenth century due to a little known, extremely bizarre event, the apostasy of Sabbatai Zevi. At that moment the god-complex inherent to Jewish theocracy collapsed, and out of its ruins arose another complex. In the aftermath of the Sabbatean-Frankist heresy, as scholars call it, anticipation of the messianic king who would raise the Hebrews to lordship over all nations utterly disintegrated. Strangely, this psychotic breakdown in Jewish faith aggravated the ancient anomaly of Israelite kingship so that it resurged in a different form. After centuries of awaiting the messiah, the Chosen People assigned to themselves the status of the exclusive messianic force in the world – and that was to be a superhuman status."

– John Lamb Lash[93]

"The psychology of the radical Sabbateans was utterly paradoxical ... true faith must always be concealed ... this theme of a secret, hidden, or occult identity became part of this evolving religious philosophy ... like the true faith, the true act was concealed, for only through concealment could it negate the falsehood of what is

explicit. Through a revolution of values, what was formerly sacred became profane and what was formerly profane had become sacred."

– Robert Sepehr[94]

"Sabbatian-Frankism, Satanism, human sacrifice religions of Sumer and Babylon fuse into one force within the Hidden Hand and stalk and control the corridors of global power."

– David Icke[95]

We will pick up the thread of the 'chosen ones' in the next century, the 1600s, when a highly interesting dual phenomenon occurred: two self-proclaimed 'messiahs' arose. The first was in the Middle East. His name was Sabbatai Zevi (also spelt many ways such as "Shabbetai" and "Sevi," "Zvi" or "Tzvi") and he attracted over one million followers in his lifetime. At the time (mid-17th century), this was around half the world's Jewish population, so to say this was a giant occurrence in the history of Judaism would be a massive understatement. His followers were called Sabbateans. Note that the words Sabbatai, Sabbath, Shabbat (Hebrew for Sabbath), Sabbatean and Saturday all etymologically stem from the same root: Saturn, god of time, harvest, tyranny and death. Saturn in turn is connected to Satan, the opposer. None of this is coincidence.

Sabbatai Zevi was a Turkish mystic and ordained rabbi. He was reportedly extremely charming and charismatic as he simultaneously suffered from mental illness. Robert Sepehr in *1666 Redemption Through Sin* writes that *"Sabbatai showed signs of what modern scholars would likely call manic-depressive psychosis ... on the other hand, some scholars and modern day followers ... have argued that his behavior did not point to psychosis, but rather, was simply what one should expect from ... a religious mystic, such as a Sufi:*

Image #11: Sabbatai Zevi, the manic-depressive or even psychotic charlatan who claimed he was the 'messiah' and that good was evil and evil was good. He had visions of leading the Jews to the 'holy land' and building the Temple at Jerusalem

meditative chanting, prayer-trance, dancing, etc."[96] The website JewishHistory.org says Zevi *"had various flights of mood and long episodes of depressions. He practiced ascetic ways, fasting for weeks on end, only drinking water. He practiced self-flagellation, which was a common practice among the Shiite Muslims who frequented his part of the world. He would act like a hermit and go out to lonely places, like forests. He would immerse himself in ritual baths 20 or 30 times a day ... in light of the messianic expectations of 1648, this triggered in his mind the idea that he could be the Messiah. In his dreams, he had an apocalyptic vision of himself actually taking revenge against the Cossacks for their terrible mistreatment of the Jews. He had dreams of leading the Jewish people to the holy land, rebuilding the city of Jerusalem and the Temple."*[97] In 1666, Zevi abolished the fasting days commemorating the destruction of the First and Second Temples, saying that since the messiah (himself) had come, the Temple in Jerusalem would be rebuilt the next year. It is here we can find some of the roots of the current Zionist fixation on capturing Jerusalem and building the Third Temple which will be discussed later in this book (see chapter 19).

Rabbi Marvin Antelman in *To Eliminate the Opiate Volume 2*[98] wrote that *"The Illuminati has a kind of precursor, known as the "Sabbatian" movement. Historically, Sabbatians have been involved in radical, and Masonic-type movements. Others were prominent in finance in nineteenth century Europe. Most known Sabbatians live in Turkey, although there are undoubtedly followers of the cult elsewhere. They keep a very low profile. Perhaps one reason is that they practice wife swapping with the deliberate intent of creating "illegitimate" offspring. It is their goal to produce from these illicit unions the reincarnation of the founder of their cult, Messianic pretender Shabbetai Zvi ... [who] died in Albania three hundred years ago after starting a movement that perverted everything Judaism stood for."*

Antelman is a very well-known source for the topic of Sabbatai Zevi, his followers the Sabbateans and his successor Jacob Frank. Antelman was an American rabbi who was trying to alert people about the way Judaism had been overtaken by a radical cult. Being an orthodox Jew and a rabbi, he had strict dogmatic views about morality and life, and I certainly don't agree with everything he said, especially his negative view of Gnosticism and the fact he was a self-professed avid Zionist. However, he was earnest in exposing what he saw as the denigration of Judaism; he even led a Supreme Rabbinical

Council as Chief Justice in 1976 that excommunicated Jew Henry Kissinger.[99] Kissinger, for those who don't know, was a key Cult operative, NWO insider, Bilderberg Group steering committee member and Satanist who ran US foreign policy for decades, especially during the Nixon Administration years. He was a war criminal responsible for untold thousands of deaths due to US foreign meddling in other nations. He directed coups, assassinations and wars, such as the famous Chile coup of 1973 that installed dictator Pinochet. Kissinger authored the nefarious NSSM 2000 in 1974 that called for depopulation in developing nations as part of 'US interest,' although it would be better understood as the NWO interest, since the USA has long been a tool to bring about the NWO. Kissinger was not just any old insider but, as I wrote about in my book *The International Satanic Network Exposed*, was actually considered the highest ranking (human) member of the worldwide Satanic network, even higher than the Rockefellers, due to his ability to coldly calculate and strategically plan ahead. Hence, Antelman was doing something to eradicate what he saw as the subversive figures within Judaism.

Returning to Sabbatai Zevi, the reason he became such an important historical figure is that he violated numerous Jewish religious laws, including those relating to dietary restriction and sexual conduct. Zevi's behavior got him kicked out of Smyrna around 1650, and he wandered for years around the Mediterranean and Middle East until 1965 when he met Nathan of Gaza. Nathan was the rabbi who persuaded him that he was indeed the messiah to usher in a new age. Zevi followed the Jewish Kabbalah (and within it the Zohar) not the Torah nor Talmud. The Kabbalah places great emphasis on the supernatural relationship between events and time, as well as the importance and hidden meaning of numbers. The Kabbalah is full of gematria, the study and interpretation of the numerical value of words and verses. Influenced by this, Zevi chose the year of 1666 to proclaim that he was the messiah.

Zevi's philosophy was that, since he was the messiah, he and everyone else were now living in 'messianic times' which meant that the normal rules didn't apply. In other words, Sabbatai and his followers reasoned that because they were now in the time of the great messianic revolution, all bets were off; they freely violated Jewish laws and customs. In fact, everything was reversed: the holy became wicked, the wicked became holy and fasts became feasts. Zevi not only promoted disobeying Jewish religious dietary laws, which to non-Jews may seem like a relatively minor issue, but he and his followers engaged in religious sexual orgies and wife sharing or swapping. They were accused of ritual incest. According to Jerry Rabow, author of *50 Jewish Messiahs*, Sabbatai's prayer was *"praised be he who permits the forbidden."*[100] Zevi and the Sabbateans believed that whenever you sinned, you used up all the evil in the world, and thus hastened the arrival of the messiah. This seems utterly batshit crazy and nothing more than an excuse to be evil (psychology shows that the human mind is excellent at inventing reasons or excuses to justify what it desires to do anyway), but apparently they deluded themselves with this idea. This source states that several hundred *"12-year-old children were married to each other 'in order to incarnate the rest of the yet unborn souls in accordance with the Kabbalistic superstition and to remove the last obstacle to the messianic times.' Sceptical rabbis were expelled."*[101] Sepehr writes that *"it is thought by some scholars that Zevi had deeper connections with the Bektashi Sufi order. Some similarities between the Sabbatean Donmeh and Bektashi practice include the deliberate violation of kashrut/halal, ritualistic group sex or wife swapping, ecstatic singing or chanting, mystical Kabbalah, and belief in an occult (hidden) reading of Torah/Quran."*[102] I will introduce the concept of the Donmeh shortly. All the writers I have seen covering this topic simply talk about Zevi committing adultery, and leave it at that. However, if we are to be completely fair here, we need to look at the question of consent. If we look at this issue from a libertarian perspective, without any prudishness or dogma, there is nothing inherently or morally wrong with an orgy, as long as everyone involved is a consenting adult. It is people associating freely exploring their sexual energy. However, problems immediately arise when minors are involved (who cannot legally give consent) since then the line is crossed into pedophilia, or when incest occurs, or when any participant is coerced and/or when Satanic elements are introduced, such as torture, abuse and sacrifice. It is unclear to what degree these things were happening with Zevi, but with his successor Jacob Frank, who we will get to shortly, the evidence is damning that all of these abusive, coercive and Satanic elements were exactly what was happening. The Satanic Cult is all about the misuse of sexual energy and using ritual for black magical rather than white magical purposes.

Zevi had strong support among the Jewish people, but the leading rabbis of Jerusalem didn't believe his messianic claims, telling him to get out of the city or be excommunicated. He returned to Türkiye (then the Ottoman Empire) where news of his claim had travelled ahead of him and had already reached the Sultan. The story goes that the Sultan eventually gave him an ultimatum – "your head or the turban" – meaning that Zevi had to take the turban (i.e. convert to

Islam) or be killed. Zevi chose the turban. Amazingly enough, his number one advocate Nathan managed to spin this conversion in such a way that Zevi didn't lose all his followers, although many did stop following him in dismay and disgust. What did Nathan say? To understand that, you have to understand some core Kabbalistic concepts. One such concept is that the material world contains divine sparks of light trapped within physicality. Nathan explained that Zevi's conversion represented the descent into the dense physical world (the 'klippotic realm') to reclaim the lost sparks to repair the world.

The other way he kept his followers was based on the concept of outward but not inward conversion. Many who continued to be loyal to Zevi also converted to Islam while secretly maintaining their Jewish identity and customs. This practice of hiding the real or true inside, while displaying the fake or false on the outside, is a key Cult theme. I cannot stress enough how extremely important this theme is; it explains the Cult modus operandi. It's a strategy relying on covert stealth rather than overt assault for its means of conquest. This exact theme underpins the world's secret societies, such as the Order of the Illuminati (which we will get to soon) and Freemasonry, where the true aims, agendas and motivations of the inner circles are not revealed to outsiders, or even to lower initiates, but only known to those at the very highest levels. The nefarious agenda is clothed in pretty, gaudy and noble-sounding language on the outside so as to disguise the evil within. It's also the exact same theme which forms the foundation of the UN Agenda 2030 manmade climate change hoax that trumpets propaganda about sustainability and saving the planet while secretly plotting to control everyone by corralling them into 15-minute Smart Cities or prisons.

Those followers who did convert to Islam were called 'Donmeh' from a Turkish word meaning 'to turn.' Sabbateanism arose not that long after the Inquisition of 1478, when many Western European Jews from places like Spain and Portugal (called 'marranos' or 'conversos') were forced to convert to Christianity. It is here that the concept of the 'crypto-Jew' or hidden Jew arose. This helps to explain why many Jews accepted Zevi's conversion, since they had already been used to living double lives as religious Jews on the inside and Christians on the outside, having to hide their identity to survive. Interestingly enough, it was crypto-Jew Ignatius of Loyola, the man who founded the Jesuit Order (Society of Jesus), who was also a member of another secret society called the 'Alumbrados' that is Spanish for the 'illuminated ones.' The Alumbrados were the forerunners to the Order of the Illuminati discussed next chapter. This explains why both the Jesuits and Zionists are implicated in the NWO conspiracies today – they spring from a similar source, and have both been Cult creations from the start.

After Zevi died in 1676, many Sabbatean sects flourished, continuing to practice religious sexual orgies, wife swapping and incest. To understand what prompted this behavior, we have to again look at the religious texts and beliefs they were following for clues. Sepehr writes that the Sabbatean sects *"said that the violation of the Torah had become its fulfillment, which they illustrated by the example of a grain of wheat that rots in the earth. In other words, just as a grain of wheat must rot in the earth before it can sprout, so the deeds of the believers must become truly rotten before they could germinate the redemption. This metaphor, which appears to have been extremely popular, converted the whole of sectarian Sabbatean psychology in a nutshell: in the period of transition, while the redemption was still in a state of concealment, the Torah in its explicit form must be denied, for only thus could it too become concealed and ultimately 'renewed.'''*[103] Redemption through wickedness, salvation through sin – it's the same deluded idea I exposed above: an excuse to be evil. Although he had many followers, Zevi died as a reviled figure to orthodox Jews, who considered him an apostate and fake messiah. The Sabbateans' belief in the holiness of sin was an affront to the average Jew. However, even the outlandish and extreme behavior of the Sabbateans was to be dwarfed by who and what was to come next. Jacob Frank, and his interpretation which became known as Frankism, took the 'salvation through sin' idea to the next level.

Jacob Frank

Born in Poland in 1726, fifty years after Zevi's death, Jacob Frank extended Zevi's paradoxical teaching that the messianic age allowed adherents to break religious laws. However, while Zevi had mostly taught that breaking the rules was permitted, Frank went beyond that and taught that breaking the rules was obligated. According to Frank, engaging in debauchery and sin was the path to redemption. It was a necessity. It was therapeutic. It was purification through transgression. And, what's more, it would hasten the coming of the messiah. According to Antelman, Frank urged his followers to sin, reasoning that if salvation could be gotten through purity, it could also be achieved through sin. This was based on a passage from the Talmud which stated that the Messiah would come only in an age that was completely guilty or completely innocent (Sanhedrin 98a). The Frankists reasoned that 'since we cannot all be saints, let us all be sinners.' This is yet another example among gazillions of how a person can justify almost any desire or behavior – which they want

Image #12: Jacob Frank, Satanist and psychopath extraordinaire, taught that one could only truly be free by committing the most wicked acts of all

to do anyway no matter what – frequently using religious scripture as some sort of authority or excuse.

Just as Zevi had done earlier, Frank convinced his followers that the only way for their special form of Judaism to survive was if they concealed their true identity. While Zevi outwardly became a Muslim, Frank outwardly became a Christian. Antelman writes that the "*Donmeh in Turkey officially converted to Islam in 1683, and the*

Frankists in Europe to Catholicism in 1759. However, their conversion to these religions was for the purpose of imitating the Sabbatian role models as well as for subverting and destroying these faiths."[104] Frank had encountered the Donmeh earlier in his life while he traveling as a salesman in Türkiye.

Frank claimed he was both the reincarnation of Zevi and the biblical Jewish patriarch Jacob. According to Antelman, Frank was thrown into prison for 13 years in Poland from 1760 to 1773 *"because it was discovered that the Godhead of the Frankist cult was not the Trinity, but included members of the sect."*[105] Antelman believed that Frank had, in fact, declared himself a god or at least thought of himself as a god due to a special Judaic coin he found where Frank had inscribed his own name (the name or nickname Dobrushka he had taken when he was released from prison) alongside three others – Elijah the Prophet, Sabbatai Zevi and Rabbi Jonathan Eibeschutz – as part of a Frankist "Quaternary" not Trinity. In Jewish legend, the original Hebrew coin was inscribed with Abraham, Sarah, Isaac and Rebecca.

Frank was not just an extremist but a nihilist. He sought to turn everything upside down and indulge in every single thing that was forbidden, immoral, wrong and sinful. As Sepehr writes, *"According to Frank, one had to free oneself of all laws, conventions and religions, to adopt every conceivable attitude and to reject it, and so follow one's leader step by step into the abyss. The annihilation of every religion and positive system of beliefs was the true way he expected his believers to follow. Jacob Frank taught that in order to ascend one must first descend ... Frank went on to explain that the descent into the abyss required not only the rejection of all religions and conventions, but also the commission of strange acts, which in turn demanded voluntary abasement, so that libertinism (disregard of authority), and the state of utter shamelessness, which led to a tikkum (fixing/rectification) of the soul, became one and the same thing."*[106]

For Frank, there was seemingly no act that he wouldn't do. The Frankists performed public burnings of the Talmud; Antleman wrote that thousands of books of the Talmud were burned in the city of Kaminetz on the last day of the Hebrew month Marach Shevan (Cheshvan) in 1757. He also said that the Frankists enticed women to leave their husbands and to join their orgies, thus breaking up families. Frank slept with his followers and even his own daughter, Eve Frank, who served as a central figure in the sexual Satanic rituals the Frankists participated in. He pimped her out to attract more followers to his cult. He insisted that incest, rape, child sacrifice and the drinking of blood were perfectly acceptable and necessary religious rituals. Frank was all about following the Kabbalah not the Talmud. Rabbi Hayyim Samuel Jacob Falk was Frank's father-in-law since he was the father of one of Jacob Frank's wives; Falk was the Baal Shem of London (in Judaism, the title of Baal Shem is bestowed upon men who allegedly cured people and 'worked wonders' – such as performing exorcisms). Another writer on the topic of Jacob Frank was Gershom Scholem, an Israeli philosopher and historian who was regarded as the founder of modern academic study of the Kabbalah and the first professor of Jewish mysticism at the Hebrew University of Jerusalem. Scholem wrote that Frank was a thoroughly corrupt and degenerate man who *"will always be remembered as one of the most frightening phenomena in the whole of Jewish history."*[107] He also wrote:[108]

The nihilistic mystic descends into the abyss in which the freedom of living things is born; he passes through all the embodiments and forms that come his way, committing himself to none; and not content with rejecting and abrogating all values and laws, he tramples them underfoot and desecrates them, in order to attain the elixir of Life ... from the standpoint of the community and its institutions, such mysticism should have been regarded as demonic possession. And it is indicative of one of the enormous tensions that run through the history of Judaism that this most destructive of all visions should have been formulated in its most unrestrained form by one who rebelled against the Jewish law and broke away from Judaism.

Frank perfectly fit the definition of a psychopath and Satanist – a person with little to no empathy for the wellbeing of others, who could be regarded as demonically possessed and who believed it was right, and necessary, to engage in rituals involving rape, blood drinking and human sacrifice. This exact kind of personality repeats itself time and again in the inner circle of the NWO. This is the mindset of the people at the very highest level who run the world. This is why those who claim the NWO is being run by Jews are only half right. The Cult is first and foremost Satanic, not Jewish. The idea of salvation through sin is Satanic. The idea of inverting traditional morals is Satanic. Satanism inverts. For the Sabbatean-Frankists, shamelessness is holy, but not in the good way of shedding unnecessary shame, but of shedding all shame, including healthy shame. This is equivalent to shedding all empathy and compassion, so that you don't feel any compunction, scruples or remorse in carrying out the most evil acts imaginable, including raping children and murdering people. It's the anything goes mentality; the more perverted, the more esteemed within the ranks of Satanism.

The Cult of Sabbatean-Frankism

The figures of Sabbatai Zevi and Jacob Frank played a tremendous part in hijacking traditional Judaism, taking it in a radically different direction by preaching salvation through sin and holiness via depravity. Their form of 'Judaism' was so extreme that it bears little resemblance to what orthodox Jews practiced at the time, although as discussed in the first three chapters, the seed of Judaism was still within their teachings – the idea of a messiah and the idea of salvation or redemption. Without these sine qua non elements, these two men could not have amassed the followers they did. What propped them up was the belief that a 'messiah' would come who would in some way 'redeem' those who believed in him. The belief in a coming messiah is still a massive part of Judaism today, and hence the scam continues (and ditto for Christianity whose messiah has come but 'through whom' Christians must go for 'salvation'). Looking outside to someone or something to save you necessarily means absolving yourself of some responsibility and giving away some (or much) of your power, no matter how you twist it. A hallmark of any cult, whether the cult of Sabbatean-Frankism or any other, includes the worship and deification of its leader(s) as superhuman. Scholem proposed that there were five distinguishing elements that made one into a Sabbatean, which were the apostasy of the messiah, the rejection of the standard Torah (and acceptance of a mystical Torah called the Torah of Atzilut), the understanding that the 'God of Israel' was not the Supreme Being/Creator, that 'God' could take a human form (which allows for cult leaders to be incarnated as God) and finally that the follower must not appear to be as he really is. This last element was what authorized the Sabbatean-Frankists to live double lives by hiding their true identities and motivations. This will become an extremely important point as we move on to the next chapter to explore the rise of the Rothschild family who met – and funded – Jacob Frank when he moved to Germany in the last years of his life. It is no coincidence that the Rothschilds, the principal NWO banking and bloodline family who have largely ruled the world since their ascent in the late 1700s, would be associated with Frank and his Satanic ways.

While there doesn't appear to be a direct connection between the warlike Khazars and the stealthy Sabbateans, it is curious that both the Khazars and the Sabbateans chose Judaism as a kind of shield – for the Khazars, as a defensive tactic to avoid getting invaded, and for the Sabbateans, as a cover to hide their activities, some of which were Satanic.

I will finish this chapter with a quote from David Icke, who writes that *"Sabbatai Zevi promised his followers they would 'return' to their Jewish homeland on the alleged site of ancient Israel and this ambition was pursued to ultimate success by the Death Cult."*[109] The effects of this promise and ambition, which has had grave and lethal implications for the indigenous Arabs (Palestinians) who own the land there, will be explored in the coming chapters.

Sources

[93] Not in His Image, pg. 61

[94] 1666 Redemption Through Sin, pg. 15

[95] The Trigger, pg. 579-580

[96] 1666 Redemption Through Sin, Pg. 6

[97] https://www.jewishhistory.org/sabbatai-zevi/

[98] To Eliminate the Opiate, pg. 149

[99] https://www.bibliomania.ws/pages/books/100618/rabbi-marvin-s-antelman-supreme-rabbinic-court-of-america-chief-justice/the-excommunication-of-henry-a-kissinger

[100] 50 Jewish Messiahs, 2002

[101] https://www.jhi.pl/en/articles/the-false-messiah-who-was-sabbatai-zevi,4472

[102] 1666 Redemption Through Sin, pg. 16

[103] 1666 Redemption Through Sin, pg. 16

[104] To Eliminate the Opiate, pg. 97

[105] Ibid. pg. 91

[106] 1666 Redemption Through Sin, pg. 22

[107] The Messianic Idea in Judaism: And Other Essays on Jewish Spirituality

[108] The Messianic Idea in Judaism: And Other Essays on Jewish Spirituality

[109] The Trigger, pg. 620

CHAPTER 5: THE RISE OF THE ROTHSCHILDS

"Money is the god of our times, and Rothschild is his prophet."

– Heinrich Heine[110]

The Sabbatean-Frankist Cult that arose in the 1600s and 1700s got a massive boost of money, power and influence once the infamous Rothschilds came onto the scene. For those that don't know, the Rothschild family is the wealthiest family on earth. They have done a brilliant job of hiding that wealth so as to conceal their true power. You won't see their name on any Forbes or Bloomberg billionaires list; they realized long ago that hiding in the shadows served their agenda much better. However, the true scale of their wealth is astonishing, and if it could ever be calculated – which would be difficult given how much is tied up in trusts, foundations, corporations, stocks, shares and ownership interests – it would have to be calculated in at least the quadrillions, if not more.

The Rothschilds started their ascent to power when Mayer Amschel Bauer (1744-1812), who lived in Frankfurt, Germany, got into the money lending business and became a banker. He changed his name to Rothschild because of the red sign hanging above his door ('rotes schild' is German for red sign). Some say it was the red Star of David (two triangles pointing in different directions and intersecting) which has come to represent Judaism, although the symbol is an ancient one, existing before the world's current mainstream religions. It is actually a symbol merging the masculine (upwards pointing triangle) and the feminine (downwards pointing triangle), and since it makes a hexagon, it is also represents Saturn, the sixth planet in our solar system. A Saturnian connection to the founder of the Rothschild dynasty … just a coincidence, right?

Image #13: Mayer Amschel Bauer started the dynasty after changing his name to Rothschild. He would later fund the Satanic Jacob Frank

Mayer Amschel Rothschild learnt the trick discussed in chapter 3 of fractional reserve banking, i.e. the lending of money that doesn't exist to make interest that does exist. *"Give me control of a nation's money and I care not who makes its laws"* is the idea or quote that is frequently attributed to him. Rothschild soon learnt that lending money to governments and kings gave him more power than being the overt political leader, and was also more profitable than lending it to private individuals. Not only were the loans bigger, but they were secured by the nation's taxes. After building his banking empire in Germany, he trained all of his five sons in the secret techniques of money creation and manipulation, then sent them out to the major capitals of Europe to open branch offices for the family banking business. He sent four of his sons to other major European cities – London, Paris, Vienna and Naples – while keeping one with him in Frankfurt. After his death, his will directed that one son in each generation was to rule the family business as the patriarch or baron. Their task was to replicate the job of their father by establishing a banking institution in their area. His will also directed that the family intermarry with their first and second cousins. Ostensibly, this motivation could be assumed to be with the aim of keeping the fortune in the family, or due to elite snobbery, however as David Icke has pointed out in his research over the last three decades, this could also be due to a desire to keep a high percentage of reptilian genetic material within the bloodline.

The Rothschild empire went from strength to strength. A key event which propelled them to even more wealth was the Battle of Waterloo in 1815 where the Duke of Wellington defeated Napoleon Bonaparte. Nathan Mayer Rothschild, the head of the British branch of the Rothschild banking dynasty, knew the value of fast, accurate information. As the story goes, he had set up a private courier system with shipping agents in Dover, Calais and Ostend with speedy ships that could sail at a moment's notice. He had horses that could quickly carry messages from the channel to London and a farm on the coast of Hythe for courier pigeons. He got the news of Napoleon's defeat 24 hours after the battle on Monday June 19th 1815, while Wellington's official messenger didn't arrive in London until two days later. Nathan knew that a victory by Wellington would send prices high (since the British Government would be less likely to default or need to borrow more money for war), while a victory by Napoleon would have devastated Britain's financial system. He positioned himself in his usual place next to an ancient pillar in the stock market. Knowing he would be keenly observed, he hung his head and began openly selling large numbers of British Government Bonds. Onlookers, thinking this meant that Napoleon must have won, started imitating him; this behavior spread around and everyone started to sell their British Bonds as well. Everyone that is except for Rothschild's secret agents, who then went around and bought up all the hugely devalued bonds when the market crashed and the prices went to near zero. Overnight, Rothschild had just massively grown his wealth to even larger amounts.

By 1815, they had risen to such wealth and power they were setting their sights on the grand prize – the prize that has been the aim of the NWO ever since its inception: a one world dictatorship, with themselves at the helm, of course. Due to their incessant warring, the European nations were heavily in debt to the Rothschilds, whose Vienna plot was to collude with Austrian Prince Metternich and British Lord Castlereagh to trick the rest of Europe into endorsing the Rothschilds' plot for world government, but Tsar Alexander I, not beholden to a Rothschild central bank, refused to play along. As Mees Baaijen writes:[111]

After the defeat of France and Napoleon in 1815, the Rothschilds invited all European rulers to assemble at the Congress of Vienna. They presented a plan for a supra-European body, to prevent the rise of another European power, by creating a "balance of power", sometimes called the Concert of Europe. Any power revolting against the new order – controlled by the British Empire and the Rothschild-led banking syndicate – would be attacked by all others. And of course, the ever-growing debt of the European nations could be used as a lever. The plan failed because Tsar Alexander I of Russia saw through it (there's a rumor that the Rothschilds became so angry that they vowed to destroy the Tsar's whole family, which indeed happened through Jewish hands, in 1918).

The Concert of Europe or Concert of Nations was the same basic idea which manifested later as the League of Nations (launched in

1919) and the United Nations (launched in 1945). All three are attempts to bring nations together under one umbrella via the pretext of promoting peace and avoiding future wars. It's a noble goal, of course, however that is just the story used to sell it. The covert aim is to produce a totalitarian world government that absorbs and ultimately eliminates all nations. The very fact that the Rothschilds had enough clout to bring European leaders together and suggest such an idea in the year 1815 shows the immense power they had already accumulated. Now, as I write these words, we are over 200 years later, and they have only accumulated even more power.

By the mid-1800s, the Rothschilds dominated all European banking and were certainly the wealthiest family in the world. They built the first European continent-wide banking network, which gave them a tremendous advantage in business, because they could know conditions in each country or market (such as government policy, whether a price may rise or fall, etc.), then relay that information to their other branches. As an international banking group, they held a great advantage over purely national banks engaging in fractional reserve banking. If one nation's policies went against their interests, they could simply do more lending elsewhere. Only they knew where their gold and other reserves were located, so they were shielded from governmental seizures. Their international reach made them into an entity more powerful than a national government. The Rothschilds set up a system of communication and information sharing better than some of the governments of the time; it was networks like these that became the forerunner to intelligence agencies like the Mossad (see later chapters, especially 12 and 14). Before long, the Rothschilds became the bankers for governments, royalty and the Pope.

They went on to fund or be financially involved in many different companies, operations and projects. They provided huge loans to establish monopolies in various industries. In America, they financed the monopolization of oil and railroads via John D. Rockefeller and his behemoth Standard Oil. Hence, the Rockefellers were entwined with the Rothschilds from the start of their rise to wealth, too. One of their most prolific agents was Jacob Schiff, who had been born in the Rothschild house in Frankfurt. Others included J.P. Morgan and Kuhn, Loeb and Company (where Schiff was on the board). Under Lionel de Rothschild (1808-1879), the Bank of England financed the British government's 1875 purchase of Egypt's interest in the Suez Canal. They funded the rise of Cecil Rhodes, who went to South Africa, then bought out many small mining concerns to quickly gain a monopoly. Although Rhodes has been credited with transforming the De Beers Consolidated Mines into the world's biggest diamond supplier, his success was largely due to Rothschild backing. Nathaniel Mayer Rothschild (1840-1915) held more shares in the company than Rhodes himself. Rhodes, a white supremacist, went on to become a very famous and influential man who made his fortune on the backs of African tribes and slaves. His Rhodes scholarship program still runs today, attracting bright young minds worldwide, however what many people don't realize is that the program's real purpose is to recruit young people and indoctrinate them into the NWO system – to train them to think like globalists and to administer an international dictatorship. Rhodes was all about expanding the British Empire and 'civilizing the natives' in other parts of the world, an ultra racist narrative that still endures today as the basis for any supremacist mindset, whether based on race, skin color, religion, gender or anything else. Remember the 'chosen people'?

Carroll Quigley in *Tragedy and Hope* and *The Anglo American Establishment* comprehensively laid out how Rhodes was the frontman whose influence and wealth spawned further organizations, the most influential of which was the Round Table group of think tanks that came to rule the world. Rhodes considered Lord Alfred Milner his closest confidant and a man who completely echoed his thoughts, desires and mindset. Milner became the principal manager of the Rhodes Trust and took over the Rhodesian mission after Rhodes died, i.e. to create a British-led world empire. Rhodes arranged his organization in concentric circles, or circles within circles, with only those in the innermost circle knowing the true agenda. This theme is repeated throughout the worldwide conspiracy, since the Rothschilds and the Sabbatean-Frankists used this method when they infiltrated existing groups, so that to lower members of the group or to anyone on the outside, they would look part of the group – remember Jacob Frank's dictate to 'be one thing on the outside, another thing on the inside.'

The inner circle of the Round Table Group was called the "Society of the Elect" and originally consisted of just four men: Cecil Rhodes, Alfred Milner, William Stead and Reginald Baliol Brett. However, Quigley later revealed there were actually six men, including … a Rothschild. Of course! Quigley wrote that *"... we can be certain that six were initiates. These were Rhodes, Lord Rothschild, Johnston, Stead, Brett and Milner."*[112] The Rothschild referred to here was Nathaniel Mayer Rothschild, mentioned earlier, who was also the designated patriarch of the family, the 1st Baron Rothschild and great-grandson of Mayer Amschel Rothschild. The outer circle was called the "Association of Helpers" and also included key movers and shakers of the world. One name with particular significance in this circle was Arthur Balfour (author of the now famous Balfour Declaration which was used to force Zionist Israel on Palestine), who will be discussed in chapter 6.

The Rothschilds purchased the media long ago – according to the late Eustace Mullins, they purchased Reuters in the late 1800s, along with two other European news agencies, Wolff and Havas.[113] Their agent Jacob Schiff set up the Anti-Defamation League (ADL) in 1913, an organization that exists just to protect Israel, Zionism and ultimately the Rothschilds, while pretending to serve Jews as a whole and stop antisemitism. While it claims to fight defamation, it actively defames those who expose Israel's criminality. The ADL is behind the many reports of the last two decades that spuriously claim that antisemitism is on the rise when in fact it is not, but rather is being manufactured to give the appearance of such to justify draconian censorship laws against those who criticize Israel and the crypto-Jewish Sabbatean-Frankist Cult that runs the world. A common theme running through the so-called 'rise of antisemitism' is Jewish men and women spraying graffiti swastikas on doors and walls, then playing the victim … until they get caught and investigators realize it is not neo-Nazis doing this but rather Jews themselves (see chapter 16). Interestingly, in America in that very same year of 1913, the Internal Revenue Service (IRS) and the Federal Reserve ('the Fed') were created, two tools of oppression foist upon the American public which persist to this day (see chapter 7). Although it's a closely guarded secret, Dean Henderson's research shows that the Rothschilds are one of eight banking families that owns shares in the Fed, the private banking cartel which pretends to be part of the US Government but which is not, and which controls the money supply.

Image #14: Evelyn de Rothschild pokes (then Prince) Charles. If you can poke royalty on the chest like you own them, you may be a Rothschild

Upon first seeing a Rothschild mansion, Wilhelm I reportedly uttered *"Kings couldn't afford this. It could only belong to a Rothschild!"*[114] Frederic Morton observed that the Rothschilds had *"conquered the world more thoroughly, more cunningly and much more lastingly than all the Caesars before ..."* and he was 100% correct. Their conquering was so cunning and so thorough that they have been able to not only maintain but actually expand their power since the 1800s, largely on account of the fact that the majority do not understand the danger inherent in the current systems of banking and money creation – and therefore do not see the prison walls. The Rothschilds do a masterful job of hiding their wealth and constantly using puppets to do their bidding while they remain in the shadows.

The Rothschilds were also at the heart of the deadliest events in recorded human history – the Russian Revolution of 1917, the 1st World War of 1914-1918 and the 2nd World War of 1939-1945 just to name a few. This will all be discussed in the coming chapters. We will finish this section with a quote attributed to Gutle Schnapper Rothschild, wife of Mayer Amschel Rothschild:

"If my sons did not want wars, there would be none."

The Birth of a New Death Cult: The Unholy Alliance of Rothschild and Frank

So much for the power of the Rothschilds. Entire books could be written about just this topic, and have been, but that is beyond the scope of this book. For now, we will return to the key period of around 1760-1780, and we will return to the repulsive character of Jacob Frank. During this period, in Germany, some very significant things happened. Jacob Frank got out of prison in Poland and moved to Germany. There, as fate would have it, he came into contact with the head of the Rothschild dynasty, none other than Mayer Amschel Rothschild himself. Did Frank with all his Satanic ways influence Rothschild? It would appear so, given the involvement of the Rothschilds in the international Satanic network up to this day. Many current Satanic network survivors have gone public with eyewitness testimonies detailing how they were forced to attend rituals of torture, rape, sacrifice and cannibalism. Some, such as Arizona Wilder (Jennifer Greene/Kealey), specifically stated that members of the Rothschild family were present at these Satanic rituals, often in a leading role.

The Rothschild goal of controlling the money of the planet, combined with the Frankist goal of supplanting Judaism and overthrowing morality, led to the formation of a dangerous new cult – a Satanic cult, a death cult, a cult bent on total world domination.

Many people associate the year 1776 with the founding of the USA, however another very important historical event also occurred in that year. On May 1st 1776, the Bavarian Order of the Illuminati was formed – the original Illuminati. This particular order has become so infamous that many truthseekers starting their research in the field of conspiracy have referred to the NWO ruling class as the 'Illuminati' before it became more fashionable to call them the 'Deep State.' Technically, however, the Illuminati is not the only secret society around, but is one of many secret societies that has infiltrated freemasonry, religion, politics, the military, etc. Did you know that Illuminati spelt backwards is "itanimulli" – and that, at the time of writing, if you go to the website itanimulli.com[115] you will be redirected to the NSA (National Security Agency) of the US, one of the most secretive and powerful military intelligence agencies worldwide, which goes to great lengths to be above the law?

Image #15: Adam Weishaupt, founder of the original Order of the Illuminati

The Order of the Illuminati was formed by Jesuit-educated Adam Weishaupt, the son of a Jewish Kabbalist rabbi in Bavaria who formed an alliance with Mayer Rothschild. As mentioned earlier, the Kabbalists are heavily into numerology, gematria and the hidden significance of numbers, which is why Weishaupt chose the date of May 1st 1776 (May is the fifth month of the year, so if all the digits are separated and added, that date can be written as 5 + 1 + 1 + 7 + 7 + 6 = 27, which is equivalent to 3 x 9, a number Kabbalists associate with power). Since the Illuminati was trying to gain control of society, its chief aims were the abolition of monarchies and religion, a logical objective, since the strongest centers of power in European society at that time were the governments (ruled by royal families or monarchs) and the Church (whether Catholic or Protestant).

The Illuminati Infiltrates Freemasonry

Weishaupt perceived that Freemasonry was the organization most fit for infiltration by the Illuminati, apparently writing in his dairy that the public was already accustomed to the three lower degrees of Freemasonry and so took little notice of it.[116] The Illuminati were able to achieve the infiltration of Freemasonry just 18 years after their 1776 formation. Sepehr writes that *"the Duke of Brunswick, Grand Master of Germany, said in 1794 that the Illuminati controlled the Masonic lodges."*[117] Antelman wrote:[118]

> *When attempts were made by the Illuminati, Jacobins and Frankists to infiltrate the Masons, their infiltration did not mean that they harbored any particular love for Freemasonry. On the contrary, they hated it with a passion, and only wished to utilize the cover of Freemasonry as a means of spreading their revolutionary doctrines.*

As the Illuminati rapidly penetrated all of Freemasonry, it began to direct it in a similar fashion as described earlier with the inner and outer circles of the Rhodesian Round Table. The highest degrees were reserved for those truly in the know, while those in the lower degrees were kept in the dark; the organization and goals they thought they were serving were completely different to the real ones. As 33° freemasonic Grandmaster Albert Pike admitted, *"Masonry, like all the Religions, all the Mysteries, the Hermeticism and Alchemy, conceals its secrets from all except the Adepts and Sages, or the Elect, and uses false explanations and misinterpretations of its symbols to mislead those who deserve only to be mislead; to conceal the Truth, which it calls Light, from them, and to draw them away from it. Truth is not for those who are unworthy or unable to receive it, or would pervert it ... So Masonry jealously conceals its secrets, and intentionally leads conceited interpreters astray."*[119] The mindset encapsulated by this quote is typical of the Cult that believes itself more special, worthy and 'illuminated' than anyone else, and therefore somehow possessing the authority to appoint itself as the ruler and treat everyone else as the slaves.

Overall, the Illuminati were spectacularly successful, however they did receive some serious setbacks. On June 22nd 1784, the Bavarian authorities caught wind of the machinations of the secret societies, and the Duke of Bavaria issued an edict prohibiting all secret societies not expressly authorized by the government. On July 10th 1785, lightning struck and just happened to kill an Illuminati member, Johann Jakob Lang (or Lanz), in whose pockets were found incriminating evidence of the Illuminati's existence and clandestine operations, in spite of the prohibition. The police also found on him a list of member names, which led to the first arrests of the Illuminati. The next year, in October 1786, the Bavarian police raided the Munich house of Franz Xavier von Zwack, a lawyer and inner member of the Illuminati. Zwack had been warned in time and had left Bavaria, but didn't have time to hide or destroy his extensive Illuminati documentation. The police confiscated it and subsequently learnt who founded and directed the order, which up until then the authorities had not definitively known. They also seized letters from Weishaupt to Zwack and documents such as notes praising suicide and atheism, the plan for founding a women's initiatory order, and instructions on how to prepare invisible ink, false seals and poisons.[120] Despite this, however, the Illuminati did go on to achieve a lot of their mission.

Having taken on the Frankist desire to destroy religion, and having created and funded the original Illuminati as one of many tools to achieve this aim, Mayer Amschel Rothschild proceeded further with his devilish plan. Sepehr writes that *"Mayer Rothschild summoned 12 affluent men to Frankfort, and asked them to pool their financial resources. He then presented a 25-point plan that would enable them to gain control of the wealth, natural resources and manpower of the entire world. This plan included instructions on how to preach 'Liberalism' to usurp political power, initiate class warfare, dismantle and reconstruct all existing institutions, and remain invisible until the very moment when the Illuminati had gained such strength that no cunning or force can undermine it. Other highlights of their plan included the use of mob psychology to control the masses ... they planned to use the press for propaganda to control all outlets of public information, while remaining in the shadows ... the plan called for the masses to be made to believe that they had been the prey of criminals, and then they would restore order and to appear as the saviors."*[121]

Creating the problem then providing the solution, or being the perpetrator while posing as the savior, is a quintessential Cult

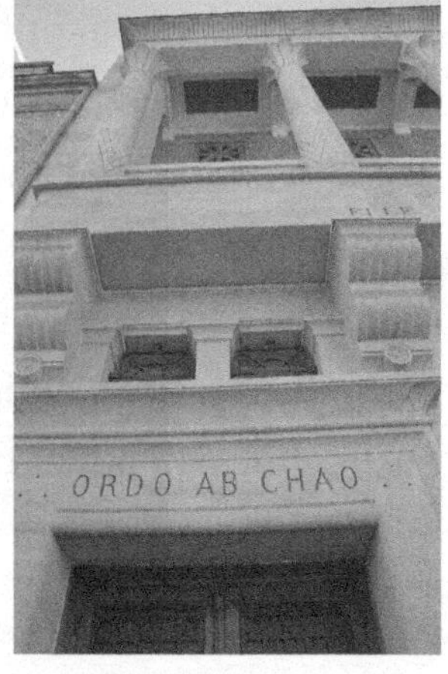

technique. After all, the motto of the Scottish rite of freemasonry is 'Ordo Ab Chao' which is Latin for 'order out of chaos' which signifies the Hegelian dialectic of thesis-antithesis-synthesis. David Icke has named it 'problem-reaction-solution.' In plain English, this means that you create problems, chaos and disorder to stir up trouble (often putting people into emotional reactivity and fear), which softens them up and prepares the way for your 'solution' which was actually just your plan all along.

Rothschild's 25-point plan brings to mind other key NWO accounts or documents which form a blueprint for total world control. I discussed these in my book *Break Your Chains* and also in articles such as this one (*Top 3 Most Chilling Conspiracy Documents or Accounts Ever)*.[122] The three I highlighted were the Protocols of the Learned Elders of Zion, the 1969 verbal account by Dr. Richard Day and Silent Weapons for Quiet Wars. The Protocols uses overt Jew vs. non-Jew/gentile/goy language to describe how the rulers would subjugate those outside them, making them into slaves, although as discussed in the last chapter, this language stems from the group of crypto-Jews that arose in the wake Sabbatean-Frankism and who hijacked Judaism and Jewish identity for their own manipulative, sadistic and Satanic interest. As for the second one, Dr. Richard Day was a Rockefeller insider – and the Rothschilds and Rockefellers have been the two dominant NWO bloodline families for centuries. In the third one, the Rothschilds are actually mentioned by name, when the text reveals how Rothschild induced people to trade real wealth (e.g. gold) for fake wealth (paper money in the form of a promissory note), and thus was able to control the currency of society like controlling energy in an electrical circuit. Thus, in totality, we have a crypto-Jew-Rockefeller-Rothschild thread running through all three! What follows are quotes from each of them.

This is from the Protocols of the Learned Elders of Zion:

"NOT A SINGLE ANNOUNCEMENT WILL REACH THE PUBLIC WITHOUT OUR CONTROL ... All our newspapers will be of all possible complexions— aristocratic, republican, revolutionary, even anarchical ... every one of them will have a finger on any one of the public opinions as required."

"WE SHALL SO WEAR DOWN THE "GOYIM" THAT THEY WILL BE COMPELLED TO OFFER US INTERNATIONAL POWER OF A NATURE THAT BY ITS POSITION WILL ENABLE US WITHOUT ANY VIOLENCE GRADUALLY TO ABSORB ALL THE STATE FORCES OF THE WORLD AND TO FORM A SUPER-GOVERNMENT."

Here are some key points from the account of Dr. Richard Day:

- Sex would be redirected; procreation would be separated from sex and would begin to only be done by the State;
- Cancer cures would be suppressed as a means of population control;
- The controllers running the conspiracy would induce heart attacks as a form of assassination to kill political opponents and dissenters;
- Alcohol and drugs would be pushed to weaken the will and mental clarity of the masses;

- The controllers would consolidate their grip on the media and restrict the flow of information;
- The ability of the ordinary person to travel freely would be limited;
- All the world's religions would be combined into a One World Religion;
- Euthanasia would be encouraged via a 'demise pill' (i.e. a suicide pill);
- Weather modification would be used by the State against foreign and domestic enemies; and
- Everything would have two goals: the stated goal and the real goal.

That last one echoes the same principle of the Sabbatean-Frankists – hide the real identity and intention under a fake outer veneer. This is from Silent Weapons for Quiet Wars:

"[T]he simplest method of securing a silent weapon and gaining control of the public is to keep the public undisciplined and ignorant of the basic system principles on the one hand, while keeping them confused, disorganized, and distracted with matters of no real importance on the other hand.

This is achieved by:

- *Disengaging their minds; sabotaging their mental activities; providing a low-quality program of public education in mathematics, logic, systems design and economics; and discouraging technical creativity.*
- *Engaging their emotions, increasing their self-indulgence and their indulgence in emotional and physical activities, by:*

- *Unrelenting emotional affrontations and attacks (mental and emotional rape) by way of constant barrage of sex, violence, and wars in the media – especially the T.V. and the newspapers.*
- *Giving them what they desire – in excess – "junk food for thought" – and depriving them of what they really need.*

- *Rewriting history and law and subjecting the public to the deviant creation, thus being able to shift their thinking from personal needs to highly fabricated outside priorities.*

These preclude their interest in and discovery of the silent weapons of social automation technology.

The general rule is that there is a profit in confusion; the more confusion, the more profit. Therefore, the best approach is to create problems and then offer solutions."

Infiltration is the Name of the Game

Sabbatean-Frankism infiltrated everything. It infiltrated Christianity via the Jesuits, Islam via the Donmeh, and secret societies like Freemasonry via the Illuminati.

Antelman noted[123] that the Frankists no longer called themselves by that name, and instead called themselves the 'Cult of the All-Seeing Eye' which would explain the ubiquitous NWO symbolism of the eye, especially atop a pyramid, frequently seen in corporate logos and governmental seals. Antelman mentioned that the Frankists dominated the ADL and B'nai B'rith, which is true, since they are some of the many Cult organizations which pretend to represent all Jews when actually they just represent the interests of the Cult.

Thus, the crossing of paths of Jacob Frank (the second fake 'messiah' of Sabbatean-Frankism) and Mayer Amschel Rothschild (founder of the Rothschild dynasty) could fairly be called one of the most catastrophic events in human history. Frank contributed the Satanism, the incest, the rape, the total disregard of empathy, conscience and morality, the idea of infiltration, the concept of the crypto-Jew and many other things, while Rothschild provided the wealth to propagate this unholy ideology throughout the entire world via created orders such as the Illuminati and numerous proxies and agents such as Adam Weishaupt, Jacob Schiff, J. P. Morgan and others.

Sources

---

[110] https://www.laphamsquarterly.org/about-money/point-order

[111] The People vs. The Predators, pg. 74

[112] The Anglo American Establishment, pg. 40

[113] The Secrets of the Federal Reserve, Estate Mullins, pg. 60

[114] https://www.linkedin.com/pulse/rise-rothschilds-m-m-lawan

[115] itanimulli.com

[116] https://freemasonrywatch.org/illuminati.html

[117] 1666 Redemption Through Sin, pg. 26

[118] To Eliminate the Opiate Vol. 1, pp. 104-5

[119] Morals and Dogma of the Ancient and Accepted Scottish Rite of Freemasonry, Albert Pike, pg. 104-5

[120] https://bitterwinter.org/3-the-political-turn-of-the-bavarian-illuminati/

[121] Ibid. pg. 27

[122] https://thefreedomarticles.com/3-most-chilling-conspiracy-documents-accounts/

[123] To Eliminate the Opiate Vol. 1, pg. 113

CHAPTER 6: THE CULT LAUNCHES ZIONISM AND PLOTS TO STEAL PALESTINE

"Zionism is but an incident of a far-reaching plan: it is merely a convenient peg on which to hang a powerful weapon."

– Lawyer for Rothschild agent bankers Kuhn-Loeb, Louis B. Marshall[124] (as quoted by Guy Carr)

As I have said before, the Cult is playing the long game. It thinks and plans in terms of decades and centuries because it is run by a nonhuman Archontic mindset. The insanity of the Cult, whose origins can be traced at least back to the Zaddikim, reemerged with a vengeance in the 1600-1700s with the appearance of Zevi and Frank, then continued to grow in power with the rise of the Rothschilds who directed the Sabbatean-Frankist-Illuminati. However, while they proved to be excellent at infiltrating organizations, religions and countries – hijacking them for their own purposes – a natural limit on their power was that they did not possess their own country. This may have been the motivation for the next phase in their evil agenda: the plot to steal Palestine. With this plan in motion, the Cult schemed to create their own nation in the heart of the Middle East, at a key place, on a key intersection of three great continents.

The idea of a Jewish homeland had been around awhile in Judaism, but as covered in chapter 1, many strict and religious Jews viewed this is a spiritual homeland not a physical one. Others however became obsessed with conquest and temple-building. The

17th and 18th century Sabbatean-Frankism continued the 12th and 13th century Knights Templar obsession of building a 'Solomon's Temple' on the exact point of Dome of the Rock/Al-Aqsa Mosque which the Jews call Temple Mount, despite there being no physical or archeological evidence that a man called Solomon ever existed, nor that a temple in his name ever existed. It was in the 19th century when the movement to create a physical Jewish homeland began gathering momentum and coalesced into a determined crusade. This movement came to be known as Zionism, and its initial planning stages culminated in 1897 in the inaugural congress of the Zionist Organization (the "First Zionist Congress") which was held in Basel, Switzerland. We will get to this shortly. However, the Zionists knew that appropriating or stealing an entire swathe of land to create a country was not going to be easy, since it meant displacing the people already there, plus stopping the neighboring countries from attacking and wiping out the new nation. The Cult knew it would need the help of some 'big' countries if it were to pull this off, and it was already looking ahead to a time when the title of the world's superpower would shift from Britain to America. Thus, it needed to ensure both of these nations would support the coming Zionist project. But how? Britain and America were predominantly Christian, so why would their populations support a Jewish homeland in Palestine? The answer the Cult came up with was devilishly cunning and typical of its modus operandi. It would infiltrate Christianity (just as it had infiltrated so many other organizations) to get Christians on board with the Zionist agenda by brainwashing them into thinking that being a good Christian equated to supporting the political state of Israel. How? By rewriting their holy book, the Bible. This it did, and continues to do in an ongoing transformation of history, and thus was born Christian Zionism.

Planting the Seeds of Christian Zionism: Enter Rothschild Agents Darby and Scofield

For a long time since the advent of the Christian religion, Christians had traditionally viewed Jews as the persecutors of Jesus and his early followers, including the orchestration of his crucifixion. Therefore, America's churches in the early 1800s would not have supported a Jewish occupation of Jesus' homeland. The Rothschilds, along with their growing army of employees, agents and proxies – plus natural allies they recruited whose interest was also served by having a future colonial outpost in Palestine – initiated a scheme to alter the Christian view of Zionism by creating and promoting a pro-Zionist subculture within Christianity.

Before going any further, we need to define some key terms. Interestingly enough, all of these terms are based upon what Lash calls the redeemer complex (discussed in chapter 2), with its four elements of the creation of the world by a father god, the trial of the chosen people, the coming of a messiah to save the world and the final judgment.

Millennialism is the belief that a messianic age will be established on Earth prior to a 'final judgment.' This contains at least one of the four elements of the redeemer complex: a last judgment. The variation premillennialism is the notion that Jesus will physically return to the Earth (the second coming) before this thousand-year messianic age of peace begins. The tribulation is another belief that accompanies this theme, and can be divided into futurism (a short period of great hardship before the end of the world and second coming of Christ) or preterism (that advocates that the tribulation has already occurred). These all contain the third element, the belief in a messiah. Dispensationalism is a way of interpreting the Bible which divides history into (usually) seven eras called 'dispensations' between creation and the 'final judgment.' Some believe that one of the dispensations is the 'rapture' which consists of an 'end of the world' event when believers will rise into the clouds to meet Jesus in the air. Again, we have elements of the redeemer complex with the trials of the chosen people, the coming or reappearance of the messiah and the idea of 'end times' or 'end of the world' which always seems to be accompanied by a judgmental divine father figure. You are forgiven if you think that the entire load of all these terms and concepts is utter nonsense, yet somehow, much of it has become entrenched in modern-day Christianity in America. Dispensationalism, promoted by John Nelson Darby and the Plymouth Brethren in the 1830s and beyond, then later via Cyrus Scofield and his Scofield Reference Bible, has become an essential element of American evangelicalism so popular and widespread in the southern states. The reason to introduce and define all these terms is that dispensationalism, considered to be the parent of Christian Zionism, is one of the most influential theological systems in Christianity. It is based on the principle that the Bible is always to be interpreted literally. It has shaped the beliefs of evangelical, fundamentalist, pentecostal and other denominations regarding Israel and Palestine over the past 150 years.

With all those terms out of the way, we can now look at two key figures who helped the Rothschilds plant the seeds of Zionism in the West, especially in the United States. The first is John Nelson Darby (1800-1882). Darby was the youngest son of a wealthy Anglo-Irish merchant, born in London into a world of commerce and privilege. He was very connected to the British and American ruling classes, and therefore the Cult. His mother Ann Vaughan was the daughter of

Image #20: John Darby

Samuel Vaughan, a sugar plantation owner from Philadelphia who was an acquaintance of George Washington and a vice president of the American Philosophical Society that was founded by Benjamin Franklin in 1743. Darby's uncle Benjamin Vaughan was a close friend of Franklin and a peace negotiator at the conclusion of the War of Independence in 1782-83. Another of his uncles was British Admiral Sir Henry D'Esterre Darby, who fought under Admiral Lord Nelson against Napoleon's fleet at the Battle of the Nile in 1798. Darby was given his middle name in honor of Lord Nelson, who was his godfather.[125] Darby's family owned Leap Castle, renowned as a sinister Irish castle.

Darby later became a freemason. He was an occultist who used Kabbalistic and theosophical language throughout his doctrinal writings,[126] showing his familiarity with these schools of thought. Some say he was also a Satanist. According to John Coleman, author of *The Committee of 300*, Darby was a *"servant"* (employee?) of the British East India Company,[127] an infamous and sinister company founded in 1600, dissolved in 1874 and operated by the Rothschilds. The British East India Company was the world's original multinational corporation. It extracted wealth from British colonies and third world nations on behalf of the Cult. It took control of Hong Kong and many parts of India, and was involved in the notorious Opium Wars which brought China to its knees during its so-called

"Century of Humiliation" (1839-1945). At its peak, the East India Company was the largest corporation in the world – it even had its own armed forces of approximately 260,000 soldiers, which was twice the size of the British Army at certain times.

Darby created the movement of dispensationalism by writing about a series of so-called dispensations. The first began with Adam and extended to the great flood. The second stretched from Noah to Abraham, including the giving of the law to Moses. Remember, as discussed in chapter 1, none of these characters were real people, since the Jews were given their history around 270 BC. However, where this becomes very interesting and relevant to Zionism is in his dispensation regarding Israel. This dispensation contained three subdispensations (law, priesthood and kingship). Darby taught that Israel and the Church were separate entities belonging to different dispensations. He pushed the notion of a heavenly Church and an earthly Israel, and that God's intention was the establishment of Israel as a literal kingdom on Earth.[128] I don't know whether the Rothschilds influenced this way of thinking, or merely opportunistically seized upon it, but either way, the idea of a political-military nation called Israel, distinct from a religious or spiritual place, emanated from Darby's teachings, spurred on by the force of his personality and his popularity.

The next phase in this story revolves around the figure of Cyrus Scofield (1834-1921), the man most responsible for spreading Darby's dispensationalism and thus amplifying the idea of an earthly, political nation of Israel. The Cult needed someone with credentials as a theologian (even if such credentials were invented) who was not a Jew, and Scofield perfectly fit the bill. Scofield studied law in St. Louis, Missouri and was admitted to the Kansas bar in 1869,

Image #21: Cyrus Scofield

however was dogged by numerous scandals such as allegations of accepting bribes from railroads, stealing political contributions and forgery. He may have been jailed for forgery. A Civil War veteran, Scofield himself confessed that he was a heavy drinker, and left his wife (and two daughters) who later divorced him on grounds of desertion. During the early 1890s, Scofield went by the name "Rev. C. I. Scofield, D.D." however there is no record of any academic institution having given him a Doctor of Divinity degree. According to this source, in 1881, the Topeka Daily Capital published this about him:[129]

Cyrus I. Schofield [sic], formerly of Kansas, late lawyer, politician and shyster generally, has come to the surface again, and promises once more to gather around himself that halo of notoriety that has made him so prominent in the past. The last personal knowledge that Kansans have had of this peer among scalawags, was when about four years ago, after a series of forgeries and confidence games, he left the state and a destitute family and took refuge in Canada. For a time he kept undercover, nothing being heard of him until within the past two years when he turned up in St. Louis, where he had a wealthy widowed sister living who has generally come to the front and squared up Cyrus' little follies and foibles by paying good round sums of money. Within the past year, however, Cyrus committed a series of St. Louis forgeries that could not be settled so easily, and the erratic young gentleman was compelled to linger in the St. Louis jail for a period of six months.

Scofield biographer Joseph M. Canfield wrote that the *"very sudden dropping of the criminal charges without proper adjudication suggests that Scofield's career was in the hands of someone who had clout."*[130] The Cult has your back when you advance their agenda. Scofield studied Darby's teachings and made rapid progress in his new ecclesiastical profession despite having no religious education. In 1881 he was already pastoring in St. Louis, then next moved to Dallas' First Congregational Church. Reverend John S. Torell wrote:[131]

There were a number of wealthy and political power brokers in the membership of the First Congregational Church in Dallas . . . I do know that most churches in the United States are heavily infested with Freemasons. George Bannerman Dealey was a member of the Westminster Presbyterian Church in the later part of his life. But he was also heavily involved in the occult, majoring in the Scottish Rite of Masonry with a 33rd degree and active as a Shriner, and was also a member of the Red Cross of Constantine. Most likely he had a hand in getting Cyrus into Masonic circles and particularly the Lotos Club in New York.

This source claims Scofield was a Freemason.[132] Remember, by the 1880s, the Illuminati had been around for over a century, so had had ample time to infiltrate Freemasonry worldwide.

Scofield rewrote the most popular Bible in America at the time, the King James Version. The Scofield Reference Bible was not just another translation, but something that radically changed the context and meaning of the terms. Scofield inserted Zionist propaganda notes in the margins and on the bottoms of the pages, between verses and chapters, which reinforced a fake biblical basis for a modern state of Israel. These explanatory notes, based on Darby's interpretation of scripture, created a false sense of authority. The Rothschilds used a European book publisher which they owned (the Oxford University Press) to publish, distribute and promote the book. With their funding, it became a best-selling Bible in America and has remained so ever since, undergoing many new updates. With each new update, the Rothschild Oxford University Press is free to keep changing history, omitting and adding little changes here and there to buttress the idea of modern Israel being promised to 'the Jews' by 'God' (promised to the Khazarian-Sabbatean-Frankists by Satan might be closer to the truth). Who controls the present, controls the past, as Orwell wrote. Scofield may have been just another Rothschild pawn in a long line without knowing why he was put into the position he was; this source states that there was *"little reason to believe that Scofield knew or cared much about the Zionist movement, but at some point, he became involved in a close and secret relationship with Samuel Untermeyer, a New York lawyer whose firm still exists today and one of the wealthiest and most powerful World Zionists in America."*[133] The Zionist and Cult operative Untermeyer is mentioned in the next chapter.

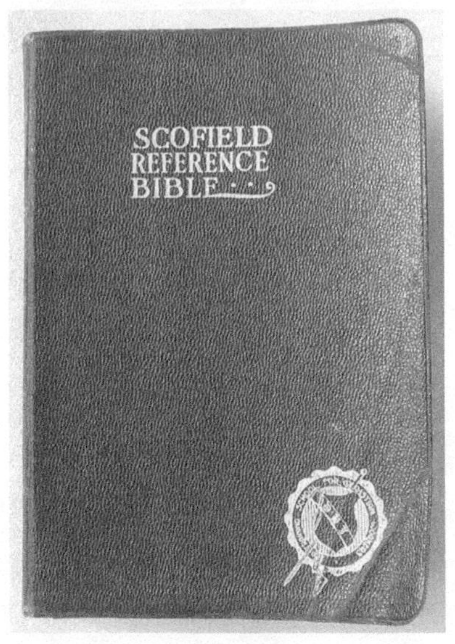

Image #22: the Scofield Reference Bible

Here are some examples of the changes the Oxford University Press (i.e. the Rothschilds) have made since Scofield died:[134]

Oxford edited the former 1945 Edition of SRB in 1967, at the time of the Six Day War when Israel occupied Palestine. The new footnotes to the King James Bible presumptuously granted the rights to the Palestinians' land to the State of Israel and specifically denied the Arab Palestinians any such rights at all. One of the most brazen and outrageous of these NEWLY INSERTED footnotes states:

"FOR A NATION TO COMMIT THE SIN OF ANTI-SEMITISM BRINGS INEVITABLE JUDGMENT." (page 19-20, footnote (3) to Genesis 12:3.) (our emphasis added)"

The Oxford 1967 Edition continues on page 19:

"(2) GOD MADE AN UNCONDITIONAL PROMISE OF BLESSINGS THROUGH ABRAM'S SEED (a) TO THE NATION OF ISRAEL TO INHERIT A SPECIFIC TERRITORY FOREVER"

It's important to remember that there was no modern state of Israel when Scofield was writing his original notes in the first version that was published in 1909. The modern state of Israel did not come into existence until 1948. The Cult knows it cannot completely transform the Bible in one fell swoop, since people would recognize that, so it uses one of its favorite techniques, known as the frog in the boiling pot, to slowly change history one term or one phrase at a time. By changing history, it therefore changes reality.

In addition to Darby and Scofield, the Rothschilds were also able to recruit key figures in the upper British elite, many of whom were also part of the secret society networks (including the Illuminati-infiltrated Freemasons), to get behind the Zionist project. Stephen

Sizer, who has closely studied the phenomenon of Christian Zionism, points to Lord Shaftesbury (1801-1885), who he says *"became convinced that the restoration of the Jews to Palestine was not only predicted in the Bible, but also coincided with the strategic interests of British foreign policy. Others who shared this perspective, in varying degrees and for different reasons, included Lord Palmerston, David Lloyd George and Lord Balfour ... Lord Shaftesbury argued for a greater British presence in Palestine and saw this could be achieved by the sponsorship of a Jewish homeland on both religious and political grounds. British protection of the Jews would give a colonial advantage over France for the control of the Middle East; provide better access to India via a direct land route; and open up new commercial markets for British products."*[135]

He mentions that Lord Palmerston, at a time when he was UK Foreign Secretary, married Shaftsbury's widowed mother-in-law, which cemented their alliance. Palmerston, born Henry John Temple (1784-1865), was Grand Patriarch of Grand Orient Freemasonry. He dominated British foreign policy from 1830 to 1865 (when Britain humiliated China via the Opium Wars), and was British PM from 1855 to 1858 and again from 1859 to 1865. This was the era when Britain was at the height of her powers (only because the Cult banking cartel wanted it that way, of course). Webster Tarpley's speech "Lord Palmerston's Multicultural Human Zoo"[136] that you can get in written form is entertaining listening or reading if you want to get an idea of the ruthlessness with which Lord Palmerston administered the British Empire, treating other leaders as puppets and other nations as resources to be exploited.

David Lloyd George became British PM in 1916. He was another self-confessed Zionist, which shows the powerful way the Cult had already promoted Zionism and pushed Zionist agents into the highest positions of power in mighty countries. George appears to have admitted to some kind of arrangement he made with influential Polish-born chemist and Jew Chaim Weizmann (1874-1952), who was a Zionist Organization president and later the first president of Israel. George joked that *"acetone converted me to Zionism,"* a reference to how Weizmann had assisted the British government by developing acetone as a new kind of explosive. Weizmann, well known in British munition production circles, had launched a massive Zionist lobbying campaign. British support for a Jewish Palestine was the reward. Another so-called Christian who tremendously helped the Zionist movement was William Hechler (1845-1931), an Anglican priest who became chaplain to the British Embassy in Vienna in 1885. Sizer writes that *"Hechler's advocacy and diplomacy marked a radical shift in Christian Zionist thinking away from the views of early restorationists like Irving and Drummond who saw restoration to the land as a consequence of Jewish conversion to Christianity. Now, Hechler was insisting instead, that it was the destiny of Christians simply to help restore the Jews to Palestine."*[137]

This notion that an event or scheme is divinely destined or fated is a clever way to dilute opposition to the idea. Think of the ideas from sci-fi films, such as Star Wars when Darth Vader says to Luke Skywalker that *"It is your destiny"* and Star Trek when the Borg declare that *"Resistance is futile."* By claiming that something is fated, you appeal to divine providence and imbue your plan with more authority than it otherwise has. In a religious context, when combined with ideas of prophecy, this can be become a very manipulative tool, since it assumes an aura of hypnotic suggestion –

'*IT IS WRITTEN.'* The promoters of Zionism have not only seeded into religious texts but have also inculcated the notion into people's minds that modern-day Israel is some sort of divinely issued plan when it is nothing of the sort.

The Cult tampered with the Bible to make it seem God himself had promised that the 'Jews' could claim Palestine as their own nation, despite the fact that anyone can become a 'Jew' and that modern-day Ashkenazi Jews are descendants of Turkic-Caucasian Khazarians, not a Semitic race. The level of manipulation here is truly staggering. Christian Zionism is an oxymoronic scam that fools some into believing that 'God' really, really, really wants to secure a great value real estate deal on some beachfront property in the Middle East.

The Rothschilds Begin the Colonization of Palestine

While the Rothschilds were busy setting things up to manipulate history through Darby, Scofield and others, they were also directly doing what they could to acquire land in Palestine, either through buying it or stealing it. For many centuries, including during the 1800s, Palestine was under the control of the Ottoman Empire, which was based in modern day Türkiye. While some sources state that the Rothschilds didn't begin actively colonizing Palestine until much later, there are reports from newspapers in 1829 that the Rothschilds were already either buying land or attempting to buy land there. The Asiatic Journal and Monthly Miscellany, Volume 29, July-December 1829[138][139] reports that the Rothschilds offered the Ottoman Sultan 35,000,000 piastres to obtain Jerusalem and Palestine, an offer that was rebuffed by the Sultan.

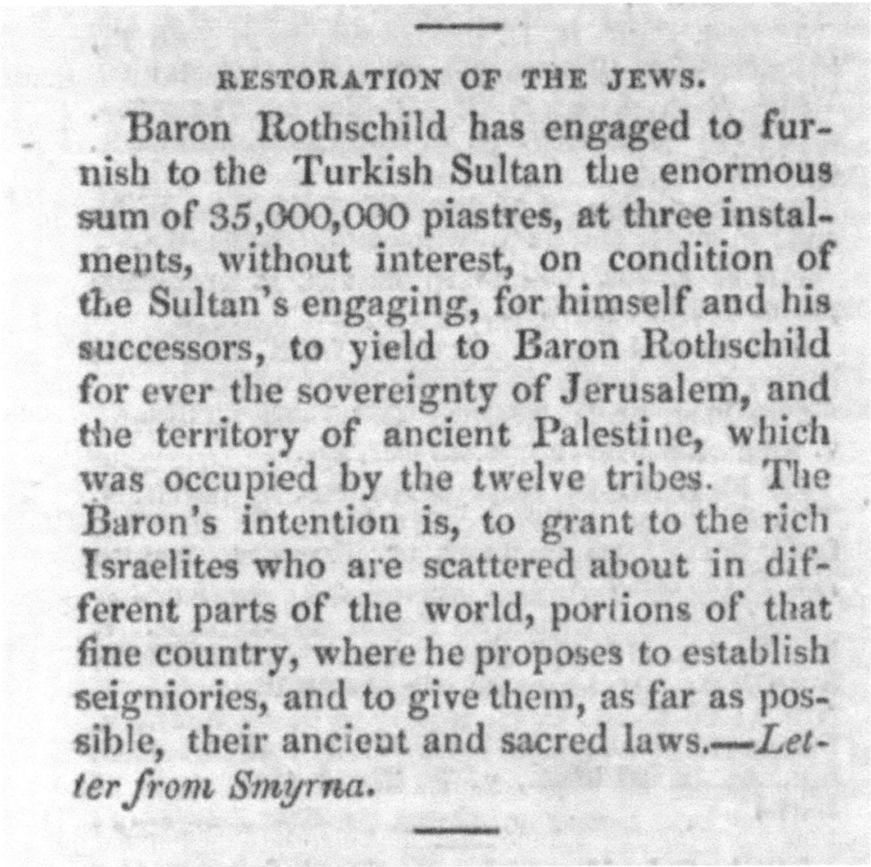

RESTORATION OF THE JEWS.

Baron Rothschild has engaged to furnish to the Turkish Sultan the enormous sum of 35,000,000 piastres, at three instalments, without interest, on condition of the Sultan's engaging, for himself and his successors, to yield to Baron Rothschild for ever the sovereignty of Jerusalem, and the territory of ancient Palestine, which was occupied by the twelve tribes. The Baron's intention is, to grant to the rich Israelites who are scattered about in different parts of the world, portions of that fine country, where he proposes to establish seigniories, and to give them, as far as possible, their ancient and sacred laws.—*Letter from Smyrna.*

Image #23: as this 1829 Asiatic Journal newspaper clipping shows, the Rothschilds tried to buy the land of Palestine, but when that didn't fully work, they resorted to other methods.

This Turkish source (www.Sabite.org)[140] claims that the oldest Jewish colony in Palestine was a Jewish agricultural school called Mikveh Israel, founded in 1870 in Jaffa, opened by Alliance Israélite Universelle (Universal Israelite Alliance) founded by French Jews in 1860. It states that the 750 acres of land used by the school was leased from the Ottoman Government. This source[141] claims the Rothschilds only began taking an active interest in buying Palestinian land in 1882. It reveals how Jewish settlers were allowed to live there but they had to answer to Baron Edmond James de Rothschild (1845-1934) who was not the actual 'baron' or patriarch of the House of Rothschild despite being called 'Baron.' It notes that *"the Baron's philanthropic regime demanded total obedience from the settlers, and their lack of independence and the friction created by bureaucratic domination led to several revolts in the colonies."* At the end of 1899, the settlements were transferred to the JCA or ICA (Jewish Colonization Association; both abbreviations are used), still controlled by Rothschild but under a different name, along with some fifteen million francs. The JCA was later reorganized by Rothschild as the Palestine Jewish Colonization Association (PJCA) with his son James appointed as president for life.[142] Other early Zionist colonization organizations included the Jewish Colonial Trust, the Colonization Commission and the Palestine Land Development Company. The same Sabite source closely tracks the advancement of Jewish colonies from the 1880s onwards, noting how the Ottoman Empire was becoming increasingly wary of the Judaization of the region, worrying that it could upset the balance of the population living there. In 1882, it issued a resolution to ban all entrance of Jewish strangers into Palestine except pilgrims, but Zionist Jews continued to settle under the guise of pilgrimage. In 1884, it issued legislation that Jews had to get their passports approved in foreign Ottoman embassies to be granted entrance into Palestine, but Zionist Jews got around that by using fake passports (see chapter 12 for today's Mossad – nothing has changed). In 1887, it limited Jewish pilgrims to a one-month stay, requiring they pay a deposit to enter. Visiting was one thing, but buying land was another. At that time, foreigners could purchase land anywhere except Hejaz, which enabled Zionists to purchase as much land as they wanted in Palestine. In 1883, the Ottoman Government passed a law permitting only Ottoman citizens to purchase land, but the Zionists got around this ban by using Ottoman Jews, who purchased the land and then transferred it to non-Ottoman Jews. This led to a law in 1892 that decreed that no Jew – regardless of nationality – could purchase any land in Palestine.

In typical Rothschild style, they had their agents there doing their dirty work. Joshua Ossovetski confiscated about 74 acres of land under false pretenses in the district of Safed in the Acre province.[143] Ossovetski settled Jews there who were encouraged to build housing on top of old Muslim cemeteries, a Zionist settling technique that is still in use to this day. The Jewish settlers who think they are returning to their 'biblical homeland' (pure hogwash) are just useful tools to the Cult, and pawns in this geopolitical game of control. Local officials were also bribed:[144]

In a letter of complaint written by Sheik Mustafa el-Abdullah in 1898, it was emphasized that the lands of villagers in Haifa were taken forcefully and sold to Jews by Sadık Pasha. Moreover, it was remarked that the governor of Acre disseized a public land in order to sell it to Jews. Another document shows that Jerusalem Treasury Accountant took the property of people illegally and under false pretenses for personal gain. Similarly, it was understood that Jericho Town Principal Ali Efendi disseized and confiscated the people's land and then, sold this land to foreigners.

In a desperate attempt to reverse reality, and as part of its ongoing hasbara (propaganda) initiatives, Israel now tries to claim it is not a colonizer, that Israelis were indigenous to the land and that it is the Palestinians who are the invaders!

Image #24: there are many Jews opposed to Zionism such as Neturei Karta, which is a positive thing, however by believing in the Torah they still subscribe to Jewish supremacy on some level

The First Zionist Congress of 1897 in Basel, Switzerland

Zionism has always been a political philosophy or national movement and, as such, is entirely distinct from Judaism, which is a religion. Zionism is about the founding of a legal-political-national-military entity for a certain group of people, and the acquisition of land that such an endeavor entails. While it drapes itself in religion, there is nothing inherently religious about it; religion is just a useful cover for it to achieve its purposes. This is why many traditional and orthodox Jewish Groups, such as True Torah Jews and Neturei Karta, have vehemently opposed Zionism and have stated that it is diametrically opposed to true Judaism. Neturei Karta (website nkusa.org) proudly proclaims itself to be anti-Zionist and pro-Palestine.

The Zionist movement coalesced in 1897 when it launched the First Zionist Congress in Basel, Switzerland. It had originally been planned to be held in Munich, Germany, but massive and widespread opposition from the local rabbis there resulted in anti-Zionist Jewish leaders signing a document stating that they would not accept a

Zionist conference in their city.[145] Even the Jewish Virtual Library[146] admits that significant opposition from the local Jewish community there, both Orthodox and Reform, made it so that it was transferred to a location less hostile. This in itself is an interesting historical footnote, because it shows the lengths to which Rothschild Zionist leaders had to go to convince Jews to get on board with Zionism when many were naturally opposed to it or skeptical of it. The movement was led by the Austro-Hungarian Theodore Herzl, a man who had contempt for ordinary Jews and believed that *"the wealthy Jews rule the world. In their hands lies the fate of governments and nations."*[147] According to Jerry Klinger, President of the Jewish American Society for Historic Preservation,[148] Herzl did not consciously know about Jacob Frank and the Frankist Cult that had arisen barely a hundred years earlier in his own backyard of the Austro-Hungarian Empire … but he was nonetheless a key agent pushing a key Cult agenda item.

It was at the turn of the century that the Zionist movement became a highly visible entity and political force; Herzl even managed to finagle his way into meetings with many world leaders such as the Ottoman Sultan and the Pope. In the next chapter, we shall turn our attention to the 20th century, when the Cult really flexed its muscle and showed its true power in being able to break up empires to mold them to its will. The Cult set its sights on conquering Eurasia, which would entail breaking up or subduing all of the Russian, Prussian, Ottoman and Austro-Hungarian Empires. The period of 1900-1945 was when the Cult greatly accelerated its agenda, lifting up or taking down countries like playthings to make way for its new pet project, the creation of the modern-day state of Israel.

Sources

---

[124] Pawns in the Game, Guy Carr, chapter 9, https://www.heritech.com/yamaguchy/library/carr/pawns_09.html

[125] https://www.chafer.edu/CTS-Journal-For-Zions-Sake-Darby-and-Christian-Zionism-by-Paul-Wilkinson

[126] https://libertytothecaptives.net/darby_writings_occult.html

[127] The Committee of 300, John Coleman, pg. 16, https://www.cia.gov/library/abbottabad-compound/4A/4A92FD2FB4DAE3F773DB0B7742CF0F65_Coleman.-.CONSPIRATORS.HIERARCHY.-.THE.STORY.OF.THE.COMMITTEE.OF.300.R.pdf

[128] https://reformedreflections.org/articles/th-dispensationalism-d-s.pdf

[129] https://fortheloveofhistruth.com/2013/09/07/scofield-bible-part-3-c-i-scofield-dispensational-scalawag/

[130] https://proliberty.com/observer/20090507.htm

[131] https://kolbecenter.org/kolbe-report-11-25-23/

[132] https://theologyonline.com/threads/the-freemason-and-dispensationalist-connection.40545/

[133] https://christianobserver.net/the-scofield-bible-its-powerful-effect-on-modern-christianity/

[134] https://www.reformedontheweb.com/eschatology2/scofield-heresy-kevin-a-lehmann.pdf

[135] https://balfourproject.org/the-road-to-balfour-the-history-of-christian-zionism-by-stephen-sizer-2/

[136] http://american_almanac.tripod.com/palmzoo2.htm

[137] https://balfourproject.org/the-road-to-balfour-the-history-of-christian-zionism-by-stephen-sizer-2/

[138] https://archive.org/details/asiaticjournala27unkngoog/page/758/mode/2up

[139] https://babel.hathitrust.org/cgi/pt?id=mdp.39015058342257&seq=997

[140] https://www.sabite.org/judaization-of-palestine

---

[141] https://www.jstor.org/stable/4282496

[142] https://sursockhouse.com/rothschild-land-purchases-and-early-israel/

[143] https://www.sabite.org/judaization-of-palestine

[144] Ibid.

[145] https://www.posenlibrary.com/entry/protest-against-zionism

[146] https://www.jewishvirtuallibrary.org/first-to-twelfth-zionist-congress-1897-1921

[147] https://www.jewishvoiceforlabour.org.uk/article/theodor-herzl-founder-of-zionism-not-quite-what-you-might-imagine/

[148] https://www.jewish-american-society-for-historic-preservation.org/images/The_longing_makes_the_Messiah.pdf

CHAPTER 7: THE CULT FOMENTS REVOLUTIONS, INSTALLS CENTRAL BANKS AND IGNITES A WORLD WAR

"From the days of Spartacus-Weishaupt to those of Karl Marx, and down to Trotsky (Russia), Bela Kun (Hungary), Rosa Luxembourg (Germany), and Emma Goldman (United States), this world-wide conspiracy for the overthrow of civilisation and for the reconstitution of society on the basis of arrested development, of envious malevolence, and impossible equality, has been steadily growing. It played, as a modern writer, Mrs. Webster, has so ably shown, a definitely recognisable part in the tragedy of the French Revolution. It has been the mainspring of every subversive movement during the Nineteenth Century; and now at last this band of extraordinary personalities from the underworld of the great cities of Europe and America have gripped the Russian people by the hair of their heads and have become practically the undisputed masters of that enormous empire ... There is no need to exaggerate the part played in the creation of Bolshevism and in the actual bringing about of the Russian Revolution by these international and for the most part atheistical Jews. It is certainly a very great one; it probably outweighs all others. With the notable exception of Lenin, the majority of the leading figures are Jews."

– From *Zionism vs. Bolshevism*, an article by former UK PM Winston Churchill[149]

"Zionism is a political program for the conquest of the world ... Zionism destroyed Russia by violence as a warning to other nations. It is destroying the United States through bankruptcy, as Lenin advised. Zionism wants another world war if necessary to enslave the people."

– Anti-Zionist Jewish attorney Henry H. Klein (1879-1955)[150]

"[The United States was railroaded into] that war [WWI] merely so that the Zionists of the world could obtain Palestine."

– From a 1961 speech by Benjamin Freedman[151]

Revolutions and wars are key ways that society is thrown into chaos, turned upside down and transformed. Changes occurs violently – and rapidly. It should come as no surprise, then, that the Cult has been the force behind major world revolutions and wars, including the French Revolution of 1789, the Young Turk Revolution of 1908 and the Russian Revolution of 1917, as well the War of 1812, the American Civil War (1861-1865) (which was an international war despite the name) and, most definitely, WWI (World War I). In the case of the French Revolution, the Cult influenced the rise of the Jacobins who instituted a 'Reign of Terror' with thousands of guillotine deaths. For more detailed information on this, see Antelman's book *To Eliminate the Opiate Volume 1*. In this chapter, we will look briefly at the Cult's meddling in the affairs of the young USA, its orchestration of the Ottoman/Turkish and Russian Revolutions, and the way it maneuvered the pieces into place years in advance so it could ignite WWI.

The Rothschilds vs. Andrew Jackson, Abraham Lincoln and a Young USA

Ever since the US broke away from England and declared its independence, the Rothschilds were intent upon establishing a private bank there with themselves as the principal owners or shareholders. Indeed, the entire history of the US for over a century – from around the 1780s to 1913, including all of the 19th century – can be best understood as the battle between the forces wanting a privately-owned central bank and the forces opposing it. All the wars and assassinations (successful or not) that went on during this period resulted from this foundational struggle. A good overview of this period can be found in the book *The Suppressed History of American Banking* by Xaviant Haze.

One of the first skirmishes occurred in 1811 when Congress chose not to renew the Charter of the First Bank of the United States, a decision mainly motivated by the fact that the Rothschilds owned 80% of the bank. In typical fashion, the Rothschilds attempted to punish the US; European investors withdrew more than $7 million from the bank, which threw the US into a recession. It also precipitated the next war, the War of 1812, which was to last around 3 years until 1815. The Rothschilds had achieved a temporary victory; in 1816, the Second Bank of the United States, also partially owned by the Rothschilds, was given a 20-year charter. The Rothschilds lost no time in creating one of their famous boom-bust cycles, whereby they increased the money supply in the years 1816-1818, then restricted it in 1819, leading to lots of people unable to pay their debts and losing their land. This event was called the Panic of 1819. It lasted until 1824 and is often referred to as America’s first financial crisis.

The Rothschilds had many agents in America. One of the prominent ones at that time was Nicholas Biddle, who became president of the Second Bank in 1822. Conversely, there were some aware people who saw the scale of enslavement that a central bank would bring, and resisted it vociferously. Among these were Thomas Jefferson (author of the Declaration of Independence and third American president) and Andrew Jackson (seventh American president). Jackson was a military commander who became a national hero. Despite his openly racist attitude towards Native American Indians, Jackson understood better than almost any other American alive during the 1820s that a privately-owned central bank had to be stopped if America were to be a free and successful country. Such was Jackson's determination on this point that he made it the central pillar of his campaign when he ran for president in 1824; he won the popular vote but not the electoral majority. Henry Clay (who had been recruited by Rothschild agent Biddle) helped to ensure that John Quincy Adams was elected, who, after he won, then invited Clay to join his cabinet. However, such was Jackson's popularity that he won the presidency in 1828 and even formed a new political coalition in the 1830s that

Image #25: the controversial Andrew Jackson who keenly understood and opposed the power of private central banking

was to become the Democratic Party, one of the two main political parties in America today. Haze writes:[152]

The Rothschilds' worst fears would now come true as Jackson began with the intent of removing all those who favored the bankers. During his first term Jackson was successful in cleaning out the Rothschilds' many minions from government service and fired more than half of the federal government. Jackson also began an investigation of the Rothschilds' central bank located at the Second Bank of the United States. The president soon discovered that the bank was privately owned, mostly by foreign stockholders with political agendas that were not in America's favor.

On July 4th 1832, Congress passed a bill to extend the central bank's charter for another 15 years, but Jackson vetoed it, laying out his reasoning in a carefully-worded veto message to Congress. However, the battle between Jackson and the Rothschilds (and their frontman Biddle) was just beginning. In October 1833, Jackson announced federal funds would not be deposited in the Second Bank and instead went to 23 state-chartered banks. Over the next two years, Jackson and the Rothschilds fought furiously; Jackson fired two Treasury secretaries and made sure no governmental funds went to the central bank, while Biddle put a squeeze on lending and demanded all loans be repaid. The Rothschilds were doing everything they could to cause financial hardship and calamity for all Americans to punish Jackson for his audacity. In January 1835, Jackson paid off the national debt, the only time in US history that this has ever been accomplished. Finally, things reached the point where the Rothschilds turned to one of their favorite Cult techniques: assassination. They hired a mentally unstable and unemployed painter named Richard Lawrence to eliminate Jackson. Lawrence approached Jackson near the steps of the Capitol building and shot, but somehow, his gun miraculously misfired. Jackson, then 67 years old, confronted the assassin and clubbed him to the ground; then Lawrence grabbed a second pistol and tried to shoot, but it also misfired! Jackson survived the assassination attempt, the first ever on an American president, and Lawrence was sentenced to life imprisonment; he would die in jail, but not before admitting that powerful people in England had hired him to kill the president. By 1836, the American economy was booming. Jackson's vice president Martin Van Buren was elected president in 1836. Jackson famously said to Van Buren that *"The bank is trying to kill me ... but I will kill it!"*[153]

As America moved into the 1840s and 1850s, the Rothschilds, still bitter from their defeat in the War of 1812 and for losing to Jackson in the bank war, had been scheming for a way to conquer America. Their plan was to instigate a civil war. They had plenty of agents in both the South and North; they maintained close business ties with the South's cotton-growing aristocracy, and they had a banking agent August Belmont, whose wife was the niece of John Slidell,

Image #26: Abraham Lincoln, another US president who resisted the Rothschilds' attempts at a central US bank. Unlike Jackson, he did not survive assassination

a partner with Judah P. Benjamin (on whom more shortly) in a law firm in New Orleans. They believed the slavery issue was America's Achilles heel and the ideal way to pit North against South and brother against brother. They managed to ignite the American Civil War a month after President Abraham Lincoln took office in March 1861. Interestingly enough, Haze suggests the possibility that Lincoln, like other famous historical figures (e.g. Adolf Hitler, see next chapter), was a Rothschild bastard, i.e. an illegitimate and undeclared child of the Rothschild family. This would certainly make sense in light of the Cult modus operandi of placing their agents in key positions, because it would mean placing their family and offspring in these positions. At any rate, the Rothschilds backed both sides, the Union (the North) and the Confederacy (the South), just as they had done with previous wars in European nations, hoping to bankrupt the American government so that it would come begging to them for financial help. This is exactly what happened. Lincoln met with the Rothschilds, and they laid out their terms to him: 35% interest on all money owed to the US, plus a new charter for another central bank! Haze writes:[154]

Lincoln held a poker face during the meeting and once it ended told them that he would be in touch. What Lincoln did next made the Rothschilds angrier than Jackson had made them. Recognizing the Rothschild hijacking for what it was, and furious about the high level of interest they attempted to gain from him, Lincoln made his boldest presidential move yet – he printed his own debt-free money.

These new banknotes were called greenbacks. Lincoln also introduced state loans that the Rothschild bankers couldn't touch, thus financing the Civil War on state-issued credit. He knew he would be a targeted man after that. Lincoln oversaw the National

Banking Acts of 1863 and 1864 which were designed to keep the Rothschilds in check by including a nationally regulated private banking system that could issue cheap credit to build industries not reliant on the Southern plantation system. To stop Lincoln's highly successful governmental paper money experiment, the Rothschilds orchestrated it so Britain had troops in Canada (waiting to invade New York), while both France and Spain had troops in Mexico (ready to invade from the south). Confederate leader Jefferson Davis even offered Louisiana and Texas to France in exchange for their military support against the North. Lincoln was in deep trouble. It was then that Tsar Alexander II of Russia stepped in. Here is Haze again:[155]

Russia shared a good economic relationship with America, which had inspired them to end serfdom and emulate the American practice of private farming ... when Lincoln learned that Alexander II had also rejected the Rothschilds' continual attempts to set up a central bank in Russia he saw that the two leaders were in the same boat, and so he asked for the Tsar's help during the Civil War. The Tsar obliged and sent his fleet across the Atlantic with a specific warning to the Rothschilds that an attack on America would be considered an attack on Russia as well.

Lincoln won his war with the Rothschilds, thanks to his greenbacks and the Tsar's Russian Navy, but he lost his final battle to them. He was assassinated on April 15th 1965, a month before the American Civil War ended, by John Wilkes Booth, a very famous actor at the time. Booth was connected to Rothschild agent Judah Benjamin, the Confederate Secretary of State, who was the most influential person in the Confederacy after Jefferson Davis (President of the Southern Confederacy) and General Robert E. Lee. Infiltration is the name of the game for the Cult. The Jewish Benjamin had been selected by the Rothschilds and installed as the first adviser to Davis. Benjamin was known as 'the brains of the revolt.' Booth had coded messages in his trunk, the key to which was found in Benjamin's possession.[156] Benjamin escaped to England where he later died. There is some evidence Booth was Jewish:[157]

Asia Booth Clarke, the sister of acclaimed actor John Wilkes Booth who shot Lincoln, stated in her 1882 memoir that their father, Junius Brutus Booth, attended synagogues along with other houses of worship: "In the synagogue, he was known as a Jew, because he conversed with rabbis and learned doctors, and joined their worship in the Hebraic tongue. He read the Talmud, also, and strictly adhered to many of its laws." Asia Booth Clarke is not the only source for this; her other brother Edwin Booth, also an actor, reportedly told Rabbi Isaac Mayer Wise that his father was Jewish. It's not at all clear how accurate the Booths' statements are, but it's certainly interesting that Junius Brutus Booth wanted it to be thought that he descended from Jews, and that two of his children believed him.

Lincoln had valiantly pushed off the Rothschilds and a privately-owned central bank on US soil, but the Cult is persistent, and it would be back around half a century later, in 1913, to finally complete its objective of enslaving America.

Isolating Germany

By 1900, the Round Table and Milner's Kindergarten operatives running the British Empire were starting to get quite nervous. Britain had been the world's superpower for quite some time, and had amassed an incredible amount of colonies as part of their "Commonwealth," killing or enslaving the natives and stealing their lands along the way. This was all being done on behalf of the Cult, of course. However, at this point in time, Britain was looking to the European continent with apprehension. The young nation of Germany, newly formed in 1871, was rising quickly to great heights. Germany was no longer just a buyer of British products but was becoming a world class manufacturer, industrial power and military force in her own right. Germany wanted to gain direct access to the oil fields of the Middle East, so came up the idea of constructing the Berlin-Baghdad Railway, which was started in 1903. The plan was to connect Berlin with Baghdad (current day Iraq, but then under Ottoman rule), and then to Basra, so that the Germans could establish a port on the Persian Gulf. The Germans were starting to build a navy that could rival that of Britain – and Britain had relied upon her navy for world domination. As Guido Preparata writes:[158]

[I]f Germany and Russia united in one form or another, the Eurasian Embrace would come into existence: that is, a concrete Eurasian empire at the center of the continental landmass, which would come to rest on an enormous Slav army and German technological mastery. And that ... would have mortally threatened the supremacy of the British Empire.

He also writes:[159]

Britain had to favor the line of least resistance, and single out Germany as the proximate adversary because: (1) the Reich was the dynamic half of the Russo-German threat, and, (2) it could be surrounded and blockaded by an entente of neighboring parties with somewhat greater ease, hence Britain's forthcoming rapprochement with Russia, her traditional antagonist.

Thus, the Cult-controlled British decide to embark on a strategy that can still be seen today whereby they aimed to ensure that no German-Russian alliance could be forged. This foreign policy objective was one of the main drivers for both WWI and WWII where, in both cases, Germany was manipulated into joining alliances or axes that would form the losing side. As we shall see, this dovetailed into the Cult Zionist agenda to use Germany to help set up their new country in the Middle East.

The Young Turk Revolution: Overthrowing the Ottoman Sultan

While the British were isolating Germany, the Rothschilds were busy moving the global chess pieces around to make the Zionist dream a reality. As detailed in the previous chapter, they had been on a quest for decades trying to colonize Palestine, and although they were making considerable headway, they also faced significant opposition from the Ottoman Sultan, who saw that the particular kind of Jews moving to Palestine – Zionist settlers being funded and/or controlled by the Rothschilds – were destabilizing the region.

The founding father of Zionism, Theodor Herzl, went to Istanbul five times between the years of 1896 and 1902 to try to convince the Ottoman Empire to allow the Jews to set up a state in Palestine. On one occasion, Herzl offered 20 million sterlings for Palestine to Sultan Abdul Hamid II via Polish aristocrat Count Philipp de Newlinsky, but the Sultan rejected the offer. On a subsequent occasion, Herzl met the Sultan and offered financial support to save the Ottoman Empire from economic dependency on the West – in exchange for Jewish settlements in Palestine. This time, the Sultan did not completely turn down Herzl's offer, but asked him to come up with a plan to consolidate the Ottoman debt. Herzl then presented a plan whereby the crypto-Jew Cult bankers would pay off all

Ottoman debt to Europe in a couple of years, and establish an Ottoman-Jewish company to improve business and industrial life in Ottoman Empire – all under the condition that Jews could establish a state within Palestine. In some of the meetings with the Sultan, he offered about 20 million Ottoman Lira to improve the economy and another 20 million to build Palestine, however the Sultan repeatedly rejected any plan that would give Palestine to the Cult.[160]

The Cult then used its resources to overthrow the Sultan in 1908 – the first of many major revolutions that would occur in the 20th century. The Cult funded a group known colloquially as "The Young Turks" and officially as the "Committee for Union and Progress" (CUP) to get rid of the Sultan. Ultimately their plan was to dispossess the Turks of Palestine entirely, thus putting it in the hands of the British whose government they controlled. However, before that would happen, they used their adherents, the Donmeh, whom we discussed in chapter 4. You may recall that 'donmeh' (also written as 'dönme') is a Turkish word meaning to turn, and it was the original term used to describe the followers of Sabbatai Zevi who 'turned' to Islam on the surface but remained Jewish underneath. This article *The Dönme: Jewish Converts, Muslim Revolutionaries, and Secular Turks* states:[161]

Most important, several Dönme were leading members of the Committee for Union and Progress, the revolutionary party known as the Young Turks, who in 1908 forced the Sultan to grant a constitution. The Dönme, like Jews and Freemasons, sympathized with the CUP's scientific, reformist program, though Baer emphasizes that the CUP was not a Dönme party – any more than the Russian Bolsheviks, though they included many Jews, were a Jewish party. Even so, some prominent Young Turks were Dönme, including the editor of the Party's newspaper and the finance minister in the new CUP government.

Mustafa Kemal Atatürk was a Donmeh[162] and a Grand Orient Mason[163] at the Lodge of Salonica where he was born. It was he who spearheaded the Young Turkish Movement that led to the Young Turkish Revolution. Later on, the Young Turks would carry out the Armenian Genocide (1915-1917) that resulted in the murder of around one million Armenians, who were made to undergo death marches to the Syrian Desert. Approximately 100,000 to 200,000 Armenian women and children were forcibly converted to Islam and integrated into Muslim households. The Cult achieved its aim: the new Republic of Türkiye that was established in 1923 was much more sympathetic to Jewish interests in Palestine than the Sultan had been.

Image #27: crypto-Jew and Donmeh Mustafa Kemal Atatürk overthrew the Ottoman Empire for the Cult

The Russian Revolution

The Russian Revolution was an event of far-reaching consequences whose effects are still felt today. Not only did the Cult manage to orchestrate it during a world war (in 1917, when the First World War was still being fought), but they managed to overthrow the monarchy in the world's largest nation (in terms of land area). Russia was no mere country but an empire that sprawled all the way from East Asia to Europe. The reign of Communism in that country officially lasted another 74 years until 1991, and even though Russia is no longer officially Communist, the features of centralized authority, and the expectation of the people that the government will/should provide everything for its dependent citizenry, still live on today.

Researchers such as Antony Sutton who wrote *Wall Street and the Bolshevik Revolution* did the research to show that the international bankers (he focused on men like John D. Rockefeller, J.P. Morgan, Max Warburg, Paul Warburg and Jacob Schiff) were the ones pulling the strings. This is true, however the Rothschilds were behind all of these names (as mentioned earlier, the Rothschilds and Schiffs shared a double house in Frankfurt)[164], not to mention the Round Table figure Milner, as well as Skull and Bonesman Averill Harriman (a friend of Prescott Bush) via Guaranty Trust. This group arranged for Leon Trotsky (real name Lev Bronstein), who was earning very little money, to have enough funds as he was transported all over the world, eventually getting an American passport (due to the intervention of then US President Woodrow Wilson) so that he could enter Russia. David Icke writes:[165]

John Schiff, Jacob's grandson, said in the New York Journal American *in 1949 that his New-York based grandfather gave some $20 million ($1 billion today) to fund the Russian Revolution ... Another big funder of Trotsky was Britain's Lord Alfred Milner according to anti-Communist Russian general Arlene de Goulevitch.*

It was also arranged for Vladimir Lenin to get into Russia. Sutton wrote:[166]

Image #28: Leonid Trotsky, a Cult-funded implant into Russia to lead the 'people's revolution'

In April 1917 Lenin and a party of 32 Russian revolutionaries, mostly Bolsheviks, journeyed by train from Switzerland across Germany through Sweden to Petrograd, Russia. They were on their way to join Leon Trotsky to "complete the revolution." Their trans-Germany transit was approved, facilitated, and financed by the German General Staff. Lenin's transit to Russia was part of a plan approved by the German Supreme Command, apparently not immediately known to the kaiser, to aid in the disintegration of the Russian army and so eliminate Russia from World War I. The possibility that the Bolsheviks might be turned against Germany and Europe did not occur to the German General Staff.

On the face of it, isn't it incredibly strange that a 'Russian' revolution would be led by foreigners? Yes, unless you understand that the Cult directs these events and thus the event was not really Russian. It took place in Russia, but only because the Cult had carefully analyzed and selected Russia as the target, after softening it up for decades prior with Marxist ideology. The same softening up has been happening to many Western countries via the Cult-

Image #29: Vladimir Lenin, another Cult-funded implant into Russia who said the political power comes from the point of a gun

concocted cultural Marxism which later led to political correctness and woke ideology.

To onlookers, it appeared that most of those leading the Russian Revolution were 'Jewish' however hopefully by now it is becoming clear that this is the usual scam and way that the Cult hides itself. The leaders were not Jewish but rather Sabbatean-Frankist crypto-Jews. David Icke says *"There were many other prominent 'Jews', too, when the Jewish population of Russia was no more than five percent."*[167] Both Icke and Sutton mention the State Department Decimal File (861.00/5339) dated November 13th 1918, which states that Jacob Schiff, Kuhn, Loeb & Company, Felix Warburg, Otto H. Kahn, Mortimer L. Schiff, Jerome J. Hanauer, Guggenheim, Max Breitung and Isaac Seligman were all Jews involved in organizing the Russian Revolution. Sutton rejects the idea that the Russian Revolution was a 'Jewish' plot (without understanding Sabbatean-Frankism) however Icke gets the point: these people are hiding behind the facade of Jewishness to do their evil work. British war Prime Minister Winston Churchill, quoted at the start of this chapter, wrote that the *"international and for the most part atheistical Jews"* were behind the Russian Revolution which I interpret as his way of highlighting that it was the crypto-Jews from whose ranks the "international" banking cartel developed and who are definitely "atheistical" from the standpoint of not following a good and healthy divine figure – although they are clearly not areligious altogether, since they follow a Luciferian or Satanic religion. Churchill's reference to Spartacus-Weishaupt is none other than Adam Weishaupt (whose code name was Spartacus according to Antelman)[168], the founder of the original Order of the Illuminati in 1776, mentioned in chapter 5. Although Churchill correctly identified that the Cult was the source of *"of every subversive movement during the Nineteenth Century"* he doesn't mention the term "Sabbatean-Frankism." It is questionable how much this awareness displayed by Churchill mattered, since he was thoroughly owned by the Cult and acted as a puppet playing his part when WWII came around.

In *Conjuring Hitler*, Guido Preparata describes how the Round Table or Cult operatives that ran the Western Powers (Britain, France and the US) not only helped the brutal Bolsheviks come to power in Russia, but also cemented their grip on power over the entire landmass by siding with the Bolshevik 'Reds' against the Czarist 'Whites.' However, while doing this, they had to publicly pretend they supported the Whites against the godless communist Reds, so they made a show of sending a small amount troops to 'assist' the Whites while double crossing them and continuing to covertly fund the Reds. By 1922, the Reds had defeated the Whites in a bloody civil war and Russia became the USSR. For the Cult, ensuring that a regime diametrically opposed to the one about to take shape in Germany was the most essential thing, no matter how many millions of lives had to be sacrificed, because this would ensure the Russians and Germans could be played off against each other in the next coming war.

Aleksandr Solzhenitsyn was a famous Russian novelist and historian who survived the gulag under Stalin. He won the Nobel Prize in literature in 1970 for books such as *Gulag Archipelago* and was finally expelled from the USSR in 1974. Towards the end of his life, some of his controversial 'antisemitic' writings never saw the light of day in the West, but in essays like *200 Years Together* he alludes to the force behind the Bolshevist takeover. He exposed that the nine-member Presidium of the CEC, which contained five Jews and only one ethnic Russian, was the source of real power in the USSR: it *"was they who had in fact ruled over Russia."*[169] Russian President Vladimir Putin himself said that the composition of the first Soviet government was around 80-85% Jewish.[170] So much for the 'Russian' Revolution.

The 1913 Double Blow to America: The IRS and The Fed are Born

During this period from around 1900 to 1920, the Cult was working its devilish magic worldwide. While it was fomenting war and revolution in Eurasia, as well as shoring up support for a Jewish state in Palestine, it was simultaneously entrenching its grip on power in the United States. The year 1913 was a phenomenal year for the Cult and a horrific one for ordinary Americans. It was the year that the IRS was established in violation of the US Constitution which expressly forbade a graduated income tax until the 16th Amendment was fraudulently passed (see the work of Bill Benson and 'the law that never was').[171] It was also the year that the banksters finally got their claws deep into the heart of their prey via the founding of their permanent central bank. Those who have researched the IRS closely have discovered that the entire

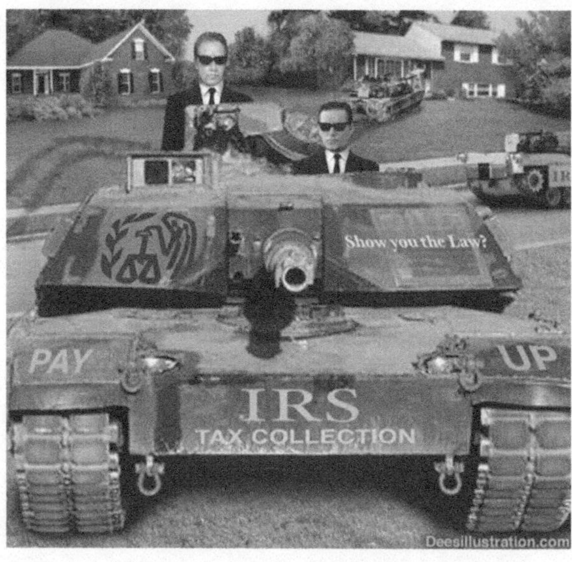

organization basically exists to siphon off the wealth of common Americans, since the US Federal Government was doing just fine funding itself from 1789 to 1913 without a federal income tax. Although you might think that the income tax would work against the ultra rich international banksters, because they might have to fork over large sums of money, think again. The international banksters (i.e. the Cult) wrote the legislation! They ensured there were sufficient loopholes so that they wouldn't have to pay. God forbid the thought. Paying tax is just for ignorant little slaves, after all. They included clauses that allowed foundations to become tax-exempt. This allowed them to not only avoid income tax but also to channel their funds into foundations that then funded education (universities, educational curricula, etc.) which furthered their purpose of opinion-molding. This is one of the reasons for the massive foundations of the early 20th century robber barons – organizations like the Rockefeller Foundation, the Carnegie Foundation, the Ford Foundation, etc. which persist to this day. The bankers then paid PR (Public Relations) firms to paint them in a good light as 'philanthropists' when the opposite was true – they were total misanthropists. According to G. Edward Griffin, the bankers called this "philanthropy with efficiency."

Close investigation reveals the IRS is, in fact, a Puerto Rican trust, deliberately set up in a US Federal Government territory (not one of the 50 states) so that it is domiciled within federal jurisdiction, and can therefore legally call many people outside its jurisdiction "aliens" and thus (absurdly) claim that the income tax it collects only applies to nonresident aliens, i.e. normal Americans living in the 50 states.[172] Many people, including ex-IRS employees like Joe Bannister and Sherry Jackson, have exposed how the agency has failed to produce evidence of a law on the books that shows it has the right and authority to tax ordinary Americans' income.

G. Edward Griffin tells the behind-the-scenes story of how the central bank of the US was formed in his book *The Creature from Jekyll Island.* It is called the Federal Reserve, although it is neither federal (since it is privately not publicly owned, thus not a part of the US Federal Government), nor does it contain a reserve (since it uses fractional reserve banking as discussed in chapter 3, thus does not need much in the way of reserves to create money out of thin air). As far as who own the Fed, it was for a long time a closely guarded secret, but thanks to various researchers, we know there are eight main families. Researcher and author Dean Henderson summarized the evidence as follows:[173]

J. W. McCallister, an oil industry insider with House of Saud connections, wrote in The Grim Reaper that information he acquired from Saudi bankers cited 80% ownership of the New York Federal Reserve Bank – by far the most powerful Fed branch – by just eight families, four of which reside in the US. They are the Goldman Sachs, Rockefellers, Lehmans and Kuhn Loebs of New York; the Rothschilds of Paris and London; the Warburgs of Hamburg; the Lazards of Paris; and the Israel Moses Seifs of Rome.

CPA Thomas D. Schauf corroborates McCallister's claims, adding that ten banks control all twelve Federal Reserve Bank branches. He names N.M. Rothschild of London, Rothschild Bank of Berlin, Warburg Bank of Hamburg, Warburg Bank of Amsterdam, Lehman Brothers of New York, Lazard Brothers of Paris, Kuhn Loeb Bank of New York, Israel Moses Seif Bank of Italy, Goldman Sachs of New York and JP Morgan Chase Bank of New York. Schauf lists William Rockefeller, Paul Warburg, Jacob Schiff and James Stillman as individuals who own large shares of the Fed. The Schiffs are insiders at Kuhn Loeb. The Stillmans are Citigroup insiders, who married into the Rockefeller clan at the turn of the century. Eustace Mullins came to the same conclusions in his book The Secrets of the Federal Reserve, in which he displays charts connecting the Fed and its member banks to the families of Rothschild, Warburg, Rockefeller and the others.

The representatives of each of these families got together on a little island off the coast of Georgia in southern USA, where they hatched the scheme to introduce a central bank. They wrote the legislation and got their man in Congress, Senator Nelson Aldrich, to promote the bill. Central to the way this was passed was the recruitment and installment of Woodrow Wilson as US President. The banksters knew they could manipulate Wilson, since he had a large ego and didn't understand how much power one has if one has the power to create the money that all of society must use. Joe Plummer, author of *Tragedy and Hope 101*, writes:[174]

... there is at least one reference, provided by Sigmund Freud, where Wilson drops all rhetorical subterfuge: 'God ordained that I should be the next President of the United States. Neither you nor any other mortal or mortals could have prevented it.' Additional

quotes further clarify the strength of Wilson's ego. For instance, in his confidential journal, he wrote: 'Why may not the present generation write, through me, its political autobiography.'

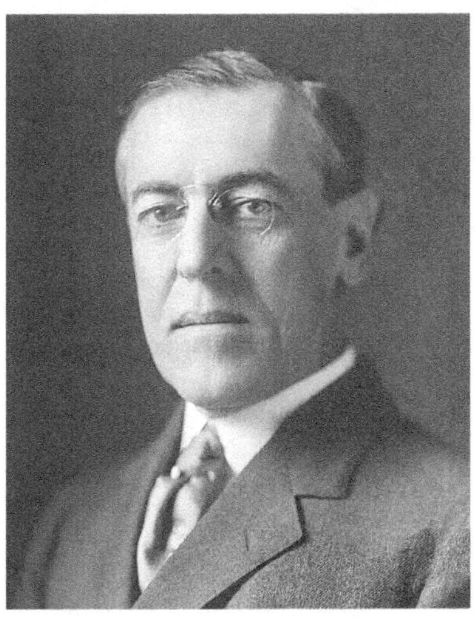

Image #31: Woodrow Wilson, the self-absorbed US president who approved the creation of the Cult private banking network, The Federal Reserve

Servando Gonzales summed up the final equation perfectly: 'Wilson was a man intoxicated with the sense of his own importance and historical relevance' and, as such, he could be 'easily manipulated by a trained intelligence officer (like Edward Mandell House).'

Wilson himself was aware of the power of the Cult at some level. In his book *The New Freedom*, he wrote:[175]

Since I entered politics, I have chiefly had men's views confided to me privately. Some of the biggest men in the United States, in the field of commerce and manufacture, are afraid of somebody, are afraid of something. They know that there is a power somewhere so organized, so subtle, so watchful, so interlocked, so complete, so pervasive, that they had better not speak above their breath when they speak in condemnation of it.

However, his awareness evidently wasn't enough to avoid getting duped by the Cult in various ways. He later regretted his decision to sign the bill allowing the Federal Reserve to become law:[176]

I am a most unhappy man. I have unwittingly ruined my country. A great industrial nation is controlled by its system of credit. Our system of credit is concentrated. The growth of the nation, therefore, and all our activities are in the hands of a few men. We have come to be one of the worst ruled, one of the most completely controlled and dominated Governments in the civilized world - no longer a Government by free opinion, no longer a Government by conviction and the vote of the majority, but a Government by the opinion and duress of a small group of dominant men.

The Cult likes to work by installing easily-controllable puppet politicians in the limelight while manipulating them from the shadows. In the case of Wilson, his handler or puppet master was Colonel Mandell House, part of the Round Table Group, who always found the 'right' advisors to guide Wilson whenever he 'needed' help. The secret meeting of the conspirators wasn't discovered until much later. As Plummer writes, *"Unfortunately, the Jekyll Island story didn't leak until 1916, years after the damage had already been done. And even after it was exposed, 'educators, commentators, and historians' continued to deny that the meeting ever took place."*[177] Such has been the power of the international banksters to confuse people, including so-called educated people and academics, about the power and nature of money creation. Frank A. Vanderlip, president of the most powerful New York bank at the time (National City Bank of New York, now Citibank) admitted the following in 1935:[178]

There was an occasion near the close of 1910, when I was as secretive—indeed as furtive—as any conspirator ... I do not feel it is any exaggeration to speak of our secret expedition to Jekyll Island as the occasion of the actual conception of what eventually became the Federal Reserve System ... Discovery, we knew, simply must not happen, or else all our time and effort would be wasted. If it were to be exposed publicly that our particular group had got together and written a banking bill, that bill would have no chance whatever of passage by Congress...although the Aldrich Federal Reserve plan was defeated, we had together laid the essential, fundamental lines which ultimately took the form of 1913's Federal Reserve Act.

Image #32: Edward Mandell House, manipulator of Woodrow Wilson

The Cult was also able to get its people into positions in the US judicial branch. Benjamin Freedman, whose mind-blowing 1961 speech I will get to shortly, was a prominent Jewish man with a conscience who blew the whistle on the conspirators' plans. According to this source,[179] Freedman claimed that lawyer Samuel Untermeyer (an ultra Zionist who played an active part in preparing the Federal Reserve Act) visited Wilson in the White House to blackmail him. Untermeyer allegedly threatened Wilson with a 'breach of promise' lawsuit on behalf of the wife of a Princeton professor with whom Wilson was allegedly carrying on an affair. Wilson himself was a former Princeton professor. Apparently, he had offered to marry this woman. According to Freedman, Untermeyer's client wanted $40,000 that Wilson did not have, so Untermeyer offered to pay his client off if Wilson would allow Untermeyer to choose the next available Supreme Court nomination. In the end, this position went to Louis Brandeis, the first American Jew appointed to the US Supreme Court, who also was a leader of the American Zionist movement and a key figure in acquiring US support for the Balfour Declaration. He was rumored to have been a descendent of a Frankist family.[180] This is yet another example of how the Cult operates – blackmail, infiltration and hijacking – to ensure it gets its agents in key positions of power.

Igniting WWI, Dragging in the US and Getting Britain to Authorize the Land Grab of Palestine

Freedman is well-known among conspiracy researchers and truthseekers for his 1961 speech where he exposed the true reasons that the US entered WWI. To understand how this horrific war began, we need to pick up the thread introduced earlier regarding the suspicion and apprehension with which the British Round Table manipulators were regarding the ascent of Germany. Their worldview was well summed up by Sir Halford MacKinder, a British geographer, academic and politician. In 1904 he put forth his paper *The Geographical Pivot of History* at the Royal Geographical Society in which he introduced his Heartland Theory, often considered a founding moment in the history of geopolitics. Mackinder's key idea was that the continents of Europe, Africa and Asia – all connected by land – constituted the "World Island" and were strategically more important to control than the outer continents of the Americas and Australia. Thus, whoever could gain control of the World Island could rule the world. Mackinder believed that the way to hegemony over the World Island was through the "Heartland" (i.e. Russia) and the way to the Heartland was through Eastern Europe (where Prussia or Germany had become the dominant power). His most famous concept is:[181]

Who rules East Europe commands the Heartland; Who rules the Heartland commands the World Island; Who rules the World Island commands the World.

His ideas were interpreted to mean that Germany and Russia must be stopped from forming an alliance at all costs, because such an alliance would be so strong that it would surely become the most dominant power in the world, overshadowing Britain. Thus, in the years leading up to the outbreak of war in 1914, a series of secret talks occurred among Britain, France and Russia, resulting in a secret threeway alliance or Triple Entente in 1907. As James Corbett said, *"the details of Britain's military commitments to Russia and France, and even the negotiations themselves, were deliberately kept hidden from Members of Parliament and even members of the cabinet who were not part of the secret society. It wasn't until November 1911, a full six years into the negotiations, that the cabinet of Prime Minister Herbert Henry Asquith started to learn the details of these agreements, agreements that had been repeatedly and officially denied in the press and in Parliament."*[182]

The idea was to isolate Germany, which was targeted and had already been designated as the eventual loser of the war – both the coming first war and also the second war. Although it may be difficult for the average person to understand this, the Cult plans events decades in advance. Its operations are marked by a ruthless, cunning, stealthy, coldhearted and longterm calculation that is distinctly nonhuman in nature. So WWI began in 1914, and Freedman relays the story that around two years into it, Germany was clearly winning. Britain was in big trouble. Instead of going in for the kill, Germany magnanimously offered Britain a peace deal on a status quo ante basis, meaning that everything would be as it was before the war started. Britain was seriously considering this offer, when in stepped the Cult representatives, who had been planning this for a long time. Their moment had arrived. They were going to use Britain's helplessness at that moment, alongside the fact it was still the world's superpower (though not for much longer), to force them into authorizing an audacious land grab in the Middle East – Palestine, to be precise. As Freedman said:[183]

The Zionists in London went to the British war cabinet and they said: 'Look here. You can yet win this war. You don't have to give up. You don't have to accept the negotiated peace offered to you now by Germany. You can win this war if the United States will come in as your ally.' The United States was not in the war at that time. We were fresh; we were young; we were rich; we were powerful. They [the Zionists] told England: 'We will guarantee to bring the United States into the war as your ally, to fight with you on your side, if you will promise us Palestine after you win the war.' In other words, they made this deal: 'We will get the United States into this war as your ally. The price you must pay us is Palestine after you have won the war and defeated Germany, Austria-Hungary and Turkey.

Now England had as much right to promise Palestine to anybody, as the United States would have to promise Japan to Ireland for any reason whatsoever. It's absolutely absurd that Great Britain – that never had any connection or any interest or any right in what is known as Palestine – should offer it as coin of the realm to pay the Zionists for bringing the United States into the war. However, they made that promise, in October of 1916.

Freedman, though being Jewish himself, was able to see through the Cult's Zionist propaganda. He knew that Britain had no right to give Palestine to anyone, since Britain itself was a settlor and colonizer of lands that were not theirs. So how did the Cult manage to drag the US into a European war when American public opinion was strongly against getting entangled in Europe's conflict? Using the same technique they always did – the tried and true false flag operation, or false flag op for short.

The Lusitania False Flag Operation and the Balfour Declaration

The Lusitania was sailing full of American passengers when it sunk by German U-boats. The Cult was planning this as the episode which would get both Woodrow Wilson and the American public behind the US Military entering WWI. James Perloff writes:[184]

On May 2, 1915 – five days before the Lusitania was sunk – Page wrote to his son: 'If a British liner full of American passengers be blown up, what will Uncle Sam do? That's what's going to happen.' Edward Mandell House was in England at this time as Wilson's emissary. On the morning of the fateful 7th, House met with Edward Grey ... Britain's foreign minister. House recorded: 'We spoke of the probability of an ocean liner being sunk, and I told him if this were done, a flame of indignation would sweep across America, which would in itself probably carry us into the war.' Later that day, House and Grey met with King George V at Buckingham Palace. House wrote: 'We fell to talking, strangely enough, of the probability of Germany sinking a trans-Atlantic liner. . . . He [the king] said, 'Suppose they should sink the Lusitania, with American passengers on board?'' (These quotes appear in Houses's official biography, The Intimate Papers of Colonel House.) These remarks betrayed foreknowledge that cannot be dismissed as coincidences chanced upon in casual conversation.

It should be noted that Germany sunk the Lusitania not to kill women and children (as Cult propaganda claimed), but in an attempt to prevent tens of tons of war munitions from reaching Europe that would be used against them. The Cult was illegally using a passenger boat to transport weapons (humans shields, anyone?). So, the US entered the war and helped the Allies achieve a decisive victory. However, the year before the war was over in 1918, the Zionists managed to get a very important document out of the British Government. This document was probably the most important document in the history of events leading up to the 1948 declaration of modern Israel. It was the 1917 Balfour Declaration, written by none other than Arthur Balfour of the Rhodes and Milner Round Table. Small world, isn't it? And guess who this declaration or letter is made out to? A Rothschild – Lord Rothschild! At this point in history, the lord or patriarch of the Rothschild family was Lionel Walter Rothschild, the 2nd Baron Rothschild. Notice how the Palestinians' rights even then are only recognized as "civil and religious rights" not political or national rights – an indication that even then the plan was to make sure the Palestinians would never have their own nation, and thus would be much easier to dispossess.

As it turns out, Balfour had no intention of consulting with the indigenous Arab population. He wrote the following in a memorandum to Lord Curzon on August 11th 1919:[185]

For in Palestine we do not propose even to go through the form of consulting the wishes of the present inhabitants of the country ... the Four Great Powers are committed to Zionism. And Zionism, be it right or wrong, good or bad, is rooted in age-long traditions, in present needs, in future hopes, of far profounder import than the desires or prejudices of the 700,000 Arabs who now inhabit that

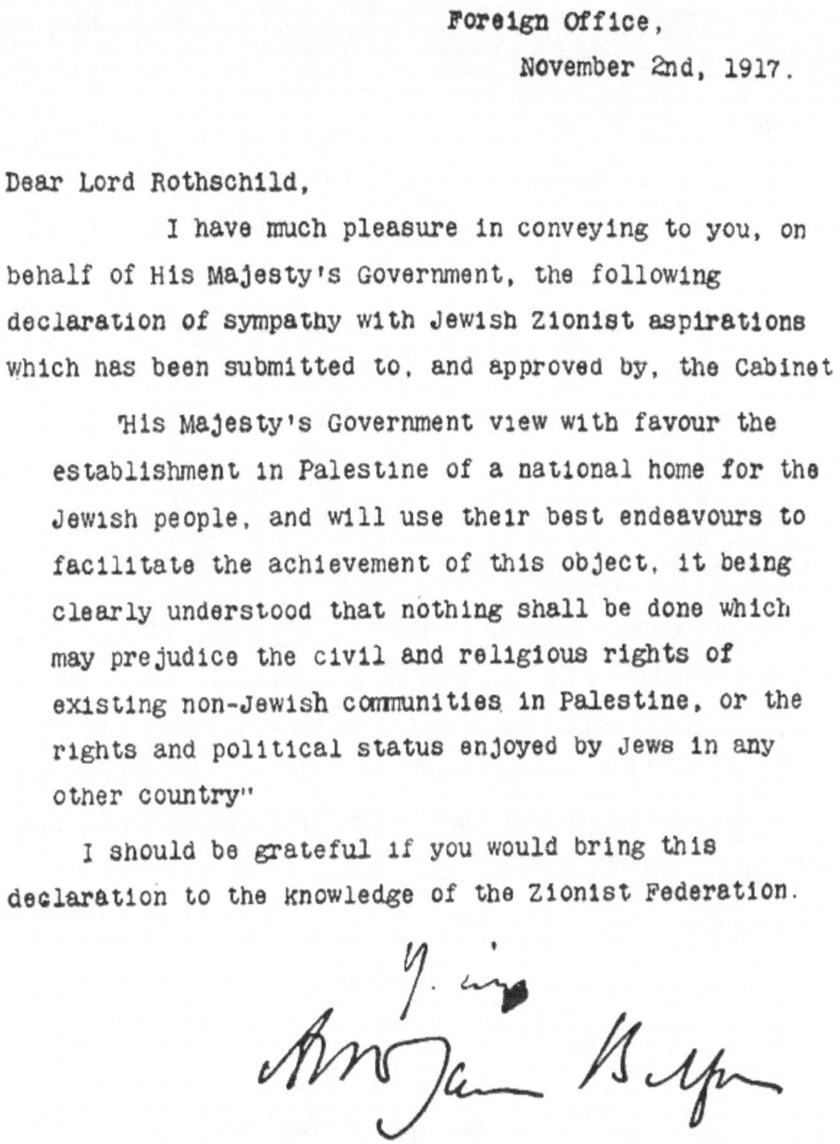

Foreign Office,
November 2nd, 1917.

Dear Lord Rothschild,

I have much pleasure in conveying to you, on behalf of His Majesty's Government, the following declaration of sympathy with Jewish Zionist aspirations which has been submitted to, and approved by, the Cabinet

"His Majesty's Government view with favour the establishment in Palestine of a national home for the Jewish people, and will use their best endeavours to facilitate the achievement of this object, it being clearly understood that nothing shall be done which may prejudice the civil and religious rights of existing non-Jewish communities in Palestine, or the rights and political status enjoyed by Jews in any other country"

I should be grateful if you would bring this declaration to the knowledge of the Zionist Federation.

Image #33: the Balfour Declaration

ancient land ... I do not think that Zionism will hurt the Arabs ... in short, so far as Palestine is concerned, the Powers have made no statement of fact which is not admittedly wrong, and no declaration of policy which, at least in the letter, they have not always intended to violate.

The four "Great Powers" he refers to at that time were Britain, France, Italy and the United States. Notice how flippantly Balfour brushes off the rights and needs of the 700,000 Arab Palestinians already living there who owned the land. Notice too how the Rothschild-led Cult had already infiltrated the four influential nations to the point where they not only favored Zionist needs over Arab needs, but also were prepared to lie and deceive for the Zionist cause. Such is the grip of power the Cult has had, and continues to have, over the mightiest nations in the world, which to it are just like branches of a giant multinational corporation that it owns.

Famous British historian Carroll Quigley, author of two books which detailed the schemes of the Anglo-American NWO establishment, said that the so-called 'Balfour' Declaration should have been called the 'Milner Declaration' because he claimed that Milner was the actual draftsman and that this was not made public until July 21st 1937. Quigley wrote:[186]

At that time Ormsby-Gore, speaking for the government in Commons, said, 'The draft as originally put up by Lord Balfour was not the final draft approved by the War Cabinet. The particular draft assented to by the War Cabinet and afterwards by the Allied Governments and by the United States ... and finally embodied in the Mandate, happens to have been drafted by Lord Milner. The actual final draft had to be issued in the name of the Foreign Secretary, but the actual draftsman was Lord Milner.

The Cult was moving quickly on multiple fronts. In the Middle East, T. E. Lawrence (Lawrence of Arabia) tricked the Palestinian

Arabs into revolting against the Ottoman Empire, promising them the land, but later reneged on that promise as the Balfour Declaration came forth that promised some of Palestine to the Jews. By 1923, Cult agent Atatürk had risen to power in Türkiye, and as a Donmeh, he naturally had no problem granting parts of Palestine to the Jews.

The Lopsided Treaty of Versailles: Laying the Groundwork for WWII

The 1919 Treaty of Versailles was overseen by Cult agents, naturally. They planned the whole war, and now they were swooping in to rearrange the world more to their liking. They had their puppet Wilson, who had served them so well for years at this point, promote the League of Nations that, as mentioned earlier, was essentially a Rothschild pretext or stepping stone to world government. According to Icke, all the Versailles leaders were advised by the Rothschilds.[187]

Additionally, the conspicuous thing about the Treaty of Versailles was how brutal the victors were on Germany, who was after all only one of several losers of the war. Germany was severely punished and financially crippled – intentionally. The Cult was thinking decades in advance and here, in the ashes of the most destructive and murderous war in humanity's history, they were already laying the groundwork for the next war to come. They pushed Germany so hard knowing it would create unbearable poverty and resentment – fertile ground for a nationalist movement to rise up and push back. As the pendulum swings one way, so it swings the other way, for every action has an equal and opposite reaction. Preparata writes:[188]

Economist John Meynard Keynes ... assessed the reparations load at 40 million dollars: a figure equal to three times the Reich's pre-war income, which, he affirmed, was beyond the paying capacity of vanquished Germany ... Then Lloyd George chanced upon the clever device of leaving the final figure unnamed, deputizing the task to a commission of experts, which was scheduled to deliver an estimate in two years – by May 1921. The explosive mixture was skillfully inoculated in the text of the Treaty by John Foster Dulles – a New York lawyer connected in high places – in the form of the infamous Article 231 ... Germany was coerced to accept the responsibility, and thus sign a 'blank check.'

Cult operative John Foster Dulles would later become US Secretary of State and his brother Allen Dulles the head of the Central Intelligence Agency (CIA) during the MK Ultra mind control experiments and the Kennedy assassination, of which he was the mastermind (see chapter 11). The Cult drafters of the Versailles Treaty also added clauses to ensure Germany was likely to rebel, by insisting the Rhineland must be demilitarized and cutting off a part of Germany (Danzig) from the rest of the nation so it would only be accessible by going through Poland. Freedman makes the point that the Germans felt especially betrayed when they learnt it was the Jews – actually the Sabbatean-Frankist crypto-Jewish Cult, but to most Germans, just 'the Jews' – who did this to them. They believed it was the Jews who got America into the war and ultimately defeated Germany, all for the sake of a piece of Middle Eastern real estate. He said:[189]

When the Germans realized this, they naturally resented it. Up to that time, the Jews had never been better off in any country in the world than they had been in Germany ... When Germany realized that the Jews were responsible for her defeat, they naturally resented it. But not a hair on the head of any Jew was harmed ... Now, the Jews sort of tried to keep the lid on this fact. They didn't want the world to really understand that they had sold out Germany ... So [the Germans] did take appropriate action against them [the Jews]. They . . . shall I say, discriminated against them wherever they could? They shunned them.

This is a good place to end this chapter, because what happened next is as horrific as it is hidden. The Cult selected a man who they thought would be a good fit to remilitarize Germany and push an aggressive foreign policy against its neighbors. The time has come to learn the truth about another infamous Cult dupe – the Rothschild bastard Adolf Hitler – as well as reveal his promoters, business partners and funders.

Sources

[149] ZIONISM versus BOLSHEVISM: A STRUGGLE FOR THE SOUL OF THE JEWISH PEOPLE, 1920

[150] Zionism Rules the World, pp. 6-7, https://ia801700.us.archive.org/26/items/klein-henry-h.-zionism-rules-the-world_202012/Klein%20Henry%20H.%20-%20Zionism%20rules%20the%20world.pdf

[151] https://highlanderjuan.com/wp-content/uploads/2019/06/Benjamin-H-Freedman-Speech-at-the-Willard-Hotel-1961.pdf

[152] The Suppressed History of American Banking, pg.54

[153] https://archive.org/details/cu31924024892709/mode/2up

[154] Ibid., pg. 140

[155] Ibid., pp. 144-6

[156] https://saxonmessenger.christogenea.org/article/lincoln-and-rothschilds

[157] https://forward.com/culture/217871/was-john-wilkes-booth-jewish/

[158] Conjuring Hitler, pp. 7-8

[159] Conjuring Hitler, pg. 12

[160] https://www.sabite.org/judaization-of-palestine

[161] https://www.webcitation.org/5ukCn6F22?url=http://www.tnr.com/print/book/review/the-other-secret-jews

[162] https://hetq.am/en/article/50143

[163] https://www.universalfreemasonry.org/en/famous-freemasons/mustafa-ataturk

[164] To Eliminate the Opiate, Volume 1, pg. 72

[165] The Trigger, pg. 603

[166] Wall Street and the Bolshevik Revolution, pg. 18

[167] The Trigger, pg. 604

[168] To Eliminate the Opiate, Volume 1, pg. 49

[169] https://www.theoccidentalobserver.net/2011/05/10/during-1917-chapter-14-of-solzhenitsyns-200-years-together/

[170] https://www.timesofisrael.com/putin-first-soviet-government-was-mostly-jewish/

[171] https://thelawthatneverwas.com/

[172] https://www.weissparis.com/nonresident.html

[173] https://www.globalresearch.ca/the-federal-reserve-cartel-the-eight-families/25080

[174] https://www.joeplummer.com/tragedy-and-hope-101-3

[175] The New Freedom, Woodrow Wilson, 1913, pg. 13

[176] Ibid.

[177] Tragedy and Hope 101, pg. 79

[178] https://www.saturdayeveningpost.com/2021/08/our-best-reporting-from-farm-boy-to-financier-stories-of-railroad-moguls/

[179] https://archive.org/details/benjamin-h.-freedman-speech-unedited-version-1961

[180] https://www.jewish-american-society-for-historic-preservation.org/images/The_longing_makes_the_Messiah.pdf

[181] Democratic Ideals and Reality: A Study in the Politics of Reconstruction, H. J. Mackinder, 1919

[182] https://corbettreport.com/wwi/, https://www.corbettreport.com/cache/nov1911.pdf

[183] https://highlanderjuan.com/wp-content/uploads/2019/06/Benjamin-H-Freedman-Speech-at-the-Willard-Hotel-1961.pdf

[184] https://jamesperloff.net/false-flag-at-sea/

[185] https://www.un.org/unispal/history2/origins-and-evolution-of-the-palestine-problem/part-i-1917-1947/

[186] The Anglo-American Establishment, pg. 169

[187] The Trigger, pg. 625-6

---

188 Conjuring Hitler, pp.74-5

189 https://archive.org/details/benjamin-h.-freedman-speech-unedited-version-1961

CHAPTER 8: THE CULT CONCOCTS HITLER AND FORGES THE SECOND WORLD WAR

"Revolutionary nihilists – the so-called Bolsheviks commanded by the intellectual radical Lenin – were transferred to Russia ... with the expectation that out of such an inflow would emerge a despotic regime, whose polarity (materialist, anti-clerical, and anti-feudal) was the inverse of that of the German Reich."

– *Conjuring Hitler*, Guido Preparata[190]

World War II, the bloodiest war in the history of humanity, was another engineered event that was decades in the making. It served two main purposes: for the Anglo-Americans to utterly destroy Germany (and prevent any possible German-Russian alliance) and for the state of Israel to be created within Palestine. When I use the term 'Anglo-Americans' I am of course referring to the group that ran (and still runs) those nations, namely the Round Table network, and the inner circle which ran the Round Table, which was – you guessed it by now – the Rothschild-led Sabbatean-Frankist Cult. There are different ways of looking at this event. Some authors look at it through the lens of individual nations and geopolitics, and as such, discuss the machinations of England. That is valid, however it must always be remembered who ran and runs England. When I discuss the 'machinations of England' in this chapter, it is the Cult working through the British Empire.

Image #34: a banknote from the 1923 Weimar Republic for 50,000,000,000 (fifty billion) marks

So, let's begin by looking at the first purpose, the scheme to pit Germany against Russia in mortal combat so as to completely eliminate any possibility of an alliance. After the Great War (i.e. WWI), Germany was in a poor state, which was only exacerbated by the Weimar Republic, whose infamous stories of wheelbarrows full of cash to buy bread are often told to highlight the danger and absurdity of hyperinflation. Saddled with unpayable debt, the nation was floundering. The Cult lost no time in moving from one phase (ending of one war) to the next (creating conditions to start the next war); as soon as the Treaty of Versailles was ratified, they began incubating the Nazi movement, which sprung onto the center stage at the lowest point of the crash of the German mark in the winter of 1923. As inflation raged, the price of basic food staples became denominated in the millions, leading to rampant unemployment, poverty, malnutrition and prostitution. The existence of a banknote of 50 billion marks, one of the highest notes given out, dated November 1923, is a testament to this sad state of affairs. Not only was

Germany struggling with hyperinflation, but also with invasion; at one point in 1923, France actually invaded Germany to demand reparations in coal (which was her right by the Treaty). During this period, American companies bought up prime German real estate and key ownership interests in German corporations for pennies on the dollar. Once Germany passed through their nadir at the end of 1923, the Cult introduced them to the next phases: two five year plans.

The Dawes and Young Plans: Five Year Plans to Re-Arm Germany

So-called 'five year plans' were around before the Cult introduced Communism to Russia and China. They also used them to aid the rise of fascism. The Cult plan was always to re-arm Germany so that it could rise up and become a formidable enough force to fight another large war. Thus, after the ultra harsh conditions of the Treaty of Versailles were implemented, the Cult banksters then began to allow Germany to wipe out its debt and to begin to re-arm. They achieved the former by allowing hyperinflation to wipe out the old German mark, which took around 3-4 years until the end of 1923; they achieved the latter by secretly allowing Germany to sign the Treaty of Rapallo with the Red Army in 1922. This incredible agreement, signed by two nations who would fight each other to the death less than two decades later, normalized German relations with the Soviets, mutually canceled all territorial and financial claims both sides had with each other after WWI, fostered military cooperation and allowed Germany to circumvent the restrictions of Versailles. Rapallo included clauses that allowed Germany to secretly train its military personnel and develop military technology inside the Soviet Union, which technically got around the limitations to which they were subjected under Versailles.

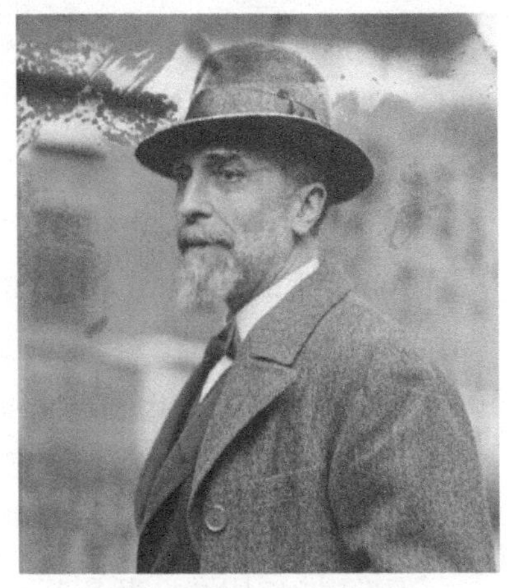

Image #35: private central banker and manipulator extraordinaire, Montagu Norman

After the mark had been wiped out, a new one was introduced, and thus began the influx of capital from America and England. Bank of England Governor Montagu Norman (Rothschild agent), in close contact with the banking house of J. P. Morgan (Rothschild agents), began pumping Germany full of money to rebuild her under schemes such as the Dawes Plan or Dawes Bailout, the first of Germany's five year plans from 1924-1928, and later the Young Plan, the second of Germany's five year plans from 1929-1933. Both Charles Dawes and Owen Young, after whom the respective plans were named, were linked with J. P. Morgan. Dawes was connected with GE (General Electric), a J. P. Morgan entity, and Owen Young was a deputy chairman of the Federal Reserve Bank of New York and a director of International General Electric. Some of the Dawes and Young Plan money was earmarked to go into giant German corporations such as I. G. Farben which was later extremely pivotal in supplying the Nazi war machine with synthetic rubber (buna), dyestuffs, poison gas, plastics, explosives, gunpowder, synthetic gasoline and jet fuel. The engineers of another major German corporation, Krupp, were secretly given the task of designing advanced military equipment.

There was extensive American-German technical and military collaboration behind the scenes, *"shielded by complex corporate contracts,"*[191] such as the cooperation between Rockefeller's

Standard Oil and I. G. Farben. It was quite a misnomer when in 1933 US President Roosevelt invoked the "Trading with the Enemy" Act since 'Funding, Establishing and Collaborating with the Enemy' would have been a more accurate description of the situation. It was the American companies associated with the Morgan-Rockefeller banking cartel (itself funded by the Rothschilds) that pumped up the Nazi's incredible industrial and military growth. In *Wall Street and the Rise of Hitler*, Sutton noted that Standard Oil-I. G. Farben cooperation for the production of synthetic oil from coal gave the I. G. Farben cartel a monopoly on German gasoline production during World War II. Two of the basic elements of modern warfare – synthetic gasoline and explosives – were in the hands of massive 'German' companies (really multinational corporations funded by Wall Street loans). Sutton wrote:[192]

Moreover, American assistance to Nazi war efforts extended into other areas. The two largest tank producers in Hitler's Germany were Opel, a wholly owned subsidiary of General Motors (controlled by the J.P. Morgan firm), and the Ford A. G. subsidiary of the Ford Motor Company of Detroit. The Nazis granted tax-exempt status to Opel in 1936, to enable General Motors to expand its production facilities. General Motors obligingly reinvested the resulting profits into German industry. Henry Ford was decorated by the Nazis for his services to Naziism. Alcoa and Dow Chemical worked closely with Nazi industry with numerous transfers of their domestic U.S. technology. Aviation, in which the J.P. Morgan-controlled General Motors firm had a major stock interest, supplied Siemens & Halske A. G. in Germany with data on automatic pilots and aircraft instruments. As late as 1940, in the 'unofficial war,' Bendix Aviation

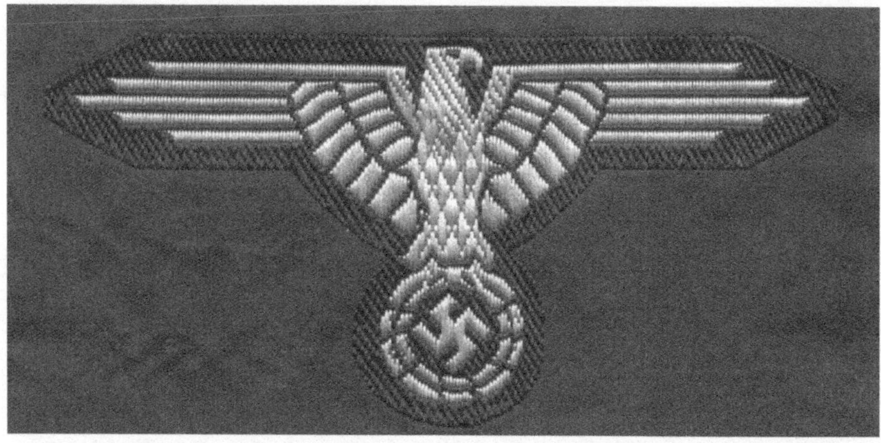

Image #36: the eagle has been a continuous symbol of empire throughout the ages, used by the Romans, the Nazis and the current US Empire (all Cult-controlled)

supplied complete technical data to Robert Bosch for aircraft and diesel engine starters and received royalty payments in return.

Incubating the Nazis

The word Nazi is an abbreviation from the two words 'National Socialist,' which were put at the front of a small political party originally called the German Worker's Party, so it became the National Socialist German Worker's Party (NSDAP). The Nazis were far more than just another political party; they were a transformational movement that exists even to this day in all corners of the world (e.g. the 'useful' Nazis used by the CIA in Ukraine to fight Russia, as well as the Nazis that escaped to Antarctica), but even that doesn't describe them in totality. Behind the scenes, they were connected to and strongly influenced by the Thule and Vril secret societies, which provided them with their vision, ideology, notions of racial purity and their now infamous emblem of the swastika. The Nazis were steeped in the occult. At first blush, it may seem incongruous or even impossible that the Cult would launch a movement that was so virulently antisemitic, but we have to remember that the Cult is run by Sabbatean-Frankist crypto-Jews, who are Jewish in name only. They don't care about ordinary Jews. In fact, as we shall see most clearly in the following chapters, they willingly sacrificed ordinary Jews because they wanted to create sympathy for their upcoming Zionist project.

It appears that Hitler was first noticed in 1922 by Anglo-American agents. Hitler was an Anglophile who hated Jews and who saw France and Russia as the enemy – exactly the man the British needed for their plan to divide Germany permanently from Russia and to create Israel within Palestine. The Cult made sure it surrounded Hitler with its agents from the start. There are at least four names worth mentioning in this regard. Two of them were Captain Truman Smith and Ernst Haenfstangl. Smith was an American intelligence officer or spy who officially worked in Berlin as a military attache (a diplomat for the US Military) between 1920 and 1924. He was sent down to Munich in November 1922 to scope out the burgeoning Bavarian movement including the SA (Sturm Abteilung), the brutal Nazi paramilitary force known as the brownshirts. He later reported that Hitler was a 'marvelous demagogue' with extraordinary oratorical skills who was convinced that only a dictatorship could restore Germany.

Ernst Hanfstaengl, nicknamed 'Putzi,' was a half-American, half-German art dealer who rubbed shoulders with the Anglo-American elite, including then US President Roosevelt. Putzi was born in Munich, Bavaria, spending most of his early years in Germany before moving to the United States and attending Harvard. He was a gifted pianist who composed several songs for Harvard's football team, tunes that he would allegedly later use as Nazi anthems such as 'Sieg Heil.' Putzi returned to Germany in 1922 and first heard Hitler speak in a Munich beer hall. Later on, to show how connected the American elite were, a member of Harvard's Hasty Pudding Club who worked at the US Embassy in Germany asked Hanfstaengl to assist spy Truman Smith in observing the Nazis. Subsequently, Putzi became very close to Hitler; he participated in the failed 1923 Munich Beer Hall Putsch where Hitler got injured. After this attempted coup, Hitler sought refuge in Hanfstaengl's home outside Munich, and Putzi's wife Helene allegedly talked Hitler out of committing suicide. Hitler was the godfather of Hanfstaengl's son Egon. Sutton wrote that Putzi Hanfstaengl's role in the early Nazi days, up to the mid-1930s, was an *"informal link between the Nazi elite and the White House."*[193]

Image #37: Putzi (left) with Hitler (center)

Hitler would never have risen through the ranks of the upper German elite, making important contacts with industrial leaders (some of whom later became ardent Nazi supporters), were it not for Hanfstaengel's help throughout the 1920s. Putzi even helped to finance the publication of Hitler's famous book *Mein Kampf* and the official Nazi newspaper, the *Völkischer Beobachter* (*People's Observer*). Given how close Putzi was to Hitler, and how much assistance he rendered Hitler while also maintaining close connections with Churchill and Roosevelt (before they became leaders of their respective nations), is it more likely that Putzi was just a friend of Hitler … or his handler? Putzi eventually fell out of favor with Hitler by the mid-1930s and had to leave Germany. In 1942, he was turned over to the Americans, where he worked for President Franklin Roosevelt's "S-Project," giving them plenty of information on Nazi leaders. Sutton maintains that Putzi, as well as Goering and Goebbels, were the men responsible for the false flag Reichstag fire which was blamed on the Communists to suspend constitutional rights and centralize Nazi power:[194]

There was only one way a group with flammable materials could have entered the Reichstag — through a tunnel that ran between the Reichstag and the Palace of the Reichstag President. Hermann Goering was president of the Reichstag and lived in the Palace, and numerous S.A. and S.S. men were known to be in the Palace ... Putzi — by his own admission — was in the Palace room at the other end of the tunnel leading to the Reichstag. And according to The Reichstag Fire Trial, Putzi Hanfstaengl was actually in the Palace itself during the fire ... According to Nazi Kurt Ludecke, there once existed a document signed by S.A. Leader Karl Ernst — who supposedly set the fire and was later murdered by fellow Nazis — which implicated Goering, Goebbels, and Hanfstaengl in the conspiracy.

A third Cult agent who gained access to Hitler and his inner NSDAP circle was Baron William (Bill) Sylvester de Ropp, a British spy who posed as a journalist for The Times. De Ropp's role was to act as a pipeline between London and Berlin. At this point, some readers may be wondering why Hitler allowed all of this. Wasn't he, or those close to him, suspicious of all this funding he was getting?

Hitler appears to have ignored it all to his detriment, as Paul Cudenec writes:[195]

Why did Hitler – a penniless, shabbily-dressed minor agitator – imagine that this upper-class socialite, who was regularly invited to play piano at the White House and is said to have been a friend of Winston Churchill, would want to invite him into his life? Did he really fall for the fib that Hanfstaengl, along with powerful figures in the US and the UK, supported him in his hatred of communism and that those states would therefore back him, or at least not oppose him, in his war on the USSR? Or maybe he didn't care. Flattered by all the sudden attention; enchanted by Hanfstaengl, his wife and child, who became his godson; installed in a posh new home; chauffeured around the place in a Mercedes limousine – little Adolf from Austria wasn't going to ask too many questions.

The book *Financial Origins of National Socialism* or as it is also called *Hitler's Secret Backers*[196] is one of the most extraordinary historical documents of the 20th century. Sutton analyses this book in chapter 10 of his book *Wall Street and the Rise of Hitler* and doesn't appear to think much of it, however I consider it to be highly revealing and valuable. This book is written under the pseudonym of 'Sidney Warburg.' In Germany, Max Warburg was a director of I. G. Farben, and in the United States, his brother Paul Warburg (father of James Paul Warburg) was a director of American I. G. Farben. Sidney may have been the son of Paul Warburg. Regardless of who the author was, the information contained is mindblowing. The book exposes who gave Hitler his immense international financial backing that got him into power, naming the American bankers and industrialists that channeled funds to him and detailing how much they gave. Specifically, it mentions "Rockefeller" (John D.

Rockefeller II), “Carter” (John Ridgley Carter, married Alice Morgan, connected to Morgan interests in Paris, US ambassador) and “Deterding” (Henri Deterding, head of Royal Dutch Shell). This book was published in 1933 in Holland, but only remained in book stalls for a few days. Then every copy (except three accidentally surviving ones) was purged. This story was silenced – almost. It was branded a forgery, but many German Foreign Ministry files (now public) and Nuremberg Trial documents affirm its key points. The book contains a couple of passages that bring you face-to-face with the most infamous demagogue in history! Here are some quotes from it:

Rockefeller himself had read a short essay in a German-American leaflet about the Nationalist movement led by this man Hitler (he said "Heitler"). It had been decided at the earlier meeting to make contact with "this man Hitler" and to try to find out if he were amenable to American financial support. Now the question was clearly addressed to me: would I be prepared to go to Germany, get in touch with him, and take the necessary steps to arrange this financial aid? It must be taken care of quickly, because the sooner the Nationalist group in Germany could be built up the better. It should be emphasized in my negotiations with Hitler that an aggressive foreign policy was expected of him, he should stir up the Revanche-Idee against France. The result would be fear from the French side, and consequently greater willingness to ask for American and English help in international questions involving eventual German aggression.

[Hitler speaking] "I don't trust a single German bank. The money must be deposited in a foreign bank, where I can then have it at my disposal." He looked again at the figures on the plate and said

imperiously, as if he were handing down a strict order: "One hundred million marks" ... On my way back to the hotel I figured out that one hundred million marks was about twenty-four million dollars.

I noticed again the emptiness of his reasoning, as I had during our conversation. Never a sign of logic, short, powerful sentences, abrupt and screamed out, political tactics of demagogy, persistent rabble-rousing. I sympathized with the journalists who were there to write reports for their papers. It seemed to me that no report could be made of a speech like that. Hitler didn't speak about the movement, nor about the platform, or of reforms he and his followers expected to carry out. He attacked every government since 1918, the large banks, Communists, Social Democrats, Jews, big department stores. His speech was full of words like traitors, thieves, murderers, unscrupulous men, repressors of the people, those who besmirch the

German spirit, etc. He mentioned no facts. He was always vague and general, but ... it worked.

In his groundbreaking 1999 book *The Biggest Secret,* David Icke asserts that Hitler was actually a bastard Rothschild, basing this on the work of Walter Langer, author of *The Mind of Hitler*, who had researched Hitler's family origins. According to Langer, Adolf's father Alois Hitler was the illegitimate son of Maria Anna Schicklgruber. It was assumed that the father of Alois was Johann Georg Hiedler ("Hiedler" became "Hitler" as a certain point), however Langer got information from a high-level Gestapo officer named Hansjurgen Koehler. Koehler wrote about the investigations of an Austrian Chancellor named Dolfuss, who due to the fact he was the leader of Austria at one point was in a position to access the birth records regarding Hitler's family tree, since Hitler was born in Austria. Koehler was able to look at the Dolfuss documents given to him by SS officer Reinhard Heydrich which showed that Schicklgruber worked at a Rothschild mansion in Vienna at the time she conceived. The only Rothschild living at the Vienna mansion was Salomon Rothschild. Icke notes that the Rothschilds and many of the NWO bloodline families have bastard children out of wedlock who are brought up under other names in different families. He writes:[197]

And Hitler's mother, a young girl working under the same roof would not have been the subject of Salomon's desire? And this same girl became pregnant while working there? And her grandson becomes the Chancellor of Germany, funded by the Rothschilds, and he started the Second World War which was so vital to the Rothschild-Illuminati agenda? And the Illuminati are obsessed with putting their bloodlines into power on all 'sides' in a conflict? And the Rothschilds are one of their most key bloodlines? And it is all a coincidence? ***Hitler was a Rothschild!***

People talk of Germany's 'economic miracle' during this time of 1933-1939 as though Hitler and the Nazis somehow magically got everyone working and virtually eliminated unemployment because Hitler issued debt-free currency. This is not at all why Germany recovered from the depths of the Weimar Republic. As already mentioned, they recovered because they were made to recover. They recovered because the banksters pumped them up. They were being set up to become a powerful military nation to fight Russia, so that when they fell again, this time German soil itself would be occupied and taken. The Cult maneuvered a fourth Cult agent, Freemason Hjalmar Schacht, into the position of Hitler's economic minister and president of the Reichsbank. Schacht stepped away from the Nazis in 1930 then stepped back in 1933 when they came to political power. He had worked for the Dresdner Bank in Berlin (linked to the Morgans/Rothschilds). Schacht was a close friend of Putzi Hanfstaengl, was a member of the international financial elite and knew the 'human spider' Montagu Norman well, and so played a vital role connecting the Nazi inner circle with foreign financiers. He also knew John Foster Dulles (the Cult agent and lawyer discussed in the previous chapter who played a key role at Versailles) who channeled funds from America to Germany in the 1930s. At Sullivan & Cromwell, Dulles floated bonds for weapons manufacturer Krupp among many other things. In an article entitled *History: Hitler was Financed by the Federal Reserve and the Bank of England*, Yuri Rubtsov writes how Norman and the Dulles brothers were meeting with Hitler to ensure the Nazis got funded:[198]

On January 4th, 1932, a meeting was held between British financier Montagu Norman (Governor of the Bank of England), Adolf Hitler and Franz Von Papen (who became Chancellor a few months later in May 1932). At this meeting, an agreement on the financing of the Nationalsozialistische Deutsche Arbeiterpartei (NSDAP or Nazi Party) was reached. This meeting was also attended by US policy-makers and the Dulles brothers, something which their biographers do not like to mention. A year later, on January 14th, 1933, another meeting was held between Adolph Hitler, Germany's Financier Baron Kurt von Schroeder, Chancellor Franz von Papen and Hitler's Economic Advisor Wilhelm Keppler took place, where Hitler's program was fully approved.

The truth almost came out via Schacht at the Nuremberg Trials, but it was squashed:[199]

Even the Nuremberg Trials could not suppress the evidence of the once close, friendly and good relations between English-American capital, its governments and Hitler, in spite of the efforts of the court to guard zealously that this side of the issue was never raised, by declaring statements about it "irrelevant and immaterial." Schacht in particular mentioned this critical subject. When Schacht brought up again the relations of foreign powers to the National Socialist regime and the assistance they bestowed upon it, the court decided that this information had nothing to do with the issue, and was therefore inadmissible ... Schacht had let representatives of foreign powers convince him they should support the National Socialist government in its infancy. The court refused to admit all these statements (NZZ no.758, May 2, 1946).

From Republic to Reich

It took some time for the Nazis to gain enough support among the German public that they could be considered a party that could realistically garner enough votes to rule. Things escalated for them in 1930-1. During an election in 1932, the Nazis got 37% of the vote (the highest they ever achieved), and in a subsequent election, they got 33%. These percentages represent roughly one third of the votes, which is far from a majority, however it was enough for Hitler to be invited by President Hindenburg to become Chancellor. The Nazis lost no time in staging a false flag operation – the burning of the Reichstag (German Parliament building) – to consolidate their power. The Nazis blamed the Communists, quickly introducing legislation (the "Enabling Act") which gave them unprecedented emergency powers and permitted the merging of the positions of President and Chancellor into one position, thus creating a dictatorship. The republic had become a 'Reich' (German for 'empire'). Hitler had no qualms in killing his political opponents, and later on, even killing those within his own ranks that he suspected of disloyalty, treachery or treason. Many terrible atrocities occurred under Hitler's authoritarian rule, including Kristallnacht ('Crystal Night' or the Night of Broken Glass), a pogrom against Jews carried out by the SA and SS, along with some participation from the Hitler Youth and German civilians, on November 9-10th 1938.

As Preparata notes, World War II was a play directed by England; they were running the show. The Nazis were incubated for over a decade before finally gaining power in 1933, then after that, the stage was set for war to break out, for the Nazis to gain land, to invade and overtake some minor countries (and even some major ones like France), before being set against the Russians. Step by step, Hitler was led into a trap without knowing it. After 1933, with the Nazis fully ensconced at the helm of the Third Reich, all the violations of the Treaty of Versailles, and all the escalations towards war, were fully allowed – and even encouraged – by Britain. Preparata writes that *"not a single maneuver on the path to war was the fruit of Hitler's strategy or imagination; the schemers of Versailles had prepared the route for him long ago, and the British stewards were now facilitating the progression."*[200] This includes the Nazi rejection of further reparations payments, the militarization of the Rhineland, the annexing of Austria (the 'Anschluss'), the invasion of Czechoslovakia and the invasion of Poland and Danzig. At any point, Britain and France could have stepped in to enforce the Versailles provisions relating to reparations or remilitarization, or the USSR could have stepped in once Hitler took Czechoslovakia, but they didn't. Consider the message that Lord Halifax (Edward Wood), a British cabinet minister, gave to Hitler to egg him on; it reads as though he was telling the Nazis what to do next, couching the language as though the British would be fine IF the Nazis happened to choose this course, when really the message was instructional:[201]

In synthesis, Halifax told Hitler that: (1) Britain considered Germany the bastion against Communism; (2) Britain had no objection to the German acquisition of Austria, Czechoslovakia, and Danzig; and (3) Germany should not use force to achieve her aims in Europe.

Given that the Treaty of Versailles forbade the German acquisition of Austria, Czechoslovakia and Danzig, what else was this other than overt encouragement to the Nazis? The whole label of 'appeasement' that was used to describe this period of Nazi expansionism is a complete misnomer. Allowing Germany to invade neighboring nations and annex land was a logical continuation of the British plan; it was not an appeasement but rather a setup. A final point to consider is that during the whole period from 1933 to the outbreak of war in 1939, the British cabinet had the same members that were shuffled around as part of the deception, to give both the Nazis and the British public the impression that there were genuine 'appeasement' and 'pro-war' camps within the leadership, while the plan had been scripted long before. Churchill was kept in the back during the 'appeasement' (i.e. setup) phase then rotated forward during the 'war' phase to play his role. Historian David Irving characterized Churchill as a drunken homicidal maniac and stated that then US President FDR called Churchill *"a drunken bum."*[202] Churchill lived beyond his means, almost losing his house to bankruptcy before being bailed out by a Jewish millionaire, and was therefore capable of being bribed. The whole thing was a stage with actors playing their parts. After all, as Shakespeare wrote in *As You Like It*, *"All the world's a stage, And all the men and women merely players; They have their exits and their entrances; And one man in his time plays many parts ..."*

England was playing a dangerous game. The Nazis could perhaps have launched a more devastating air invasion of the British isles, or even a ground invasion. However, the British knew they had a couple of aces up their sleeve … if things really got bad, they could always call in the Americans (or even the Russians). Overall, whether it was the UK in the West or the USSR in the East, the Nazis were fully supported to maturity. England gave support via Bank of England and American loans, and appeasement; the USSR sabotaged the German Left opposition and provided vital materials in the run-up to the war. The part played by the Bolsheviks was also important:[203]

None of this would have been possible without the unreserved collaboration of Soviet Russia. The Soviets worked in unison with the anti-German directives of Britain as if they were her most faithful ally; they, like Britain, appeased the Fuhrer, and contributed abundantly to the Nazi war machine, shipping carloads of provisions to Germany throughout the entire length of the Nazi rearmament.

If the British did that then, who's to say they are not doing the same thing now, or their heir apparent the USA is not engaging in the exact same tricks today?

Meanwhile … What About Hitler and the Jews?

So far in this chapter I have covered the destruction of Germany and the prevention of any possible German-Russian alliance; now, it's time to discuss the other main purpose of World War II which was equally as important: laying the foundation for the creation of Israel. You may have noticed by now that the Cult likes to imbue its conflicts with the seeds of future conflicts. Just as the Treaty of Versailles (Rhineland militarization, Danzig land separation, punitive reparations, etc.) seeded the next war, so did the end of WWII with the creation of Israel in 1948 seed many future wars which are still ongoing to this day.

Hitler was a NWO dupe who served many purposes. The entire time that England was playing the Nazis like a violin with diplomatic cunning, there was another aspect that was taking place: the '*judenfrage*' or the Jewish Question. In the previous chapter, I quoted from the 1961 speech of Jew Benjamin Freedman who pointed out how the Jews had betrayed the Germans in WWI by getting America into the war on the side of Britain, France and Russia. This naturally caused German resentment against the Jews in the aftermath, creating fertile ground for nationalist and antisemitic movements like the Nazis to arise.

ballito STOCKINGS — BUY BRITISH

Daily Express

NO. 10,258. — FRIDAY, MARCH 24, 1933. — ONE PENNY.

St Ivel CHEESE Aids digestion 2d., 6d. & 8½d. each.

JUDEA DECLARES WAR ON GERMANY

JEWS OF ALL THE WORLD UNITE

BOYCOTT OF GERMAN GOODS

MASS DEMONSTRATIONS

"Daily Express" Special Political Correspondent.

A STRANGE AND UNFORESEEN SEQUEL HAS EMERGED FROM THE STORIES OF GERMAN JEW-BAITING.

The whole of Israel throughout the world is uniting to declare an economic and financial war on Germany.

Hitherto the cry has gone up: "Germany is persecuting the Jews." If the present plans are carried out, the Hitlerite cry will be: "The Jews are persecuting Germany."

SUTCLIFFE AND PAYNTER OUT FOR "DUCKS."

CHRISTCHURCH (N.Z.), Friday, March 24.

There was a thrilling start to the first Test between England and New Zealand here to-day.

Sutcliffe and Paynter opened the innings, but within a few minutes were both out for "ducks."—Sutcliffe caught by James and Paynter bowled by Smith.—Reuter.

Late Scores: Stop Press.

Canon Shot At Prayer

SISTER FINDS HIM KNEELING AT

THE SOVIET AMBASSADOR ENTERTAINS

AN ALL-RED TALKIE FOR ALL-WHITE DIPLOMATS

MISSING GUESTS

"Daily Express" Special Representative.

THE Soviet Ambassador and Mme. Maisky gave a reception last night in the Russian Embassy at Harrington House, Kensington Palace-gardens.

Many of the diplomatic representatives of foreign Powers, together with many of London's

Mr. Churchill's Withering Attack On Premier

Officer Describes The Girl

DAYS OF LOVE IN BERLIN

"Daily Express" Special Representative.

SUMMER days and nights of love in Berlin through a fortnight of hectic pleasure; and then, when the holiday was over, stolen, hurried meetings in Holland.

One party to this romance, a pretty German girl of wealth, to whom money apparently meant nothing—the other, an officer of the British Army, who was content to allow the girl to pay him for his company and favours.

'MONEY "A PRESENT"

That, in brief, was the story which Lieutenant Norman Baillie-Stewart, of the Seaforth Highlanders, told in defence before the court-martial which is trying him on charges of attempting to betray his country to a foreign Power for

'BROUGHT US NEARER TO WAR'

FOUR YEARS' WORK WITHOUT ANY SUCCESS

OUR DON QUIXOTE

By Our Parliamentary Representative

THE House of Commons, which has grown mealy-mouthed since the crisis of eighteen months ago, was shocked into reality last night by one of the most withering personal attacks of recent years.

The attack came from Churchill. It fell like a thunderbolt on Ramsay MacDonald.

GRAVE CHARGE

Amid the ridicule and contempt which Mr. Churchill obviously enjoyed heaping on the Prime Minister there was a charge of the utmost gravity. The charge was that the Prime Minister's conduct of foreign affairs has brought Great Britain nearer to war.

"The Prime Minister's interventions in foreign affairs," said

Mrs. George Lansbury Dead

A boy-and-girl romance which began at fifteen, ended last night with the death of Mrs. George Lansbury, wife of the Parliamentary Leader of the Socialist Party. Their fifty-three years of happy married life began in the deepest poverty and endured through a disappointing emigration to Australia. The dramatic story of this perfect domestic partnership is told on Page Thirteen.

STOP PRESS
Telephone: Central 8000

Image #39: the famous 1933 headline where Cult-aligned Jews attacked Germany, in preparation for WWII

The fact is that in 1933, a group of international Jews declared war on Germany by using their economic clout to institute a boycott on German goods in an attempt to cripple the Nazi economy. But here again, we must be very careful to distinguish between 'Jews' and 'Zionists.' Many innocent Jews were caught up in this political intrigue, only to later lose their lives.

While they might appear to be mortal enemies, the truth is that the Nazis and the Zionists had a lot in common and had mutual objectives. Being Cult creations, both were driven by the same mindset, by the concept of supremacy, whether racial, religious or otherwise, thinking of their clan or nation as superior to others around them, and feeling justified in using deception and violence against those 'lesser peoples' – the *untermenschen* and *goyim* subhumans. Both Nazism and Zionism wanted a 'ethnically clean' state. They were both attempting to build ethno-nationalist countries where one class would have more rights than other classes. In 1933, the purveyors of the 'Aryan Race' and the 'Chosen People' mythologies also had a very practical thing in common: they both wanted Jews out of Germany. The Nazis wanted them out for obvious reasons, and the Zionists wanted as many Jews as possible to populate Palestine, in order to boost their chances of successfully establishing a Jewish State there, so they saw the opportunity to grab German Jews and ship them off to the Middle East. Thus began on August 25th 1933 the official Nazi policy of German Jewish immigration to Palestine under the Transfer Agreement or Ha'avara Agreement, named after the Tel Aviv company where the funds were transferred. In 1934, Goebbels minted a coin *"Ein Nazi fahrt nach Palastina"* ("A Nazi travels to Palestine") to commemorate the deal (see image #40). In order for the agreement to be made, Hitler had demanded that the Zionists reject the worldwide Jewish boycott on German goods, and the Zionists had agreed. Thus, Adolf Hitler became the chief sponsor of the State of Israel, setting into motion the migration of Jews needed to later make Israel a

Image #40: a German coin inscribed with the following message: "A Nazi travels to Palestine"

viable reality. This is not an irony, because again, the Cult was orchestrating the entire event of WWII, exerting influence and control over all sides.

Hitler's Jewish Soldiers

To what degree was Hitler's antisemitism real? Did he genuinely hate all Jews, or was he using the Jews as a convenient scapegoat to score political points with his fanbase, as politicians are wont to do? Consider the following:

1. Hitler set up the Ha'avara migration project for rich German Jews;

2. The Nazis allowed major Zionist opposition activities within Germany when almost all other political opposition (often at the point of a gun) was banned. The German Ministry of Propaganda banned all Communist and left-leaning organizations from publishing a newspaper but allowed the Zionists to publish the *"Judische Rundschau"* ("Jewish Review") from 1933 to 1939;

3. Hitler never named his international backers, who were either Jewish bankers themselves or very, very closely connected to them (there is only a hair's breadth from the Rockefellers and Morgans to the crypto-Jewish Warburgs and Rothschilds); and

4. Many (at least a quarter but perhaps a half of the) people in the Nazi organization were Jewish.

It is an understatement to say that Hitler's views on the Jews were highly irrational and inconsistent. Dr. Bryan Mark Rigg, author of *Hitler's Jewish Soldiers: The Untold Story of Nazi Racial Laws and Men of Jewish Descent in the German Military*, reveals that despite strict Nazi ideology, many men whom the Nazis considered

Jews became German soldiers. According to the Nazi racial laws in effect at the time, the Nazis designated these partial Jews as *"mischlinge"* (either full Jew, half Jew or quarter Jew). Hitler granted personal exemptions to many of these soldiers so they could serve in the armed forces; Rigg calculates that the actual number was 150,000 men (60,000 half Jews and 90,000 quarter Jews) who received exemptions from Hitler. Some of these soldiers were high-ranking officers including generals and admirals! If Hitler truly thought the Jews were the source of all evil, why would he allow them to be in command like this? On the one hand, there is evidence that Hitler was so obsessed by 'the Jews' that he sometimes placed it above winning the war by firing important generals in 1944, but on the other hand, there is also evidence that Hitler overlooked 'the Jewish question' in order to get strong men of fighting age into the Nazi armed forces.

Of course, what the Nazis were coming up against was the biological reality of the situation which trumped the mythological propaganda. As discussed in chapter 1, there is no Jewish race, and despite the Nazi's best, most thorough and most scientific methods, they could not accurately prove 'Jewishness' biologically or genetically. Shlomo Sand remarked in a 2009 Russia Today interview with Paula Slier[204] that Hitler and the Nazis could never define, nor find, Jewish blood despite their best efforts. Hitler would give the impression that he could look at someone and determine their 'Jewishness' but it was nonsense; on one occasion, Goebbels used Nazi propaganda to recruit 'the most Aryan looking soldier' and when Werner Goldberg won the competition, they subsequently discovered that his father was 'Jewish' under Nazi racial laws![205]

Image #41: extensive Nazi-Zionist collaboration shows that they are both Cult creations

Nazi-Zionist Collaboration and the Kastner Train Incident

To understand the situation fully, you have to understand that the top Nazis and the top Zionists were in close contact with each other – and were, in fact, **collaborating**. The attitude of the Zionists towards Nazi antisemitism was one of warm embrace. The Zionists, in contrast to the rest of the ordinary Jews, were doing everything they could to **support** the Nazis, not oppose them. Many states or nations offered that the Jews being expelled from Germany could be resettled in their land, such as Australia, the USSR, Japan, Alaska and Madagascar, but the Zionists adamantly refused; they only cared about founding an Israel within Palestine, even if it meant more ordinary Jews had to be sacrificed to achieve this goal. This uncompromising Zionist attitude even continued during the last years of the war from 1942 to 1945 when Jews were being sent to concentration camps.

In 1937, the leader of an infamous Jewish terrorist group Haganah (more on this in later chapters), Feivel Polkes, met in Berlin with top Nazi Adolf Eichmann (SS officer and organizer of the Holocaust). Polkes told Eichmann that he was interested above all in *"accelerating Jewish immigrants to Palestine, so that the Jews would attain a majority over the Arabs in his country. For this purpose, he worked together with the secret services of England and France and he also wanted to cooperate with Hitler's Germany."*[206] For *"secret services of England and France,"* substitute 'Cult intelligence agencies and Cult agents' and you'll have the plain truth right there.

This kind of close communication and cooperation between the Nazis and Zionists was typical of the entire period of WWII. One of the most telling examples of Nazi-Zionist collaboration – which completely destroys the simplistic narrative that the Nazis wanted to hinder and kill all Jews – is the Kastner Train incident. In April 1944, the aforementioned Adolf Eichmann made an offer to Joel Brand, the head of the Hungarian Aid and Rescue Committee, that the Nazis would spare the lives of one million Jews in exchange for 10,000 trucks and others goods from the Allies. Stefan Moore writes that, *"Brand immediately flew to Istanbul to present the proposal to the Jewish Agency which, as Brand later said, lacked any sense of urgency, since it was more focused on Jewish emigration to Palestine than the slaughter in Europe."*[207]

However, the real kicker came when Eichmann offered a similar deal to a Zionist leader named Rudolph Kastner, a colleague of Brand's from the Committee. Eichmann proposed that in exchange for USD $1,000 each (USD $25,000 in today's money), the Nazis would allow the departure of 1,684 mostly affluent Jews – including Kastner's family and friends – to escape to Switzerland by train. This by the way was typical of what occurred in WWII with Switzerland, which pretended to be neutral on the surface, but which was in reality implicated in helping the Nazis. The deal was that Kastner was to not tell the Hungarian Jews that they would be sent to the Nazi concentration camps. Moore notes that in the subsequent months from May to July 1944, 437,000 Jews were transported to Auschwitz, which was almost the entire rural Jewish population of Hungary. He writes:[208]

In 1954, an Israeli judge ruled that Kastner had 'sold his soul to the devil' by negotiating with Eichmann to save some Jews, while 'paving the way for the murder of Hungarian Jewry.' He was assassinated on 15 March, 1957 by members of the Lehi, Israel's right-wing militia, for collaborating with Nazis. Kastner was later rehabilitated as a hero in Israel.

Pick a Side Dammit – the Nazis or the Jews!

There is a certain segment of truthseekers and of the Alternative Media who believe that Hitler was not a villain but a hero fighting 'the evil Jews.' This is false, although to be fair, Hitler was made out to be a far worse monster than what he actually was by the Zionist owned media at the end of WWII. This is the cunning of the Cult, who rule by the control of money and the control of the mind, i.e. the control of information, narrative and perception. They are masters of introducing ideologies to seduce truthseekers, freedom fighters and patriots to lead them astray, as well as masters of introducing false dichotomies where they control both sides, or where supporters of either side advance the Cult agenda. They masterfully create opposing sides to play them off against each other using the classic 'divide-and-conquer' technique. Examples are Communism vs. capitalism, left vs. right, progressivism vs. conservatism, socialism vs. fascism, feminism vs. men's rights, Hamas vs. Israel, etc. The latest iteration in America is woke ideology (or wokeism) versus MAGA (Make America Great Again) ideology, which can be loosely defined as the ideology of diehard Trump supporters.

The 'Nazi vs. Jew' dichotomy is another fake binary to be aware of, for as I have showed in this chapter and will show more in the chapters to come, the people at the top were on the same side. They were collaborating. It was the Cult pulling the strings of both puppets on the stage. The Zionists welcomed Hitler's Nazi Germany and its rabid antisemitism; the Nazis encouraged the Zionist push to emigrate German Jews to Palestine. If we want to understand the full truth of history, or any current situation, and if we want to promote true freedom, we need to assiduously avoid the pitfalls of shallow thinking and false dichotomies, and refuse to 'pick a side' when both are Cult-controlled.

Hitler was "Fighting the New World Order"?! Give Me a Break

In a similar vein, another popular but false idea floating around patriot and Alternative Media circles is that Hitler was a hero gallantly fighting the NWO, in particular the bankers. As I write these words in 2025, for those of us in the USA who have just lived through another excruciating presidential cycle and (s)election, the identical theme occurred with the political marketing of Donald Trump, who many people tell us was 'fighting the Deep State.' However, it's pretty hard for you to drain the swamp when you are a swamp dweller and swamp creature yourself (see chapter 12 for a closer look at sexual predator Trump, best buddy for decades with Israeli intelligence asset Jeffrey Epstein).

Hitler was most definitely not fighting the NWO. In fact, he used the almost identical term "New Order" (*"Neuordnung"* in German) in his speeches, for instance when he first proclaimed a *"European New Order"* on January 30th 1941. Hitler's idea of a New Order was different to the commonly accepted definition of the New World Order, meaning a totalitarian world government with a one world army/police force, one world currency and a society of just two classes (rulers and slaves). Hitler's concept was of an ethno-state structured to the benefit of a perceived Aryan-Nordic master race, which the Nazis would force on Europe and the rest of the world. It eugenically asserted that this so-called master race had the right to suppress and/or kill 'inferior' ethnicities deemed 'unworthy of life.' This 'worthy-unworthy' and 'ruler-slave' theme is the Cult mindset. Hitler's NWO may have been different than the one that is planned for humanity right now, but hardly less horrific or dictatorial.

Was Hitler as evil as Stalin? Probably not, however that doesn't make him a hero. This period of human history was full of actors that were all deceitful monsters who committed grave crimes – including Churchill, Roosevelt, Truman, Eisenhower, Stalin and Hitler. There were no 'good guys.'

If someone was truly fighting the NWO, they would stand for the opposite of what the NWO entails: they would promote values like freedom, truth, honesty, sovereignty, decentralization and peace. Instead, Hitler and the Nazis self-evidently promoted centralization of power (via the Enabling Act after the false flag Reichstag fire), murder of political opponents, suppression of alternative viewpoints or dissent, censorship (book burning), deception, propaganda, gun control, state-controlled education, militarization of society and war (aggressive foreign policy).

The entire drama of WWII – and it was a drama, like a Shakespearean play, with 'actors' playing their parts in the 'theater' of war – was an orchestrated event with two main purposes, to bring Germany to its knees (and thus split Germany and Russia for a long time) while getting a large number of Jews into Palestine, and generate sympathy, for the coming modern-day state of Israel. There were psychopathic agents on all sides; the Cult infiltrated and directed all the main players. The English leadership was highly manipulative, as was the leadership of America and Russia. The Nazis were an authoritarian regime that ruled through terror, manipulating public perception via propaganda, false flag events and the silencing and killing of political opposition. However, the story didn't end there; in typical Cult fashion, WWII was yet another stepping stone on the way to further aspects of the NWO agenda, with the creation of the United Nations or UN (planned basis of a One World Government) and the state of Israel to follow shortly thereafter.

Sources

[190] Conjuring Hitler, pg. 1

[191] Conjuring Hitler, pg. 169

[192] Wall Street and the Rise of Hitler, pg. 14

[193] Wall Street and the Rise of Hitler, pg. 86

[194] Wall Street and the Rise of Hitler, pg. 84

[195] https://substack.com/home/post/p-161946680

[196] https://cdn.preterhuman.net/texts/history/nazi/Hitlers%20Secret%20Backers%20Warburg.pdf

[197] The Biggest Secret, pg. 513

[198] https://www.globalresearch.ca/history-of-world-war-ii-nazi-germany-was-financed-by-the-federal-reserve-and-the-bank-of-england/5530318

[199] Ibid., pg. 46

[200] Conjuring Hitler, pg. 239

[201] Conjuring Hitler, pg. 238

[202] https://odysee.com/@DavidIrving:0/David_Irving_on_Winston_Churchill_The_Drunken_Homicidal_Maniac:3

[203] Conjuring Hitler, pg. 204

[204] https://www.youtube.com/watch?v=Uinft1c5KQ8

[205] https://ww2gravestone.com/werner-goldberg-german-half-jewish-ancestry-whose-image-appeared-berliner-tageblatt-ideal-german-soldier-copy/

[206] Journal of Palestine Studies – The Secret Contacts: Zionism and Nazi Germany 1933-1941, pg.72

[207] https://consortiumnews.com/2024/06/24/the-treachery-of-the-nazi-zionist-alliance/

[208] Ibid.

CHAPTER 9: THE CULT RIDES THE WAVE OF ANTISEMITISM WITH THE HOLOCAUST LEGEND

"What Zionist propaganda for years could not do, disaster has done overnight."

– David Ben-Gurion[209]

"The anti-Semites will become our most dependable friends, the anti-Semitic countries our allies."

– Theodor Herzl[210]

"The Zionist approach that Jewish blood is the anointing oil needed for the wheels of the Jewish state is not a thing of the past. It remains operable to this very day."

– Rabbi Moshe Shonfeld[211]

Antisemitism became an entrenched phenomenon in Europe in the period from around 1875-1900, especially in Russia, France, the Austro-Hungarian Empire and Germany. In Russia during this time, for example, there were pogroms which targeted and killed many Jews. Although it appeared that Zionism arose as a natural reaction to this antisemitism, it is more accurate to say that the Zionists used it as the wind behind their sails on their way to steal Palestine. Zionist Theodor Herzl repeatedly declared that the Jewish problem in Europe needed to be handled and solved on an international level.

To understand the concept of the Zionists using antisemitism to their advantage, I must again stress the distinction I have been emphasizing this entire book – the distinction between the Cult 'Jews' (crypto-Jews) and the rest of the Jews. Many people make the mistake of assuming that Jewish people are one homogenous unit who all think and act in the same way. This is not true. The Jews are as heterogenous as any group, be it religious, ethnic or national, all the more so because their identity has been hijacked by the Cult. This chapter will focus on how the Khazarian Sabbatean-Frankist crypto-Jews not only allowed the Holocaust, but encouraged it, because it was the fuel they needed to acquire massive worldwide sympathy for their singleminded goal of stealing Palestine. They could easily paint the authoritarian, expansionist and eugenicist Nazis as 'evil' (even though they had incubated and installed them, then made deals with them throughout their time in government). They could easily paint Nazi victims as 'poor' Jews, even though these Cult Zionists had just as much contempt for the non-Cult Jews as the Nazis did. To the Cult, these Jews were just cannon fodder or human meat to be sacrificed for the cause of the establishment of Israel, but a very convenient pretext behind which to hide their true agenda. To understand the callousness with which the Cult was prepared to sacrifice the Jews, it is useful to go back in time a little – because the idea of a 'holocaust' (which means 'sacrifice' or burnt offering) was prophesized (and therefore predicted and planned to happen) long before 1941-1945, and thus on a mental and energetic level was MADE to happen by directing the attention of religious adherents towards the event.

<u>The Holocaust Legend</u>

The point of this chapter is to maximize truth, not to minimize suffering. There is no doubt ordinary Jews were blanketly targeted and, sadly, incurred massive oppression during WWII. Every life lost in this time period, Jewish and all other, is one life too many as far as I am concerned, since the entire conflict was orchestrated by the Cult, hiding behind the curtains and directing all the 'sides' on the public stage to slaughter each other. They ruthlessly sacrificed ordinary Jews for their own demented and criminal agenda, then controlled the coverup afterwards, so they could exaggerate and lie about it to mold perception of the event. Some of the ways they did this included their influence over the Nuremberg Trials, control of the history books, control of the educational curriculum and the creation of Holocaust Museums in every corner of the world.

The Holocaust happened. Period. It is, clearly, an historical event that took place. However, the official story of the Holocaust is full of gigantic exaggerations and outright falsifications. Esteemed British author and researcher David Irving said that he prefers to call it the 'Holocaust Legend' not the Holocaust Lie, because it has the feeling of a religion. With all the occult significance and symbolism behind this event, it was absolutely driven by religious and occult extremism, and on top of that, the Holocaust has become a kind of state religion within Israel, the means by which they justify almost any of their criminal behavior, including their current genocide of the Palestinians. It's also the way Israel shuts down any criticism of its crimes and plays the eternal victim while being the aggressor. Let's recall what former Israeli minister (MK or Member of Knesset) Shulamit Aloni admitted in 2002 when asked about the phenomenon of people being labeled antisemitic:[212]

Well, it's a trick. We always use it. When, from Europe, somebody is criticizing Israel, then we bring up the Holocaust. When, in this country, people are criticizing Israel, then they are antisemitic.

There it is, straight from the horse's mouth. The terms 'antisemite' and 'Holocaust denier' are ad hominem attacks and quick insults designed to shut down critical debate and genuine inquiry into historical events and current affairs. Through massive propagandistic efforts since 1945, the Cult has managed to mold a popular perception that Hitler was the worst villain ever and that the Holocaust was the worst evil ever done – despite the close Nazi-Zionist collaboration covered in the previous chapter.

Many Jews and Israelis can see the truth that the Holocaust has become a weapon for Israel to use today against anyone who dare criticize it. Tom Segev, an Israeli historian and author of the book *The Seventh Million: The Israelis and the Holocaust*, has talked about the Zionist attempt to transform the Holocaust story into state religion, unquestionable and untouchable. He writes that the Holocaust history has been manipulated in accordance with the ideological requirements of the state, which is identical to the ideological requirement of the Cult, since the state of Israel is the Cult's pet project.

6,000,000 Symbolism: Hoping for a Holocaust

Before starting this topic, let me make one thing clear: the brutality of the Nazis against the Jews is a provable fact of history, as were the existence of Concentration Camps and slave labor. What I am about to write is no way excusing, exonerating or condoning that.

The Holocaust happened. Period. However, evidence shows that nowhere near 6 million Jews died during the Holocaust or in all of WWII, and evidence shows that the Nazis did not kill Jews in gas chambers. These are the two main falsifications.

We've probably all heard the official story repeated ad nauseam that six million Jews were killed (by being gassed to death) by the Nazis in WWII. Would it surprise you to learn that the six million number was being bandied around in the 1800s? The six million number was being used in all sorts of contexts long before WWII. The excellent documentary *"The First Holocaust - The Surprising Origin of the Six Million Figure"*[213] shows some of the copious evidence. Many of the examples to follow are from this documentary. In 1850, 1866, 1869 and 1889, there were various Christian publications, and then also the NYT (New York Times), that reported that there were 6,000,000 Jews living in Europe. What is weird is that the number never changed! Apparently, there were the same number of Jews living in Europe in 1850 as in 1889 – or editors were just blindly repeating the same number over and over. In 1891, there were reports of 6,000,000 Jews living in Russia; in 1903 during and after the Russian pogroms, Russia was blamed for murdering Jews in a holocaust; from 1905-1911, there were reports that 6,000,000 Jews were to be expelled from Russia. This is the exact same story as WWII, except that WWI hadn't even happened, and the villain in this narrative was Russia not Germany!

During WWI from 1914 to 1918, the NYT kept reporting that there were 6,000,000 Jews in the war zone. In 1900 in the NYT, Rabbi Stephen Wise wrote: *"There are six million living, bleeding, suffering arguments in favor of Zionism."* In 1933 and 1935, there were again reports of 6,000,000 Jews living in Europe; in 1936, Cult agent Chaim Weizmann (discussed in previous chapters) said that six million Jews from Eastern Europe needed to emigrate to Palestine. On June 25th 1940, a newspaper from Palm Beach, Florida, quoted Zionist Nahum Goldman as saying that six million Jews would be doomed. On December 13th 1942, the NYT reported that two million were killed, which was one third of the Jews in *"Hitler's Domain"* (if two million is one third, the total therefore is six million). In February 1943 in the Reader's Digest, Jewish-Hollywood writer Ben Hecht again peddled the six million Jewish lives motif. On March 10th 1943, the NYT reported that two million had been killed and that four million were to be killed! On May 14th 1943, the Canadian Jewish Review used the six million figure; the same thing happened on May 15th 1943, in the Australian newspaper *The Advertiser* (Adelaide), in May 1944 with Rabbi Chaim Michael Dov Weissmandl, and in November 1944 with a newspaper in Ohio, USA. Finally, in December 1944, on January 4th 1945, and on March 15th 1945, the Soviet propagandist Ilya Ehrenburg wrote about six million dying.

How could they have known?

None of this makes any sense unless you realize that the 6,000,000 figure is not an accurate historical count of any number of Jews, dead or alive, in Europe, Germany, Russia or anywhere else. It's symbolism! It's code. Mainstream German historian Martin Broszat of the Munich Institute for Contemporary History called the six million figure a *"symbolic figure"* while testifying in a German court of law.[214] The Cult is steeped in the occult, especially old texts or schools of thought such as the Kabbalah, which places heavy significance on gematria. Therefore, the choosing of numbers is deliberately done to produce maximum effect. Every number has a different frequency; to give you a very basic example, the number 4 has a different frequency to the number 6. The number 4 is connected to the square and rectangle; in English we say 'all square' when things are even and talk of someone fair and just as having good moral "rectitude." The number 6 is connected to the hexagon; it also represents incompleteness (since it is one less than seven). 6 is connected to Saturn, since Saturn is the sixth planet in the Solar System, and Saturn also has a hexagon at its pole. As mentioned earlier, Saturn, the god of harvest, time, law, tyranny and death, is a very important god to the Cult. When the number 6 occurs three times, as it does in many symbols, it becomes 666, the infamous number associated with evil. It is highly probable, therefore, that the six million number was calculatedly chosen because of the frequency. Reporter Greg Reese narrated a video entitled *"Antisemitism and the Origin of Hate Speech"* in which he alluded to the symbolism of six million, connecting it with two thirds and the Sabbatean-Frankist idea of sacrifice to hasten the messianic era:[215]

Six million is a six followed by six zeros. And so it can represent sixty-six. Sixty-six is also two-thirds. The Hebrew prophet Zechariah wrote that two-thirds of the nation of Israel will be cut off and die. Many believers of biblical prophecy believe that this mass blood sacrifice is necessary in order for their messiah to return.

An official plaque from 1948 stated that four million died at Auschwitz (not necessarily all Jews), but later in 1991, a Russian

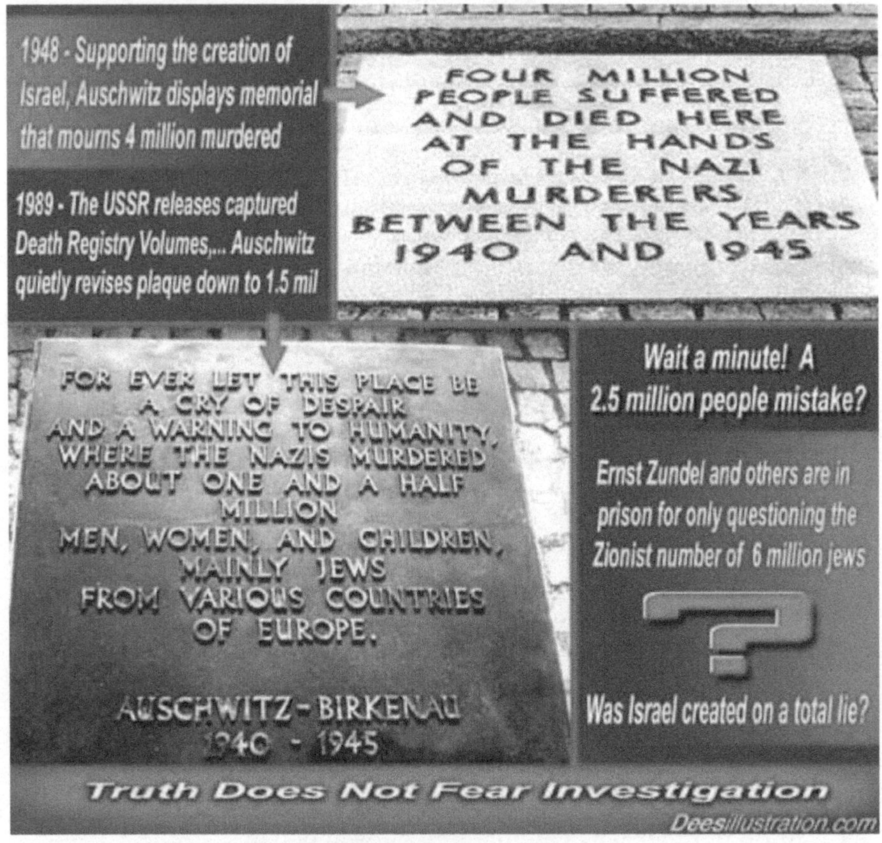

Image #43: the six million figure got downgraded to four million, then to one and a half million

plaque stated the combined number at Auschwitz-Birkenau was one and a half million. What all this means is that the Cult was not only predicting or prophesizing but absolutely obsessing over the symbolic Kabbalistic 6,000,000 figure, doing whatever they could to bring it about and make it happen. It was planned. The crazy Jewish religious fundamentalists who were pushing this didn't even care whether it was Russia or Germany doing the killing; they just wanted their mass sacrifice because they somehow believed it was necessary in order to establish Israel and hasten the arrival of the messiah (control via narrative).

The number of murdered Jews was at one time as high as 11 million due to Simon Wiesenthal *inventing* another five million; he was called out for lying by Israeli historian Yehuda Bauer.[216] This even became an official 'fact' in 1979 when then US President Jimmy Carter issued an executive order, but this was eventually overturned when challenged by other Jews like Elie Wiesel and Deborah Lipstadt. As this Rense article shows, the number has been steadily downgraded over time.[217] In 1990, the Polish Auschwitz State Museum reduced the figure to one million that were killed at Auschwitz;[218] however others like historian Jean Claude Pressac, on his third revision, suggested that the figure may be around 630,000 to 711,000.[219] This was just Auschwitz however so the total number for the whole war may be higher.

At this point some may ask: why does the number matter, anyway? Wasn't there a lot of murder and carnage? Fair question, and in many senses, I agree. The Nazis, whether through methodical killing or general brutal treatment, murdered many Jews or caused them to be killed. However, the number matters in a few senses: it shows that the event was prophesized (i.e. planned), it reveals the sheer lunacy behind the religious fanatics who believed they needed a mass sacrifice, and it also matters in a legal-financial sense, because Israel extracted approximately USD $86.8 billion from Germany for Holocaust reparations (from 1945 to 2018, so it only ended 7 years ago).[220] The reparations were supposed to be compensation to Holocaust victims and their heirs, however Jew Norman Finkelstein (whose parents were both Holocaust survivors) has emphatically stated that the scheme is a shakedown by *"a repellent gang of plutocrats, hoodlums and hucksters"* chasing massive legal damages and financial settlements from Germany and

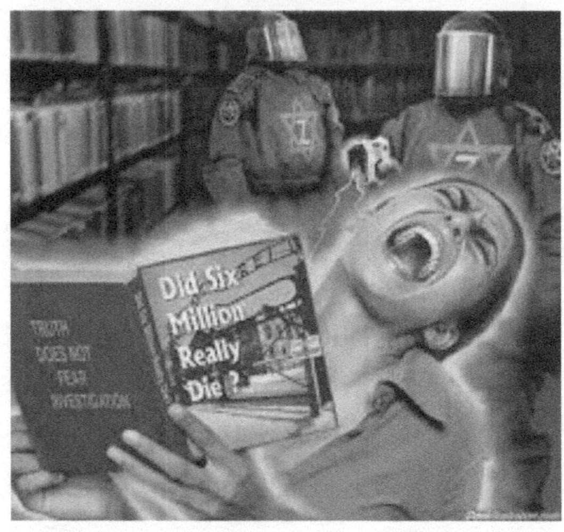

Image #44: the official narrative of the Holocaust, unlike any other single historical event, is for some reason unquestionable and untouchable

Switzerland, money which then goes to the lawyers and institutional agents involved in procuring them rather than actual Holocaust survivors.[221] In other words, it was a racket, just like the Versailles reparations forced on Germany after WWI. While the racket was going, it was quite lucrative – the Holocaust Industry was worth around a billion dollars a year. Researchers have found that some of the claimed Holocaust survivors are liars who completely fabricated their stories to generate more atrocity propaganda for the Zionist cause and to cash in on the Holocaust reparations,[222] an outrageous affront to the actual Holocaust survivors who lived through Nazi oppression.

True freedom means freedom of speech, freedom of expression and freedom of thought. We need to be able to look at ANY historical event and question it, regardless of when and where it happened, or who the actors involved were. Holocaust denial is actually a crime in some countries in Europe, which is to say that the lawmakers there are so sure of their version of history that they won't even allow citizens to conduct their own research and investigation! This is the very definition of tyranny: we decided what happened and how it happened. Shut up and don't question it.

'Holocaust denier' has become a smear term devoid of true meaning and designed to evoke anger and loathing. The truth is that it is entirely possible to take an objective look at the Holocaust and:

1. Have compassion for all the Jews that were oppressed and killed, regardless of the exact number;
2. Understand that Jews were persecuted during WWII;
3. Understand that the treatment of the Jews was unjust;

while still, at the same time, to see through the lies revolving around the symbolic six million figure and the invention of murderous gas chambers.

Gas Chamber Fakery

A very important point to remember about the Cult is that all its high-up agents are sociopaths or psychopaths. One characteristic of psychopaths is that they have limited to no empathy, and thus they feel no scruples in exploiting others. Another key characteristic is their ability and willingness to lie, if they think they can gain something from it or that it will advance their interests in some way. You may have noticed certain politicians that lie as easily as they speak. How do you know if these people are lying? Easy – they're talking. For them, spreading outrageous lies is no big deal at all.

The gas chamber topic is another 'holy cow' kind of topic that people fear to touch due to the social stigma of being branded an antisemite, or simply just being called insensitive. In point of fact, it is actually being more sensitive to the many Jewish victims of the

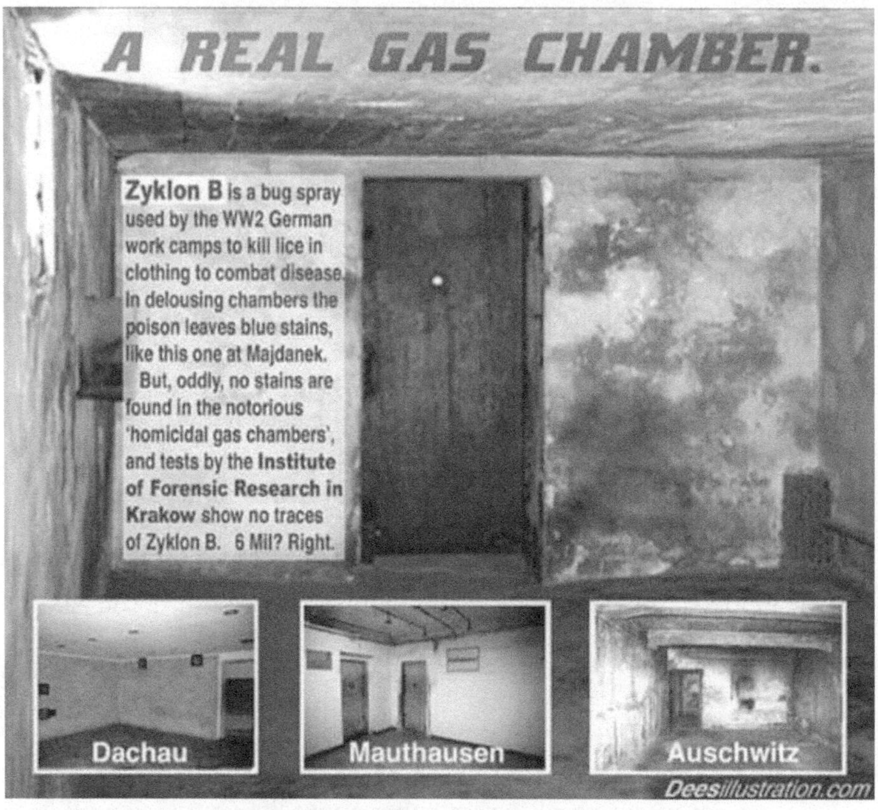

Image #45: there is no evidence that there were homicidal gas chambers to kill Jews en masse, though the Nazis certainly killed Jews in other ways

Nazis (and Jewish victims of the Zionist Cult) to investigate the issue and arrive at the truth, so we can learn from what happened and expose the ongoing deception to warn others. During the trial between David Irving and Deborah Lipstadt, Irving presented groundbreaking scientific, forensic evidence from the Leuchter Report. This report, written by gas chamber expert Fred Leuchter after a careful investigation of the Auschwitz, Birkenau and Majdanek concentration camps, concluded that there was no possible way that Jews were gassed in gas chambers in the way described in the 'official' version of history. Here are a few of its most salient points:

- **No seals or gaskets:** none of the so-called gas chambers contained seals or gaskets that a standard gas chamber would have to keep in the gas;
- **Windows:** some of the alleged gas chambers, improbably enough, contained windows (which could have been broken by desperate prisoners trying to escape);
- **Gaps under the doors:** some of the doors had gaps (in terms of inches) under them;
- **No provision to exhaust gas mixture:** the so-called gas chambers were not designed with a way to let out the gas mixture. How could anyone have gone in to clean up the dead bodies without being poisoned?
- **Standard (and not explosion proof) lighting in chambers:** the light bulbs and light globes in the alleged chambers were not explosion proof;
- **No provision to protect operating personnel:** there was no way to stop the gas spreading out and killing the operators;
- **No provision to stop gas spreading to crematoria:** there was no way to stop the gas from spreading to the crematoria;
- **No traces of Zyklon B (hydrogen cyanide) on the walls:** the official narrative claim is that Jews were gassed by Zyklon B (hydrogen cyanide), which necessarily leaves a stain on brick and cement walls, even after decades. Leuchter sent the samples to a lab, and after a careful, forensic analysis, it was reported that there were *no significant levels of cyanide* in the samples. If millions of Jews were gassed, one would expect copious amounts;

- **68 years would have been required to gas six million Jews:** according to Leuchter, it is ludicrous and insulting to imagine that with the facilities available, the Germans could have managed to kill and cremate six million Jews in the space of less than five years (at the rate of over 3,200 bodies per day, every day, without fail) with the facilities they had on hand at the time.

You can find additional proof of Leuchter's expert forensic analysis in a paper written by scientist Germar Rudolf, who worked at the prestigious Max Planck Institute. Rudolf authored the *Report on the formation and verifiability of cyanide compounds in the Auschwitz gas chambers*[223] which concluded the collected and analyzed samples from the walls of the alleged gas chambers in the Auschwitz concentration camp contained only insignificant and non-reproducible traces of cyanide compounds.

Here is yet more evidence:

- **Gas chamber built after WWII:** Jewish historian David Cole captured on film[224] an admission by Franciscek Piper, senior curator and director of archives at Auschwitz, that "Krema I", the alleged gas chamber, was in fact reconstructed after the war (watch from the 25 minute mark);

- **Not a single German wartime document to be found:** Meticulous historian David Irving, who has gone through more German wartime documents than anyone else alive today, states that there is not a single German wartime document to be found that mentions gas chambers or gassing of the Jews;

- **British-cracked secret code:** During WWII, the British cracked German top secret codes and discovered that deputy Fuehrer Rudolf Hess (commander at Auschwitz) reported back to the German hierarchy in Berlin. The Hess reports contained the following data:

- 1. Number of prisoners that had arrived at Auschwitz in the last 24 hours;
  2. Number of prisoners that had left Auschwitz in the last 24 hours;
  3. Number of prisoners on hand;
  4. Fatalities in the last 24 hours.
  Of the last piece of data (fatalities), there were 3 subcategories:
  4a. Deaths due to epidemics and disease;
  4b. Deaths due to prisoners being shot;
  4c. Deaths due to prisoners being hanged.
  There was no reference to gassing in the data. The numbers 4b and 4c were far below, magnitudes below, the numbers of 4a;

- **Aerial shots from the British archive:** according to Irving, aerial shots of Auschwitz at that time show no piles of bodies or coke (an agent necessary for cremation) outside the crematoria, no mass graves and no long waiting lines. Irving claims that Russian documents reveal that, from start to finish, 2188 kilograms of coke were delivered and used at Auschwitz, enough to cremate only 70,000-80,000 bodies total. Tens of thousands of tons of coke didn't exist which would have been needed.[225]

<u>US and Other Western Nations Shut their Doors to Jews During WWII</u>

So, while the wholesale oppression of ordinary Jews was taking place at the hands of the brutal Nazis (six million or not, gas chambers or not), what were other nations doing, particularly the richer ones like the USA? Were they doing everything they could to accept Jewish refugees? No. Far from it. In fact, the US deliberately closed its doors many times to fleeing Jews. On one occasion, it turned away 900 of them in 1939[226], and on another occasion, it turned away thousands in 1942, using the excuse they were 'Nazi spies.'[227] This was done at the behest of American Zionist Jews who exerted a powerful influence over then President Roosevelt. The Zionists only cared about the establishment of the state of Israel; Jews escaping to America didn't fit their plans. Disgustingly, they either wanted all emigrating Jews to go to Palestine (to boost the numbers of a future Jewish state) or to remain in Europe and be sacrificed to anoint the wheels of a future Jewish state, as Rabbi Moshe Shonfeld said (quoted at the start of this chapter). The same thing happened with Canada[228] and other nations.

The Cult agenda was to create a mass sacrifice, and sadly, other nations played their part in allowing the Nazis to do this up to a certain point, at which time the script required that they step in to defeat the Nazis and end the war. None of the WWII Allied Powers cared about ordinary Jews, but they were able to claim after the war that they did, which made for good PR and allowed them to pat themselves on the back and reassure themselves that they were the 'good guys' in the fight.

Zionist Militias Try to Recruit Nazis to Come to Palestine to Fight the British

Yes, that sub-heading you just read is correct. Read it again!

Another staggering fact from this period is that the early Zionist militias (Haganah, Irgun and Lehi, who eventually went on to merge into the IDF when Israel became a state) actually asked for help from … the Nazis! Israeli newspaper Haaretz reported[229] in 2023 that Lehi attempted to enlist the aid of Nazi Germany against the British in Palestine. Declassified Israeli documents revealed that Efraim Zetler, a member of Lehi or the Stern Gang (which splintered off from Irgun), was kidnapped by Haganah militants in 1942. Zetler confessed to the rival militia Haganah that Lehi was asking the Nazis to come help them fight the British in Palestine. He said, *"We will communicate with any military power ready to help with the establishment of the kingdom of Israel, even if it's Germany. If Germany agrees to help us fight enemy number one, the English, we'll team up with it. It's not an enemy of the Jews in Israel."* The documents also reveal that Avraham Stern (the man who created Lehi out of Irgun, which was why Lehi was also called the Stern Gang) had suggested seeking Nazi support. Lehi representatives went as far as meeting a German Foreign Ministry official in Beirut in 1940. Haaretz cites the declassified document stating that *"the establishment of the historical Jewish state on a totalitarian national basis, in an alliance relationship with the German Reich, is compatible with the preservation of German power."* Top Nazi spy Reinhard Gehlen became quite close to Israeli intelligence after the war. Israeli writers Dan Raviv and Yossi Melman note in their book, *Every Spy a Prince*, that Gehlen was *"the engineer of the special relationship between the Jewish state and the 'new' Germany"* and that Gehlen *"established a deep professional relationship with Israel."*

Wow. What a headshaker! Along with the Kastner train incident described in the previous chapter, this is more overwhelming proof that the Zionists and the Nazis were indeed collaborating at the highest level. Any Jews that were not part of the Cult were simply pawns in the game to be exploited and sacrificed as the Cult psychopaths saw fit.

Even One Innocent Person Killed is One Too Many (Jew or Not)

To round off this chapter, let's remember that even one innocent person killed is one too many, Jew or any other group. Pointing out the continuous Zionist-Nazi collaboration, the Cult's coldhearted sacrifice of Jewish lives, its obsession with the symbolic six million and the way it lied and exploited the Holocaust is in no way minimizing the suffering and death that all the Concentration Camp inmates went through. Again, the point is to maximize truth, not to minimize suffering, so that all the fifty-five million or more who died in WWII didn't only die in vain – that maybe we can actually learn from this horrendous episode in history and raise our collective consciousness enough to not repeat it. That has to necessarily require we know the truth about it.

Some may read my words and scream 'Holocaust denier!' from the top of their lungs. But since when is asking questions or conducting investigations a crime? The slur of 'Holocaust denier' is a reflection on those speaking the words and their attitude towards honest research. I am interested in the truth; Jewish deaths are no more or less important than any other deaths in WWII. We are all one human race, and we are all equal, regardless of race, religion, gender or any other divider.

Victors write the history books. The ubiquitousness of a story is no indication of its veracity, especially when Hollywood can churn out Holocaust movies like *Schindler's List* (directed by the Jewish Steven Spielberg) that get watched by hundreds of millions. At this point the Holocaust Legend has become so deeply ingrained in the Jewish psyche, and in our collective consciousness, that many people unknowingly repeat and defend it without doing their due diligence and research.

Israel's Treatment of its Holocaust Survivors

You would think that Israel would elevate its Holocaust survivors to the status of national celebrities, given how important the Holocaust is for its PR purposes. But, think again. The Zionist Regime doesn't care about its Holocaust survivors, just as it doesn't care about most Jewish people. The 2017 article "How the State of Israel Abuses Holocaust Survivors" revealed that around $31 billion (40%) of the compensation and reparations for survivors of Nazi persecution was allocated to Holocaust victims in Israel, but the funds got channeled through the Israeli government and the Jewish Claims Conference, an agency founded in 1951 to administer payments to Holocaust survivors worldwide:[230]

According to the Holocaust Survivors Rights Authority, the Israeli governmental agency entrusted with the issue of Holocaust survivors, there are about 200,000 Holocaust survivors living in Israel, nearly a third of whom live below the poverty line. Last April, Israel's welfare minister, Haim Katz, released a scathing report revealing that more than 20,000 survivors in Israel had never received the government assistance owed to them. The undelivered rights and benefits amounted to more than $30 million.

I will end this chapter with a quote that reinforces one of the central messages of this book: the Cult secretly hates Jews while pretending to represent them. Chabad Lubavitch Rebbe Menachem Schneerson said the Holocaust was good because it got rid of a disease-ravaged limb of the Jewish people to cleanse them of their sins:[231]

So it is not impossible for the physical destruction of the Holocaust to be spiritually beneficial. On the contrary, it is quite possible that physical affliction is good for the spirit ("Mada Ve'emuna," Machon Lubavitch, 1980, Kfar Chabad).

Yehuda Bauer writes:[232]

Schneerson goes on to compare God to a surgeon who amputates a patient's limb in order to save his life. The limb "is incurably diseased ... The Holy One Blessed Be He, like the professor-surgeon ... seeks the good of Israel, and indeed, all He does is done for the good ... In the spiritual sense, no harm was done, because the everlasting spirit of the Jewish people was not destroyed." The Rebbe's stance, therefore, is clear: The Holocaust was a good thing because it lopped off a disease-ravaged limb of the Jewish people — in other words, the millions who perished in the Holocaust — in order to cleanse the Jewish people of its sins.

So, in other words, mass human sacrifice is good. What further proof do you need that the Demiurge, Archons and Satanism at play here?

Sources

[209] Rebirth and Destiny of Israel, pg. 41

[210] Herzl's diary entry on June 12th 1895, *The Complete Diaries of Theodor Herzl, Vol.1*, 1960, edited by Raphael Patai, translated by Harry Zohn, p. 83-84

[211] https://ia600906.us.archive.org/29/items/ShonfeldMosheTheHolocaustVictimsAccuse_201903/Shonfeld_Moshe_-_The_Holocaust_victims_accuse.pdf

[212] https://www.bitchute.com/video/F8jt0FfoQwAO

[213] https://www.bitchute.com/video/PM7KvaK78emm

[214] https://www.bitchute.com/video/PM7KvaK78emm

[215] https://gregreese.substack.com/p/antisemitism-and-the-origin-of-hate

[216] https://barnesreview.org/simon-wiesenthal-lied-and-admitted-it-says-top-israeli-holocaust-historian/

[217] https://rense.com/general62/auch.htm

[218] https://www.upi.com/Archives/1990/07/17/Poland-lowers-official-Auschwitz-toll/1039648187200/

[219] https://ihr.org/journal/v21n3p24_weber-html

[220] https://www.state.gov/reports/just-act-report-to-congress/germany/

[221] https://nymag.com/news/intelligencer/41838/

[222] https://www.bitchute.com/video/zqo7aXVlkhUw/

[223] https://germarrudolf.com/germars-views-2/302-the-rudolf-report/

[224] https://www.bitchute.com/video/M3IN4a0qDyOf

[225] https://www.bitchute.com/video/ynVnqmoBB3ng

[226] https://www.theatlantic.com/politics/archive/2017/01/jewish-refugees-in-the-us/514742/

[227] https://www.smithsonianmag.com/history/us-government-turned-away-thousands-jewish-refugees-fearing-they-were-nazi-spies-180957324/

[228] https://www.canada.ca/en/canadian-heritage/services/canada-holocaust/history.html

[229] https://www.haaretz.com/israel-news/2023-06-21/ty-article-magazine/.highlight/zionist-military-org-efforts-to-recruit-nazis-in-fight-against-the-british-are-revealed/00000188-d93a-d5fc-ab9d-db7ae0ea0000

[230] https://www.tabletmag.com/sections/israel-middle-east/articles/israel-abuses-holocaust-survivors

[231] https://forward.com/life/10856/the-rebbe-and-the-shoah/

[232] Ibid.

CHAPTER 10: THE CULT ACQUIRES ITS OWN COUNTRY - AND ITS OWN NUKES

"Palestine was hardly Britain's to give away."

– Former US President John F. Kennedy (JFK) in a letter to his father in 1939[233]

"If I were an Arab leader, I would never sign an agreement with Israel. It is normal; we have taken their country. It is true God promised it to us, but how could that interest them? Our God is not theirs. There has been Anti-Semitism, the Nazis, Hitler, Auschwitz, but was that their fault? They see but one thing: we have come and we have stolen their country. Why would they accept that?"

– First Israeli Prime Minister David Ben-Gurion[234]

"If the basic problem faced by Diaspora Jews is how to survive as a minority, then the basic problem of Zionism in Palestine is how to eliminate the original population and make the Jews as the majority."

– Israeli scholar Benjamin Beit-Hallahmi[235]

When WWII finally finished in 1945, the world stopped and took a collective gasp. Over 55 million people from many continents had been murdered in the bloodiest battle in human history. The Cult banksters were delighted by the carnage, since their profits were through the roof, however their bigger agendas beyond just money were the reorganization of the world into a post-WWII order (a New

Image #46: 33° Freemason Franklin Delano Roosevelt (center)

World Order) – with the US and USSR as the world's undisputed superpowers – and the establishment of their coming headquarters in the Middle East in the form of a new country, the state of Israel. The wave of antisemitism that had spread through Europe, led by the Nazis, had propelled the emigration of many Jews to Palestine and had engendered massive international sympathy towards the plight of the Jewish people. Now was the time for the Cult to strike while the iron was hot – and it struck in more ways than one.

Towards the end of the war, then US President Roosevelt, a 33° Mason who had served the Cult very well with his confiscation of gold from the American public and his deception in allowing (with full knowledge) Japan to attack Pearl Harbor, may have outlived his usefulness. The official story is that he died of natural causes, but

Joseph Stalin himself told FDR's son Elliott Roosevelt that his father Delano Franklin was poisoned by the 'Churchill Gang.' What did Stalin mean by the 'Churchill Gang'? Almost without doubt, he meant the inner core of the Cult, the international bankers from the City of London who had brought the Bolsheviks to power in Russia and had manufactured both world wars. Some have suggested it was because FDR was not in favor enough of using an atomic bomb, supporting the establishment of Israel and allowing Britain to keep all her colonial possessions. Other suggest that FDR wasn't pro-Jewish enough; the Saudi king Abd al-Aziz Ibn Saud at the time got assurances from FDR that he would *"do nothing to assist the Jews against the Arabs and would make no move hostile to the Arab people."*[236] Here is what Colonel Fletcher Prouty wrote about FDR's death – or murder:[237]

Because Elliott had met Stalin in Tehran with his father in 1943, in late 1946, Gardner Cowless, publisher of LOOK magazine asked him to go to Moscow to interview Stalin. Roosevelt accepted this offer and did interview Stalin there. At the end of a long interview, he turned to the Generalissimo and asked one more question, "Why is it that my mother has never been permitted to visit Moscow even though she has made three very formal applications for the trip?"

Stalin glared at Elliott and said, "You don't know why?"

Elliott replied, "No!"

Quickly, Stalin responded, "Don't you know who killed your father?"

Roosevelt – shocked – answered, "No."

Stalin rising from his chair, continued, "Well, I'll tell you why I have not invited her here. As soon as your father died, I asked my ambassador in Washington to go immediately to Georgia with a request to view the body." Stalin believed that if Gromyko could see the body he would confirm that the cerebral hemorrhage that had caused his death had caused extensive discoloration and distortion.

Elliot responded that he knew nothing about that and then Stalin said, "Your mother refused to permit the lid of the coffin to be opened so that my ambassador could see the body." Adding "I sent him there three times trying to impress upon your mother that it was very important for him to view the President's body. She never accepted that. I have never forgiven her."

This forced Elliott to ask this last question, "...but why?"

Stalin took a few steps around the office, and almost in a rage roared, "They poisoned your father, of course, just as they have tried repeatedly to poison me."

"They, who are they?" Elliot asked.

"The Churchill gang!" Stalin roared, "They poisoned your father, and they continue to try to poison me ... the Churchill gang!"

The man to succeed FDR was another 33° Freemason, Harry Truman, who famously authorized the dropping of two nukes over Japan. Truman also went on to oversee the setting up of the backbone and infrastructure of the US MIC (Military Intelligence Complex) which has gone on to completely dominate American society, and indeed the world. In 1947, Truman authorized the National Security Act which established the CIA; then in 1952, he officially formed the National Security Agency (NSA) which was so secret for awhile that

Image #47: out goes 33° Mason Roosevelt, in comes 33° Mason Truman (3rd from left)

it was jokingly known as 'No Such Agency.' These two agencies have intruded so massively into peoples' lives with their mass surveillance that there are very few secrets anymore. Along with the Defense Intelligence Agency (DIA), National Reconnaissance Office (NRO) and National Geospatial-Intelligence Agency (NGA) they form the big five spying agencies of the MIC. According to his diary entires, Truman was not a huge fan of the Jews:[238][239]

That situation is insoluble in my opinion. I have spent a year and a month trying to get some concrete action on it. Not only are the British highly successful in muddling the situation as completely as it could possibly be muddled, but the Jews themselves are making it almost impossible to do anything for them. They seem to have the same attitude toward the "underdog" when they are on top as they have been treated as "underdogs" themselves. I suppose that is human frailty.

The Jews have no sense of proportion, nor do they have any judgment on world affairs ... The Jews, I find, are very, very selfish. They care not how many Estonians, Latvians, Finns, Poles, Yugoslavs or Greeks get murdered or mistreated as displaced persons, as long as the Jews get special treatment.

Was it this reluctance to do what the crypto-Jews wanted – support the Zionists against the Arabs, and especially support the founding of modern-day Israel – that led some of the Zionist terrorists groups to attempt to assassinate Truman? In her biography of her father, entitled simply *Harry S. Truman*, Truman's daughter Margaret described how the Stern Gang tried to assassinate her dad by mail:[240]

In the summer of 1947, the so-called Stern Gang of Palestine terrorists tried to assassinate Dad by mail. A number of cream-colored envelopes about eight by six inches, arrived in the White House, addressed to the President and various members of the staff. Inside them was a smaller envelope marked "Private and Confidential." Inside that second envelope was powdered gelignite, a pencil battery and a detonator rigged to explode the gelignite when the envelope was opened. Fortunately, the White House mail room was alert to the possibility that such letters might arrive. The previous June at least eight were sent to British government officials, including Foreign Secretary Anthony Eden. The British police exploded one of these experimentally and said it could kill, or at the very least maim, anyone unlucky enough to open it. The mail room turned the letters over to the Secret Service and they were defused by their bomb experts. The Secret Service still screens all our mail.

The Cult wanted their own country. They wanted a formal partition of Palestine. Thus, they sought UN recognition for their pet Zionist project which would require a two thirds majority in the UNGA (UN General Assembly). However, on November 26th 1947, it became apparent to the Zionists that the UNGA vote wouldn't go their way. So what did they do? What they always do, of course; they filibustered for a postponement and then dished out the bribes and threats – the carrot and stick method. They bribed the Latin American delegates by saying the Pan-American Highway construction project would be more likely to happen if they voted in favor of the partition plan; they bribed delegates' wives with mink coats (although the wife of the Cuban delegate returned hers); they reportedly bribed Costa Rica's President Jose Figueres with a blank checkbook; they bribed Haiti with economic aid. Zionist Supreme Court Judge Felix Frankfurter, in addition to ten senators and Truman domestic advisor Clark Clifford, threatened the Philippines at a time when there were seven bills pending in US Congress regarding the Philippines. Before the vote, the Filipino delegate had given a passionate speech denouncing the idea of partition, defending the rights of a people to preserve the territorial integrity of their native land. One day later, the delegate buckled under the pressure and voted 'Yes' on the partition plan.[241]

The Cult knows that if the carrot of bribery doesn't work, next comes the stick of threats. They threatened smaller nations such as Greece (that had planned on voting against the partition) into changing its vote. They went all the way to the top and threatened Truman himself by stating they would withdraw Jewish support for him in the upcoming presidential election if he didn't support the partition plan vote. Truman wrote:[242]

The facts were that not only were there pressure movements around the United Nations unlike anything that had been seen there before, but that the White House, too, was subjected to a constant barrage. I do not think I ever had as much pressure and propaganda aimed at the White House as I had in this instance. The persistence of a few of the extreme Zionist leaders — actuated by political motives and engaging in political threats — disturbed and annoyed me.

There were many different Cult agents threatening people of power. Former DOJ lawyer John Loftus (a former Army intelligence officer with NATO Cosmic clearance) became well known for his books on the topics of Bush-Rockefeller-Nazi connections, and the links between the CIA and former Nazis. Loftus revealed that Reuven Shiloah (at that time a Haganah agent sent by Ben-Gurion) blackmailed Nelson Rockefeller into creating the State of Israel. He writes:[243]

[B]efore World War II, Allen Dulles and his brother John Foster Dulles set up a series of front companies to disguise the fact that their client, Nelson Rockefeller, had invested heavily in the Third Reich industrial complex and was supplying Hitler with oil. Prescott Bush, father of future president George Herbert Walker Bush, did as he was told and agreed to become the American fall guy, sitting on the boards of half a dozen Nazi front companies as a placeholder for Rockefeller.

Prescott Bush had nothing to fear. The Dulles brothers were the best lawyers in the world at hiding illegal investments, or so they thought.

You see, their sister, Eleanor Dulles, knew all her brothers' dirty secrets.

Eleanor was the "family scandal." She had married a Jewish professor. Having a Jew in the Dulles family created a bad image for their German clients. Eleanor always blamed her brothers for driving her Jewish husband to commit suicide. So she started making copies of the records concerning her brothers' front companies for Nazi money laundering, including some of the Nazi codes. According to my sources, she gave them all to a man named Reuven Shiloah.

Apparently, the deal went something like this: Nelson Rockefeller told Shiloah that he would help get the Latin American votes at the UN for Israel to become a country on the condition that he, the Rockefellers, Prescott Bush, etc. were not prosecuted for investing in Nazi Germany. Shiloah was the founder of the Mossad, the nefarious Cult Israeli intelligence agency that will become extremely important in the coming chapters.

When the UN vote was finally taken, the Zionists just got over the line to gain a two thirds majority: 33 countries voted in favor, 13 opposed and 10 abstained. On May 14th 1948, just 11 minutes after Israel declared itself a country, Truman rushed to recognize it. The USA was thus the first country in the world to recognize Israel as a nation. Why? Because the Cult had bribed Truman to the tune of two million dollars. Gore Vidal wrote a foreword to Israel Shahak's book where he relayed that JFK had said to him, *"That's why our recognition of Israel was rushed through so fast."*[244] This move by Truman disgusted many of those around him; some, such as then Secretary of State Dean Acheson, warned that the West would pay a high price for Israel. How right he has proven to be. He stated:[245]

I did not share President's view on the Palestine solution ... the number that could be absorbed by Arab Palestine without creating a grave political problem would be inadequate, and to transform the country into a Jewish state capable of receiving a million or more immigrants would vastly exacerbate the political problem and imperil not only American but all Western influence in the Near East.

He also saw that the Middle East would become a tinderbox:[246]

Throughout the Near East lay rare tinder for anti-Western propaganda: a Moslem culture and history, bitter Arab nationalism galled by Jewish immigration under British protection and with massive American financial support, the remnants of a colonial status, and a sense of grievance that a vast natural resource was being extracted by foreigners under arrangements thought unfair to those living on the surface. This tinder could be, and was, lighted everywhere ...

A tinderbox indeed. That has always been one of the points of Israel. Just as the Cult set things up for WWI, manipulated that event into being, then at its conclusion set things up for WWII, so has it set up another region of the world for almost endless conflict that could turn into WWIII, if for example Israel or the US get into a sustained regional war with Iran.

Numerous US officials fiercely opposed the partition plan, and the US State Department strenuously opposed it, considering Zionism to be contrary to both fundamental American principles and US interests. The head of the State Department's Division of Near Eastern Affairs, Gordon P. Merriam, warned against the partition plan on moral grounds, as quoted by activist Alison Weir: *"U.S. support for partition of Palestine as a solution to that problem can be justified only on the basis of Arab and Jewish consent,"* adding that without consent, *"bloodshed and chaos"* would follow, a tragically accurate prediction.[247] An internal State Department memorandum accurately predicted how Israel would be born through armed aggression masked as defense:[248]

[T]he Jews will be the actual aggressors against the Arabs. However, the Jews will claim that they are merely defending the boundaries of a state which were traced by the UN... In the event of such Arab outside aid the Jews will come running to the Security Council with the claim that their state is the object of armed aggression and will use every means to obscure the fact that it is their own armed aggression against the Arabs inside which is the cause of Arab counter-attack.

Truman's Secretary of State George Marshall, a former WWII general and author of the Marshall Plan, thought support of the partition plan would damage US presidential dignity. Commander E. H. Hutchison, who chaired the Jordan-Israel Armistice Commission after the 1948 Arab-Israeli War, said that every step in the establishment of a Zionist state was a challenge to justice. Loy Henderson, Director of the State Department's Office of Near Eastern and African Affairs, wrote a memo to the Secretary of State warning that *"the active support by the Government of the United States of a policy favoring the setting up of a Jewish State in Palestine would be contrary to the policy which the United States has always followed of respecting the wishes of a large majority of the local inhabitants with respect to their form of government. Furthermore, it would have a strongly adverse effect upon American interests throughout the Near and Middle East."*[249] Another US official who will become important in the next chapter, Secretary of

Defense James Forrestal, revealed that *"the methods that had been used ... to bring coercion and duress on other nations in the General Assembly bordered closely onto scandal."*[250]

The apparently bitter Cold War enemies – the ideological opponents of the United States and the Soviet Union – stood together to fully endorse the creation of the Zionist state within Palestine. This is unsurprising, since by this point in time, the Cult had well and truly gained control of both superpowers. The USSR in particular was a Cult creation out of Russia, as discussed earlier. At the final vote on November 29th 1947, despite the Zionists' best immigration efforts, the Arabs had a majority. This source (Report of Sub-Committee 2 of the United Nations Special Committee on Palestine) states that in December 1946, there were 1,364,000 Palestinians and 608,000 Jews in Palestine.[251] Yet, the United Nations Partition Plan for Palestine gave Jews around 56% and the Arabs around 43% of the land, with Jerusalem becoming an international zone. Those looking at the situation logically could see that the Palestinians had absolutely nothing to do with WWII in Europe, the Nazis or the Holocaust. So why should they be dispossessed of their land? However, the decision to create the colonial outpost of Israel in the Middle East, promoted and administered by White, Caucasian, Khazarian 'Jews' with Eastern European names, had nothing to do with logic, fairness or justice, and everything to do with the Cult's agenda. Israelis only comprised 5-8% of the new population. The more unjust a decision, the more violence which results against it.

David Icke has referred to Israel as 'the fiefdom of the Rothschilds' since their monetary contribution to its infrastructure is immense. Baron Edmond James de Rothschild has the Tel Aviv Rothschild Boulevard named after him. David Livingstone writes:[252]

The main building of the Knesset, the state legislature, completed in 1966, was financed by his son, James de Rothschild, as a gift to the State of Israel. James married Dorothy Mathilde Pinto, a close friend of Chaim Weizmann. Dorothy was the first chairperson of the Yad Hanadiv ("The Rothschild Foundation"), who donated the building for the Supreme Court of Israel, which features a Masonic-inspired pyramid. The foundation memorializes her husband's father, Edmond James de Rothschild.

Jewish Terrorism and the Palestinian Nakba

Just as the Jews had their 'Shoah' (the Hebrew word for the Holocaust), so too did the Arabs have their 'Nakba' (the Arabic word for 'the catastrophe'), which describes the period starting around November 1947, and continuing through 1948 (and technically is ongoing to the present day), when the Palestinians were violently driven off their land and killed by Zionist terrorists and militias. Later, once Israel had declared itself a nation, these Zionist terrorists and militia became Israel's national military. The Nakba concept also encompasses the broader way in which the Palestinians were 'ethnically cleansed' (a horrible euphemism) and deprived of their culture, rights, national aspirations and identity. A typical Zionist retort today is that Palestine was never a nation and that there were no such people as the Palestinians before Israel became a nation in 1948. The kind of mindset that underlies these statements is one that completely denies Palestine and seeks to eradicate all Palestinian identity. For instance, Golda Meir, one-time Israeli PM, said the following: *"How can we return the occupied territories? There is nobody to return them to."*[253]

During the Nakba, around 750,000 people (about half of Palestine's population at the time) were expelled from their homes.

There were numerous instances of massacres which completely destroyed entire villages, towns and urban neighborhoods, which were then colonized by the Zionist invaders who gave the areas new Hebrew names. Israel used biological warfare by contaminating Palestinian wells; "Cast Thy Bread" was a top secret operation conducted by Haganah (and later the IDF) during the 1948 Palestine War where Israeli terrorists used typhoid bacteria to contaminate the wells.[254] By the end of 1948, 78% of the area of Mandatory Palestine was under Israeli control. The Nakba was brutal genocide. One example that stands out among all the killing is the Deir Yassin massacre on April 9th 1948. Zionist terrorists murdered at least 107 Palestinians, including women and children, despite the fact that the village had agreed to a non-aggression pact with the Zionists.

The newly created state of Israel lost no time in forming a state army out of the many militia organizations that had already been operating there to terrorize the local Arab Palestinians: Haganah (including Palmach), Irgun, Lehi/the Stern Gang and the Hebrew Resistance Movement. Some of the soldiers and commanders of these groups would later go on to become high-up Israeli officials, including being Prime Minister, such as Menachem Begin, Yitzhak Shamir and Yitzhak Rabin. The father of current Israeli PM Benjamin Netanyahu, Benzion Netanyahu, was the personal assistant of Benjamin Azkin, the secretary of Revisionist Zionist and terrorist Ze'ev Jabotinsky. Here is what Jabotinsky had to say:[255]

A voluntary reconciliation with the Arabs is out of the question either now or in the future. If you wish to colonize a land in which people are already living, you must provide a garrison for the land, or find some rich man or benefactor who will provide a garrison on your behalf. Or else, give up your colonization, for without an armed force which will render physically impossible any attempt to destroy or prevent this colonization, colonization is impossible, not difficult, not dangerous, but IMPOSSIBLE!... Zionism is a colonization adventure and therefore it stands or falls by the question of armed force. It is important... to speak Hebrew, but, unfortunately, it is even more important to be able to shoot – or else I am through with playing at colonizing.

Theodore Herzl wrote this in his dairy in 1895:[256]

We shall try to spirit the penniless population across the border by procuring employment for it in the transit countries, while denying it any employment in our country. The property owners will come over to our side. Both the process of expropriation and the removal of the poor must be carried out discretely and circumspectly.

British Zionist Israel Zangwill was the one who came up with the impudent Zionist slogan *"A land without a people for a people without a land."* In 1904, he also wrote that *"we must be prepared either to drive out by the sword the tribes in possession as our forefathers did, or to grapple with the problem of a large alien population, mostly Mohammedan and accustomed for centuries to despise us."*[257] He later admitted that Palestine was not a land without people, but this lie is still repeated today.

Ben-Gurion admitted:[258]

We were not just working – we were conquering, conquering, conquering land. We were a company of conquistadors.

Israel was always about colonization and theft under the cloak of religion. What is especially sad about the situation is that the Palestinians let them in and helped them, only to be stabbed in the

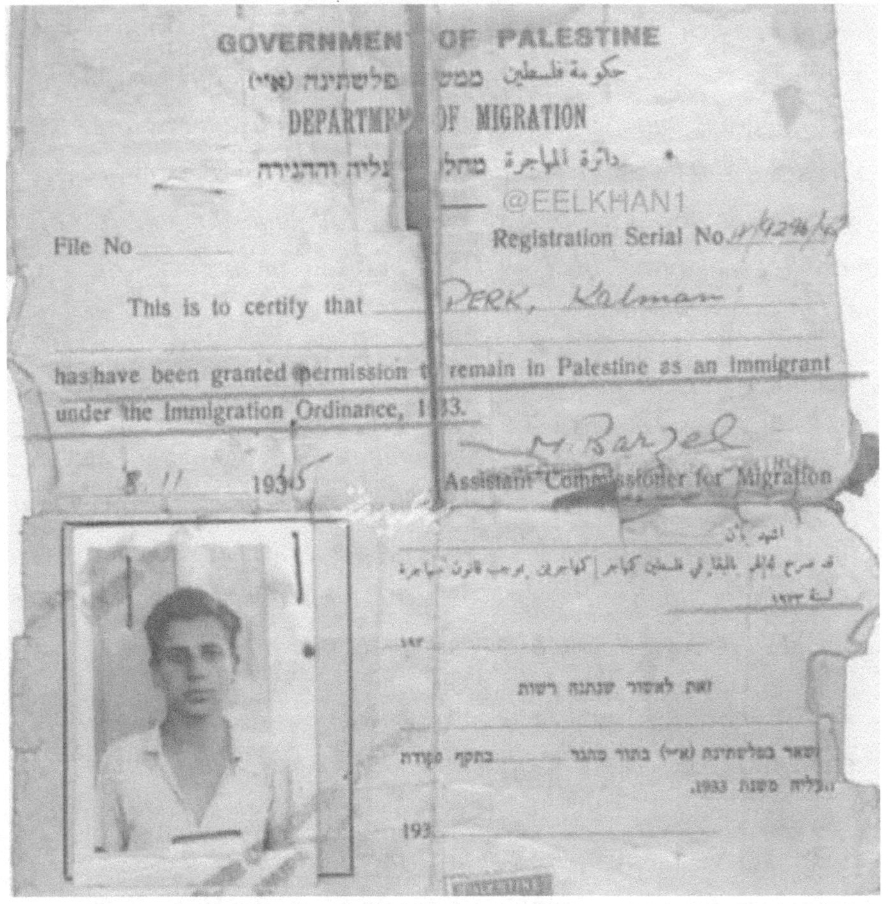
GOVERNMENT OF PALESTINE

DEPARTMENT OF MIGRATION

File No

Registration Serial No.

This is to certify that PERK, Kalman

has/have been granted permission to remain in Palestine as an immigrant under the Immigration Ordinance, 1933.

M. Barzel

Assistant Commissioner for Migration

8. 11 1935

זאת לאשר שנתנה רשות

193

Image #48: the Government of Palestine's Department of Migration issues permission for an immigrant to remain in Palestine

back. As image #48 shows, immigrants were given permission by the Government of Palestine.[259]

Why Israel Wages War with its Archeologists

In addition to waging war against its Middle Eastern neighbors in more obvious ways – spying, hacking, assassination, false flag operations (see chapter 12) and direct invasion (see chapter 17) – Israel also wages war by way of archeology, using its archeologists to find 'evidence' of a previous Jewish civilization in Palestine. Israel uses archaeology as a tool of colonization, narrative control and perception management, a means by which it attempts to legitimize its occupation of Palestine. As discussed in earlier chapters, this goes back a long way; Ben-Gurion was an otherwise secular politician who made many religious statements after becoming leader, espousing archeology as the way to connect current Israeli Jews to an 'ancient Jewish people' and thus strengthen the bond between the nation and the 'mystical homeland.' George Orwell wrote that whoever controls the present controls the past, and that whoever controls the past controls the future. Israel, via its current military domination of the Palestinians (and Lebanese, and many others) in the present, is able to fabricate 'evidence' of the past, just as the ruling party did in 1984 via use of the Memory Hole and the constant updating of newspapers. Then, with a new 'past' established, it attempts to legitimize its future. This kind of Zionist propaganda is not only used on non-Jews but especially on Israelis themselves, such as those fighting in the IDF:[260]

According to Toprak, the ancient mountaintop fortress of Masada in southeastern Israel is one example of Tel Aviv using archeology as a tool for occupation and colonization. In the 1960s, (Israeli) Commander Yigael Yadin reminded people of the Jews who resisted against the Romans at the fortress of Masada. He talked about how hundreds of people resisted and chose to commit suicide instead of surrendering to the Roman soldiers, thereby making history. "The slogan 'Masada shall not fall again' is still used by soldiers in Israel against Arabs. Yadin conducted excavations here to prove the legend, but only 25 graves were reached. No instances of suicide were found in any of them."

It was reported in November 2024[261] that an Israeli settler (in other words, someone living on stolen Palestinian land) and researcher named Ze'ev Erlich was killed by Hezbollah in an ambush after accompanying IDF troops into Lebanon without approval. His area of research was trying to make a connection between Arab villages and ancient Jewish communities. He was accused of having authored numerous falsified studies on the topic.[262]

There are many Israelis, not aligned with the current rightwing and fascist Israeli Likud government, who oppose this weaponization of archaeology. Haaretz journalist Nir Hasson wrote that Israel's attempt to extend the jurisdiction of the Israel Antiquities Authority (IAA) over stolen land *"officially turns Israeli archaeology into a pickaxe with which to dig for the sake of furthering apartheid."*[263] Israeli archeologist Raphael (Rafi) Greenberg exposes how the Zionist regime uses antiquities to acquire real estate. He says:[264]

In Israel, most of the antiquities that you see are probably not Jewish. If you walk through the countryside and see a ruined building or a castle, it's likely to be Islamic, Christian or something else ... Most sites are eclectic; they have stuff predating Judaism by thousands of years. They have stuff after the times of Jewish independence in [ancient] Palestine, from different Islamic dynasties and Christian control. If you take any slice of the history of Israel-Palestine, at any point in time, you will not find a single homogenous culture across the landscape. There's no time in which everyone in this country was Jewish, Islamic, Christian or anything else. Archaeology in its essence does not provide that kind of certainty and purity that ethnocratic right-wing government ministers might want. So they have to invent it.

It is not surprising that this kind of biblical archaeology[265] became well known in America due to the funding of Cult operative, Rothschild agent and Jew Jacob H. Schiff, named in chapter 7 as one of the men owning shares in the private banking system of the US, the Federal Reserve. The more you research this, the more you realize that it's one closely connected Cult circle at the top that has its fingers in every pie.

The Cult Acquires Nuclear Weapons for Israel

From its inception in 1948, Israel went on the rampage and war path, plundering, marauding and killing its way to as much land as possible. Some months after the Six Day War ended on June 10th 1967, Israel returned some of the land it had stolen from Egypt (the Sinai peninsula) in exchange for peace. (Incidentally, regarding the Six Day War, Israeli leaders acknowledged that Egyptian President Nasser's deployment of two divisions along the border was defensive; it was Israel that attacked Egypt not vice versa.) However, since the 1950s, Israel had been working on a project that would mean it would never again have to play second fiddle to its Arab neighbors – a project so clandestine it would involve the acquisition of the most dangerous and powerful weapon in the world at that time (at least, the most most powerful publicly known one, excluding the underground weapons tied up in secret black military operations).

Here's how the Israeli nuclear weapons program started. Israel and France had a close relationship in the 1950s. Israel provided intelligence to France (on Algeria) in exchange for weaponry. Israeli PM Ben-Gurion sent Shimon Peres, Moshe Dayan and Yehoshafat Harkabi (military intelligence) to France in 1956 when France agreed to give Israel nuclear technology and build a nuclear plant at Dimona in the Negev Desert. As a cover to deflect curiosity, they built the plant as a textile factory, but American U2 planes spotted it.

Israeli-American writer, historian, and professor Avner Cohen, author of the 1999 book *Israel and the Bomb*, revealed a lot of about the inner workings of the mind of David Ben-Gurion. There is no doubt that Ben-Gurion became increasingly paranoid that Israel would be obliterated by its Arab neighbors. He writes that Ben-Gurion was consumed by fears for Israel's security, and although he didn't mention the Holocaust much publicly, he repeatedly referenced it in private communications with foreign leaders. When exchanging letters with JFK, he compared the Arabs' attitude towards Israel with Hitler's hatred of the Jews. Cohen writes:[266]

Anxiety about the Holocaust reached beyond Ben-Gurion to infuse Israeli military thinking ... Israeli military planners have always considered a scenario in which a united Arab military coalition launched a war against Israel with the aim of liberating Palestine and destroying the Jewish state. This was referred to in the early 1950s as mikre hkol, or the 'everything scenario.' This kind of planning was unique to Israel, as few nations have military contingency plans aimed at preventing apocalypse. Ben-Gurion had no qualms about Israel's need for weapons of mass destruction ... Ben-Gurion's determination to launch a nuclear project was the result of strategic intuition and obsessive fears, not of a well-thought out plan. He believed Israel needed nuclear weapons as insurance if it could no longer compete with the Arabs in an arms race.

Ben-Gurion was the key driver in Israel obtaining nukes and his fear-based mindset dominated Israeli military and foreign policy long after he stepped down and died. The same kind of thinking can be found in Israel's current PM Benjamin Netanyahu. Ben-Gurion said

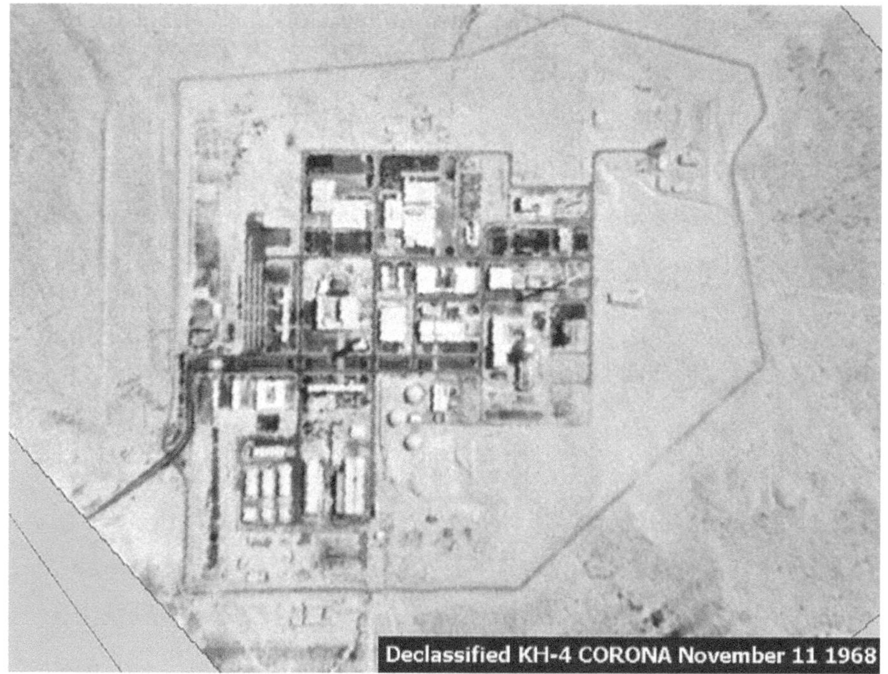

Image #49: aerial photograph of nuclear weapons plant at Dimona, Israel

that the Arabs were constantly declaring that they wished to terminate Israel, and that therefore, Israel must have the bomb to defend itself. Thus, the so-called nuclear option was both at the core of Ben-Gurion's worldview and Israeli national security policy. Famous journalist Seymour Hersh, author of the 1991 book *The Samson Option*, writes that this paranoid military policy involves a last resort option where they detonate a nuclear bomb to blow up the region, themselves included. *If you try to kill us, we'll take everyone down.* This name refers to the biblical Israelite character 'Samson' who, after being captured by the Philistines, pushed over the pillars of Dagon's Temple in Gaza, bringing down the roof and killing both his enemies and himself. Cult-owned Israeli officials are willing, if necessary, to blow everything up in order to destroy the Arabs they hate so much. Time and again we see the pattern of the Cult blaming others (projection) for the very thing it does itself, when others are innocent of it. The Cult is a death cult, so it's unsurprising that Israel would be the biggest 'suicide bomber' of all, and it's also unsurprising that Islamic terrorist suicide bombers like Al Qaeda, ISIS, etc. are all Cult-Israeli-CIA-Mossad creations anyway. Israeli military historian Martin van Creveld was quoted in David Hirst's 2003 book *The Gun and the Olive Branch* as saying:[267]

We possess several hundred atomic warheads and rockets and can launch them at targets in all directions, perhaps even at Rome. Most European capitals are targets for our air force. Let me quote General Moshe Dayan: "Israel must be like a mad dog, too dangerous to bother" ... Our armed forces, however, are not the thirtieth strongest in the world, but rather the second or third. We have the capability to take the world down with us. And I can assure you that that will happen before Israel goes under.

So refreshing to hear such sanity coming from a nuclear-armed nation. One of John F. Kennedy's great missions was to stop the spread of nuclear weapons, which is why he was championing the Nuclear Non-Proliferation Treaty (NPT). JFK was determined to make sure that both America and the USSR would limit their stockpiles, and that no new countries would get nuclear weapons. Hence, when he caught wind of a possible Israeli nuclear project at Dimona, he insisted the Israelis allow US inspectors there to check it out. Ben-Gurion did his best to procrastinate and refuse; he even ordered the creation of a fake 'Potemkin village' facade to hide the real operations there. JFK and Ben-Gurion kept exchanging letters, but JFK was adamant; in a telegram on May 18th 1963,[268] JFK essentially issued him an ultimatum, though diplomatically worded: allow American inspections at Dimona under international law, or US support and aid to Israel would be jeopardized. In response to this, Ben-Gurion resigned on June 16th 1963 in order to not receive the letter, which appears to have been a dallying tactic to buy Israel time. JFK picked up the issue with the next PM, but it was only several months later when Kennedy was assassinated, and the incoming man, President LBJ, was as already mentioned 100% owned by the Zionists, so he naturally let the matter drop and allowed the tiny nation of Israel to go on its merry way and acquire nuclear weapons.

And go on its merry way it did. In his documentary *NUMEC: How Israel Stole the Atomic Bomb and killed JFK,*[269] Ryan Dawson details the history of how the Zionists, mainly Haganah, focused on the US War Assets Administration (WAA) to smuggle weapons into Israel. They used the US-based Sonneborn Group (and its front group charity the Sonneborn Institute), financing via Jewish organized crime and transportation via third party countries as a stopping point from US to Palestine. The Mossad also smuggled 200 tons of yellowcake uranium from Europe in 1968. However, the bulk of the theft came from NUMEC (Nuclear Materials and Equipment Corporation) in Apollo, Pennsylvania, USA. It was owned by the parent holding company Apollo Industries that was full of Zionists. Its chairman was Zalman Shapiro, who was also the Pennsylvania chapter president of the Zionist Organization of America (ZOA). As chairman for NUMEC, Shapiro oversaw the theft of massive amounts of nuclear material in Pennsylvania to Israel. The US Atomic Energy Commission chairman Glenn Seaborg was also in on it, hiding the theft away from JFK while he was still president. The CIA later found highly-enriched uranium near Dimona in 1968 that could only have come from America; NUMEC and Nautilus (the first nuclear-powered submarine) was the only program in the world with that level of enrichment. At one point the FBI was investigating Zalman Shapiro, but Jewish mafia gangster Meyer Lansky (who played a big part in the JFK assassination, chapter 11) blackmailed FBI chief Edgar Hoover, threatening to release photos of him having gay sex with Clyde Tolson, so the FBI dropped their investigation of Shapiro. Another excellent source for this topic is Grant Smith, director of the Institute for Research: Middle Eastern Policy in Washington DC, who has authored books such as *Divert!: Numec, Zalman Shapiro and the Diversion of US Weapons Grade Uranium Into the Israeli Nuclear Weapons Program*. All in all, between 1957 to 1978, over 300 kilograms of highly enriched u-235 (uranium 235, the isotope needed for nuclear production) went missing from the Apollo plant.

Another figure in this sordid affair was billionaire Arnon Milchan, an Israeli super-spy. Milchan was a big Hollywood movie producer and a leading Israeli arms dealer. In addition to funding Oliver Stone's movie *JFK*, he produced Hollywood movies that foreshadowed 9/11, another giant false flag operation executed by Israel (e.g. *Medusa's Touch* – see chapter 14). Stone's movie *JFK* told half-truths about the assassination; the point was to cover Israel's role, of course. Arnon Milchan was the man who helped Shimon Peres and others further the Israeli nuclear program via LEKEM or LAKAM (ha-Lishka le-Kishrei Mada, Hebrew for "Bureau of Scientific Relations"), an Israeli intelligence agency headed by Benjamin Blumberg and Rafi Eitan which collected scientific and technical intelligence. It was disbanded in 1987 after Jonathan Pollard's arrest who was caught spying for Israel (more on this in chapter 12). In a 2011 unauthorized biography, authors Meir Doron and Joseph Gelman revealed that Milchan was a LAKAM agent.[270]

Interviewed regarding Milchan's intelligence activities, Peres stated:[271]

Arnon is a special man. It was I who recruited him... When I was at the Ministry of Defense, Arnon was involved in numerous defense-related procurement activities and intelligence operations. His strength is in making connections at the highest levels... His activities gave us a huge advantage, strategically, diplomatically and technologically.

Israel went on to develop hundreds of nuclear weapons, and were it not for the bravery of an Israeli insider, we may not know that much about it. Mordechai Vanunu is a former nuclear technician who became a whistleblower and peace activist. While working at Dimona, he secretly took photographs of the inside of the facilities, then went public with them. You can see them at this website.[272] Interestingly enough, when he tried to sell them, he reached out to the British Press in 1986, some of which was owned by Robert Maxwell, an Israeli spy and an early mentor of Jeffrey Epstein (covered more in chapter 12). He was also the father of Ghislaine Maxwell who became Epstein's lover and the recruiter of young girls into his pedophile blackmail ring.

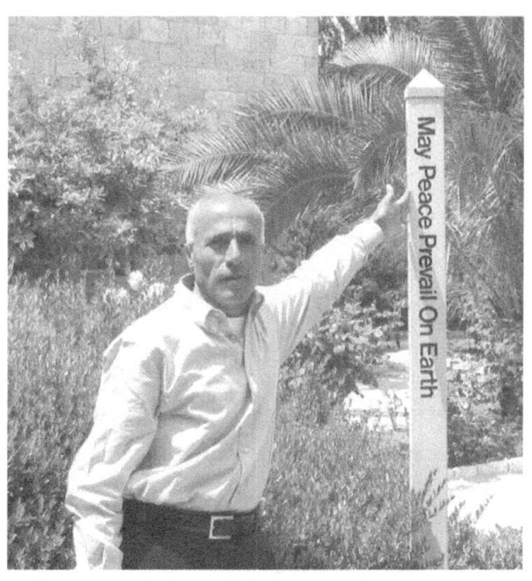

Image #50: Israeli Mordechai Vanunu, a man with heart and conscience, blew the whistle on the Israeli nuclear program

Maxwell based himself in London and owned a publishing empire. According to Seymour Hersh, it was Maxwell and his editor Nick Davies who put the Mossad onto Vanunu; they lured him to Italy with a romantic interest, but it was a honeypot trap. Once the Mossad agents got him, they drugged and abducted him, taking him back to Israel where he was convicted in a trial held behind closed doors. He spent 18 years in prison (of which more than 11 were in solitary confinement) and when he was released from prison in 2004, he was forbidden from giving interviews to foreign journalists and attempting to leave Israel. Vanunu has been characterized by Israel as a traitor, but it was his conscience and his opposition to weapons of mass destruction that led him to expose the Israeli nuclear program.

To this day, Israel has adopted a policy of 'nuclear ambiguity' which is an Orwellian term. It is patently obvious to anyone who looks closely that Israel has nuclear weapons; in fact, a Joint Atomic Energy Intelligence Committee (JAEIC) report from December 1960, declassified just recently in December 2024,[273] confirms that the JAEIC knew that Dimona included a reprocessing plant for plutonium production and was weapons related, even if it took other US Intelligence agencies several more years to catch on. However, by the late 1960s, the entire US MIC knew that the Zionists had reached the threshold of nuclear weapons capability. US President Nixon and Israeli PM Meir reached an agreement in 1969 that the US would not push Israel to declare its arsenal nor join the NPT as long as Israel maintained a low profile. This is yet another example of how the Cult helped the Cult; Cult-controlled America helped Cult-controlled Israel avoid declaring its nuclear capability, being the only country in the world to hold such a position. Israel's possession of nukes makes its constant hype about Iran's supposed nuclear ambitions all the more absurd and hypocritical. The US MIC has repeatedly concluded, over and over, that Iran has no nuclear weapons nor is pursuing the path to make them ("*We continue to assess Iran is not building a nuclear weapon and that Khamenei has not reauthorized the nuclear weapons program he suspended in 2003 ...* ")[274], yet every few years Israel keeps banging the war drums over the issue in a classic case of psychological projection. Israel in fact used the excuse of an imminent Iranian nuclear weapon as a casus belli when they aggressively and in unprovoked fashion struck Iran on June 12th 2025 (the start of the 12-Day War) in Operation Rising Lion.

Israel not only secretly acquired nuclear tech, but also secretly spread nuclear tech. In October 1964, the Chinese performed a nuclear test explosion that was actually a joint Chinese-Israeli operation. Both Seymour Hersh and Michael Piper laid out the evidence that it was in fact a joint Chinese-Israeli operation. Piper claims to have found evidence that JFK wanted his staff to draw up a plan for a US Air Force (USAF) raid on a Chinese nuclear site with the intention of stopping a potential Chinese nuclear weapons project. In support of this idea, Piper sourced intelligence historian Richard Deacon, author of the 1978 book *The Israeli Secret Service*, who stated that nuclear bomb production *"has been one of the spheres in which the Israelis and the Chinese have actually helped one another—not officially, but discreetly through Secret Service channels."*[275] Is it really surprising that Israel would spread nuclear tech to other nations (outside the Middle East, where it wants to be the regional hegemon)? Milchan claimed *"to have used connections to promote the apartheid regime in South Africa in exchange for it helping Israel acquire uranium."*[276]

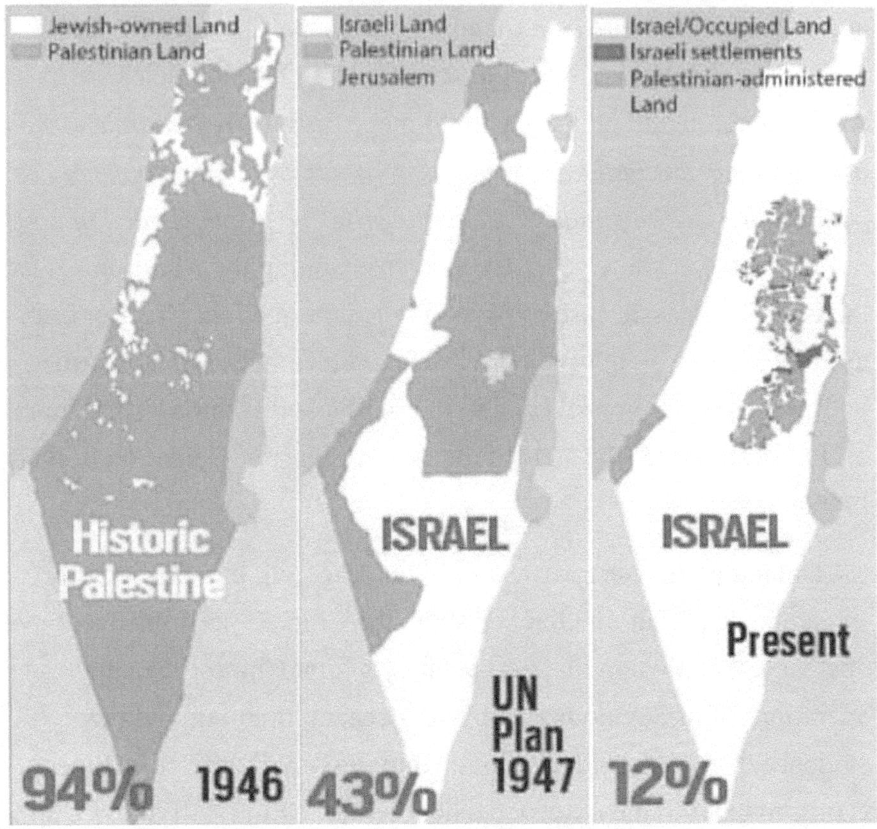

Image #51: the Israeli monster swallows historic Palestine

<u>Can a Country Even Have a Right to Exist?</u>

Interestingly enough, these days we hear so much about Israel's right to exist – but hang on a minute. Since when do countries have a right to exist? People have a right to exist. States don't have a right to exist. States come and go with the rise and fall of civilizations and the tide of history. The Cult Zionists have turned the issue on its head by outrageously claiming that Palestine never existed but that Israel always existed, or by insisting that Israel's right to exist must never be questioned, and that Jews have a 'right to return' to the region,

عيسى داود العيسى
يوسف حنا
داود بندلي العيسى

فلسطين
FALASTIN

The Zionist Crocodile to Palestine Arabs :-

تمساح الصهيونية لعرب فلسطين :-
لا تخافوا !!! سأبلعكم بسلام..

لا كان التحسين
ولا التجميل
اذا كانت هذه اساليبه !!

Image #52: the Zionist crocodile promises peace to the Palestinian Arabs

while Palestinians are denied that same 'right of return' despite the fact they were the existing inhabitants of the land prior to the 1880s, 1920s and 1940s, when European, Caucasian, Ashkenazi (Khazarian) Jews were pumped in for decades to bring the Jewish numbers up. Yet, as image #51 shows, Palestine as a nation, land and region has been systematically eradicated since the Cult Israeli project began. Some Palestinians could see it coming. The Palestinian Christian-owned Falastin newspaper featured a caricature in its June 18th 1936 edition[277] (image #52) depicting Zionism as a crocodile under the protection of the British. The headline reads: *"Don't be afraid!!! I will swallow you peacefully."*

Zionism has always been colonization at the tip of a sword and the point of a gun. In the next chapter, we will look at how Israel in the 1960 began to emerge as a serious world power with the ability to infiltrate mighty nations like the USA … and to kill their presidents (and presidential candidates).

Sources

[233] https://www.jfklibrary.org/asset-viewer/archives/jfkpof-135-001#?image_identifier=JFKPOF-135-001-p0001

[234] As quoted by Nahum Goldmann in *Le Paraddoxe Juif* (The Jewish Paradox), pp. 121-122.

[235] Beit Hallahmi, 1993:23, as quoted by Retno Winarni in From Palestine To Palestine: The Jewish Strategy In Establishing Israel Country on Palestine, https://pdfs.semanticscholar.org/d609/caecedd90167d8a4f2360edd762b5a810d02.pdf

[236] https://history.state.gov/historicaldocuments/frus1945v08/d2

[237] https://www.prouty.org/comment1.html

[238] Truman quoted in *A Life*, by author by Robert H. Ferrell, 1994, pg. 307

[239] https://catalog.archives.gov/id/5859986

[240] https://dcdave.com/article5/120510.htm

[241] https://ummid.com/news/2024/september/16-09-2024/deception-bribery-and-blackmail-how-israel-was-born.html

[242] https://www.einpresswire.com/article/237353389/israel-s-modus-operandi-blackmail-bribery-and-bullying

[243] https://amimagazine.org/2021/02/10/blackmailing-rockefeller/

[244] https://www.jstor.org/stable/j.ctt183q63d.3

[245] https://en.wikiquote.org/wiki/Dean_Acheson#Middle_East

[246] Ibid.

[247] https://www.palestinechronicle.com/the-real-story-of-how-israel-was-created/

[248] https://history.state.gov/historicaldocuments/frus1948v05p2/d210

[249] https://history.state.gov//historicaldocuments/frus1945v08/d711

[250] https://www.winterwatch.net/2024/11/take-downs-of-america-firsters/

[251] https://www.jewishvoiceforpeace.org/wp-content/uploads/2016/06/Khalidi-Revisiting-the-1947-UN-Partition-Resolution_Jl-Pal-Studies_1993pdf1.pdf

[252] Zionism: History of a Jewish Heresy, pg. 572

[253] As quoted in the NYT, https://palcit.net/article-958-return-the-occupied-territories-there-is-nobody-to-return-them-to

[254] https://www.tandfonline.com/doi/abs/10.1080/00263206.2022.2122448

[255] https://buildingthebridge.eu/common-ground/general/our-friday-news-analysis-what-the-world-reads-now/1841

[256] https://palcit.net/article-652-both-the-process-of-expropriation-and-the-removal-of-the-poor-must-be-carried-out-discretely

[257] https://palcit.net/article-738-be-prepared-either-to-drive-out-by-the-sword-the-tribes-in-possession-as-our-forefathers-did

[258] https://palcit.net/article-901-we-were-a-company-of-conquistadores

[259] https://x.com/DrLoupis__/status/1924163430379897072

[260] https://www.aa.com.tr/en/middle-east/israel-uses-archaeology-to-legitimize-occupation-of-palestine-says-scholar/2969072

[261] https://thecradle.co/articles/israeli-researcher-killed-by-hezbollah-after-accompanying-troops-into-lebanon-without-approval

[262] https://www.presstv.ir/Detail/2024/11/24/737823/Settler-archaeologist-exploits-archeology-to-justify-pro-settlement-agenda

[263] https://www.haaretz.com/israel-news/2024-07-11/ty-article/.premium/allowing-israel-antiquities-authority-to-operate-in-west-bank-is-equivalent-to-annexation/00000190-a32c-ddf1-abb6-efedbd390000

[264] https://www.972mag.com/israel-archaeology-annexation-rafi-greenberg/

[265] https://www.jstor.org/stable/23887932#references_tab_contents

[266] Israel and the Bomb, pp. 10-14

[267] The Gun and the Olive Branch, pg. 227

[268] https://nsarchive.gwu.edu/document/18727-national-security-archive-doc-28-department

---

[269] https://rumble.com/v1a6xdr-numec-how-israel-stole-the-atomic-bomb.html

[270] https://web.archive.org/web/20130803053831/https://www.nytimes.com/2011/07/18/business/global/new-book-tells-tale-of-israeli-arms-dealer-in-hollywood.html?_r=0

[271] http://fourwinds10.com/siterun_data/history/zionism/jews-judaism/news.php?q=1448379225

[272] https://www.vanunu.com/uscampaign/photos.html

[273] https://nsarchive.gwu.edu/briefing-book/nuclear-vault/2024-12-17/1960-intelligence-report-said-israeli-nuclear-site-was

[274] https://www.dni.gov/files/ODNI/documents/assessments/ATA-2025-Unclassified-Report.pdf

[275] Final Judgment, pg. 409

[276] https://www.theguardian.com/world/2013/nov/26/arnon-milchan-israeli-spy-past

[277] https://x.com/WTAFRich/status/1978130036751270213

CHAPTER 11: THE CULT KILLS THE KENNEDYS

"We now have plenty of money – our new backers are Jews – as soon as 'we' (or 'they') take care of Kennedy."

– Alleged comment by Cuban exile Homer Echeverria the day before the JFK assassination, as recorded in a declassified US Secret Service document[278]

"Fundamentally, the founding fathers of U.S. intelligence were liars ... the better you lied and the more you betrayed, the more likely you would be promoted ... Outside of their duplicity, the only thing they had in common was a desire for absolute power. I did things that, in looking back on my life, I regret. But I was part of it and loved being in it."

– James Jesus Angleton, as quoted by David Talbot[279]

"John Kennedy was assassinated because he was about to give our most vital secret to the Soviets ... the alien presence."

– CIA agent E. Howard Hunt[280]

The key to understanding the JFK assassination lies in understanding two extremely powerful, and simultaneously, extremely psychopathic men: Allen Dulles and James Angleton. This entails understanding who they were, the power they held (occupying the apex of the iniquitous CIA), the mindset they embodied and, crucially, the factions with which they aligned themselves outside of the CIA. Both were Cult agents of the highest degree; Angleton in particular stood at the intersection of two highly influential factions,

Image #53: John Fitzgerald Kennedy – the last American president to meaningfully stand up to the Cult

the Israeli faction and UFO/ET (Extraterrestrial) secrecy faction. Both of these factions were prepared to kill anyone who seriously obstructed them.

John F. Kennedy, though one of the best presidents in US history, was not a perfect man. He was a womanizer with seemingly little or no restraint over his sexual desires who surrounded himself with officials and advisors from the Bilderberg Group and the CFR (Council on Foreign Relations). Seeing the Jewish lobby and the Mob as necessary evils he needed to court to get elected, he made deals with them, but once in office, he reneged on these agreements, refusing to let Israel run his foreign policy and going after the Mafia. He championed equal rights for all including black people, he was threatening to remove the oil depletion allowance which angered the rich Texas oilmen, he refused to provide air cover for the failed CIA Cuban invasion, he would not let Israel push him around and he was doing his best to rein in the CIA and its splinter group MJ-12 that had possession of the most important knowledge and technology in the world. In short, he made a lot of enemies.

For a very long time now, it has been patently obvious that JFK was not killed by a supposed lone wolf. Some books have pushed 'the Mafia did it' theory while other books such as Douglass's *JFK: The Unspeakable* pushed 'the CIA did it' theory which greatly influenced the public, including people in the Kennedy family themselves, such as the current Secretary of Health and Human Services (HHS), and son of RFK, Bobby Kennedy Jr. These are all partially true; a lot of people had the motivation to kill him. However, the key question that often gets overlooked is not whether the Mafia or CIA did it – because they were both indisputably involved – but who gave the order. Who hired whom? Who were the downstream lackeys, and who were the upstream masterminds?

The Official JFK Story: Nonsense and Impossibility

Many people doubt the official JFK story, and with good reason. It is the source of the famous 'magic bullet' theory in which we are somehow meant to believe that a single bullet went through President Kennedy's neck into Texan Governor John Connally's chest, then through Connally's right wrist to finally embed itself in Connally's left thigh. To believe this is to deny common sense and copious evidence. In the video footage, you can clearly see JFK's head get knocked back and to the left, which indicates at least some of the shots (and the most forceful ones) were from the front and to his right, and probably from below, yet the official Warren Commission concluded he was only shot from behind and up high from the Texas School Book Depository (TSBD) building. Lee Harvey Oswald, the designated fall guy, was characterized by the Soviets as *"a poor shot when he tried target firing in the USSR."*[281] In his superb documentary *Rush to Judgment*,[282] lawyer Mark Lane interviewed people that knew from firsthand experience that Oswald was a poor shot, such as Sergeant Nelson Delgado. Delgado served in the Marine Corp with Oswald and said he couldn't shoot very well, and even appeared as a witness before the Warren Commission, but said that when he was questioned about it by FBI agents, they tried to get him to change his statement: *"The way they were throwing the questions at me – they were trying to twist my testimony around."* Oswald had no credible motive to kill JFK, and when he was arrested and dragged off, he even shouted out that he was the patsy!

Before going any further, let's look at some of the key milestones that have occurred since 1963 to further our understanding of the assassination. At the start of 2025, Trump decided to release more JFK files, which did reveal a few more things, including existing documents with less redaction. However, in typical style, the Cult ensured it would be a limited hangout; they orchestrated it so the fox would yet again be guarding the henhouse. Zionist Jew and US Congresswoman Anna Paulina Luna was put in charge of the 2025 JFK Files release. This was similar to how David Marwell and his assistant on the Assassination Records Review Board (AARB), Douglas Horne, left it to go on to work for the US Holocaust Memorial Museum in Washington DC, which, as Michael Collins Piper wrote, is *"very closely cooperating with the Israeli government (and the Mossad) in a variety of ventures of interest to the worldwide Jewish community."*[283] It was Piper who deciphered the truth about Israel's involvement in the JFK assassination back in the 1990s. He published his book *Final Judgment* in 1993 where he outlined Israel's major role in great detail. With extensive research, Piper brilliantly tied together Israel, the CIA, the Mafia (dominated by the Jewish crime syndicate led by Meyer Lansky, not by Italians as you may think), the French OAS (Organisation Armée Secrète or Secret Army Organisation, the French paramilitary and terrorist group founded in 1961 that wanted Algeria to remain French), the right-wingers and the FBI, showing how they all had a hand in it. However, he did not understand the UFO/ET angle.

One year later in 1994, David Icke wrote his book *And The Truth Shall Set You Free*, published in 1995, which highlighted Piper's work and wove together other important threads, such as the insight of James Shelby Downard who wrote the essay *King Kill 33°* also in 1994. Downard was very knowledgeable on the topic of what he called 'mystical toponomy' or the esoteric significance of place names. He understood the power of the secret societies (including of course Freemasonry, which was infiltrated by the Illuminati, as described in chapter 5) and their obsession with gematria and numerical symbolism. It was Downard who pointed out that Kennedy was the 'Sun King' who was sacrificed at Dallas, on the 33rd parallel, on November 22nd (November is the 11th month, so 11 + 22 = 33), hence 'king kill' 33°. Bill Cooper was another researcher who saw how the murder of Kennedy was the esoteric sacrifice of the Sun King; he deeply understood how the mystery schools or secret societies ran the world, using occult symbology as a coded language that only the initiated could understand, and practicing black magic in their rituals to gain further power over the world. However, Cooper was wrong in his assessment that Secret Service driver William Greer turned around and shot Kennedy; he was basing that on the Zapruder film which had been greatly altered. Other great sources over the years who have helped uncover the truth about the JFK assassination include attorney Mark Lane (who challenged Earl Warren, leader of the Warren Commission, to his face), and Robert Morningstar, who brought to light the killing of Dallas police officer J. D. Tippit (who bore an uncanny resemblance to JFK) and the body swap that occurred with his body and JFK's body.

In 2013, Michael Salla Ph. D. published his book *Kennedy's Last Stand: Eisenhower, UFOs, MJ-12 and JFK's Assassination*, an outstanding piece of research. In *Break Your Chains*, I highlighted Salla's work in which he lays out the compelling evidence that JFK, mentored by former Secretary of Defense James Forrestal, was doing his best to wrest control of the ET issue away from Majestic Twelve (MJ-12), the CIA splinter group formed by Truman in 1947 to oversee the extremely sensitive issue of ET visitation and technology.[284] Salla uncovers a series of documents which lay out a paper trail from the time Kennedy entered office at the start of 1961 up until his death before the end of 1963. They demonstrate the power struggle going on between the office of the US President and the directorship of the CIA, showing the initiatives Kennedy undertook to wrest control back from the rogue agency. I will present the evidence as clearly as possible in this chapter that Allen Dulles, CIA director up until Kennedy fired him in November 1961, engineered a solution, in equal parts ingenious and nefarious, to ensure JFK was killed when the time was right, even if Dulles himself was not in the CIA anymore. The assassination directive was dutifully carried out by his protégé Angleton.

When we combine all of the above authors and other great sources, we can finally get a clearer understanding of how and why the Cult killed John Kennedy – and Robert Kennedy, and other Kennedys too. First, I am going to look at JFK assassination from the Israeli angle, then from the UFO/ET angle, then tie it all together, but crucially, let's set the stage by remembering that Kennedy was in a high stakes power struggle with the CIA.

Splinter the CIA in a Thousand Pieces and Scatter it to the Winds

Since its inception in 1947 as the agency of succession after the Office of Strategic Services (OSS), the CIA has always been a Cult-controlled spy agency involved in the most evil acts in the world – drug running, weapon running, regime change, coups, assassinations, mind control and wars. To understand the context of JFK's murder, you need to understand the young president had locked horns with the rogue agency in a battle that would end up costing him his life. This erupted into a crisis after he signed on to a limited attack on Cuba in April 1961 that became known as the Bay of Pigs fiasco and which ended in disaster. Kennedy is recorded to have said that he wanted to *"splinter the CIA in a thousand pieces and scatter it to the winds."* After the unsuccessful and embarrassing attack on Cuba, JFK had advisors submit ideas of how to reorganize the US Federal Government. One of these was Arthur Schlesinger Jr., who submitted a memorandum entitled "CIA Reorganization" on June 10th 1961. In it, he exposes how the CIA was already out of control, pursuing its own interests and agenda that superseded the US President, US Department of State, US ambassadors and US foreign policy:[285]

The contemporary CIA possesses many of the characteristics of a state within a state. CIA operations have not been held effectively subordinate to United States foreign policy ... 47 percent of the political officers serving in United States embassies were CAS — agents working under diplomatic cover known as Controlled American Sources. Sometimes the CIA mission chief has been in the country longer, and has more money at his disposal, wields more influence (and is abler) than the Ambassador ... Often he has direct access to the local Prime Minister. Sometimes ... he pursues a different policy from that of the Ambassador.

We talk about the CIA and the Mafia as though they are two separate entities, but the truth is that, at the highest level, it's the same thing! Government is organized crime. In fact, pre-CIA US intelligence agencies were making deals with the Mafia way back in the 1940s. In 1942, when a bomb exploded on the French ocean liner Normandie (docked in New York), the Office of Naval Intelligence cut a deal with Mafia boss Lucky Luciano, who was in prison. His men controlled the New York docks. Luciano later helped US intelligence during the invasions of Sicily and mainland Italy; after WWII, Luciano and other mobsters including Vito Genovese formed an anti-Communist alliance with US intelligence. Walter Herbst writes:[286]

When the CIA wanted to create underground armies in eastern Europe in the late 1940s to contain the spread of communism, the operation had to be funded without the knowledge of the U.S. government, because the Senate would never have approved it. They turned to Luciano once again. He had opium from southeast Asia sent to the Corsican Mafia in France, where it was processed into heroin, forwarded to Cuba, and sent distributed in the inner cities of America, and the CIA obtained the financing they needed. The Mafia would become involved with the CIA again in the 1950s in mind control drug experimentation on unsuspecting individuals. And by the late 1950s the CIA was hiring mobsters to try and kill Fidel Castro.

The Mafia was indubitably involved in killing JFK on the operational level. Now, let's take a look at which forces were calling the shots, and we will begin with none other than Cult-owned Israel.

The Motive for Israel to Kill JFK

There were some people who knew from the start that Israel was involved in it. This declassified NSA document dated November 25th 1963 spells it out (see image #54):[287]

The assassination of the great President Kennedy was a shock to Palestinians. Please convey our sincere sympathy to the Kennedy family and to the people of the United States.

Behind the mysterious crime is a carefully plotted Zionist conspiracy. Review of the secret and overt Zionist criminal conspiracies against Lord Moween Bernandotte, the Egyptian and German scientists, as well as the terrorist method adopted in kidnaping EICHMAN and many others, provides the evidence to question the position of their secret organizations. The late President

TOP SECRET DINAR

MINIMUM DISTRIBUTION
REPRODUCTION PROHIBITED WITHOUT PRIOR NSA APPROVAL

WS 7114 3/O/[redacted]/T1785-63
IS 2 Dec 63 P
Dist: HCO Plus

PRESIDENT KENNEDY'S ASSASSINATION A ZIONIST CONSPIRACY

25 Nov 63

The assassination of the great President KENNEDY was a shock to Palestinians. Please convey our sincere sympathy to the KENNEDY family and to the people of the United States.

Behind the mysterious crime is a carefully plotted Zionist conspiracy. Review of the secret and overt Zionist criminal conspiracies against Lord MOWEEN BERNANDOTTE, the Egyptian and German scientists, as well as the terrorist methhod adopted in kidnaping EICHMAN and many others, provides the evidence to question the position of their secret organizations. The late President was likely to win the coming presidency elections without supplicating the Zionist sympathy or seeking the Jews votes. Aware of the fact that their influence and power in the United States are based upon the Jews votes, the Zionists murdered the courageous President who was about to destroy that legend of theirs. His assassination is a warning to the rest of the honorable leaders.

Reveal their conspiracy to the supreme judgement of the world. Be careful, you are the hope of the Palestinians.

MS 974 TI --

3/O/[redacted]/T1785-63

THIS DOCUMENT CONTAINS 1 PAGE

TOP SECRET DINAR

Image #54: proclamations of a Zionist conspiracy were already being issued on November 25th 1963 *was likely to win the coming presidency elections without supplicating the Zionist sympathy or seeking the Jews votes. Aware of the fact that their influence and power in the United States are based upon the Jews votes, the Zionists murdered the courageous President who was about to destroy that legend of theirs. His assassination is a warning to the rest of the honorable leaders.*

Reveal their conspiracy to the supreme judgement of the world. Be careful, you are the hope of the Palestinians.

Before we go any further, some readers may be wondering: would Israel be prepared to actually murder a sitting American president? The answer is an emphatic "Yes!" We have proof of it, because ex-Mossad agent Victor Ostrovsky, who I quote liberally throughout this book, affirmed as much. Ostrovsky worked for the Mossad (Hebrew for "The Institute," an abbreviation for "Institute for Intelligence and Special Operations") which has become a highly feared and lethal agency with its own assassination unit. Ostrovsky reveals in his 1994 book *The Other Side of Deception* that the Mossad formulated a plot to assassinate then US President George Bush in 1991 due to the pressure he was putting on Israel to negotiate peace with the Palestinians.[288] The scheme was to kill Bush, release three Palestinian 'assassins' at the scene, and then kill these Palestinians on the spot. In signature Israeli false flag style, the crime was to be blamed on the Palestinians (see next chapter for a deeper look at this phenomenon). Ostrovsky got a call from a trusted Mossad agent informing him of the plot, urging him to make it public so as to ensure it didn't happen. Ostrovsky met with US Congressman Paul McCloskey, made the plot public and the assassination was averted. Israel, via the Mossad, had the ability and the lack of moral scruples to do the job (sorry, the words Mossad and moral don't belong in the same sentence).

So, what were Israel's motives? What pushed the Zionist regime to have a hand in the assassination? The answer is that JFK was attempting to thwart Israeli interests at every turn. Here are three examples. Firstly, he promoted the right of return of the 750,000 Palestinian refugees expelled from their neighborhoods and villages during the Nakba in the period from 1947 to 1948. On November 20th 1963, the US delegation to the UN called for the implementation of Resolution 194 (adopted by the UNGA) which reads as follows:[289]

... refugees wishing to return to their homes and live at peace with their neighbours should be permitted to do so at the earliest practicable date, and that compensation should be paid for the property of those choosing not to return and for loss of or damage to property which, under principles of international law or equity, should be made good by the Governments or authorities responsible.

Secondly, knowing how influential the Jewish lobby had become in US politics by the 1960s, JFK attempted to get the American Zionist Council (AZC) to register as a foreign agent under the Foreign Agents Registration Act (FARA) as was dictated by law. On November 21st 1962, the DOJ (led by US Attorney General and brother of JFK, Bobby Kennedy) ordered the AZC to register under FARA after it was found to be laundering tax exempt Jewish agency funds into US lobbying and PR campaigns.[290] Another Israeli lobby group, the Zionist Organization of America (ZOA), ignored seven FARA orders from 1938-1960.[291] In October 1963, he again had Bobby attempt to force them to register as a foreign agent; the DOJ gave AZC a 72-hour deadline to register as a foreign agent.[292] The

AZC dealt with this by spinning off American Israel Public Affairs Committee (AIPAC), currently the most powerful lobby in America, to create a legal separation of AZC and AIPAC. AIPAC has evaded FARA to this day. Alan Dershowitz, lawyer and associate of pedophile, sex trafficker and Israeli intelligence agent Jeffrey Epstein, actually told the truth when admitted that *"my generation of Jews ... became part of what is perhaps the most effective lobbying and fund-raising effort in the history of democracy."*[293]

The third – and the strongest, most obvious way that JFK obstructed Israel – was to put immense pressure on them to disclose their nuclear program and allow American inspectors in to see it, the idea being to force Israel to sign the NPT and stop them getting the bomb. Thus, Kennedy became the man that might have prevented the Zionist Regime from getting nuclear weapons. Israel wanted the bomb – at any cost. True or not, rational or not, Zionist leaders such as Ben-Gurion (as explained in the previous chapter) had whipped themselves up into such a paranoia that they believed the nuclear issue was existential for Israel; they believed that without the bomb their Arab neighbors would destroy them. This kind of thinking is exactly part of the core problem of the Zionist Cult; it's a mindset of denial and is all about avoiding taking responsibility for oneself, or doing self-reflection to perceive one's full self, both light and dark, good and bad. The Zionist regime would rather lie, cheat, steal, destroy and murder that actually look at itself and change its behavior for the better so that its Arab neighbors would have no reason to want to destroy it. As mentioned in the previous chapter, Kennedy had been pressuring Ben-Gurion ever since meeting him in person in New York in 1961 over Israel's nuclear program at Dimona. He and Ben-Gurion had been exchanging letters back and forth which culminated in the resignation of Ben-Gurion, which was most likely a tactic to buy time for Israel, so that Kennedy would have wait longer to take the matter up again with the next Israeli Prime Minister.

I will be going into more depth on this topic next chapter, however for now, I need to bring up a crucial point: Israel has developed itself into a lethal assassination machine. From the early days when Jewish terrorists invaded Palestine, through the days when they became 'official' killers in the Israeli armed forces, Israel has shown that assassination is its favored policy tool almost above anything else – above diplomacy, dialogue and even open war. Cult Israeli leaders follow the idea of 'rise and kill first,' a quote from the Talmud which was the inspiration for Ronen Bergman's book, also discussed next chapter. Netanyahu repeatedly proclaims this idea to excuse Israel's targeted killings or preemptive attacks, such as in September 2024 when Israel killed Hezbollah leader Hassan Nasrallah.[294] By 1963, Israel was already very willing, experienced and adept at political assassination on foreign soil; it had already formed assassination divisions within its military intelligence agencies, such as the Mossad's Caesarea division which houses the Kidon (Hebrew for 'tip of the spear'), an elite group of assassins.

Enter James Jesus Angleton, the Biggest Zionist in Washington

At this point, it's time to introduce James Jesus Angleton. His spying career began in 1943 in Italy in the P2 Masonic lodge and the X-2, the Italian arm of the OSS, the forerunner to the CIA. He was stationed in Rome during and after WWII. He excelled at spying, codebreaking and intelligence work, some of which was monitoring the number of Jews that were being transferred from Germany to Palestine. He began to develop sympathy for the Jews and to create a network of contacts with leading Zionist figures. In 1947 with the creation of the National Security Act, Angleton joined the CIA. Angleton was a typical Cold Warrior who saw the Communist Soviet Union as America's number one enemy. He was initially concerned that the USSR (the first country to recognize the state of Israel in 1948 alongside the US) would flood Israel with Russian immigrants, and then use Israel to catapult spies into the West. In 1954, he became Counterintelligence Chief, with direct access to the CIA Director and all foreign UFO intelligence from the Intelligence Advisory Committee (IAC) which had been established to look into national security implications involving the UFO phenomenon. In 1956, Angleton became a CIA legend when he got a copy, courtesy of Israeli intelligence, of the secret speech Nikita Khrushchev gave to the Russian Parliament criticizing the cult of Stalin. Declassified JFK assassination documents[295] establish that Angleton had two separate responsibilities at the CIA – one as

Image #55: James Jesus Angleton, JFK assassination mastermind

Image #56: Cult asset to his core, Allen Dulles issued the directive to have Kennedy killed

Counterintelligence Chief and the other as the controller of the "Israeli Account."

Angleton's bosom buddy and mentor from OSS days was none other than Allen Dulles, CIA head from 1953-1961. You may recall from chapter 7 that Allen Dulles was the brother of John Dulles who drafted the Treaty of Versailles with the tremendously and deliberately unfair punitive measures for Germany. Allen was a corporate lawyer and partner at Sullivan & Cromwell before he become CIA director in 1953. He was steeped in criminal Cult activities for a long time before he led the CIA, such as helping the Rockefellers funnel money to the Nazis during WWII. The Dulles brothers Allen and John were instrumental in US policy throughout the 1950s, as CIA Director and Secretary of State respectively. Allen Dulles was the one who pushed Kennedy to sign off on the disastrous Bays of Pigs operation but was fired by Kennedy, leaving the CIA in November 1961. Dulles just so happened to end up on the Warren Commission investigating the JFK assassination! Dulles was clearly a psychopath. David Talbot, author of *The Devil's Chessboard: Allen Dulles, the CIA, and the Rise of America's Secret Government* quoted at the start of this chapter, said the following about Dulles:

You have to be unfeeling to a certain extent to send people to their death in war and take the kind of actions that men and women in power routinely have to take. But with Dulles, I think he went to the next step. His own wife and mistress called him 'the Shark.' His favorite word was whether you were 'useful' to him or not. And this went for people he was sleeping with or people he was manipulating in espionage or so on. He was the kind of man that could cold-bloodedly, again and again, send people to their death, including people he was familiar with and supposedly fond of.[296]

As head of Counterintelligence, Angleton occupied the third most powerful CIA position. He was in theory meant to report directly to the CIA director, but Dulles give Angleton free reign, and subsequent CIA heads gave Angleton just as much leeway as Dulles had, including Richard Helms, another Angleton mentor. Directing Counterintelligence meant Angleton had the responsibility and freedom to hunt for infiltrators and moles within the agency. According to Peter Dale Scott, Angleton was running a second CIA within the CIA, sealed from scrutiny and accountable to no one, yet supported by an almost unlimited budget. This is doubly ironic given Schlesinger's quote above which talked about the CIA running *"a state within a state."* So here we have a man in a very high position, empowered to spy on just about anyone in the US or abroad who could claim that his spying was for the protection of his agency and country (even if it wasn't), who was running his own operation, without oversight from the director, who was already at the top of a rogue agency without oversight from the US Executive, Judicial or

Legislative Branch! This is the Cult modus operandi – extreme secrecy, extreme hoarding of knowledge, extreme evasion of accountability and an unlimited license to kill. To give you an insight into Angleton's above-the-law mindset, here is a snippet of testimony he gave before the 1975 Church Committee, which was a US Senate select committee created to investigate abuses by the CIA, FBI, NSA and the IRS:[297]

It is inconceivable that a secret intelligence arm of the government has to comply with all the overt orders of the government.

Angleton, in addition to being in charge of both Counterintelligence and the Israeli account, also had control over the FBI's liaison relationship with the CIA as *"Bureau Informant 100."*[298] He was wiretapping everyone. The well-known idea that knowledge is power is never more true than in the spy world. That world is run via a strict hierarchical pyramid where everyone is on a 'need-to-know' basis with those at the top having the most information or ammunition to use against anyone else, friend or foe. Lisa Pease, long time researcher of the 1960s assassinations, writes:[299]

Thomas Braden, a CIA media operative was confronted by Dulles over a remark Braden had about one of Dulles' professional relationships. Wise recounted what followed:

"You'd better watch out," [Allen] Dulles warned him. "Jimmy's got his eye on you." Braden said he drew the obvious conclusion: James Angleton had bugged his bedroom and was picking up pillow talk between himself and his wife, Joan. But Braden said he was only mildly surprised at the incident, because Angleton was known to have bugs all over town.

Braden described how Angleton would enter Dulles's office 'first thing in the morning' to report the take from the overnight taps:

He used to delight Allen with stories of what happened at people's dinner parties ... Jim used to come into Allen's office and Allen would say, 'How's the fishing?' And Jim would say, 'Well, I got a few nibbles last night.' It was all done in the guise of fishing talk.

More to the point, Braden was upset because "some senator or representative might say something that might be of use to the Agency. I didn't think that was right. I think Jim was amoral." It would not be beyond belief that Angleton routinely used information gathered through clearly illegal taps to blackmail people into supporting his efforts. No wonder some of his Agency associates feared him.

The CIA was aware of Soviet espionage rings operating in the US; the main task of the Counterintelligence division was to foil any attempt to acquire technical and scientific information on advanced technologies which would give an advantage to the Soviet Union. In other words, he had to prevent any penetration by moles or double agents. Angleton biographer Tom Mangold described[300] how Angleton set up a small elite unit consisting of eight of his most trusted people called the Special Investigation Group (SIG). SIG was so secret that many Counterintelligence staff didn't even know it existed, and nearly everyone was denied access to it. Over the years, the true function of this group became hidden until it reached a point where only a few insiders actually understood its purpose. Secret units within a secret unit was a hallmark of Angleton's (and the Cult's) operating procedure. By the late 1950s, there was resentment within the CIA over Angleton's methods and SIG, as secret policemen. When the situation called for it, Angleton could go around proper channels to obtain data on anyone within the CIA and other agencies, even if it violated the CIA charter and FBI jurisdiction. The end justified the means. This approach of extreme secrecy and this desire to protect classified information at any cost is extremely relevant to the JFK assassination, as we are about to find out.

So what was Angleton's relationship with Israel? According to Jefferson Morley,[301] author of the book *The Ghost: The Secret Life of CIA Spymaster James Jesus Angleton*, and who interviewed a former Mossad head Efraim Halevy, in the early years of the 1950s, the CIA and the Mossad began to develop a close relationship. At that time, Israeli PM Ben-Gurion came to Washington to meet with then US President Truman, Allen Dulles and James Angleton. Morley states that Halevy (the 9th director of Mossad and the 3rd head of the Israeli National Security Council) personally told him the purpose of these meetings:[302]

... to clarify in no uncertain terms that notwithstanding what had happened between Israel and the Unites States in 1948, and not withstanding that Russia had been a key factor in Israel's survival, Israel considered itself part of the Western world and would maintain the relationship with the United States in this spirit ... Angleton became the CIA's exclusive liaison with the Mossad in 1951. Angleton returned the favor by traveling to Israel often. He was introduced to Amos Manor, chief of counterespionage for Israel's domestic security service known as Shabak or Shin Bet ... "They told me I had to collect information about the Soviet bloc and transmit it to them," Manor recalled ... from such arrangements, the CIA-Mossad relationship began to grow.

Angleton was the man who fostered the CIA-Mossad relationship such that they became virtual twins. Angleton began to develop closer and closer ties with Israel, frequently visiting the occupied territories, passing Israel loads of sensitive information and using his position to give Israel the best available intelligence. Angleton oversaw numerous CIA-Mossad joint operations during the 1950s and 1960s, some of which were assassination plots that didn't succeed or were never carried out, such as the plan to kill Egyptian President Nasser.[303]

Image #57: Meir Amit (left, Mossad head 1963-68), dressed as a cowboy, with James Angleton, right

In 1963, Meir Amit became the chief of Mossad, and he called Angleton *"the biggest Zionist in Washington."*[304] Angleton didn't grow up as a Jew but became a staunch Cult Zionist nonetheless. Morley reveals that *"Angleton liked nothing better than to leave the cramped office politics of Washington for the austere frontier of the Holy Land. On his visits, Angleton stayed in Ramat Gan, on the suburban coastal plain north of Tel Aviv, the home to many Israeli intelligence officers and diplomats."*[305] The aforementioned Mossad agent Halevy, who was later Mossad's liaison officer to the CIA in Tel Aviv in the early 1960s, told Morley that Angleton would come to Israel to get briefings from the Mossad, and would also meet with Ben-Gurion whom he knew very well; in fact, Angleton knew him so well he went down to Sde Boker, Ben-Gurion's home in the Negev Desert.

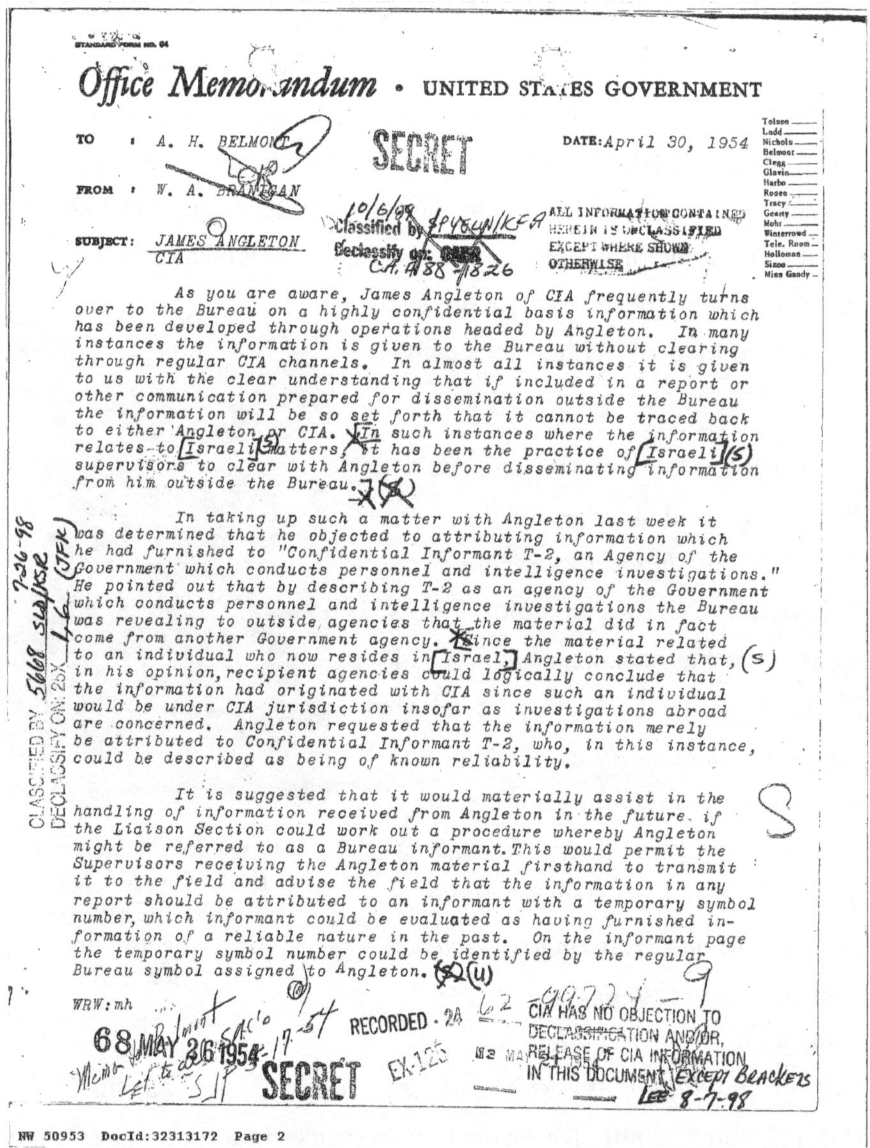

STANDARD FORM NO. 64

Office Memorandum • UNITED STATES GOVERNMENT

TO : A. H. BELMONT

FROM : W. A. BRANIGAN

SUBJECT: JAMES ANGLETON CIA

SECRET

DATE: April 30, 1954

10/6/98 Classified by SP4 SUNIKER Declassify on: OADR CA#88-1826

ALL INFORMATION CONTAINED HEREIN IS UNCLASSIFIED EXCEPT WHERE SHOWN OTHERWISE

Tolson, Ladd, Nichols, Belmont, Clegg, Glavin, Harbo, Rosen, Tracy, Gearty, Mohr, Winterrowd, Tele. Room, Holloman, Sizoo, Miss Gandy

As you are aware, James Angleton of CIA frequently turns over to the Bureau on a highly confidential basis information which has been developed through operations headed by Angleton. In many instances the information is given to the Bureau without clearing through regular CIA channels. In almost all instances it is given to us with the clear understanding that if included in a report or other communication prepared for dissemination outside the Bureau the information will be so set forth that it cannot be traced back to either Angleton or CIA. [In such instances where the information relates to [Israeli] (S) matters, it has been the practice of [Israeli] (S) supervisors to clear with Angleton before disseminating information from him outside the Bureau.] (S)

In taking up such a matter with Angleton last week it was determined that he objected to attributing information which he had furnished to "Confidential Informant T-2, an Agency of the Government which conducts personnel and intelligence investigations." He pointed out that by describing T-2 as an agency of the Government which conducts personnel and intelligence investigations the Bureau was revealing to outside agencies that the material did in fact come from another Government agency. [Since the material related to an individual who now resides in [Israel,] Angleton stated that, (S) in his opinion, recipient agencies could logically conclude that the information had originated with CIA since such an individual would be under CIA jurisdiction insofar as investigations abroad are concerned. Angleton requested that the information merely be attributed to Confidential Informant T-2, who, in this instance, could be described as being of known reliability.

It is suggested that it would materially assist in the handling of information received from Angleton in the future if the Liaison Section could work out a procedure whereby Angleton might be referred to as a Bureau informant. This would permit the Supervisors receiving the Angleton material firsthand to transmit it to the field and advise the field that the information in any report should be attributed to an informant with a temporary symbol number, which informant could be evaluated as having furnished information of a reliable nature in the past. On the informant page the temporary symbol number could be identified by the regular Bureau symbol assigned to Angleton. (S)(U)

WRW:mh

CLASSIFIED BY 5668 SLD/KSR 7-26-98 DECLASSIFY ON: 25X 1,6 (JFK)

RECORDED - 24 62-99724-9

68 MAY 26 1954

EX-125

SECRET

CIA HAS NO OBJECTION TO DECLASSIFICATION AND/OR RELEASE OF CIA INFORMATION IN THIS DOCUMENT EXCEPT BRACKETS LEE 8-7-98

NW 50953 DocId:32313172 Page 2

Image #58: a declassified file showing Angleton was in charge of Israeli matters at the CIA. Up until recently, the words in square brackets were redacted to hide the Israeli connection

Angleton even visited Ben-Gurion at Ben-Gurion's home after the Israeli leader had stepped down as prime minister. A top spy from one country visiting the home of a former primer minister in another country? What was going on here? What were they discussing?

Prior to the Trump Admin 2025 release, many previous batches of declassified JFK files contained an interesting feature: just one word was redacted from certain documents – "Israel" (or in some case the terms "Israeli" or "Israeli Intelligence Services"). Now in 2025 at the time of writing, we can see that word or term unredacted as it was originally typed. Note in the bottom right corner of the image (#58) how it says *"CIA HAS NO OBJECTION TO DECLASSIFICATION AND/OR RELEASE OF CIA INFORMATION IN THIS DOCUMENT EXCEPT BRACKETS"*[306][307] where the word in the brackets was Israel, Israeli or Israeli Intelligence Services. Angleton wasn't just sharing intel with Israel, but acting as a gatekeeper to obscure Israel from any scrutiny when it came to obtaining sensitive information. Although (as described in the previous chapter) Zalman Shapiro, Glenn Seaborg and NUMEC were heavily involved in stealing nuclear knowhow and material from America and handing it off to Israel, would it surprise you to learn that there was another major figure coordinating this? It was none other than … James Jesus Angleton.

Some years after much of the nuclear material had been stolen from NUMEC, there was a journalist Tad Szulc who wrote a 1975 article referencing that the Eisenhower Administration wanted to assist Israel in obtaining nuclear weapons, and stating that it was Angleton's responsibility to provide that assistance. Angleton denied the claim by saying that it was *"totally false"*[308] however later on (under the same questioning by lawyer Chief Counsel Frederick

Schwarz) he admitted that *"technical assistance"* may have been involved, while still denying the transfer to the Israelis of *"fissionable material."* How was the knowhow given to the Israelis? It was given via six CIA officers who obtained Q clearances in mid-1962, halfway through President Kennedy's term, that allowed them access to nuclear weapons design material.[309] The words of Angleton themselves are highly revealing:[310]

There is always a question of whether a democratic country is capable of having an intelligence service of any great merit, simply because of the built-in inhibitions. It usually takes a national crisis, or a Pearl Harbor, for people [to] then understand what survival means. But you don't have to be a great, or large, or wealthy country, to have a good intelligence service, as long as you have the norms, as long as you have the disciplines, as long as you have the motivation, the singleness of purpose, you can be a small service, have one great penetration and you can move the world.

Note the references to:

- Controlling people through (manufactured) crises like Pearl Harbor
- A small county (Israel) with a small service (Mossad) with one great penetration (Angleton himself acting for the cause of Israel)
- A singleness of purpose (Cult mindset willing to kill for the Zionist cause)
- The ability to move the world (with infiltration, surveillance, espionage, blackmail, etc.)

As if that wasn't enough – being the CIA head of Counterintelligence, being the CIA head of the Israeli account and being the CIA point man to the FBI – Angleton was also the central figure in the coverup of the assassination. He was the top CIA agent in control of exactly what information was fed to the Warren Commission, and thus could ensure that it would fail to get to the root cause of the assassination and that it would conclude that the designated patsy Lee Harvey Oswald did it.

Speaking of Oswald, it was Angleton who had been carefully nurturing him for years, orchestrating that Oswald would be sent to certain places (like the USSR) to build up a profile that would paint him in a bad light. Morley reveals how Angleton had collected a 198 page file on Oswald, but several CIA officials lied about this under oath. It was Angleton who appointed Jew Reuben Efron to spy on Lee Harvey Oswald and read all his mail.[311] Oswald was being 'sheep dipped' or given an alternate identity, a common practice in intelligence circles where agents are assigned ordinary jobs in order to disguise their true identity. Piper wrote that *"The Senate Intelligence Committee reported that at a meeting in late December of 1963, Angleton had requested that he be allowed to take over CIA responsibility for dealing with the Warren Commission probe ... Angleton suggested that his own Counterintelligence Division take over the investigation and [Richard] Helms acceded to this suggestion ... What's more, Angleton's close friend (and FBI source), William Sullivan, number three man at the FBI, was detailed as the FBI's liaison with the Warren Commission."*[312]

The Warren Omission

The Warren Commission (or Warren Omission) was a 7-man committee that was solely designed to provide a ridiculous cover story to exonerate the Cult of its guilt in the assassination. The whole point was to put out the 'lone nut' narrative, replete with an absurd 'magic bullet' invented by the young Jewish lawyer Arlen Specter. The commission, named after Chief Justice Earl Warren, was comprised of the following members:

1. Earl Warren

2. Richard Russell Jr.

3. John Sherman Cooper

4. Hale Boggs

5. Gerald Ford

6. Allen Dulles

7. John J. McCloy

Almost all of these men, if not all, were connected to the Cult in one way or another. What else do you expect? Warren was a 33° Mason; politician Gerald Ford, a Bilderberg attendee and future US president, has been named as a serial rapist by Cathy O'Brien; Allen Dulles as already mentioned was the psychopath and CIA head sacked by JFK after the Bay of Pigs (and much more, as we will come to shortly); and John McCloy was another Bilderberg attendee and the chairman of the CFR, one of the key NWO think tanks and Round Table institutions of North America. Piper wrote:[313]

Facts are facts: of the 22 Warren Commission staff attorneys, nine were Jewish. Another was married to a Jewish woman. Several others had ties to the Israeli lobby. What's more, one of the commission's most active members—Gerald R. Ford—was the protégé of a figure long linked to both the Mossad and the Lansky Crime Syndicate. Another commission member, John McCloy, was intimately associated with some of the most powerful families in the Jewish elite.

Furthermore, Gerald Ford had links to Israel via his handler Max Fisher, who was a business partner of longtime Mossad figure Tibor Rosenbaum, the driving force behind the Permindex corporation (to be discussed shortly). Piper wrote:[314]

In 1957, in partnership with Tibor Rosenbaum's Swiss-Israel Trade Bank, Fisher bought a controlling interest in Israel's Paz conglomerate—long owned by the Rothschild family of Europe—which maintained a monopoly over Israeli oil and petrochemical interests ... [Max Fisher] would 'tell the president what to do and when to do it.' And in light of his status in Ford's rising political fortunes, we do know that in 1963—when Ford was appointed to the Warren Commission, Fisher likewise was then in a position to tell Ford 'what to do and when to do it.' So who is Max Fisher? Here's how Gerald Ford described Fisher in his own memoirs. Fisher, he said, was "a prominent Detroit businessman who was chairman of the Jewish Agency for Israel. Max was a lifelong Republican and a close friend. He had served as an unofficial ambassador between the United States and Israel for years, and his contacts at the highest levels of both governments had often helped us bridge over misunderstandings."

Piper believed Warren never had any idea of the real depth of the issue:

Warren himself probably never had any idea as to the real truth—or even part of the truth—as to what really happened or where the assassination conspiracy originated. Any effort by Warren to probe deeper would no doubt have been scuttled immediately ...

Additionally, Warren was also under the influence of his close friend, syndicated columnist Drew Pearson, himself an asset and longtime collaborator of Israel's propaganda and intelligence arm in this country, the Anti-Defamation League of B'nai B'rith. It was Pearson who floated the blatantly fraudulent story that Fidel Castro had been the prime mover behind the JFK assassination.

The establishment of the Warren Commission was also due to Cult Zionist and Jewish American legal scholar Eugene Rostow. Donald Gibson, author of *The Kennedy Assassination Cover-up*, wrote that the Warren Commission could more accurately have been called the 'Rostow Commission' or the 'McCloy-Dulles Commission.'[315] It was Rostow who called Assistant Attorney General Nicholas Katzenbach three times on the afternoon of Sunday November 24th 1963, two days after the assassination, pushing him to create a Presidential Commission. Katzenbach was obviously friendly to Zionist interests, since he was the one who let the AZC get away with not registering under FARA after JFK died.

Katzenbach wrote a memo entitled *"Memorandum For Mr. Moyers"*[316] (known as the Katzenbach Memo, images #58 and #59) which was disseminated on Monday November 25th 1963, the day of the Kennedy funeral. The memo clearly advocates a political course and outlines the blueprint for the coverup, including an FBI report and possible Presidential Commission of *"unimpeachable personnel to review and examine the evidence and announce its conclusions."* Katzenbach wrote that *"The public must be satisfied that Oswald was the assassin; that he did not have confederates who are still at large; and that evidence was such that he would have been convicted at trial."* He also suggests a quick public announcement to *"head off speculation or Congressional hearings of the wrong sort."* Corrupt

FBI head J. Edgar Hoover was already on board with this memo; there is an account of him calling White House aide Walter Jenkins and at the end of the call noting the need to have *"something issued so we can convince the public that Oswald is the real assassin."*[317] Nothing to see here. Move along!

To return to Angleton, the Mossad's man inside the CIA tried to blame the Soviet KGB defector Yuri Nosenko (the KGB case officer who handled Lee Harvey Oswald during his time in Russia), however that narrative never stuck. The Cult desperately wanted this, because blaming Russia would have created the perfect enemy and deflected people from investigating Israel. The same tactic was used throughout the Cold War, and even in the 2016 US presidential elections, when sore loser Hillary Clinton and the Democrats invented the whole RussiaGate hoax to try to smear Donald Trump (and I say that as absolutely no Trump supporter). In summary, from 1951-1974, Angleton was the head of the CIA's Israeli account. For that entire time, he was the only US intelligence official authorized to talk to the Israelis. He created a position where he ran operations how he wanted, essentially without any oversight or accountability. He oversaw the monitoring and setting up of Oswald as the Russian patsy. Under his tenure, Israel executed Operation Susannah (the false flag Lavon Affair) in 1954, invaded Egypt in 1956, attacked the USS Liberty in 1967, initiated the Six Day War in 1967 and stole nuclear material and technology from America (which Angleton aided and abetted). During the Warren Commission coverup, Angleton decided which documents the CIA would provide to the commission. According to Sam Parker:[318]

Angleton made dozens, perhaps more than a hundred trips to Israel. And was friends with all sorts of powerful Israelis, including

Teddy Kollek – the first mayor of Jerusalem – and Yitzhak Rabin, eventual Prime Minister of Israel. When Angleton died in 1987, the Israelis held a special tree-planting memorial service for him attended by the following notable figures: then Defense Minister Yitzhak Rabin (who was in Dallas the day JFK was shot); the then current heads of the Mossad and Shin Bet; former Mossad chiefs Meir Amit ... Zvi Zamir and Yitzhak Hofi; former Shin Bet Chiefs Avraham Ahituv and Amos Manor; and former Military Intelligence chiefs Aharon Yariv, Shlomo Gazit and Binyamin Gibli.

Some say that Angleton's obsession was stopping Communism, like many American military and intelligence officials of his day during the Cold War, and that he only liked Israel inasmuch as it helped him against the USSR. This is not the full truth. Time and again we find that the Communism bogeyman was used to divide and conquer, as well as to cover the real force orchestrating world events – the Cult, operating out of Israel, that invented Communism. Cult agent and Jew Roy Cohn (more on him in the next chapter) sat alongside Senator Joseph McCarthy during his 1950s red scare, promoting the whole Communist witch-hunt which terrorized America. Zionists like Angleton and Cohn used Communism to deflect attention away from Israel that was always the source of the deepest crimes.

So, I have now outlined Israel's motivation to kill JFK and given an overview of the characters of Angleton and Dulles. In the next few subsections, I will show how key people, companies and organizations involved in the 'how' of the JFK assassination (the actual carrying out of the murder) were connected to Israel/Mossad.

Permindex

November 25, 1963

MEMORANDUM FOR MR. MOYERS

It is important that all of the facts surrounding President Kennedy's Assassination be made public in a way which will satisfy people in the United States and abroad that all the facts have been told and that a statement to this effect be made now.

1. The public must be satisfied that Oswald was the assassin; that he did not have confederates who are still at large; and that the evidence was such that he would have been convicted at trial.

2. Speculation about Oswald's motivation ought to be cut off, and we should have some basis for rebutting thought that this was a Communist conspiracy or (as the Iron Curtain press is saying) a right-wing conspiracy to blame it on the Communists. Unfortunately the facts on Oswald seem about too pat—too obvious (Marxist, Cuba, Russian wife, etc.). The Dallas police have put out statements on the Communist conspiracy theory, and it was they who were in charge when he was shot and thus silenced.

3. The matter has been handled thus far with neither dignity nor conviction. Facts have been mixed with rumour and speculation. We can scarcely let the world see us totally in the image of the Dallas police when our President is murdered.

I think this objective may be satisfied by making public as soon as possible a complete and thorough FBI report on Oswald and the assassination. This may run into the difficulty of pointing to inconsistencies between this report and statements by Dallas police officials. But the reputation of the Bureau is such that it may do the whole job.

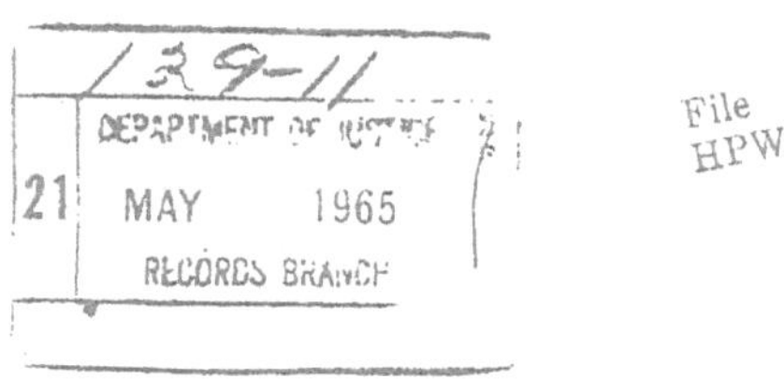

Image #59: the Katzenbach Memo, first page

The only other step would be the appointment of a Presidential Commission of unimpeachable personnel to review and examine the evidence and annouace its conclusions. This has both advantages and disadvantages. It think it can await publication of the FBI report and public reaction to it here and abroad.

I think, however, that a statement that all the facts will be made public property in an orderly and responsible way should be made now. We need something to head off public speculation or Congressional hearings of the wrong sort.

Nicholas deB. Katzenbach
Deputy Attorney General

Image #60: the Katzenbach Memo, second page.
It provided the outline for how the coverup would proceed

Piper did an excellent job highlighting the role of Mossad front company Permindex in the assassination. “Permindex” is an acronym that stood for PERmanent INDustrial EXpositions. It was a subsidiary of Centro Mondiale Commerciale (CMC), Italian for "World Trade Center” based in Rome. Permindex linked the key players of the JFK assassination together: the Mossad, the CIA, the Meyer Lansky organized crime syndicate and the French connection. Clay Shaw, a longtime CIA asset, was on the Permindex board, hence was both CIA and Mossad. Shaw was the only man to have ever been charged with a role in the JFK assassination; he was involved in the New Orleans aspect of the conspiracy where Lee Oswald was being prepared. One of the chief shareholders of Permindex was Banque de Credit Internationale (BCI) of Geneva, established by Tibor Rosenbaum, who supplied the Mossad. BCI was also Meyer Lansky’s main money laundering bank in Europe.

One of the key figures involved with Permindex was its leader Louis Bloomfield. He was a Canadian by birth but was hired by the FBI as a recruiter in their counterespionage division, Division Five. Bloomfield became a working partner of the head of Division Five, the aforementioned William Sullivan – the number three man at the FBI and a close friend of Angleton. Piper wrote that *“Bloomfield was also given an officer's rank in the U.S. Army during World War II and assigned to the Office of Strategic Services (OSS)—just as had been the American who ultimately became his fellow Permindex director, Clay Shaw.”*[319]

According to Piper, Bloomfield was just a henchman for Sam Bronfman, a Lansky syndicate figure. The Russian-Jewish Bronfman family became rich from bootlegging alcohol during the prohibition era of the 1920s. The Bronfmans are another key Cult Zionist family whose name also comes up again in connection with pedophile Jeffrey Epstein (see next chapter). Piper wrote, *"... new evidence indicates that Dallas mob figure Jack Ruby was actually on the Bronfman payroll. In addition, while another Bronfman associate in Dallas, oilman Jack Crichton, functioned as a "translator" for Lee Harvey Oswald's widow after the JFK assassination, another Bronfman functionary—"super lawyer" John McCloy ... —served on the Warren Commission. McCloy was a director—and Crichton served as vice president—of the Empire Trust, a financial combine controlled in part by the Bronfman family ... Allen Dulles ...—later the CIA director fired by JFK and also a Warren Commission member—served as an attorney involved in the private business ventures of Bronfman's daughter Phyllis."*[320]

Meyer Lansky

A super important player in the JFK assassination saga was Jewish mobster Meyer Lansky. Although many think of Lansky as 'Mafia' and think of Mafia as Italian, Lansky was not Italian. He was Khazarian. Born Maier Suchowljansky in the Russian Empire (now Belarus), he was Polish-Jewish and considered Poland his home country. He immigrated to the US as a child. It would be most accurate to call what he created – and led – an 'Organized Crime Syndicate' rather than the Mafia. Lansky was a gigantic figure in the international criminal underworld, and was extremely closely connected to Israel. The Zionist state was established, in major part, through the political and financial assistance of Lansky and his mobster underlings. Lansky's interests and Israel's interests were synonymous. As mentioned above, his principal European money laundering bank was BCI, run under the auspices of Mossad officer Rosenbaum. Lansky was involved in drug weapons running to

Haganah via the Sonneborne Institute, as explained in chapter 10. Lansky was the kingpin; other Mafia criminals such as Giancana and Roselli played second fiddle to him.

As with many other criminals, Lansky escaped to Israel in 1970 under the law of return. Like Jack Ruby (coming up), Lansky was 'kosher nostra' rather than cosa nostra. Just as the plain 'the CIA did it' theory falls short in explaining why and how JFK was killed (unless it takes into account the forces controlling the men at the top of the CIA), so too does 'the Mafia did it' theory fall short since it fails to take into account the multi-ethnic nature of the organized crime syndicate. Piper warned that *"anyone who attempts to view the JFK assassination as a "Mafia hit" is making a big mistake, failing to calculate in the role of Mossad-connected Meyer Lansky, his Chicago associate Hyman Larner, and their allies in Israel's Mossad."*[321]

The French Connection

In his book Piper also wrote a lot about the so-called 'French Connection' which was really an Israeli connection. Kennedy and then French President Charles de Gaulle had many things in common, one of which was their desire to see Algeria as free and sovereign nation, not as a French colony. However, there were elements within French society and intelligence that strongly disagreed with that idea. Israel also opposed it, because they calculated that another free Arab country in the region would be worse for their security than a controlled French colony. For this reason, the Israelis funded a secret French organization called the OAS. The Mossad-backed OAS didn't just target American politicians with strikes; it also targeted French ones. Piper wrote that *"(f)ollowing an investigation of one attempt, in 1962, French*

Image #61: Lyndon Johnson, a man involved in the JFK assassination up to his neck

intelligence (the SDECE) charged that Permindex laundered money into the OAS coffers to finance the attempt on de Gaulle's life."[322]

The Mossad had obtained a key contact in French intelligence, Colonel Georges deLannurien, who became the primary conduit between the Mossad's Yitzhak Shamir and the CIA's James Angleton. Later on, when writing the fifth edition of *Final Judgment*, Piper revealed one of his sources, former French intelligence officer Pierre Neuville. As it turned out, seven years before the Kennedy assassination, deLannurien had tried to frame Neuville and use him as a patsy in a Mossad plot to kill Egyptian President Nasser in October 1956, just prior to the Israeli invasion at Port Said during the Suez Crisis. On that occasion, when Neuville realized he was about to be utilized as a patsy in a Nasser assassination plot, he gave himself up to Egyptian intelligence at Cairo International Airport.[323]

LBJ = 100% Zionist Puppet

Angleton may have been the mastermind of the JFK assassination, but Lyndon Baines Johnson, the man who succeeded JFK as president, was in on the plot. LBJ was a ruthless killer and simultaneously a spineless Zionist puppet up to his neck in all sorts of shady shenanigans. He was an ardent Zionist who was also quite possibly America's first 'Jewish' president (following the standard convention of [falsely] believing the Jews are a race, Johnson's mother was Jewish). His aunt Jessie Johnson Hatcher, who had a major influence on him, was a member of ZOA and had nurtured LBJ's desire to befriend Jews. According to historian James M. Smallwood, as a congressman, LBJ got hundreds of Jews into Texas during the 1940s, using Galveston as the entry port, and – both legally and illegally – hiding them in the Texas National Youth Administration. One source states that Johnson was illegally shipping weapons to Zionist terrorists in Palestine in boxes marked "Texas Grapefruit."[324]

Johnson lost no time in reversing JFK's policies towards Israel. He refused to stop Israel from gaining the knowledge and materials it needed to gain nuclear weapons, looking the other way when it came to its nuclear program. He also refused to pressure the AZC to register under FARA, dropping the matter entirely, which has had grave ramifications for current American politics, since AZC became AIPAC, undisputedly the most powerful lobby in Washington DC. Johnson did everything the Cult Zionists wanted. He assured the Israelis that the US would always provide them with a military edge over the Arabs, thus making America Israel's chief arms supplier. He refused to follow the advice of his aides to make America's delivery of nuclear-capable F-4 Phantoms conditional on Israel's signing the

NPT. As discussed in the previous chapter, he even allowed the Israelis to attack and sink a US ship (the USS Liberty). Foreign aid to Israel went from $40 million (FY [Fiscal Year] 1964) to $130 million (FY 1966). The US abandoned its position as mediator in the Middle East and abandoned the 1950 Tripartite Declaration, which was a joint statement by the US, UK and France that had guaranteed the territorial status quo determined by the 1949 Arab–Israeli Armistice Agreements. American interests become entwined with Israeli interests in an unholy alliance unprecedented in American history; never before had the US entered into a political and military marriage like this. From the moment LBJ ascended to the presidential throne, the Israelis began to act like they had an intrinsic and unalienable right to American aid. Seymour Hersh revealed that LBJ did not want then CIA director Richard Helms to tell him about Israel's bomb – as once he acknowledged and accepted that information, he would have had to act upon it in some way. Instead, Johnson chose to deliberately stay uninformed about it, since the last thing in the world he wanted to do was to confront Israel.

LBJ was a womanizer with many mistresses. He was controlled in particular by one of his mistresses, Zionist Mathilde Krim, who had at one point been married to Irgun terrorist David Danon, exiled by the British from Palestine for his terrorism. Danon recruited people for Irgun and carried out secret operations in Western Europe, using Mathilde to transport explosives across international borders bound for Palestine. She later married a man called Arthur Krim. The Krims were among Johnson's very closest friends; they had a room in the White House and even built a house in the Texas hill country close to LBJ's ranch in Stonewall. Johnson would stay at their New York house. Madeleine Duncan Brown (1925-2002), a longtime mistress of Johnson, revealed she had a son by him. In an interview[325] she stated that Johnson had emerged from a meeting in Texas on November 21st 1963, the night before the assassination. This meeting was at the house of Texas oilman Clint Murchison, and many people in on the conspiracy allegedly attended, including J. Edgar Hoover, Clyde Tolson, Richard Nixon and E. Howard Hunt. Brown said that after the meeting, LBJ was in a rage and grabbed her by the arm, saying, *"After tomorrow, these SOBs [sons of bitches, i.e. the Kennedy brothers] will never embarrass me again. That's no threat; that's a promise."*

Political operative Roger Stone, author of the book *The Man Who Killed Kennedy: The Case Against LBJ*, states that former US President Richard Nixon told him that the Warren Commission was *"the biggest goddamn hoax in American history"* and also that *"Lyndon Johnson and I both wanted to be president – the difference was, I wasn't willing to kill for it."*[326]

Jack Ruby = Jacob Rubenstein

Another player in the JFK murder drama was 'Jack Ruby' whose real name has been deliberately hidden from widespread public knowledge. His real name was Jacob Rubenstein and he was a Jew – not just any ordinary Jew, but one prepared to kill and die for Israel, so in other words, a Cult crypto-Jew with diehard allegiance to Israel. Rubenstein was part of the mob, but the Jewish Mafia, not the Italian Mafia. As with Lansky, he was kosher nostra. He clearly had foreknowledge since he asked an FBI informant on the morning of November 22nd 1963 if he'd *"like to watch the fireworks"* in Dallas.[327] Rubenstein was apparently given the role to kill the patsy Oswald before Oswald could speak, but ironically, must have known he was also in the scapegoat position himself. Jack Ruby was quite a blabbermouth, given his statements like this one:[328]

Everything pertaining to what's happening has never come to the surface. The world will never know the true facts of what occurred, my motives. The people who had so much to gain, and had such an ulterior motive for putting me in the position I'm in, will never let the true facts come above board to the world ... I did it to show the world that Jews have guts.

He also said the following in his testimony to Chief Justice Earl Warren who was presiding over the Warren Commission coverup:[329]

Mr. RUBY: *"But I won't be around, Chief Justice. I won't be around to verify these things you are going to tell the President."*

Mr. TONAHILL: *"Who do you think is going to eliminate you, Jack?"*

Mr. RUBY: *"I have been used for a purpose, and there will be a certain tragic occurrence happening if you don't take my testimony and somehow vindicate me so my people don't suffer because of what I have done."*

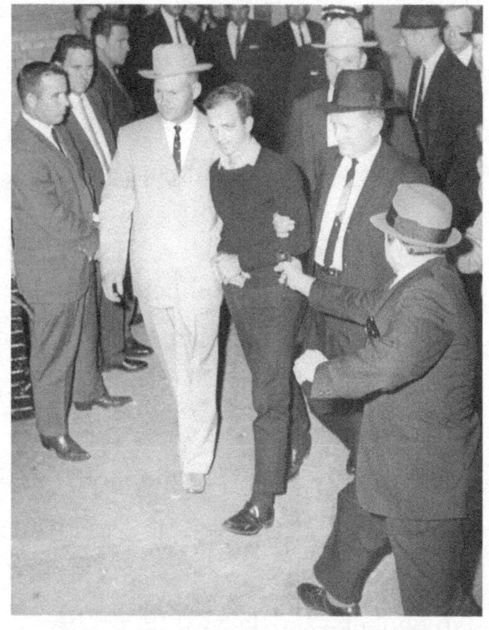

Image #62: Mossad-linked Jacob Rubenstein (aka Jack Ruby) steps forward to kill patsy Lee Oswald on live TV

Freedom of Information Act (FOIA) records confirm

that, as mentioned earlier, Yitzhak Rabin, a future Israeli PM and then deputy chief of staff for the IDF, was in Dallas on November 22nd 1963.[330] This was first mentioned in an autobiography written by Rabin's widow in 1997. Rabin, along with seven or eight associates, suspiciously left Dallas in a hurry. Was Jack Ruby reporting to him? Ironically enough, Rabin also met his death later on as Israeli PM when he was assassinated in 1995.

At the highest or deepest level, all of the world's conspiracies interconnect. It is no surprise, therefore, that Jack Ruby was declared insane by none other than MKUltra mind control psychiatrist and CIA contractor Jolyon West. West was implicated in assisting the international Satanic network by playing a role in convincing victims that they had 'false memories' when they were recalling true events of Satanic Ritual Abuse. MKUltra mind control techniques seem to have been clearly used on Sirhan Sirhan, the patsy used in the RFK assassination (more on this later in this chapter).

Cult agents are sacrificed when their usefulness has run out. When the script shows that they have no more lines to say or parts to play, it's time for them to go. This could mean they are killed, but sometimes, they are whisked away to Israel, given a new identity and removed from public view forever. This is almost certainly what happened with Epstein (see next chapter); it may also have been what happened with Ruby. Piper wrote that a woman named Grace Pratt thought that she saw Jack Ruby photographed boarding a plane for Israel, and that he (Piper) knew that she never told the story publicly or sought recognition.[331] Despite being used by the Cult, Ruby covered up for the Zionists.

In summary, like Meyer Lansky, Jack Ruby was more 'Mossad' than 'Mafia' but the Cult-owned American MSM deliberately covered that up by emphasizing that he was a Mafia agent. Ultimately, both Oswald and Ruby were two men who were separately used by the same power. Piper writes that *"after they were arrested and jailed, both men said they had been manipulated. 'I'm a patsy,' said Oswald. 'I've been used for a purpose,' said Ruby."*[332]

George H. W. Bush

Image #63: George Herbert Walker Bush, a serial rapist, Cult Satanist and criminal directly involved in both the JFK assassination and the 9/11 operation

The crimes of lifelong manipulator George H. W. Bush are large enough to fill a giant book. Bush, whose father Prescott (along with the Dulles brothers and some of the Rockefellers) was involved in funding the Nazis, got involved in Cult activities at a young age via the Skull and Bones Secret Society at Yale University that has been caught on tape practicing Satanic ritual. He soon joined the CIA and became its head in 1976, as well as the Director of Central Intelligence, which was a different position at one time. He was US Vice President under Reagan from 1981-1989, then US President from 1989-1993. Mind-controlled sex slave survivor Cathy O'Brien has detailed how he abused her and her daughter Kelly, repeatedly raping and torturing them. She also reveals that she witnessed him order a man to jump off a plane without a parachute to his death. Bush tried to claim he joined the CIA much later than he really did. A declassified document shows a 'George Bush' worked there however he tried to claim it was another George Bush.[333] Bush absurdly claims he doesn't remember where he was on the day of JFK's assassination, despite this being such a highly significant day in history where virtually everyone remembers where they were, even those living outside the USA. In his film *Dark Legacy*,[334] filmmaker John Hankey connects the pieces of evidence showing that Bush was likely at Dealey Plaza when the murder occurred. Researcher Robert Morningstar[335] also revealed something that he was told directly by Ed Grimsley, a former Texas state champion marksman who is now deceased. Grimsley said that Bush approached him at a Texas firing range, telling him that he was a great shot and that he'd had his eye on him for a long time. Bush invited him to his office, then offered him a job for $2 million.

Grimsley: *"What do I have to do for $2,000,000?"*

Bush: *"You have to kill someone, of course."*

Grimsley: *"Who?"*

Bush: *"John F. Kennedy."*

At that point, Grimsley declined and left. Bush told him not to tell anyone about the offer he had given him. Grimsley kept the secret for decades until finally telling Morningstar in the 1990s.

It should be noted here that just because the Mossad targeted Bush in the early 1990s does not mean that Bush was not also part of the Cult. It's one big club at the top, somewhat like the traditional Italian Mafia which bands together to enforce their criminal rackets, but which also undergoes periodic infighting as families jostle for power.

<u>Other Characters: Clay Shaw, Guy Banister, David Ferrie, Cord Meyer, Frank Sturgis and E. Howard Hunt</u>

There were many minor characters involved in the JFK assassination. Clay Shaw, Guy Banister and David Ferrie were all involved in the New Orleans aspect where they were managing the future patsy Oswald. As already discussed, Shaw was connected to the CIA/Mossad. According to Piper, FBI agent and private investigator Banister did contract work for the ADL (the aforementioned Anti-Defamation League, a Rothschild front created to weaponize antisemitism and use it to silence any criticism of Israel and the Cult). Banister was closely associated with Kent and Phoebe Courtney, who Piper showed were essentially ADL assets, doing the usual Israeli trick of being vehemently anti-Communist to hide their Zionist connections, as so many on the political right do. Banister was also an FBI agent assigned to the UFO matter, which will become very significant, as we are about to see. David Ferrie, a CIA contract agent, was standing alongside mobster Carlos Marcello in a New Orleans courtroom when JFK was shot. Shaw, Banister and Ferrie were all manipulating Oswald to make him appear as a 'pro-Castro agitator.' Piper wrote that *"Banister and Ferrie were also involved in the machinations outside New Orleans at Lake Pontchartrain of CIA operative (and Mossad asset) Frank Sturgis. Oswald is said to have trained at this camp."*[336]

As if he didn't have enough enemies already, JFK also made enemies by sleeping around. He was famous for his many affairs, one of which was with Mary Meyer, ex-wife of CIA agent Cord Meyer. Mary was married to Cord from 1945-1958. Cord was president of the United World Federalists, an organization he helped to fund, which pushed international socialism and world government. It is important to remember that socialism and Communism are Cult ideologies that promote the centralization of power and the abolition of individual rights. According to Deborah Davis in her 1979 book *Katharine the Great: Katharine Graham and the Washington Post*,[337] Meyer became the "principal operative" of Operation Mockingbird, a widespread CIA project which infiltrated (Cult style) the American media landscape and had many famous news anchors and reporters directly on its payroll. The Cult has been greatly able to mold perception via the CIA and this particular long running project, which gives rise to the phrase Mockingbird Media and explains why the MSM is so pathetic and untrustworthy. Cord worked directly under … James Angleton, who also knew Mary as part of the Washington DC intelligence clique.

Another minor character worth mentioning was longtime Mossad asset Frank Sturgis. Piper revealed that *"Sturgis had ties to Israel's Mossad, going back fifteen years prior to the JFK assassination. Writing in the July 1975 issue of Argosy magazine, F. Peter Model reported that Sturgis was a 'Haganah mercenary during the first (1948) Israeli-Arab war,' and that Sturgis also had a girlfriend in Europe in the 1950s who worked for Israeli intelligence and with whom he worked. Sturgis himself is quoted by JFK assassination researcher A. J. Weberman as having said that he assisted his girlfriend as a courier in Europe in a number of her endeavors on behalf of the Mossad."*[338] Sturgis, who also doubled as a CIA contract agent, met with E. Howard Hunt and Ruby in Dallas the day before the assassination. According to Piper, *"Sturgis told Marita Lorenz, that he had been involved in the assassination itself. Looking at Sturgis alone, we can thus say, without qualification, that a known Mossad asset has thus confessed to have played a direct part in the president's murder."*[339] Piper revealed that, according to the testimony of Marita Lorenz (one time girlfriend of Fidel Castro), there was a group of anti-Castro Cubans with Sturgis who arrived in Dallas on November 21st 1963 to meet with E. Howard Hunt and Jack Ruby. Piper revealed that *"during the heyday of the CIA's anti-Castro operations in Miami with which Sturgis and E. Howard Hunt were so closely associated, some 12 to 16 Mossad agents worked out of Miami under the command of Mossad Deputy Director Yehuda S. Sipper ..."*[340]

Miami is in Florida, and interestingly enough, Florida was a hotbed of Mossad activity pre-9/11 as they were preparing to pull off that operation (chapter 14).

E. Howard Hunt, quoted at the start of the chapter in regards to JFK and ET disclosure, was undoubtedly involved in the assassination, but most likely as a lower level player who was in the dark about key aspects of it. Piper showed it was Angleton (yet again) who was responsible for framing Hunt in a limited hangout operation. The idea was to throw a bone to the 'CIA did it' crowd without revealing the Israeli or MJ-12 connection. Hunt was involved in the Watergate burglary, which damaged his reputation, so he was hung out to dry while the real conspirators in the shadows escaped. In a so-called deathbed confession, Hunt admitted he was a "benchwarmer" for the real assassination team.[341]

Part of the way the operation was pulled off was to create smoke and mirrors, decoys and fallback positions – a forerunner of what was to come with the Zionist false flag op of 9/11. On that fateful day of November 22nd 1963, Dallas was filled with all kinds of nefarious characters. In fact, following on from the information about Sturgis and Hunt above, there appears to have been at least one, and possibly several, dummy assassination operations in effect, whose purpose was to muddy the waters so that the real shooters and orchestrators could avoid detection. Michael Milan, author of the book *The Squad*, exposed his role as part of a secret FBI team collaborating with the Lansky crime syndicate. He said there were people in Dallas who thought they were there to kill Governor Connally.[342]

The How

I am intentionally focusing here on 'the why' and 'the who' of the JFK assassination much more than 'the how,' because these are much more important questions. I will take a similar approach when analyzing the 9/11 false flag operation in chapter 14. If we understand why a US president was murdered in broad daylight – with not even the pretense of it being an accident – we can understand what issues matter the most to the people running the world. We can understand their pressure points. We can understand what we need to focus on in order to be free. If we understand who, and what forces 'the who' represented, we gain a clearer comprehension of who really runs the world behind the political puppet show and facade of democracy.

Having said that, I can offer the following pieces of information which I think best describe how it was actually done. For starters, it's vital to keep in mind the words of L. Fletcher Prouty who served as Chief of Special Operations for the Joint Chiefs of Staff in JFK's administration. After the assassination, Prouty went on to become a specialist in assassination security and analysis. He wrote:[343]

No one has to direct an assassination – it happens. The active role is played secretly by permitting it to happen.

This happens in all assassinations and it happened in this one: you can watch the video footage online[344] where the two Secret Service agents (Donald Lawton and Clint Hill),[345] who were the bodyguards on either side of the presidential vehicle, were ordered to stand down, right before the car turned from Houston Street onto Elm Street (where JFK was killed). This prevented them from doing their job as human shields to the president, and allowed the multiple assassins a clear shot.

Image #64: the CIA's Operation 40 squad, including Porter Goss (left, with glasses) who also cropped up in the 9/11 operation (see chapter 15)

For those interested in ascertaining the names and positions of the gunmen, I recommend researching Operation 40,[346] an elite team of assassins composed of around 40 crack CIA agents, created in the late 1950s by President Eisenhower and Vice President Nixon. It was behind many of the most famous high-profile assassinations that began in the 1960s and continued in the following decades. Interestingly enough, in the photograph of Operation 40 members taken in January 1963 (image #63), you can find Porter Goss, sitting on the left wearing glasses, who has strong links to the 9/11 false flag operation.

Image #65: J. D. Tippit

Another aspect of the how worth mentioning is Dallas police officer and JFK lookalike Jefferson Davis Tippit. Researcher Robert Morningstar discovered that Tippit so resembled Kennedy that even his friends called him 'JFK.' Tippit was killed shortly after JFK so the conspirators could perform a body switch! The JFK assassination was, in fact, a triple assassination or triple sacrifice in the open-air temple of Dealey Plaza. Kennedy, Oswald and Tippit were all murdered for different reasons. Patsy Oswald was murdered by Ruby so that he wouldn't spill the beans and declare what he knew of the plot. Tippit, who was friends with Ruby, was murdered because the conspirators had decided they needed his exact corpse to do the body switch with JFK's body – and he looked so similar they thought they could do the switch without anyone noticing. JFK's bloody body was taken from Parkland Hospital in Dallas, Texas, and against state law, was transferred to Bethesda Naval Hospital in Maryland – the same place his mentor James Forrestal died, as we about to find out. It was during this transfer that the body switch was performed.

Abraham Zapruder and the Zapruder Film

The Zapruder film became famous for capturing the moment JFK was killed. However, the film was clearly altered by the insertion of a black frame. I guess Zapruder was just really lucky to be standing there, at that time, in that place, with video camera ready. Just a lucky coincidence … or is there much more to this character?

Did you know that Abraham Zapruder was a Ukrainian born Jew, i.e. a Khazarian? That he was a Freemason and an Inspector-General (33°) of the Scottish Rite?[347] That he also had an office in the Dal-Tex building where he ran a clothing business, the same business Israel falsely claimed was the purpose of the Dimona nuclear plant? Zapruder had a business partner named Jeanne LeGon de Mohrenschildt, who just so happened to be the wife of CIA asset and Oswald best friend (and handler) George de Mohrenschildt. Notable JFK assassination researchers such as Jim Garrison and L. Fletcher Prouty used audio, video and ballistics studies to prove the Dal-Tex Building was one of the locations from which the shots were fired – specifically the third and fourth floors. Guess who happened to have an office on the fourth floor? Abraham Zapruder.

Hopefully, at this point, I have provided enough evidence to show Israel's motivation and means to kill Kennedy. Now, it's time to move on to the next aspect of the assassination which is even more fundamental in explaining why it occurred. I refer to the Cult operation known as MJ-12, the guardian of UFO and ET affairs, over which JFK was, in vain, trying to gain control.

The UFO/ET Issue is the Highest Level of Secrecy

In military intelligence, the issue that carries that highest level of classification and secrecy – which reflects how important it is to the Cult that controls the world's intelligence agencies – is the UFO/ET issue. It is higher even than anything related to nuclear energy or nuclear weapons programs. The reason for this is that the issue of UFOs and ETs cannot be separated from the issue of advanced technology and free energy. One inevitably leads to the other; once the mass public accepts the truth that otherworldly UFO craft fly above us and have landed here, and that otherworldly aliens have visited here, it will begin to wonder how such craft operate and question the energy and propulsion systems involved. This would in turn lead to a mass awakening regarding the existence of free energy, a.k.a. over-unity energy or zero point energy, which is energy produced essentially for free in abundant quantities, so that scarcity would become a thing of the past. This would be a disaster for the power-hungry Cult, whose control of nations and continents depends on its control of oil, gas, coal, etc. and its suppression of alternative energy which could be produced very cheaply or for free. Nikola Tesla found this out the hard way when his investor, bankster and Cult agent J. P. Morgan, pulled the rug from under Tesla's feet after 1901 once he discovered that Tesla, via his Long Island Wardenclyffe Tower project, was intending to give the world free wireless energy, something from which Morgan could not personally profit.

The Cult guards its UFO and free energy secret extremely closely and is prepared to kill to protect it. To understand how JFK came to obstruct this, we have to go back in time a little – to the 1940s, starting with the story of James Forrestal, whom Bill Cooper described as a very idealistic and religious man. Forrestal had a highly successful career, doing well as a financier on Wall Street before becoming Undersecretary of the Navy in 1940, then Secretary of the Navy in May 1944, then Secretary of Defense (the first one ever in US history, since it was a newly created cabinet level position) in September 1947. Significantly, Forrestal was one of the first senior public officials to cultivate a young JFK, recognizing his potential. Kennedy developed a very strong friendship with Forrestal,

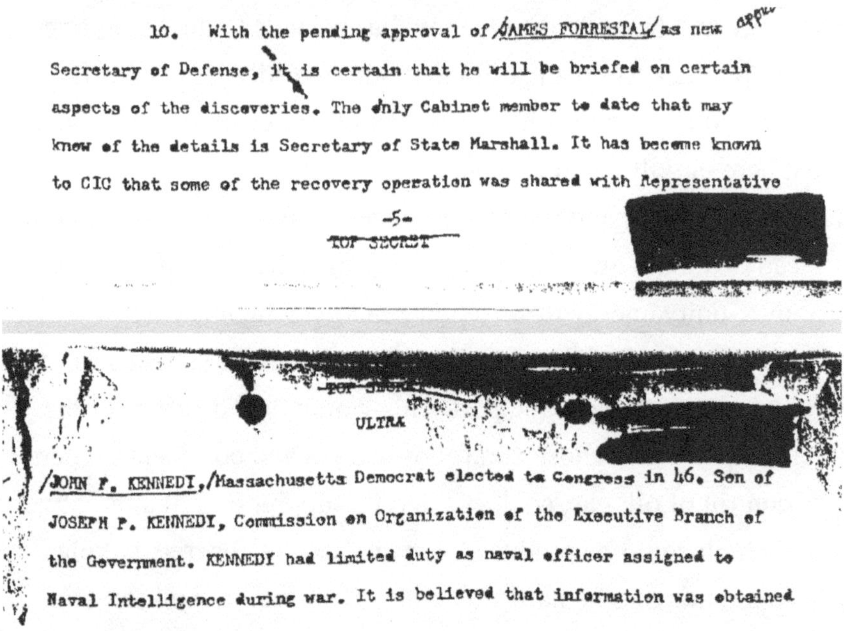

10. With the pending approval of /JAMES FORRESTAL/ as new Secretary of Defense, it is certain that he will be briefed on certain aspects of the discoveries. The only Cabinet member to date that may know of the details is Secretary of State Marshall. It has become known to CIC that some of the recovery operation was shared with Representative

-5-

TOP SECRET

TOP SECRET

ULTRA

/JOHN F. KENNEDI,/Massachusetts Democrat elected to Congress in 46. Son of JOSEPH P. KENNEDI, Commission on Organization of the Executive Branch of the Government. KENNEDI had limited duty as naval officer assigned to Naval Intelligence during war. It is believed that information was obtained

Image #66: a document from July 22nd 1947 showing that JFK, though only a congressman, knew about the Roswell UFO crash recovery

who became one of his mentors. Importantly, Forrestal and Kennedy saw eye-to-eye on many issues. They were ideological allies, especially regarding wanting to maintain America's good relations with the Arab world and wanting to share the truth concerning UFOs and ETs with the public. Salla believes that JFK may have been privy to classified information from the 1942 Battle of LA where UFOs flew over Los Angeles, but for sure there is documented proof that he was briefed about the July 1947 UFO crash in Roswell, New Mexico (see image #66):[348]

It has become known to CIC that some of the recovery operation was shared with Representative John F. Kennedy, Massachusetts Democrat elected to Congress in 46. Son of Joseph P. Kennedy, Commission on Organization for the Executive Branch of the

Government. Kennedy had limited duty as naval officer assigned to Naval Intelligence during war.

CIC stood for Counter Intelligence Corps, an elite army counter intelligence team responsible for 'interplanetary phenomena.' The extraordinary nature of that event prompted then President Truman to set up a new committee which would, from that point on, handle the UFO/ET affair. In a September 1947 memo (image #67) to his new Secretary of Defense Forrestal, Truman wrote that *"[h]ereafter this matter shall be referred to only as Operation Majestic Twelve."*[349] Truman set things up so that any further consideration of the matter would rest with the president, after consultation with the Secretary of Defense, Director of Central Intelligence and a man named Dr. Vannevar Bush (no relation to Prescott and George Bush). However, that year 1947 was to be a highly significant year in terms of Cult control over America, just as 1913 was, but only worse. Truman signed the National Security Act of 1947 which reorganized the US military and intelligence establishment, and created the CIA. It was the year that the Cult got its foot in the door and really began to exert its dominance over America. While Truman was busy overtly creating new military-intelligence structures and agencies, he covertly created Majestic Twelve, which was also referred to as MJ 12, MJ-12 and/or Majic in subsequent documents. A tradition began where the newly created position of Director of Central Intelligence, which headed the newly created CIA, would also sit as director on the 12-person committee of MJ-12. Each member was given a designation from one through twelve; the head of MJ-12 was MJ-1. Due to his position as Secretary of Defense, Forrestal was an original member of MJ-12 (MJ-3), however apparently he was in the minority position on the issue of 'disclosure,' i.e. whether to tell the American public about UFOs and ETs.

TOP SECRET
EYES ONLY
THE WHITE HOUSE
WASHINGTON

September 24, 1947.

MEMORANDUM FOR THE SECRETARY OF DEFENSE

Dear Secretary Forrestal:

As per our recent conversation on this matter, you are hereby authorized to proceed with all due speed and caution upon your undertaking. Hereafter this matter shall be referred to only as Operation Majestic Twelve.

It continues to be my feeling that any future considerations relative to the ultimate disposition of this matter should rest solely with the Office of the President following appropriate discussions with yourself, Dr. Bush and the Director of Central Intelligence.

Harry Truman

TOP SECRET
EYES ONLY

Image #67: a letter dated September 24th 1947 from then President Truman to then Secretary of Defense Forrestal launching Majestic Twelve or MJ-12

In fact, Forrestal was consistently at odds with (Cult-controlled) Truman so much so that Truman fired him from his Secretary of Defense position – then somehow managed to have him committed to a medical facility at Bethesda Naval Hospital for having a 'nervous breakdown' despite the official records not describing his condition as such. I mentioned Forrestal previously in chapter 10 regarding his opposition to the nascent Israeli state. Forrestal crossed the Cult once by adamantly opposing the creation of modern Israel, and he crossed the Cult again by advocating disclosure. Forrestal believed the public should be told and could handle the truth. Apparently, crossing the Cult twice was not good for his health; Forrestal died in May 1949 under highly suspicious circumstances. The official story is that he jumped out a window, however according to many such as UFO researcher Richard Dolan, Forrestal did not kill himself, but rather was strangled and thrown out the window. One extremely interesting piece of information is that then congressman Lyndon Johnson was one of the few people that managed to gain access to Forrestal, who had been denied all visitors. Salla writes that *"according to one of Forrestal's aides, Marx Leva, Johnson managed to gain entrance to the suite, against Forrestal's wishes. This is a very significant revelation. It suggests Johnson was part of a group of public officials pressuring Forrestal to remain silent about something."*[350] As already discussed, LBJ was prepared to kill for the presidency and was a faithful Cult agent. It would have been completely in character for Johnson to have bullied or even murdered Forrestal. Was Johnson part of the group that was prepared to kill to maintain UFO/ET secrecy?

After Truman left office, he was succeeded in 1952 by Eisenhower, the war general who had led American forces in Europe during WWII. As US Army Chief, Eisenhower was certainly well aware of the UFO/ET issue. Eisenhower ran as a Republican. The Republican Party in US politics is the rightwing or conservative party, and at least historically or theoretically, is supposed to favor the ideology of smaller central government with a larger corporate role. Eisenhower invited Nelson Rockefeller of the infamous NWO Rockefeller bloodline family to lead a committee advising him on government re-organization. As mentioned in other parts of this book, the Rockefellers and the Rothschilds are probably the two most powerful bloodline families on the planet. They have since intermarried so much that the Rockefellers, whilst not originally being Zionists like the Rothschilds, are nonetheless very closely connected to the Zionist agenda by virtue of being Cult agents. It is no stretch of the imagination at all to conclude that Nelson Rockefeller 'advised,' or rather persuaded, Eisenhower, against a backdrop of Republican 'large corporate power, small government power' ideology, to allow control of the UFO/ET issue to be put in private hands. The main argument used by those in military intelligence is that black world projects (ultra secretive, off-the-book, off-record projects) have to be strictly separated from white world projects (publicly visible) to ensure operational efficiency, long-term planning and a degree of insulation from meddling politicians who are here today, gone tomorrow. Some black ops can be further divided into Special Access Programs (SAPs) and Unacknowledged Special Access Programs (USAPs), with the latter being programs that don't officially exist. With all of them, you strictly cannot know about them unless you have 'need to know' security clearance. Eisenhower agreed to the logic of keeping the matter out of the public eye, and did indeed sign off on Rockefeller's recommendation to hide MJ-12 deep in the world of black projects and covert operations. Rockefeller had managed to get Eisenhower to set things up so that MJ-12 could conduct its business in total secrecy without interference from prying or ambitious politicians – even from the president himself, as Eisenhower was about to find out.

Part of the deal Eisenhower granted MJ-12 was that it could have its own protected area to run its operation. The area chosen was a remote part of the Nevada desert that belonged to the US Department of Energy. The CIA was given authority for security of the area which became known as Area 51, just south of Groom Lake, a dry salt bed in the desert. In true Cult fashion, the CIA/MJ-12 decided to hide yet another layer within an already secretive layer, and they oversaw the construction of another facility in the area called S4, right near Papoose Lake; this meant that Area 51 could be a cover for S4. According to whistleblowers who have worked at Area 51 or S4, or have been part of MJ-12, such as Dr. Michael Kruvant Wolf, the merely Top Secret and Above Top Secret stuff would be at Area 51, while the Umbra Top Secret stuff would be at S4.[351] The man given the responsibility for acquiring Area 51 for the CIA was Richard Bissell, the "mayor of Area 51," who was in charge of the CIA's Directorate of Plans (covert ops) from 1959-1962. He became the number two man at the CIA (the Deputy Director). Bissell was in charge of the USAF's Project Blue Book that purported to give the public the full truth about UFO sightings but was little more than a glorified PR exercise. It was Bissell who took the brunt of the blame for the failed Bay of Pigs invasion, for which he and director Dulles would get fired by Kennedy. At the same time, JFK also fired General Charles Cabell. In an uncanny synchronicity, Charles's brother Earle Cabell would be mayor of Dallas when JFK was later killed there. Was this just a coincidence or proof that Cult agents were in key positions of power to kill a president and get away with it?

Those on the MJ-12 board who were committed to absolute secrecy were happy with the arrangement for the CIA to run security at Area 51 instead of any of the traditional US Military branches (Air Force, Navy or Army), because the CIA already had autonomy outside the traditional political/military structure that allowed it to operate out of the system with minimal accountability and oversight. Salla writes that Dulles, as Director of the CIA when Area 51 became operational, became MJ-12 head (MJ-1), and that Angleton, as Director of Counterintelligence, would have been in charge of security of Area 51 and been the official gatekeeper of the CIA's UFO secrets. He had an extensive international spy network at his fingertips for learning about UFO and ET activity anywhere in the world.

Dulles and Angleton … those same two men, again.

It wasn't long at all, however, until Eisenhower deeply regretted his decision to reorganize the government by giving the UFO/ET issue to MJ-12 via the CIA. He felt as though he had lost control of the matter and could not get the information he wanted as leader, president and commander-in-chief of the military. MJ-12 told him he didn't have jurisdiction. So, he came up with a novel idea that aptly suited his talents and experience – he threatened to invade Area 51! That's right; according to a whistleblowing ex-CIA agent that came forward in 2013 (with only a few months to live),[352] Eisenhower was fed up with being denied access and told this CIA agent to fly to Nevada and give MJ-12 a message: that if they didn't report to him in Washington by the end of the week, he would grab the First Army out of Colorado, march onto the base, take it over and *"rip this thing apart."* MJ-12 must have considered Eisenhower's threat quite credible, because it did reveal some things to him after that, however

Eisenhower was deeply worried. He had achieved a tactical victory over MJ-12, but not a strategic one, and he left office soon thereafter … to make way for the incoming 43-year-old president, John F. Kennedy.

Given Eisenhower's famous farewell speech on January 17th 1961, where he warned the American public about *"the acquisition of unwarranted influence, whether sought or unsought, by the military-industrial complex,"*[353] it is highly probable that Eisenhower would have warned the young JFK of the urgent need for the office of the US president to reign in the CIA and MJ-12, which had begun to grow dangerously out of control. JFK lost little time in doing so; on February 19th 1961, he issued an Executive Order (EO), number 10920,[354] to abolish the Operations Coordinating Board (in charge of psychological operations or psy ops), bringing it back under the control of the National Security Advisor and Department of State, both of whom answered directly to the president. One of the points of this was to begin wresting control away from MJ-12, since it used psychological warfare in its operations. On June 28th 1961, JFK sent a memo (see image #68) to Dulles requesting a summary of MJ-12 "Intelligence Operations" as they related to "Cold War Psychological Warfare Plans."[355]

That same day, Kennedy also issued three National Security Action Memoranda (NSAMs) which strictly limited clandestine or paramilitary operations, putting them back under control of the Joint Chiefs of Staff and out of CIA hands.[356] This was not just about MJ-12 and UFOs, but also in response to the disastrous and failed April 1961 Bay of Pigs invasion of Cuba which resulted in a US defeat and retreat. Kennedy was furious at the CIA for dragging him into a war and resented how much power the agency had, including

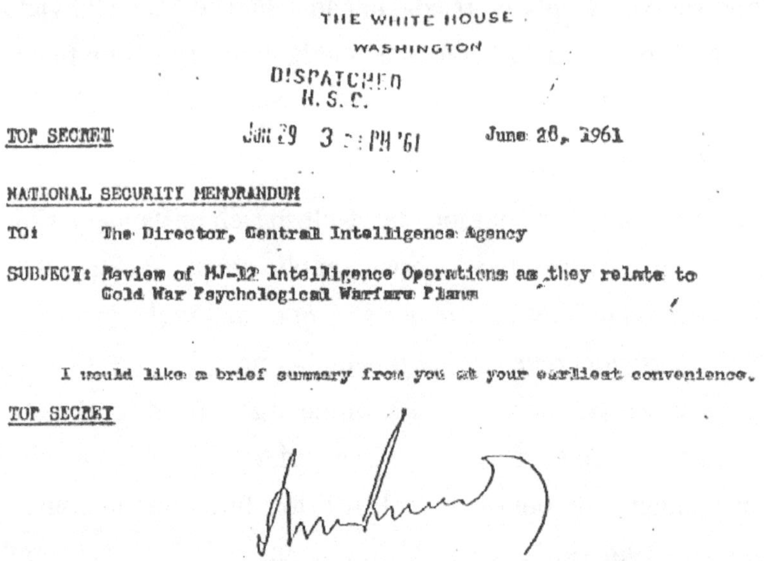

THE WHITE HOUSE
WASHINGTON

DISPATCHED
N. S. C.

TOP SECRET JUN 29 3 : PM '61 June 28, 1961

NATIONAL SECURITY MEMORANDUM

TO: The Director, Central Intelligence Agency

SUBJECT: Review of MJ-12 Intelligence Operations as they relate to Cold War Psychological Warfare Plans

I would like a brief summary from you at your earliest convenience.

TOP SECRET

Image #68: on June 28th 1961, Kennedy writes a terse memo to CIA Director Dulles, asking for a review of MJ-12 intelligence operations

its own paramilitary force with the ability to stage coups and topple foreign governments, as had happened throughout the 1950s with Operation Ajax in Iran (1953) and Operation PBSUCCESS in Guatemala (1954). The point of these EOs, NSAMs and memoranda was, broadly, to limit CIA power and bring both the CIA's and MJ-12's activities back under presidential purview.

This, however, was something that Dulles as MJ-1 would never allow. Fortunately, due to the intervention of an anonymous CIA agent, we can piece together what happened next. James Angleton left the CIA in 1974 after then Director Colby asked him to leave. When Angleton died in 1987, his successors decided to burn his voluminous files so that nothing sensitive could be revealed. A CIA agent who was one of Angleton's counterintelligence underlings claimed to be present at the burning of these files and, when some papers caught his eye, he quickly and quietly grabbed them from the fire. He then sent these files to UFO researcher Timothy Cooper who made them public. The documents are both uniquely fascinating and damning.

There are two burned memos in particular which provide the smoking gun evidence to solve the JFK assassination. According to Dr. Robert Wood and Ryan Wood, considered the top experts on Majestic documents, the documents are genuine. The first[357] is a memo (image #69) written from MJ-1 (or CIA Director Dulles) addressed to MJ-2, MJ-3, MJ-4, MJ-5, MJ-6 and MJ-7. It lays out the situation that Kennedy had been inquiring about their activities, that they could not allow this, and that they needed to find the best way to respond. Dulles had a sense of urgency in his tone; the Woods assess that document was drafted in September (i.e. of 1961), while Dulles requests an answer by no later than October. We can speculate that Dulles was writing to a majority of the committee (the next six members in terms of seniority) so that he could bypass the full committee and get an answer that would win a majority vote if it ever needed to. Dulles presents 8 "tabs" at the bottom of the memo; importantly, one of the "tabs" at the bottom of the memo is called "Project ENVIRONMENT" which comes up in the next memo.

The other burned memo,[358] if genuine as it appears to be, is smoking gun evidence of the hit order given by Dulles. It is a cryptic assassination directive. It is the "Project ENVIRONMENT" referred to previously. Here is what the memo literally says (image #70):

Directive Regarding Project ENVIRONMENT

When conditions become non-conducive for growth in our environment and Washington cannot be influenced any further, the weather is lacking precipitation ... it should be wet.

Salla writes, *"Dr. Robert Wood who is the foremost expert in analyzing MJ-12 documents using forensic methods, has concluded that the burned document is an assassination directive. In an interview disclosing the burned document, he points out that the cryptic phrase 'it should be wet' originates from Russia where the phrase 'wet works' or 'wet affairs' denotes someone who had been killed and is drenched with blood."*[359] The strange wording is a security precaution to insulate against leaks and provide a case for plausible deniability, but a CIA veteran like Angleton – whose responsibility it was to execute the order – would have known exactly what it meant. We do not have any record of what the other MJ-12 members replied to Dulles, but the paper trail can be picked up again on November 5th 1961[360] (see image #71), when Dulles replied to Kennedy by giving little tidbits of information mixed with propaganda and lies, and additionally, an outright refusal to divulge more sensitive data *"for reasons of security."* This letter is a great demonstration of the power struggle that was going on between Kennedy and Dulles, showing that Dulles was unafraid to directly deny presidents information. It must be said that MJ-12 included other operations in addition to UFO/ET matters, including covert operations, psychological warfare and even spin-off projects such as the now famous MK-ULTRA mind control program, with 153 sub-projects, all of which would have been affected had Kennedy gained access. For many reasons such as the Bay of Pigs fiasco and his clear insubordination, Dulles was fired, and left the CIA shortly thereafter on November 28th 1961. He had, however, cunningly set into place the gears of mortal execution that were to manifest around two years later in November 1963, even though he would officially be out of the CIA from that point on.

How does Angleton play into this? According to famous ET abductee and UFO researcher Whitley Strieber, Angleton was the CIA's UFO gatekeeper. It was his job to enforce the secrecy and to ensure no one who was not approved by MJ-12 got access. This aligns exactly with what we know of Angleton as a ruthless mole-hunter within the CIA who was paranoid and constantly on the lookout for 'Soviet moles' who had infiltrated the agency. A document which implicates Angleton directly and shows his involvement with the MJ-12 assassination directive is this one[361] which is dated November 12th 1963 (image #72). It is a memo that Kennedy had written to the new CIA director John McCone, but on the bottom is the handwriting of William Colby, then CIA chief for Far East Asia, but later CIA Director. It states: *"Angleton has MJ-12 directive. 11/20/63"* Given that the date of the memo was 10 days before the assassination, and Colby's handwritten date was 2 days before the assassination, this is suggestive that Angleton did indeed have the Project ENVIRONMENT assassination directive, and was the one tasked with carrying it out.

In 1961 and 1962, Kennedy did his best to find out the truth about extraterrestrial life on earth. Since Kennedy was not a 5-star general as Eisenhower had been, he could not credibly take the same blunt approach that Eisenhower did of threatening to march upon Area 51 with an army. JFK approached the problem from a different angle. Any US president or commander-in-chief would have been denied access if they showed up at Area 51/S4, because it was under CIA security, not military control, but what the president could do is visit any normal US military base and demand access as the highest-ranking officer. According to Salla, JFK had great success in gaining access to numerous military facilities in New Mexico and Texas where he personally witnessed UFOs and met with ETs. Further evidence of this comes from Lt. Col. Philip Corso who wrote the 1997 book *The Day After Roswell* about his involvement in seeding advanced ET technology into private corporations. Corso reveals how he personally briefed RFK, John's brother and US Attorney General, about a crashed UFO of extraterrestrial origin whose technology was being reverse engineered. Bobby was extremely close to John, so briefing Bobby was like briefing John.

The famous actress Marilyn Monroe also got caught up in this. Her well-known affair with JFK apparently led to him divulging UFO secrets to her. We know that right before her death Monroe had threatened to hold a press conference where she would tell everything, including on the topic of *"things from outer space."* We know this because a CIA wiretap summary[362] (see image #73) that was signed by Angleton himself contains a conversation between two people that knew Monroe – reporter Dorothy Kilgallen and her close friend Howard Rothberg. Kilgallen, who used to publish gossip and rumor news, also had sources in high places and had thus gained knowledge of the UFO/ET affair. We can be quite certain the document is genuine since the CIA had a chance to legally challenge it but did not:[363]

This is a CIA document that appeared sometime in the early 1990s and has been (unwittingly) authenticated by the CIA itself, in that when Dr. Donald R. Burleson, author of UFOs and the Murder of Marilyn Monroe, filed his appeal of the CIA's refusal to release transcripts of government wiretaps on Marilyn Monroe's telephones, the appeal, which was based largely on the 3 August 1962 document in question, was accepted; ultimately no transcripts were released, but the acceptance-of-appeal process did demonstrate that the document is of authentic CIA provenance.

Salla writes that RFK was desperate to get Monroe to be quiet and even visited her on the day of her death, trying to get her diary of secrets, and that unbeknown to RFK, one of the two agents accompanying him to visit Monroe that day worked for Angleton (Angleton ultimately got Monroe's diary and prevented it from being made public). If it's true that Angleton had an agent with Bobby Kennedy that day, it would have allowed Angleton to blackmail RFK, because he could have spread plausible rumors that RFK was responsible for murdering her.

Despite the 1961 Bay of Pigs fiasco and the perilous 1962 Cuban Missile Crisis, Kennedy's desire for peace and strong intention to cooperate with the Russians ultimately broke through the icy American-Russian Cold War relations. A leaked NSA document reveals that JFK and Soviet leader Nikita Khrushchev were discussing UFOs (see image #74);[364] his son Sergei Khruschev confirmed that finally Nikita had decided to accept Kennedy's offer of joint lunar cooperation in early November 1963 around a week before his assassination.[365] It was on November 12th 1963, just 10 days before JFK's life would end, where JFK finally made the moves that precipitated his murder. On that day, JFK issued two extremely important memos. The first was NSAM #271, entitled *"Cooperation with the USSR on Outer Space Matters,"*[366] (see image #75) and instructed James Webb, head of NASA, to develop a program of close cooperation with the Soviet Union on outer space matters. That same day, we have a draft memorandum from Kennedy addressed to

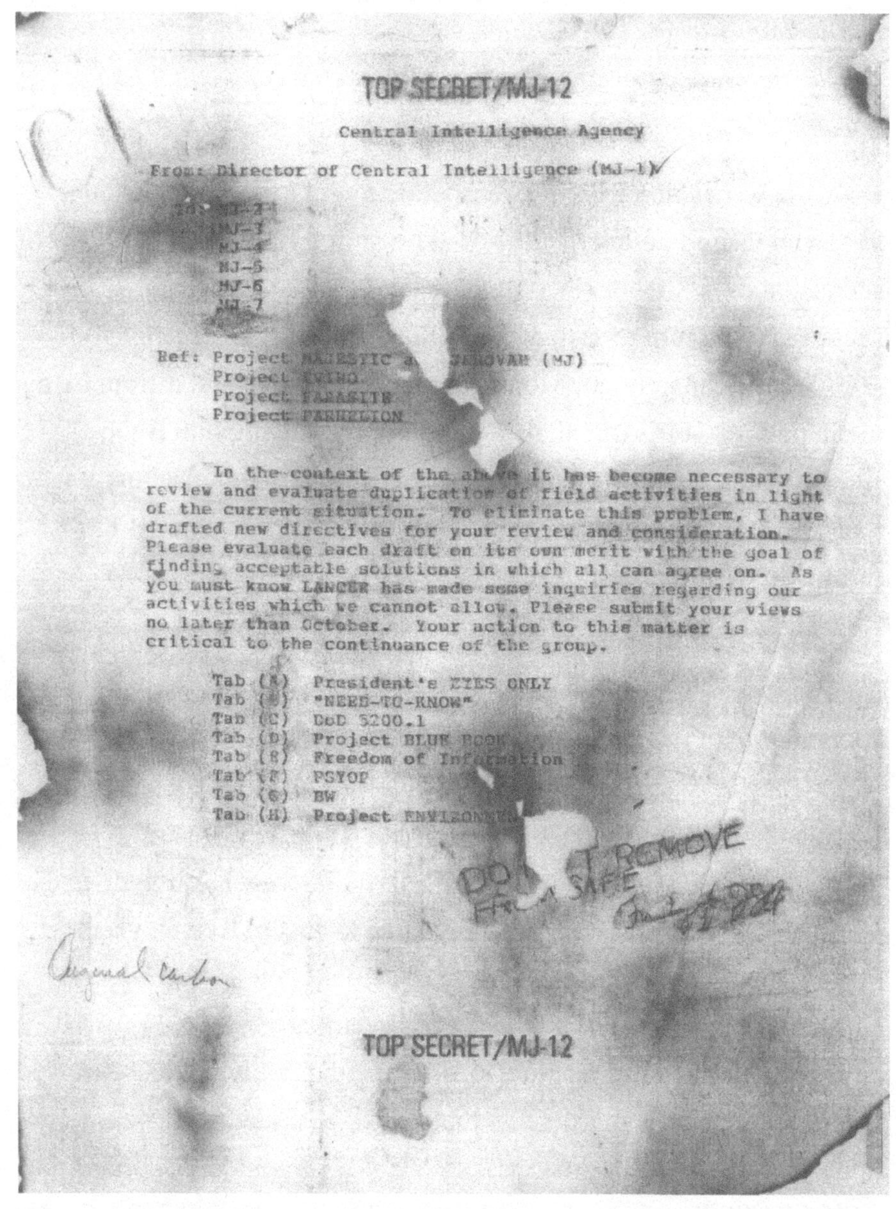

TOP SECRET/MJ-12

Central Intelligence Agency

From: Director of Central Intelligence (MJ-1)

To: MJ-2
MJ-3
MJ-4
MJ-5
MJ-6
MJ-7

Ref: Project MAJESTIC a[illegible] JEHOVAH (MJ)
Project [illegible]
Project PARASITE
Project PARHELION

In the context of the above it has become necessary to review and evaluate duplication of field activities in light of the current situation. To eliminate this problem, I have drafted new directives for your review and consideration. Please evaluate each draft on its own merit with the goal of finding acceptable solutions in which all can agree on. As you must know LANCER has made some inquiries regarding our activities which we cannot allow. Please submit your views no later than October. Your action to this matter is critical to the continuance of the group.

Tab (A) President's EYES ONLY
Tab (B) "NEED-TO-KNOW"
Tab (C) DoD 5200.1
Tab (D) Project BLUE BOOK
Tab (E) Freedom of Information
Tab (F) PSYOP
Tab (G) BW
Tab (H) Project ENVIRON[illegible]

DO NOT REMOVE FROM SAFE

Original carbon

TOP SECRET/MJ-12

Image #69: Dulles (MJ-1) writes to 6 other members on MJ-12 Committee (MJ-2 to MJ-7) to get their opinions on how to handle JFK's (Lancer's) probing

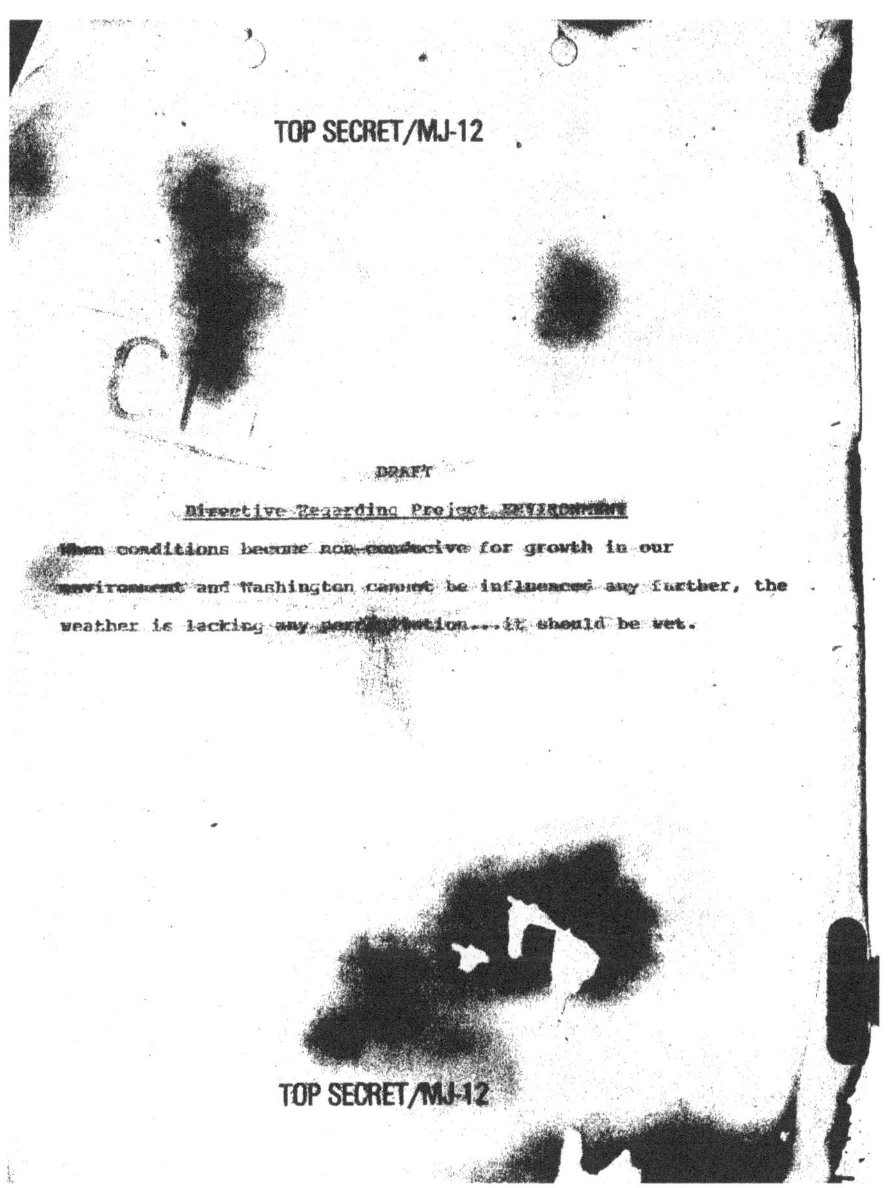
TOP SECRET/MJ-12

DRAFT

Directive Regarding Project ENVIRONMENT

When conditions become non-conducive for growth in our environment and Washington cannot be influenced any further, the weather is lacking any perturbation....it should be wet.

TOP SECRET/MJ-12

Image #70: the draft memo of the assassination directive

RECEIVED
JUL 21 2000
5-1

TOP SECRET

SENSITIVE

5 November 1961

Operations Review
by Allen W. Dulles

THE MJ-12 PROJECT

The Overview. In pursuant to the Presidential National Security Memorandum of June 28, 1961, the U.S. intelligence operations against the Soviet Union are currently active in two broad areas; aircraft launch vehicles incorporating ELINT and SIGINT capabilities; and balloon borne decoys with ECM equipment.

The Situation. The overall effectiveness about the actual Soviet response and alert status is not documented to the point where U.S. intelligence can provide a true picture of how Soviet air defenses perceive unidentified flying objects.

Informational sources have provided some detail on coded transmissions and tactical plans whose reliability is uncertain, and thus, do not give us precise knowledge of Soviet Order of Battle. Current estimates place Soviet air and rocket defenses on a maximum alert footing with air operations centered on radar and visual verification much the same as ours.

Future psychological warfare plans are in the making for more sophisticated vehicles whose characteristics come very close to phenomena collected by Air Force and NSA elements authorized for operations in this area of intelligence.

Basis for Action. Earlier studies indicated that Americans perceived U.F.O. sightings as the work of Soviet propaganda designed to convince U.S. intelligence of their technical superiority and to spread distrust of the government. CIA conducted three reviews of the situation utilizing all available information and concluded that 80% of the sighting reports investigated by the Air Force's Project Blue Book were explainable and posed no immediate threat to national security. The remaining cases have been classified for security reasons and are under review. While the possibility remains that true U.F.O. cases are of non-terrestrial origin, U.S. intelligence is of the opinion that they do not constitute a physical threat to national defense. For reasons of security, I cannot divulge pertinent data on some of the more sensitive aspects of MJ-12 activities which have been deemed properly classified under the 1954 Atomic En[illegible] of 1954.

I hope this clarifies the necessity to keep current operations w[illegible]A activities in sensitive areas from becoming official disclosure. From time to time, updates will be provided through NIE as more information becomes available.

(Signed) Allen W. Dulles

This document contains information affecting the national defense of the United States within of the Espionage Laws, Title 18, U. S. C., Section 793 and 794. The transmission or the revelation of its contents in any manner to an unauthorized person is prohibited by law. Exempted from automatic regrading: DoD 5200.10

This document contains____ pg
Copy No. of copies

Image #71: Dulles writes back to Kennedy, giving him little, and claiming he could not divulge certain data "for reasons of security"

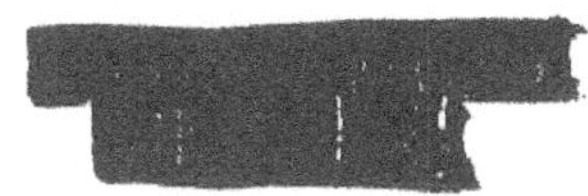

TOP SECRET

November 12, 1963

MEMORANDUM FOR
The Director, Central Intelligence Agency

SUBJECT: Classification review of all UFO intelligence files affecting National Security

As I had discussed with you previously, I have initiated and have instructed James Webb to develop a program with the Soviet Union in joint space and lunar exploration. It would be very helpful if you would have the high threat cases reviewed with the purpose of identification of bona fide as opposed to classified CIA and USAF sources. It is important that we make a clear distinction between the knowns and unknowns in the event the Soviets try to mistake our extended cooperation as a cover for intelligence gathering of their defence and space programs.

When this data has been sorted out, I would like you to arrange a program of data sharing with NASA where Unknowns are a factor. This will help NASA mission directors in their defensive responsibilities.

I would like an interim report on the data review no later than February 1, 1964.

/S/ John F. Kennedy

Image #72: Kennedy writes to the CIA, asking them to separate the "knowns" and "unknowns" (i.e. manmade UFOs vs. extraterrestrial UFOs). At the bottom, William Colby writes that "Angleton has MJ directive" and dates it 11/20/63, just 3 days before JFK's death

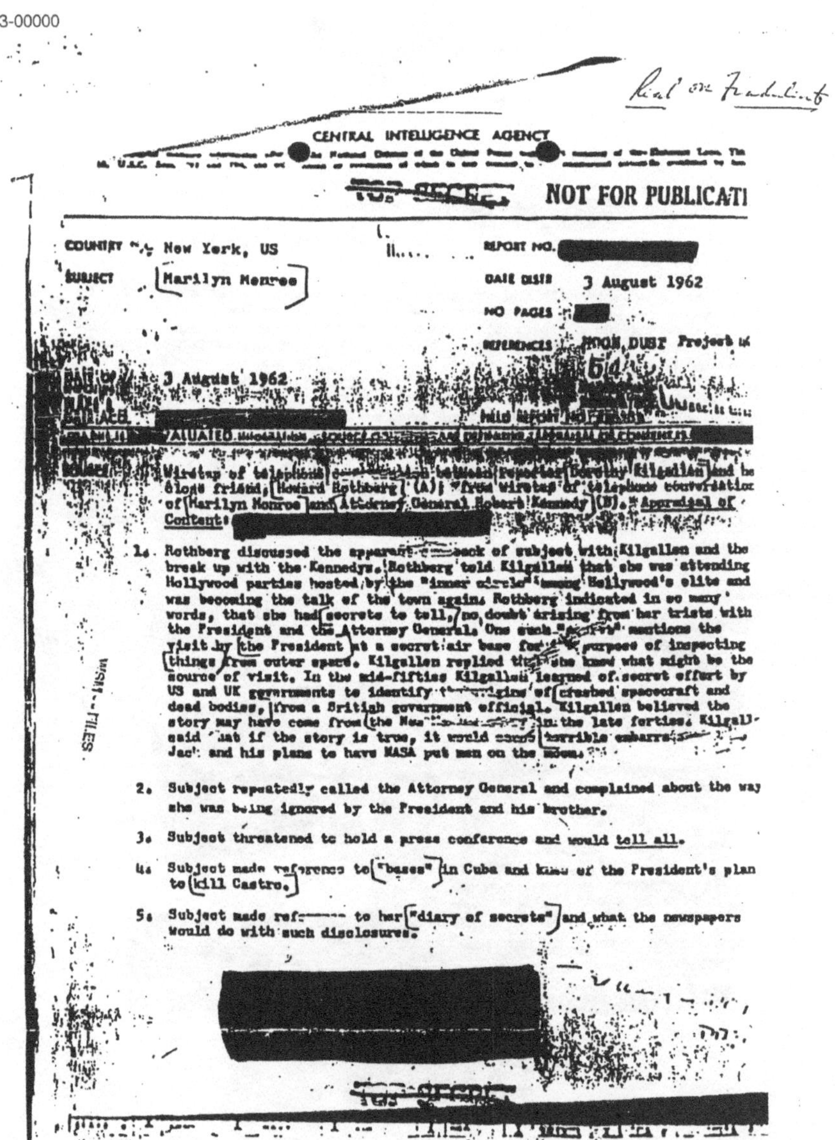

13-00000

CENTRAL INTELLIGENCE AGENCY

NOT FOR PUBLICATI

COUNTRY New York, US

SUBJECT Marilyn Monree

REPORT NO.

DATE DISTR 3 August 1962

NO PAGES

REFERENCES MOON DUST Project

3 August 1962

Wiretap of telephone [illegible] between reporter Dorothy Kilgadlen and her close friend, Howard Rothberg (A); "from wiretap of telephone conversation of Marilyn Monroe and Attorney General Robert Kennedy (B)." Appraisal of Content:

1. Rothberg discussed the apparent [illegible]back of subject with Kilgallen and the break up with the Kennedys. Rothberg told Kilgallen that she was attending Hollywood parties hosted by the "inner circle" among Hollywood's elite and was becoming the talk of the town again. Rothberg indicated in so many words, that she had secrets to tell, no doubt arising from her trists with the President and the Attorney General. One such "[illegible]" mentions the visit by the President at a secret air base for [illegible] purpose of inspecting things from outer space. Kilgallen replied that she knew what might be the source of visit. In the mid-fifties Kilgallen learned of secret effort by US and UK governments to identify [illegible] origins of crashed spacecraft and dead bodies, from a British government official. Kilgallen believed the story may have come from the New [illegible] in the late forties. Kilgallen said that if the story is true, it would cause terrible embarrass[illegible] Jack and his plans to have NASA put men on the moon.

2. Subject repeatedly called the Attorney General and complained about the way she was being ignored by the President and his brother.

3. Subject threatened to hold a press conference and would tell all.

4. Subject made reference to "bases" in Cuba and knew of the President's plan to kill Castro.

5. Subject made ref[illegible] to her "diary of secrets" and what the newspapers would do with such disclosures.

Image #73: the CIA wiretap summary of Marilyn Monroe, signed by Angleton

TOP SECRET
UMBRA

NSA INTERCEPT OF THE "HOT LINE"
COMSEC FILE DATED 11/12/63

ETCRRM TX HOURLY TEST
FROM: OOTP
TO :PUSSR
SUBJ : UFO WORKING GROUPS

WHCA
SOD
DCIA
DNSA
NMCC
CJCS
SECSTATE
NSC

"Mr. Premiere a situation has developed that affects both our countries and the world and I feel it necessary to convey to you a problem that we share in common."

"Mr. President I agree."

"As you must appreciate the tension between our two great nations has often brought us to the brink of showmanship with all the tapestry of a Greek comedy and our impasse last year was foolish and deadly. The division that separates us is through misunderstanding, politics, and cultural differences. But we have one thing in common which I would like to address to your working group on the UFO problem."

"Yes, yes...I agree with your assessment. We nearly tied the knot that divides us permanently. Our working group believes the same way as yours. The UFO problem presents grave dangers to our

Image #74: NSA intercept of conversation about UFOs between Kennedy and Khrushchev

the CIA Director (McCone), whose subject is *"Classification review of all UFO intelligence files affecting National Security"* (image #71) which contains Colby's handwriting about Angleton having the MJ-12 directive. In this memo, JFK refers to the memo he had just issued earlier that day to James Webb of NASA, and directs McCone to separate the UFO cases of extraterrestrial origin and the ones of terrestrial origin, the former being *"bona fide"* and the latter being *"classified CIA and USAF sources."* Kennedy wrote that it was important to make *"a clear distinction between the knowns and unknowns."* What he was essentially requesting here was a classification review of all the UFO files, which would necessarily give him as president access and more control over the matter – couching the request in the context of needing it in order to proceed with a lunar cooperation program with the Soviets. Kennedy undoubtedly knew that there were two sets of UFO files, and that the USAF's Project Blue Book was a sham. JFK was directly confronting the CIA.

On the morning of November 22nd 1963, JFK was on his way to give a speech at the Trade Mart in Dallas. In a 2024 interview/documentary entitled *JFK: The Final Speech*,[367] Daniel Liszt (a.k.a. Dark Journalist) reveals a ton of connections between the JFK assassination and the aerospace industry, which is inseparable from the military/armaments industry. Remember, it was Eisenhower in the 1950s who approved the guardianship of advanced technology, supervised by MJ-12 and gleaned from alien craft, passing into the hands of private corporations. This meant the likes of giant corporate defense contractors like Lockheed Martin, Boeing, Northrop Grumman, Raytheon Technologies and General Dynamics. These are the companies that hold the secrets today. The censors have done their best to scrub JFK's final speech from history, so we don't have the exact text of it, but Liszt speculates that JFK's final speech was going to be on the topic of a joint moon mission with Russia or relating to UFO files. A purported JFK final speech showed up in 1969 but it was a pro-war, pro-nuclear speech[368] that sounds absolutely nothing like Kennedy, so it's clearly a decoy. We can glean some information on what this final speech may have been about from the notes of Lloyd Berkner, who was to have met JFK at the Trade Mart and who was, also, an initial member of MJ-12! Berkner is an interesting character; he went to Antarctica at the age of 22 and was friends with Admiral Richard Byrd who wrote a foreword/note of thanks to him. Byrd was the famous explorer who led an expedition to Antarctica from December 1946 to February 1947 called Operation Highjump. The 4700 man-strong expedition ended abruptly after 6 weeks as Byrd was forced to beat a hasty retreat. This has given rise to a lot of speculation about the strength of the force that caused him to withdraw so rapidly and unexpectedly; there is credible evidence that either the Nazis or an ET force using advanced technology (including UFOs) repelled Byrd's armada, but whatever the case, Byrd apparently saw something so top secret that he was ordered to keep silent about it. Whatever Byrd saw there, it would have been relayed back to James Forrestal, who was Secretary of the Navy at the time. Berkner, whom Byrd took under his wing (pun intended), went on to create the International Geophysical year in 1957-58. Berkner wrote that JFK was *"to have made a major national and international address at Dallas"*[369] however it appears the genuine speech is lost to history. Although Berkner was part of MJ-12, he was, like Forrestal, part of the group that believed in sharing the UFO/ET truth, not hiding it with lethal protection. Berkner and Forrestal were supportive of

2

 November 12, 1963

NATIONAL SECURITY ACTION MEMORANDUM NO. 271

MEMORANDUM FOR

The Administrator, National Aeronautics and Space Administration

SUBJECT: Cooperation with the USSR on Outer Space Matters

I would like you to assume personally the initiative and central responsibility within the Government for the development of a program of substantive cooperation with the Soviet Union in the field of outer space, including the development of specific technical proposals. I assume that you will work closely with the Department of State and other agencies as appropriate.

These proposals should be developed with a view to their possible discussion with the Soviet Union as a direct outcome of my September 20 proposal for broader cooperation between the United States and the USSR in outer space, including cooperation in lunar landing programs. All proposals or suggestions originating within the Government relating to this general subject will be referred to you for your consideration and evaluation.

In addition to developing substantive proposals, I expect that you will assist the Secretary of State in exploring problems of procedure and timing connected with holding discussions with the Soviet Union and in proposing for my consideration the channels which would be most desirable from our point of view. In this connection the channel of contact developed

Image #75: NSAM #271 where Kennedy directs NASA head James Webb to start a program of information sharing with the USSR

JFK's efforts to learn and spread the truth, while other members of MJ-12 were not. The members who were prepared to kill for UFO secrecy were obviously Allen Dulles and may also have included Detlev Bronk, who had connections to the NWO bloodline Rockefeller family and became president of Rockefeller University from 1953 to 1968.[370]

It is beyond coincidence that the JFK assassination keeps leading back to Antarctica. This in turn leads back to hidden advanced technology at Antarctic bases, going back to at least the 1930s when the Germans began taking expeditions – before the outbreak of WWII, the Nazi's acquisition of super high-tech weapons and Operation Highjump. In addition to Berkner's connection to Antarctica, here is another one: when Oswald got a job at the TSBD, the owner of that building was David Harold Byrd (the cousin of Admiral Byrd). What are the chances of that? David Byrd funded an Antarctica expedition and even had a mountain range in Antarctica (Harold Byrd Mountains) named after him. According to Liszt, he also invested $3 million into LTV, Ling-Temco-Vought, an aerospace company. The UFO/ET matter is inextricably connected to advanced technology and free energy. Those in possession of this knowledge are prepared to kill for it, not just because of aliens themselves, but because they don't want the public to know about the science of advanced ET civilizations and demand that knowledge for themselves.

In another video, Liszt interviews Douglas Caddy, who was briefly the lawyer for the five Watergate burglars as well as two other men involved in the Watergate scandal, E. Howard Hunt and Gordon Liddy. He revealed a startling piece of information he was told by ex-

CIA agent Hunt, quoted at the beginning of this chapter. The conversation went like this:[371]

Caddy to Hunt: *"Why was John Kennedy assassinated?"*

Hunt: *"John Kennedy was assassinated because he was about to give our most vital secret to the Soviets."*

Caddy: *"What was that?"*

Hunt: *"The alien presence."*

Conclusion: Who Killed JFK?

In summary, the evidence shows that Dulles gave the ultimate directive to kill Kennedy, while Angleton carried it out as the mastermind who aligned with Israel to take care of the implementation and coverup. The MJ-12 group's assassination directive gave Angleton a license to kill. With Angleton at the CIA in charge of deciding what information the Warren Commission would get, and LBJ as president in the White House, the Zionists had people in key positions of power during the post mortem investigations. They seeded the JFK operation with numerous patsies and decoy events so as to muddy the waters. They made sure that whatever narrative was amplified to explain the event – the absurd 'lone nut' and 'magic bullet' theory of the Warren Commission, the 'Castro did it' theory, the 'Nazis did it' theory, the 'Soviets did it' theory and the 'Mafia did it' theory – that none of them led back to Israel.

Nonetheless, the truth has been out for a long time. It was the hero whistleblower Mordechai Vanunu (introduced in the last chapter) who was quoted in a 2004 interview as saying that there were *"near-certain indications"* that JFK was killed due to the *"pressure he exerted on then head of government, David Ben-*

Gurion, to shed light on Dimona's nuclear reactor." He went on to say that *"we do not know which irresponsible Israeli Prime Minister will take office and decide to use nuclear weapons in the struggle against neighboring Arab countries ... what has already been exposed about the weapons Israel is holding can destroy the region and kill millions."*[372] Former Libyan leader Muammar Gaddafi gave a 2009 speech to the UN in which he said that JFK was killed by Israel due to the struggle over the Dimona inspections.[373]

When we weave it all together, we make a tapestry that can be summarized as follows: JFK was sacrificed at a certain place on a certain day in a public black magic ritual, carried out by the Mob/ Mafia, French assassins, the CIA and the Mossad/Israel, covered up by the FBI, ultimately due to his pressure on Israel and his insistence on gaining control over the UFO/ET issue. Many of the actors involved were Masons. The Cult had their agents inside the key positions of power locally and federally to ensure that both the murder and the coverup could be executed without the true masterminds or even the hitmen getting discovered or arrested. There are even more UFO/ET-Israeli connections to be made for curious researchers in this field. For example, John Lear asserts that Ben Rich, engineer at Lockheed Martin's secretive Skunk Works division that develops stealth aircraft (based on reverse engineered technology taken from crashed UFOs), said that Rich was a Mossad agent.[374] If true, this shows the interlocking nature of the Cult at the very highest levels.

RFK

The murder of RFK was another Zionist Cult operation. What distinguishes this assassination is that it was the first time that Israel carried out its signature false flag operation – committing a crime

Image #76: Robert F. Kennedy

then framing an Arab or Muslim as the guilty party – on American soil. I discuss this signature false flag operation more in chapter 12. The unfortunate patsy who took the blame was the innocent and mind-controlled Sirhan Sirhan, a Christian Palestinian man originally from Jerusalem.

The motive for Israel to kill RFK was not quite as strong as it was for JFK, however RFK was massively popular and on his way to becoming president. The Kennedy brothers were incredibly close and loyal to each other; John made Robert not only his Attorney General but also his most trusted adviser, even on matters outside of the purview of Attorney General, including foreign policy and military affairs. As previously discussed, at John's direction, Bobby was pushing AZC/AIPAC to register under FARA and pursuing prosecutions of mob and organized crime agents, many of whom were linked to Zionist kingpin Meyer Lansky. Robert was strongly pro-peace and was speaking out against the Vietnam War, which had become increasingly unpopular. RFK was not afraid to criticize Israeli interests and dual loyalty publicly, as in this interview published in 1988 by the John F. Kennedy Library, where he refers to Myer Feldman. Robert recalled that John *"had valued Feldman's work"* but then added his opinion that *"His [Feldman's] major interest was Israel rather than the United States."*[375] Unsatisfied with the Warren Commission report, there can be little doubt that Robert would have done everything in his power to investigate – and avenge – the murder of his elder brother. This the Cult could not allow.

Israel has put out a lot of propaganda, both then and now, that Bobby Kennedy was pro-Israel. This is a Cult tactic to give Israel an alibi and make it appear as though RFK was Israel's friend, in which case Israel would have had no motive to kill him. It bolsters the cover story that Sirhan was the beginning of Islamic terrorism in America … despite this story being nonsensical, since Sirhan was Christian not Muslim. It is true that RFK had promised to give Israel 50 fighter jets during his presidential campaign (as mentioned by Sirhan in a 1989 interview[376]), but American politicians say lots of things during election season to get votes. That is just how the game is played in American politics.

An interesting difference between RFK and JFK was that RFK had already been befriended by Chabad Lubavitch, the orthodox and ultra-Zionist messianic sect of Judaism described earlier. Chabad wields extraordinary influence worldwide and in America. Its former leader Rebbe Menachem Mendel Schneerson (see chapter 2 for his Jewish supremacist quotes) influenced many US politicians, including Robert Kennedy. In fact, according to a tweet by RFK Jr. himself,[377] his father considered the Rebbe *"a spiritual mentor and sought his advice on diverse issues of morality and ethics. He once visited the Rebbe at 2 o'clock in the morning!"* On the Chabad website, you can see a picture of Bobby Kennedy wearing a yarmulke (Jewish religious cap) sitting down in conversation with the Rebbe.[378]

Nonetheless, the evidence points strongly in the direction that it was Israel who killed RFK. The patsy Sirhan was not the one who fired the fatal bullet. According to the autopsy report by Chief

Medical Examiner-Coroner Thomas Noguchi, RFK succumbed to fatal wounds received from bullets fired from behind the right ear at point blank range following an upward angle, yet Sirhan was in front of Kennedy at all times and was five to six feet away from his target when he fired. The Pruszynski recording,[379] released in 2004, was an audio recording made by freelance newspaper reporter Stanislaw Pruszynski, who accidentally turned his recorder back on after taping RFK's California Primary victory speech. It found that 13 bullets in total were fired at RFK, including five bullets from a second gun, but Sirhan's revolver only carried eight. Witnesses claimed there were two shooters. The second shooter was Thane Eugene Cesar, hired by Jew Junius Myer Shine of the Ambassador Hotel. Cesar's gun was never inspected; he was never interrogated; he was known to have hated the Kennedys; and he sold his gun after the assassination. Another key point is that RFK was never meant to take the route he took through the kitchen. A member of RFK's team repeatedly insisted that Kennedy exit the hotel this way. Who? Jew Frank Mankiewicz, who had started his career at the LA office of the ADL of B'nai B'rith.

In her book *A Lie Too Big to Fail: The Real History of the Assassination of Robert F. Kennedy*, Author Lisa Pease showed the ballistics evidence was clearly manipulated and concealed to promote the absurd official narrative, as well as photos, door jambs and ceiling tiles being destroyed. Pease recently stated in November 2023 that *"if you want to make the case for the Mossad killing a Kennedy, there's a stronger case to be made that they were involved in the RFK assassination. The patsy [Sirhan Sirhan] (who is firing blanks, not bullets, in a hypnotic state, thinking he was firing at targets on a range) was Palestinian. One of the on-site organizers at the*

Ambassador Hotel was purportedly from Israel. James Angleton, the Mossad contact in the CIA, ended up with a set of the RFK assassination autopsy photos. The other shooters, except for the security guard, who was CIA, bore a resemblance to Sirhan and could've come from the Middle East as well."[380]

In his 1988 book *The Senator Must Die*, ex-CIA contract agent Robert Morrow put forward the theory that the RFK assassination was a CIA contract hit executed by the SAVAK (Bureau for Intelligence and Security of the State), the secret police of the Shah of Iran. The SAVAK was an intelligence agency created in 1957 by the CIA, the SDECE and the Mossad in the 1950s, shortly after the CIA had pulled off the Operation Ajax coup d'état in 1953 to oust Prime Minister Mohammad Mosaddegh and install the Shah. Although it was formally disbanded in 1979 after the Shah was deposed and Iran underwent an Islamic revolution, Mossad still retains very close ties to current Iranian intelligence – despite the Israeli-Iranian tension and 12-Day War of June 2025 which was more performative and symbolic than a real war (see chapter 18). Israel and Iran continued their strong connections behind the scenes during the 1980s when Israel covertly sold arms to Iran to help it during its 8-year long war with Iraq. The two countries share a strong suspicion and dislike of the Arab nations on their borders. Piper wrote:[381]

In charge of the CIA's training of SAVAK operatives was an operation known as the International Police Academy in Washington. This academy also played a major part in training operatives of Israel's Mossad. The academy was run by one Joseph Shimon, a man with additional interesting connections. Shimon counted among his close friends Chicago Mafia boss Sam Giancana and the Mafia's roving ambassador, Johnny Roselli ...

The truth is that Sirhan was not the 'first instance of Islamic terrorism on American soil' but rather one of the first instances of a mind-controlled assassin on American soil. In my previous books I have discussed how the use of mind-controlled assassins and sex slaves sprung from the CIA's MKUltra program that ran (officially) from 1953 to 1971. Many have thought up until recently that it was the Nazis, brought en masse to the US under Operation Paperclip, who joined the CIA and ran the MKUltra program. But was it the Nazis inside the CIA … or other forces? The Cult is brilliant at obfuscation and misdirection; Jewish power frequently hides behind 'evil Nazis' or 'evil Communists' to avoid detection. Kudos to Laurent Guyénot[382] for pointing out that it was actually Dr. Sidney Gottlieb, son of Hungarian Jewish immigrant parents, who was running MKUltra, where the CIA was researching to what extent a hypnotized subject could be commanded or controlled to perform a particular action, such as kill another human being, then forget about it completely.[383] The CIA indeed demonstrated this and many other similar things were entirely possible. If the Jewish Gottlieb was running MKUltra for so long, and Israel already had men inside the CIA like Angleton who were Zionist moles, what are the chances that they didn't gain access to this mind control knowhow?

Mind control works by establishing new personalities or 'alters' in the mind of the victim, often via drugs, abuse or torture. These alters are then programmed to be completely separate from each other, compartmentalized by an amnesiac barrier, like files in a filing cabinet. In this way, when one alter is activated by a trigger (which could be a word, a smell, a sound, a symbol, or anything at all), the other alters are deactivated and take a backseat while the triggered or activated alter runs the show. Then, it is deactivated and another one is brought forth, all without the person knowing. It is literally like different people are inside of the one person, which is why mind control victims are said to suffer from MPD (Multiple Personality Disorder) or DID (Dissociative Identity Disorder). Their core personality and identity has been attacked and hijacked. To make matters worse, the victim can be programmed with amnesia (to forget or deny real memories) while simultaneously believing that implanted false memories (inserted by the handlers) actually happened. This destroys their sense of reality and makes it very difficult for them to know the truth of who they are and what actions they committed. This very much played out in the case of Sirhan who claims to have no memory of things leading up to the shooting. There was a notebook found in Sirhan's bedroom that contained repetitive lines which Sirhan recognizes as his own handwriting but does not remember writing. This is suggestive of hypnotically induced automatic writing. Guyénot writes:[384]

In 2008, Harvard University professor Daniel Brown, a noted expert in hypnosis and trauma memory loss, interviewed Sirhan for a total of 60 hours, and concluded that Sirhan, whom he classified among 'high hypnotizables,' acted involuntarily under the effect of hypnotic suggestion: "His firing of the gun was neither under his voluntary control, nor done with conscious knowledge, but is likely a product of automatic hypnotic behavior and coercive control."

There is some evidence of Israeli foreknowledge of the RFK assassination. Israeli tour guides told American tourists that RFK had been assassinated months before he actually had been, although they stated the places were Milwaukee and Nebraska, not Los Angeles where he was actually killed.[385] An astonishing piece of noteworthy evidence comes from Bergman's *Rise and Kill First: The Secret*

History of Israel's Targeted Assassinations. He reveals that Israel in the 1960s was indeed devising plans to take Palestinians and turn them into mind-controlled assassins. He writes that an Israeli military psychologist called Benyamin Shalit carried out a plan in May 1968 where he took a Palestinian member of Fatah, then, based on the 1962 film *The Manchurian Candidate*, tried to *"brainwash and hypnotize him into becoming a programmed killer"* aimed at Yasser Arafat.[386] This occurred just one month before RFK was killed!

Sadly, the Cult long ago got to RFK Jr., son of RFK and nephew of JFK. RFK Jr. briefly ran for president in 2024 before joining the Trump campaign and accepting a cabinet position as Secretary of HHS. One of his first priorities as the health minister was to … combat antisemitism. Antisemitism a problem for health? You can't make this stuff up. RFK Jr. blames 'the CIA' for the murder of his uncle, but chooses to ignore the all-important truth of Mossad influence over the CIA. He believes Sirhan is innocent, and blames Thane Eugene Cesar alone for the murder of his father, overlooking the Israeli orchestration of the entire assassination. The case of RFK Jr. is a stellar example of the deeply sinister and sick nature of the Cult. They befriended and brainwashed him from a young age to see Israel as 'the only democracy in the Middle East' and to falsely equate all Palestinians with Hamas – while killing his father and uncle. Even today, with all the information about these events online and in books for those who want the truth, RFK Jr. apparently doesn't realize the real force that killed his dad beyond the name of Thane Eugene Cesar.[387]

JFK Jr

There is no such thing as a 'Kennedy curse' which is superstitious nonsense put out by the Cult to obscure their role in killing JFK and

RFK – as well as JFK's son, John Kennedy Jr. JFK Jr. died in a plane crash in 1999. Strangely enough, or not, he took an interest in internal Israeli politics, which signaled that he may well have suspected the real force behind his father's death. He was publishing his magazine called *George* and, in one issue, he published a letter written by the mother of the assassin of Israeli PM Yitzhak Rabin who was murdered in 1995. Piper found evidence that the Mossad was involved in the 'accidental' plane crash of JFK Jr.:[388]

Image #77: John F. Kennedy Jr.

Adams reported that writer C. David Heymann had told her that ten days before the fatal crash, he and JFK Jr. had spoken and that JFK Jr. had expressed misgivings about the upcoming airplane flight (even though, by all other accounts, young Kennedy was quite enthusiastic about his new hobby). What created the buzz about possible Mossad involvement was the report by both The New York Post and USA Today that Heymann was a U.S.-Israeli dual citizen who said that he had told young Kennedy, some years ago, that during the 1980s he (Heymann) had actually worked for the Mossad. It was for this reason that Kennedy had approached Heymann about doing a story for George on the Mossad —according to Heymann.

Adding to the confirmation of Mossad involvement in this is the fact that Peter Goelz, later head of the National Transportation Safety

Board (NTSB), was the one investigating the JFK Jr. crash.[389] Goelz was the NTSB spokesman after 9/11, which reveals an interesting connection between one of the Kennedy assassinations and the 9/11 false flag operation. The NTSB officially investigates the cause of air crashes, so why wouldn't the Cult have an agent in that organization, given how much they like to knock people off via 'accidental' plane crashes? Researcher Christopher Bollyn discovered that Goelz was linked to Israeli military intelligence agent Ehud Mendelson, and was vice president of Mendelson's US Aviation Technology company that specialized in … aircraft remote control technology (this will become highly relevant in chapter 14).

Watergate: The Same Force that Killed the Kennedys also Dethroned Nixon

There is an interesting connection between the JFK assassination and Watergate: some of the Watergate burglars (E. Howard Hunt and Frank Sturgis) were also involved in the JFK assassination. Going deeply into Watergate is beyond the scope of this book, but there is every indication that the same force that took out JFK also dethroned Nixon, only this time, they decided rather than killing him to force him to resign, a far less risky and conspicuous operation. Like many US presidents before and after him, Nixon did a lot of things to help Israel. However, the Cult doesn't care about your past record. At a certain point Nixon, like Kennedy before him, was perceived to be an impediment to Israel's wellbeing and survival. Therefore, the Watergate operation was set into motion to remove him from the White House. Once he sensed trouble, Nixon tried to blackmail the CIA, threatening then Director Richard Helms that he (Nixon) would expose the CIA's involvement in the JFK assassination if Helms didn't use his influence over the FBI to call off the investigation into the Watergate burglars.[390] As CIA chief, Helms had more power than a US president, and he wasn't about to let Nixon tell the public about the CIA's role in the murder.

Netanyahu Invokes the "Grassy Knoll"

In a story from 2014, Mondoweiss reported that Netanyahu gave a speech in Hebrew where he was defending himself against an Obama Administration official who had called him *"chickenshit."* Here is how a certain paragraph of his speech was translated:[391]

Netanyahu told Knesset: 'When there are pressures on Israel to concede its security, the easiest thing to do is to concede. You get a round of applause, ceremonies on grassy knolls, and then come the missiles and the tunnels.'

In America, the phrase 'grassy knoll' means one thing: Dealey Plaza and the assassination of JFK. No one uses that very unique and colloquial term to mean anything else. It's part of the American lexicon. What are the chances that Netanyahu, who grew up partly in the US and speaks impeccable English, didn't know this? The chances are 0%. Was this a veiled threat against another US president by Cult mouthpiece and agent Netanyahu?

The Very Word Secrecy is Repugnant in a Free and Open Society

In investigating the JFK assassination, it is inadequate to simply say 'the CIA did it' without explaining the interconnectedness between the Mafia and CIA, and the Mossad and the CIA, and without explaining the motivations and power of the factions controlling the CIA. In this chapter I have shown that the interests and agenda of two powerful factions – Israel and MJ-12 – coincided, then coalesced into the plan to kill Kennedy. The men representing these dark forces and responsible for the ultimate decision and implementation to eliminate JFK were Allen Dulles and James Angleton. History demonstrates that the people opposed to Israeli objectives and UFO secrecy (Forrestal and Kennedy) were the killed, while the people who supported Israeli objectives and UFO secrecy (Angleton and Johnson) were the killers.

JFK didn't like secrets being kept from the public – as he said in his speech he called *The President and the Press*:[392]

The very word 'secrecy' is repugnant in a free and open society; and we are as a people, inherently and historically, opposed to secret societies, to secret oaths and to secret proceedings.

The *"monolithic and ruthless conspiracy"* to which JFK alluded got him in the end. It's high time to end the secrecy and expose what force really murdered him. At the highest level, the Kennedys' killers are still on the loose.

Sources

[278] https://www.maryferrell.org/showDoc.html?docId=10490#relPageId=363

[279] The Devil's Chessboard: Allen Dulles, the CIA, and the Rise of America's Secret Government

[280] https://www.youtube.com/watch?v=z-x5XNET4to

[281] https://www.archives.gov/files/research/jfk/releases/2025/0318/104-10014-10064.pdf

[282] https://www.youtube.com/watch?v=N33kgE2ToSo

[283] Final Judgment, pg. 424

[284] https://majesticdocuments.com/pdf/truman_forrestal.pdf

[285] https://nsarchive.gwu.edu/document/32910-1-arthur-schlesinger-jr-president-kennedy-cia-reorganization-secret-june-10-1961-5

[286] https://www.reddit.com/r/Mafia/comments/u0ievt/lucky_luciano_the_mafia_and_the_cia/

[287] https://www.nsa.gov/portals/75/documents/news-features/declassified-documents/jfk/jfk00067.pdf

[288] The Other Side of Deception, pg. 280

[289] https://www.unrwa.org/content/resolution-194

[290] https://www.israellobby.org/AZCDOJ/P6100127redorder/default.asp

[291] https://www.israellobby.org/zoa/DOJ-149-1603-ZOA/default.asp

[292] https://www.israellobby.org/AZCDOJ/

[293] https://mondoweiss.net/2022/08/theres-a-long-tradition-of-describing-israel-lobbys-power-so-long-as-you-dont-criticize-it/

[294] https://www.israelnationalnews.com/news/396877

[295] https://www.archives.gov/files/research/jfk/releases/2022/docid-32423393.pdf

---

[296] https://www.motherjones.com/media/2015/10/book-review-devils-chessboard-david-talbot/

[297] https://www.maryferrell.org/showDoc.html?docId=1164#relPageId=78

[298] https://www.archives.gov/files/research/jfk/releases/2025/0318/124-10326-10103.pdf

[299] https://www.kennedysandking.com/john-f-kennedy-articles/james-jesus-angleton-and-the-kennedy-assassination-part-1

[300] https://web.archive.org/web/20051022001739/ajweberman.com/nodules2/nodulec5.htm

[301] https://www.youtube.com/watch?v=zi9JIctV-Hk

[302] https://www.youtube.com/watch?v=zi9JIctV-Hk

[303] https://www.cia.gov/readingroom/docs/CIA-RDP91-00561R000100090036-3.pdf

[304] The Ghost: The Secret Life of CIA Spymaster James Jesus Angleton, Jefferson Morley

[305] The Ghost: The Secret Life of CIA Spymaster James Jesus Angleton, pg. 171

[306] https://www.archives.gov/files/research/jfk/releases/2025/0318/124-10326-10100.pdf

[307] https://www.archives.gov/files/research/jfk/releases/2025/0318/124-10326-10104.pdf

[308] Ibid, pg.92

[309] https://www.linkedin.com/pulse/jfk-2022-documents-cias-james-angleton-running-covert-cruickshank

[310] https://x.com/KarlGolovin/status/1911586604193394942

[311] https://www.timesofisrael.com/new-jfk-documents-reveal-assassins-cia-monitor-was-jewish-spy-reuben-efron/

[312] Final Judgement, pg. 225

[313] Final Judgment, pg. 333

---

[314] Final Judgment, pg. 341

[315] https://earthnewspaper.com/mark-r-elsis/israel-assassinated-president-john-f-kennedy-by-mark-r-elsis/

[316] https://ia801207.us.archive.org/26/items/nsia-KatzwinkelAnita/nsia-KatzwinkelAnita/Katzenbach%20Nicholas%20deB/Katzenbach%20Nicholas%20DeB%2007_text.pdf

[317] https://www.maryferrell.org/pages/Walkthrough_-_Formation_of_the_Warren_Commission.html

[318] https://x.com/BasedSamParker/status/1902461124970475683

[319] Final Judgment, pg. 193

[320] Final Judgment, Photo Section (pg. 558 of eBook)

[321] Final Judgment, pg. 146

[322] Final Judgment, pg. 199

[323] Final Judgment, pg. 446

[324] https://www.jpost.com/features/a-friend-in-deed

[325] https://www.bitchute.com/video/AeNAeJZgDcDJ

[326] https://x.com/RogerJStoneJr/status/1902170097982099696

[327] https://www.archives.gov/files/research/jfk/releases/docid-32149267.pdf

[328] https://www.jfk-assassination.net/russ/testimony/ruby_j1.htm

[329] Ibid.

[330] https://cairnsnews.org/2024/12/21/so-what-was-yitzak-rabin-doing-in-dallas-the-day-of-jfks-assassination/

[331] Final Judgment, pg. 182-3

[332] Final Judgment, pg. 176

[333] https://www.cia.gov/readingroom/docs/CIA-RDP99-01448R000401580066-9.pdf

[334] https://www.bitchute.com/video/fRsk6DDWgfSY

---

335 https://www.youtube.com/watch?v=ViFo2D4KFHg

336 Final Judgment, pg. 299

337 https://archive.org/details/katharinegreatka00davi/page/n5/mode/2up

338 Final Judgment, pg. 235

339 Final Judgment, pg. 300

340 Final Judgment, pg. 236

341 https://www.bitchute.com/video/GcZEtPIyLP3L

342 The Squad: The US Government's Secret Alliance With Organized Crime, 1990, Michael Milan

343 https://ratical.org/ratville/JFK/introAB.html

344 https://www.youtube.com/watch?v=F1FVZksUiZw

345 https://www.c-span.org/clip/qa/user-clip-secret-service-confusion-at-love-field-explained/3997797

346 https://spartacus-educational.com/JFKoperation40.htm

347 https://freemasonry.bcy.ca/biography/zapruder_a/zapruder_a.html

348 https://majesticdocuments.com/pdf/ipu_report.pdf

349 https://majesticdocuments.com/pdf/truman_forrestal.pdf

350 Kennedy's Last Stand, pg. 25

351 https://www.bibliotecapleyades.net/sociopolitica/esp_sociopol_mj12_4_1.htm

352 https://www.youtube.com/watch?v=JlP1fqyzGv8

353 https://www.bitchute.com/video/duiiMADIbvcE

354 https://www.presidency.ucsb.edu/documents/executive-order-10920-revoking-executive-order-no-10700-february-25-1957-amended

355 https://majesticdocuments.com/wp-content/uploads/2022/08/kennedy_ciadirector_1.pdf

356 https://www.jfklibrary.org/asset-viewer/archives/jfknsf-330-007

[357] https://majesticdocuments.com/pdf/burnedmemo-s1-pgs1-2.pdf

[358] https://majesticdocuments.com/pdf/burnedmemo-s1-pgs3-9.pdf

[359] Kennedy's Last Stand, pg. 121

[360] https://majesticdocuments.com/pdf/mj12opsreview-dulles-61.pdf

[361] https://majesticdocuments.com/pdf/kennedy_cia.pdf

[362] https://www.archives.gov/files/research/jfk/releases/2022/104-10338-10005.pdf

[363] https://www.reddit.com/r/UFOs/comments/1amcvhc/an_august_3rd_1962_cia_document_possibly_proves/

[364] https://majesticdocuments.com/pdf/umbra.pdf

[365] https://www.spacewar.com/news/russia-97h.html

[366] https://www.jfklibrary.org/asset-viewer/archives/jfknsf-342-015#?image_identifier=JFKNSF-342-015-p0003

[367] https://www.bitchute.com/video/otENXuVCCZc7

[368] https://www.scribd.com/document/233187424/The-Unspoken-Speech-of-John-F-Kennedy

[369] https://magazine.utdallas.edu/the-jfk-connection/

[370] en.wikipedia.org/wiki/Detlev_Bronk

[371] https://www.youtube.com/watch?v=z-x5XNET4to

[372] https://www.indymedia.org.uk/en/2004/07/295523.html?c=on

[373] https://www.bitchute.com/video/xwaOkXkHljr9

[374] https://www.bitchute.com/video/rpjZ49Vfbu8r

[375] https://mondoweiss.net/2008/11/rfk-accused-jfks-deputy-counsel-of-dual-loyalty-his-major-interest-was-israel-rather-than-the-united-states/

[376] https://web.archive.org/web/20131114222307/https://www.nytimes.com/1989/02/20/us/sirhan-felt-betrayed-by-kennedy.html

[377] https://x.com/RobertKennedyJr/status/1831511198539657236

[378] https://www.chabad.org/news/article_cdo/aid/4053159/jewish/50-Years-Later-Robert-F-Kennedy-and-the-Rebbe.htm

[379] https://justiceforrfk.com/evidence/audio-recording.html

[380] https://x.com/lisapease/status/1724102667134505099

[381] Final Judgment, pp. 777-8

[382] https://www.unz.com/article/did-israel-kill-the-kennedies/

[383] https://www.wanttoknow.info/bluebird10pg

[384] https://www.unz.com/article/rfks-false-flag-assassination-and-the-forgotten-palestinian-patsy/

[385] https://www.ynetnews.com/article/skztazbyxg

[386] Rise and Kill First, pp.118-9

[387] https://www.sfchronicle.com/opinion/openforum/article/Robert-F-Kennedy-Jr-Sirhan-Sirhan-didn-t-16686114.php

[388] Final Judgment, pg. 585

[389] https://oneillandassoc.com/associate/peter-goelz

[390] https://www.politico.com/news/magazine/2022/06/05/nixon-helms-cia-jfk-assassination-00037232

[391] https://mondoweiss.net/2014/10/netanyahus-respond-chickenshit/

[392] https://www.jfklibrary.org/archives/other-resources/john-f-kennedy-speeches/american-newspaper-publishers-association-19610427

CHAPTER 12: CULT SPECIALITIES: SPYING, HACKING, BLACKMAIL, SEX RINGS, TERRORISM, ASSASSINATION AND THE SIGNATURE FALSE FLAG OP

"(The) resultant breakdown of moral order and humanity are a direct result of the kind of megalomania that characterizes the operation of the Mossad. That's where it all begins. This feeling that you can do anything you want to whomever you want for as long as you want because you have the power."

– Ex-Mossad Agent Victor Ostrovsky[393]

"He'd cut the non-prosecution deal with one of Epstein's attorneys because he had 'been told' to back off, that Epstein was above his pay grade. "I was told Epstein 'belonged to intelligence' and to leave it alone ..."

– Journalist Vicky Ward, writing about lawyer Alexander Acosta who cut Epstein a sweetheart non-prosecution plea deal in 2007[394]

"See, fucking around is not a crime. It could be embarrassing, but it's not a crime. But fucking a fourteen-year-old girl is a crime. And he [Epstein] was taking photos of politicians fucking fourteen-year-old girls – if you want to get it straight. They [Epstein and Maxwell] would just blackmail people."

– Ex-Aman (Israeli Military Intelligence) Agent Ari Ben-Menashe[395]

The Cult had its own country, but things were not without difficulty. Manipulating a country as a special interest group is one thing, but surviving as a country in the big league, among other countries, is another thing. Israel was surrounded by large countries – large in terms of geographical land area, population and power – who took a very dim view of its blatant dispossession and murder of the Palestinians. The Zionists ruling Israel attempted to change this in all three areas. Right from the start, even before Israel declared itself a nation in 1948, they set about gaining as much land as possible, which necessarily meant stealing it from the Palestinians. Population-wise, they encouraged as many Jews as possible from Europe to emigrate; their fixation was upon building a 'Jewish state' with a Jewish majority. Israel did allow some Palestinians and Arabs to become Israeli citizens, but they have always been second class citizens. Their great fear has been that Israeli Arabs would outnumber Israeli Jews, and hence that the Zionists would become a minority in 'their' own country, which they could not allow. They have always wanted to give the appearance of being a 'Jewish, democratic country' even though behind the scenes they have manipulated the population demographics to ensure the Jews retain a majority and thus political control.

The last area – power – is the most interesting, and is the focus of this chapter. Being small in terms of land area and population has forced Israel to invest its money, efforts and talent into increasing its power. That way, despite being small in other areas, it would still be a force to be reckoned with. In chapter 10, I already covered how this obsession with power led to Israel acquiring nukes. In chapter 11, I covered how this obsession with power led to Israel developing the will and ability to assassinate world leaders. In this chapter, we will look at how Israel developed itself into a powerhouse, now having the dubious distinction of becoming a world leader, or the world leader, in spying, hacking, blackmail (especially sexual blackmail), pedophilia, assassinations and false flag operations. With little or seemingly no restraints on its behavior, Israel has gone on to terrorize nations nearby and manipulate larger ones farther away to elicit the ire of almost the entire world.

1. Spying Galore

Israel has several intelligence agencies: Aman (military intelligence, part of the IDF), Shin Bet (a.k.a. Shabak, internal security) and the Mossad. Aman contains units within it such as the infamous Unit 8200 (the Central Collection Unit of the Intelligence Corps or Israeli SIGINT [Signals Intelligence]). Shin Bet functions in a similar way to the American FBI where it covers internal matters and is not (in theory anyway) supposed to be involved with foreign spying or operations. In the previous chapter, I discussed how the Mossad began its special relationship with the CIA when Israeli leaders asserted that they aligned with the US and the West, not with Russia. They then started feeding the US secret intelligence on the Soviets under the condition that they would never reveal their sources.

Image #78: the logo and motto of the Mossad: by way of deception, thou shalt do war

The feeding of intelligence in certain ways, at certain times, to certain nations is the art of using knowledge as a weapon. It is no surprise that the nefarious Rothschilds are and always have been at the center of this. Australian Roland Perry, author of the 1990 book *The Fifth Man: The Soviet Super Spy*, revealed that it was none other than the third baron of the manipulative Rothschild family, the late Victor Rothschild, who was the 'fifth man' of the Cambridge spy group. Rothschild died in 1990, was a member of British House of Lords and was a high level MI5 intelligence agent. Perry's extensive research shows that Rothschild was a super spy who sabotaged Western intelligence for 20 years after WWII. A Cold War is only possible with a balance of powers; to achieve that stalemate, both sides need to have the same technology. It was Rothschild who was behind the transfer of the world's most secret technology (nuclear weapons) to the USSR. In true Rothschild fashion, he got Stalin to support Israel, because the Rothschild-controlled West had done so much to help the Soviets during WWII.

Meanwhile, despite the US-Israeli intelligence relationship beginning in a mutually beneficial way, Israeli espionage soon reached epic proportions, and it was unafraid to bite the hand that fed it. In chapters 10 and 11, I discussed how Israel stole both nuclear technological secrets and nuclear material from NUMEC (with the help of Angleton) – directly from the United States, its chief benefactor. From the 1960s onwards, Israeli spying continued and intensified. In the 1980s, Israel was involved in at least two big profile episodes or scandals. The first involved a piece of software called PROMIS that was developed by a company called Inslaw led by former NSA software programmer Bill Hamilton. PROMIS was an acronym formed from Prosecutors Management Information System and was a case management system for use in law enforcement record keeping. PROMIS could read and integrate different programs and databases simultaneously regardless of operating system. PROMIS was an early software forerunner of what companies today like Palantir are trying to do – build massive centralized databases that track every aspect of a person's life. Palantir is partially owned by Cult agent Peter Thiel – the same Peter Thiel who is a Bilderberg Steering Committee member and funder of James Vance, Trump's vice president. Thiel exerts a ton of influence/ control over the Trump Administration. According to this source,[396] it was Barry Kumnick who programmed a backdoor into PROMIS before it got stolen, unbeknown even to the owners of Inslaw, Bill and Nancy Hamilton. In January 1991, NSA agent Alan Standorf who allegedly discovered a connection between PROMIS and the Bank of Credit and Commerce International (BCCI) was found dead. PROMIS became too successful for its own good. An article on ConsortiumNews.com by Richard Fricker states:[397]

The Reagan administration was very taken with the Inslaw version of PROMIS. In March 1982 Inslaw was awarded $9.6 million to install the program in 20 U.S. Attorney's offices, with further installations in the remaining 74 offices, if successful. This would be the last government contact the Hamiltons would receive, not because the system failed quite the contrary, it was too successful. Hamilton explained, 'We developed it originally just for prosecutors. But some of our users wanted to have it shared with the courts and the police. So, the software was engineered to make it adaptable. In making it highly adaptable, a byproduct was to make it useable for non-prosecutor tracking and that made it adaptable totally outside the criminal justice system.'

U.S. Department of Justice

Office of the Associate Attorney General

Washington, D.C. 20530

March 16, 1994

Dr. Joseph Ben-Orr
P.O. Box 1143
Jerusalem, Israel 91010

Dear Dr. Ben-Orr:

This letter shall constitute a receipt for the materials provided by you to Neil MacNeil of the American Consulate in Jerusalem on behalf of the United States Department of Justice. I have asked Mr. MacNeil to provide this letter to you upon receiving a magnetic tape which you claim to have received from the Department of Justice in 1983 and which purportedly contains a software program known as PROMIS.

Furthermore, at your request, the Department of Justice waives any claims it may have against you arising from or related to your possession of the above referenced tape.

Sincerely,

John C. Dwyer
Assistant Associate Attorney General

Image #79: some of the evidence trail showing how the Israelis got their hands on PROMIS

It became obvious with the latest round of modifications any data system could be integrated into PROMIS. And those data systems could interact that is, combine with each other forming a massive tracking data base of people via government documents such as birth and death certificates, licenses, mortgages, lawsuits or anything else kept in a data base. PROMIS could also track banking transactions, arms shipments, communications, airplane parts ...

Inslaw sued the DOJ in 1986, alleging that the Feds had conspired to put Inslaw out of business through deceit by withholding payments to them – and then pirating their software. Inslaw ultimately lost the case after 12 years. Coincidentally (or not), then US Attorney General Bill Barr was involved, whose name crops up later in connection with sex trafficker Jeffrey Epstein. What links Israel to Inslaw/PROMIS is that the DOJ gave a pirated copy to the Israelis – to Rafi Eitan, who was at that time head of Lakam (who had also been in the Haganah and the Palmach), mentioned in chapter 10. Lakam collected foreign scientific and technical intelligence abroad, particularly for Israel's nuclear program, but was disbanded in 1986 after the second scandal – the spying and theft of Jonathan Pollard (more on this shortly). Journalist Danny Casolaro was 'suicided' in 1991 for getting too close to the truth on this matter after he received information from Hamilton and also from Michael Riconosciuto, who alleged that backdoors had been inserted into the software so that whoever bought or received a copy of it from the DOJ could be spied upon. But of course – this is exactly why Israel wanted the software! Declassified DOJ documents released by the National Archives confirm that a copy of PROMIS software was given to a 'Dr. Joseph Ben-Orr' which, upon closer examination, turned out to be an alias for Rafi Eitan.[398]

In his book *Profits of War: Inside the Secret U.S.-Israeli Arms Network*, Ari Ben-Menashe adds further firsthand knowledge about what PROMIS could do and how it was spread to the world with trap doors added:[399]

A nation's spy organization would buy Promis and have it installed in its computers at headquarters. Using a modem, the spy network would then tap into the computers of such services as the telephone company, the water board, other utility commissions, credit card companies, etc. Promis would then search for specific information. For example, if a person suddenly started using more water and more electricity and making more phone calls than usual, it might be suspected he had guests staying with him. Promis would then start searching for the records of his friends and associates, and if it was found that one had stopped using electricity and water, it might be assumed, based on other records stored in Promis, that the missing person was staying with the subject of the investigation ... Rafi Eitan did not want to risk having a trap door developed in Israel. Word might leak back that the Israelis had been bugging software and then handing it out to others. He didn't even suggest that the NSA develop the trap door because he had a great sense of national pride. As far as he was concerned, it was Israel's idea and would remain so. Yet it still had to be kept secret. Eitan decided it would be best if a computer whiz could be found outside the country ... The CIA group that was to use Promis had not handed the program back to the NSA to have the trap door fitted by them for the simple reason that they didn't want the NSA to know about it – interagency competition was fierce. Only this small CIA group, headed by Robert Gates – who was to become head of the Central Intelligence Agency in October 1991 – was in on the secret. So we now had a small group in Israel and a small group in the U.S. that knew about the trap door. The next step for both Israel and the United States was to find a neutral company through which the doctored Promis program could be sold. It was agreed that the head of the company had to be a man who could be trusted to keep intelligence secrets, who had contacts with both Western and East Bloc countries and who had a respected businessman's image. The man they came up with was Robert Maxwell.

In a nutshell, PROMIS was a spy's dream come true, a piece of software that could read and integrate multiple sources of data from multiple programs. The Reagan Administration seeded PROMIS throughout the world so that the Cult's top agencies (the CIA and Mossad) could have backdoors to all other nations. PROMIS is the perfect software to run in banks and for cryptocurrency – who knows just how far this software has infiltrated the world's computer systems?

The second Israeli spying scandal of the 1980s involved the American Zionist Jonathan Pollard, a former US Navy intelligence analyst who got caught selling or giving massive amounts of classified information in 1984 to various countries, chiefly Israel. Some of this material included the NSA's ten-volume manual detailing how the US gathers its SIGINT. He was busted in 1985, and then in 1987 was sentenced to life in prison. Israel tried many times to get the US Government to release Pollard early, but to no avail, until 2015, when he was finally released. In 2020, when his parole expired and all restrictions were eliminated, Pollard subsequently emigrated to Israel and settled in Jerusalem, renouncing his US citizenship. His chief handler was Rafi Eitan. Surprisingly, many top US officials didn't blindly toe the Israeli line, maintaining that the damage done to US national security by Pollard was devastating and more severe than acknowledged publicly. The Israeli Government partially acknowledged its role in Pollard's espionage in 1987, but did not admit to paying him till 1998. However, as Chris Menahan of Information Liberation notes, *"President Trump, in an act of utter humiliation both for himself and our country, on his last day in office [referring to the end of his first presidency, i.e. January 20th, 2020] also pardoned Israeli colonel Aviem Sella, the handler of Pollard who never faced justice because he fled to Israel after Pollard got arrested and Israel refused to extradite him."*[400]

In the 1990s, Israel continued its spying antics, using White House intern Monica Lewinsky to seduce Bill Clinton so that it could then later blackmail the American president. *The Times of Israel* reported[401] in 2014 that Netanyahu was specifically trying to use these 'Lewinsky tapes' to secure the release of the aforementioned Jonathan Pollard. Welsh author Gordon Thomas did a lot of research on this, using two key sources, the aforementioned Israeli intelligence agents Rafi Eitan and Ari Ben-Menashe. Thomas was able to discover that the Mossad had amassed some 30 hours of phone sex conversations between Lewinsky and Clinton; he claimed they were using it either for blackmail or to defend an embedded mole in the White House whose code name was 'Mega.' Thomas also claimed that the Mossad was responsible for the deaths of Robert Maxwell (as mentioned above, seller of PROMIS software – more on him to come), Princess Diana and the 241 American marines killed in a 1983 barracks explosion in Lebanon (see end of chapter).

Israel has continued its spying on Congress and the White House all throughout the last decades, regardless of which political party or president has been in power. Even pro-Israel Trump was not spared; in 2019 *Politico* revealed that tiny surveillance devices known as 'StingRays' (International Mobile Subscriber Identity-catchers or IMSI-catchers) were found surrounding the White House. They work by mimicking normal mobile phone towers to fool mobile phones into transmitting location and identity information (metadata); they also can capture the contents of calls (the data itself). The article stated that the USG had concluded that within the past two years that *"Israel was most likely behind the placement of cellphone surveillance devices that were found near the White House and other sensitive locations around Washington, according to three former senior U.S. officials with knowledge of the matter. But unlike most other occasions when flagrant incidents of foreign spying have been discovered on American soil, the Trump administration did not rebuke the Israeli government, and there were no consequences for Israel's behavior, one of the former officials said."*[402] Cult-controlled Israel does whatever it wants, consequences be damned. It rarely even gets a slap on the wrist. The US Government Accountability Office (GAO) reported in 1996 that Israel *"conducts the most aggressive espionage operation against the United States of any U.S. ally. Classified military information and sensitive military technologies are high-priority targets for the intelligence agencies of this country. [Israel] seeks this information for three reasons: (1) to help the technological development of its own defense industrial base, (2) to sell or trade the information with other countries for economic reasons, and (3) to sell or trade the information with other countries to develop political alliances and alternative sources of arms."*[403]

A 2024 article on Information Liberation by Chris Menahan revealed that former UK PM Boris Johnson wrote in his book *Unleashed* that a bugging device was found in his personal bathroom on the *"thunderbox"* – after it was used by Netanyahu during a 2017 visit! Hopefully the Israeli spies got some good information from that device above all the sounds of farting and flushing.

One of the most comprehensive insights into the inner workings of the Mossad comes from ex-Mossad agent Victor Ostrovsky who worked there from 1984 to 1986. The Mossad trained him as a 'katsa' or case agent. Ostrovsky wrote two books, *By Way of Deception* and

The Other Side of Deception, exposing how the Mossad is structured, how it operates and even what historical events it was behind, including several false flag operations described later in this chapter. Ostrovsky revealed a lot about the Mossad's kidon assassination unit. He writes that many assume that the Mossad does not operate in the US, but that they are wrong:[404]

Pollard was not Mossad, but many others actively spying, recruiting, organizing, and carrying out covert activities – mainly in New York and Washington, which they refer to as their 'playground' – do belong to a special, super-secret division of the Mossad called simply Al, Hebrew for 'above' or 'on top.' The unit is so secretive, and so separate from the main organization, that the majority of Mossad employees don't even know what it does and do not have access to its files on the computer. But it exists, and employs between 24 and 27 veteran field personnel, three as active katsas. Most, though not all, of their activity is within U.S. borders.

The Mossad has risen to become one of the deadliest agencies in the world, if not the most. This is partially due to its espionage ability (the ability to extract information without anyone knowing how it got that information), partially due to its ability and willingness to kill and also partially due to the pressure the Cult puts on nations that foil its plans and capture Mossad agents. The Cult makes those nations look the other way and clear a path. Israel loves to boast about the 'long arms' of the Mossad but it's certainly not infallible. Mossad agents are absolutely willing to murder anyone they deem standing in the way of the Israeli cause. Ostrovsky was able to see, unlike a lot of his colleagues and superiors in the Mossad and upper power echelons of Israeli society, that America was giving Israel a lot, and that Israel needed to be more humane and grateful:[405]

The general attitude about the Americans was: 'Hey, they wanted to stick their nose into this Lebanon thing, let them pay the price.' For me, it was the first time I had received a major rebuke from my Mossad superior, liaison officer Amy Yaar. I said at the time that the American soldiers killed in Beirut would be on our minds longer than our own casualties because they'd come in with good faith, to help us get out of this mess we'd created. I was told: 'Just shut up. You're talking out of your league. We're giving the Americans much more than they're giving us.' They always said that, but it's not true. So much of Israeli equipment was American, and the Mossad owed them a lot.

His final verdict on the Mossad and the Zionist regime is stunning, and also very impressive, given that he moved in those circles and was thus inundated with 'we are the best' and 'we are the chosen ones' supremacist propaganda. Here he refers to the first Palestinian uprising ('intifada') that occurred in 1987:[406]

This is what happens after years and years of secrecy; of 'we're right, let's be right, no matter what'; of keeping the officials deliberately misinformed; of justifying violence and inhumanity through deceit, or, as the Mossad logo says: 'by way of deception.' It's a disease that began with the Mossad and has spread through government and down through much of Israeli society. There are large elements inside Israel who are protesting this slide, but their voices are not being heard. And with each step down, it gets easier to repeat, and more difficult to stop.

Other Mossad agents openly boast of their god-like powers. As mentioned previously, two anonymous agents came forward to CBS News to explain how they infiltrated Hezbollah's supply line with the front company BAC Consulting, sold them explosive-rigged pagers/

phones, then remotely detonated the devices in a September 2024 operation that killed 42 people (including 12 civilians) and injured an estimated 4000. This is what they said:[407]

We create a pretend world ... We write the screenplay, we're the directors, we're the producers, we're the main actors ... the world is our stage.

The Mossad were the key players involved in carrying out the JFK assassination, and as we shall see in chapter 14, they were also the key players in carrying out the 9/11 operation.

The Sayanim

The 'sayan' (singular) is an essential element of the international Zionist spying network. The 'sayanim' (plural) are another piece of evidence that what we are dealing with here is a cult. One of the characteristics of a cult is that its members are indoctrinated to develop a blind loyalty and obedience to the cult mission and leaders, which would include funding it, lying for it, cheating for it, and supporting it in any way as demanded – even killing or dying for it. Israel is the Cult's chosen nation and Jews are the Cult's chosen people. The sayanim are Jews around the world, living outside of Israel, who believe in the Zionist cause enough that they will actively help the Israeli Government, the Mossad, Shin Bet or any similar agency carry out its (usually unethical and illegal) missions. The USA has a Jewish population of around 7.5 million,[408] and quite a portion of these Jews would be sayanim, willing to jump into service if tapped by the Mossad and elevate their loyalty to Israel over any group or nation, including their home country of America. Many have since birth been propagandized and indoctrinated by fanatical

Zionist parents, relatives, teachers and rabbis; they have thus become Zionist zealots. Many are dual US-Israeli citizens.

It is the sayanim that help Israeli intelligence to be so effective. Imagine how much time, effort and money it saves to be able to have an international network whose services you can tap anytime you have a mission in a foreign land and need some help. Ostrovsky writes:[409]

... the sayanim [are] a unique and important part of the Mossad's operation. Sayanim — assistants — must be 100 percent Jewish. They live abroad ... There are thousands of sayanim around the world. In London alone, there are about 2,000 who are active, and another 5,000 on the list. They fulfill many different roles. A car sayan, for example, running a rental agency, could help the Mossad rent a car without having to complete the usual documentation. An apartment sayan would find accommodation without raising suspicions, a bank sayan could get you money if you needed it in the middle of the night, a doctor sayan would treat a bullet wound without reporting it to the police, and so on. The idea is to have a pool of people available when needed who can provide services but will keep quiet about them out of loyalty to the cause. They are paid only costs ... You have at your disposal a nonrisk recruitment system that actually gives you a pool of millions of Jewish people to tap from outside your own borders.

Ostrovsky also mentions that *"the Mossad regards the whole world outside Israel as a target, including Europe and the United States"*[410] – another clue of the Cult mindset.

Hacking Galore

Hacking is a natural bedfellow of spying. Spying is the art of knowing what your allies or adversaries know, preferably without them knowing that you know. In today's increasingly digital age, with so much information stored on computers, hacking has become a sine qua non element of modern espionage. The Cult regime in Israel has made a point of becoming an extremely advanced hacking force – arguably the best in the world. To understand this, we have to go back to the point made at the start of this chapter. Israel is a tiny country, surrounded by larger and more populous nations on many sides with militaries far greater. So, how did it position itself so that it could survive, and thrive, in a potentially hostile Middle Eastern environment? It focused first on outsmarting (not out-muscling) its neighbors. It focused on gaining advantages that would secure its dominance in the long run (acquiring nukes and developing state-of-the-art spying and hacking capabilities) that were not dependent on having a large military force, a large land mass, a large deposit of minerals or a large amount of natural resources. That has been Israel's strategy, and it has achieved spectacular success. All the brouhaha over supposed Russian hacking is just a smokescreen (projection) to cover the real hacking from Israel.

Aman, the Military Intelligence Directorate, is part of the IDF, and in turn has many subdivisions. One such subdivision is Unit 8200, the Israeli SIGINT National Unit (as you may recall, SIGINT is an abbreviation/acronym for Signals Intelligence). Unit 8200 is responsible for hacking (code decryption), counterintelligence, cyberwarfare, military intelligence and surveillance. The unit has risen to become the world's preeminent technical intelligence agency, on a par with the NSA, except that it is much smaller. However, as

Netanyahu boasted in this speech at Cybertech 2019 in Tel Aviv, Israel has now surpassed the other supporting nations to America in the Five Eyes network (US, UK, Canada, Australia, NZ) to become the second leading nation in the world despite its size:[411]

You know the five eyes? Israel is the second eye ... The cyber is the real domain of power ... It's giving us powers we never had before ... with the click of a button, you can bring down nations to their knees very rapidly if you so desire.

Image #80: current Israeli PM Benjamin Netanyahu, a liar, warmonger and bona fide psychopath, willing to commit genocide and trying his best to steal Arabian land for the Cult agenda of Greater Israel

Netanyahu bragged that even though the US was approximately 42 times the size of Israel in terms of population (not quite accurate, as it's about 340 million vs. 9-10 million, but his point remains), the NSA was only about 5-10 times the size of Unit 8200. So, per capita, Israel has the largest SIGINT and hacking agency for its size in the entire world. Those who train and work at Unit 8200 and then later leave (Unit 8200 alumni or graduates) have become very well known for their integration into Silicon Valley. Unit 8200 graduates, more than alumni from any other spy agency worldwide, have gone on to form highly successful companies that often get bought out by Big Tech (the really big players in the technological arena, such as Alphabet [parent company of Google],

Microsoft, Meta [Facebook, Instagram], X [Twitter], etc.). Unit 8200 startup companies are everywhere. What this means is that a large chunk of US intelligence uses cyber software or systems developed by Unit 8200. I say 'developed' but a better verb may be 'owned' since if Unit 8200 agents put backdoor access into the software, they can then access data from whoever ends up using that software. This is exactly what happened with PROMIS in the 1980s so why would it not be magnified now in the technological age? Israel creates software with backdoors only it can access, builds Fortune 500 tech companies, disseminates that software out to the world then spies upon all the end users of that software, including corporations and their customers, and other governments and their citizens. This source has a list of Unit 8200 apps which you might prefer to avoid using, such as Moovit, Call App, Gett and Facetune.[412]

At this point some may object and say that Israel, as America's supposed 'greatest ally,' would never do that. If that what's you think, is there not enough evidence in this book to show that Israel's leaders couldn't care less about the US or any other country that is foolish enough to help them? The USS Liberty incident where Israel killed 34 Americans in cold blood happened over 58 years ago in 1967! Some may object by saying that the US Intelligence Community would not allow Israel to gain a technological advantage over the US that would harm the average American, but that would be completely naive. Remember how the CIA and Mossad started in the 1940s/1950s and then became joined at the hip (chapter 11)? Remember how Ben-Menashe revealed what happened with PROMIS and its backdoors, with the CIA fully in the know? Remember how the Cult works. Infiltration is the name of the game. Israel already had the CIA under control in the 1950s and 1960s thanks to men like Angleton in key positions. Why would they not have all these agencies and organizations under their control now?

For the Cult, there are no countries or borders. There's one giant world that it wants to control, so it is constantly trying to erode national sovereignty and destroy borders so there's no protection against its predation. History rhymes, to paraphrase Mark Twain. Just as big corporations like I. G. Farben and IBM were essential to boost the war efforts of Nazi Germany, so too are today's giant corporations essential in helping Israel sustain its apartheid and genocide of the Palestinians. Numerous Big Tech multinational corporations cooperate very closely with Israel; Intel and Microsoft have offices in Israel with a massive number of employees there.[413][414] It is questionable whether these companies could even be called American anymore; they are at least American-Israeli and

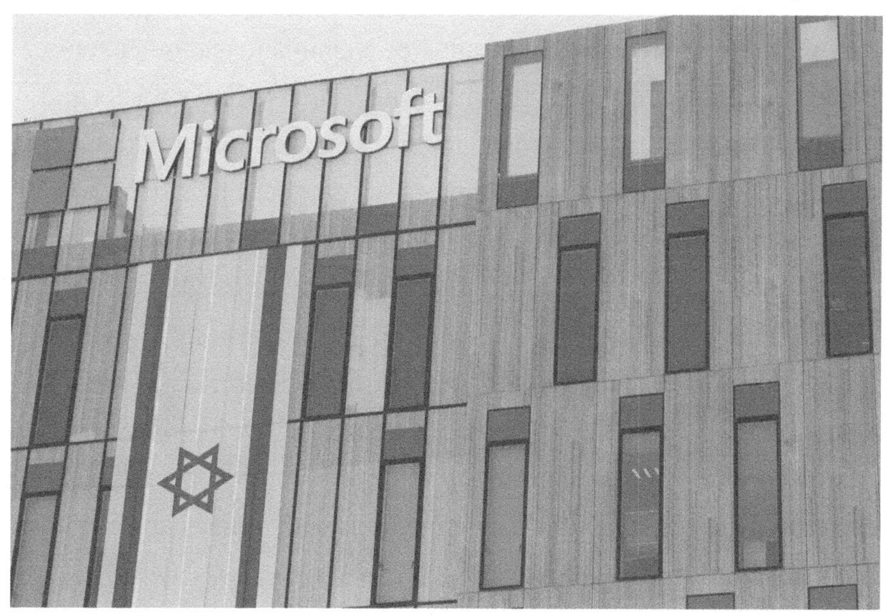

Image #81: Microsoft is one of many Big Tech companies joined at the hip with Israel

perhaps one day may be just Israeli. Big Tech willingly collaborates with Israel in developing new autonomous weapons and testing them out on the Palestinians, using them as human guinea pigs. The way they are attacked today (constant surveillance, invasive biometrics, drone assassinations, etc.) is the way that all people in the West – and the world – will be attacked tomorrow. We are all Palestinians. Palestine is the open air prison where the Cult tests its new weapons and methods of control. Israel has maliciously orchestrated things so the Palestinians still don't officially have their own country at the time of writing (although that may change with recent nations like the UK, Portugal, Canada and Australia recognizing Palestine in September 2025), and thus have no official armed forces.

In the case of Microsoft, it's hard to tell where Microsoft ends and the Israeli state begins. Microsoft disabled the email account of the chief prosecutor of the International Criminal Court (ICC) Karim Khan after he issued arrest warrants for Netanyahu and other senior Israeli officials. Microsoft employs over 1,000 ex-IDF soldiers and intelligence agents inside Israel, and dozens of ex-IDF at its worldwide headquarters in Seattle and at its offices in Miami, San Francisco, Boston and New York. Microsoft has purchased 17 Israeli tech companies since the year 2000. Microsoft Azure (Microsoft's cloud computing platform) maintains an AI system called 'Rolling Stone' which is essential in allowing Israel to enforce its apartheid state on the Palestinians.[415] Microsoft employees work closely with the specific units in Israeli military to develop products and systems.[416] Azure, armed with almost limitless storage capacity, gave Unit 8200 millions of mobile phone calls made every day by Palestinians in Gaza and the West Bank at the rate of around a million calls an hour.[417]

Numerous examples could be given of the close cooperation between other American Big Tech companies and Israel over the last 10 years. Here are a few:

– The Alphabet/Google Acquisition of Wiz: in April 2025, Google announced it would acquire Israeli-American cloud security firm Wiz for $32 billion, which is 65 times Wiz's annual revenue, which will further cement the close relationship between Google and the Israeli military;[418]

– Project Nimbus: a joint contract signed in 2021 between Google and Amazon to provide cloud computing infrastructure, AI and other tech services to the Israeli Government and military;

– OpenAI: an AP (Associated Press) investigation, whose results were published in February 2025,[419] revealed that Israel's use of Microsoft and OpenAI technology massively accelerated after the October 7th Hamas attack (covered in chapter 17). Microsoft, very embedded in Israel, is the biggest investor in OpenAI. Microsoft gave Israel extensive access to OpenAI's GPT-4 language model, the engine behind ChatGPT;

– Dell: *The Electronic Intifada* got their hands on internal documents that reveal that Dell supports the Israeli military. Dell provides hardware (laptops) for Unit 8200 and Elbit Systems Land & C41 (the Israeli arms manufacturer's military communications technology arm). Dell also provides servers that enable Israeli AI company AnyVision's facial recognition systems which target Palestinians. The founder and CEO of the company, Michael Dell, said at the Dell Future Ready Conference in May 2016 that Dell is *"deeply committed to Israel."*[420]

– Palantir: led by Bilderbergers Peter Thiel and Alex Karp, data analysis and surveillance behemoth Palantir announced a strategic relationship with Israel in January 2024 whereby Palantir would allow Israel to use its AI models for war missions.[421] Thiel is linked to the notorious Jeffrey Epstein (more on him shortly) who invested a substantial sum into a company that Thiel had co-founded, Valar Ventures, to the tune of $40 million.[422] Palantir is literally building the NWO surveillance control grid and is greatly assisting Israel with advanced AI-enabled operations such as Gotham which is a decision-making AI. It selects objects to destroy and people to kill on the battlefield, then makes suggestions to human operators. Unfortunately, it won't be long before these 'suggestions' become 'decisions' and 'commands.'[423] This January 2025 Guardian article based on leaked documents show how Microsoft, Apple, Google and Open AI all deepened ties with Israel to support its Gaza genocide; the leaked documents include commercial records from Israel's defense ministry and files from Microsoft's Israeli subsidiary:[424]

... the IDF has become increasingly dependent on the likes of Microsoft, Amazon and Google to store and analyse greater volumes of data and intelligence information for longer periods ... In recent years, documents show, Microsoft has also provided the Israeli military with large-scale access to OpenAI's GPT-4 model – the engine behind ChatGPT – thanks to a partnership with the developer of the AI tools which recently changed its policies against working with military and intelligence clients. However, in a war that has become known for the IDF's application of novel systems on the battlefield – including AI-driven target recommendation tools such as The Gospel and Lavender – the role played by major US-

headquartered tech companies to support Israel's operations in Gaza has, until now, largely remained out of sight.

Palantir is starting to embed itself not just inside the US and Israeli governments, intelligence agencies and militaries, but also in many other organizations worldwide. A salient example is from the Israel-Iran 12-Day War where Israel used an International Atomic Energy Agency (IAEA) report to claim that Iran was on the verge of making a nuclear bomb. Israel's claim was nonsense – Netanyahu is the boy who cried wolf for over 30 years, always claiming that Iran is just about to get the bomb – but what made this different was that Israel co-opted IAEA chief Rafael Grossi and used predictive analysis from a Palantir AI called Mosaic. Since 2015, the IAEA has used Mosaic, a $50-million AI system that collects 400 million data points (satellite imagery, social media, personnel logs, etc.) to predict nuclear threats. Mosaic doesn't just analyze but predicts, turning monitoring into pretext; it can infer hostile intent from indicators which are not confirmed evidence. One of the big problems, as with all AI, is bias, and we know for sure that Palantir's code and algorithms favor Israel, since even its founder Peter Thiel admitted that his *"bias is towards Israel."*[425]

Palantir is another classic case of the CIA outsourcing its dirty work to a non-governmental company which removes public accountability and oversight. Palantir grew out of the Total Information Awareness (TIA) program established by DARPA in January 2002. Funded by In-Q-Tel, the CIA's venture capital arm, Palantir's ambition is to dominate military AI infrastructure and to set up a massive surveillance grid combining millions of points of information about each and every citizen in the world.

Tight US-Israeli cooperation is corporate/private and governmental/public. As already stated many times in this book, American and Israeli intelligence are joined at the hip. This 2013 document[426] shows that the NSA provides the Israeli SIGINT National Unit (ISNU) with SIGINT data – raw, unredacted phone and email communications between Palestinian Americans in the US and their relatives in the occupied territories. However, despite this relationship, the Zionists' loyalty is not to the USA, which is receding as a superpower. The NWO Cult controllers are shifting power away from the West to the East, specifically to China/Russia, who will become the new superpower bloc. Israel uses America like a parasite uses a host; they'll be ready to move on once America crumbles. There have already been Likud members in the Israeli Knesset (Parliament) who have called for Israel to abandon America and instead ally with China and Russia. For example, during Biden's time as president, Knesset member Ayoob Kara threatened that Israel was prepared to ditch America and partner with China and Russia if Biden reneged on America's recognition of Israeli sovereignty over the Golan Heights, or if he signed a nuclear deal with Iran.[427]

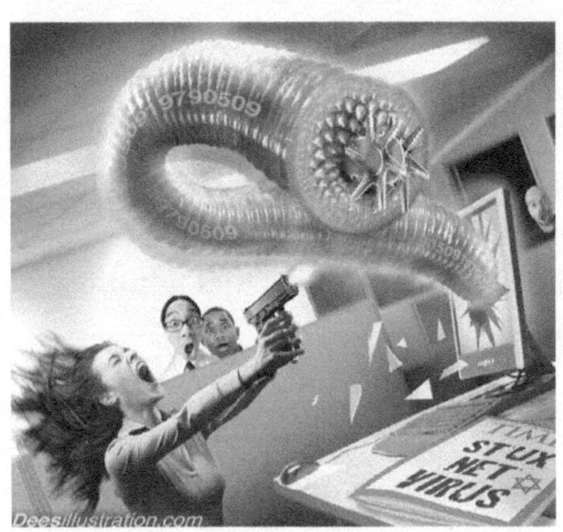

Image #82: Israel's Unit 8200 and the USA' NSA cooperated to create the computer virus Stuxnet, which later infected Iran

Despite this threat from the more extremist factions of Israeli society, Israel and the US – or rather their intelligence agencies – often work together on top secret projects. A famous example of this was Stuxnet, a highly destructive computer virus that whistleblower Edward Snowden assessed was a joint Unit 8200/NSA production.[428] Stuxnet was developed to sabotage the Iranian nuclear plant at Natanz where uranium enrichment is or was being done. The virus was known as a 'zero day' exploit meaning that there have been zero days to prepare for it; it's a cyberattack that takes advantage of an unknown or unaddressed security flaw in computer software or hardware. Stuxnet was introduced to the target environment via an infected USB flash drive, since the Iranian computers controlling the centrifuges were air-gapped. Stuxnet reportedly destroyed around 20% of Iran's nuclear centrifuges,[429] infecting over 200,000 computers and causing 1,000 machines to physically degrade.[430]

The extent of Israeli technological control over the world is difficult to ascertain – but its reach could be truly staggering. As mentioned earlier, there are many American companies that have become de facto Israeli companies, such as Intel, who specialize in microprocessors or semiconductor chips – the brain or controlling system of a computer. Technically, Intel is headquartered in the Silicon Valley in Santa Clara, California, but a lot of its product development is done in Haifa and a lot of its manufacturing is done in a plant near Jerusalem. Australian researcher Brendon O'Connell points out that through

Image #83: Does Israel have a backdoor to virtually every computer on Earth via the Intel Management System and the Arc processor?

the combination of two Intel products and systems – the Intel Management System and the Arc processor – Israel has a backdoor into every computer on Earth:[431]

... this is the ultimate backdoor of backdoors, and it was designed and fabricated in Israel as the basis of the new core series of Intel CPUs integrated between 2006 and 2008. These are the same CPUs that all server files all over the world use, every Google server file, Facebook, corporate, public and private. The NSA insisted on a patch that could switch off the Intel Management System for sensitive systems. No such luck for us mere mortals. The Intel Management engine cannot be switched off and is a wide open hardware backdoor for Israel to get into any and all computer systems around the world.

2. Blackmail Galore

From spying and hacking naturally flows blackmail. Once you have access to people's private communications, you can then learn all sorts of things about them – their past or present crimes, their wounds, their weaknesses, their desires, their fantasies and the skeletons in their closet. Then, you can use these things against them. Everyone has things they are ashamed of or would rather not air in public. The Cult aims to learn and exploit those things. However, to make sure its blackmail is really effective, it needs to get people doing illegal and immoral things – horrific things – then record them doing so, either in photo or on video, so it has cold hard evidence. This is where sexual blackmail rings come into the picture, and it's no surprise that Israel is heavily involved.

Although many people now know about the Jeffrey Epstein saga, there is still a shockingly high number who don't understand that Epstein was an intelligence agent … for Israel. There are many people who still haven't connected the dots to realize that Epstein was getting all that dirt on politicians and celebrities around the world so they could be blackmailed … by Israel. The entire Epstein network and operation was a Cult Israeli operation! Additionally, the Epstein saga is a microcosm of the New World Order agenda of manipulation, abuse of power, pedophilia, psychopathy, Satanism, transhumanism and eugenics.

For those who have never heard of Epstein, here is a brief summary. Epstein, who had two sets of Russian-Jewish grandparents, would recruit young girls who were broken, vulnerable, naive and/or without much money, then groom them for the role of being a sex slave, at first by forcing them to give sexualized massages. He, and his main partner in crime Ghislaine Maxwell, would use both the carrot and stick on girls for manipulation, offering to pay for their education and threatening to destroy their careers (or even kill them) if they didn't submit and obey. Teenage girl victims have also reported that Epstein not only wanted them to have sex with powerful men, but also wanted them to report back to him what the fetishes of these men were. The Epstein case had many similarities to the Savile case; British pedophile Jimmy Savile found kids for the British Royals, and when he got caught, the Establishment scurried to cover it up since it went all the way to the very top. Epstein was close friends with (former Prince) Andrew Mountbatten Windsor; likewise, Jimmy Savile was close friends with Prince (now King) Charles.

According to ex-Aman agent Ari Ben-Menashe,[432] the Epstein sex-trafficking ring started as follows. Mossad agent and billionaire Robert Maxwell (real name Jan Ludvik Hyman Binyamin Hoch) based himself in London and built a publishing empire. He was born in then Czechoslovakia in a little town called Solotvyno, now

Ukraine – another Khazarian Cult asset. He owned or controlled Macmillan Publishing, Pergamon Press, the Berlitz language group and The Mirror newspaper in London. It was Maxwell and his editor Nick Davies who were the same men involved in passing the location of whistleblower Mordechai Vanunu to the Mossad, as covered in chapter 10. They were also smuggling weapons to Iran on behalf of Israel (the Iran Contra affair). They met Epstein but were apparently unimpressed with him, considering him *"not very competent."* Maxwell's daughter Ghislaine fell in love with Epstein, which was probably the main factor prompting Maxwell to decide to bring Epstein into the 'family business' – i.e. Israeli intelligence. At some point after Epstein was introduced to Robert Maxwell, although Ben-Menashe doesn't specify what year, Epstein and Ghislaine Maxwell began their sexual blackmail operation on behalf of Israeli military intelligence. Ben-Menashe's opinion is that they weren't seen as 'agents' because they weren't that competent, so they found themselves a niche: blackmailing (mostly American) politicians and celebrities. In the same interview with Zev Shalev, Ben-Menashe said that *"later on [Ghislaine] got involved with Israeli Intelligence with [Epstein] but not in this arms deal with Iran."*[433]

Robert Maxwell played a role smuggling weapons into Israel in the 1948 Israeli-Arab War. He later persuaded the Czechoslovakian Government to sell weapons to Israeli terrorists who were killing Arabs to establish the Jewish state. Maxwell served the Cult all his life, but there is no honor among thieves; despite all he did to advance the Cult agenda and the Israeli cause, he came to an inglorious end. The Cult won't hesitate to kill you no matter how loyal you've been if you cross them. Maxwell 'fell' naked overboard off his yacht to his death. Tellingly, although he spent all his life in

Czechoslovakia and London, he was buried in Jerusalem. After his death, he was given a state funeral in Israel. At his funeral, six former and current heads of Israeli intelligence attended while then Prime Minister Yitzhak Shamir (discussed in the previous chapter) eulogized: *"He has done more for Israel than can today be said."*[434]

The evidence that Epstein was an agent for Israeli intelligence is overwhelming. Firstly, the kind of honeypot/honeytrap sexual blackmail operation that Epstein and Ghislaine Maxwell were running was a signature Israeli intelligence op. Secondly, Ghislaine's father Robert Maxwell was a known Mossad agent. Thirdly, we have explicit Ben-Menashe testimony in this interview by Narativ's Zev Shalev:[435]

Interviewer (Zev Shalev): "*Would you say she [Ghislaine] was an agent as well?"*

Ari Ben-Menashe: *"Yes."*

Interviewer: *"Military intelligence as well?"*

Ari Ben-Menashe: *"Yes, yes."*

Vicky Ward was a journalist exposing the Epstein case. She claims her 2003 story was censored by then-Vanity Fair editor Graydon Carter,[436] who met Epstein personally and agreed to not run the story. Vanity Fair was owned by Condé Nast, which was owned by Macmillan Publishers, owned by … Robert Maxwell. Ward claims Epstein also got Conrad Black (her ex-husband's former boss)[437] to stop her from publishing. Apparently Epstein even threatened Ward's baby[438] (she was pregnant at the time) by telling her he knew which hospital she was in. Ghislaine Maxwell, daughter of Robert Maxwell and Epstein's lover-recruiter, acted like a pimp for his underage girls. She was a key part of the operation, because she would literally go around and find underage girls then lure them into Epstein's web. Ghislaine would also rape them herself. Surprisingly, Ghislaine got caught, put on trial in federal court in New York City and sentenced in 2022 to twenty years' imprisonment. Ghislaine was a socialite and seemed to know everyone. She was captured at the wedding of Chelsea Clinton (see image #84), daughter of Bill Clinton, whose name was in the flight logs having flown at least 26 times to Epstein's private Caribbean island aboard what has been dubbed the 'Lolita Express,' Epstein's private jet. Bill Clinton was specifically targeted by the Israelis because they were concerned that he would push for Israel to make peace with the Palestinians, just as former president Jimmy Carter had – something the diehard Cult Zionists wanted to avoid at any cost. Ben-Menashe makes the connection between peace with the Palestinians, Clinton and Epstein:[439]

Mr. Carter ... as in President Carter ... the Israelis feared that Mr. Clinton, when he was campaigning for President, will be a repeat of Mr. Carter. He wanted to press them for peace with the Palestinians and all that stuff. They feared ... Clinton wasn't that ... but they feared he was that ... And I think Mr. Epstein was sent early on to catch up with President Clinton.

Ben-Mensahe also revealed that Israeli intelligence had dirt on both Clinton and then Israeli leader Ehud Barak. When they were meeting with Palestinian leader Yasser Arafat, and were on the verge of making a deal for a two-state solution, Israeli intelligence used Epstein blackmail against both of them to stop them![440] This shows many things, among which are that the Cult is fundamentally opposed to a two state solution and that the Cult is not afraid to blackmail Israeli leaders just as much as any others. Other Israeli leaders linked to Epstein include Shimon Peres (who introduced Barak to Epstein) and Ehud Olmert (named as an Epstein associate by the Virgin Islands).[441]

Epstein's island was dubbed Pedo Island and Orgy Island by locals, but its real name is Little St. James Island. Firstly, Epstein bought an island that is part of the *Virgin* Islands; the name virgin itself is not coincidental given the fact he was running a sex-trafficking ring composed of children. This connects to the obsession with virginity and child abuse running through the secret societies, and which for instance is etymologically behind the name Virginia (a US State). Epstein's temple was topped with a golden dome, reminiscent of the Al-Aqsa Mosque or Dome of the Rock in Jerusalem, Palestine, considered to be the third holiest place in Islam. There exists a longstanding Zionist plan to destroy the Islamic Dome

Image #84: Ghislaine Maxwell (circled, on right) attends the wedding of Chelsea Clinton

of the Rock and build a Jewish Temple Mount in its place, which will be elaborated on in chapter 19.

The Epstein case's connections to Kirkland and Ellis law firm are beyond mere coincidence. This law firm has produced lawyers such as Alex Acosta, Jay Lefkowitz, William Barr, Kenneth Starr and Alan Dershowitz, who all have connections to Jeffrey Epstein in one way or another. Acosta, quoted at the start of the chapter, was forced out of Trump's cabinet and resigned as US Secretary of Labor in 2016 due to public scrutiny that he gave Epstein a sweetheart deal when he prosecuted him in 2007. Epstein was being criminally defended by Lefkowitz. Acosta and Lefkowitz met over breakfast before the ruling to reach a deal, which involved Epstein only being charged under a Florida state statute (not a federal one), and being given day leave. Barr has long-time connections to Epstein; in 1973, Epstein was hired as a mathematics teacher due to Barr's father, Donald Barr, being the headmaster at Dalton School. His New York Times obituary notes that Donald Barr belonged to the OSS, forerunner to the CIA.[442] William Barr, who himself spent years at the CIA, helped cover up the Iran-Contra scandal by approving the pardons of Elliott Abrams and other officials who were caught in illegal activity. The Cult is one big club, and the CIA is never more than a couple of centimeters away from the center.

Starr and Dershowitz both represented and defended Epstein at one point or another. Starr was the lawyer who prosecuted Bill Clinton (closely connected to Epstein) over his affair with the (Jewish) Monica Lewinsky. As discussed earlier, Lewinsky, with no experience, was given a job as a White House intern, deliberately placed there to seduce Clinton so that Israel could blackmail him to release Pollard. Ardent Zionist Alan Dershowitz is a nasty individual, a Cult agent and an attack-dog lawyer quick to threaten people with lawsuits to try to shut them up. He represented Epstein on many occasions and was evidently dispatched by the Cult to mop up the PR disaster caused when Epstein's network (the Cult network) became front page news. Virginia Roberts Giuffre stated that Dershowitz raped her. Unsealed documents from January 3rd 2024 totaling 943 pages from the lawsuit brought by Giuffre, who died this year in April 2025 by 'suicide' around one month after being hit by a bus, include the anonymous female victim "Jane Doe #3" asserting that Epstein "required" her to have sexual relations with Dershowitz on multiple occasions.[443] Dershowitz admits to getting a 'massage' at Epstein's but vociferously denies raping anyone, despite writing a 1997 article in the LA Times arguing that statutory rape is an outdated concept and that the age of consent should be lowered to 15.[444] Epstein's little black book, first released to the public by Nick Bryant in 2015, features Dershowitz, and flight logs[445] indicate Dershowitz flew the Lolita Express to Little St. James. Dershowitz's name appears almost as many times as Bill Clinton's. According to this source, Virginia Giuffre's diary contained the following admission: *"I used to be watched by Epstein's hidden cameras, which I have seen myself. The FBI have the archive footage showing me being abused by other men, used as blackmail."*[446]

Although the diehard MAGA (Make America Great Again) crowd love to promote Trump as their hero and savior, the truth is that current US President Donald Trump (a Republican) was just as connected to Epstein as former US President Bill Clinton (a Democrat) – which makes sense, since the Cult has owned both political sides in the US for a very long time. Trump wasn't on the flight logs of Lolita Express only because he has his own jet. The

Cult's ownership of Donald Trump goes back a long way. Trump has always chosen Jewish criminals as his friends. His father Fred Trump rubbed shoulders with the rich and influential Jews of New York during all his real estate deals. In the end, Fred Trump donated the plot of land for the Brooklyn Beach Haven Jewish Center and contributed money towards its construction.[447] Early on in his business career, Donald Trump was mentored by Jew Roy Cohn, who was connected to Mafia boss Meyer Lansky and a corporate investor in the Mossad's Permindex operation – hence there are at least two ways Cohn was connected to the JFK assassination. Trump later chose Jew Michael Cohen as his lawyer, hence both Trump lawyers were Jews and political fixers. Although Cohn was Trump's personal attorney from the early 1970s to his death in 1986, Cohn's role in Trump's life was far beyond that. Cohn was Trump's closest advisor and friend. According to this source, *"Cohn was an eminent legal 'fixer', among the most connected men in New York, and facilitated Trump's entry into the rarefied stratosphere of Manhattan commercial real estate by embedding him in social and political networks with profound national and transnational power ... [Cohn] became Donald's mentor, his constant advisor on every significant aspect of his business and personal life. — Trump biographer Wayne Barrett."*[448] People love wearing red MAGA hats … is it just a coincidence that 'maga' and 'magus' are the fifth degree in the hierarchy of the Church of Satan?[449]

The Trump family bloodline is intermixed with the Eastern European/Ashkenazi/Khazarian blood. Trump's eldest daughter and Jewish convert, Ivanka Trump, is married to Jared Kushner. Jared's father Charles Kushner is a wealthy New Jersey real estate mogul, so it's not surprising Trump married his daughter into that family.

Zionist Charles Kushner is a big donor to the Democratic Party and to Israeli causes, including having donated to illegal settlements in the occupied West Bank. The Kushners have deep personal ties to Benjamin Netanyahu. Charles Kushner financed Netanyahu's early political ambitions; when Netanyahu visited the US, he would stay at the Kushner residence where he slept in Jared's bedroom while Jared had to sleep in the basement.[450]

Trump took over the Mossad and CIA-linked front company Resorts International (formerly the Mary Carter Paint company) after its head James Crosby died. It was set up to launder money from the profits of drug trafficking, gambling and other illegal activities. When he was working at *The Spotlight*, Piper reported in 1978 that the main investors of Resorts International were Meyer Lansky, Tibor Rosenbaum, William Mellon Hitchcock, David Rockefeller and Baron Edmond de Rothschild.[451] What a collection of Cult agents right there! I discussed the role of Lansky, chief financier of the underworld gambling syndicate, in the JFK assassination and in weapons smuggling programs to Israel, in the previous chapters. I also discussed Rosenbaum, the Mossad's Swiss-based financier running covert arms as well as the head of the BCI of Geneva, the Lansky syndicate's European money laundry. William Mellon Hitchcock was one of the heirs to the Mellon family, a super rich NWO bloodline family. Then we have the leaders of the two quintessential NWO bloodline families: David Rockefeller, at that time head of the Rockefeller empire, and Baron Edmond de Rothschild, at that time head of the Rothschild empire. Piper wrote:[452]

Resorts International expanded by leaps and bounds and soon became one of the most profitable of all the gambling enterprises, and by 1970 the underworld figures who were running the casinos (in league with their behind-the-scenes partners) began moving to expand casino gambling in the United States. Mob chief Lansky called a high-level meeting of gambling syndicate figures in Acapulco, Mexico and there the assembled mobsters pinpointed the fading resort of Atlantic City as their first new target. (Prior to that time, of course, the mob had already established Nevada as the only outpost of legalized gambling on U.S. soil.) ... up-and-coming young New York real estate tycoon Donald Trump stepped into the picture and bought Crosby's interest in the gambling empire. Trump soon became a household name ... But while the name "Trump" appeared in the headlines, the names of the real movers behind Resorts International remained hidden from public view.

In the 1980s, Trump got into financial trouble with his casinos. It was Rothschild agent Wilbur Ross, who managed bankruptcy restructuring at Rothschild & Co in New York, who helped bail him out. In return, Trump made Ross Secretary of Commerce in his first administration. Thus, Trump has been beholden to – and owned by – the Rothschilds and the Cult for decades, long before he stepped onto the political scene. Trump has been an extremely loyal Zionist both before and during his time in the White House, giving Israel everything it wanted – and then some more. Trump is unafraid to boast about the blatant way he has been bribed by Israel; he said this in reference to Zionist mega-donors and billionaires Miriam and Sheldon Adelson:[453]

Miriam and Sheldon would come into the White House probably almost more than anybody outside of people that worked there. They were always after it ... As soon as I'd give them something, oh it's for Israel. As soon as I'd give them something, they'd want something else. I said, 'Give me a couple of weeks, will you please!' But I gave them the Golan Heights, and they never even asked for it.

Trump was well acquainted with Jeffrey Epstein long before Epstein was outed as a pedophile. Trump wasn't just 'friends' with Epstein; he was highly involved with Epstein in all his shenanigans. They were best friends. Trump hung out on Robert Maxwell's yacht (see image #85); he partied with Epstein in Florida and New York. In 2002, Trump was quoted by the *New York Magazine* as saying about Epstein: *"I've known Jeff [Epstein] for fifteen years. Terrific guy. He's a lot of fun to be with. It is even said that he likes beautiful women as much as I do, and many of them are on the younger side."*[454]

Anonymous victims filed lawsuits against Trump in which they accuse him of the exact same actions as Epstein – pedophilia, rape and threatening the victim with her life if she didn't keep quiet. One suit alleges that Epstein and Trump argued over who should get to rape the 13-year-old girl first to take her virginity. One lawsuit filed by a "Katie Johnson" was dismissed by a judge in May 2016 but filed again in June 2016, then withdrawn some months later. A third version of it was

ST. LOUIS POST-DISPATCH

WEDNESDAY, MAY 17, 1989 7W

On Their Toes

One thing about the party aboard British media mogul **Robert Maxwell**'s yacht: Everybody, but everybody, had to doff their shoes before boarding the plush-carpeted "Lady Ghislaine." Maxwell insisted and his guests cooperated, including **Donald Trump** (minus **Ivana**) who has a much bigger yacht and was happy to compare them with Maxwell. Guests sipped champagne, nibbled caviar flown in from Paris on the Concorde, and salmon served from the vessel's stores by shoeless waiters. There was **John Tower**, former senator and thumbed-down defense secretary; ex-Navy secretary **John Lehman**, now with Paine, Webber; lawyer **Tom Bolan**; literary agent **Mort Janklow**; U.N. envoy **Thomas Pickering**; **Peter Kalikow**, owner of the New York Post; Maxwell's daughter, **Ghislaine**, and Max' niece, **Helene Atkin** of Macmillan, the publishing house Maxwell recently took over.

Maxwell, who weighs about 300 pounds, went over the guest list personally. No one could tell who didn't make the final invitation list but we do know that **Martha Smilgis** of Time was invited and then disinvited. She wrote the profile of Maxwell for the mag, which he apparently did not like.

Robert Maxwell

Image #85: newspaper report of Donald Trump aboard the yacht of Mossad spy Robert Maxwell

Image #86: best buddy sexual predators Donald Trump (left) and Jeffrey Epstein (2nd from right at front) with their respective spouses or partners, Melania Trump (2nd from left) and Ghislaine Maxwell (right at front)

filed in September 2016 under the name of Jane Doe but was also dropped months later. The plaintiff accused both Epstein and Trump of sexually assaulting her many times at a series of parties at Epstein's New York townhouse in 1994 when she was 13 years old. The plaintiff was scheduled to appear in a press conference six days before the 2016 US presidential election, but abruptly canceled; her attorney stated that the woman had received credible death threats.[455][456] Although Trump and Epstein had a falling out over a real estate deal, that in no way diminishes the extent of their very cosy relationship; it just gave Trump a convenient excuse to distance himself from the predator and blackmailer with whom he used to commit rape and horrific crimes. American author Michael Wolff describes Jeffrey Epstein showing him polaroids of Trump with underage girl victims.[457] Trump did a good job of hiding his Cult credentials during his presidential campaigns, but he is owned to the core, even before any sexual blackmail footage was taken of him. Trump even visits the Rebbe's grave.[458] Wolff, who has written a lot on Trump, had a long-standing journalistic relationship with Epstein. Wolff says he urged Epstein to release information he had on Trump, but that Epstein appeared concerned about what Trump would do to him. *"He said, 'I may be a pervert, but I'm not crazy.'* He then said, *'Trump is a man without any scruples.'"*[459] If Epstein thinks you have no scruples, you're in trouble.

Epstein drew many top celebrities or famous people into his network, such as Kevin Spacey and Richard Branson. Photos exist of members of the NXIVM multi-level marketing company and sex trafficking cult with Branson on Branson's private island (Necker Island) in 2010. Branson is pictured with Sara Bronfman (daughter of the billionaire Edgar Bronfman Sr) who was a funder and leader of NXIVM. The Bronfman connection with the JFK assassination was covered in the previous chapter, but they are also connected to Epstein in several ways. One way was via his benefactor buddy Les Wexner, who helped Charles Bronfman set up the Mossad-linked Study Group or Mega Group in 1991, which pushed Israel first policies. Some of the members of Mega included the aforementioned Max Fisher (benefactor of Gerald Ford) and Hollywood film director Steven Spielberg. Also, Epstein's little black book had an entry for Edgar Bronfman. It's one big club at the top!

Epstein, working for Israeli intelligence, was naturally also connected to Israeli politicians. At one point, Epstein was in business with former Israeli PM Ehud Barak whose name was in the little black book and on the Lolita Express flight manifests. Barak is the exact same man who was propagating the misdirection and cover story that 'Bin Laden did it' on BBC right after the towers fell (see chapter 14).[460] He is strongly suspected to be the 'Prime Minister' mentioned by Giuffre in her memoir *Nobody's Girl* (released posthumously in 2025) whom she accuses of raping her so violently she had to beg for her life, however for fear of retribution, she didn't name him there, although she had previously named him as one of her abusers according to court records.[461]

For some time now, and especially since Trump and the MAGA movement got into power in January 2025, people have been screaming for the 'Epstein List' or his 'Client List' – but there is no such list. Rather, the evidence is comprised of:

– Epstein's little black book;

– Flight logs/manifests on Epstein's private jet; and

– Testimonies of his victims, some of whom brought lawsuits against him and Ghislaine.

There is also the circumstantial evidence of Epstein's donations, and his personal and business connections. Additionally, there are testimonies of ex-intelligence agents. That's it. There's not a master list floating around that detailed all his clients, but we already know due to victim testimony who many of the people are that Epstein entrapped.

Finally, it's important to note there's a fundamental Epstein connection to Satanism and eugenics. Epstein's temple on Pedo Island was surrounded by owls, reminiscent of the Bohemian Club/ Grove, the secretive place in Northern California where a certain male-only segment of the NWO come together to practice black magic and conduct fake (or not) sexual, sacrificial and Satanic ritual in front of a giant, 40-foot owl called Moloch. A Chicago contractor and engineer, James Both, made this comment about the locking bar on the outside of Epstein's former temple: *"What makes it peculiar is that if you wanted to keep people out, the bar would be placed inside the building, [but the] locking bar appears to be placed on the outside ... as if it were intended to lock people in."*[462] Another way the Epstein saga is linked to Satanism is via Leslie Wexner, the man who 'sold' Epstein his New York townhouse (valued at a minimum of $50 million) for … $1.00. Wexner was the super wealthy owner of Victoria's Secret and very much part of Epstein's network, since Epstein would entice girls by promising them a modeling career there. Wexner admitted to being tormented by an archontic 'dybbuk' or inner demon that would drive him to do evil acts. Whitney Webb writes:[463]

He told New York magazine that his dybbuk makes him 'wander from house to house', 'wanting more and more' and 'swallowing companies larger than his own.' In other words, it compels him to accumulate more money and more power with no end in sight. Wexner later describes the dybbuk as an integral 'part of his genius.'

Epstein victim Juliette Bryant recalls waking up at Zorro Ranch, Epstein's New Mexico property, on some kind of operating table that looked like it was in a science lab.[464] She wondered if she was being operated on or whether there was some scheme to steal her eggs. Epstein was recorded to have stated that he had the goal of inseminating hundreds of women to perpetuate his DNA.[465]

Victims

Epstein was a pedophile, but above all, was a psychopath. He became a master manipulator. He and Ghislaine would lure girls into their network with promises of modeling careers, fame, glory and riches. Victims like South African Juliette Bryant reveal how Epstein had a way of making his whole operation *"look legit"* by talking about his connection with Leslie Wexner (owner of Victoria's Secret) and leaders of the modeling industry, as well as famous people in general. Epstein could easily impress teenage girls or young women in their early 20s by having Bill Clinton walk into the room. Then, once the girls' trust was won over, Epstein would fly them off to his island where he would immediately begin abusing them. Much of this was happening before the widespread use of mobile phones, so many of the girls had no easy way of escaping. Once he had the girls in his grip, Epstein would do things like lie to them, telling them that he was CIA and threatening that if they ever reported him to the police, he would track them down and have them killed. Some victims went to the New York Police Department (NYPD) and FBI, who both did nothing with their complaints. Then they went to Vanity Fair – and this was the aforementioned story that was famously suppressed by Vanity Fair editor Graydon Carter over the protests of journalist Vicky Ward. It was reported that Epstein may have intimidated Carter by leaving a bullet and a dead cat's head outside his door. Epstein victim Maria Farmer stated that Ghislaine retaliated in response to the Farmer girls (Maria and Annie) trying to go public by saying that she (Ghislaine) was going to burn Maria's paintings and blacklist her from the New York art world. Later on, Ghislaine issued a veiled death threat:[466]

Image #87: former Prince Andrew Windsor with a 17-year-old Virginia Roberts, who mysteriously died in April 2025

You're going out to jog on the West Side Highway every day, and I know this. You need to be very careful because there's so many ways to die there. So you have to be really careful. Look over your shoulder.

Maria specifically states that Ghislaine *"was raping just as many children"* as Epstein, and that Epstein's Jewish friends said to Ghislaine: *"Maria is not a Jew. She is a nobody."*[467] This is the same Jewish supremacy theme first introduced in chapter 1. There are at least hundreds if not many thousands of Epstein victims from all over the world. The late Virginia Roberts Giuffre was one of the most high-profile victims due to her allegations (and subsequent lawsuit claims) that she was raped by Epstein and Andrew Windsor (former Duke of York). Giuffre revealed that Epstein promised her money for an education to lure her in. Andrew Windsor knew about Virginia (with whom he had sex when she was 17). He publicly denied ever meeting Virginia, yet a leaked email shows he emailed Ghislaine on January 3rd 2015 telling her he had questions about Virginia Roberts.[468]

Other victims like Sarah Ransome revealed that *"Ghislaine - she tortured me daily. I mean, she tortured me every time I saw her. She starved me. She forced me into Jeffrey's room to be raped."*[469] She also said that *"It makes me sick to my stomach that Ghislaine is claiming to be innocent and claiming to be a victim, because she was the chief orchestrater. She was the engineer."*[470] Ransome explains how Epstein claimed he could get her into the Fashion Institute of Technology and pay for her schooling, but it was all a lie. After Epstein raped her repeatedly, she was manipulated into recruiting young girls who were all around 14-15 years old. She says that Epstein wanted as many girls as she could get him, that it was never enough, and that together mastermind manipulators Epstein and Maxwell fooled the entire world. Another anonymous Epstein victim (Jane Doe #15) said that *"Epstein wielded great villainous power in his ability to make victims feel ashamed of their backgrounds to the point where we felt grateful for any attention or invitation into his inner billionaire playground, no matter the trauma it brought upon us. It was the weight of Epstein's wealth, the isolation to which he subjected me and his discussion of his social connections that crushed me into submission, far more than his physical strength."*[471]

The meme "Epstein didn't kill himself" became famous after the public was told that the sexual predator committed suicide in his prison cell in 2019. Photos clearly show that the 'Epstein' we were shown who 'killed himself' was not the same Epstein who went into prison, given many facial differences such as ear shape and length. A former mobster who served seven months on that tier and in those cells in the exact jail where Epstein died (or disappeared), Michael Franzese, said there was *"just no way"* Epstein could have killed himself.[472] Nonetheless, MAGA appointees Kash Patel (owned by Israel) and Dan Bongino (Director and Deputy Director of the FBI respectively) tried to claim in May 2025[473] that they had seen the video showing that Epstein killed himself … presumably the same video that was later released to the public with a missing minute that proves nothing anyway. I thought Trump and MAGA were supposed to save us from the corruption? Besides, these days with the advent of AI deep fakes and AI mimicry, anything can be generated, and it is very difficult or impossible to tell the difference between fake and real footage. One way or another, the Epstein character was written out of the script; it is entirely possible that he is sitting on the beach somewhere in Israel with a reconstructed face.

Although Jeffrey Epstein has become infamous for his pedophilic, predatory and criminal behavior, it was another Cult Zionist agent who ran the original Jewish pedophile sexual blackmail operation before Epstein inherited it. I refer to the aforementioned Roy Cohn, Trump mentor and McCarthy assistant. David Livingstone, author of *Zionism: History of a Jewish Heresy*, writes that *"Cohn admitted to NYPD detective James Rothstein that he was part of an elaborate sexual blackmail operation that compromised politicians with child prostitutes, carried out as part of an anticommunist crusade. According to Rothstein, 'Cohn's job was to run the little boys. Say you had an admiral, a general, a congressman, who did not want to go along with the program. Cohn's job was to set them up, then they would go along. Cohn told me that himself.'"*[474]

3. Sex Rings and Pedophilia Galore

Blackmail is part of the Cult modus operandi, and sexual blackmail is probably the most effective form, since there are few things regarded as more immoral, criminal and disgusting than raping young children. However, Cult agents don't just use pedophilia to trap others; many of them actively practice it themselves. As David Icke says, at the highest level, pedophilia and Satanism are the cement that holds the global conspiracy together. Given this, it is unsurprising that Israel is home to more pedophiles than any other nation.

Israel takes advantage of the cultivated confusion around Jewish identity to allow 'Jews' from anywhere in the world to return to their supposed 'homeland' of the occupied territories of Palestine. Israeli citizenship can thus be obtained by declaring yourself to be a Jew (under the law of return), sometimes referred to as 'making aliyah' thereby gaining automatic citizenship (for both applicants and their families) with minimal barriers. Many pedophiles have used this feature to their advantage by escaping the law in one country (e.g. the USA or Australia) to flee to Israel to gain protection. While criminal background checks exist, offenders can bypass these requirements in various ways to evade capture. Several media reports from the last 5-10 years expose how widespread this has become. Some of the reports mention an American organization called Jewish Community Watch (JCW) which doesn't appear to exist anymore. However, it was apparently a group that tracked the movement of pedophiles to Israel. One report states that since JCW started tracking accused pedophiles in 2014, over 60 fled from the US to Israel.[475] Haaretz reported in 2022 that around 100 rabbis, teachers and other people who had been accused, charged or convicted of sexual abuse successfully took refuge in Israel after fleeing from other nations.[476] The Jerusalem Post reported in 2020 that tens of thousands of pedophiles operate in Israel every year, leading to about 100,000 victims annually, citing the Matzof Association, an Israeli pedophile monitoring organization.[477] Earlier this year in 2025, Israeli official Tom Alexandrovich was arrested in America in a child predator sting, but the Trump Admin on behalf of its master Israel intervened to let him escape back to Israel.[478]

The aforementioned Chabad Lubavitch sect was embroiled in sex scandals in Australia. In Melbourne, numerous pedophiles were operating at the yeshivah school in East St. Kilda. One of them was David Kramer, a young American rabbi who began molesting children in 1989. He was later sentenced to seven years in prison in St. Louis, Missouri, for molesting children at a youth camp. The head of the Lubavitch sect in Melbourne, Rabbi Yitzchok Groner, bought Kramer an airplane ride to Israel, on the condition he leave Australia immediately – the same strategy just discussed above. Later, another pedophile came on the scene, David Cyprys, who abused many boys. Despite raping many boys, Cyprys was only charged with indecent assault and fined AUD$1,500 in 1992. Many parents confronted Groner, only to get the same message: the yeshivah authorities were dealing with it, there was nothing to worry about and don't go to the police. In this way, senior figures covered up the crimes and allowed them to continue through inaction, in an almost identical way to how the Catholic Church has refused to deal with its massive and monstrous pedophilia problem. As is so common in cults or cult-like religions, Groner was revered as an unimpeachable and impeccable leader who could do no wrong. Additionally, there was the Jewish concept of 'mesirah' which meant not ratting out your religion or community if wrongdoing was occurring, but rather, keeping it in the family so to speak. These two factors made it so pedophilia flourished there, although as this Guardian article notes,[479] some Jewish rabbis did not agree with this, making it clear that the religious prohibition of mesirah did not apply to child abuse.

Members of the Jewish cult of Lev Tahor were arrested in Guatemala in 2024 for child trafficking. The group follows its own atypical interpretations of Jewish law, including practices such as arranged marriages between teenagers and head-to-toe black coverings for girls and women beginning at the age of three, showing a similarity to Islam.[480] Interestingly, some Jews refer to the Lev Tahor leader Rabbi Shlomo Helbran as the 'Sabbatai Zevi' or false messiah of our times. According to Guatemalan authorities, Lev Tahor engages in child sexual abuse, pedophilia and rape. A 2024 statement from the US Attorney's Office in the Southern District of New York reads: *"Yoil Weingarten, Yakov.Weingarten, and Shmiel Weingarten, leaders of Lev Tahor, an extremist Jewish sect based in Guatemala, have been found guilty of kidnapping a 12-year-old boy and a 14-year-old girl and transporting the 14-year-old girl outside the United States to continue a sexual relationship with her adult male 'husband.' With this verdict, all nine Lev Tahor leaders and operatives charged for these heinous crimes have been held accountable. The defendants' conduct – which included forced child marriages, physical beatings, and family separations – is unthinkable and has caused irreparable harm to children in their formative years."*[481]

Pedophilia, child marriages, rape and sexual abuse run through many organized religions, not just Judaism, however it is certainly very prevalent in Cult-affiliated groups. Ultimately, the attitude of

Cult members can be summed up by Rabbi Manis Friedman whose own son was accused of sexually abusing children.[482] Friedman compared child sex abuse to diarrhea by saying that *"it's embarrassing but nobody's business"*[483] in an attempt to shield official investigation. He also wrote the following about Israel's ongoing genocide of the Palestinians:[484]

I don't believe in western morality, i.e. don't kill civilians or children, don't destroy holy sites, don't fight during holiday seasons, don't bomb cemeteries, don't shoot until they shoot first because it is immoral. The only way to fight a moral war is the Jewish way: Destroy their holy sites. Kill men, women and children (and cattle) ... Living by Torah values will make us a light unto the nations who suffer defeat because of a disastrous morality of human invention.

'Torah values' can mean anything, just as 'Judeo-Christian values' can (see chapter 13). It's a subjective term that allows the speaker to avoid accountability. I'm guessing that many people outside the Khazarian Cult, including many good Jews, would be disgusted by this view and interpretation that 'Torah values' equate to mercilessly destroying and killing one's 'enemy.' Whether it's the Torah or the Talmud, all sorts of depravity can be justified with some holy verse. The difficulty is that, as previously mentioned, all three holy books – Torah, Talmud and Kabbalah – promote Jewish supremacy, so it's hardwired into the Jewish religion. Jewish supremacy lives on through current Israeli policy; Israel doesn't consider drug dealers and slave traders criminals, if the victims are non-Jews.

If all of this is not bad enough, Israel has also been implicated in organ harvesting. In 2009, Alison Weir reported that Palestinians believed Israel was seizing young Palestinian men and using them for their organs.[485] In December 1968, an Israeli hospital took a heart from a living patient, Avraham Sadegat, for use in a heart transplant. The hospital explained that it had abided by Israeli law, which allowed organs to be harvested without the family's consent. In 2001, the parents of a young killed IDF soldier Ze'ev Buzgallo filed a petition with the Israeli High Court of Justice pressing criminal charges against Dr. Yehuda Hiss, who was the director of the Abu Kabir Forensic Institute. The Israeli media reported that in a previous case *"Hiss removed the heart and other body parts from [another] body, using them for commercial purposes. In that case, a settlement was reached by which the forensic institute made a compensatory payment to the family."*[486]

4. Terrorism Galore

As discussed in chapter 10, Israel has been a nation of terrorists right from the start. On May 26th 1948, David Ben-Gurion transformed the Zionist terrorist groups – Haganah, Palmach, Irgun and Lehi (the Stern Gang) – into what became the 'Israeli Defense Forces' (IDF). However, no cover of legitimacy, official emblems or State standards has been able to erase the terroristic roots of the IDF, which behaves as it always has, causing serious injury or death to civilians in the pursuit of political, military and ideological goals, which is the very definition of terrorism. Israel's continuing military operations against Gaza, the West Bank, Lebanon, Syria, Yemen and Iran – not to mention its previous attacks against Egypt, Jordan, Tunisia and Sudan – demonstrate a blatant disregard for international law, human rights and moral principles.

One of the earliest leaders of the Zionist terror gangs was the Ukrainian Ze'ev Jabotinsky, who called for militarizing Zionism to defeat the indigenous Palestinians and drive them off their land.

Jabotinksy founded Irgun, and as previously mentioned, the assistant to his secretary was the Polish Benzion Netanyahu, father of current Israeli Psychopath-in-Chief, Benjamin Netanyahu – or if you remember from chapter 1, Benjamin Mileikowsky. Along with the Polish David Ben-Gurion, these were some of the leading men fighting militarily to regain 'their' land in the Levant. I don't remember learning in geography that Poland and Ukraine were part of the Middle East, but it must be my mistake, I guess. What a farce this whole thing is!

Israel's history is full of Jewish terrorists. There was a group of Jewish militants called Nakam (meaning 'avengers') who sought revenge against the Nazis after WWII. Their first plan (Plan A) was to poison the water supply of five German cities: Hamburg, Nuremberg, Frankfurt, Weimar and Munich. Their fallback plan (Plan B) was to poison Nazi prisoners of war. In mid-1945, the Nakam avengers, disguised as engineers, infiltrated the waterworks of each target city. They studied how the water supply was pumped into German homes. Renowned Jewish chemist Chaim Weizmann, later Israel's first president, managed to procure a poison that was lethal in milligrams. Nakam didn't carry their plan all the way through, but it certainly demonstrated the murderous Zionist mindset.[487]

Later on, in 1973, terrorist Menachem Begin (from Irgun) and terrorist Yitzhak Yezernitsky or Yitzhak Shamir (Stern Gang/Lehi) formed the right-wing political party Likud that has dominated Israeli politics for much of the time since its inception. This is Netanyahu's party. Likud brings together under one umbrella all the ultra-conservative, hard-core and fundamentalist Zionists, united in their belief that Israel should own all the land and that the Palestinians should be obliterated. Begin, who went on to become Israeli PM (yet another certified terrorist to hold Israel's leading political office), once boasted that he was *"the father of terrorism in all the world."*[488] In a great case of Satanic inversion, this is the very same man who won the 1978 Nobel Peace Prize! Shamir, another Israeli PM, was as you may recall from the previous chapter intimately involved in the JFK assassination since he was in charge of Mossad's kidon or assassination unit. Shamir sanctioned assassination of Lord Moyne in 1944, performed the King David bombing in 1946 and was involved in the Deir Yassin massacre and the Folke Bernadotte assassinations of 1948. Lovely chaps. Even the now deceased Queen Elizabeth was wary of the Zionists; former Israeli President Reuven Rivlin admitted that the *"relationship between [Israel] and Queen Elizabeth was a little bit difficult, because she believed that every one of us was either a terrorist or a son of a terrorist."*[489]

Is it any wonder with this kind of history and these kind of people – literal terrorists at the helm – that the Zionist regime running Israel has become the monster that it is?

5. Assassinations Galore

At this point, you may be wondering if there is any evil act that Israel wouldn't do. No, there isn't. When you are run by a Death Cult that believes salvation comes from sin, there is nothing too low. That is precisely why Israel has become the master of murder. The Cult via Israel has taken the tool of assassination to the extreme. Although the dual assassinations of the Kennedy brothers (covered in chapter 11) are arguably the most famous Israeli extrajudicial murders, there are many other high-profile examples. Many governments, groups and agencies are willing to kill, but few if any have developed the willingness and capacity to kill as Israel has – anywhere in the world.

The Zionist regime has absolutely established itself as the most prolific and skillful practitioner of assassination as a tool of control, surpassing the exploits of the Order of Assassins – the small band of lethal Muslim killers who terrorized the Middle East a thousand years ago. No other nation has Israel's experience in carrying out international assassination operations. According to Israeli journalist Ronen Bergman, author of *Rise and Kill First*, Israel has conducted over 2,700 assassinations since World War II. Since he is an Israeli Jew, Bergman has been able to get direct access to Mossad chiefs and other high-up sources to acquire his information. Bergman describes the mindset of those running Israel's notorious assassination program:[490]

And when they spoke, many of them repeated—and they were, of course, completely disconnected from or not synchronized with each other, but they repeated one sentence, one quote from the Babylonian Talmud, which says, 'If someone comes to kill you, rise up and kill him first.' And I think this was said not as an alibi or justification; this was said as to explain a mindset ... because these people, the people that they have killed, are considered to be threat to the sole existence of the nation, to a possible risk for a second annihilation ... when they want to eliminate you or call for your destruction ... Israelis were left with one conclusion: Rise and kill first, paying very little tribute to international law, international norms, and building these two sets of law, one for regular matters and one for the intelligence community and the military.

Bergman was able to see that, for Israel, although the assassinations were tactically effective, they were strategically ineffective, because it reinforced the idea that you could just use force – murder – as a way to solve all problems. Hence, Cult-owned

Israel doesn't develop its statesmanship or diplomacy to have a real discourse with its adversaries. It just kills them.

Support for assassination is high in Israel, not just among Cult agents, diehard Zionists or the political ruling class, but even among society in general. In 1997, after a botched assassination attempt by Israel in Jordan, The Washington Post reported that *"Israelis are dissecting every tactical, technical and procedural flaw in the affair. Strikingly absent from the debate, however, is a question that might be expected elsewhere: Should the government be in the business of dispatching assassins to kill its enemies abroad? For Israeli Jews, profoundly insecure still in their 50th year of statehood, the answer appears to be self-evident."*[491] A self-evident *"of course,"* that is.

Zionist terrorists have never been afraid to kill anyone, from any walk of life, if they perceived that person got in the way of the Zionist cause. Even before Israel was founded in 1948, Jewish terrorists killed European peacemakers visiting Palestine. One of the most egregious examples is the assassination of Folke Bernadotte, a Swedish diplomat who had negotiated the release of about 450 Danish Jews and 30,550 non-Jewish prisoners from a Nazi concentration camp during WWII. Bernadotte was a United Nations Security Council mediator in the Arab–Israeli conflict from 1947 to 1948. His assignment as mediator was to bring about a ceasefire, then a permanent resolution, between the Palestinians and the Zionists. When Bernadotte was visiting West Jerusalem on September 17th 1948, four members of Lehi attacked his UN convoy and murdered him in cold blood, afraid that the Israeli leadership would agree to Bernadotte's peace proposals. The hit was signed off by the Lehi leadership, one of whom was, as mentioned before, Yitzhak Shamir.

In 1947, as covered in chapter 10, Israel sent a letter bomb to target Harry Truman. Later on in the 1960s, it used letter bombs to target former Nazi German scientists helping Egypt develop rockets. In 1997, Netanyahu (who was then serving his first term as Israeli PM), ordered Israeli spies to kill Meshaal, a Hamas founder who was living in Jordan. The Mossad team of assassins entered Jordan posing as Canadian tourists and attacked Meshaal outside the Hamas political office in Amman. They sprayed a toxin into his ear, causing Meshaal to fall into a coma, but some of the assassins were captured by Jordanian authorities – after which Jordan threatened to end its peace treaty with Israel. Then US President Bill Clinton successfully pressured Netanyahu to send his Mossad chief Danny Yatom to Amman with the antidote that ended up saving Meshaal's life. This is one of many examples showing that the Mossad is far from invincible.

In 1972, there was the deadly Palestinian militant attack by a group known as Black September on Israeli athletes at the Munich Olympics which killed 11 people. In response, then Israeli PM Golda Meir *"ordered Israeli spies to hunt down and kill all Palestinian militants involved in the attack. The covert campaign was dubbed Operation Wrath of God and became the subject of an Oscar-nominated 2005 Steven Spielberg movie. Israeli assassins spent 20 years hunting those linked to the Munich attack. They killed Palestinians in France, Italy, Greece, Cyprus and Lebanon. They used a remote-controlled bomb hidden inside a phone in France and used guns with silencers to kill targets in the streets of Rome. Among those to take part in the yearslong effort was Ehud Barak, then a young Israeli commando who went on to become prime minister."*[492]

This is the same Ehud Barak alleged to have violently raped Virginia Giuffre and to have taken pleasure in watching her beg for her life.

This article on the Cradle.com website entitled *"A terror state through time: from Ben Gurion to Netanyahu"* discusses Israel's terroristic history, and how early Zionist militants actually used it as a weapon to scare nonviolent Jews into fleeing to Palestine, thereby increasing the Jewish population there:[493]

The Irgun's violent reach extended beyond Palestine, as in 1946, when Jewish terrorists bombed the British embassy in Rome, frustrated by what they saw as British hesitation to expedite Jewish immigration to Palestine. This attack helped stoke anti-Jewish sentiment in Britain and encouraged further Jewish immigration to Palestine, a tactic reminiscent of Zionist plots in Egypt, Iraq, and Syria to target and terrorize Jewish minorities, inciting violence and societal strife that would ultimately force them into fleeing to Palestine. The term "Zionist terrorism" was common in the official British discourse, including in the rhetoric and correspondence of the mandate authority in Palestine. This was especially the case in the 1930s, before World War II, and after the outbreak of the 1936–1939 Great Palestinian Revolt, when the indigenous Arab population rose against the British occupation authorities and the unchecked inflow of foreign Jewish settlers.

The Cult has never been shy to kill its own if they wander off the reservation. In 1995, then Israeli PM Yitzhak Rabin was assassinated, many believe for getting too close to peace with the Palestinians. The Cult has also never been shy to combine people from supposedly opposite teams, provided they had the right mindset, because as already explained, the Cult operates beyond political and national groupings, which are mostly for public consumption. We covered

Zionist-Nazi collaboration in chapters 8 and 9, and here's another example. Did you know that the Mossad tracked down and hired Nazi Otto Skorzeny?[494] Skorzeny, a tall and adventurous SS commando leader with a prominent dueling scar on his face, was personally rewarded by Hitler after he led a daring operation to rescue then Italian leader Benito Mussolini in 1943. Amazingly enough, the Mossad managed to get to Skorzeny to help them against Egypt, which had recruited Nazi scientists to develop advanced rocketry.

In 2004, longtime Palestinian Liberation Organization (PLO) and Fatah leader Yasser Arafat was poisoned. Israel had been trying to kill Arafat for decades. However, it has become an Israeli trademark to be completely silent after attacking an enemy:[495]

According to Ismat Mansour, a Palestinian expert on Israeli affairs, Israel tends to commit two different kinds of assassination. In the first kind, he said, Israel publicly takes credit for the assassination with a view to bolstering confidence in the Israeli security forces ... The second kind of assassination remains undeclared, Mansour explained, 'like the murder of late Palestinian leader Yasser Arafat, who was poisoned by an unseen assassin.'

Between 2010 and 2020, five Iranian nuclear scientists were assassinated by Israel as part of their agenda to stop Iran acquiring nuclear weapons, despite the fact that Iran has repeatedly stated they have no intention of developing nuclear weapons, that Islamic law forbids such development and that the US Intelligence Community has consistently assessed that Iran is not doing so.[496][497] In 2011 and 2012, Iranian authorities arrested a number of Iranians who had been recruited by Mossad to assist in the extrajudicial killings. In typical fashion, Israel neither confirmed nor denied its role in the assassinations, although then Israeli Defense Minister Moshe Ya'alon made Israel's involvement abundantly clear when he said, "*... one way or another, Iran's military nuclear program must be stopped. We will act in any way and are not willing to tolerate a nuclear-armed Iran. We prefer that this be done by means of sanctions, but in the end, Israel should be able to defend itself.*"[498]

Israel has assassinated many Palestinian resistance leaders. One example is the 1996 killing of Yahya Ayyash, a leader of the armed wing of Hamas, the Qassam Brigades, and the mastermind behind numerous operations against Israel. Shin Bet used a small explosive hidden in a portable device to carry out the attack.[499] The same tactic of supply chain infiltration of mobile phones and pagers was used in the aforementioned 2024 attack against Hezbollah.

Cult advocates and apologists may attempt to argue that Israel's assassinations, though murdering people, are at least targeted, only killing the intended victims. However, this is not true; Israel's assassinations and false flag operations kill many people other than the intended targets. For instance, the Hezbollah pager/mobile phone operation killed many innocent civilians, women and children. Who knows how many people have been caught up as 'collateral damage' in total in all these operations?

6. The Emergence and Perfection of the Signature Zionist False Flag Operation

The Cult, being the hidden hand behind the British Empire, the Nazis, the Bolsheviks and the Zionists, among numerous other movements, organizations and nations, had demonstrated its affinity for false flag operations many times over. However, once Israel became its own nation, the Cult developed a particular flavor of false flag – the signature Zionist false flag operation or what I call ZioIslamic Terrorism™.

A false flag operation is where one group destroys or kills an innocent group while disguised as a second group (or making it look like the second group was the perpetrator). The end goal is to frame the second group so that the first group elicits sympathy for itself, or to prompt other uninvolved groups to condemn and attack the second group, or to simply get away with a crime by setting up another group to take the fall. The term 'false flag' comes from old military language in which a ship would fly a flag of their enemy while committing certain criminal acts, so that observers would believe that enemy was committing those acts. However, there are many sophisticated ways that false flag ops can be conducted. I have been describing many of them in various chapters throughout this book. In general, the false flag operation has three key variations:

1. The perpetrator fully and/or directly does the attack then blames it on the target group; or
2. The perpetrator allows and/or encourages the attack to happen by the target group (having full foreknowledge but letting it happen anyway); or
3. The perpetrator fabricates an attack out of thin air, pretending something happened when there was no attack at all.

An example of the first type was the 1933 Nazi-orchestrated fire that burned down the Reichstag, which Hitler then used to blame on the Communists.

Examples of the second type would be the way that the Cult engineered US entry into WWI (enticing an enemy to act first so that they look like the aggressor, so that a subsequent attack on them [the plan all along] can be justified as 'self-defense') and US entry into

WWII (this time enticing Japan rather than Germany to attack the US).

An example of the third type was the 1964 Gulf of Tonkin incident, the concocted 'firing' on a US ship which never happened as it was invented out of thin air. This third type of false flag incident is what David Icke calls a "No Problem-Reaction-Solution" scenario whereby there is no problem, followed by an engineered reaction, then followed by a solution which is the plan all along. The most striking example ever of the No Problem-Reaction-Solution scenario was the fact that there never was a SARS-CoV-2 virus during the entire COVID scamdemic from 2019-2023 as I analyzed in detail in *Break Your Chains*.

The signature Zionist false flag operation is to stage a terror attack and blame it on Arabs or Muslims. The Zionists long ago cunningly mastered the art of executing horrific bombings on various targets, then quite convincingly making it look like the Arabs did it. Well, quite convincingly on the surface, but not to those who have seen through their deceit. This theme is absolutely imperative to grasp if you want to understand what's been happening in the world in the last approximately 80 years since Israel's founding in 1948 – and imperative context to understand to decode events such as the JFK assassination, the 9/11 operation and the Hamas attack on October 7th 2023.

In his book *The Profits of War: Inside the U.S.-Israeli Arms Network*, ex-Aman agent Ben-Menashe specifically outlines how the Zionist false flag op works: fund "*Israeli controlled 'Palestinian terrorists' who would commit crimes in the name of the Palestinian revolution, but were actually pulling them off, usually unwittingly, as part of the Israeli propaganda machine.*"[500] Piper reported on this phenomenon for decades in his career first at *The Spotlight* and later at *American Free Press. Final Judgment* contains footnotes to old issues of *The Spotlight* (e.g. from the 1980s) where Piper follows the breadcrumb trails that lead back to Zionist terrorism/the Mossad for many bombings.

In 1954 and 1967, two significant Zionist false flag ops occurred. The first was called Operation Susannah and is colloquially known as the Lavon Affair after the then Israeli Defence Minister Pinchas Lavon who was forced to resign because of the incident. Aman Unit 131 of the IDF recruited Egyptian Jews for the operation, which targeted cinemas, libraries and American educational centers belonging to the UK, US and Egypt. The targets were bombed and the blame was put on Egyptian Arabs, including the Muslim Brotherhood, itself another Cult organization that was created in 1928 and was being funded and used by the British during the 1940s and 1950s.[501] The UK and its superpower heir the US have always found radical and fundamentalist religious movements to be extremely useful, since many can easily be convinced to use violence to achieve their goals and will thus become 'terrorists' – the perfect ready made enemy. Specifically, the hit was to be blamed on the regime of Egyptian President Gamal Abdul Nasser, who at that time was becoming a very powerful leader in the Arab world with his movement of pan-Arab nationalism and secularism. Israel was hoping to alienate the US and Britain from Egypt, and thus prevent the Egyptian nationalization of the Suez Canal. The Egyptians quickly caught wind of the plan, then rounded up and arrested a 13-man spy ring, concluding that the operation was ordered by Lavon. Although the operation was unsuccessful as far as the Israelis were concerned, it was the first of numerous attacks to follow – many of

which would accurately hit their targets and successfully fool the public concerning the identity of the true orchestrators.

In 1967, Israel executed another false flag attack codenamed Operation Cyanide, which was essentially a rework of Operation Northwoods (the never-actualized plan to conduct a false flag attack on US soil and blame Cuba). Israel again attacked a Western target (the American Naval technical research and intelligence ship, the USS Liberty) and again tried to make it look as though Egypt were the culprit. On June 8th 1967, during the Six Day War where Israel attacked and stole land from Egypt, Syria and Jordan (claiming it was in defense), Israeli jets that had covered up their Star of David markings sunk the Liberty, putting napalm on the bridge of the ship, killing 34 and wounding 172 Americans. The attack with 12-18 aircraft lasted as long as the attack on Pearl Harbor. The coverup was

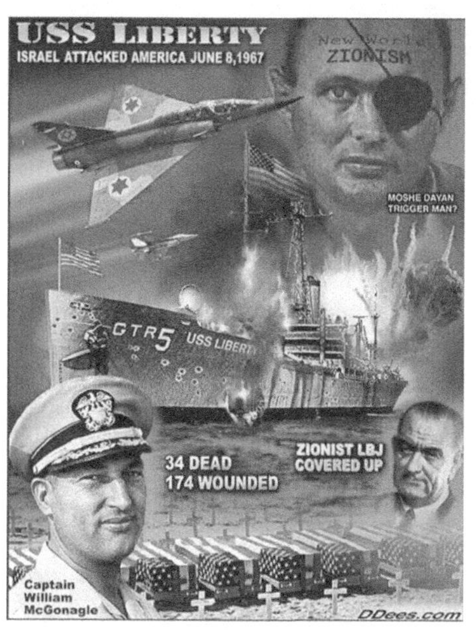

a joint conspiracy which went all the way to the very top brass. Admiral John McCain Sr. (the father of the late senator and presidential candidate John McCain) hid the truth on behalf of LBJ. McCain ordered the investigation to be completed within one week, an impossible task showing the intent to obfuscate. As revealed last chapter, Lyndon Johnson was controlled by his Zionist handler and mistress Mathilde Krim who was connected to Irgun. It was actually Russia who saved the USS Liberty – despite Israel trying to destroy lifeboats of escaping US soldiers! As survivor Phil Tourney told his sons who entered the US military, *"If you enlist, there's only one place you're fighting for and dying for: Israel."*[502] It is completely reasonable to assume that if Israel had succeeded in sinking the Liberty without witnesses, it would have attributed the crime to Egypt, and there would have been no one around to disprove this accusation – which could have led to the US entering into war against Egypt on behalf of Israel. During this Six Day War against Egypt, Israel committed all sorts of war crimes. For example, Israeli soldiers attacked and killed 14 Indian peacekeeping soldiers flying the UN flag on their way to Gaza; one Indian officer described this as a *"deliberate, cold-blooded killing of unarmed UN soldiers."*[503] The Israelis had captured some Egyptians and were holding them in the town of El Arish. By June 8th, they were tired of holding the prisoners, since the Israelis had nowhere to imprison them and inadequate forces with which to guard them. So, they decided to kill them en masse. They lined up 60 unarmed Egyptians with their hands tied behind their backs and murdered them in cold blood with machine guns. They also forced some Egyptian prisoners to dig graves for the dead and then shot them. Israeli army historian Aryeh Yitzhaki said that Israeli soldiers, including future Israeli PM Ariel Sharon (originally Scheinerman), slaughtered about 1,000 Egyptian prisoners in the Sinai.[504] Israeli officials later admitted that Egypt was not going to attack Israel, and that the Zionists were lying to feign self-defense; for example, Israel's coalition cabinet member during the Six Day War, Mordechai Bentov, admitted that the *"entire story of the danger of extermination was invented in every detail, and exaggerated a posteriori to justify the annexation of new Arab territory."*[505]

Here are more examples of the many Zionist false flag operations that the Cult has carried out:

– King David Hotel bombing, Jerusalem, 1946: Two years before Israel declared itself a nation, the Zionist terrorist group Irgun attacked the King David Hotel in Jerusalem, targeting the British administrative headquarters in the southern wing. 91 people were killed, including Arabs, Britons and Jews. Irgun terrorists disguised themselves as Arab workmen and hotel waiters. The motivation was that Irgun wanted to destroy recently seized documentation, held by the British in their headquarters, that incriminated the other main Jewish terrorist group at the time (Haganah) who were leading the Jewish insurgency against Britain.

– Rue Saint Anne bombing, Paris, 1978: Israeli agents exploded a bomb planted under a small car in Rue Saint Anne, killing Mohammed Boudia, an organizer for the PLO. Piper wrote that,

"Immediately afterward, Paris police received anonymous phone calls accusing Boudia of involvement in narcotics deals and attributing his murder to the Corsican Mafia. A thorough investigation subsequently established that Mossad special-action agents were responsible for the terrorist killing."[506]

– Cruise Ship MS Achille Lauro, Mediterranean Sea, 1985: this was a classic example of the 'Palestinian terror' that wasn't. Muhammad Zaidan, a.k.a. Mohammed Abul al-Abbas, of the Palestine Liberation Front (PLF), hijacked the Italian Achille Lauro liner off the coast of Egypt. He was getting paid millions from Israeli intelligence officers posing as Sicilian dons. Ben-Menashe describes how the Israeli-owned terrorists were told to *"make it bad, to show the world what lay in store for other unsuspecting citizens if Palestinian demands were not met. As the world knows, the group picked on an elderly American Jewish man in a wheelchair, killed him, and threw his body overboard. They made their point. But for Israel it was the best kind of anti-Palestinian propaganda."*[507] .

– Attempted Blowup of El Al Plane, London, 1986: this operation is also detailed by Ben-Menashe. The Mossad wanted to discredit the Syrians and implicate the Syrian Embassy in London in terrorism, so Rafi Eitan used Radi Abdullah, a former Jordanian colonel who was being paid as a Mossad informant. Radi had a 35-year-old cousin, Jordanian Nezar Hindawi, who lived in London. Hindawi lied to his girlfriend with an unwanted pregnancy, Ann-Marie Murphy, and convinced her to fly to Palestine. The plan was that she would take aboard a hidden bomb without knowing it and blow up the entire plane. Airport security found her and stopped the plot. Ben-Menashe writes: *"[Hindawi] spilled the beans and told them that a Syrian intelligence officer had asked him to carry out the task. But Radi was not implicated. He was under MI-5 protection. As a result, Margaret Thatcher closed down the Syrian Embassy in London. Rafi Eitan had had his way, Hindawi was jailed for 45 years ..."*[508]

– Operation Trojan, Tripoli, Libya, 1986: Mossad agents got a communication device on shore in Tripoli called a Trojan because it would take communications from the Israelis (an IDF boat in Mediterranean waters) and then rebroadcast them on what appeared to be official Libyan communication channels. This would give the appearance that the broadcast was coming from the Libyan Government or Libyan intelligence when it was not. In this way, the Israelis framed the Libyans to make it look like they were plotting terrorist attacks when they were not. Several nations such as the US and UK intercepted the communications and fell for this trick, believing the communications to be genuine Libyan communications, since they also coincided with Mossad reports about planned Libyan terrorism – here we have the Zionist signature false flag element again, framing Arabs for crimes they did not (or did not plan to) commit. France and Spain didn't fall for it, reasoning that the Libyans had been careful in the past not to plan or perform terrorism, and that the language used in the intercepted Libyan communications matched some of that used in the Mossad reports. Busted! However, unfortunately for Libya and Gaddafi, the Americans attacked them based on this fake 'intelligence' even though France refused to allow American planes to use its airspace for the operation.[509] This event is recounted by Ostrovsky in his second book, *The Other Side of Deception*. There is a reason why both of Ostrovsky's book titles about his Mossad misadventures contain the word 'deception' and why this very same word also features in Mossad's motto. This operation also involved the Mossad bombing a German discotheque, the Labelle Club in West Berlin on April 5th 1986. Piper reported that *"West Berlin police director Manfred Ganschow, who took charge of the investigation, cleared the Libyans, saying, 'This is a highly political case. Some of the evidence cited in Washington may not be evidence at all, merely assumptions supplied for political reasons.'"*[510] Then US President Reagan was convinced it was a Libyan attack, and retaliated by bombing Libya. Decades later, in 2011, Libyan leader Muammar Gaddafi would be killed after NATO bombed his country – the same Gaddafi who opposed Greater Israel, who supported pan-Arab pushback against Zionist expansionism, who warned that JFK was killed by Israel due to the nuclear issue (as revealed in the previous chapter), that 9/11 was not done by Osama bin Laden[511] and that all the Arab nations would by militarily picked off by the US/Israel Cult alliance, just as they were once friends with Iraqi leader Saddam Hussein before they turned on him and murdered him.[512]

– World Trade Center (WTC) bombing, New York, 1993: Piper found evidence of Mossad involvement in the earlier attack on the WTC in 1993. He revealed that the Mossad, who often recruits informants and agents from among the ranks of petty criminals, found a man called Ahmad Ajaj, whom they allegedly tasked to infiltrate radical Palestinian groups operating outside Israel. Piper wrote that, *"After Ajaj's deportation from Israel, he showed up in Pakistan, in the company of the Mujahideen rebels who were fighting against the Soviets in Afghanistan. And this, in itself, could point to further evidence that Ajaj was working for the Mossad. The copy of the infamous volume—described as 'the Al-Qaeda Terrorist Training Manual'—that received widespread publicity following the events of 9-11 had been uncovered in the possession of Ahmad Ajaj, the*

Mossad undercover informant in the first WTC attack."[513] In his second book *The Other Side of Deception*, ex-Mossad agent Ostrovsky reveals how the Mossad was supervising the supply line for the Mujahideen: *"a large portion of the Mujahideen's weapons were American-made and were supplied to the Muslim Brotherhood directly from Israel, using as carriers the Bedouin nomads who roamed the demilitarized zones in the Sinai."*[514]

– Israeli Embassy bombing, England, 1994: Former MI5 agent Annie Machon revealed how the Mossad bombed its own embassy in London in 1994, framing two prominent Palestinian activists to take the blame (Samar Alami and Jawad Botmeh), who received 20 year sentences for a crime they didn't commit.[515]

I will end this chapter with more evidence of Zionist false flag operations, this time against the Jewish population itself in Iraq. British-Israeli historian Avi Shlaim wrote a 2023 autobiography entitled *Three Worlds: Memoirs of an Arab-Jew*, in which he details his childhood as an Iraqi Jew and subsequent exile to Israel. During the period from 1950 to 1951, there was a mass exodus of 110,000 Jews from Iraq to Israel. Shlaim states he has proof of Zionist involvement in several 1950s attacks on Iraqi Jews, claiming that Mossad pulled off the bombings to drive Jews out of Iraq and get them to migrate to Israel. His experience was that *"we were conscripted into the Zionist project"*[516] and that, for the majority of Iraqi Jews, the migration to Israel was not some 'biblical homecoming' or other such Zionist nonsense, but rather a deeply traumatic experience of being uprooted from their home nation and forced to adapt to a new life elsewhere.

Finally, I will say this in response to those who say, like Ben-Gurion and all the other hardcore Zionists that have come after him, that the 'Jewish state' must have nuclear weapons (while disallowing anyone else around it to have them) and must attack its enemies preemptively and aggressively because its neighbors are determined to 'wipe Israel off the map.' How often have we heard this claim? Firstly, the truth is almost always the reverse due to the psychological phenomenon of projection. It is Israel that has planned and is executing the 'Greater Israel' project which involves completely overtaking many Arab countries and ruling an area from the Nile to the Euphrates. Secondly, the Zionists have a habit of outright lying. How do we know such claims are true? Thirdly, the Zionists are experts at conjuring their enemies so they have the excuse to attack. Fourthly, if some Arab or other Muslim leaders did get angry and say such things, it was in response to Israeli threats and aggression, not preceding it. Thus, Israel has the power to change its actions and therefore to not elicit such a response, which would be a better guarantor of their safety rather than continuing with their theft and aggression. Author Zeev Maoz, an expert on the Israeli security establishment and Middle Eastern scholar, wrote a 2008 book entitled *Defending the Holy Land: A Critical Analysis of Israel's Security and Foreign Policy*, in which he shows that almost all of the wars in which Israel has been involved (with the possible exception of the 1948 War of Independence) were, in his own words, entirely avoidable and *"the result of deliberate Israeli aggression, flawed decision-making, and misguided conflict management strategies."*[517]

Lorraine Day MD attributes this quote to Admiral and former CIA Deputy Director, Bobby Inman: *"Israeli spies have done more harm and have damaged the United States more than the intelligence agents of all other countries on earth combined ... They are the gravest threat to our national security."*[518] It is no exaggeration to say that, since its creation, the psychopathic Mossad has executed 70+ continuous years of sabotage, assassinations and false flag operations. Their whole world is their playground; the whole world is their target. They are the *"engine of policy in Israel"* as Ostrovsky writes; together with the CIA and other Cult intelligences agencies like the MI5, MI6 and the Russian FSB, they run the world. The Mossad is indeed the quintessential Cult 'Institute.' In the coming chapter, we will explore just how far this control has extended into Western institutions and agencies.

Sources

[393] By Way of Deception, Victor Ostrovsky, pp. 335-36

[394] https://web.archive.org/web/20250507113035/https://www.thedailybeast.com/jeffrey-epsteins-sick-story-played-out-for-years-in-plain-sight/

[395] https://www.narativ.org/p/blackmail-factory

[396] https://www.bitchute.com/video/qCfTTZzds43i

[397] https://consortiumnews.com/2013/07/11/prisms-controversial-forerunner/

[398] https://archive.org/details/Dr.JosephBenOrr-Inslaw/page/n5/mode/2up

[399] Profits of War: Inside the Secret U.S.-Israeli Arms Network, pp. 129-135

[400] https://www.informationliberation.com/?id=62044

[401] https://www.timesofisrael.com/netanyahu-said-to-have-offered-lewinsky-tapes-for-pollard/

[402] https://www.politico.com/story/2019/09/12/israel-white-house-spying-devices-1491351

[403] https://www.gao.gov/assets/t-nsiad-96-114.pdf

[404] By Way of Deception, pg. 262

[405] Ibid., pg. 322

[406] Ibid., pp. 335-36

[407] https://www.cbsnews.com/news/israeli-mossad-pager-walkie-talkie-hezbollah-plot-60-minutes/

[408] https://www.pewresearch.org/religion/2021/05/11/the-size-of-the-u-s-jewish-population/

[409] By Way of Deception, pp. 86-7

[410] Ibid., pg. 88

[411] https://www.bitchute.com/video/jQPeghtWmluG

[412] https://www.donotpanic.news/p/the-best-selling-apps-made-by-israeli

---

413 https://www.intel.com/content/www/us/en/corporate-responsibility/intel-in-israel.html

414 https://www.whoprofits.org/companies/company/7371

415 https://www.donotpanic.news/p/how-microsoft-became-a-hub-for-israeli

416 https://www.972mag.com/microsoft-azure-openai-israeli-army-cloud/

417 https://www.theguardian.com/world/2025/aug/06/microsoft-israeli-military-palestinian-phone-calls-cloud

418 https://www.mintpressnews.com/oogle-wiz-cybersecurity-data-deal/289413/

419 https://apnews.com/article/israel-palestinians-ai-weapons-430f6f15aab420806163558732726ad9

420 https://electronicintifada.net/content/dells-complicity-israels-genocide/50824

421 https://www.palantir.com/assets/xrfr7uokpv1b/3MuEeA8MLbLDAyxixTsiIe/9e4a11a7fb058554a8a1e3cd83e31c09/C134184_finaleprint.pdf

422 https://www.nytimes.com/2025/06/04/business/jeffrey-epstein-peter-thiel-estate.html

423 https://www.palantir.com/assets/xrfr7uokpv1b/3A0y10xksgXENvRMNaAsUu/ed8f7f1ed534c0101f64536a85f7297b/Gotham_AI-Enabled_Operations_White_Paper.pdf

424 https://www.theguardian.com/world/2025/jan/23/israeli-military-gaza-war-microsoft

425 https://www.bitchute.com/video/GJCRxxdakOQS

426 https://www.theguardian.com/world/interactive/2013/sep/11/nsa-israel-intelligence-memorandum-understanding-document

427 https://www.informationliberation.com/?id=62044

428 https://web.archive.org/web/20130708153028/https://www.spiegel.de/international/world/interview-with-whistleblower-edward-snowden-on-global-spying-a-910006.html

---

429 https://web.archive.org/web/20140509020404/http://www.businessinsider.com/stuxnet-was-far-more-dangerous-than-previous-thought-2013-11

430 https://web.archive.org/web/20170904015230/https://www.mac-solutions.net/en/news/129-sheep-dip-your-removable-storage-devices-to-reduce-the-threat-of-cyber-attacks

431 https://rumble.com/v4vfc8q-israels-arc-intel-processor-the-backdoor-to-the-world.html

432 https://archive.org/stream/0000-00-00-00-whitney-webb-00/2019-10-02_Former%20Israeli%20Intel%20Official%20Claims%20Jeffrey%20Epstein%2C%20Ghislaine%20Maxwell%20Worked%20for%20Israel_djvu.txt

433 https://x.com/ZevShalev/status/1746286233146314900

434 https://www.unz.com/isteve/jeffrey-epstein-and-foreign-intelligence/

435 https://x.com/ZevShalev/status/1746286233146314900

436 https://x.com/vickypjward/status/1148241562251517954

437 https://x.com/VickyPJWard/status/1128883871611801600

438 https://www.youtube.com/watch?v=G6X69JirzkU

439 https://www.mintpressnews.com/ari-ben-menashe-israel-relationship-jeffrey-epstein/263465/

440 https://x.com/mrally/status/1952581498340581682

441 https://www.jpost.com/israel-news/politics-and-diplomacy/article-844177

442 https://accuracy.org/release/epstein-protected-because-he-is-a-spy-a-backgrounder/

443 https://uploads.guim.co.uk/2024/01/04/Final_Epstein_documents.pdf, pg. 457

444 https://www.newspapers.com/article/the-los-angeles-times-statutory-rape-is/42705087/?locale=en-US

---

445 https://embed.documentcloud.org/documents/1507315-epstein-flight-manifests/

446 https://x.com/zerohedge/status/1942794543474286929

447 https://www.israelhayom.com/2020/10/16/fred-and-donald-trumps-jewish-connection/

448 https://pikulexpedition.substack.com/p/trump-timeline-of-an-israeli-asset

449 https://churchofsatan.com/hierarchy/

450 https://www.timesofisrael.com/when-netanyahu-slept-at-the-kushners-and-other-media-tales-of-trumps-jewish-confidantes/

451 https://silview.home.blog/2021/05/30/the-trump-rothschild-rockefeller-connections/comment-page-1/

452 https://silview.media/2021/05/30/the-trump-rothschild-rockefeller-connections/

453 https://rumble.com/v6soy23-caitlin-johnstone-its-all-out-in-the-open-find-link-to-source-document-belo.html

454 https://nymag.com/intelligencer/2019/08/trump-epstein-friendship-ended-over-mansion-report.html

455 https://www.politico.com/f/?id=00000158-267d-dda3-afd8-b67d3bc00000

456 https://www.scribd.com/doc/316341058/Donald-Trump-Jeffrey-Epstein-Rape-Lawsuit-and-Affidavits#fullscreen?platform=hootsuite

457 https://x.com/TomJChicago/status/1941251068316483740

458 https://www.jewishpress.com/news/jewish-news/chabad-2/trump-praises-lubavitcher-rebbe-one-of-the-most-dynamic-and-influential-faith-leaders-in-modern-history/2025/06/29/

459 https://x.com/Acyn/status/1951780402684985535

460 https://www.bitchute.com/video/hpgb0p4gx687

461 https://x.com/jkbjournalist/status/1275510424084021249

---

[462] https://www.businessinsider.com/jeffrey-epstein-private-island-temple-2019-7

[463] https://unlimitedhangout.com/2022/06/reports/leslie-wexners-inner-demon/

[464] https://www.youtube.com/watch?v=FRb0KLo9d1U

[465] https://www.nytimes.com/2019/07/31/business/jeffrey-epstein-eugenics.html

[466] https://www.vanityfair.com/news/2019/11/hunt-for-jeffrey-epstein-alleged-enabler-ghislaine-maxwell

[467] https://www.bitchute.com/video/Gwb0Bo9SZ6zA

[468] https://www.theguardian.com/uk-news/2020/oct/23/prince-andrew-asked-ghislaine-maxwell-about-accuser-documents-suggest

[469] https://www.npr.org/2021/12/17/1065083182/sarah-ransome-writes-about-jeffrey-epstein-abuse-allegations-in-silenced-no-more

[470] https://abcnews.go.com/US/epstein-accuser-ghislaine-maxwell-chief-orchestrator/story?id=81589520

[471] https://www.bbc.com/news/world-us-canada-50471342

[472] https://www.westernjournal.com/former-mobster-housed-epsteins-cell-says-no-way-killed/

[473] https://thefreedomarticles.com/patel-and-maga-agents-join-the-club/

[474] https://ordoabchao.ca/articles/the-profumo-affair-a-real-life-case-of-eyes-wide-shut

[475] https://www.cbsnews.com/news/how-jewish-american-pedophiles-hide-from-justice-in-israel/

[476] https://www.haaretz.com/israel-news/2022-07-25/ty-article/.premium/tip-of-the-iceberg-how-foreign-sex-offenders-find-refuge-in-israel/00000182-3532-d7e9-af96-3d73c52c0000

[477] https://www.jpost.com/israel-news/tens-of-thousands-of-pedophiles-operate-in-israel-every-year-637393

[478] https://www.informationliberation.com/?id=65013

[479] https://www.theguardian.com/australia-news/2015/feb/19/rabbis-absolute-power-how-sex-abuse-tore-apart-australias-orthodox-jewish-community

[480] https://web.archive.org/web/20220731071452/https://www.haaretz.com/2012-03-09/ty-article/pure-as-the-driven-snow/0000017f-dbc7-d3ff-a7ff-fbe74a1b0001

[481] https://www.justice.gov/usao-sdny/pr/statement-us-attorney-damian-williams-convictions-three-lev-tahor-leaders-child

[482] https://jewishchronicle.timesofisrael.com/day-school-teacher-suspected-of-sexual-abuse-in-pittsburgh/

[483] https://www.smh.com.au/national/sex-abuse-victims-sue-rabbi-over-comments-20130131-2dnks.html?js-chunk-not-found-refresh=true

[484] https://www.nefariousrussians.com/p/biblical-war-chabad-style

[485] https://www.counterpunch.org/2009/08/28/israeli-organ-harvesting/

[486] https://www.israelnationalnews.com/flashes/12699

[487] https://allthatsinteresting.com/nakam-abba-kovner

[488] https://www.wrmea.org/2009-march/russell-warren-howe-1925-2008.html

[489] https://www.jewishnews.co.uk/former-israeli-president-claims-queen-elizabeth-saw-israelis-as-terrorists/

[490] https://www.democracynow.org/2018/11/21/did_israel_kill_yasser_arafat_stunning

[491] https://www.washingtonpost.com/archive/politics/1997/10/12/for-many-israelis-assassination-is-only-as-bad-as-its-execution/adf20330-4c3a-458b-a507-ca8d5f7d0661/

[492] https://archive.is/cxK57

[493] https://thecradle.co/articles/a-terror-state-through-time-from-ben-gurion-to-netanyahu

[494] https://newlinesmag.com/review/the-nazi-fugitives-hired-by-israel/

---

[495] https://www.aa.com.tr/en/middle-east/israels-longstanding-policy-of-extrajudicial-murder/1058177

[496] https://apnews.com/article/us-iran-nuclear-intelligence-b506d130e474c00f6bd653d3d5a8d31a

[497] https://www.dni.gov/index.php/newsroom/congressional-testimonies/congressional-testimonies-2025/4061-ata-hpsci-opening-statement-as-delivered

[498] https://www.jpost.com/Middle-East/Iran/Israel-behind-assassinations-of-Iran-nuclear-scientists-Yaalon-hints-411473

[499] https://idsf.org.il/en/history-en/deadly-attacks/

[500] The Profits of War: Inside the U.S.-Israeli Arms Network, pg. 123

[501] https://archive.org/details/secretaffairsbri0000curt/page/n451/mode/2up

[502] https://www.youtube.com/watch?v=QCDjoc7FBbk

[503] Body of Secrets, Anatomy of the Ultra-Secret National Security Agency From the Cold War Through the Dawn of the New Century by James Bamford, Doubleday, New York, 2001, pg. 201

[504] Ibid., pp. 201-203

[505] https://palcit.net/article-977-all-this-story-about-the-danger-of-extermination-has-been-a-complete-invention

[506] Final Judgment, pg. 23

[507] The Profits of War: Inside the U.S.-Israeli Arms Network, pg. 124

[508] Ibid., pp. 124-5

[509] The Other Side of Deception, pp. 114-117

[510] Final Judgment, pg. 23

[511] https://www.youtube.com/watch?v=5INSyV_Wk_E

[512] https://www.bitchute.com/video/qkLiU9uu7oFf

[513] https://www.unz.com/book/michael_collins_piper__false-flags/

[514] The Other Side of Deception, pg. 199

[515] https://x.com/Kahlissee/status/1838518302143823872

[516] https://www.youtube.com/watch?v=TMqJQE9yoe0

[517] https://press.umich.edu/Books/D/Defending-the-Holy-Land

[518] https://www.goodnewsaboutgod.com/studies/spiritual/home_study/immigration_wars.htm

CHAPTER 13: CULT CONTROL OF WESTERN POLITICS AND MEDIA

"Believing with absolute certitude that now, with the White House, the Senate and much of the American media in our hands, the lives of others do not count as much as our own."

– Israeli journalist Ari Shavit, The New York Times, May 27th 1996[519]

"Every time we do something, you tell me Americans will do this and will do that. I want to tell you something very clear: don't worry about American pressure on Israel. We, the Jewish people, control America, and the Americans know it."

– Then-Israeli PM Ariel Sharon to former Israeli PM Shimon Peres, October 3rd 2001, as reported on Kol Yisrael radio[520]

The degree to which Israel has taken over key centers of power in society is staggering and frightening. Israeli control over many aspects of life is similar in many Western nations, whether it be the USA, UK, France, Canada or Australia. In this chapter, I will focus just on the US as a microcosm, and just on Israeli control over politics and media, although the control extends much further than that.

Israeli Control of Congress

Israeli control over US politics used to be more covert, but it seems to have become more overt, probably because the Cult realizes just how entrenched its power has become, and so it can afford to become more brazen. Last year in 2024, during the US presidential elections, a man called Matt Brooks (Executive Officer of the Republican Jewish Coalition) stepped out onto the stage at the Republican National Committee (RNC). He immediately commanded the crowd, *"Let me hear you cheer if you support Israel!"*[521] and said the same sentence again, this time with more urgency. You would be forgiven if you thought you were in Israel instead of the USA. It is now a very common sight to see flags which are a combination of the US and Israeli flags stitched together. Israel invests a huge amount of energy in perception and narrative control, and in this case, what it wants you to believe is that American interests are the same as Israeli interests. It wants as many Americans as possible conjoining the two things in their mind, so that there are less questions when it comes to the ongoing financial, military, political and cultural support of Israel, which costs the US billions of dollars per year – at a time when America's infrastructure is crumbling, when homeless Americans sleep on the streets, when the cost of living is rising and robbing people's standard of life, and when the middle-class is vanishing.

Image #90: the United States of America? Or the United States of Israel?

Another brazen example of Israeli control of Congress came when current US Congressman Brian Mast, a representative from

Florida, decided to wear his old IDF uniform to Congress in October 2023![522] Mast is a dual US-Israeli citizen who had previously fought in the IDF before fighting in the US Army. In what other country would it be even remotely acceptable to wear the military uniform of another nation to that country's parliament, congress or official political assembly? US Department of State spokesperson Tammy Bruce let her true colors shine when she said that *"America is the greatest country on Earth ... next to Israel."*[523]

US politicians are owned by Israel. Recall the example from the previous chapter where Donald Trump actually boasted how he gave Israel (via Sheldon and Miriam Adelson) more than what they asked for! According to the website TrackAIPAC.com at the time of writing,[524] Trump has received $230+ million from pro-Israel interest groups, including $14+ million from the aforementioned Republican Jewish Coalition (an AIPAC ally) since 2020. By far the biggest donation, or better put, bribe, has come from Miriam Adelson's Preserve America PAC, which has bought Trump off with $215+ million.

Former Congresswoman Cynthia McKinney was one of the brave few politicians who refused to go along with the Cult Israeli agenda. Years ago she exposed how US politicians running for Congress were given 'The Pledge' by Jewish lobby agents to assess whether they were on board with the Israeli agenda:[525]

"Every candidate for Congress at that time ... was given a pledge to sign ... the Pledge has Jerusalem as the capital city, the military superiority of Israel."

"American Congresspeople have to sign this pledge?"

"Yes ... If you don't sign the pledge, you don't get money."

Israel controls almost all US politicians via two principal methods: bribery and blackmail. This is why child sex rings, like Epstein's, are such an important tool to them, because they need to catch and record US politicians committing crimes (like pedophilia and rape) so that they have something on them.

Israel has such massive control over America that it doesn't just control federal politics; it also controls state and local politics. There is no rational reason why Israel should concern a state or local politician, since they are not in charge of US foreign policy, but that doesn't matter to the Cult – it seeks total domination. Therefore, its infiltration of US politics extends to all levels. To see this, you just need to look at the words and actions of some of the state governors. For instance, take Florida Governor Ron DeSantis, who ran for the presidency in 2024. Guess where he decided to sign a piece of legislature – state legislature? In Israel! That's right. He was the sitting governor of Florida, and he decided to sign an antisemitism bill in Israel[526] to demonstrate his allegiance and fealty to the Jewish state. Talk about an example of a captured politician and a captured system. DeSantis, like Trump, is 100% owned by Israel; during his presidential bid he vowed that if he were president he would go after third world countries that have become *"hotbeds of antisemitism."*[527] He also dined with Miriam Adelson and other Republican Party megadonors in Jerusalem.[528] Another former US state governor, former South Dakota Governor Kristi Noem, signed an antisemitism bill in 2023, boasting that she had signed the *"strongest"* hate crime bill in America that would be *"model legislation that other states can implement to stand with our Jewish brothers and sisters and stand with our ally Israel."*[529] Noem was apparently promoted for her loyalty by becoming Department of Homeland Security (DHS) head

Image #91: Trump, owned by Israel, will do pretty much whatever Bibi wants. But he's 'anti-establishment' right?

in the MAGA Trump Admin. Noem had earlier in 2020 signed an executive order[530] prohibiting state offices from conducting business with companies boycotting Israel. It is the right of citizens or businesses to choose with whom they want to do business, or to exercise their right to not do business with certain groups or nations (boycotting), which why the Boycott, Divest, Sanction (BDS) movement has been so successful. Israel has for some time now been pushing US politicians to pass anti-BDS legislation.

DeSantis and Noem were great during the COVID scamdemic when they pushed back against unconstitutional and human right-destroying COVID rules and restrictions, but as soon as the topic comes around to Israel … forget about unalienable and inherent human rights. This pattern of US politicians, journalists and media influencers appearing to be pro-freedom and pro-individual rights while secretly being beholden to Israel has come up repeatedly in US politics since the end of the scamdemic.

<u>Control of the Entire US Government</u>

It's not just Congress that Israel controls; it's virtually every branch, agency and aspect of the entire US Government. The White House or Executive Branch is teeming with Zionists, including in very high-up positions, such as Secretary of Defense (now called Secretary of War) Pete Hegseth and Secretary of State Marco Rubio. Former National Security Advisor Mike Waltz was such a Zionist he was actively collaborating and making war plans with Netanyahu; this was too much even for Trump so Waltz was fired.

Israel doesn't just use proxies; sometimes it tries to insert actual dual citizens into positions of power. In April 2025, a woman called Merav Ceren was appointed as the director for Israel and Iran affairs at the National Security Council. Guess what? Ceren had previously worked with the Israeli Ministry of Defense! Talk about conflict of interest and blatant corruption. She was removed from her position in May. The Zionist media tried to hide her past, however according to this article on Al-Monitor, *"According to her biography on the foundation's website, Ceren worked at the Israeli Defense Ministry before beginning the fellowship. In that capacity, she participated in negotiations between the Israeli government and the Palestinian Authority at the ministry, according to the biography, which was last updated in 2016."*[531] Ceren is a "National Security Fellow" at the Foundation for Defense of Democracies, one of many Zionist think tanks and nonprofit organizations in America with noble sounding names that appeal to freedom, democracy and human rights but whose mission destroys these things in service of the Cult's Israel first agenda.

Israel also exerts control over the US National Institutes of Health (NIH). Journalist Green Greenwald pointed out[532] that, according to an NIH April 2025 announcement,[533] *"medical researchers will have all funds terminated if they support a boycott of Israel. They can support a boycott of any other country, or even other US states – just not Israel."* More in-your-face tyranny. The notice was later rescinded,[534] perhaps due to bad publicity. As elaborated in previous chapters, Israel ensures it maintains control over the CIA; nothing has changed in this regard since Angleton left. I quoted Bobby Ray Inman at the end of last chapter. Piper related a story about a run-in Inman had with the Israeli lobby:[535]

Inman described how in 1981 when the Israelis had bombed Iraq's nuclear reactor, he (Inman) discovered that the Israelis had been able to carry out their act precisely because they had gained access to high-level Pentagon satellite reconnaissance files. At that juncture, Inman, then serving as acting CIA director during CIA director William Casey's absence from the country, gave orders limiting Israeli access to such strategic national intelligence. In response, according to Inman, 'The [Israeli] defense minister, General Sharon, was so furious he came to the U.S. to protest to [Secretary of Defense] Weinberger.' But Weinberger—himself a critic of Israel—stood behind Inman. Then, after CIA Director Casey returned to the United States, William Safire—a longtime friend and a former campaign manager for Casey when Casey made an unsuccessful bid for Congress—complained to Casey who countermanded Inman's decision. According to Inman, 'from that point on, if you will trace the [media] coverage [of Inman], it's been hostile.'

Control of key institutions within the US Federal Government obviously gives Israel control of US foreign policy. Here is what then-Senator J. William Fulbright said on CBS' "Face the Nation" on April 15th 1973:[536]

Israel controls the US Senate. The Senate is subservient to Israel, in my opinion much too much; we should be more concerned about US interests, rather than doing the bidding of Israel. The great majority of the Senate of the US – somewhere around 80 percent – are completely in support of Israel; anything Israel wants, Israel gets. This has been demonstrated time and again, and this has made [foreign policy] difficult for our government.

Israel controls America to such an extent that it is even able to control US policy towards other third party nations regarding those nations' conduct towards Israel. An example from June 2025 is when Chile, in response to the ongoing Gaza genocide committed by Israel since the October 2023 Hamas attacks, announced plans[537][538] to diversify its military purchases to reduce dependence on Israel, as well as to ban the importation of Israeli settlement goods. In response, Israel was trying to get the US to punish Chile; this source states that America *"is weighing a series of retaliatory measures against Chile in response to the Boric government's deteriorating ties with Israel, The Media Line has learned from a source within President Donald Trump's administration. The warning comes after Chile withdrew its military attachés from Tel Aviv, citing Israel's conduct in the war in Gaza ... According to the source, "everything is on the table." Among the options being discussed in Washington: canceling Chile's participation in the US Visa Waiver Program, increasing tariffs on Chilean exports, suspending student visa interviews, and even closing the US consulate in Santiago."*[539]

Israel's control also extends to international organizations such as those under the auspices of the UN. A recent example mentioned in the previous chapter was Israel's ability to co-opt the IAEA. Iran claims, very plausibly, that Israel was able to obtain information from the IAEA regarding the names and locations of various Iranian scientists working on Iran's nuclear program. With that information, Israel then launched one of it nefarious decapitation or assassination campaigns to murder at least 14 Iranian nuclear scientists.[540] In other words, Israel got information from what is supposed to be a neutral governing body and used it militarily.

Under Trump, the US Citizenship and Immigration Services (USCIS) announced in August 2025 that it would screen immigrants for "antisemitic ideologies"[541] while in Germany, a new 2024 German citizenship test includes questions on holocaust denial and when Israel was founded.[542] This is to become a *German* citizen!

The Sprawling Israeli Lobby Network: AIPAC, ADL, 'Jewish Friends' Organizations and More

To say that the Israeli lobby network in America is extensive would be the understatement of the millennium. The network is easily the most powerful in America. It is composed of many separate organizations, think tanks, agencies, associations, councils and Political Action Committees (PACs), all working towards the singular goal of advancing Israeli interests at any cost, above American interests if need be. The most influential of them all is AIPAC which, as mentioned in chapter 11, was the spin off successor to the AZC. It is no secret that AIPAC funds devoted American Zionists with as much money as they need to win election or re-election, while withdrawing funds and simultaneously funding opponents if Congresspeople refuse to toe the Israeli line. Veteran Vermont Senator Bernie Sanders admitted that AIPAC controls how politicians vote:[543]

But if you stand up you're going to find that AIPAC and other billionaire-funded Super PACs are going to go to war against you, putting huge amounts of money in a primary in your general election ... There are many members of the Senate who will come to you privately and say 'My God, what Netanyahu is doing is outrageous! I just can't vote because money is going to come and destroy my political career' ... People can't vote their conscience. People can't vote their intelligence.

Thomas Massie is one of the very few Congress members left with integrity. He spelled it out very clearly when he said that virtually all members have an 'AIPAC babysitter' who is *"always talking to you ... They're probably a constituent in your district, but they are firmly embedded in AIPAC ... when they come to DC, you go have lunch with them. They've got your cell [phone] number ... I've had four members of Congress say 'I'll talk to my AIPAC person ... my AIPAC guy, and see if I can get him to dial those ads back' ... they've basically got a buddy system with someone who's representing a foreign country."*[544]

Massie makes the point that there is no other country in the world – not Britain, not Australia, not Germany – who has a lobby that is anything like Israel's. After all, countries like Britain, Australia and Germany are natural US allies, so why would they need a huge lobby to convince the US? The very fact that Israel invests so much money and energy into its lobby network shows how fragile the US-Israeli connection could be, if more Americans realized that it's not in their best interest to support Israel to this degree. Massie points out that Israel, which receives a minimum of $4 billion of US aid every year (plus all the extra money it gets, such as in 2023-24 when it got at least $17.9 billion[545]), is sucking off the American teat in a way that other nations are not. When Massie was asked on a podcast what exactly the US gets from Israel to justify this enormous drain on American finances, he replied, *"We get a lot of countries that hate us."*[546]

Another vector of Jewish power in America is the loathsome ADL, formerly known as the Anti-Defamation League of B'nai B'rith, which was set up by Rothschild agents in 1913 in New York – the same year as the IRS and Fed were set up as covered in chapter 7. The ADL is a Cult Rothschild Israeli front, named in an Orwellian fashion to hide its true objective. While it claims to oppose defamation (and fight antisemitism), it actually defames those who criticize the Cult, Jewish power, Jewish supremacy and Israel's criminal actions. It split off from the B'nai B'rith early on. Its first job was to do damage control in the case of Leo Frank, President of the local B'nai B'rith chapter, director of the National Pencil Company and a wealthy Jewish pedophile. Frank raped and murdered a 13 year old girl named Mary Phagan who worked at his factory. Frank and his lawyers appealed the case, which went all the way to the US Supreme Court, but he lost and was sentenced to death by hanging, a sentence which was subsequently commuted to life imprisonment. Frank's conviction was upheld by thirteen courts and judges in his thirteen appeals.[547] The case attracted a lot of media, and two years later in 1915, Frank was kidnapped from jail, taken to Marietta, Georgia (Mary Phagan's hometown) and murdered – by hanging. The ADL has unsuccessfully tried to claim the trial was marred by mob antisemitism, but it did succeed in 1986 in convincing the Georgia State Board of Pardons and Paroles to issue a pardon in recognition of the state's failures. Notably, however, the board took no stance on Frank's guilt or innocence. Frank, a white man, blamed the black janitor, characterizing him in a very racist way.

The ADL, like the Cult, is afraid of open discussion, since it would lose control of the narrative in a straight and honest debate.

Therefore, it relies on intimidation and (ironically) defamation to get people censored and shut them down. A favorite tactic of the ADL is to claim that an author or speaker is 'antisemitic' or 'inciting hate' and that their presentation or event could lead to a breach of public peace and should therefore be cancelled. The ADL first pressures hosts of venues that have invited certain authors or researchers to speak, trying to force them to cancel the event. It engages in massive smear campaigns to sully the reputation of genuine truthseekers who have gotten close to the truth about the Cult that has hijacked Judaism. It treated Michael Collins Piper this way for decades before his death, and still treats David Icke this way. The moral to the story is that if you are a truthseeker who is getting attacked by the ADL, you must have touched a nerve and be on to something true and important.

Al Jazeera released two revealing documentaries which gave an inside look into how Israel blatantly interferes in US and UK politics, both entitled *"The Lobby."* Often the strategy is to set up front groups which appear to be grassroots with sappy names (Friends of Israel, Labour Friends of Israel, Conservative Friends of Israel, We Believe in Israel, etc.). These groups are really funded and supported via the Israeli Embassy and other groups, which are in turn funded from Israel itself and Cult intelligence agencies. In addition to the aforementioned AIPAC, Republican Jewish Coalition and ZOA, there are Jewish lobbies and influential organizations everywhere – here is a partial list of just the groups in the US alone:

- CUFI (Christians United for Israel)
- J Street
- AJC (American Jewish Committee and American Jewish Congress)

- AJPA (American Jewish Press Association)
- AZM (American Zionist Movement)
- AFSI (Americans For a Safe Israel)
- ADL (Anti-Defamation League)
- B'nai B'rith International
- Birthright Israel Children of Jewish Holocaust Survivors
- Conference of Presidents of Major American Jewish Organizations
- EMET (Endowment for Middle East Truth)
- Hadassah – Women's Zionist Organization of America
- HODS (Halachic Organ Donor Society)
- ARZENU (International Federation of Reform and Progressive Religious Zionists)
- JTA (International Jewish News Service)
- IAC (Israeli-American Council)
- JCPA (Jewish Council for Public Affairs)
- JDL (Jewish Defense League)
- JFNA (Jewish Federations of North America)
- JNF (Jewish National Fund)
- RZA (Religious Zionists of America)
- UCI (Unity Coalition for Israel)

Then there are Zionist think tanks such as the Brookings Institution, the Foundation for Defense of Democracies, the Heritage Foundation, the Washington Institute for Near East Policy, the Foreign Policy Research Institute and many many more. The network is massive, well-organized and incredibly well-funded. And if these aren't enough for you, you can always go to your local school for some 'Israel first' flavoring: Beverly Hills in Los Angeles will now display Israeli flags in public schools.[548]

<u>The Targeting and Removal of Anyone who Criticizes Israel</u>

The Cult has developed into a finely-oiled machine with an array of tools at its disposal – bribery, blackmail, reputation smearing, impeachment and assassination to name a few. When bribery and blackmail don't work to get politicians to toe the Israeli line, the Cult will target them, and find a way to either prevent them from accessing office or remove them from their current position. You can see how politicians in Washington DC are deeply scared to speak out against the Cult for fear of losing their jobs, their careers or their lives. Everyone, no matter how loyal they have been, is expendable to the Cult if they wander off the plantation.

This has been going on a long time – ever since the 1950s, with the establishment of the CIA and the Mossad and their tight-knit connection. In the 1960s they were assassinating American presidents; in the 1970s they were arranging for American presidents to be impeached or resign. In his book (pages 377-382), Piper provides some other examples. He highlights how the Israeli connection can be found in scandals that plagued Spiro Agnew, John Connally and Gary Hart. The 'scandal' that took down Agnew was super contrived: Barnet Skolnik, a liberal Jewish prosecutor, made a deal with Lester Matz, a prominent Jewish businessman, who was under investigation for paying kickbacks to public officials in Maryland. Matz claimed that he had paid bribes to Agnew. Two years after getting kicked out of office, Agnew was criticized for pointing out the preponderance of Israeli sympathizers in the media. Later

Agnew would write, in a private letter, that the advent of his difficulties sprang from his confrontation with this lobby. When John Connally (the Texas Governor sitting in front of JFK when he was shot) ran for the presidential nomination in 1980, he challenged Israeli power in a controversial speech. In reaction to this, Israeli educator and philosopher Emmanuel Rackman, president of Bal Ilan University, called for Connally to be stopped at any cost, even if it meant assassination. Are you seeing the pattern by now? Rackman hysterically compared Connally to Hitler and also to 'Amalek,' the ancient Jewish enemy of the Bible. This appeal to 'Amalek' is often used by Cult Israeli officials to control their citizens or soldiers by way of inciting hate and dehumanizing the opponent – see chapter 17 where Netanyahu did exactly the same thing as he launched the Gaza genocide in 2023. Here is what Rackman wrote, as quoted by Piper:[549]

The American Jewish community must be alerted. If only we had stopped Hitler early enough, millions of Jews would still be alive. And Connally must be stopped at all costs. He must not even get near the nomination! He must be destroyed, at least politically, as soon as possible. It is sufficiently early to make Connally look ridiculous and destroy him politically without bloodshed ... Perhaps I am overreacting, but if I have learned anything especially from the rabbinic view of Biblical history it is that we are less fearful and more forgiving of enemies who at least accord us a modicum of respect than we are of enemies who treat us with disdain, with contempt. That makes Arafat more acceptable than Connally ... Remember Amalek ... Eradicate him from the face of the earth.

Piper also mentioned the case of Senator Gary Hart, who was running for the 1988 Democratic Presidential nomination. Hart had been at the forefront of inquiries into the JFK assassination and the Mafia in general. Piper wrote that Tampa mob boss Santo Trafficante, underling of Meyer Lansky, once said about Hart that *"We need to get rid of the son of a bitch."*[550] Hart's campaign was derailed after the Jewish-owned media made a big fuss about his supposed affair with his campaign aide Donna Rice.

Ostrovsky was explicit about the power of the Mossad. 'The Institute' has ways to control who makes it to the US Presidency and Vice Presidency, as well as to remove presidents and shuffle vice-presidents into the top position, if they are deemed to be better for Israel:

Any time a president was not on the best of terms with Israel, the Jewish organizations were instructed to cozy up to the vice president. That was the case with Dwight Eisenhower, whom Israel regarded as the worst president in history (although, ironically, the vice president they regarded as a friend, namely Richard Nixon, himself became an enemy once he was president). It was what lay behind the strong support Israel and the Jewish community gave to Lyndon Johnson, who almost doubled aid to Israel in his first year as president, after John Kennedy had come down hard on the Israeli nuclear program ... That strategy was behind their hatred for Nixon and their admiration for Gerald Ford.[551]

Although you may think that all US officials are pro-Israel, that is not the case. Colonel Nathan McCormack was on the Joint Chiefs of Staff's J5 planning directorate before he was removed from his position in June 2025. To his credit, McCormack saw right though Israeli propaganda, and on his semi-private social media account, called Israel America's *"worst ally"* which provides the US with *"literally nothing"* other than the *"enmity of millions"* worldwide.[552]

In another post, he explicitly called Israel a *"death cult"*[553] and in another post stated that *"Netanyahu and his judeosupremacist cronies are determined to prolong the conflict for their own goals: either to remain in power or to annex the land."*[554] What a refreshingly awake and honest American official!

Despite the Cult's domination of US politics, there are those who have pushed back. Former US Congressman James (Jim) Traficant was brave and bold. He was a former sheriff who emphasized that it was America's one-sided handling of Middle Eastern affairs (totally favoring Israel) that incited hatred against her across the world. Traficant saw firsthand for 17 years in Congress how Israel totally dictated US foreign and domestic policy. He had the distinction of being the only American in history to have defeated the DOJ in a RICO (Racketeer Influenced and Corrupt Organizations) trial pro se (without a lawyer)! The Cult went after him; he was framed and imprisoned for nearly 8 years for a crime he didn't commit, but he did walk free eventually. He died in 2014.

Current Republican Congressman Matt Gaetz successfully fended off a failed blackmail attempt by Israeli agent Jake Novak in 2023, in what appeared to be a $25 million extortion plot targeting Gaetz's wealthy father.[555] Was this why Trump did not pursue asking Gaetz to join his administration after initially tapping him – that he wasn't pro-Israel enough and wasn't able to be blackmailed?

<u>Control of Media: The MSM, The Rightwing and the MAM</u>

The MSM (Mainstream Media) was bought long ago by the Cult. In chapter 5 regarding the rise of the Rothschilds, I mentioned that the Rothschilds bought Reuters and AP, two of the biggest media companies in the world. The MSM underwent lots of consolidation in the 1990s and 2000s where it got to the point that a handful of gigantic corporations controlled 90% of TV and radio stations. At the top of them are all ultra Zionists; to give one example out of many, Time magazine, which has promoted the official story of the JFK assassination, is owned by the mega-rich Bronfman family (mentioned in both the previous two chapters in connection to the JFK assassination and to Jeffrey Epstein).

Since that time, with internet media becoming more a part of people's everyday lives, the Cult, ever hungry to control the narrative, had to figure out how to take over the new media. One of the ways it did this was by infiltrating the political right and its rightwing media outlets. As usual, it was very cunning. As the political left became increasingly extreme during the 2010s, with the rise of the transgender agenda and woke ideology, the right started to look sane by comparison. Many rightwing media outlets were speaking out against the manmade climate change hoax, the idea that people can choose what sex they are and the idea that jobs should be given not on the basis of merit but on where you fall in the woke/ oppression hierarchy. Since they were on the side of freedom and individual rights, they gained a lot of support. Then, during the COVID scamdemic, the issue became politicized, and again the rightwing came out on the side of freedom and individual rights. So the rightwing again came out smelling like roses. However, for those paying attention, there was something dark lurking under the surface; virtually all these popular rightwing outlets were secretly funded, or had strong connections, to Israel. However, it wasn't that apparent to the average person until Israel was in the news (e.g. after the October 7th 2023 Hamas attack), since Israel wasn't being discussed that much. Michael Tracy commented on Twitter/X that *"The number of right-wing media outlets that are systematically, fanatically 'pro-Israel' is actually astonishing,"* providing his own list:[556]

- Fox News
- Daily Wire
- Newsmax
- The Post Millennial
- PragerU
- Breitbart
- Washington Free Beacon
- Rebel News
- Epoch Times
- Babylon Bee
- New York Post
- National Review
- WorldNetDaily
- Washington Times
- Washington Examiner
- One America News
- Real America's Voice
- Christian Broadcasting Network
- The Blaze
- Daily Mail
- The Free Press
- The Federalist
- Gateway Pundit
- Salem Radio Network
- Right Side Broadcasting Network

- Western Journal
- Human Events
- RedState
- PJ Media
- Hot Air
- Twitchy
- Townhall
- Drudge Report
- Daily Caller

From Israel's perspective, creating, financing or supporting these media organizations to get viewers in their corner is a cunning way to win the information war. You think the left is crazy? So do we! Now come support Israel and its genocidal wars!

Some of the Israeli involvement in the media outlets has not been all that subtle. Israel has been prepared to use its actual agents. For instance, the CEO of PragerU, Marissa Streit, is a (former) member of Israeli intelligence – Aman's Unit 8200. As discussed last chapter, Unit 8200 alumni are spread throughout the media landscape, and it's hard to say how much they are really 'former' workers there. Likewise, Ben Shapiro of the Daily Wire is also Israeli intelligence, as confirmed by his former Breitbart colleague Charles Johnson, who wrote the following in a tweet now taken down:[557]

I want to be fully on record that I saw Ben Shapiro receive tasking from Israeli intelligence connect[ing] to Netanyahu when I worked next to him at Breitbart.com. When I asked him about it he said he always kept close ties. It's time for Ben to register under FARA.

Shapiro ran cover for the Mossad and hilariously tried to claim that it doesn't matter who shot JFK.[558] The new media landscape is now soaked with these Israel first outlets which are mostly rightwing but in theory could be anywhere on the political spectrum. The whole point is to suck people in with content they like, while indoctrinating them with the Zionist perspective and instilling Islamophobia or anti-Arab, anti-Iran sentiment. In 2023, David Icke coined the term "Mainstream Alternative Media" or MAM to describe these new media outlets and reporters, many of whom are utterly clueless when it comes to understanding the force that really runs the world. Many blindly supported Trump during his 2024 presidential bid, helping him get elected, only then to turn around and express frustration or disappointment when Trump did what he was always going to do – put Israel first at any cost, even if it meant starting wars with Israel's enemies by attacking Yemen and Iran. One MAM member Tim Pool even secretly met with Netanyahu to *"to discuss 'anti-semitism' in pro-Trump spaces"*![559] Meanwhile, Alex Jones, who ceased being credible a very, very long time ago (at least by 2016 when he became all pro-Trump and fell headlong in the fake left-right paradigm), was said to have been visited by the Mossad and told to leave the topic of Israel alone, according to Nick Fuentes.[560] Recently it was reported that Israel is paying US social media influencers thousands of dollars per post to improve its image, around $7,000 per post according to the information[561] based on this document.[562] Whatever it could have been or should have been, the MAM is now no better than the MSM, and is similarly compromised and infiltrated. It's more important than ever to check your sources carefully when selecting from which media outlets to get your news.

<u>The Death or Disappearance of Charlie Kirk</u>

The Cult is absolutely ruthless when it comes silencing its opposition – even from its own agents. Conservative MAM podcaster Charlie Kirk was either murdered or whisked away on September 10th 2025. These days with AI video fakery, false flag hoaxes and advanced holographic technology the public doesn't even know exists, it's impossible to say what really happened. It could have been a death, or it could been a disappearance; Kirk was written out the script just as Epstein was. After slavishly defending Israel for most of his career, Kirk was beginning to push back in quite a few ways, including questioning the October 7th false flag operation (see chapter 17), questioning rich Jewish donors funding leftwing causes like mass migration and marxism, and pointing out how Israel was on the verge of a civil war before the Hamas attack (Netanyahu was trying to change the Constitution of Israel to strip power from the judicial branch). Kirk was Israel's investment, and no criticism would be tolerated. He had to go.[563]

Why did the Cult write Kirk out of the script? There are at least four reasons:

1. To reassert control over the narrative. Charlie was pushing back against Israel too much. This includes taking over TP USA (Turning Point USA) with Erika Kirk. Max Blumenthal (The Grayzone) did great journalism to uncover how Cult Zionists like Bill Ackman[564] and Robert Shillman[565] were badgering Charlie into even more diehard support for Israel or cutting his funding. To his credit, Kirk refused bribery ($150 million funding offer for TP USA) and 're-education' (a visit to Israel) in the last few weeks before his death/disappearance. Shillman is actually a very appropriate name since he also funds other Zionist shillmen and

shillwomen such as Tommy Robinson, Ben Shapiro and Laura Loomer.

2. To use and capitalize upon the death/disappearance of Kirk to promote government, voting, rightwing politics, conservatism, Jesus/Christianity (and unreasonable forgiveness/humility along with that, to make people more docile). This includes trying to make Charlie into a Jesus figure/martyr like they tried to with Trump and his two fake assassinations, which were also hoaxes.[566]

3. To potentially start a Civil War in America between the left and the right.

4. To distract from other important topics such as the further investigation and uncovering of the Epstein network, including Epstein's connection to Trump and many other NWO figures.

The official Charlie Kirk story is another magic bullet scenario just like the JFK assassination. We're supposed to believe that a .30-06 bullet pierced Kirk's left shoulder but didn't exit his body? These bullets go through steel plates. The abnormalities, inconsistencies and impossibilities with this incident abound. Why was no autopsy performed? Why was there no blood and flesh splattered all over the canopy? Why was there blood on the table and chairs, but not on the grass? Why are so many 'Tylers' involved in this incident, when in Freemasonry, the Tyler or Tiler is the officer in charge of guarding the lodge's door on the outside? Why did Erika flash the devil's horn sign? Why was the crime scene not cordoned off? Why was it quickly paved over? Why was there a trap door right near where he sat? Why did the same men who signaled before the shot move his body? Why does the crime scene resemble a menorah?

Why did the patsy Tyler Robinson reassemble his gun? Why did the official video only show the patsy running on the roof not taking the shot? Why did FBI head Kash Patel fire the top Salt Lake City FBI branch leaders beforehand? Why did Patel say he would meet Charlie *"in Valhalla"*[567] when the word Valhalla is code for the US federal Witness Protection Program? Why was the Kirk memorial not a funeral but a high-vibe rally with fireworks? Why did Charlie get an exceptionally strange dignified transfer (flying in an official governmental jet), usually reserved only for military, presidents or congressmen? Was Kirk a Cult CIA-Mossad asset all along? Why was the Charlie Kirk show hosted by US VP James Vance (linked to Thiel/Palantir) and Ben Shapiro (Mossad) for the first days after the death/disappearance? Do the USG and Mossad own his show?

Finally, how do we explain the Israeli foreknowledge of the event? Chief Rabbi of Israel, David Yosef, sent a letter of condolences to Charlie Kirk's family dated September 2nd – ten days before the psyop date![568] Netanyahu tweeted about Kirk's death on X/Twitter at 11:21am, over an hour before the official time of 'death' at 12:23pm.[569]

The Capturing of TikTok

When the USG claimed it needed to ban TikTok because China was spying on Americans, it was yet another op motivated by the Cult. China was just the convenient enemy and excuse; the point was to censor criticism of Israel. Unfortunately for Israel, genocides are normally not good for PR. In a leaked recording, ADL CEO Jonathan Greenblatt admitted that Israel had *"a TikTok problem"* and a *"Gen Z problem"* because the number of people who thought that Hamas' attack was justified was high.[570] He stressed it was a generational, young vs. old problem, not a left vs right problem. Is Israel truly struggling to keep ahold of the narrative with the next generation? We can only hope so. Time will tell. Greenblatt said:[571]

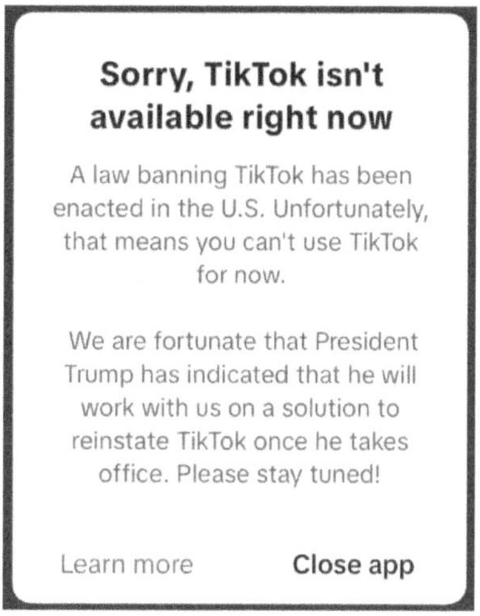

We must, you must, take this deadly seriously. Pushing extremists off Wikipedia might not seem equal to the challenge of pushing Hezbollah north of the Litani River. Capturing Tiktok might seem less meaningful than holding on to Mount Hermon. Libelous tweets certainly might seem less deadly than missiles from Yemen. But this is urgent, because the next war will be decided based on how Israel and its allies perform online as much as offline.

Sorry, TikTok isn't available right now

A law banning TikTok has been enacted in the U.S. Unfortunately, that means you can't use TikTok for now.

We are fortunate that President Trump has indicated that he will work with us on a solution to reinstate TikTok once he takes office. Please stay tuned!

Learn more   **Close app**

Image #92: TikTok has come under close Zionist control since Israel realized it had a "Gen Z" problem and was losing the narrative

The Cult was quick to install former IDF soldier Erica Mindel as 'Public Policy Manager of Hate Speech' (an Orwellian euphemism for 'Censorship Czar'). Afterwards, the White House announced that the Tiktok algorithm had been "secured, retrained and operated" under a new system run by Oracle, owned by the very pro-Israel Larry Ellison.[572] So predictable. Ellison has given lots of money to the Friends of the Israel Defense Forces (FIDF).[573] Ellison, in fact, vetted current Cult agent Marco Rubio for Israel in 2015.[574] TikTok, like other social media companies, has been infiltrated with large numbers of Unit 8200 propagandists.[575]

'Judeo-Christian Values' – More Nonsense

Israeli leaders, and Netanyahu in particular, love to talk about 'Judeo-Christian values' as though they are a definable thing. It's pure nonsense. It's part of the desperate attempt by the Cult Zionists to push the equivalence and/or alliance of America and Israel. Yet, applying critical thinking to this topic shows that the US and Israel are completely different. The US went through a long period of allowing slavery and segregation that eventually led to the civil rights movement, culminating in the 1960s with Martin Luther King Jr. and the 1964 Civil Rights Act. This forced America to grow as a nation and to look at its internal racism, and therefore its notion of supremacy, since all racism is based on supremacy. Has Israel done the same? Not at all. Not in any way. Segregation is celebrated and legalized in Israel. It's an apartheid state. Israel enforces its segregation daily via military checkpoints. In 2018, Israel voted to be a 'Jewish' state by passing its Nation-State law, downgrading its Arab citizens to second class citizens, making self-determination exclusive to Jews and demoting Arabic from being an official language.

All this talk of Judeo-Christian values and a Judeo-Christian alliance is doubly ironic and absurd given what some Israelis are doing. Israeli settlers are burning Christian villages in occupied Palestine,[576] Israel is targeting churches in Gaza[577] and some Jews continue the old 'tradition' of spitting on Christians (defended by the psychopath Ben-Gvir, naturally).[578] And we're meant to believe there is a strong Judeo-Christian alliance? For those Jews who really espouse Jewish supremacy, anyone outside their group, definitely including Christians and not just Muslims, is not as worthy.

Many people are still blind to the obvious truth that Israel treats America like a resource to be exploited. Is Israel America's greatest ally … or worst enemy? Remember the 1983 Lebanon incident, where a truck bomb struck the US marine barracks in Beirut. Ostrovsky stated that the Mossad had detailed foreknowledge of the event but it chose to only give the Americans general information which was useless and resulted in the death of 241 marines.[579] They don't care! Just recently, Netanyahu bragged about defying the US with impunity when talking about future military strikes or wars against its Arab neighbors: *"with or without [US] approval, it doesn't matter."*[580] The propagandists love to read the mantra 'Israel is our greatest ally' to Americans over and over ad nauseam, but this is evidence itself that the statement is probably untrue. The truth just is; you don't have to repeat it incessantly. Propaganda, on the other hand, has to be drummed in (or catapulted in as George Bush Jr. once said). The 'Israel is our greatest ally' lie is similar to the lie told to American school children: 'You're free.' If you're truly free, why would you need to be persuaded or convinced of it?

<u>Cult Values</u>

The rhetoric of Judeo-Christian values is a cover for the Cult's values: theft, murder, control and sadism. These values manifest in land grabs, assassination, war and genocide. Sometimes Cult agents justify it using the Talmud[581] – 'rise and kill first' or preemptively strike your enemy – using a selective interpretation. Sometimes Cult agents justify it using the Torah[582] – kill the seed and blot out the memory of Amalek. These are the values espoused by Israeli Knesset Member Tally Gotliv:[583]

I believe in the value of revenge ... stop being afraid to talk about revenge ... blot out the memory of Amalek. This is my moral command, my code of values, my heritage.

Behind all the window dressing of Israel as a civilized, advanced democracy surrounded by barbarian Arabs there lurks under the surface fundamentalist religious extremism and a dangerous, evil Cult. But what would happen if Israel stopped letting its Jewish supremacists make its law and shape its policy? What if it listened to other citizens, people like Haaretz journalist Gideon Levy, an Israeli Jew who saw through Israeli propaganda and programming. In this presentation,[584] he reveals how he used to work for Shimon Peres for four years. Peres was a 'leftwing' politician who had great rhetoric but did the exact same thing as the rightwing would have (continued the occupation and building settlements on stolen land). In Israel, the government is pro-occupation and pro-genocide, no matter which wing is in power. Levy exposes how Israeli supremacists have at least three core values underlying the occupation:

1. We are the chosen people
2. We are the only victims (even though the Israeli occupation is so brutal and cruel)
3. The Palestinians are not equal human beings to us

Levy states that the brainwashing, ignorance and denial is so deep with the average Israeli that it is very difficult for them to overcome it. This kind of denial comes out when the IDF shoots a typical Palestinian civilian teenager, and the Israeli government and media claim she fell off her bike. It takes a lot of awareness to rise above it, but some Israelis have managed to do so. This can be seen by the Israelis who were protesting Netanyahu's attempt to strip the judiciary of power. It can be seen by the Israelis who protested their 'Hannibal Government' (see chapter 17). It can be seen in the many aware current and former Israelis, and good Jews, like Norman Finkelstein (fierce critic of Israeli policy who was banned from Israel for 10 years in 2008), Gilad Atzmon (author and musician who called out how the Cult manipulates people with Jewish identity confusion), David Sheen (investigative journalist who exposes Zionist lies), Ilan Pappé (Israeli historian who exposed the 1948 Nakba genocide campaign against the Palestinians), Antony Loewenstein (Australian Jew, journalist and author who exposes how Israel treats the Palestinians as lab rats), Jeff Halper (Israeli-American Jew who opposes the occupation and is the director of the Israeli Committee Against House Demolitions) and Efrat Fenigson (independent journalist who saw through the October 7th deception). I have quoted Israeli Jew Shlomo Sand and Israeli-Canadian Jew Victor Ostrovsky extensively throughout the book. There are also several former Israeli soldiers who have broken the propaganda spell and gone on to stand for peace, including Benzion Sanders, Ariel Bernstein, Yonatan Shapira (who says Israel is led by *"Jewish supremacist Nazis"*[585]), Eran Efrati and Miko Peled.

There are many good Jews, both inside and outside of Israel, who are horrified at the direction and actions of the current Zionist regime and are horrified at the crimes being committed under the banner of Judaism. Whenever someone says "It's all the Jews" we have to absolutely reject this kind of black-and-white thinking. It's not all the Jews. It's the Cult hiding behind Judaism using ordinary, well-meaning Jews as shields. Jewish people above all need to realize what is being done in their name, so please give this book to any Jew you know who is open-minded so we can spread the truth. Humanity has to wake up to this essential truth and rise above supremacism and racism if we are to halt the enslavement agenda planned for ALL OF US. We have to cleanse the doors of perception, as poet William

Blake once wrote, and see the force that is manipulating us into limited hangouts and perceptual cul-de-sacs.

Israel is a tiny nation of around 10 million people which is also geographically far smaller than most European nations and US states. The world Jewish population is estimated at around 16 million, which is about 0.2% of the current estimated world population of 8 billion. Yet, their breadth of influence and control is truly astonishing. This network has the power to intimidate and silence virtually any criticism of Israel via various means of censorship. Historian David Irving spoke of it when he tried to defend the factual findings he presented in his books. Almost every single one of these Zionist organizations exists NOT to serve or protect Jews, Judaism or Jewishness; it's all about pushing the cause of Zionism (and behind that, the Cult) and whitewashing the crimes of Israel. In the US, Congress is full of dual US-Israeli citizens; those not loyal are controlled by AIPAC, and those outside their reach are controlled by the ideology of Christian Zionist evangelism.

There are successful cases of when people push back against Cult censorship or cancellation. One example is the Australian journalist Antoinette Lattouf who won a legal case against the ABC (Australian Broadcasting Corporation) after she was unfairly dismissed … because she shared a (truthful and accurate) post (footnoted here[586]) and added the sentence *"HRW [Human Rights Watch] reporting starvation as a tool of war."* The judge ruled that ABC contravened the Fair Work Act by firing her, including for reasons of holding a political opinion opposing the Israeli military campaign in Gaza. The judge also concluded that external pressure from 'pro-Israel lobbyists' was a factor in her getting sacked.[587] It was a victory against the Jewish Lobby. May there be many more to come.

Sources

[519] https://web.archive.org/web/20191016104009/https://www.nytimes.com/1996/05/27/opinion/how-easily-we-killed-them.html

[520] https://www.wrmea.org/from-our-archives/sharon-to-peres-don-t-worry-about-american-pressure-we-control-america.html

[521] https://www.bitchute.com/video/RIKP3wVKaviV

[522] https://www.informationliberation.com/?id=64043

[523] https://www.bitchute.com/video/LQAHJUDg6vRI

[524] https://www.trackaipac.com/trump

[525] https://x.com/abierkhatib/status/1799281313054122122

[526] https://www.jewishpresstampa.com/articles/desantis-signs-antisemitism-bill-while-in-israel/

[527] https://www.informationliberation.com/?id=63896

[528] https://www.informationliberation.com/?id=63732

[529] https://x.com/KristiNoem/status/1766122440814416267

[530] https://www.middleeastmonitor.com/20200116-south-dakota-governor-signs-anti-bds-executive-order/

[531] https://www.al-monitor.com/originals/2025/04/white-house-denies-staffer-merav-cerens-ties-israeli-defense-ministry-what-know

[532] https://x.com/ggreenwald/status/1914738413451833355

[533] https://grants.nih.gov/grants/guide/notice-files/NOT-OD-25-090.html

[534] https://grants.nih.gov/grants/guide/notice-files/NOT-OD-25-124.html

[535] Final Judgment, pg. 362

[536] http://pdfs.jta.org/1973/1973-04-17_075_Passover.pdf

[537] https://www.riotimesonline.com/chile-turns-to-brazil-india-and-turkey-to-cut-military-reliance-on-israel/

[538] https://www.i24news.tv/en/news/international/latin-america/artc-chile-breaks-off-diplomatic-relations-with-israel-over-gaza-war

---

539 https://themedialine.org/top-stories/exclusive-to-tml-us-mulls-sanctions-on-chile-as-santiago-signals-possible-break-with-israel/

540 https://apnews.com/article/israel-iran-nuclear-science-attacks-e298f00ba261debba4499a48c9df8b3d

541 https://www.uscis.gov/newsroom/news-releases/uscis-to-consider-anti-americanism-in-immigrant-benefit-requests

542 https://www.middleeasteye.net/news/germany-new-citizenship-test-includes-questions-holocaust-founding-israel

543 https://x.com/Resist_05/status/1878437511480975494

544 https://www.bitchute.com/video/2booHjxBlp0G

545 https://www.ap.org/news-highlights/spotlights/2024/us-spends-a-record-17-9-billion-on-military-aid-to-israel-since-last-oct-7/

546 https://x.com/DelGroyp/status/1937472202691215500

547 https://littlemaryphagan.com/wp-content/uploads/2024/10/Phagan-Family-Newsletter-13.pdf

548 https://www.informationliberation.com/?id=65022

549 Final Judgment, pg. 381

550 Ibid., pg. 382

551 The Other Side of Deception, pg. 278

552 https://archive.ph/2025.06.17-203813/https://x.com/mick_or_mack/status/1777077484426543148

553 https://archive.ph/2025.06.17-203639/https://x.com/mick_or_mack/status/1798729267196711319#selection-589.0-589.30

554 https://archive.ph/2025.06.17-203737/https://x.com/mick_or_mack/status/1926700593134915740#selection-589.4-589.154

555 https://www.informationliberation.com/?id=63606

556 https://x.com/mtracey/status/1787751207437472229

557 https://www.naturalnews.com/2023-10-26-ben-shapiro-receive-tasking-from-israeli-intelligence.html

---

[558] https://pjmedia.com/benshapiro/2025/03/20/why-does-it-matter-who-shot-jfk-n4938101

[559] https://www.informationliberation.com/?id=64903

[560] x.com/ShaykhSulaiman/status/1963340728395858045

[561] https://responsiblestatecraft.org/israel-influencers-netanyahu/

[562] https://efile.fara.gov/docs/7652-Exhibit-AB-20250926-1.pdf

[563] https://thefreedomarticles.com/the-evidence-israel-murdered-charlie-kirk/

[564] https://thegrayzone.com/2025/09/15/bill-ackman-israel-intervention-charlie-kirk/

[565] https://thegrayzone.com/2025/09/22/israel-tpusa-donor-terminated-kirk/

[566] https://thefreedomarticles.com/20-key-questions-exposing-the-trump-assassination-hoax/

[567] https://www.bitchute.com/video/7xFoJuPmGm5L

[568] https://seemorerocks.substack.com/p/did-the-chief-rabbi-of-israel-sent

[569] https://x.com/netanyahu/status/1965888327938158764?lang=en

[570] https://www.instagram.com/texasforpalestine/reel/DE_sFQdML8N/

[571] https://www.bitchute.com/video/jbRLrY3cS5Ml

[572] https://thecradle.co/articles/pro-israel-tech-firm-to-take-control-of-us-tiktok-algorithm

[573] https://www.jta.org/2017/11/05/united-states/record-53-8-million-raised-for-idf-soldiers-at-beverly-hills-gala

[574] https://www.dropsitenews.com/p/larry-ellison-vetted-marco-rubio-israel-hacked-emails-ron-prosor

[575] https://www.mintpressnews.com/288710-tiktok-isnt-anti-israel-its-hired-unit-8200-agents-to-run-its-affairs/288710/

[576] https://x.com/JaydaBF/status/1938140238452576287

[577] https://www.aa.com.tr/en/middle-east/timeline-israel-strikes-3-churches-in-gaza-since-start-of-war/3634109#

[578] https://www.middleeasteye.net/news/israel-spitting-christians-jerusalem-not-criminal-ben-gvir

[579] By Way of Deception, pp. 321-22

[580] https://www.informationliberation.com/?id=65009

[581] https://steinsaltz.org/daf/sanhedrin72/

[582] https://jewishstudies.duke.edu/news/destroying-amalek

[583] https://x.com/SuppressedNws/status/1960158089048375785

[584] https://www.youtube.com/watch?v=MPt8c_93zM0

[585] https://www.youtube.com/shorts/rEofzQ4fPU4

[586] https://www.instagram.com/reel/C1An_t_uOiN/?hl=en

[587] https://www.abc.net.au/news/2025-06-26/antoinette-lattouf-won-abc-what-happens-next/105459628

CHAPTER 14: THE CULT CARRIES OUT THE CRIME OF THE CENTURY: 9/11

"[The Mossad is a] wildcard [and] ruthless and cunning. Has capability to target U.S. forces and make it look like a Palestinian/ Arab act."

– Original quotation from a 68-page paper at the US Army's School of Advanced Military Studies (SAMS), reported by The Washington Times on September 10th 2001, the day before 9/11[588]

"The truth is, there is no Islamic army or terrorist group called Al Qaida. And any informed intelligence officer knows this. But there is a propaganda campaign to make the public believe in the presence of an identified entity representing the 'devil' only in order to drive the TV watcher to accept a unified international leadership for a war against terrorism."

"Al-Qaida, literally "the database", was originally the computer file of the thousands of mujahideen who were recruited and trained with help from the CIA to defeat the Russians."

– Former UK Foreign Secretary Robin Cook[589] [590]

"It is 100% certain that 9/11 was a Mossad operation ... If Americans ever know, ever know, that Israel did this, they're going to scrub them off the Earth ... The Zionists are playing this as truly an all-or-nothing exercise."

– Dr. Alan Sabrosky, Director of Studies at US Army War College, 2010[591]

The attacks against America on September 11th 2001, which have come to be known simply as 9/11, constitute one of the biggest crimes of the 21st century. 9/11 was nothing at all like it appears. It was the ultimate false flag event – and it was also the most daring example of the signature Zionist false flag op. The entire event was decades in planning and built upon the framing of Arabs and Muslims which the Zionists had been practicing ever since the 1940s (as covered in previous chapters), including a dry run bombing of the WTC (World Trade Center) in 1993. However, the event gave the Cult the excuse to create the new purported abstract enemy of 'Islamic terrorism' like never before, the new purported enemy group of 'Al-Qaeda' and the pretext to launch the 'War on Terror' which laid down the fake justification for the Israeli-led US military to invade numerous Middle Eastern nations. Before we get into the who and how of 9/11, we need to set the context. For those wanting more information than what is contained in this chapter, please see great sources such as David Icke, Chris Bollyn, Dr. Judy Wood, Rebekah Roth, Wyatt Peterson (of the website TruthBlitzkrieg.com) and the International Center for 9/11 Justice which published an incredibly comprehensive 9/11 timeline on their website.[592]

Neocon = Zionist

To understand who did 9/11 and how they did it, we first have to understand the groups that were in power at that time. The administration of George Bush Jr. was run by 'neoconservatives' or 'neocons' as they are widely known. Shockingly, there are a lot of media analysts who still use the terms neoconservative or neocon without realizing the crucial implication: neocons are Zionists! They are 'Israel firsters' who cover their fanaticism with rightwing politics and policies. The standard definition of neoconservatism is that it's a political movement that started in the US in the 1960s which advocates interventionism, or in other words, foreign meddling and war. This belligerence is usually covered up with Orwellian euphemisms such as the 'promotion of democracy,' the 'responsibility to protect' and 'peace through strength' as they invade and bomb other nations to smithereens. The neocons became very politically influential during Republican presidential administrations, especially during the 8 years under Bush Jr. The neocons oversaw the 9/11 operation, the start of the War on Terror and the US invasion of Middle Eastern nations Afghanistan (2001) and Iraq (2003).

Two of the key founders of neoconservatism are Irving Kristol (Cult Zionist) and Norman Podhoretz (Cult Zionist). Both had sons that carried on the neocon Zionist cause. Irving's son William or Bill Kristol went on to found the Project for a New American Century (PNAC), a Cult organization to its very core which was absolutely brimming with Zionists, which I will discuss shortly. Norman's son John Podhoretz wrote a stunningly hate-filled article in 1999 after the death (or murder) of JFK Jr. which Piper thought fit to reproduce in full in the fifth edition of *Final Judgment.* The fictional article is entitled *"A CONVERSATION IN HELL"*[593] and is written from the point of view of the devil talking with family patriarch Joe Kennedy, with whom he made a deal: the devil would allow one, and only one, of Joe's sons to be president, but the devil would kill some of his other children and grandchildren. It reads simultaneously like an admission of guilt and unadulterated bragging that Israel killed the Kennedys.

Neoconservatism was, essentially, Israel's way to hijack US foreign policy. In 1996, a group of American-Jewish neocons published a report called *A Clean Break: A New Strategy for Securing the Realm*. The group was led by Richard Perle at the behest of newly-elected Israeli PM Benjamin Netanyahu. The report advocated that the US aggressively defend Israel's interests in the Middle East, including conducting a regime change operation in Iraq to topple CIA asset Saddam Hussein, engage and contain Syria through proxy wars, support an alliance between Israel, Türkiye and Jordan against Iraq, Syria and Iran, and reject any two-state solution to the Israeli-Palestinian conflict. All of this later came true. The report also contained ideas from pro-Israel right-wingers and affiliates of Netanyahu's Likud party, such as Douglas Feith.

The PNAC think tank was launched in 1997 by Bill Kristol and Robert Kagan. Kagan – a classic Khazarian name – is another Cult Zionist whose wife Vicky Nuland played a big role in the Ukrainian Maidan coup of 2014 that toppled the democratically elected, pro-Russian president Viktor Yanukovych and brought the Neo-Nazis to power. Russian President Vladimir Putin himself considers this coup the real start of the Russo-Ukraine War which officially began in February 2022. Kagan was also a senior figure at the Brookings Institution which analyzed how the US and Israel could defeat Iran in the 2009 report *Which Path to Persia?*[594] Both Iran and Russia have been in the Cult crosshairs for a long time, but at the same time the Cult has long controlled them in its own way, via infiltration, positioning them on the international geopolitical chessboard to be future enemies of the US and Israel in a geopolitical strategy of tension and war (see chapter 18).

PNAC disbanded in 2006. Prominent members, in addition to Kristol and Kagan, included Paul Wolfowitz, Paul Bremer, Elliott Abrams, Richard Perle, Douglas Feith, James Woolsey, Robert Zoellick, John Bolton, Jeb Bush, John Negroponte and and David Horowitz (all Cult Zionists). Some of these men held positions in either the Bush Sr. or Bush Jr. Administration. In 1991, Wolfowitz wrote the *Defense Planning Guidance of 1992* that came to be known as the Wolfowitz Doctrine and later the Bush Doctrine. It advocated that the US deter potential competitors from arising, and when necessary, use force unilaterally; allies might be nice but America, as the preeminent world military superpower, no longer needed them. It doesn't take much to see how the neocon philosophy directly reflected the Cult mindset of 'attack preemptively' and 'control everything.'

Although George Bush Sr., Dick Cheney and Donald Rumsfeld did not self-identify as Zionists, they all held very high positions of power in the 1990s and 2000s, and they all toed the Zionist line in their support for Israel, promotion of American influence in the Arab world and launching the War on Terror (despite the Mossad's hypothetical plans to terminate Bush). Bush Sr. was an ex-CIA director, involved in the JFK assassination, an ex-US president, Satanist and serial rapist according to mind control victim Cathy O'Brien, who was abused by him and Cheney along with her daughter Kelly. Cheney was an ex-US vice president, Satanist and another serial rapist. Rumsfeld sold weapons to Iraq's Saddam Hussein in 1983 during the Iraq-Iran War and, as president and CEO of Searle, suppressed news that Searle's key product, aspartame, was toxic. GMO and glyphosate-pushing Monsanto bought Searle in 1985, which gives you some idea of what kind of company it was.

PNAC became infamous among the conspiracy research community for its publication *Rebuilding Americas Defenses* in the year 2000, which featured the crucial and now notorious sentence, *"Further, the process of transformation, even if it brings revolutionary change, is likely to be a long one, absent some catastrophic and catalyzing event – like a new Pearl Harbor."*[595] The choice to refer to Pearl Harbor is very fitting, because like 9/11, Pearl Harbor was an event that was allowed and made to happen in order to get the US into WWII. After 9/11, the Cult got its catastrophic and catalyzing event, and the world was plunged into a series of horrific conflicts and never-ending war against an imaginary enemy.

The Bush-Bin Laden Connection

The Bush crime family goes way back to at least Prescott Bush, father of George Sr. and grandfather of George Jr., who along with the Cult NWO bloodlines the Harrimans and Rockefellers, helped fund the 1917 Russian Revolution as discussed in chapter 7.[596] George Bush Sr. funded Saddam before the Cult-controlled US decided Saddam was the 'bad guy' and turned around to fight him in the First Gulf War of 1990. It's important to mention here too that the shadowy figure of Osama bin Laden wasn't just pulled out of nowhere to be the patsy. Would it surprise you to learn that the Bush crime family had ties to the 'royal' bin Laden Saudi family going way back? The Bushes and bin Ladens were longtime business partners. In 1978, George W. Bush and Osama's brother Salem bin Laden founded a Texas-based oil company called Arbusto Energy; both families have been investors in the Carlyle Group where Bush Sr. was an advisor. In fact, the Bushes and bin Ladens met the day before 9/11 in New York City[597] when the Carlyle Group met at the Ritz Carlton Hotel. In attendance were George Bush Sr. and Shafiq bin Laden, another brother of Osama. Unbeknownst to many Americans, Osama bin Laden was on the CIA payroll in the 1980s during the Soviet invasion of Afghanistan when the US backed the mujahideen; Robin Cook wrote in The Guardian:[598]

Bin Laden was, though, a product of a monumental miscalculation by western security agencies. Throughout the 80s he was armed by the CIA and funded by the Saudis to wage jihad against the Russian occupation of Afghanistan.

Netanyahu's War on Terror

Current Israeli PM Benjamin Mileikowsky or Netanyahu is a genuine psychopath who couldn't care less about Palestinian suffering. Netanyahu was delighted with 9/11 because it was good for Israel. The New York Times quoted him as saying *"It's very good"* after which he caught himself and said, *"Well, not very good, but it will generate immediate sympathy."*[599] The Israeli newspaper Haaretz quoted him elsewhere as saying, *"We are benefiting from one thing, and that is the attack on the Twin Towers and Pentagon, and the American struggle in Iraq,"* and that the 9/11 event *"swung American public opinion in our favor."*[600]

The War on Terror™ has become such a hackneyed phrase that it's worthy of being trademarked and corporatized, if the Military Industrial Complex hasn't done so already. Think of how much carnage, death and destruction have been wrought in the name of fighting the War on Terror™ and ZioIslamic Terrorism™ – millions of people killed in Afghanistan, Iraq, Libya, Lebanon, Yemen, Syria, Palestine and more. The phrase itself doesn't make any sense. Terror is a consequence of war. How can you have a war on terror when war produces terror? In other words, how can you fight something (terror) with a method (war) that produces that very thing? How can you wage a war on something which is a consequence of war? This in itself is a clue that the phrase is a catchy slogan, like 'Peace through Strength,' designed to bypass people's filters and critical thinking, and manipulate them into supporting wars against Israel's enemies.

As far back as 1979, Netanyahu was promoting the idea on the world stage with terrorist Israeli PM Menachem Begin (both of the Likud party) at the Jerusalem Conference hosted by the Netanyahu Institute. Netanyahu later wrote a 1995 book about terrorism. His main arguments throughout the decades have been that:

- Israel is a democracy whereas all its other Arab and Muslim neighbors are dictatorships;
- Israel is therefore a Western state with Western values, unlike its neighbors;
- Israel is only defending itself when it attacks its neighbors;
- When Israel gets attacked, the real target is the USA;
- There is no equivalence between the State of Israel's 'official' and 'governmental' military attacks and the 'unofficial' and 'non-governmental' military attacks ('terrorism') of its neighbors like Palestine, Lebanon, etc.;
- Therefore, the US should help Israel and attack its neighbors for the sake of the Jewish State, freedom and democracy.

The whole ideology is driven by Jewish supremacy. As discussed earlier, one of the key points the scam turns on is convincing people of 'Judeo-Christian values' that underpin a 'Judeo-Christian civilization.' It is purely designed to get the West, chiefly America, to fight Israel's enemies. In America, the War on Terror followed on from the War on Poverty, the War on Cancer and the War on Drugs of earlier decades which also had disastrous results. We are still in spiritual kindergarten if we think we can solve problems by going around and declaring war on them. It's a fundamental truth that whatever you fight, you become. You take on the frequency of something you hate because you psychologically attach yourself to it in a very intense way. If you truly want to eradicate a thing (e.g. poverty), you need to focus on its opposite (e.g. wealth). You need to put more energy into creating the thing you want rather than opposing the thing you don't want. Look how much energy has gone into fighting drugs and cancer. Has there been any improvement? No. There are just as many drugs around and there are still a lot of people dying from cancer. However, these things are not meant to be won; they are meant to put the government on a permanent war footing, just as George Orwell said.

Sadly, the War on Terror isn't meant to end until the Cult has achieved its goal of Greater Israel and has expanded its territory from the Nile to the Euphrates, clearing all non-Jewish inhabitants from the region.

The Crypto-Jew Saudis, Best Friends with Israel

Saudi Arabia's connection to 9/11 seems important, given that 15 of the 19 (supposed) hijackers originate from there, as did bin Laden. However, the actual role of the country in the attacks seems to be minimal. Saudi Arabia was involved by at least allowing itself to be used as a 'bad guy' in the official narrative. This stems from the snug, cozy relationship between Israel and Saudi Arabia. At first glance, it admittedly seems extremely odd that the Zionist regime of

Image #93: Saudi Arabia and Israel are both equally owned by the Sabbatean-Frankist Cult

Israel, holding such an antagonistic presence towards Arabs in the Middle East, would be friends with one of the most powerful Muslim nations in the region (alongside Iran and Türkiye). However, things are not always what they seem. The truth is that these two nations have the same geopolitical aims and allies, despite the recent rapprochement between Saudi Arabia and Iran – and also a linked Jewish history.

To understand the relationship between Israel and Saudi Arabia, you first need to know how Saudi Arabia became a country. The Kingdom of Saudi Arabia (KSA) as it is formally called remains the only nation on the entire Earth to be named after and ruled by a single family. After the British defeated the Ottoman Empire in WWI, there were three distinct authorities in the Arabian peninsula: Hussein bin Ali, the Sharif of Hijaz (in the west), Ibn Rashid of Ha'il (in the north) and Emir Ibn Saud of Najd (in the east) and his religiously fanatical followers, the Wahhabis. Of these three, Britain got the most help during WWI from Hussein who led the Arab Revolt against the Turks and helped the British defeat them. After the war, Hussein was hoping the British would keep their word (as he saw it) and agree to the establishment of a single Arabian country from Gaza to the Persian Gulf. However Britain, as it has done many times in the past, did not keep its promises. Instead, along with France, it drew up the Sykes-Picot agreement in 1916 and issued the Balfour Declaration in 1917. The Sharif was not happy and told the British that he would never sell out Palestine to the British Empire by acquiescing to the establishment of Zionism in Palestine, nor accept the new random borders carving up Arabia by British and French imperialists.

At this point T. E. Lawrence (Lawrence of Arabia) was dispatched to bribe and buy Hussein. When this didn't work, he turned to threats, which were also echoed by Winston Churchill, who was then Colonial Secretary. Both men threatened to unleash Ibn Saud and his Wahhabis (whom they were arming and funding), which they did first against Ibn Rashid of Ha'il. Ibn Saud defeated Ibn Rashid. Then, the British unleashed Ibn Saud and his armies on Hijazi territory. By September 1924, Ibn Saud had overrun Hussein, and Ibn Saud's Wahhabis committed their customary massacre, slaughtering women and children as well as going into mosques and killing traditional Islamic scholars. They captured the holiest place in Islam, Mecca, in mid-October 1924. Sharif Hussein was forced to abdicate and went into exile. Ibn Saud, ancestor of the current Saudi lineage, attacked Jeddah in January 1925. The city finally surrendered in December 1925. The British officially recognized Ibn Saud as the new King of Hijaz in February 1926. The new unified Wahhabi state was rebranded in 1932 as the Kingdom of Saudi

Arabia. As you can see, right from the start, the man who opposed a Zionist state in Palestine as a matter of principle was kicked out, and the man who was willing to let it happen was paid off handsomely and given an entire new country to rule.

But that's not all; the Saudi clan is also connected to Sabbatean-Frankism via the Donmeh Jews (the first crypto-Jews covered in chapter 4). There is the research of Mohammad Sakher who recounts the story about how a Jewish man disguised himself as an Arab and seeded the Saudi lineage. Sakher was apparently the subject of a Saudi contract murder hit for exposing the Zionist-Saudi roots. He includes a quote he states is from then King Faisal Al-Saud on September 17th 1969 in the Washington Post:[601]

WE, THE SAUDI FAMILY, are cousins of the Jews: we entirely disagree with any Arab or Muslem Authority which shows any antagonism to the Jews; but we must live together with them in peace. Our country (ARABIA) is the Fountain head from where the first Jew sprang, and his descendants spread out all over the world.

There is other evidence that Muhammad bin Saud (founder of modern day Saudi lineage) and Muhammad bin Abdul Wahhab (the founder of the violent Wahhabi sect of Islam) may have been Jewish. This DIA document from September 24th 2002, entitled "The Birth of Al-Wahabi Movement And it's Historic Roots", states as follows (AI-Dawnamah = Dönmeh = Donmeh):[602]

The original Arabic sheikhs of Najd as well as the scientific resources, confirm that Muhammad bin 'Abd-al-Wahab is from a Jewish family from "AI-Dawnamah" in Turkey. The Dawnamah here refers to those Jews who have declared their Islam for the purpose of harming Islam and save themselves from the chase by the Ottoman Sultans.

Reporter and ex-NSA agent Wayne Madsen commented on this report by remarking that a lot of the information in this DIA study was from the memoirs of a "Mr. Humfer," a British spy who used the name Mohammad, claimed to be an Azeri who spoke Turkish, Persian and Arabic, and who made contact with Wahhab in the mid-18th century with a view to create a sect of Islam that would precipitate an Arab revolt against the Ottoman Empire and pave the way for the introduction of a Jewish state in Palestine. Madsen also refers to a book called *The Dönmeh Jews* by D. Mustafa Turan, who claims that Wahhab's grandfather, Tjen Sulayman, was actually Tjen Shulman, a member of the Jewish community of Basra, Iraq.

Israel and Saudi Arabia work together closely behind the scenes. Three examples of many which demonstrate this are then Saudi King Salman helping to finance the election campaign of Netanyahu in 2015 to the tune of $80 million, as revealed by Isaac Herzog, then member of the Knesset but now Israeli President (Herzog cited the Panama Papers leak).[603] Secondly, Saudi Arabia covertly blocked Iranian drones from entering Israel during the 12-Day War between Israel and Iran earlier this year, despite publicly condemning the Israeli attack on Iran. According to this report, the Saudi Arabian air force scrambled helicopters to shoot down Iranian drones crossing airspace over Iraq and Jordan – all to protect Israel![604] Thirdly, during the Gaza genocide (see chapter 17), Genoa dockworkers decided to block a Saudi arms shipment bound for Israel[605] in protest. Why would Saudi Arabia help Israel in its genocide against the Palestinians? Because they're both controlled by the Cult.

Former Reagan administration official Paul Craig Roberts offers a key point about the role of Saudi Arabia in the 9/11 operation as a fallback position to prop up the official narrative and deflect attention away from Israel. He got this idea from speaking directly to none other than … James Angleton:[606]

James Jesus Angleton, head of CIA counterintelligence for three decades, long ago explained to me that intelligence services create stories inside stories, each with its carefully constructed trail of evidence, in order to create false trails as diversions. Such painstaking work can serve a variety of purposes. It can be used to embarrass or discredit an innocent person or organization that has an unhelpful position on an important issue and is in the way of an agenda. It can be used as a red herring to draw attention away from a failing explanation of an event by producing an alternative false explanation. I forget what Angleton called them, but the strategy is to have within a false story other stories that are there but withheld because of "national security" or "politically sensitive issues" or some such. Then if the official story gets into trouble, the backup story can be released in order to deflect attention into a new false story or to support the original story. Angleton said that intelligence services protect their necessary misdeeds by burying the misdeed in competing explanations.

Roberts suggests that the so-called 'revelation' that 9/11 was financed by the Saudi Government is a fallback position. It bolsters the sagging official story while simultaneously trying to satisfy those who know something is off. Alleged Saudi financing restores the credibility of the original story, and the credibility of the hijackers (even though they have none), as it directs American anger at the

Saudis for underwriting the attacks. Meanwhile, the real culprit (Israel) hides in the shadows.

Operation Northwoods, the 1993 WTC Bombing and the 1995 Oklahoma City Bombing

There are three important things to cover in this subsection to set the context to properly understand 9/11: a set of plans for false flag operations that were thankfully not acted upon, as well as two bombings that occurred in America in the 1990s in the lead up to 2001, including the 1993 bombing of the WTC itself.

The first one is Operation Northwoods. It is noteworthy that as far back as the 1960s, official governmental plans were hatched to hijack civilian or commercial planes, to remotely control them from the ground, and then to steer and crash them into buildings. Northwoods was a 1962 false flag operation plan that was actually authorized by the US Joint Chiefs of Staff and presented to then President Kennedy by chairman Lyman Lemnitzer. The chairman of the Joint Chiefs of Staff is the third highest ranking military officer in the US, second only to the Secretary of Defense and the President! Northwoods called for the CIA to conduct acts of terrorism against American targets, then blame them on Cuba to justify launching a war against the small Caribbean nation. One of the proposed scenarios was the remote control of civilian aircraft which would be secretly repainted as USAF planes. JFK was apparently disgusted with the scheme and rejected it, moving Lemnitzer out of his position. The existence of the Northwoods plot proves that the CIA not only knew about remotely controlling aircraft but was prepared to actually participate in such a diabolical scenario.

The second one is the time the WTC was bombed before 9/11, which occurred in 1993 as a result of an FBI sting operation. For those who don't know, a sting operation in law enforcement is defined as a deceptive operation where undercover agents pose as criminals or victims in an attempt to catch someone committing a crime, however what usually happens is that the undercover agents actually encourage and facilitate the crime – which would not have happened otherwise. In other words, the FBI commits entrapment by inducing someone to commit a crime. This first WTC bombing was another signature Zionist false flag op. The official narrative placed the blame on Muslims, some of whom were Palestinian, including Ahmed Ajaj (mentioned earlier), Ramzi Yousef, Mahmud Abouhalima, Mohammed A. Salameh, Eyad Ismoil, Nidal Ayyad and Abdul Rahman Yasin. Emad Salem built the bomb that exploded, yet as Icke reveals, Salem was an informant on the FBI payroll, and the bomb was *"planted in a truck with a rental agreement including the phone number and address of notorious Mossad agent, Josie Hadas!"*[607] In his essay 'Fifty Years of the Deep State,' researcher Mark Gorton reveals that the 1993 bombing created the conditions so that Israeli-owned companies like Kroll Associates could move in to grab security contracts for the WTC:[608]

The 1993 WTC bombing created the necessary pretext for a massive engineering upgrade of the WTC complex. The purpose of the 1993 WTC bombing was not to bring down the WTC. A truck bomb could not bring down a structure as large as the WTC. The purpose of the 1993 WTC bombing was to create a rationale for a "security upgrade" of the WTC complex. And for this purpose, the 1993 WTC bombing succeeded perfectly. According to Alan Reiss, the PANYNJ's [Port Authority of New York and New Jersey] World

Trade Center Director, "After the 1993 bombing, we implemented a ten-year redevelopment program. We were spending a half a billion dollars on upgrades. It was an engineer's dream." After the 1993 bombing, the PANYNJ brought in Kroll Associates to do a "complete security analysis."

The third one was the Oklahoma City Bombing of 1995 which was initially blamed on Muslims then later on a pair of US 'lone nutters.' Muslims and lone nutters as the guilty parties … now where have I heard that before? This was another false flag attack which sought to inject fear into American society and blame the US Christian Patriot movement. Timothy McVeigh was the chosen patsy. The official narrative defied the laws of physics, as it seems to every time, by claiming that a truck bomb did all the damage when pillars closer to the truck did not fall while others further from the truck did fall. Numerous witnesses testified that they heard a second bomb and the seismographic record at the Oklahoma

Image #94: the 1995 Oklahoma City bombing was said to be caused by a truck bomb out the front of it. As with 9/11 and the twin towers, we are supposed to believe this kind of damage occurred with no preplanted bombs in the building

Geological Survey at the University of Oklahoma recorded two separate seismic events at the time the Alfred P. Murrah Building was hit.

The Official 9/11 Story Makes Less Sense than a Fairy Tale

Before we go any further in analyzing the who and how of 9/11, let's take a look at the official narrative which is so far beyond absurdity and fantasy that it makes a fairy tale looked based in concrete facts by comparison. In fact, I wouldn't want to slander fairy tales by comparing the official 9/11 narrative to them. Here's what they want you to believe: there were once 19 cocaine-snorting, alcohol-drinking, pork-eating Islamic terrorists who were devout and pious Muslims, who, according to their flight instructors, flew planes so badly that they had absolutely no clue what the plane's controls did and were totally wasting the air school's resources. These 'Muslim' hijackers, led by two different men playing Mohammed Atta, hijacked four planes, flying some of them for as long as 45 minutes before turning them around to hit their targets, despite presumably knowing that the civilian Federal Aviation Administration (FAA) would tell the military North American Aerospace Defense Command (NORAD) to scramble jets from nearby air bases and have them airborne in a couple of minutes to intercept. For some reason, fighters were not scrambled from Andrews Air Force Base (AFB) even though the base was extremely close by. In the case of the Pentagon, they chose to turn the plane around 270° in a very difficult and low maneuver to hit a side that just so happened to be recently reinforced. In New York City, three buildings fell in perfect symmetrical collapse, despite only two being hit and despite the fact that jet fuel cannot burn at temperatures above 750°F whereas steel needs temperatures of around 2500°F or higher to melt. It also takes around one hour for such structural steelwork to attain an elevated temperature of 1100°F. The hijackers flew the aircraft super fast while super low, even though planes cannot fly that low and maintain structural integrity due to air resistance; experienced pilots have stated that they could not have pulled off that kind of maneuver. The aluminum planes completely pierced the concrete and steel of WTC towers 1 and 2 despite the planes' nose cones being hollow and made of plastic. They fully penetrated the WTC towers' concrete and steel without shattering to pieces, and in the case of the Pentagon, fully penetrated the bricks reinforced with Kevlar (a strong, heat-resistant synthetic fiber) and steel. Meanwhile, you are told that many victims made calls while being hijacked in the air, despite the fact that cell phones don't work at that altitude and Boeings at that time not having air phones. Despite all the fire and smoke in New York City, somehow one of the hijacker's passports magically survived intact and was discovered, even though the plane parts were not. Finally, you are told that a man in a cave in a third world nation with a scary turban and beard

Image #95: jet fuel cannot burn above 750° F (398° C), but steel requires at least 2500° F (1371° C) to melt

masterminded the whole thing. The facial features of this same man kept changing in video to video, and he was later killed at least twice. US leaders declared him guilty yet the FBI never charged him and did not list 9/11 as one of the terrorist acts for which Osama bin Laden was wanted. When asked why, head of FBI investigative publicity, Rex Tomb, said that the FBI had no hard evidence connecting Bin Laden to 9/11![609]

Because Western politicians and the Western public swallowed the official narrative, the US-led West went to war with many nations including Iraq. David Icke notes that *"Hidden Hand lapdog Tony Blair read a 'dossier' to a compliant House of Commons in support of Britain joining the US invasion and he began: 'This document does not purport to provide a prosecutable case against Osama bin Laden in a court of law.'"*[610] Indeed, the entire flimsy official story wouldn't stand up to any scrutiny in a court of law.

Diverting the Planes to Westover AFB for the Phone Calls

Rebekah Roth is a flight attendant with decades of experience and knowledge of FAA protocols. After intensive research involving a lot of FOIA data, she wrote a 5-part book series: *Methodical Illusion, Methodical Deception, Methodical Conclusion, Methodical Exposure* and *Methodical Agenda.* Her area of speciality is exposing the fake phone calls. As a flight attendant, she was very aware of what mobile or cell phone technology was capable of – and what it was not capable of – when it came to making calls from high-altitude flights. Her research shows that American Airlines (AA) had deactivated all air phones on 757s by January 2001. Cell phone calls are impossible above 1500 feet; she reveals how tests have shown that cell phones don't work at 8,000 feet (so clearly they cannot work at 35,000 feet). Even if they did, the transfer of calls from one receiving station to another (handoffs) is very difficult at high speeds (planes normally travel at 500 mph or 804 kph). Simply put, she knew that cell phones wouldn't work in the air, so she knew that the official calls were either completely fabricated, or else, if made by real passengers, must have been from the ground – presumably with cue cards and their captors holding them at gunpoint. In a sense, these captors were the real hijackers, and they were Middle Eastern, but not Arabian – they were Israeli.

Roth highlights the following suspicious aspects of the official 9/11 calls:

– Some of the phone calls went on a long time and never dropped. How is this possible?

– There were six calls from flight attendants to family or friends. This completely broke protocol and would have been the very last thing that a trained flight attendant would do.

– One passenger (Mark Bingham) introduced himself to his mother with his first and last name. Who does this?

– One passenger said *"we think we might be hijacked."* How could you not know for sure?

– All the passengers spoke in a calm way, yet if the calls were made in the air during a real hijacking, the plane would have been undergoing a steep descent. This would have been very alarming to the average person and thus have affected the voice tone and background noise made by the passengers, yet none is heard. Is this realistic?

– One of the calls features a flight attendant allegedly saying to her supervisor, *"Listen, and listen to me good."* Roth remarks that no attendant would speak to their supervisor like that.

– Another of the calls features someone saying *"You did great"* at the end. Is this more proof that Israeli soldiers or assassins were supervising the calls at gunpoint, complimenting the speaker before they were killed?

– One of the calls features a flight attendant called Betty Ong who says *"I think there's mace ... that we can't breathe"* which Roth says is highly suspicious. From her knowledge and experience as a flight attendant, Roth said that if mace were sprayed into the pressurized cabin of a plane, everyone would be breathing it, no matter what class they were in. How could Ong be correct about the mace and still have made a call over 25 minutes long?[611] Additionally, how could any of the passengers, flight attendants or not, be allowed by the hijackers in a genuine hijacking to make a call for 25 minutes without being killed?

– One of the flight attendants named CeeCee Lyles whispers at the end of her call *"It's a frame."* Was she hinting that the whole thing was framed or set up?[612]

– One of the people on board the hijacked planes was American-Israeli Danny Lewin, a millionaire tech entrepreneur who was also an assassin. Lewis was an IDF captain who served in the Sayeret Matkal, an elite special forces unit within Aman, specializing in hostage rescue and assassination. Apparently Lewin could bench press 315 pounds and squat almost 500 pounds, and was trained to kill people with a credit card or pen. The official account says Lewin was the first to be killed on his flight, even though with his skills he would easily have overpowered the thinly built hijackers and used any knifes or boxcutters against them. In another interesting coincidence, Lewin was sitting in row 9 on flight 11, and a photo of him in the year 2000 shows him wearing a Swatch Watch model called 'Hijacker' with the hands all set to 11.

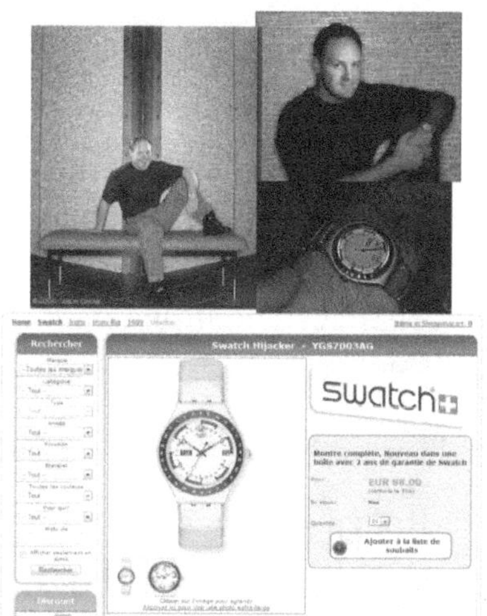

Image #96: tech entrepreneur, IDF captain and premier black ops assassin Danny Lewin was in seat 9B of Flight 11. Here he is a year earlier pictured against a backdrop resembling two grey towers

– Another of the calls was from the Jewish woman Barbara Olson to her husband Ted Olson, who was legal counsel to then President Reagan during the Iran-Contra scandal in the 1980s where the US was selling arms to Iran. Ted Olson also defended traitor, diehard Zionist and convicted Israeli spy Jonathan Pollard, who stole secrets for Israel, as covered in chapter 12. Say it again slowly after me ... C. O. I. N. C. I. D. E. N. C. E.

Roth concludes that the passengers were taken to Westover AFB, around 79 miles west of Boston, Massachusetts. She got confirmation from someone near this base who saw a United flight circling above the air base, very low, so that the passengers could be seen through the windows. Westover reservists (military officers) had been evacuated that morning and were housed for the next few days in hotels. Westover is likely where the 'official' 9/11 calls were made from. The suspicious Israeli-linked passengers on board were there to facilitate the remote electronic hijack of the plane, to ensure the pilots and flight attendants did not interfere with the Cult operation. The flight calls began at the exact time at which planes would have landed after having been taken to Westover.

There can be little doubt that the people on board were murdered after they made the calls and had been forced to play their part in this grand and gruesome psychological operation.

Roth also suggests that the intelligence agencies may have infiltrated American and/or United Airlines by getting some of their flight attendants on the CIA/Mossad payroll. It would have been relatively easy for the agencies to hide this (because flight attendants can have unpredictable schedules, so if they had to suddenly leave it would not arouse the suspicion of their friends/family) and would have given the CIA/Mossad access to corporate airline protocol for hijackings, which they needed to have known just as they knew the FAA/NORAD protocols. Roth believes that 'Speckled Trout' (the name given to a highly advanced US military plane reserved for the top US military brass, which was being used that day by the Joint Chiefs of Staff chairman General Hugh Shelton) was the operations center from which the 9/11 attack was fully or partially run. The timeline offered by Shelton cannot be true and is contradicted by other accounts.[613] Roth agrees with the theory, discussed shortly, that at least some if not all of the planes did not hit the WTC towers or the Pentagon, nor crash into an empty field in Shanksville, Pennsylvania. Dr. Kevin Barrett writes:[614]

Among the airline industry whistleblowers who have contacted Roth is one who still possesses the original passenger manifests for the "hijacked flights." There are no Arab names on those manifests.

That would explain why the public versions also contain no Arab names; why no remains of any alleged hijackers were ever DNA-identified; why the US government has repeatedly refused pleas from the alleged hijackers' family members to accept DNA samples and try to identify their falsely-accused loved ones; why several of the alleged hijackers were identity theft victims with Mossad doppelgangers; why not a single authentic security camera image shows any of the alleged hijackers en route to boarding any of the four alleged attack aircraft; why no airline industry employees have ever testified about ticketing or boarding any of the 19 Arabs; why no passenger stubs have ever been produced for the 19 Arabs; and why ten of the alleged hijackers turned up alive after 9/11.

The 19 Arab hijackers were the patsies. Clearly, many innocent Arabs had their identity stolen, and many of the 'hijackers' had Mossad doppelgängers, which is why three of them were seen simultaneously on the US East Coast and the West Coast at the same time in early September 2001.[615]

The Who

To pull off an operation of the magnitude of 9/11, you must have your agents in all the positions of power to coordinate the planning, execution and coverup of the affair. In addition to all the Cult agents in the Bush Administration at that time, including all the PNAC members and other neocons listed above, there were literally Cult Zionists everywhere in key positions of power. These included people such as:

1. Larry Silverstein (friend of Netanyahu [with whom he spoke every Sunday] who purchased the WTC lease just weeks before 9/11);

2. Lewis Eisenberg (friend of Netanyahu, associated with AIPAC, worked at Goldman Sachs, US ambassador to Italy and San Marino, Chairman of PANYNJ during 9/11);

3. Ronald Lauder (associated with Roy Cohn and Jeffrey Epstein, long-time donor to Netanyahu and Israel's Likud Party, head of the World Jewish Congress, friend of Donald Trump, pushed for the WTC lease to be sold to Silverstein, headed NY Governor Pataki's New York State Commission of Privatization and the New York State Research Council on Privatization, was the man who ultimately decided that WTC 1 and 2 should become privately owned for the first time, funded a Mossad school called the Interdisciplinary Center in Herzliya where he established the Lauder School of Government, Diplomacy and Strategy);

4. Michael Chertoff (mother was a Mossad agent,[616] father was a Talmud scholar, co-author of the USA PATRIOT Act, head of the criminal division of the DOJ during 9/11 and thus was the main investigator of the entire attack);

5. Dov Zakheim (PNAC, Pentagon Comptroller during 9/11, connected to a company called System Planning Corporation that conducted remote control of aircraft systems by using the Flight Termination System. Dov's father Jacob I. Zakheim was a member of Betar, a revisionist Zionist movement formed in 1923 in Riga, Latvia);

6. Stephen Berger (worked for two Rockefeller commissions, Executive Director of PANYNJ during 9/11);

7. Alan Dershowitz (heavily connected to Epstein as described in chapter 12, stepped in to secure release of dancing Israelis,[617] on whom more shortly);

8. Alvin Hellerstein (judge for 9/11 cases who ensured not a single one went to trial, so the public was denied information that could have come out. Judge Hellerstein's son, Joseph Hellerstein, is an Orthodox Jewish lawyer in Israel for the law firm Amit, Pollak & Matalon, who just so happened to represent the parent company of International Consultants on Targeted Security [ICTS], the very company responsible for airport security on 9/11 and a primary defendant in the tort litigation. Under normal circumstances this would've been more than enough to have Judge Hellerstein removed from the case);

9. Kenneth Feinberg (Zionist lawyer who led the 9/11 victims' compensation fund); and

10. Philip Zelikow (Executive Director of the 9/11 Commission who oversaw the coverup).

There are many more Zionists involved, of course, but that gives you an idea of how well the Cult had infiltrated important positions in America, and after all, infiltration is the name of the game for Sabbatean-Frankists. Now, with that background in place, we will take a look at how they pulled it off.

<u>The How</u>

To begin with, it's impossible to know exactly how the Cult pulled this off, unless you are an insider at the very top of the pyramid. Due to the strict compartmentalization used by the Cult and its intelligence agencies, where everything is on a need-to-know basis, even agents that participated in this giant false flag operation will not know how the whole thing was done. The op was full of smoke and mirrors, designed to create maximum confusion and deflect attention away from the essential and operative aspects of the attack. It's much more important to understand who and why, rather than how, but nonetheless, I will paint a summary of the key themes so we can better understand the devious nature of the Cult mindset and how it performs its deception, and thus become immune to it in future.

There are many aspects to the how. I will begin by noting a few things about the Mossad. By the 1990s, the relationship between the Mossad and the CIA that I described in chapter 11 now had had four decades to solidify. Colonel Lawrence Wilkerson said in a July 2025 interview that *"I watched Mossad take over the Pentagon in 2002"* and that *"Donald Rumsfeld, the Secretary of Defense, said to my boss one time, 'Hell, I don't run my building. Mossad does.'"*[618] However, the Mossad had infiltrated the USG and all its agencies long before 2002. It's important to keep in mind two key things Ostrovsky said about the Mossad – that it liked to use the 'art student' cover story to give its spies a fake identity, and that it had thousands of front companies (registered, paying taxes, with everything up to date) just waiting to be taken off the shelf.[619] Mossad has front companies galore; remember also what Israeli spy Arnon Milchan said: *"In Israel, there is practically no business that does not have something to do with defense."*[620]

We will begin with control of computer systems and software. The information in chapter 12 about the Cult theft of PROMIS, and the installation of backdoors into the software, is of crucial importance here. Israel had gotten the PROMIS software, which, as a reminder, had a distinguishing feature: it could integrate different programs and databases simultaneously regardless of operating system. This made it an incredibly useful piece of software, and all the more so when you consider that the Cult knew about a backdoor to it that even its inventor Bill Hamilton apparently did not know about. The PROMIS affair occurred during the 1980s, and with technology advancing all the time, you can imagine how much better it was even just 10-15 years later. Christopher Bollyn, relying on Michael Ruppert's From the Wilderness website, notes that a Mossad front company known as PTech *"produced software that derived from PROMIS, had an artificial intelligence core, and was installed on virtually every computer system of the U.S. government and its military agencies on September 11, 2001."*[621] PTech was a front company with an Arab (Lebanese) owner called Oussama Ziade to hide the Zionist connection. Its real owner was Michael Goff, a Mossad sayan whose father and grandfather were 32° Masons in B'nai B'rith.[622] PTech worked together with another company called MITRE that is also involved in the NWO conspiracy in other ways, such as the spraying of chemtrails in the sky as part of the ongoing geoengineering programs.[623]

Indira Singh was an IT consultant who had previously worked on a Defense Advanced Research Project Agency (DARPA) project before working for JP Morgan in risk management. After 9/11, she became a whistleblower who exposed PTech, MITRE and their sinister cooperation. In 2002, she was fired for refusing to allow PTech developer Hussein Ibrahim access to JP Morgan's proprietary software. Singh reveals that before 9/11, PTech's clients included many of the important agencies of the USG – Congress, the White

House, the Treasury Department, the IRS, Customs, the FBI, the Department of Energy, the DOJ, the Secret Service, Air Force One (the US President's plane) and – wait for it – the FAA and the US Armed Forces (DoD, Navy, Air Force, etc.)![624] PTech software was even used by IBM and NATO. This meant that the true conspirators had access to and control over all the US government computer systems they needed to create confusion and execute the coverup. Singh said:[625]

PTech was with MITRE Corporation in the basement of the FAA for two years prior to 9/11. Their specific job is to look at interoperability issues the FAA had with NORAD and the Air Force in the case of an emergency. If anyone was in a position to know that the FAA – that there was a window of opportunity or to insert software or to change anything – it would have been PTech along with MITRE.

In other words, using backdoor-enabled PROMIS software, PTech and MITRE worked inside the FAA for two years studying FAA, NORAD and USAF interoperability … so they could hinder it. The confusion between FAA and NORAD was one of the chief reasons why fighter jets were either scrambled too late, scrambled from the wrong base, scrambled and sent in the wrong direction, or not scrambled at all, as I will get to. One aspect of disrupting FAA-NORAD interoperability was to manipulate the radar screens so that agents would be overwhelmed with blips or data, and thus confused about which were real and which were exercise, drill or decoy. It would have been a piece of cake for PTech to do this. The US Government had unwittingly put itself in the position where a foreign nation (Israel) had control over its governmental and military computer systems to the point where it could control what appeared or did not appear on its screens. Other aspects of software manipulation likely included Israel hacking the AA/United reservation software to keep passenger loads on the four 9/11 planes extremely low, as reported by CNN.[626]

Software manipulation was also behind the remote hacking of the Flight Management System (FMS) and activating what is called the Flight Termination System (FTS). As mentioned earlier, it was Pentagon comptroller Dov Zakheim who was connected with a company called System Planning Corporation (SPC) that specialized in defense technologies like FTS technology which allows operators to remotely take control of flights via a Command Transmitter System.[627] SPC also refurbished commercial 767s, converting them and selling them as military refueling tankers.[628] When FTS takes over a plane, it completely prevents any plane communication with the outside world, including turning off the transponder. This explains why none of the 9/11 pilots squawked the hijack code (7500) – they were shut out of the system. To make matters worse, then NORAD commander General Ralph Eberhart, who spent the rest of his career after 9/11 trying blame the FAA for NORAD's inaction, decided to reduce the Infocon to Level 5, the lowest possible level – at 9:09pm on September 10th 2001, just under 12 hours before the attacks began![629] The Infocon threat level was established in March 1999 to be a measure of the perceived threat to DoD computer systems and networks. Different levels required different security protocols. This meant that any hackers would have had the highest possible access and lowest possible security to penetrate. Just another coincidence?

It was an SPC subsidiary called Tridata Corporation that oversaw the investigation after the 1993 WTC terrorist attack. Tridata was a small company with no web presence – how did they manage to gain the contract for WTC security over large American companies (unless they had inside help from Cult agents)? The pattern follows the way that Kroll Associates got the contract after the 1993 WTC bombing. Suspiciously, Tridata declared bankruptcy right after 9/11.[630] It is entirely reasonable to presume that their security contract gave Tridata agents access to plant bombs in the WTC elevator shafts, the crucial structural place that had to be targeted and weakened in order for the other preplanted bombs (combined with DEW) to bring down the buildings in totality.

The second aspect of 'the how' is the preponderance of drills that were taking place at the same time. The largest annual war game, Vigilant Guardian, was happening during 9/11; in fact, Webster Tarpley reported[631][632] that there were many drills or dummy wargame simulations occurring on the morning of September 11th (and 46 in total when you count before, during and after). What are the chances so many drills would just happen to be scheduled then? I suppose your answer will depend on whether you are a coincidence theorist or a conspiracy theorist. Of course, with that many drills taking place simultaneously, the screens of the FAA and NORAD agents were overwhelmed with dots and blips, making it extremely difficult if not impossible to determine where the real planes were; agents were frequently heard to be asking their supervisors, *"Is this real world or exercise?"* Another purpose of the drills was to remove fighter pilots and jets from NEADS (North East Air Defense Sector), which was the division responsible for the northeast area of the US (including Washington, Boston, New York and Pennsylvania) at the time of 9/11. The theme of the Cult pulling off a false flag operation at the same time as a drill for a very similar, or even identical, scenario,

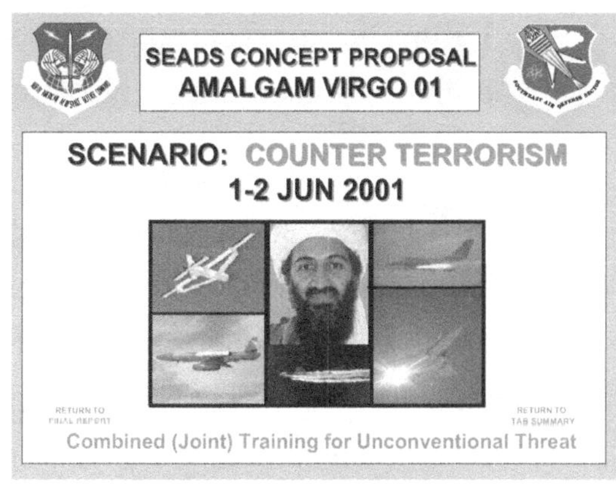

Image #97: the Amalgam Virgo wargame simulation with bin Laden as the enemy

was to continue many times after 9/11, including during the 7/7 London bombings (when Netanyahu was in London) and the many school shootings in the US between 2010 and 2020. There were also wargame simulations conducted earlier in 2001, such as the June 1st-2nd exercise called Operation Amalgam Virgo which just so happened to feature a scenario where a terrorist group would launch a missile or drone attack against the US. Guess who the 'enemy' was in the Amalgam Virgo simulation? Osama bin Laden.

The third aspect of the how is the obvious stand-down by the FAA and NORAD. Within the US, it is standard operating procedure to scramble jet fighters whenever a plane goes off course or loses radio contact. Between September 2000 and June 2001, intercepting fighter jets were scrambled 67 times, and in the year 2000 alone, it was 129 times.[633] The procedure is that FAA is meant to immediately notify NORAD (and may get transferred to one of their subdivisions, like NEADS), and NORAD is meant to immediately scramble fighters. There were at least three types of failures that day:

1. **Failure to report**: the FAA took an inordinately long time to report deviating aircraft;
2. **Failure to scramble:** NORAD didn't scramble fighter jets from the nearest military bases; and

3. **Failure to intercept:** once airborne, the fighters didn't reach or intercept their targets because they flew at small fractions of their top speeds and/or in the wrong direction.

The first failure can partially be explained by the first two 'how' points above, namely hacked software and war games. The Cult could control what blips appeared on which radar screens, or if not, could create mass confusion with multiple blips due to war games, thus slow down the normal FAA agent response time to NORAD. The delays included an 18- to 23-minute delay in reporting Flight 11 and a 39-minute delay in reporting Flight 77, depending upon which official timeline you believe out the many offered by the USG.[634] It is also revealing to note that a top security official at the FAA at that time was Michael Canavan, a specialist in US Special Operations which includes off-record black projects outside the law. David Icke writes:[635]

Canavan was Commanding General, Special Operations Command, Europe, and Commanding General, Joint Special Operations Command, at Fort Bragg, North Carolina ... this is the same Fort Bragg that provided several officers from its US Army 4th Psychological Operations (PSYOPS) Group to work in the news division at CNN's headquarters in Atlanta ... and also staffed the National Security Council's Office of Public Diplomacy (OPD), a shadowy government propaganda agency that planted stories in the US media ... a 'senior US official' [described] the OPD as a 'vast psychological warfare operation of the kind the military conducts to influence a population in enemy territory.'

How interesting, given that it was precisely the American population who were the enemy that day in a daring psychological operation. Other strange coincidences were that Jane Garvey, then

FAA head, went on to sit on the board of MITRE … and her husband Robert Garvey was then sheriff of Hampshire County where Westover AFB was located. Another piece of evidence regarding the stand-down comes from then Transportation Secretary Norman Mineta.[636] During the morning of 9/11, then Vice-President Dick Cheney, with Bush out of the way for hours (or all day) reading goat books to primary school children, was able to assume the role of president. Mineta testified that he was there when a young man kept coming up to Cheney with reports of a plane rapidly approaching the Pentagon – *"The plane is 50 miles out," "The plane is 30 miles out."* Mineta says that when it got down to the plane being 10 miles out, the young man asked Cheney:

"Do the orders still stand?"

Mineta says that Cheney whipped his neck around and said:

"Of course the orders still stand! Have you heard anything to the contrary?"

Mineta later joined the Mossad-connected ICTS board … there's that word again, coincidence.[637]

The US Government never adequately answered why the Pentagon didn't use its ground-to-air missiles anyway, being one of the most closely guarded buildings in the world. This kind of response from Cheney typifies what happened that day – the collective suspension of normal procedures and usual security protocols. It brings to mind once again the famous quote of Leroy Fletcher Prouty who was Chief of Special Operations for the Joint Chiefs of Staff under JFK and who closely studied assassinations. I will quote him again since his words are well worth repeating:[638]

No one has to direct an assassination – it happens. The active role is played secretly by permitting it to happen. This is the greatest single clue. Who has the power to call off or reduce the usual security precautions?

The second failure – that NORAD didn't scramble fighter jets from the nearest military bases – makes no logical sense. If you were truly trying to defend your cities from hijacked planes, why would you scramble jets from a base further away, making it so they have more, not less, time to intercept?

The third failure again shows deliberate intervention to subvert the standard operating procedures to make the system not function as it should have. Once airborne, the fighters didn't reach or intercept their targets because they only flew at small fractions of their top speeds. This 9/11 truth website calculated the planes' speeds as follows:[639]

Otis to the WTC

The first base to finally scramble interceptors was Otis in Falmouth, Massachusetts, at 8:52, about a half-hour after Flight 11 was taken over. This was already eight minutes after Flight 11 hit the North Tower, and just 9 minutes before Flight 175 hit the South Tower. According to NORAD, at the time of the South Tower Impact the two F-15s from Otis were still 71 miles away. Otis is 153 miles east-northeast of the WTC. That means the F-15s were flying at:

(153 miles - 71 miles)/(9:03 - 8:52) = 447 mph

That is around 23.8% of their top speed of 1875 mph.

At around 9:20 the F-15s finally reached the World Trade Center. Their average speed for the trip was:

153/(9:11 - 8:52) = 483 mph

That is around 25.8% of their top speed.

Langley to the Pentagon

The F-16s from Langley reached the Pentagon at 9:49. It took them 19 minutes to reach Washington D.C. from Langley AFB, which is about 130 miles to the south. That means the F-16s were flying at:

130 miles/(9:49 - 9:30) = 410.5 mph

That is around 27.4% of their top speed of 1500 mph.

Even if we assume the top speeds of the F-15 and F-16 are slightly lower (1500mph and 1300mph), the planes still flew way below their top speeds, somewhere between 20 and 30%. Why on earth would they do this if they were genuinely trying to defend US airspace? There were even fighter jets flying in the wrong direction out over the Atlantic Ocean! The sane conclusion here is that the pilots were given slow-down orders – someone high up the chain of command interfered to ensure the fighters would not get to the scenes of the crime on time.

Another question to ponder is this. Is it just a coincidence that Russia would fly its jets super close to US jets, and begin a major exercise in the northern Pacific area, right before 9/11? This prompted NORAD to send additional fighter aircraft to Alaska and northern Canada to monitor the exercises, thus leaving less planes to monitor US continental airspace.[640]

The fourth aspect of 'the how' is the takeover of the planes themselves. There has been a lot of debate within the 9/11 Truth Community about whether planes hit the buildings or not – the 'plane' vs. 'no plane' theory. Some of it has devolved into infighting which suits the Cult just fine (divide and conquer). There is solid evidence that CGI (computer generated imagery) graphics were used on some of the widely circulating footage after the event, where fake planes were inserted. Certainly, when you combine the pre-planted bombs in the WTC buildings and the Pentagon, along with the use of DEW (Directed Energy Weapons), both of which I will talk about shortly, there was *no need* for a plane to hit either of the twin towers to cause the observed damage, since the damage was caused by other means. One major problem the 'plane theory' has to overcome is how a plane could have entered the WTC tower like a knife through hot butter to the point where the building totally enveloped the plane; one major problem the 'no plane theory' has to overcome is to adequately explain how planes appeared on the video camcorders of private citizens and New Yorkers who filmed it from the street below (not MSM footage). It is difficult to conclude with 100% certainty that planes either did or did not hit the buildings; but regardless, it wasn't necessary for planes to do so in order for the buildings to be damaged and destroyed.

If there were planes that hit the towers, or if it were missiles, either way, they were remotely controlled. By 2001, it was a piece of cake for the Cult to remotely control planes and fly them wherever they wanted. The technology to remotely control planes from the ground has been around a very long time. The 9/11 truth site Holocausts.org quotes from an article entitled *"Thwarting skyjackings from the ground"* by Alan Staats, previously written for the organization FACSNET (Foundation for American Public Records) on October 2nd 2001, where he reveals that the US Military has had the technological capability to remotely control aircraft since the 1950s:[641]

Controlling the aircraft from the ground is nothing new. The military has been flying obsolete high performance fighter aircraft as target drones since the 1950s. In fact, NORAD (the North American Air Defense Command) had at its disposal a number of U.S. Air Force General Dynamics F-106 Delta Dart fighter aircraft configured to be remotely flown into combat as early as 1959 under the auspices of a program known as SAGE. These aircraft could be started, taxied, taken off, flown into combat, fight, and return to a landing entirely by remote control, with only human intervention needed being to fuel and re-arm them.

Additionally, on April 24th 2001, it was reported by Britain's International Television News that a robotic plane, UAV (unmanned aerial vehicle) or drone, made by US aerospace and defense contractor Northrup Grumman, with the exact wingspan of a Boeing 737, successfully flew across the Pacific from America to Australia:[642]

Image #98: the Northrup Grumman Global Hawk UAV or drone

A robot plane has made aviation history by becoming the first unmanned aircraft to fly across the Pacific Ocean. The American high-altitude Global Hawk spy plane flew across the ocean to Australia, defence officials confirmed. The Global Hawk, a jet-

powered aircraft with a wingspan equivalent to a Boeing 737 flew from Edwards Air Force Base in California and landed late on Monday at the Royal Australian Air Force base at Edinburgh, in South Australia state. It flies along a pre-programmed flight path, but a pilot monitors the aircraft during its flight via a sensor suite which provides infra-red and visual images.

Part of the coverup that day was officials pretending that the technology was far off in the future when it already existed in 2001 and, in fact, had already existed in the public arena for an extremely long time. MIC technology, often developed in secretive Deep Underground Military Bases (DUMBs) is far ahead of public sector technology.

One aspect of the Cult mindset is that rarely leaves things to chance. It's the control freak mindset; it needs to be in charge of every little detail. The remote control of planes is a key component of the 9/11 false flag operation because, this way, the Cult removed any possible human error with 'hijackers' who may or may not have been able to commandeer the aircraft and perform the necessary aerial maneuvers. In fact, from what we know of the laws of physics and expert pilot testimony, the maneuvers that day were impossible for a human pilot … but not for a machine. However, it is difficult to fully pierce the veil of deception that was created that day in September 2001, because even with the understanding that remotely controlled planes were used, there is still not a satisfactory explanation for the lack of visible plane debris and lack of impact damage to the (remotely controlled) planes as they hit the building. The footage of aluminum and plastic planes fully penetrating the towers, and being completely enveloped by them, is utterly fake.

The fifth aspect of 'the how' is the takeover of security at the WTC and the planting of explosives before the event. For a long time, Cult Israeli companies had been trying to gain control of WTC security. Atwell Security was a Tel Aviv company started by Mossad agent Shaul Eisenberg who was involved in the JFK assassination and who helped form terrorist groups Irgun and the Shanghai Betar. He also worked closely with Cult agent Henry Kissinger throughout the 1970s to run guns to Pol Pot's Khmer Rouge. The Washington Times reports that Atwell was trying to obtain the WTC security contract even in 1987.[643] This contract would also have given them control of New York's airports, ports and commuter trains – more control to execute and cover up the operation. They almost got the contract in 1987 until PANYNJ found out that Atwell director Avraham Shalom Bendor had killed two Palestinian teenagers in 1984 as head of Shin Bet. Nonetheless, Bendor went on to work for the Zionist-run Kroll Associates, who as already mentioned acquired the security contract in 1993 after the WTC bombing of that year. So much for the general security. The control of WTC electronic security was awarded to Securacom (later Stratesec), which had on its board Marvin Bush, younger brother of then President Bush! It's a small criminal world at the top. Additionally, the Cult also controlled security at some US airports during 9/11 via Mossad front company ICTS, which was based in Holland and founded in 1982 by Israelis Ezra Harel and Menachem Atzmon. It was its subsidiary Huntleigh that did 9/11 airport security.

So, with that background in place, consider this: as luck would have it, in the period leading up to 9/11, a group of Jewish 'art students' managed to obtain temporary construction passes to perform work on the 91st floor of WTC 1. These passes, in fact, granted them access to the entire WTC complex. The group called themselves Gelatin or later Gelitin which of course is not too far removed from the word gelignite (a.k.a. blasting gelatin), the explosive material consisting of collodion-cotton (a type of nitrocellulose). They claimed they were doing an art project called the "B-Thing" which involved them removing heavy WTC windows on the 91st floor and constructing a prefab balcony outside of the building. They stretched 'putty' around the windows and filmed it by helicopter.[644] They posted photos which showed boxes stacked to the ceiling labelled "BB18" on the side, which is the model number for a fuse-holder accessory sold by the company Littel.[645] The features and benefits of this product include saving space and workload in a complicated wiring situation, decreasing wiring terminations and reducing assembly time.[646] The New York Times covered the story with a photo that shows the group had removed wall and ceiling panels.[647] The impact points of the 'planes' was around the 93rd to 98th floors. To top it all off, in another spectacular coincidence, the entire WTC 1 building was powered down during an entire weekend prior to 9/11, according to IT specialist Scott Forbes.[648] During the power down, doors were open and surveillance security cameras did not work, meaning virtually anyone had access to the building. To keep this section brief, I won't go through all the evidence that there were bombs in the building, but there are multiple eyewitness accounts affirming it,[649] and we know that steel couldn't burn that hot due to jet fuel. It is therefore highly probable that Gelitin planted some or all of the bombs that were used to blow up the floors to make it look, in cartoonish style, like a soft-metal plane with a plastic nose cap had literally pierced and penetrated the building to the point where the building entirely enveloped it. Eyewitnesses including firemen also heard or experienced bombs in the basement.[650] The

Image #99: look at the sheer force, propulsion and size of those explosions. How could jet fuel have done that?

buildings fell close to free-fall speed in splendid symmetry, a telltale sign of controlled demolition. In this TV clip,[651] lucky Larry Silverstein claimed he had gotten a call from the fire department commander, and that the fire department made the decision to "pull it" which is slang for pulling the building or demolishing it in a controlled way.

However, I would suggest that in addition to bombs (at many levels) in the buildings, the sixth aspect of 'the how' can account for how the buildings actually fell – and disappeared into dust. They were pulverized or 'dustified' way beyond a normal controlled demolition. The buildings exploded and got pulverized – and only after that did they collapse. I refer to the exotic technology of DEW which was barely know to the public at the time of 2001, and is still not known to many people now, although people are starting to wake up to it. In my 2023 book *Break Your Chains*, I exposed how the Cult had been using DEW to raze entire neighborhoods to the ground under the pretense of wild fires, as happened in California to the

Images #100 & 101: look at the immense structural strength of the twin towers

Santa Rosa area (2017) and Paradise (2018). Not long after the book was published, Lahaina, Maui was hit with a DEW attack in August 2023 which virtually wiped out the entire town.[652] The same blueprint was again used in the Los Angeles area (e.g. the Palisades) in January 2025. Dr. Judy Wood, author of the 2005 book *Where Did the Towers Go? Evidence of Directed Free-Energy Technology on 9/11*, scientifically analyzed the destruction of the twin towers. She includes hundreds of photographs showing the way the towers exploded into dust that is not consistent with pancaking or collapse. People, cars and objects below in the streets were covered in thick layers of dust. An interesting piece of evidence she offers relates to the jumpers or people who were trapped in the upper stories before the building was completely dustified. In an ordinary office fire scenario, you would expect people to wear wet clothes (wet from the sprinkler system) to protect themselves against the heat, but on this occasion, many people took their clothes off. Why? Wood proposes that a microwave field, such as used in Active Denial Systems (ADS) for crowd control, was deployed. She writes that *"wet clothing intensifies the pain caused by such microwaves ... intensifie[s] the effects of the beam."*[653] Were people removing wet clothes to escape DEW or ADS?

Other striking photographic evidence are the various cars and firetrucks below whose fronts were wilted and doors were melted but bodies were intact, as well as intact paper, flags and trees. This kind of damage is not caused by ordinary fires, but can be caused by microwave fires or DEW using what Wood calls the Tesla-Hutchison effect. The use of this technology explains the lack of observable steel debris which should have been plentiful and overwhelming, but was not due to the dustification. Another thing that doesn't add up is how the fire retardant was missing from the inside of the WTC buildings so that the explosives could do their work unhindered. One possible answer is that extreme pressure was used to strip the fire retardant from the towers' steel beams. Did DEW provide this extreme pressure? Is this connected to Hurricane Erin, a category 5 hurricane over the Atlantic which could potentially have hit New York, but was most likely geoengineered and steered away? Was the hurricane created to produce pressure in Manhattan so that the buildings could more easily be destroyed?

In the WTC twin towers, there were thousands of desks, chairs, computers and phones. In an earthquake collapse, these objects are usually found – damaged, but identifiable. Why were virtually none of them found in the 9/11 debris? Were they vaporized? Here is what a first responder said:[654]

Everything was dust and metal ... there were no chairs ... there were no desks ... there were no phones ... Everything was just pulverized.

The seventh aspect of 'the how' worth consideration, though not as large as the others, is the fact that there is scant evidence that a plane hit the Pentagon or that a plane crashed in a Pennsylvanian field. In neither case was there sufficient debris to substantiate that an airliner had crashed. The damage to the Pentagon resembled something narrow and small that would more likely have been caused by a bomb or missile. In fact, in an interview one month after 9/11 in October 2001 with *Parade Magazine*, Rumsfeld said that a missile had damaged *"this building"* (meaning the Pentagon), although later claimed he had "misspoke":[655]

Here we're talking about plastic knives and using an American Airlines flight filled with our citizens, and the missile to damage this building and similar (inaudible) that damaged the World Trade Center.

The ground in Shanksville was basically just a smallish hole in the ground with virtually no debris at all. Residents and journalists nearby, and even the mayor of Shanksville himself, said that no plane crashed there. Parts or debris were found as far as eight miles from the designated crash site.[656]

The eighth aspect of 'the how' was the enormous Mossad spy ring in Florida that was uncovered by Fox News reporters. Fox is owned by Cult Zionist Rupert Murdoch so in some ways it is surprising that the story even got air time, but it was quickly taken down. Here's what happened: Fox journalist Carl Cameron reported that a gigantic, sprawling Israeli spy ring was operating in Florida,

California and New Jersey where literally hundreds of 'Israeli art students' had gained access to the offices – and homes! – of Drug Enforcement Administration (DEA) agents, IRS agents and US marshals. These 'students' turned out to be Mossad agents, body guards for generals, explosive experts, demolition experts and even experts in US Patriot missile systems. Israel's spy network was highly prominent in Florida where many of the Arab 9/11 'hijackers' were located. In other words, Mossad agents were closely watching the patsies in the lead-up to the false flag operation. Were the Arab hijackers actually on the Mossad payroll? They could well have been – remember, these devout 'Muslim' hijackers were caught drinking alcohol, eating pork, going to strip clubs and paying lap dancers in the weeks leading up to 9/11, being loud and leaving extra copies of the Koran laying around to create a trail for dummies that any investigator could easily pick up. Interestingly enough, when these 'art students' were arrested and detained, many were bailed out by … Israeli company AMDOCS (a company that specializes in software for communications and media).[657] Yes, that's right: another Israeli software company is coincidently connected to 9/11.

Foreknowledge

It is difficult to pull off a crime of the century like 9/11 without a lot of people involved, some who may accidentally spill the beans ahead of time, especially if they are trying to use that knowledge to save loved ones or to make money. Here are 14 examples of foreknowledge of the 9/11 event, in chronological order, the majority of which are directly traceable to Israel or if not to Cult corporations and agencies. A few of these examples may more fairly be described as predictive programming, a technique where the Cult seeds the idea of an event into the public consciousness, often couched in art, movies, fictional stories, etc., in the hopes that people will become accustomed to it … and subconsciously create it without realizing it. In this way, the Cult not only lessens the resistance to their planned event by getting people used to it in advance, but actually harnesses the creative potential of humanity by tricking in into helping to make the event happen. Such is the untapped power of the human mind.

The first example is from the 1978 film *Medusa Touch*, which was directed by … Arnon Milchan. Another coincidence, I'm sure. I discussed Milchan in chapter 10 regarding his work spying for Israel and helping its nuclear program. In *Medusa Touch*, the main character has the power to cause disasters simply by thinking about them. In an attention-grabbing scene, he makes a commercial jet crash into a New York skyscraper. Interestingly enough, there was another film made in that same year of 1978 called *The Trigger Effect*.[658] It looked back at the massive power blackout in the northeastern US that occurred in 1965. The blackout occurred on November 9th or 11/9 ... which is 9/11 written backwards. The documentary opened in front of the NYC WTC and persistently focused on one flight that day out of hundreds that were disrupted: Scandinavian flight 911 or SK911. As luck would have it, the flight is introduced in the documentary right around the 9:11 mark. Other examples of 9/11 predictive programming include several episodes of *The Simpsons* where 9/11 was prominently displayed, as well as big Hollywood movies like *The Matrix*, where the expiration date of the passport of the main character, Neo, was 9/11/2001.

The second example comes from 1980 and a quote from Isser Harel, considered the father of modern Israeli intelligence. Harel was Mossad director from 1952 to 1963. Jewish-American journalist

Michael Evans interviewed Harel, and recalled what Harel had said in a later Jerusalem Post article:[659]

I sat with former Mossad chief Isser Harel for a conversation about Arab terrorism. As he handed me a cup of hot tea and a plate of cookies, I asked him, 'Do you think terrorism will come to America, and if so, where and why?' Harel looked at his American visitor and replied, 'I fear it will come to you in America. America has the power but not the will, to fight terrorism...' As to the where, Harel continued, 'New York City is the symbol of freedom and capitalism. It's likely they will strike the Empire State Building, your tallest building [he mistakenly thought] and a symbol of your power.' ...Twenty-one years later, the first part of Harel's prediction came true; except, of course, that the Twin Towers of the World Trade Center were much taller than the Empire State Building.

As described above, when Atwell Security of Tel Aviv got the WTC security contract in 1987, there were two of Isser Harel's top agents, Peter Zvi Malkin and Avraham Shalom Bendor, who were working for Atwell.

The third example of foreknowledge is George Bush Sr.'s convenient purchase of Brady bonds that were about to come due on September 12th 2001, the day after the 9/11 attacks. Bush purchased $240 billion of ten-year Brady bonds on September 13th 1991 using fraudulent collateral and forged signatures, facilitated by then Secretary of the Treasury Nicholas Brady and allegedly underwritten and held by the trustee Cantor-Fitzgerald bond brokerage firm, whose offices were on the 101st to 105th floors of the north WTC tower. All the evidence and paperwork was destroyed, and thus there were no requirements to pay them back.[660]

The fourth example of foreknowledge relates to Able Danger, a classified military plan led by US Special Operations Command (SOCOM) and the DIA. Ex-DIA agent Lt. Col. Anthony Shaffer stated that Able Danger identified Al-Qaeda cells operating inside the US around one year in advance: the 'Brooklyn cell' linked to Blind Sheik Omar Abdel-Rahman, Mohamed Atta, and three other alleged hijackers. For his trouble, Shaffer's revelations were squashed, his access to classified information was revoked in 2005 and his security clearance was revoked in 2006. The coverup had to go on, unimpeded.

The fifth example of foreknowledge came in the form of predictive programming when the Fox Network planted another 'fictional' 9/11 seed in the public mind. On March 4th 2001, the first of a 13-part series called *The Lone Gunmen* aired. In the pilot episode, a computer hacker, part of a secret governmental cabal, takes remote control of a Boeing 727 commercial jet and tries to crash it into the WTC. Note how the name itself reinforces the fake Cult narrative around events (like the JFK, RFK, MLK and John Lennon assassinations that all took place in America between 1963 and 1980) where it tries to pin the blame on a lone nutter to hide the vast interconnected conspiracy in the shadows.

The sixth piece of foreknowledge is that Bill Cooper, on June 28th 2001, predicted bin Laden would be set up to take the fall for an imminent attack. Cooper was killed by law enforcement on his property on November 5th 2001. Here's what he said:[661]

Supposedly, a CNN reporter found Osama bin Laden, took a television camera crew with him, went in to Osama bin Laden's hideout, interviewed him and his top leadership ... and he came out and told everybody, "Within three weeks Osama bin Laden is going to attack the United States and Israel." Now don't you think that's kinda strange, folks? You see, because the largest intelligence apparatus in the world, with the biggest budget in the history of the world, has been looking for Osama bin Laden for years and years and years, and can't find him. Some ... reporter with a camera crew waltzes right into his hideout and interviews him. And I'm telling you, be prepared for a major attack. But it won't be Osama bin Laden; it will be those behind the New World Order.

The seventh example of foreknowledge was that the company Zim Integrated Shipping Services (ZIM), 49% owned by the Israeli Government, mysteriously vacated its 10,000 square foot office space in the north twin tower just a few days before 9/11, despite the fact its lease ran to the end of 2001, losing $50,000 in the process.

The eighth example of foreknowledge and predictive programming was the SAMS (US Army's School of Advanced Military Studies) report, a quote of which is featured at the beginning of this chapter. The 68-page paper had been released earlier, but in a piece of very coincidental timing, The Washington Times decided to publish an article about it on September 10th 2001, the day before 9/11, and the quote they used described the Mossad as a ruthless and cunning wildcard that could target America and make it look like a Palestinian or Arab act. The SAMS report also stated: *"500-pound gorilla in Israel. Well armed and trained. Operates in both Gaza [and the West Bank]. Known to disregard international law to accomplish mission. Very unlikely to fire on American forces. Fratricide a concern especially in air space management."*[662]

The ninth example of foreknowledge was the financial shenanigans that went on right before the event. In the world of finance, you can bet whether the value of a stock will increase or decrease. If you think it will increase, you can buy a call option; if you think it will decrease, you can buy a put option. Whoever planned the attacks knew the ensuing fallout would cause grave concerns about the companies in question (American Airlines and United Airlines) whose stock price would be sure to fall. In the days leading up to 9/11, 4,744 put options were bought on United Airlines and 4,516 put options were bought on American Airlines, six times the normal volumes, while other airlines did not have similar trading.[663] Investigative journalist Michael Ruppert discovered that at least one of these trades – which left an unclaimed payout of $2.5 million – was placed by the company called Banker's Trust-AB Brown, which was until 1998 managed by *"the man who is now in the number three Executive Director position at the Central Intelligence Agency"*[664] (A.B. "Buzzy" Krongard). Just a coincidence, I'm sure.

The tenth example of foreknowledge is that public figures like San Francisco Mayor Willie Brown[665] and author Salman Rushdie revealed they received calls before the event advising them to be cautious about air travel. In Rushdie's case, the original article reporting this has been removed from The London Times' website, however here is what it said according to this 9/11 truth website:[666]

On September 3 the Federal Aviation Authority made an emergency ruling to prevent Mr Rushdie from flying unless airlines complied with strict and costly security measures. Mr Rushdie told The Times that the airlines would not upgrade their security.

In other words, according to the London Times, Rushdie believed the USG knew of the imminent attack when they banned him from taking flights in Canada and the US just a week before. The Times reported that the FAA had told Rushdie's publisher that US intel had given them a vague warning of something out there without further details.

The eleventh example of foreknowledge occurred on the morning of the event involving Odigo, the Israeli instant messaging company whose US headquarters were located only two blocks from the WTC. Someone used Odigo's network to transmit a warning hours before the attacks telling its recipients to stay away from the towers on 9/11. Odigo Vice President Alex Diamandis stated: *"The messages said something big was going to happen in a certain amount of time, and it did – almost to the minute. It is possible the attack warning was broadcast to other Odigo members, but the company has not received reports of other recipients of the message."* Odigo CEO Micha Macover told Haaretz (September 26th 2001) that he had no idea *"why the message was sent…It may have been someone who was joking and turned out they accidentally got it right."* Accidentally, of course.

The twelfth example of foreknowledge is probably the most well known and quintessential smoking gun proof that 9/11 was orchestrated by people very high up on the food chain. The British Broadcasting Corporation (BBC) reported that WTC 7 (Building 7 in the WTC complex) had collapsed before it actually did! In a clip spread all over the internet for decades, reporter Jane Standley tells her audience that WTC 7 has fallen when it is, in fact, still standing and visible in the background.[667]

The thirteenth example of foreknowledge became apparent following the incident which is known as the "5 Dancing Israelis." Someone noticed five men cheering and giving each other 'high fives,' as well as making loud cries of mockery in the immediate aftermath of the planes hitting the towers. She called the police. Later that afternoon, the men were arrested in Bergen County, New Jersey, by police who discovered they were carrying boxcutter knives, multiple foreign passports, $4,700 in cash and suspiciously marked maps which connected them to the bombings of NYC. On top of that, bomb-sniffing dogs inspected the van and detected explosive residues. It turned out that two of the men (Sivan and Paul Kurzberg) were Mossad agents while the other three (Yaron Schmuel, Oded Ellner and Omer Maramari) had ties to intelligence as well. The five Israelis were arrested and held in custody[668] for 71 days then released, ultimately, by Cult Zionist Michael Chertoff. They returned to Israel where three of them appeared on Israeli TV, after which they disappeared. They said they were there to *"document the event."* Document the event?! Who told them to do that? How could they document an event unless they knew it was coming? Remember how Ostrovsky said the Mossad had many front companies sitting on a shelf just waiting to be used? Dominik Suter, the owner of Urban Moving Systems, also fled to Israel before he could face justice. The fact that the van of Urban Moving Systems was brazen enough to display a plane crashing into the towers shows you just how shameless and cocky the Cult is. The Cult did a similar thing in the London 7/7 bombing attack in 2005, when it orchestrated the event so that one of the buses that was bombed at the scene happened to have a large ad on it, which read: *"Outright Terror ... Bold and*

Image #102: the van of Mossad front company Urban Moving Systems with its mural of a plane hitting the WTC

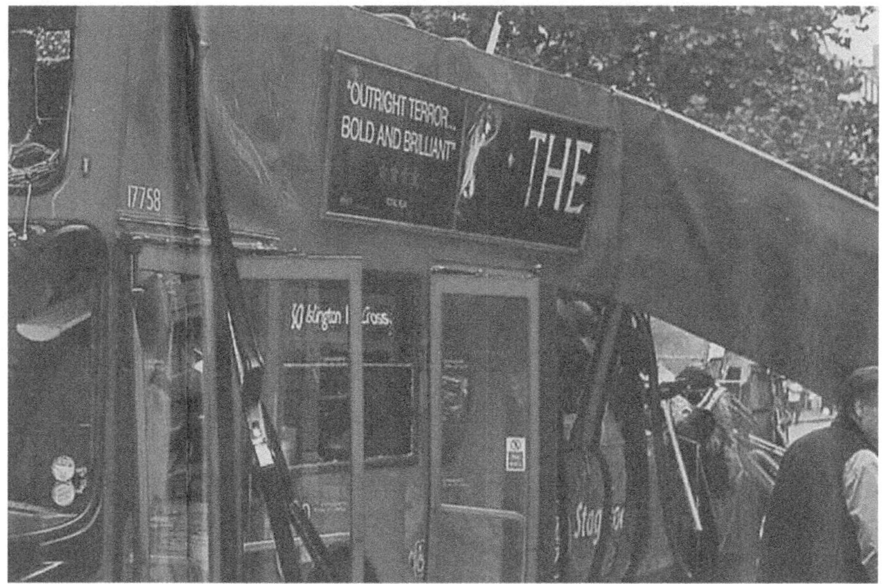

Image #103: look at the ad on the bombed bus

Brilliant." The Cult is sick, twisted and evil – and is directed by nonhuman intelligence.

The fourteenth and final example of foreknowledge that I will provide here are the reports that the USG received from its own intelligence agencies and the leaders of other nations that an attack was imminent. In 1998, the CIA told then President Bill Clinton that Al-Qaeda was planning attacks in America that might include hijacking, and Afghani Ahmad Shah Massoud, leader of the anti-Taliban Northern Alliance, said in an April 2001 speech before the European Parliament that he had limited intelligence about an imminent terrorist attack on the US. Massoud was assassinated by Al-Qaeda two days before 9/11, on September 9th 2001, the same day that Russian President Vladimir Putin called Bush to share his concern over Massoud's assassination and to warn him that *"something larger might be afoot."*[669]

I will end this subsection by bringing up the theme of symbolism, since it is connected to predictive programming. The Cult is steeped in the occult and black magic. It uses symbolism to communicate its messages for many reasons, two of which are that symbolism is a coded way to transmit information that not all people will be able to interpret or understand, and also that symbolism bypasses the conscious mind and goes straight into the subconscious, thus avoiding a conscious filter that might question or reject its effect. In other words, symbolism can be a very effective brainwashing tool.

9/11 was chosen as the date for this horrific event because a large aspect of the attack was a psychological operation. The number sequence 911 is what you dial in America when you are in an emergency or need to reach the police, ambulance or fire department, so that number is already associated with threat, danger or emergency in the minds of Americans. When George Bush was on television in the Florida classroom reading about a pet goat to children, the teacher was getting the class to repeat five words after her. Guess what they were?[670]

Kite, Hit, Steel, Plane, Must

What are the chances the children would be learning those particular words that day – a day when planes or flying objects were hitting steel buildings?

The Coverup of the Century

To cover up the crime of the century, the Cult exerted control over at least the following four aspects:

1. Control of the nascent narrative: in the immediate aftermath, seeding the official story in the public mind via mass media of the new enemies to fear and hate: Osama bin Laden, Al-Qaeda and Islamic terrorism;

2. Control of the crime scenes: controlling who could access the area while getting rid of the debris (evidence) as fast as possible;

3. Control of the investigation: censoring inconvenient information, silencing inconvenient witnesses and setting up an official Cult-controlled commission with a predetermined finding that would point the blame in other directions; and

4. Control of the long-term litigation process: control of the courts and victims' funds to obstruct legal discovery and stop the truth ever getting out via lawsuits.

Let's discuss each of these in turn. Firstly, the Cult ensured its Zionist agents were given primetime exposure on its MSM corporations so that they could seed the official narrative right away. They were going to name the patsy or bogeyman immediately, and with repetition, to drum it into the public mind. Two men interviewed on 9/11 were former Israeli PM, terrorist and close Epstein associate Ehud Barak[671] and American Paul Bremer,[672] who somehow became a de facto head of state of Iraq after the US illegally invaded that nation in 2003. Everyone had their cover story ready; according to Richard Clarke, author of *Against All Enemies*, Cheney said, *"It's an Al-Qaeda attack and they like simultaneous attacks. This may not be over."*[673] How could Cheney have known that already unless Al-Qaeda was the predesignated enemy? Right from the start, fake bin Laden videos were distributed via the Mossad-front SITE (an acronym for Search for International Terrorist Entities) led by Israeli Rita Katz, whose father was once executed in Iraq after having been caught spying for Israel. Mossad not only instigates numerous false flag terror attacks by 'Islamic terrorists,' but it also sets up a series of fake Islamic terrorism websites that 'claim responsibility' for these attacks. It's a stitch up. SITE also 'found' a guide entitled *The Arab Volunteers in Afghanistan* that conveniently told the USG all they needed to know about radical Islamic terrorism and which Katz described as *"practically the 'Who's Who of al-Qaeda.'"*[674] I'm so grateful for the fortunate discoveries made by Mossad throughout 9/11. Did any of these figures produce compelling evidence that bin Laden was guilty? Not on your life. In what become one of his most famous utterances, Bush declared *"you're either with us or against us"*[675] (polarize, divide and conquer, with no shades of grey) and on bin Laden said that *"there's no need to discuss innocence or guilt – we know he's guilty."*[676]

Secondly, it was the aforementioned Michael Chertoff who oversaw the removal of evidence at Ground Zero. He gave the job to Richard Sheirer, who ensured the more than 60,000 tons of steel was taken from the crime scene and transported to two Jewish-owned scrapyards in New Jersey where it was cut into pieces that were 60 inches (150cm) or less, mixed with other scrap metal and shipped to China – before anyone could inspect it! As Wyatt Peterson of TruthBlitzkrieg.com writes, *"The two scrapyards that handled all of the steel from Ground Zero were Hugo Neu and Metal Management. Both companies happened to be owned and operated by Zionists: Alan Ratner at Metal Management and Robert Kelman at Hugo Neu. (Metal Management's Newark-based operation had just begun recovering from Chapter 11 bankruptcy shortly before 9/11, an event that would provide windfall profits for the troubled firm.)"*[677] The *New York Daily News* reported in April 2002 that *"185,101 tons of structural steel have been hauled away from Ground Zero. Most of the steel has been recycled as per the city's decision to swiftly send the wreckage to salvage yards in New Jersey. The city's hasty move has outraged many victims' families who believe the steel should have been examined more thoroughly."*[678] The hasty removal of evidence led to the sad and absurd situation where engineers went down to the scrap yards to sift through the material like 'mountain goats,' timing their explorations so that they wouldn't be crushed, in the hope they could find something of value before it was shipped off.

Thirdly, the Cult ensured it controlled any investigation by overseeing the creation of the official 9/11 Commission and the release of the official report by the National Institute of Standards and Technology (NIST). As Chairman Thomas Kean and Vice Chairman Lee Hamilton admitted in their 2006 book *Without Precedent: The Inside Story of the 9/11 Commission,* the entire thing was set up to fail. The whole point was to direct people away from Cult power centers and agencies (Israel, the Mossad, the CIA, the MIC, etc.) and to deflect blame. Building 7 was not even mentioned, despite falling in its own footprint and not being hit by anything! Initially the Cult had wanted to appoint massive insider, war criminal and Satanist Henry Kissinger as 9/11 Commission chairman, but the public outcry was too great. The role of NIST, which may be a better acronym for National Institute of Story Telling, was to produce scientific nonsense that somehow explained away a completely symmetrical and purely vertical near free-fall implosion, despite asymmetrical impact damage and fires. The NIST reports of 2005 (WTC 1 and 2) and 2008 (WTC 7) also did not address how the lower floors and supporting structures allowed the collapse to progress as rapidly as it did, the extreme hot spots in the rubble nor the pulverization of non-metallic materials. This is because they were covering up explosives in the building and DEW dustification. In contrast to the Cult-compromised NIST, the University of Alaska Fairbanks released a 2020 report whose principal conclusion was that fire did not cause the collapse of WTC 7 and whose secondary conclusion was that *"the collapse of WTC 7 was a global failure involving the near-simultaneous failure of every column in the building"*[679] – which means pre-planted explosives or exotic weaponry. Additionally, Architects and Engineers for 9/11 Truth released a rebuttal of the NIST fairy tale where they raised 25 points which demolished the official story (pun most definitely intended), including NIST's refusal to test for explosive residue, refusal to comply with FOIA requests, falsification of models, omission of critical data and failure to follow standard fire investigation protocol.[680]

You don't have to dig too deep to discover massive corruption and conflicts of interest surrounding the 9/11 commissioners; for example, commission member Barbara Glewe was hired later on by MITRE.[681] On October 29th 2024, MITRE announced that NIST renewed their contract for another five years to operate the National Cybersecurity Federally Funded Research and Development Center, which MITRE has operated since 2014.[682] So here you have the government via NIST subcontracting to MITRE which worked with Ptech to access and subvert the computer systems pre-9/11. Why not just invite your murderer over for dinner?

Fourthly, to ensure a successful coverup, the Cult had to stop any chance of the truth getting out in open trial. To do this, it had to 'control the opposition' (as it has done for centuries) by appointing its own agents to corral the victims' families in a certain direction.

The Cult came up with its trademark evil genius idea: create a fund for victims (that would aggressively push money in exchange for silence), appoint a special mediator for victims (who would aggressively push money in exchange for silence) and appoint a judge to handle all victims' cases (who would aggressively push money in exchange for silence). With control of private banking, money is no object to the Cult; paying people off is a long-established part of its modus operandi. Enter Zionists Kenneth Feinberg, Sheila Birnbaum and Alvin Hellerstein. The Cult chose Feinberg to lead the 9/11 Victim Compensation Fund. Feinberg was a Zionist lawyer whose wife Diane Feinberg was *"an executive member of the United Jewish Appeal – the organization to which Larry Silverstein and Lewis Eisenberg both belonged – and was also on the board of governors for the Jewish Agency, an elite organization with close ties to the Mossad."*[683] As many as 97% of families immediately took the hush money. The ones who held out for trial were pressured and intimidated by Jewish lawyer and special mediator Sheila Birnbaum, who said that *"there was an emotional response and they wanted to find that someone was responsible other than the terrorists because of the grief they were feeling"*[684] or, in other words, they suspected the official government story about what happened was utter crap. Peterson notes that Birnbaum was a *"partner of the international law firm Skadden Arps (headed by Eric Friedman). Skadden Arps has very strong ties to the state of Israel. A senior partner at the firm is Kenneth Bialkin, a former national chairman of the Anti-Defamation League of B'nai B'rith."*[685] Finally, for the victims that Feinberg and Birnbaum could not silence with cash, Talmudic Jew and judge Alvin Hellerstein stepped in. He managed to drag the litigation process on for so long that eventually, one by one, all the victims agreed to drop the lawsuits and settle out of court. Hellerstein so successfully obstructed legal discovery that he became known as the 'judge of attrition.' Of the 96 families who had initially brought lawsuits forward for trial, not a single one of their cases ever reached the open courtroom. Feinberg revealed the Cult agenda when he said about Hellerstein that he *"knew from the very beginning that the cases had to settle and he got there."*[686]

Responses from Leaders and Government Officials Worldwide

Many people smelt a rat when the US presented the world with its official and absurd 9/11 story. Here are three responses that show some people were awake and unafraid to logically question the nonsense:

The deathly precision of the attacks and the magnitude of planning would have required years of planning. Such a sophisticated operation would require the fixed frame of a state intelligence organization, something not found in a loose group like the one led by the student Mohammed Atta in Hamburg.

– Eckehardt Werthebach (Former President of Germany's Verfassungsschutz or Domestic Intelligence Service)[687]

Planning the attacks was a master deed, in technical and organizational terms. To hijack four big airliners within a few minutes and fly them into targets within a single hour and doing so on complicated flight routes! That is unthinkable, without backing from the secret apparatuses of state and industry.

– Andreas von Bülow (Former Secretary of State of Defense for Germany), Tagesspiegel, January 13th 2002[688]

[Bin Laden supposedly confessed] to the Qaeda September [attack] to the two towers in New York [claiming to be] the author of

the attack of the 11, while all the [intelligence services] of America and Europe ... now know well that the disastrous attack has been planned and realized from the CIA and the Mossad with the aid of the Zionist world in order to put under accusation the Arabic Countries and in order to induce the western powers to take part ... in Iraq [and] Afghanistan.

The mastermind of the attack must have been a sophisticated mind, provided with ample means not only to recruit fanatic kamikazes, but also highly specialized personnel. I add one thing: it could not be accomplished without infiltrations in the radar and flight security personnel.

– Francesco Cossiga (former Italian President and the man who revealed the existence of Operation Gladio)[689]

Cui Bono? Who Benefits?

When investigating any crime, it's crucial to ask the age old Latin question "cui bono?" or "who benefits?" Whoever benefits the most from a crime or event is most likely its originator. So, who benefitted most from 9/11? We can point to individuals like 'lucky' Larry Silverstein, who just so happened to not go to the WTC that day like he normally did and who wound up getting a $4.55 billion insurance payout. We can point to the USG which massively expanded its power and scope via the Patriot Act and the creation of the DHS and TSA (Transportation Security Administration) – note the use of the term 'homeland' in DHS as other fascist regimes have used in the past, such as the Nazis. The MIC certainly benefitted from a bonanza of arms contracts for new wars (almost interminable wars like Afghanistan, and the endless War on Terror), especially since the American public mostly forgot the astonishing admission by

Rumsfeld on September 10th 2001 that the Pentagon could not account for a missing $2.3 trillion!

It is clear that it was Israel who benefitted the most. Israel was able to launch its War on Terror that by definition framed its opponents as the ones committing terror, despite the mass Zionist terrorism unleashed on the Arabs to even create the State of Israel, not to mention the fact that many of Israel's leaders (e.g. Menachem Begin, Ariel Sharon) have been proud Jewish terrorists themselves. Israel benefitted by increasing Islamophobia and getting the US to attack Israel's Middle Eastern enemies in all directions – *"7 countries in 5 years"* (Iraq, Syria, Lebanon, Libya, Somalia, Sudan and Iran) as General Wesley Clark famously admitted in 2007.[690] As mentioned above, Netanyahu specifically said Israel was benefitting from the attacks!

Tying it All Together: A Cult Stitch Up

9/11 was a psyop based on perception management or perception control. Remember the Archons discussed in chapter 2? The 9/11 operation was an Archontic attack to make it appear that something happened which, in fact, did not happen. This is why there are so many anomalies, coincidences and impossibilities in the story. It was an attack on your senses; it was an attack on your idea of reality.

Just as the JFK assassination was imbued with Cult symbolism, so was 9/11. The twin towers evoke the two pillars of Freemasonry, Boaz and Jachin (or Joachim), which were said to guard the entrance of sacred and mysterious places and to be the entrance to Solomon's Temple. Solomon's Temple will be discussed in chapter 19. The two pillars are a gateway into the unknown. After 9/11, the world entered a new unknown era of terror, fear, war and reduced freedom. In ancient Greece, the pillars of Hercules flanked the Straits of Gibraltar; they were said to have borne the warning 'Nec Plus Ultra' meaning 'nothing further beyond.' Was the Cult warning anyone to not go further investigating? The date of 9/11 is written in Roman numerals as IXXI which resembles the Masonic compass and square logo and which forms the sigil of Saturn, connecting the event to the god of tyranny and death.

Image #104: a Masonic lodge room with twin pillars

In the lead up to 9/11, Cult Zionists oversaw or controlled USG computer systems (FAA/civilian and NORAD/military), WTC security, airport security, the official criminal investigation, the destruction of evidence, the courts and the 9/11 Commission. It was a Zionist stitch up. In reviewing Christopher Bollyn's book *Solving 9-11: The Deception That Changed the World*, here is what Dr. Robert Sungenis had to say:[691]

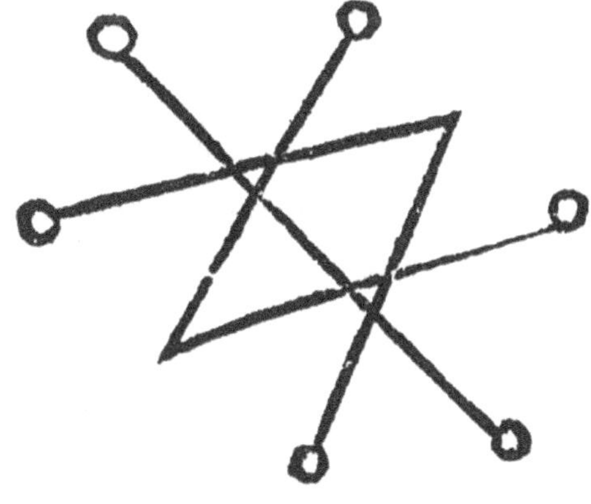

Image #105: the sigil of Saturn

Who had the power to pull it off without a hitch? Who had the most pressing motive? Who had the money to pay for it all? Who had control of the military and

NORAD to force it to stand down while four passenger planes went to their designated targets? Who knew the intricacies of US commercial flights to get around the FAA air traffic control? Who had the power, if needed, to operate planes by remote control? Who had control of the courts to make sure that no wrongful death claims went to trial? Who had control of disposal so that all the steel girders of the Twin Towers were shipped to China before they could be chemically analyzed? Who had the power to corral the NYPD and NYFD? Who had the power to allow dozens of suspects to escape to foreign countries? Who had the technology to bring down steel-girded buildings built to withstand forces much greater than aberrant planes and nominal fires? Who had the advanced computer knowledge to coordinate the attacks? Who had state of the art knowledge about explosives and detonators? Who had control of the press and media to curtail investigations? Who is most familiar with and has political control over the city at which the attacks took place? Who has a history of unprovoked attacks or even false-flag operations? Who has a network of spies operating in the US that could facilitate the attacks? Who has personnel in almost every sector of the federal government to create a massive cover up? Lastly, as any detective would ask, who benefits from the attacks?

Again, I want to emphasize that exactly how they pulled off the attack is not as important as understanding who did it and why they did it. In time, humanity will come to understand the how, but the who and why are crucial to understand right now.

Some in the 9/11 Truth Movement have framed part of the debate as LIHOP vs MIHOP ('let it happen on purpose' vs. 'made it happen on purpose') but the Cult simultaneously both let it happen and made it happen – so this distinction is unhelpful. On the lower levels, the

Cult let it happen for example by Cult agents lowering security (Eberhart and Infocon, Cheney and stand-down orders, moving the mentally deficient president out of the way to a Florida school classroom, etc.); on the higher levels, the Cult made it happen for example by Cult agents seeding the idea of the event in the public mind via film and TV, by planting bombs in the buildings, by using DEW technology to pulverize the twin towers into dust, by remotely controlling and flying the planes, and by taking control of WTC security, airport security and the computer systems of the US government and military.

The lies came thick and fast after 9/11, overwhelming the average person. Brian Michael Jenkins is the senior advisor to the president of the RAND corporation and was deputy chairman of Crisis Management for Kroll Associates from 1989 to 1998, the company as mentioned earlier that directed the PANYNJ response to the 1993 WTC bombing. Jenkins said, *"We knew there was no realistic way to protect the skyscrapers from a suicide mission. We couldn't very well mount missile batteries above the Windows on the World restaurant."*[692] This supports the widespread lie offered by many in the Bush Admin that 'we couldn't have foreseen it' – yet Operation Northwoods and the Vigilant Guardian war game on 9/11[693] planned for it and were based on it. As David Icke points out, when authorities try to bamboozle the public with events like this, they have a series of lies and fallback positions. The first lie is that there was nothing they could have done. That may convince some people, but not others, so then they resort to a second fallback position, which is that they were incompetent. This is still a lie to hide the stark truth – that they both let and made it happen by orchestrating it. The incompetence lie is easier for some people to hear rather than the painful truth that our rulers are psychopaths who willingly destroy and murder to advance their evil agenda.

So what happened in the aftermath of 9/11? More lies and more wars, of course. Then Secretary of State Colin Powell went out to brazenly assert[694] the propaganda talking point of the time, which was the buzzphrase 'Weapons of Mass Destruction' or 'WMDs' for short. When they couldn't convincingly blame Iraq for developing nukes (since Israeli jets had bombed Iraq's Osirak reactor in 1981 in an act of unprovoked aggression, thus stopping any Iraqi nuclear program dead in its tracks), they had to come up with another story, which was the equivalent of 'that bad guy over there has really bad weapons.' The propaganda is kindergarten-level stuff when you analyze it, but it is designed to evoke fear and an emotional reaction, both of which prevent people from thinking clearly and critically. Powell tried to claim the US had 'intelligence' that Iraqi leader Saddam Hussein, the same leader who the CIA backed during the 1980s and the same leader with whom Rumsfeld met in the 1980s to push US weapons sales, was now developing WMDs. It was all a blatant lie. Since 2001, numerous nations have been invaded and millions of people, mostly civilians, have died – all for the Cult cause of redrawing the Middle East on the way to a totalitarian NWO One World Government.

The 9/11 false flag operation was designed to send a very clear message to America and the Western world: you are not safe. You are in danger. You are under assault. Terrorists can strike you anywhere, anytime. Cult Zionists expressed the opinion that they were glad that America was finally getting some idea of what it was like to be under attack just as Israel had been for so long. So what did they do? They made sure America was under attack, even if they had to do it themselves! This was the psychopathic mindset driving the event, which was, after all, a psychological operation. RAND Corporation-connected Jenkins underlined the psychological nature of false flag terrorism when he said in 1974 that *"terrorism is aimed at the people watching, not at the actual victims. Terrorism is theater."*[695]

In executing this operation, the Cult inflicted another grave psychological wound upon the American psyche. The young US republic, which already fought off many attempts during the 1800s to stop a central bank, had to undergo the Cult assassination of a president (Lincoln) in 1865 and another Cult assassination of a president (JFK) in 1963. The Kennedy assassination in particular left a deep psychic scar on the nation. Now, with the 9/11 operation, the Cult had managed to add to America's collective trauma. Remember what former Mossad chief Isser Harel said in 1980 to reporter Mike Evans: *"America has the power, but not the will, to fight terrorism."* The point of the 9/11 psyop was to galvanize America against Israel's enemies, for the Cult to harness the awesome firepower of the US military – and use it for the Cult agenda, not America's best interests.

In the next chapter, we'll deconstruct the template the Cult uses for assassinations and operations. The more we understand about their methods, the less we are susceptible to their deception and manipulation.

Sources

---

[588] https://www.washingtontimes.com/news/2001/sep/10/20010910-025319-6906r/

[589] https://rense.com/general84/alq.htm

[590] https://www.theguardian.com/uk/2005/jul/08/july7.development

[591] https://www.bitchute.com/video/KxTDGU7tYnPN

[592] https://ic911.org/complete-911-timeline/

[593] https://nypost.com/1999/07/21/a-conversation-in-hell/

[594] https://www.brookings.edu/wp-content/uploads/2016/06/06_iran_strategy.pdf

[595] https://archive.org/details/RebuildingAmericasDefenses/page/n11/mode/2up, pg. 51

[596] Alice in Wonderland and the World Trade Center Disaster, pg. 35

[597] https://www.globalresearch.ca/george-w-bush-and-the-bin-laden-family-meet-in-new-york-city-one-day-before-911/5332870

[598] https://www.theguardian.com/uk/2005/jul/08/july7.development

[599] https://www.nytimes.com/2001/09/12/us/day-terror-israelis-spilled-blood-seen-bond-that-draws-2-nations-closer.html

[600] https://www.haaretz.com/2008-04-16/ty-article/report-netanyahu-says-9-11-terror-attacks-good-for-israel/0000017f-db7e-db22-a17f-ffff07ea0000

[601] https://stateofthenation.info/?p=7774

[602] https://ia803104.us.archive.org/19/items/BirthOfTheAlWahabiMovement2002/2002%20-%20Birth%20of%20Al-Wahabi%20Movement%20and%20Its%20Historical%20Roots%20-%20S.%20M.%20N.%20AI-Arniri.pdf

[603] https://muslimmirror.com/king-of-saudi-arabia-sponsored-netanyahus-campaign-panama-papers/

[604] https://www.presstv.ir/Detail/2025/07/03/750527/Iran-US-Saudi-Arabia-Israel-CENTCOM

[605] https://x.com/TheCradleMedia/status/1954484599318286384

[606] https://www.paulcraigroberts.org/2016/07/20/is-the-saudi-911-story-part-of-the-deception-paul-craig-roberts/

[607] Alice in Wonderland and the World Trade Center Disaster, pg. 323

[608] https://wikispooks.com/wiki/1993_World_Trade_Center_bombing

[609] https://ic911.org/consensus-panel/consensus-points/point-g-1/

[610] The Trigger, pg. 397

[611] https://ic911.org/complete-timeline/818-a-m-september-11-2001-flight-11-attendant-betty-ong-calls-airline-reservations-office-to-report-hijacking/

[612] Codex 9/11, https://www.youtube.com/watch?v=JlwycIbN7FM, 2 hour 13 minute mark

[613] https://www.consensus911.org/point-mc-7/

[614] https://beforeitsnews.com/9-11-and-ground-zero/2019/09/911-passengers-were-routed-to-westover-afb-cellphone-calls-military-personnel-confirm-flight-attendant-research-conclusions-capt-dave-betrand-ret-video-2442677.html

[615] https://ic911.org/complete-timeline/early-september-2001-accounts-place-three-9-11-hijackers-on-east-and-west-coasts-at-the-same-time/

[616] https://files.secure.website/wscfus/10348600/7798982/michael-chertoff-israeli-runs-dhs-involved-in-911.pdf

[617] https://ariwatch.com/Links/WhatDidIsraelKnow.htm

[618] https://x.com/MyLordBebo/status/1944690462675390900

[619] *By Way of Deception*, pg. 94

[620] https://www.nbcnews.com/id/wbna3340725

[621] http://www.hugequestions.com/Eric/TFC/Bollyn-mossad-911.html

[622] http://www.hugequestions.com/Eric/TFC/Bollyn-Ptech.html

[623] https://sarahwestall.com/why-is-no-one-talking-about-the-mitre-corporation-the-new-manhattan-project-w-peter-kirby/

624 https://corbettreport.com/ptech-and-the-911-software/

625 https://www.facts-are-facts.com/news/is-mitre-corp-the-trojan-horse-of-9-11-

626 https://edition.cnn.com/2001/US/09/19/hijacked.planes/

627 https://www.scribd.com/document/66396417/Dov-Zakheim-Systems-Planning-Corporation-and-Remote-Control-Planes-on-9-11

628 https://www.scribd.com/document/381274647/Dov-Zakheim-and-911-SPC-and-Remote-Plane-Controls-pdf

629 https://corbettreport.com/911-suspects-ralph-eberhart/

630 https://archive.org/details/1993-wtc-tri-data-investigation-dov-zakheim/page/4/mode/2up

631 https://911nwo.com/2018/02/27/the-46-drills-operations-war-games-and-exercises-of-911-webster-tarpley-interview/

632 http://tarpley.net/docs/drills_of_911.pdf

633 https://www.foreignpolicyjournal.com/2013/01/16/the-case-against-ralph-eberhart-norads-911-commander/

634 https://911truth.org/flights-11-175-77-and-93-the-911-commissions-incredible-tales/

635 *Alice in Wonderland and the World Trade Centre Disaster*, pg. 235

636 https://www.bitchute.com/video/WcIkmHS1oqjS

637 https://www.poandpo.com/who-is-promoted/icts-europe-holdings-bv-with-new-supervisory-board/

638 https://ia802900.us.archive.org/0/items/nsia-ProutyLFletcher/nsia-ProutyLFletcher/Prouty%20L%20Fletcher%2040.pdf

639 https://911research.wtc7.net/planes/analysis/norad/

640 https://web.archive.org/web/20201201190607/https://www.washingtontimes.com/news/2001/sep/11/20010911-025331-4897r/

641 https://holocausts.org/911/facsnet/aviation.php3

[642] https://web.archive.org/web/20010707000937/http://itn.co.uk/news/20010424/world/05robotplane.shtm

[643] https://www.washingtonpost.com/archive/politics/1987/04/12/israeli-firm-loses-ny-airport-award/b197ca31-2b51-4236-97d5-541f5955b4f9/

[644] https://www.youtube.com/watch?v=v20s0No32cA

[645] https://www.littelfuse.com/products/fuses-overcurrent-protection/fuse-holders-fuse-blocks-accessories/fuse-holders/dead-front-fuse-holders/powr-busbar/bb18

[646] https://www.winterwatch.net/2017/09/world-trade-centers-infamous-91st-floor-israeli-art-student-project/

[647] https://www.gelitin.net/uploaded/PDF/B-Thing/NYT180801.pdf

[648] https://www.youtube.com/watch?v=IqSpL-NUzuc

[649] https://ic911.org/toronto-hearings/report/toronto-report-ch-08/

[650] https://ic911.org/journal/articles/118-witnesses-the-firefighters-testimony-to-explosions-in-the-twin-towers-2/

[651] https://www.bitchute.com/video/Y8OquFPhXeea

[652] https://thefreedomarticles.com/aloha-dew-lahaina-maui-hit-by-directed-energy-weapons/

[653] Where Did the Towers Go?, pg. 32

[654] https://x.com/RichardGage_911/status/1958223697044738503

[655] https://www.scoop.co.nz/stories/WO0111/S00136/secretary-rumsfeld-interview-with-parade-magazine.htm

[656] https://ic911.org/consensus-panel/consensus-points/point-flt-2/

[657] https://web.archive.org/web/20020201215326/https://www.firefox.1accesshost.com/cameron.html

[658] https://www.youtube.com/watch?v=NcOb3Dilzjc

[659] https://www.jpost.com/opinion/america-the-target-602181

---

660 http://www.tomheneghanbriefings.com/Why_Bush_Sr_chose_9-11-01_as_WTC_hit_date_no_payback_on_bond_billions_for_terrorism_fund_-_Cash_payoffs_bonds_and_murder_linked_to_White_House_911_finance__2005_Tom_Flocco.pdf

661 https://www.bitchute.com/video/xlX3iOlIsqPl

662 https://holocausts.org/911/sams.html

663 https://truthout.org/articles/911-terrorists-made-millions-on-the-stock-market/

664 https://www.globalresearch.ca/9-11-attacks-criminal-foreknowledge-and-insider-trading-lead-directly-to-the-cia-s-highest-ranks/32323

665 https://www.sfgate.com/bayarea/matier-ross/article/Willie-Brown-got-low-key-early-warning-about-air-3314754.php

666 https://www.grandtheftcountry.com/facts/911/foreknowledge/rushdie.html

667 https://www.bitchute.com/video/kCKMQuz3HyP4

668 https://www.haaretz.com/2001-09-17/ty-article/5-israelis-detained-for-puzzling-behavior-after-wtc-tragedy/0000017f-db50-d3ff-a7ff-fbf0d7830000

669 https://en.wikipedia.org/wiki/September_11_intelligence_before_the_attacks

670 https://www.bitchute.com/video/HbclumiLgP1y

671 https://www.bitchute.com/video/aD6p91Vk9v5K

672 www.youtube.com/watch?v=I07XgqejVic

673 https://richardaclarke.net/wp-content/uploads/2019/05/Against-All-Enemies-Excerpt.pdf

674 https://ic911.org/complete-timeline/1999-us-government-ignores-whos-who-book-of-al-qaeda-figures/

675 https://www.c-span.org/clip/white-house-event/user-clip-youre-either-with-us-or-against-us/4985475

---

[676] https://www.theguardian.com/world/2001/oct/14/afghanistan.terrorism5

[677] https://truthblitzkrieg.com/2024/09/02/1379/

[678] https://www.nydailynews.com/2002/04/16/wtc-girder-is-key-to-collapse-puzzle/

[679] https://files.wtc7report.org/file/public-download/A-Structural-Reevaluation-of-the-Collapse-of-World-Trade-Center-7-March2020.pdf, https://ine.uaf.edu/wtc7

[680] https://www.ae911truth.org/evidence/technical-articles/articles-by-ae911truth/140-25-areas-of-specific-concern-in-the-nist-wtc-reports

[681] https://ic911.org/complete-timeline/before-august-2007-key-9-11-investigator-hired-by-cia-contractor/

[682] https://www.mitre.org/news-insights/news-release/nist-renews-five-year-contract-mitre-operate-national-cybersecurity

[683] https://truthblitzkrieg.com/2024/09/02/1379/

[684] https://www.law.nyu.edu/news/BIRNBAUM_9_11_MEDIATOR

[685] https://truthblitzkrieg.com/2024/09/02/1379/

[686] https://www.nytimes.com/2016/09/10/nyregion/judge-in-9-11-suits-feels-no-regret-that-none-ever-went-to-trial.html

[687] https://archives.globalresearch.ca/articles/BOL112B.html

[688] https://www.ratical.org/ratville/CAH/VonBuelow.html

[689] https://www.globalresearch.ca/ex-italian-president-intel-agencies-know-9-11-an-inside-job/7550

[690] https://www.bitchute.com/video/lYVJ6Eh8XP28

[691] https://www.bollyn.com/public/Review_of_Solving_911.pdf

[692] https://www.foreignpolicyjournal.com/2012/07/23/the-nexus-between-terror-propaganda-and-terrorism-bremer-and-jenkins/2/

[693] https://911research.wtc7.net/planes/defense/wargames.html

[694] https://rumble.com/v4pxmhb-colin-powell-speech-to-the-united-nations-regarding-iraq-wmd.html

---

[695] https://www.foreignpolicyjournal.com/2012/07/23/the-nexus-between-terror-propaganda-and-terrorism-bremer-and-jenkins/2/

CHAPTER 15: CULT CRIME TEMPLATE: SIMILARITIES AMONG THE JFK, RFK AND 9/11 OPERATIONS

"From the ridiculous Warren Commission Report to NIST's 'Final Report of the World Trade Center Disaster Investigations' and Philip Zelikow's '9/11 Commission Report,' Jewish Zionists repeatedly direct the investigation away from the guilty."

– Wyatt Peterson of TruthBlitzkrieg.com

In *Break Your Chains*, I described what I dubbed the false flag formula – the template which the Cult NWO controllers used to construct a false flag shooting or bombing. I focused mostly on shootings, since there seemed to be so many of them in America during the Obama years from 2008-2016. In a similar way, there is a template the Cult uses to pull off its really big events, whether they be political assassinations or spectacular false flag operations. In this chapter, we'll take a look at the pattern or template behind three giant Cult crimes, all of which left a psychological scar and an imprint of terror and grief upon the collective American and world psyche (for the exact sources to many of these points that are not endnoted here, please refer back to chapters 11 and 14).

Impossibilities in the Official Narratives

An obvious place to start is with the official story of the event in question. Any good detective would immediately ask: does it account for the means, motive and opportunity of the supposed guilty party?

Does it account for the motivations of the actors, agents, shooters, bombers, hijackers or killers? Did they have the chance to do it? Did they have the strength, intelligence, time, agility, training, skill level and technology to do it? Overall, does it make sense?

However, with events as the JFK assassination, RFK assassination and 9/11 operation, we have to take a step back and even ask: were the actions taken per the official story even possible? In every case, the answer is a resounding no. The advantage that truthseekers have with these events is that we simply need to show that the official version is impossible, while the conspirators need to actually make people believe in impossibilities, to defy logic, common sense and even their own senses, to trust what 'authority' says no matter what.

JFK assassination: we are told that Oswald shot JFK from behind from the middle floors of the TSBD. Yet, both the USSR and fellow military colleagues (such as Sergeant Nelson Delgado, who was in the Marine Corps with Oswald) attested to the fact he was a notoriously poor shot. How could one single bullet – unless it were a 'magic' bullet – have gone through JFK, exited his body, and then gone on to hit Connally?

RFK assassination: the coroner report of Thomas Noguchi concluded that the lethal bullet that killed Robert F. Kennedy came from behind, but Sirhan was in front all the time. How then did Sirhan supposedly kill Kennedy?

9/11 operation: the official narrative of 9/11 is so full of absurdity and impossibility that one could write a book on this topic alone. Here is a selection of 10 points to give you a flavor of just how far outside the bounds of possibility the official version was:

1. WTC 7 collapsed in perfect symmetry without being hit. How?

2. The passport of one of the alleged hijackers magically survived the crash and was found. How?

3. The indestructible airliner black boxes were never retrieved from any of the planes (even when paper passports were). How?

4. Virtually all the steel and concrete from WTC 1 and 2 was destroyed, but paper, flags and trees were intact surrounding the twin towers. How?

5. Jet fuel, which burns to around 750° F (398° C), purportedly managed to melt steel with a melting point of at least 2500° F (1371° C). How?

6. Boeing planes supposedly managed to fly at super high speeds despite being at super low altitudes (near sea level) as they crashed into the towers, in violation of what Boeing itself says its planes can do, as well as the known laws of physics. How?

7. The two Boeing planes, made of aluminum and with plastic nose caps, fully penetrated the twin towers like a hot knife through butter rather than shattering on impact. How?

8. Many of the hijackers were such poor pilots that they were turned away from flying schools after showing that they could barely fly a Cessna. How then were they able to handle large Boeing airliners with such skill that even experienced pilots state that they could not have performed the maneuvers as dictated by the official version?

9. After supposedly flying planes into buildings on kamikaze missions where they would have perished for their cause, many of the hijackers turned up alive after September 11th 2001. How?

10. From a cave somewhere in the mountains of Afghanistan, Osama bin Laden managed to outwit the most technologically advanced nation on Earth, coming up with a plan that included successfully bypassing long established FAA and NORAD protocols for air safety and defense. How?

Oklahoma City bombing: here's a bonus one. We are told that a truck or fertilizer bomb caused all the damage to the Alfred P. Murrah Federal Building in Oklahoma City in 1995. How did it do this when pillars closer to the truck did not fall while others further from the truck did fall? How can we account for witness testimony of a second bomb and the seismographic record at the Oklahoma Geological Survey at the University of Oklahoma which recorded two separate seismic events?

Foreknowledge

JFK assassination:

1. According to Dick Russell's biography of him, Richard Case Nagell, a US Army veteran and CIA agent, claimed to have gotten himself arrested in a Texas bank shooting in late September 1963 to avoid becoming a patsy in the pending JFK assassination. How did he know?[696]

2. US soldier (private first class) Eugene Dinkin was a cryptographic code operator stationed in France. After going AWOL from his unit on November 4th 1963, he appeared in the UN Press Room in Geneva, Switzerland on November 6th to tell

reporters he was being persecuted – and that "they" were plotting something against President Kennedy and that "something" would happen in Dallas. How did he know?[697]

3. Why did right-wing extremist Joseph Milteer tell Miami police informant William Somersett that the assassination of JFK was *"in the working,"* that the best means of killing Kennedy was *"from an office building with a high-powered rifle,"* and that *"they will pick up somebody within hours afterwards, if anything like that would happen just to throw the public off"*?[698]

4. Why did Jack Ruby (Jacob Rubenstein) ask an FBI informant on the morning of November 22nd 1963 if he'd *"like to watch the fireworks"* in Dallas?

5. Why did local British newspaper Cambridge News get an anonymous call about *"some big news"* in the US, 25 minutes before JFK was shot?[699]

RFK assassination: How were Israeli tour guides able to tell American tourists that RFK had been assassinated months before he actually had been (even if they got the place wrong)? Is it just a coincidence that Israeli military psychologist Benyamin Shalit was working on a plan in May 1968, one month before Bobby was killed, that involved taking a Palestinian Fatah member, then trying to brainwash and hypnotize him into becoming a killer?

9/11 operation:

1. Is it just a coincidence that Israeli spy Arnon Milchan in his 1978 movie *Medusa Touch* included a scene of a jet crashing into a high-rise building?

2. Is it just a coincidence that former Mossad boss Isser Harel told a reporter in 1980 that terrorists would strike America's tallest building in New York?

3. Is it just a coincidence that George Bush Sr. bought Brady bonds which were to come due on September 12th 2001, and which, due to the destruction of the financial records contained in the twin towers, never had to be repaid?

4. How was ex-DIA agent Lt. Col. Anthony Shaffer able to know about Al-Qaeda cells one year in advance via Able Danger?

5. Is it just a coincidence that Fox News decided to air a program in March 2001 called *The Lone Gunmen*, in which a computer hacker takes remote control of a plane and tries to crash it into the WTC?

6. How was Bill Cooper on June 28th 2001 able to accurately predict that Osama bin Laden would be blamed for an impending major attack?

7. Is it just a coincidence that ZIM Shipping, 49% owned by the Israeli Government, vacated its 10,000 square foot office space at the WTC just a few days before 9/11, breaking its lease and losing $50,000 to do so?

8. Is it just a coincidence that The Washington Times decided to publish an article about the SAMS report on September 10th 2001, using a quote to describe the Mossad as a ruthless and cunning wildcard that could target America and make it look like a Palestinian or Arab act?

9. Is it just a coincidence that 4,744 put options were bought on United Airlines and 4,516 put options were bought on American

Airlines, six times the normal volumes, while other airlines did not have similar trading?

10. Is it just a coincidence that San Francisco Mayor Willie Brown got a call warning him in advance? Or that author Salman Rushdie's publisher was told by the FAA that US intel had given them a warning?

11. Is it just a coincidence that someone transmitted a message on the network of Israeli instant messaging company Odigo, whose US headquarters were two blocks away from the WTC, with a warning to stay away from the towers on 9/11?

12. Is it just a coincidence that BBC reported that WTC7 had fallen before it actually had?

Image #106: Someone knew WTC7 (World Trade Center Building 7) would fall down in advance – but don't talk about it!

13. Is it just a coincidence that 5 men known as the 'Dancing Israelis' were there waiting and ready to *"document the event"* as they later admitted?

14. Is it just a coincidence that CIA and foreign leaders announced that an attack was imminent?

<ins>Preparing the Patsy</ins>

Image #107: Lee Harvey Oswald a little too conveniently poses with a rifle in a Dallas suburb, months before the JFK assassination

Preparing the patsy is a key part of pulling off a deceptive operation so that the guilty party escapes accountability. Often, the patsy is killed afterwards, as dead men tell no tales.

JFK assassination: James Angleton spent years grooming and preparing a confused Lee Harvey Oswald. Angleton had Jewish spy Reuben Efron read Oswald's mail. The CIA ensured a double of Oswald went down to Mexico City, where David Atlee Phillips was CIA station chief, to leave a trail. CIA asset George de Mohrenschildt looked closely over Oswald while CIA-connected Ruth Paine (who knew Allen Dulles personally) and Michael Paine (who worked for CIA cover organization USAID) helped to set the patsy up in Dallas and paint a credible back story for Oswald for the public to consume. Wyatt Peterson writes that in *"the spring of 1977, George de Mohrenschildt was found dead from a shotgun blast to the head after publicly* *complaining that 'the Jewish mafia' was trying to kill him for writing a memoir about his former friend Lee Harvey Oswald titled 'I Am A Patsy! I Am a Patsy!''*"[700] Additionally, Jack Ruby (who was part-patsy, part-conspirator) killed Oswald for the real conspirators, then got a visit from infamous CIA mind control handler Dr. Louis Jolyon West to ensure he wouldn't talk.

RFK assassination: as the unfortunate Palestinian patsy chosen by the Zionist Cult to commit its first ever signature Zionist false flag op on American soil (ZioIslamic terrorism), Sirhan Sirhan was suggestible and easily hypnotized. Just one month before the death of RFK in June 1968, Israeli intelligence was attempting to turn Palestinians into mind-controlled assassins, as can be seen in the case of the Israeli military psychologist Benyamin Shalit and a Fatah agent, as revealed by Bergman in *Rise and Kill First*. By 1968, the CIA's MKUltra had been running exactly 15 years, so mind control techniques were being perfected. In addition to MKUltra director Hungarian Jew Sidney Gottlieb, and the aforementioned Jolyon West, there were many other Jews involved, including John Gittinger, Harold Abramson, Harris Isbell, Ray Treichler, James Keehner, Charles Geschickter, Eugene Saenger, Lauretta Bender, Chester Southam, Albert Kligman and Robert Lashbrook, according to Peterson.

9/11 operation: in this case, we had the 'mastermind' patsies Osama bin Laden (who was relentlessly demonized before and after the event) and Khalid Sheikh Mohammed in addition to the 19 Arab hijackers. The Mossad spy ring in Florida, via the extensive use of body doubles for Atta, made sure that they left Korans lying around everywhere as a trail, even as they did very Islamic things like drink alcohol, eat pork, snort cocaine and pay for lap dances. The fake clues left behind were so obvious it wouldn't even be credible in a C-List Hollywood movie. After that, bin Laden, who seemed to have more lives than a cat, was reportedly killed multiple times. The conspirators ensured their version of the events regarding the patsies and their abilities made it to the official report. Peterson writes the following about ex-IDF soldier Eddie Shalev and Arab hijacker Hani Hanjour:[701]

[Eddie Shalev] claimed that Hanjour was a "good pilot". After 9/11, both the FBI and a staffer from the 9/11 Commission interrogated Baxter, Conner, Bernard and Shalev. Conner later claimed that he was expecting to receive a call to testify before the commission. The call never came. The 9/11 Commission final report totally ignored the testimony of Baxter, Conner and Bernard and only mentioned Shalev's testimony that Hanjour was a "good pilot" and his name once in a small end note. So ... who was Eddie Shalev? He was an Israeli who came to the states shortly before 9/11 who had previously served in the Israeli Defense Force. Was he a Mossad agent? We will never know as he was never vetted by the 9/11 Commission and has disappeared.

Suspending Normal Procedures and Protocols

As Prouty said, one of the keys to pulling off these kind of operations is to ensure the usual safety protocols are suspended, thereby allowing 'the accident' to occur.

JFK assassination: why were Secret Service agents Donald Lawton and Clint Hill called off and told to step away as the car made its final turn from Houston Street onto Elm Street? Why did Secret Service driver William Greer slow down so much, and even come to a partial stop, at the exact moment when Kennedy was shot, when that would be the last thing to do if you were protecting someone?

RFK assassination: why was RFK led away from his victory speech through the kitchen of the Ambassador Hotel? Peterson writes that *"according to a campaign volunteer who was present at the scene, Robert's Press Secretary Frank Mankiewicz insisted he go through the kitchen where Sirhan lay in wait."*[702] According to Piper, Mankiewicz started his career as a civil rights director at the ADL.

9/11 operation: why was the FAA so slow to report planes going off course to NORAD? Why was NORAD so slow to make the decision to scramble interceptor jets? Why were the jets not scrambled from the nearest military base? Why did the jets not fly at their top speed in order to intercept? Why did Cheney knowingly give, or at least aid and abet, the stand down order? Why didn't the Pentagon fire its ground-to-air missiles?

Smoke and Mirrors

All of these events contain a large psychological and perceptual element, because they are literally magic tricks – black magic tricks of the Satanic Cult. This is why we have the term 'psychological operation' and why the Cult-controlled MIC puts so much money and effort into its psy-ops divisions. As any good magician knows, the key to a successful trick is to capture and divert your audience's attention. Smoke and mirrors, whether literal or figurative, are important elements to stoke maximum confusion and deflect attention away from the functional aspects of the attack.

JFK assassination: was there one shooter or multiple shooters? One bullet, or two? Three? Four? Five? Were the bullets later swapped to prevent accurate forensic examination? Did one bullet

manage to go through Kennedy, come out his body and then enter Connally (the 'magic bullet')? How do we know JFK's body even made it to Bethesda Naval Hospital in Maryland? Was JFK's body switched with his lookalike J. D. Tippit?

RFK assassination: was there one shooter or multiple shooters? One bullet, or two? Three? 13? Which bullets were the lethal ones? Were the bullets later swapped to prevent accurate forensic examination?

9/11 operation: why were the usual leaders unavailable, including President Bush and Joint Chiefs of Staff chairman General Hugh Shelton? Who was in charge – Vice President Cheney, acting chairman of the Joint Chiefs of Staff General Richard Myers or someone else? NORAD? Why was there such confusion over the chain of command? Why were multiple official timelines released for the same event? Did planes hit the buildings, or did no planes hit the buildings? If planes hit the buildings, how did they cut through steel and concrete so effortlessly, and how did they not shatter? If no planes hit the buildings, how did they end up on privately recorded video footage of the event from citizen's camcorders?

Simultaneous Drills and Exercises

For a long time now, numerous false flag shootings and bombings have occurred at the same time as when an active shooter drill or other type of exercise was occurring, practicing for the very thing that happened to unfold. In other words, these are drills, exercises or simulations that then 'go live,' however even if they don't go live, they serve the purpose of confusing those involved and diverting skilled personnel away from the actual event.

JFK assassination: testimony by people like Marita Lorenz, E. Howard Hunt and Michael Milan show that there were dummy assassination teams in Dallas, or shooters there who mistakenly believed they were there to kill Governor Connally.

9/11 operation: the war games that were occurring during 9/11 did a tremendous job – from the point of view of the Cult – of obscuring the real planes flying that day by covering FAA and NORAD screens with dots and blips. Agents kept asking their supervisors, *"Is this real world or exercise?"* Some of the exercises practiced earlier that year involved a scenario where a plane was hijacked or crashed into a high-rise building in New York City! The war games also (purposefully) removed fighter pilots and jets from NEADS.

A Plethora of Coincidences

There are far, far too many coincidences to mention about the JFK assassination and the 9/11 operation, but here is a smattering:

JFK assassination: was it just a coincidence that Oswald got a job at the TSBD, right along the parade route, six weeks before JFK visited Dallas? Was it just a coincidence that Ruth Paine, who took the Oswalds into her Dallas home, was on personal terms with ex-CIA Director, MJ-1 and Kennedy hater Allen Dulles? Was it just a coincidence that JFK was killed in the city whose mayor at the time was Earle Cabell, the brother of General Charles Cabell at the CIA whom JFK fired because of the Bay of Pigs fiasco? Was it just a coincidence that JFK's body was taken to Bethesda Naval Hospital, the same place where James Forrestal died, when both men were opposed to Israeli control of America and Cult control of the UFO/ET affair?

9/11 operation: was it just a coincidence that Sayeret Matkal assassin Danny Lewin was sitting in row 9 on flight 11, and a photo of him in the year 2000 shows him wearing a Swatch Watch model called 'Hijacker' with the hands all set to 11? Was it just a coincidence that one of the 9/11 passenger calls was from a Jewish woman (Barbara Olson) to her husband Ted Olson, who defended diehard Zionist and Israeli spy Jonathan Pollard? Was it just a coincidence that the Infocon threat level was downgraded to the lowest level the night before 9/11? Was it just a coincidence that Jane Garvey, then FAA head, went on to join the MITRE board? Was it just a coincidence that her husband Robert Garvey was then sheriff of Hampshire County (Westover AFB) where some of the 9/11 planes were flown? Was it just a coincidence that 9/11 Secretary of Transportation Norman Mineta later joined the Mossad-connected ICTS board? Was it just a coincidence the entire WTC 1 building was powered down during a weekend prior to 9/11?

Controlling the Crime Scene

One thing is essential in successfully hiding a crime: taking control of the crime scene so incriminating evidence can be quickly removed and destroyed.

JFK assassination: why was JFK's body taken from Parkland Hospital in Dallas, against the wishes of the local doctors and police, and in violation of Texas state law (which stated that an autopsy must be performed), and rushed off to Maryland?

9/11 operation: why were over 60,000 tons of steel hastily removed from the crime scene and taken to two Jewish-owned scrapyards, where they were cut into small pieces, mixed with other scrap metal and shipped to China, before anyone could inspect it?

Controlling the Coverup

Logic dictates that if you want to successfully cover up your crime, you ensure you and your agents are the ones investigating it! Pretty simple really. Have you ever wondered why all those official special commissions that authorities like to convene never lead anywhere? What happens when the government investigates the government? Not guilty, every time!

JFK assassination: do you think the truth was going to come out when assassination mastermind James Angleton was also the very same person at the CIA in charge of deciding what information the Warren Commission got fed? Do you think the truth was going to come out when the Warren Commission was stacked with Masons (Earl Warren) and Cult agents (John McCloy, Gerald Ford)? Do you think the truth was going to come out when at least 9 of its 22 staff attorneys were Jewish? Do you think the truth was going to come out when the Warren Commission included on its 7-man team none other than Allen Dulles, drafter of the MJ-12 assassination directive? Fox. Henhouse. Need I say more?

9/11 operation: the control of the coverup was so blatant in this case that the conspirators at first even nominated war criminal and Cult insider Henry Kissinger to lead the 9/11 Commission, but after public outcry, they settled for Zionist Philip Zelikow, who dutifully toed the line. Some 9/11 commissioners reported that Zelikow seemed to have a predetermined outcome in mind, which of course he did; the commission was just window dressing and mostly for show, since the whole point was to whitewash the affair and lead people away from the Israeli connection. In the end, the 9/11 Commission Report didn't even mention WTC 7, despite the fact it fell at near free-fall speed when it didn't get hit by anything!

<u>Documenting the Event</u>

Why is documenting the event important to the Cult?

JFK assassination: is it just a coincidence that Ukrainian-born Jew and Mason Abraham Zapruder, whose business partner Jeanne LeGon de Mohrenschildt was the wife of CIA asset and Oswald handler George de Mohrenschildt, just happened to be in the right place at the right time to film the event? Is it a further coincidence that Zapruder had an office on the fourth floor of the Dal-Tex Building when ballistics studies proved that this building was one of the locations from which the shots were fired – specifically the third and fourth floors?

9/11 operation: is it just a coincidence that one of the five 'Dancing Israelis,' two of whom were Mossad agents and three of whom appeared on Yair Lapid's television show when they got released from custody and returned to Israel, admitted that *"our purpose was to document the event"*?

Peterson points out:[703]

If documenting world changing crimes is a Jewish mitzvah, it could explain why German TV presenter Richard Gutjahr was in position to film the terror attacks in both Nice, France and Munich, Germany in the summer of 2016. The attacks occurred one week and 500 miles apart, yet Gutjahr happened to be present and filming at both. Gutjahr's wife, Einat Wilf, is a former Israeli intelligence operative of Unit 8200 and a member of the Knesset. She's worked for both Ehud Barak and Shimon Peres (the father of Israel's nuclear program), and ran for President of the World Jewish Congress in 2007.

He then humorously adds:

Considering all of this we're left to wonder if perhaps somewhere there exists a 19th century daguerreotype of John Wilkes Booth, firing his .44 caliber Henry Deringer pistol into Abraham Lincoln's skull, stored away in a dusty vault in some Jew's attic.

Direct Connections

Astute readers may have noticed that some of the exact same names turned up at more than one of these operations. JFK assassination mastermind Angleton ended up with the gruesome photos of Robert Kennedy's autopsy in his safe. Peter Goelz, who played a role investigating the death of JFK Jr., ended up as president of the NTSB during 9/11 where he was looked to for accurate information on aviation safety. After personally calling Goelz, Christopher Bollyn confirmed that Goelz was connected to Ehud

Mendelson and *"said he had met with the Israeli captain from Israeli military intelligence 'two or three' times in Washington, D.C."*[704]

On the morning of 9/11, Porter Goss, a member of the CIA's Operation 40 team (the team of assassins that likely provided the multiple gunmen that shot JFK) and at one point a nominee for CIA Director, hosted a breakfast meeting on Capitol Hill in honor of General Ahmad of the Pakistani Inter-Services Intelligence, the alleged money-man behind the 9/11 hijackers. This was as a follow-up meeting to one held in Pakistan in late August 2001, barely two weeks before 9/11.[705]

Lastly, George Bush Sr., who very closely resembles a man photographed in Dallas on November 22nd 1963, and who offered Texas marksman Ed Grimsley $2 million to kill JFK, was the father of the (mentally-challenged) US President George Bush Jr. during the 9/11 operation, and was undoubtedly highly involved with the planning and coverup, especially since he was meeting with the bin Ladens the day before.

Sources

---

[696] https://www.maryferrell.org/showDoc.html?docId=3611#relPageId=155

[697] https://www.maryferrell.org/pages/Allegations_of_PFC_Eugene_Dinkin.html

[698] https://www.maryferrell.org/pages/Predictions_of_Joseph_Milteer.html

[699] https://www.bbc.com/news/uk-england-cambridgeshire-41773716

[700] https://truthblitzkrieg.com/2024/07/06/parallels-jfk-rfk-9-11/

[701] Ibid.

[702] Ibid.

[703] Ibid.

[704] Solving 9/11, Christopher Bollyn, pg. 112

[705] https://www.nadir.org/nadir/initiativ/agp//free/9-11/globalresearch/cho407a.htm

CHAPTER 16: CULT DEFLECTION WITH THE ANTISEMITISM INDUSTRY

"And he's an antisemite, because that's what we say he is. And that's one stain you cannot wash. Now, it shames me as a Jew to tell you that, but that's the fact, and it's wrong."

– Victor Ostrovsky[706]

"An antisemite used to be someone who hates Jews; nowadays an antisemite is someone Jews hate."

– Gilad Atzmon[707]

"*The anti-Semitism industry is there to protect the psychopaths from exposure by using nice and okay people as their human shield.*"

– David Icke[708]

Freedom of speech is one of the most important human rights that exist, and is particularly important when it comes to keeping totalitarianism in check. One of the first defenses against tyranny is speaking out against it. Unjust authorities don't like criticism. When free thinkers, poets, comedians, academics and artists unite in condemning those in power, it usually spells the end of their rule, because they are able to help the masses see the corruption of the rulers. If you follow the idea (rightly or wrongly attributed to Voltaire) that *'to learn who rules over you, simply find out who you are not allowed to criticize'* then pretty soon you will arrive at the doorstep of Israel – and the giant antisemitism industry it has created.

Cult-controlled Israel puts a MASSIVE amount of effort into stopping exposure of its crimes by twisting the truth and trying to claim that anyone who attacks it must be racist (or more accurately 'religion'-ist, since Jews are not a race). It takes a lot of chutzpah, lack of shame and lack of self-reflection to say this, because what the Cult is basically asserting is that anyone who criticizes Israel cannot possibly have a legitimate reason for doing so, and must necessarily be driven by prejudice and only be doling out criticism because they just inexplicably hate Jews. For no reason at all. That's the logic of it!

Image #109: the Cult has used the shield of Nazism and emotional appeals to the Holocaust to hide its murderous and genocidal ways, but people are seeing through it. Image credit: Jordan Henderson

I'm sure genuine antisemitism has existed in the past, and I'm sure some still exists today, according to the actual and historical definition of the term, which is pre-existing (i.e. pre-judging, prejudiced) hatred of Jews, just for being Jewish. However, the overwhelming majority of people being accused of antisemitism today do not have this hatred or prejudice at all. Rather, they are disgusted, horrified, sad and angry at the behavior of Cult-controlled Israel and all its appendages – the Mossad, Aman, Shin Bet, the IDF, the ADL, the Jewish lobby and so on – which as I type these words are still committing genocide in Gaza and attempting to enslave the world. The terms antisemite and antisemitism have thus become bludgeoning tools with which the Cult batters people into silence. The good news, however, is that this technique is losing its effectiveness as humanity awakens, and ever more people see through this cheap trick, which is after all nothing more than an ad hominem attack devoid of logic. It's just name-calling or insulting designed to shut an argument down before it starts. It's all about hiding to avoid open discussion and accountability.

Manipulating the Definition of Antisemitism

Part of the trick is not only using the ad hominem attack, but changing the definition of the term itself in true Orwellian fashion. This agenda was pushed by Natan Sharansky (former minister of Diaspora Affairs and Chair for Jewish Agency for Israel), who founded the Global Forum Against Antisemitism in 2004, the same year he laid out a 3-pronged test for antisemitism (the three Ds):

– Delegitimization

– Demonization

– Double standard

Sharansky defines the first one, delegitimization of Israel, as the denial of the Jewish people's right to self-determination. However, it's another trick, because those who oppose Israel's policies and behavior are not generally saying that Jewish people have no right to self-determination; it's just that such self-determination must also respect the rights of others, i.e. by not stealing their land and slaughtering their children, as Israel has done with Palestine. Israeli self-determination cannot trump Palestinian self-determination.

Sharansky defines the second one, demonization of Israel, as the use of sinister stereotypes portraying Jews in a negative light, speaking of an international Jewish conspiracy or speaking of Jewish control of the government, media and economy. This falls under the banner of collective assignment of guilt which is the problem with all types of discrimination (racism, sexism, etc.). However, there is a demonstrable international conspiracy – Sabbatean-Frankist Cultists (hiding behind the Jewish identity) are running it! Likewise, there is control of the world's governments, media and economy by a Satanic cabal, many of whom outwardly call themselves Jews. What Sharansky is really saying is: "Criticism of certain (Cult) Jews tends to be collective and imply all Jews are responsible, which they are not, so therefore, you are antisemitic if you criticize certain Jews, and you can't do it!" The solution to this is more precise speech, based on understanding the concepts I have explained in this book, i.e. the infiltrating and deceptive nature of the Satanic Cult which hides behind Judaism.

Sharansky defines the third one, that of applying a double standard to Israel, as the criticism of Israel and only Israel on certain issues, while ignoring similar actions by other countries. I agree that this is a problem – if it happens. However, what usually happens is the exact opposite – that Israel gets away with massive crimes for which other countries would be forcibly stopped or at a very minimum held to account. What other nation would have been able to attack the ship of a powerful country, the equal most or outright most powerful country in the world, and face no repercussions for the act, and continue receiving generous amounts of foreign aid from that country? This is exactly what happened with the USS Liberty. What other nation would be able to get away with mass murder and genocide that is still ongoing to this day, and not be stopped in any way, economically, politically or militarily? This is exactly what is happening with the Gaza genocide (covered in the next chapter).

The Cult built on Sharansky's 2004 definition of antisemitism to push the barometer even further. In 2016, the International Holocaust Remembrance Alliance (IHRA) released their definition of antisemitism which is as follows:[709]

1. Calling for, aiding, or justifying the killing or harming of Jews in the name of a radical ideology or an extremist view of religion.
2. Making mendacious, dehumanizing, demonizing, or stereotypical allegations about Jews as such or the power of Jews as a collective — such as, especially but not exclusively, the myth about a world Jewish conspiracy or of Jews controlling the media, economy, government or other societal institutions.
3. Accusing Jews as a people of being responsible for real or imagined wrongdoing committed by a single Jewish person or group, or even for acts committed by non-Jews.
4. Denying the fact, scope, mechanisms (e.g. gas chambers) or intentionality of the genocide of the Jewish people at the hands of National Socialist Germany and its supporters and accomplices during World War II (the Holocaust).

5. Accusing the Jews as a people, or Israel as a state, of inventing or exaggerating the Holocaust.
6. Accusing Jewish citizens of being more loyal to Israel, or to the alleged priorities of Jews worldwide, than to the interests of their own nations.
7. Denying the Jewish people their right to self-determination, e.g., by claiming that the existence of a State of Israel is a racist endeavor.
8. Applying double standards by requiring of it a behavior not expected or demanded of any other democratic nation.
9. Using the symbols and images associated with classic antisemitism (e.g., claims of Jews killing Jesus or blood libel) to characterize Israel or Israelis.
10. Drawing comparisons of contemporary Israeli policy to that of the Nazis.
11. Holding Jews collectively responsible for actions of the state of Israel.

Unsurprisingly, what the Cult wants here is protection against criticism and exposure. Some of these points are completely absurd. For example, the reason for #6 is to try to deflect the obvious truth that some Jews are more loyal to Israel than America and whatever other nation with which they hold dual citizenship. Remember what billionaire American Jew Haim Saban, who contributed millions to the US Democratic Party, said: *"I am a one-issue guy, and my issue is Israel."*[710] This same adherence to ultra Zionism – Israel first, no matter what – is exactly what qualifies you for key positions within Israel, the USA or other Western countries where Israel has a strong grip on that country. This is exactly what the Cult wants from its agents: blind allegiance and obedience to the cause (in this case, the cause of Israel), which in this case they can then manipulate by controlling Israel and its policies. Other points, such as #4 and #5, have the effect of squelching free and independent analysis on an historical event, analysis that may have nothing to do with discrimination or racism at all, but rather with an earnest desire to know the truth. What other event in history are you not allowed to question? As for #10, this is an obvious indication that the Cult wants to control perception, and not be likened to the Nazis, which it itself created (as covered in chapter 8). Even if we put aside the Nazi-Zionist cooperation that occurred before, during and after WWII, many people can clearly see that it is indeed the same mindset that ran the Nazis as runs the Zionists. They can cry wolf all they want, but the truth is still the truth. This is why the whole concept of antisemitism is empty. It has become an overused term devoid of real meaning and a catch cry by Cult agents or collaborators desperately trying to cover up their crimes.

The inversion of reality is so complete that even Holocaust survivors – yes Holocaust survivors – can now be branded as antisemites if they don't follow the Zionist agenda as dictated by the Cult. You would think Holocaust survivors would be sacred to Israel since they could be exploited to generate sympathy, but apparently no one is off limits to attack by the Cult, as the late Holocaust and Auschwitz survivor Esther Bejarano found out when she was called an antisemite for supporting the BDS movement![711]

It must also be noted that the term antisemitism is nonsensical when you consider that the true Semites were the original people of the Middle East – not the white-skinned Khazarian interlopers. Semitic most commonly refers to the Semitic languages, the most wide-spoken of which is Arabic. The term 'Semite' is much closer to meaning 'Arab' than 'Jew' which makes the whole antisemitism concept especially ironic.

Hoaxes to Ratchet Up Non-Existent Antisemitism

It wasn't enough for the Cult to twist the definition of antisemitism and change the meaning of words according to its agenda. On top of that, it then had to create and literally conjure antisemitism out of nowhere. Problem-reaction-solution only works if you have a problem or the perception of a problem, so what does the Cult do? It creates one! This is the basis for the spate of antisemitism hoaxes or Jewish hate hoaxes that have been recorded worldwide. Here are a few examples of many:

– In November 1963, five Jews were arrested for painting swastikas using a stencil and a spray gun on the front of the Israeli Consulate-General building in New York;[712]

– In January 2012, a Jewish man in New York was accused of taping notes with antisemitic symbols including swastikas on five apartment doors and in the hallway of a building in Manhattan. He also said that *"all Jews should die and go to hell."*;[713]

– In March 2017, an American-Israeli Jew was arrested in Jerusalem *"as the prime suspect in a wave of bomb threats against U.S. Jewish community centers ... [the] surprising arrest of the man, a hacker who holds dual Israeli and American citizenship, came after a trans-Atlantic investigation with the FBI and other international law enforcement agencies."*[714]

– In April 2019, a restaurant in Winnipeg, Canada, was defaced with racist graffiti and swastikas. Winnipeg police Chief Danny

Smyth said the attack was staged and was a hate hoax conducted by the Jewish owners of the restaurant. All three were arrested and charged with public mischief;[715] and

– In December 2023, German-Israeli singer Gil Ofarim admitted in court in Leipzig, Germany, that he made up a claim of antisemitism against two hotel employees in 2021. Ofarim had originally claimed that the front desk manager refused to check him in since he was wearing a Star of David necklace, saying that he had to put it away if he wanted to be checked in. It was a complete fabrication.[716]

There are websites dedicated to logging hate hoaxes, many of which are antisemitic hoaxes, such as FakeHateCrimes.org.[717] This agenda to fake antisemitism against Jews – committed by Jews – is long-running, extensive and international. It also occurs on a governmental, geopolitical level. A recent example is the late 2024 explosions at a kosher restaurant in Sydney and Adas Israel Synagogue in Melbourne. These incidents caused no injuries and little damage. In August 2025, Israel kindly provided a 'tip' to the Australian Security Intelligence Organisation (ASIO) that it was Iran who did these cowardly antisemitic attacks. This led to Australia expelling Iran's ambassador on August 26th. Iran rightfully described the claims as ridiculous and baseless, pointing out that it would have no motive to target a Jewish-owned restaurant halfway across the world.[718] As Dr. Tim Anderson wrote, the Mossad snookered the Australian government, fooling them with fake intel, and Australia swallowed the bait.[719]

Using Antisemitism to Create Severe Consequences

So the Cult constructs a new definition of antisemitism, aiming to criminalize normal human speech or behavior, and additionally creates a lot of antisemitism hoaxes. What happens next? It then lobbies the governments it controls to pass laws to punish the newly defined antisemitism. This is why this phenomenon is truly an antisemitism 'industry.'

In March 2025, Palestinian activist Mahmoud Khalil, an Algerian citizen of Palestinian origin and an American green-card holder, was arrested by Immigration and Customs Enforcement (ICE) after leading protests at Columbia University. Despite committing no crime, being a legal US permanent resident and having a wife who was eight months pregnant, Khalil was detained for 104 days at the LaSalle Detention Center in Louisiana before federal judge Michael Farbiarz ruled his detention unconstitutional.[720] Radical Cult Zionist group Betar pushed for his deportation,[721] while current US Secretary of State and Cult-owned neocon Marco Rubio declared that *"We will be revoking the visas and/or green cards of Hamas supporters in America so they can be deported"* in an attempt to link legitimate, non-violent protest with support for Hamas.[722]

It turns out that Betar makes lists of people it doesn't like, then has enough influence to get these lists into the hands of Trump Admin officials like Rubio who can then revoke their visas. Jews making lists – does anyone see the irony here? Israel used a facial-recognition technology known as NesherAI, developed by Stellar Tecs (officially registered under the name 'Stellar Defense & Cyber Intelligence LLC'), and their AI is trained to identify anonymous demonstrators who support Palestine. Stellar Tecs has designated their program as "Operation Wrath of Zion."[723]

Later in March 2025, the Trump Admin announced it would cancel $400 million in grants and contracts to Columbia University over antisemitism, the week after HHS Secretary Robert Kennedy Jr. declared that antisemitism *"kills people with lethalities comparable to history's most deadly plagues."*[724][725]

In September 2025, dual Israeli-Ameican citizen Congressman Brian Mast (the same guy who wore his IDF uniform to Congress) introduced an amendment designed to give the Secretary of State the power to revoke passports for US citizens deemed to have provided "material support for terrorism" – the same argument used by Greenblatt. Basically, it would allow the USG to punish criticism of Israel by stripping Americans of their inherent right to travel. Current Secretary of State Rubio already stripped Turkish doctoral student Rumeysa Ozturk of her visa based on an anti-Israel opinion piece she penned earlier this year. Mast later removed the measure but the incident goes to show the Cult agenda very clearly: your intrinsic human rights will be tied to your attitude towards Israel.[726]

The antisemitism witch-hunt is out of control. Israel even admits that it closely monitors all US government officials for antisemitism. According to Dillon Hosier, CEO of the Israeli-American Civic Action Network and former Political Officer for the Ministry of Foreign Affairs, State of Israel, at the Consulate General of Israel in Los Angeles, *"After Oct 7 [we implemented] an Iron Dome for Israel here in the US, where we're monitoring every elected official at every level of government. Every school board commission, from social media to press releases to official documents, we're monitoring all of it."*[727]

One of the key organizations policing antisemitism (i.e. running cover for Cult criminality) is the ADL which I have mentioned repeatedly throughout this book. The ADL tries to pretend its mission is to oppose all racism and discrimination when its actual mission is to crush any criticism of the Sabbatean-Frankists, the Satanists, Zionism, the Rothschilds and their pet project Israel. Its CEO Jonathan Greenblatt is an American Jew leading an American organization that is supposedly meant to work for American interests, but it appears he accidentally forgot that in this interview where he identified himself as Israeli.[728] Just another foreign agent not registered under FARA. Greenblatt is one of the ones leading the charge by trying to criminalize the first amendment rights to free speech and to non-violent protest, framing peaceful protests in support of Palestine as 'support for Hamas.' It's utter nonsense, especially since Israel created Hamas, as we will come to next chapter. In this interview by the New York Times, he was grilled over his attempt to frame pro-Palestine protests by Students for Justice in Palestine as 'material support' for Hamas, which is designated a terrorist group, and could therefore potentially result in 20-year prison sentences for those found guilty. When pressed by the reporter to justify the connection, Greenblatt tried to claim that the protestors used the term "Zionist Regime" instead of "Israel" as his proof! He also tried to imply that the flyers or literature the protesters were handing out may have been supplied by Hamas.[729] It would be funny if it weren't so sad and serious, but this is the angle the Cult is taking in trying to stamp out all legitimate criticism of its activities, whether such actions be theft, murder or genocide.

Other Cult Ad Hominem Attacks

It's useful to recall the admission of Shulamit Aloni whom I quoted in chapter 9:[730]

Well, it's a trick. We always use it. When, from Europe, somebody is criticizing Israel, then we bring up the Holocaust. When, in this country, people are criticizing Israel, then they are antisemitic.

The ad hominem slur of antisemite has been around a long time, but now in the year 2025, it's outlived its usefulness to a major extent, despite the quote from Ostrovsky (which was made in the 1990s) at the beginning of this chapter. The Zionists have also extracted a lot of mileage from the ad hominem insult of 'Holocaust Denier' since it is illegal in some countries (as of 2025, the list is Germany, Austria, Belgium, Canada, Czech Republic, France, Greece, Hungary, Israel, Italy, Lithuania, Luxembourg, Portugal, Poland, Romania, Russia, Slovakia, Sweden, Switzerland and Ukraine)[731] to question the historical event in any way, a privilege not afforded to any other past event in humanity's history. So the Zionists have partially achieved their aim of making antisemitism (i.e. challenging Jewish power) illegal in some parts of the world. Whether they fully succeed will depend on the rising consciousness of humanity and how well it can see through the Cult which hides behind Judaism.

There is another Zionist ad hominem attack you have may have heard – 'blood libel.' The term is defined as *"falsely accusing Jews of murdering Christians in order to use their blood in the performance of religious rituals."* Like other terms, the Cult has seized upon this one and expanded its definition so that any complaint of Israeli bombings and killings of people is twisted and thrown back at the observer. An example is the former Permanent Representative of Israel to the United Nations (2020-2024), Gilad Erdan, who accused Hamas of concocting *"a new blood libel"*[732] when it stated that an IDF strike killed over 100 Palestinians, and who also accused the ICC of *"a blood libel, a witch-hunt driven by pure Jew-hatred"* when it issued arrest warrants for PM Netanyahu and Defense Minister Yoav Gallant in May 2024.[733] Given that the Sabbatean-Frankist Cult is Satanic, that blood-drinking is part of Satanic ritual and that Jacob Frank himself was recorded as being a blood drinker, is it really that difficult to imagine the origin of this term? The term is pointing to a deeper truth about our world. I personally have no idea whether Jews murdered Christians to drink their blood, and I couldn't care less about religious infighting. What I can say is that numerous victims of Satanic Ritual Abuse, who were forced to attend – and even to participate – in Satanic ritual, have confirmed that they witnessed people being ritually sacrificed and human blood being drunk at these events (see *The International Satanic Network Exposed* for more information).

When You Have No Good Arguments, Attack the Character of the Other Person

The verbal assaults of the Cult – antisemitism, Holocaust denier and blood libel – work less well than they used to on the average person, especially in light of Israel's Gaza genocide, but there is no denying the Cult's agenda to silence people is widespread and very well funded. We know Israel's surveillance of American politicians and the public is extreme, and from the Cult perspective, silencing people through shame (you racist antisemitic Holocaust denier who commits hate crimes and blood libels!) is much easier than calling in the Sayeret Matkal or the Mossad's kidon unit to have them assassinated.

I wrote when you have no good arguments, attack the character of the other person, but it's much more than that. I could equally have written, 'When you refuse to take responsibility, attack the character of the other person.' Israel isn't singled out because it's Jewish. It's singled out because it flagrantly violates rules, norms and international laws, acts like a homicidal maniac and murderous psychopath, and partially gets away with it via control of America and other powerful nations. In many ways, the success of this silencing approach depends on how much confusion the Cult can continue to perpetuate through scrambling the idea of Jewish identity. Gilad Atzmon writes:[734]

> *How to define a Jew is a loaded topic since Jews define themselves in many different ways, some contradictory, and use those definitions to try to achieve political aims.*

The Cult has done a great job deflecting attention away from its crimes, but humanity at large is starting to awaken and notice. In the next chapter, we will look at the horrific and ongoing Gaza genocide, an atrocity which has awoken lots of people from their slumber.

Sources

[706] https://israelpalestinenews.org/former-mossad-agent-describes-planting-claims-critics-israel-antisemitic-video/

[707] https://www.theguardian.com/world/2011/sep/28/moral-obligation-and-jewish-identity

[708] The Trigger, pg. 684

[709] https://holocaustremembrance.com/resources/working-definition-antisemitism

[710] https://mondoweiss.net/2023/09/bidens-israel-policy-is-scripted-by-saban/

[711] https://electronicintifada.net/content/why-auschwitz-survivor-esther-bejarano-supports-bds/26191

[712] http://pdfs.jta.org/1963/1963-11-05_210.pdf

[713] https://www.reuters.com/article/world/us/jewish-man-arrested-for-swastikas-anti-semitic-calls-idUSTRE80F1SM/

[714] https://apnews.com/article/a6a67fb761304e3cae7497faa32dcdc9

[715] https://reason.com/2019/04/25/anti-semitic-hate-crime-winnipeg-hoax/

[716] https://www.jns.org/german-singer-to-donate-to-holocaust-charities-after-hate-crime-hoax/

[717] https://www.fakehatecrimes.org/

[718] https://thegrayzone.com/2025/09/09/israeli-tip-preceded-australian-claim-that-iran-plotted-bombings/

[719] https://counter-hegemonic-studies.site/mossad-australia-iran/

[720] https://www.informationliberation.com/?id=64869

[721] https://x.com/Betar_USA/status/1898768413301841993

[722] https://x.com/marcorubio/status/1898858967532441945

[723] https://21stcenturywire.com/2025/03/31/operation-wrath-of-zion-dox-and-deport-pro-palestinian-human-rights-activism/

[724] https://www.informationliberation.com/?id=64868

[725] https://www.informationliberation.com/?id=64864

[726] https://theintercept.com/2025/09/13/marco-rubio-revoke-us-passports-terrorism/

[727] https://x.com/infolibnews/status/1851609117237923855

[728] https://x.com/MintPressNews/status/1955302727237489016

[729] https://x.com/infolibnews/status/1954379286254670140

[730] https://www.bitchute.com/video/F8jt0FfoQwAO

[731] https://en.wikipedia.org/wiki/Legality_of_Holocaust_denial

[732] https://www.jns.org/in-what-may-be-his-last-action-at-un-erdan-says-security-council-amplifies-new-blood-libel/

[733] https://www.israelnationalnews.com/news/390275

[734] https://www.theguardian.com/world/2011/sep/28/moral-obligation-and-jewish-identity

CHAPTER 17: CULT CONQUEST OF THE MIDDLE EAST: HAMAS FALSE FLAG OP AND GAZA GENOCIDE

"In the future, the state of Israel has to control the entire area from the river to the sea."

– Benjamin Netanyahu[735]

"Yes, you are repeating what I have been saying for a long time. October 7th was an Israeli psyop."

– Former Israeli Prime Minister Ehud Olmert (asked whether Netanyahu had funded and deliberately propped up Hamas)[736]

"We are destroying everything that remains in Gaza ... the world isn't stopping us."

– Israeli Foreign Minister Bezalel Smotrich[737]

Israeli leaders like Netanyahu compared the October 7th 2023 Hamas attack on Israel with Pearl Harbor and 9/11.[738] He is right in the sense that all three events were false flag operations that were allowed and made to happen. The Hamas attack was another significant milestone in the long Middle Eastern history of conflict, assassination and war, because it has given Israel the excuse to go on a rampage of destruction ever since, accelerating its agenda for regional domination, and engaging in direct military conflict with several of its neighbors simultaneously, including Palestine, Lebanon, Syria, Yemen and Iran. Before we analyze how the attack was allowed to happen, let's take a look at the group that committed the incursion, Hamas.

Hamas – ZioIslamic Terrorists

Israel created Hamas. This is super important to realize when you hear Israeli leaders complain about Hamas terrorism or talk of the need to completely remove Hamas from Gaza. ZioIslamic terrorism,® remember? Hamas, an acronym from the Arabic name Ḥarakat al-Muqawamah al-Islamiyyah (Islamic Resistance Movement), is also the Arabic word for zeal, strength or bravery. Hamas is a Palestinian nationalist political organization with a military wing, the Qassam Brigades. It has governed Gaza since 2007.

Hamas got its start in 1987 around the time of the First Intifada (Palestinian Uprising), emerging from the 1973 Mujama al-Islamiya Islamic charity – affiliated with the Muslim Brotherhood. This connection is unsurprising given the longterm Cult Middle Eastern strategy, originally carried out via the UK and now mainly by the US, to create fundamentalist Islamic groups to divide and conquer the Arabian countries, especially those with secular and nationalist governments. Israel created Hamas as a counterbalance to the secular, leftwing PLO and Fatah parties. Brigadier General Yitzhak Segev was an Israeli military governor of Gaza in the early 1980s who admitted that he helped finance the Palestinian Islamist movement as a counterweight, confessing that the Israeli government had given him a budget. David K. Shipler, Jerusalem bureau chief of the NYT from 1979 to 1984, wrote:[739]

In 1981, Brig. Gen. Yitzhak Segev, Israel's military governor of Gaza, told me that he was giving money to the Muslim Brotherhood, the precursor of Hamas, on the instruction of the Israeli authorities. The funding was intended to tilt power away from both Communist and Palestinian nationalist movements in Gaza, which Israel considered more threatening than the fundamentalists. Judging by a distressed phone call I got later from the army spokesman, General Segev's superiors were not happy with his disclosure of a practice that did not look very clever, even at the time. They thought incorrectly — but apparently wished — that he had made his comments off the record.

Avner Cohen, a former Israeli religious affairs official who worked in Gaza for over 20 years, said in 2009 that, *"Hamas, to my great regret, is Israel's creation."*[740] Yasser Arafat himself stated that Hamas was *"a creature of Israel which, at the time of Prime Minister [Yitzhak] Shamir [the late 1980s, when Hamas arose], [who] gave them money and more than 700 institutions, among them schools, universities and mosques. Even [former Israeli Prime Minister Yitzhak] Rabin ended up admitting it, when I charged him with it, in the presence of [Egyptian President Hosni] Mubarak ... [Hamas] received financing and training from Israel. They have continued to benefit from permits and authorizations, while we (i.e. the PLO) have been limited."*[741]

So, here is what happened in a nutshell: firstly, the Israelis built up a fundamentalist, Islamist group; then, the Israelis had the enemy they wanted, that would fight back, bomb them back and even commit atrocities; so, then the Israelis claimed the justification to bomb and besiege the entire Gaza strip because since 'Hamas uses the whole civilian population as human shields, hiding everywhere' the only way to eradicate Hamas is to destroy all of Gaza.

For Israel, who needs friends when you have enemies like Hamas? Hamas is a divine gift to Israel, because it has provided them with the perfect excuse to obliterate Gaza. The +972 Israeli digital magazine ran a story entitled *"The not-so-secret history of Netanyahu's support for Hamas"* which describes the central role of Netanyahu in propping up Hamas, with funding being delivered via Qatar in suitcases stuffed with cash. Keeping the money flowing to Hamas ensures the Palestinian national movement remains splintered between Hamas in Gaza and the Fatah-controlled Palestinian Authority (PA) in the West Bank. Israeli spies infiltrated Hamas long ago so they could keep tabs on its plans. The article interviews Israeli historian and human rights activist Adam Raz, author of the book *The Road to October 7: Benjamin Netanyahu, the Production of the Endless Conflict and Israel's Moral Degradation*. Raz makes the following point:[742]

Netanyahu is the number one opponent of a two-state solution. In broad terms, Fatah and the PLO are in favor of this solution, while Hamas is against it, which means that on this very crucial point, Netanyahu and Hamas' interests align ... Since coming back to power [in 2009], Netanyahu has resisted any attempt, be it military or diplomatic, that might bring an end to the Hamas regime in Gaza ... Fast forward to 2018, when PA President Mahmoud Abbas stopped transferring money to Gaza completely, leaving Hamas on the brink of collapse. Instead of letting the PA return to Gaza [after it was kicked out by Hamas in 2006, following elections], Netanyahu saved Hamas by allowing in suitcases full of cash from Qatar. He was actually the mastermind and the architect of this Mafia-style money transfer.

Many people and countries around the world have been saying for decades that we needed a two state solution. Netanyahu and other (mostly rightwing or religious extremist) Israelis don't want that, because once Palestine is recognized as its own country, they won't be able to get away with conducting their land grab and murder as much. So, they have desperately fought to stop Palestine becoming its own country. One of the insidious ways they have done this is by blatantly expanding Israeli settlements on Palestinian land, in all directions, not concentrated in one area, meaning that it is now practically impossible to divide the land evenly between a future Israel and a future Palestine. This strategy of using Hamas to 'divide and rule' to prevent a unified Palestinian leadership was also admitted by two former heads of Shin Bet and Mossad, Ami Ayalon and Efraim Halevy, respectively.[743]

In delivering it so much cash, Netanyahu knew that Hamas was not going to use the money for infrastructure or the welfare of Gaza's children, but rather for building tunnels and obtaining weapons. Yet he still did it, given his obsession with preventing any kind of two-state solution, which in turn is based on his obsession with conquering all of Palestine … on the way to conquering Lebanon, Syria, Jordan and parts of Egypt, Saudi Arabia, Türkiye and Iraq. It's all about the Greater Israel project. In an interview on Israeli TV station i24, Netanyahu admitted he was on a *"historical and spiritual mission"* alluding to the so-called 'Promised Land.'[744] Although neither the interviewer nor Netanyahu specifically used the term 'Greater Israel' this is clearly what was being referred to. It is precisely this expansionist idea of stealing land which underpins the

Cult Zionist neocon agenda of 9/11, of driving US foreign policy in the Middle East, of getting America to fight Israel's wars, of Wesley Clark's famous admission of *"7 countries in 5 years"* and also which is mentioned in a July 2014 speech of former Syrian President Bashar Assad, who said:[745]

The occupation of Palestine, invasion of Iraq, division of Sudan and attempts to divide Iraq today are linked events.

<u>Allowing the Attack to Happen</u>

What does the Cult do when it wants to expedite its plans? It manufactures a crisis with a predetermined solution in mind, of course. The Hamas attack on October 7th 2023 is nothing more than yet another false flag operation that was both allowed and made to happen to facilitate the Cult agenda. The evidence for this is overwhelming.

To begin with, Israel's own Shin Bet admitted that certain Israeli/ Netanyahu policies paved the way for the attack. A summary of their report listed several factors, including the aforementioned acquiescence of Netanyahu to the money flow from Qatar to Hamas, a deliberate Israeli "policy of quiet" towards Hamas, a deliberate Israeli policy of dividing Palestinians by boosting Hamas at the expense of the Palestinian state, a deliberate Israeli policy of horribly mistreating Palestinian prisoners and a deliberate Israeli policy of permitting daily Jewish prayers at the compound around Jerusalem's al-Aqsa mosque, also called Dome of the Rock and known to Jews as the Temple Mount. A Guardian article notes:[746]

The prayers violate a 58-year-old understanding with Jordan that only Muslims should be allowed to pray at the al-Aqsa and the esplanade around it, but they were championed by the governing coalition's former national security minister, Itamar Ben-Gvir.

Current Israeli Minister of National Security Itamar Ben-Gvir and current Israeli Minister of Finance Bezalel Smotrich are two highly dangerous and extreme men that form part of Netanyahu's coalition government. These two psychopaths hate Arabs with a passion and would like nothing more than to see all of Gaza destroyed and all the Palestinians either displaced or murdered.

Israeli policies definitely contributed to the attack, but that's not all; like all the other false flag operations covered in this book, there were highly suspicious Israeli moves and direct foreknowledge. Here are six examples of many:

1. Detailed Hamas training videos were posted online in the weeks before the attack;[747]

2. Egypt's intelligence minister stated that Egypt warned Israeli intelligence beforehand that an explosion was coming soon;[748]

3. Someone short sold Israeli stocks (just as happened with the put options on American airline companies before 9/11) in the days before October 7th;[749]

4. In April 2022, Aman had come into possession of a Hamas invasion plan which Aman codenamed "Jericho Wall." Hamas followed this Jericho Wall blueprint with shocking precision: the document proposed Hamas use a barrage of rockets to begin the attack, deploy drones to knock out the security cameras and then invade Israeli territory en masse with paragliders, on motorcycles and on foot – all of which happened on October 7th;[750]

5. Two days before the attack, on October 5th 2023, Israeli military leadership moved two elite commando companies from Gaza to the West Bank, leaving just 600 regular IDF soldiers (conscripts) spread thinly along the Gazan border;[751]

6. The location of the electronic music Nova Festival, where many Israelis were killed, was moved right up to the Gaza border days before the attack.

The last point can be explained by the fact that Nova Festival founder Nimrod Arnin is connected to Israeli intelligence. According to Grayzone editor Wyatt Reed, Arnin helped organize the rave, is listed as a Tribe of Nova Foundation co-founder, and is on the advisory board of DOT SAGA, a company that claims to provide smartphone network connectivity anywhere on Earth and was founded by an IDF psychological warfare specialist. On October 8th 2023, the day after the false flag attack, Arnin co-founded Cobalt Complex, an Open Source Intelligence (OSINT) and Web Source Intelligence (WEBINT) operations center to support the Israeli intelligence apparatus.[752] None of this is suspicious or anything! What was it that Arnon Milchan said again? Oh, that's right – *"In Israel, there is practically no business that does not have something to do with defense."*[753]

What also makes it impossible to believe that Israeli intelligence did not foresee the Hamas attack is the level of Israel's surveillance of Gaza, which is beyond comprehensive. Israel uses high-tech drones like the Hermes 900, equipped with electro-optical and infrared sensors, thermal surveillance monitors, laser designation targeting and electronic listening devices. Iain Davis writes:[754]

In 2021 Israel was the first country to deploy an AI-controlled drone swarm to locate, identify and attack its enemies. Israel's drone surveillance of Gaza was so pervasive it led Gazans to complain of sleep deprivation due to the persistent "buzz" in the skies above their heads ... Israel's human (on the ground – HUMINT) intelligence prowess was equally formidable. Shin Bet HUMINT led the IDF to frequently intercept and shut down Hamas border tunnels. Shin Bet's infiltration of Hamas' literal underground network was so exhaustive, and Hamas so destabilised, that Hamas resorted to mass executions of suspected spies and possible collaborators.

It doesn't stop there. Israel even has a fleet of satellites (Ofeq-13 SAR systems)[755] that allow it to monitor Gaza from space, in all weather and cloud conditions, night and day, with a ground resolution of 0.5 square meters. This means that each pixel in the produced image represents 0.5 square meters on the ground. Despite all their surveillance and technology, we're supposed to believe that Israel somehow didn't see it coming.

<u>The Actual Attack and the Stand Down</u>

The October 7th false flag operation led by Hamas started around 6:30am, with approximately 3000 fighters pouring into Israeli territory and rampaging through the southern areas. The Hamas soldiers overran military positions and civilian communities. All in all, around 1200 people were killed (of which 800 were civilians), including 360 people at the Nova Music Festival, and an additional 240 people at a minimum were abducted and taken back as hostages to Gaza. In November 2023, Israeli government spokesman Mark Regev downgraded the body count from 1400 to 1200.

I am about to expose much more than meets this eye about this attack, but before I go any further, let me say that I do not support random acts of violence or terrorism. It's important not to get sucked into a polarity by choosing sides. Lots of innocent people were killed here. If you choose a side – whether it be the military Hamas or the military IDF – you are supporting the Cult, since both are Cult creations.

Right after the attacks, independent Israeli journalist, podcaster and COVID dissident Efrat Fenigson become well-known for her take on the event.[756] Like most Israelis, Fenigson was in the Israeli military when she was younger as part of the compulsory service program. She actually worked on the border fence, which is one of the most, if not the most, defended and technologically advanced walls on Earth. She reveals that the Israeli military leadership discovered that women were generally better than men at spotting abnormalities and responding to them quickly, so females were used in the spotting positions and watching the screens fed by cameras posted all along the wall. Fenigson reveals that the high-tech surveillance wall was good enough 25 years ago to detect a cat; others, such as this Israeli woman who worked as an Infantry Operations Sergeant, have suggested it's even good enough to detect a bird or a cockroach.[757] The fence was breached by Hamas in at least 15 places – which would have been utterly impossible without inside Israeli cooperation. Watching clips of Hamas fighters enter Israel on paragliders – yes, paragliders – was a large dose of the surreal. This is the most, or one of the most, technologically sophisticated walls on Earth, and yet it somehow couldn't prevent the enemy from hang-gliding over it!? What about guns attached to the walls? What about quickly dispatching drones to shoot down the fragile paragliders? Just as with the JFK assassination and the 9/11 op, the October 7th attack was a false flag operation which requires you to do away with common sense and believe in fairy tales to conform with the official narrative.

This brings us to the key point: the stand down. After Hamas had broken through and entered into Israel, what do you think the IDF did? Remember, Israel is a very small country; it's only about 500 kilometers (310 miles) from north to south, and less than 200 kilometers (124 miles) east to west. Even if Israeli leaders had made an honest mistake (which they did not, since 'Israeli leader' and 'honest' don't mix very well) by positioning too many troops near the West Bank rather than Gaza, they could still have rapidly redeployed them in an hour or two, especially with the use of helicopters. Yet, for some inexplicable reason, Hamas was allowed to freely roam around Israel, killing and capturing people, for around 6-7 hours before there was an Israeli military response! This is unthinkable in a genuine attack scenario, but the whole point was to allow the attack, and allow Hamas to kill and capture, so as to produce an emotional reaction among the Israeli citizenry and the world in general.

We have proof the stand down was ordered. Shalom Sheetrit, a soldier in the IDF Golani Brigade, testified[758][759] before the Israeli Knesset in July 2025 that he was told not to patrol the Gazan border as normal on the morning of October 7th, specifically between 5:20am and 9:00am. He was ordered to not patrol the fence until 9:00am, and that no vehicle was to go down to Burma. He found this order to be highly strange since it went against standard defensive procedure. There is also information from another source. Independent reporter Lauren Witzke, who used to work for TruNews (an organization that has done a lot of good work over the years exposing Zionist control), confirms in this video clip[760] that a stand down order was given to both the Israeli Air Force and Army. The clip features Cecily Routman, founder and president of the Jewish Pro-Life Foundation, revealing that she got the information from Israeli rabbi Chananya Weissman, who has sources among Israel's top security officials. Weissman writes:[761]

[Israel] actively collaborated on everything that went down, including dismissing warnings in the months, weeks, and days leading up to October 7, threatening and persecuting those who issued credible warnings, disarming the local communities, transferring many of the soldiers away from the border, ignoring calls for immediate help over many hours during the attacks — including from soldiers on bases that were ambushed, citizens under siege for many hours, and even the mayor of Ofakim. They also moved the ill-fated music party into harm's way just in time for the attack. The same people who were too "surprised" and "shocked" to send help weren't too surprised and shocked to institute a media blackout during the attacks ... And they declared that "now is not the time to ask questions", and floated a fascist law that would criminalize statements that could be construed as "hurting morale" in a time of war.

Weissman is referring to the law passed in January 2025 by the Knesset. Modeled after the 1986 law banning Holocaust denial,[762] Israel has now banned questioning the October 7th operation. The law criminalizes the denial, minimization or celebration of the event "with the intention of defending or identifying with Hamas" and imposes a five-year prison sentence for those who break it. This is more Cult censorship from those who rule the world who can't handle criticism and exposure of their crimes. Truth does not fear investigation.

Haaretz reported[763] that Lieutenant Colonel Haim Cohen, commander of the Gaza Division's Northern Brigade, got to the Nova Festival site at 5:30am, around an hour before Hamas attacked, and received updated intelligence warnings as he was driving to the site, but he took no preventative action – despite Aman, Shin Bet and the Israeli Army getting signs of unusual Hamas activity. Cohen claimed he was reassured by the increased police presence there, but in the end, this turned out to be woefully inadequate. This is another suggestive clue of a deliberate policy to sacrifice civilians at the Nova Festival for maximum effect.

With stand down comes cover up. Right after the attack, IDF soldiers, including relatively senior IDF officers, tried to access the standard recordings of IDF communications to discover what had happened, but to their surprise found their security clearances had been revoked and they could not access them. The Jerusalem Post reported the following on December 3rd 2023:[764]

Some of the recordings have either disappeared or were simply downloaded from the network and relocated under the directives of commanding officers. Consequently, we are unable to access them ... It seems that someone made a deliberate choice to either transfer or delete these recordings to ensure that no one could listen to them.

<u>The Hannibal Directive</u>

If you thought what the Israeli Government did so far to allow this attack was bad – funneling cash to Hamas, ignoring Hamas' obvious plan to attack, moving troops away from the Gazan border, allowing a music festival to be moved right next to the border, issuing a stand down order for 6-7 hours and all the rest of it – wait for this. This next piece of evidence proves the Zionist Regime not only allowed this attack to happen on purpose, but made it happen on purpose (LIHOP going to MIHOP), showing just how sadistic, psychopathic and Satanic the Cult decision-makers were that day. The IDF carried out what is known as the Hannibal Directive, or the killing of its own citizens. This is a military procedure which justifies the killing of Israelis by the Israeli armed forces if such Israelis could be captured as hostages and reveal information to the enemy. The directive is named after the famous Carthaginian general and leader Hannibal who fought against Rome in the Second Punic War. When defeat was imminent, Hannibal poisoned himself rather than be taken by the Roman Empire, and thus his name has come to represent militaristic suicide or self-destruction.

Colonel Nof Eraz, a senior IDF reserve helicopter pilot, admitted that the Israeli military did fire on its own citizens, telling Haaretz that *"what we saw here was a mass Hannibal"* where the pilots were apparently firing indiscriminately on everyone (Palestinian or Israeli, soldier or civilian) because *"they did whatever they could without the coordination from the ground forces."*[765] Haaretz acquired documents and testimonies proving the Hannibal Directive was operational, reporting that *"[t]here was crazy hysteria, and decisions started being made without verified information."*[766] This article on Common Dreams states that during *"the first hours of the Hamas-led attack, according to Haaretz, Israeli soldiers were given an order: 'Not a single vehicle can return to Gaza.'"*[767] Yedioth Ahronoth (Ynetnews) reported that the IDF admitted that *"Casualties fell as a result of friendly fire on October 7, but the IDF believes that beyond the operational investigations of the events, it would not be morally*

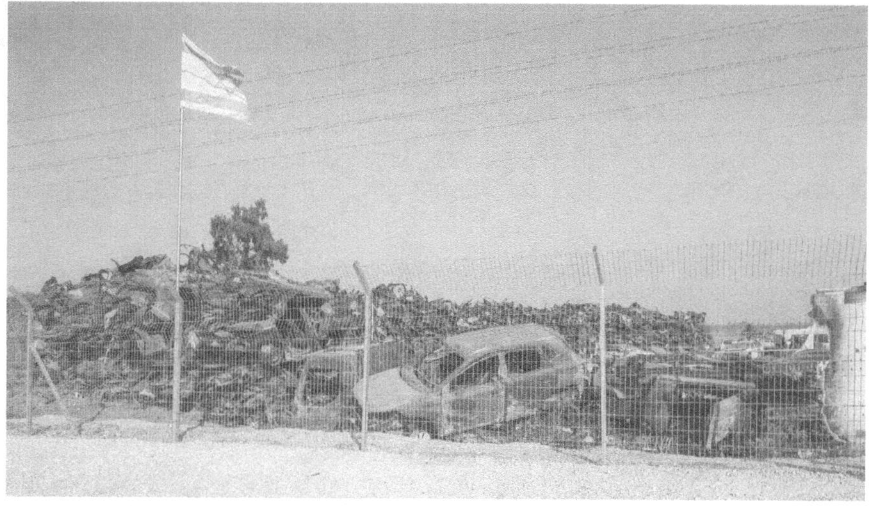

Image #110: destroyed cars on October 7th 2023. Did Israel use DEW?

sound to investigate these incidents due to the immense and complex quantity of them that took place in the kibbutzim and southern Israeli communities due to the challenging situations the soldiers were in at the time."[768] Not morally sound? Is that excuse on par with the dog ate my homework?

Meanwhile, at one of the kibbutzim in southern Israel (a kibbutz is a communal settlement based on agriculture in which all wealth is held in common), Kibbutz Be'eri, Israeli tanks were there … firing on Israeli civilians. Israeli Channel 12 conducted an investigation featuring accounts from settlers, concluding that Israeli tanks were inside the Be'eri settlement on October 7th and that they targeted houses, even when dozens of people were inside. Given that Hamas does not possess tanks, this could only have been the Israeli military. This video footage[769] from Channel 12 published on December 19th 2023 shows the tanks firing. Yasmin Porat, an Israeli woman who fled the Nova Festival and sought shelter in a nearby community when Hamas arrived, undercut the official narrative by explicitly

Image #111: "Hannibal Government" written in Hebrew outside the headquarters of the IDF in Tel Aviv

describing how the Israeli military tanks fired at houses and killed Israeli civilians inside.[770] The only other person reportedly to escape the Kibbutz Be'eri massacre alive, Tuval Escapa, told journalists that the IDF shelled houses full of people, without knowing whether they were alive or dead.[771][772] Even Israeli Lieutenant Colonel Golan Vach admitted that Israeli tanks killed Israeli civilians.[773] The Cradle reported that while Hamas militants did indeed kill some innocent people at the Nova Festival, whether deliberately or due to the chaos of battle, the evidence suggested that the majority of fatalities were carried out by Israeli security forces. They also found that Israel's Border Police was deployed at the Nova site before Hamas stumbled onto the festival – a piece of foreknowledge which fits right in with the aforementioned Israeli intelligence-connected Nimrod Arnin and the now obvious fact that this was a false flag operation.[774] Furthermore, an Israeli police investigation reported by Haaretz concluded that Hamas was likely not aware of the festival in advance, but rather were targeting Re'im, a settlement and military base located down the road on Route 232 from the Nova site.[775] Speaking of the Nova Festival, the damage inflicted on the cars there was not at all consistent with Hamas weaponry. There is some evidence of the Israelis using DEW against the Palestinians in general.[776] Was DEW used during the October 7th attack?

The truth of this horrendous operation and betrayal of its own citizenry by the Israeli Government was not lost on some Israelis, who went out to protest at the evil committed by their leaders. One such protest featured "Hannibal Government" written in Hebrew in front of the IDF's headquarters in Tel Aviv.[777] I applaud Israelis with the awareness to see through their government's deception and with the courage to take a stand against it.

Atrocity Propaganda

After the Hamas attack, the Zionist controlled media – whether the MSM or MAM – swung into full gear. Their plan was to exaggerate and lie, but mostly lie, in order to turn this event into the worst thing that had happened to the Jews since the Holocaust. It was to be Israel's 9/11. Right from the start, all areas of Israeli society were tapped to join in the propaganda war. It became a war of perception, a psychological operation, an area where Israel has historically held all the trump cards. Lying Israeli teens were used to pretend their parents were killed by Hamas, but their smirking and giggling on camera didn't exactly lend credibility to their accounts.[778] Matt Guertin did some great analysis to show that Israel released a ton of fake video footage created by AI.[779] This AI video is clearly more advanced than the CGI images from 20+ years ago in the 2000s when Israel was trying to produce fake but convincing images of the planes hitting the WTC towers, but nonetheless, a close analysis reveals repeated patterns showing the AI was 'guessing' or filling space in with pixels trying to match the surroundings. It's not real. However, Hamas also posted its own videos showing graphic images of the deaths it had inflicted, so not all the footage was faked.

The term 'atrocity propaganda' describes the way one side attempts to demonize another side by portraying them, truthfully or not, as perpetrators of horrific deeds. It's a tool to win the information/perception war and gain the upper moral ground. Israel marshaled its troops first in the Israeli media, and then in the Western media, to get in those vital first pieces of information (when peoples' perceptions are just being formed about an event). What did the Zionist regime say? It invented atrocity propaganda out of thin air, namely that Hamas militants had raped Israeli women, had chopped Israeli children's heads off and had burnt Israeli babies in ovens. The beheading accusation obviously was invented to gain a lot of attention. Remember head-chopping ISIS, another ZioIslamic® terrorist creation? The 'head-chopping' claim can be traced back to David Ben Zion, a deputy commander in IDF Unit 71, which was among the first units to arrive at the Kfar Aza Kibbutz. Ben Zion also just so happened to be the leader of the Shomron Regional Council of 35 illegal Israeli settlements in the West Bank. Ben Zion and his council were associated with a murderous attack on the Palestinian town of Huwara in February 2023 which led to house burning and the killing of 65 Palestinians, including 13 children, by the Israeli security forces and illegal settlers. Prior to the house burning and killing, Ben Zion had posted on social media that *"the village of Huwara should be erased today ... there is no room for mercy."*[780] Smotrich explicitly repeated the idea too.[781] This is the same Ben Zion that Israeli i24 News 'journalist' Nicole Zedeck used as her source when she claimed that Hamas had chopped off children's heads off at the Kfar Aza Kibbutz. It was later admitted that 10-month-old Mila Cohen may have been the only baby killed during the entire Hamas attack, and that Mila died at Kibbutz Be'eri where it is highly probable she was killed by the IDF, as covered above. In this interview,[782] Israeli reporter David Sheen states that two babies were killed by Hamas, but that none were purposefully killed, and none were decapitated. Eyewitnesses from Kibbutz Be'eri (like Yasmin Porat) stated that Hamas treated women very well and had no intention of killing civilians. However, truth is of no concern to the hasbara or propaganda disseminators. MSM outlets like CNN and the BBC ran with the beheading story, as did Netanyahu and then President Biden. The truth is that, while some photographic and video evidence from Kfar Aza shows clear signs of concentrated small arms fire, media reports also show completely destroyed dwellings that appear to have been shelled. This kind of damage, as already explained, is indicative of Israeli forces and is not consistent with Hamas forces.

One of the lies that got the most coverage was the false claim that Hamas 'mass raped women' on October 7th. The Times Of London newspaper investigated this claim and found that, after sifting through all the available photographs and footage, there was no audio or video evidence of rape. Their investigation even included hiring *"a leading Israeli dark-web researcher to look for evidence of those images, including footage"* who reported that *"none could be found."* The Times found that the mass rape claims originated from the ultra-religious group Zaka, whose men *"never saw a woman except their wife,"* who were likely repeating what they had read in religious scripture. The Times wrote that *"they (Zaka members) have read a lot of Jewish texts that depict the raping of women. These texts kind of reappear again and again in Jewish stories and they reappear every time there is a major event against Jewish communities."*[783] Moran Gez, the Israeli prosecutor focused on October 7th, admitted that *"in the end, we have no complainants"* alleging that rape occurred that day. She said her team had *"turned to women's rights groups and ... asked for cooperation,"* but were told by Israeli women that *"they were simply not approached (by Hamas)."* In January 2025, 15 months after the October 7th event, no alleged victims of rape had come forward.[784] What was happening was that Israeli leaders were using the hashtag concept of 'Believe Israeli Women' to mean 'Believe Israel,' inventing fictitious rape accounts for political advantage. While Israel could not produce evidence of Hamas raping Israeli women, the same may not be true in reverse – and even America knows it. In March 2024, a US State Department official in charge of the Israeli-Palestinian portfolio met with IDF Brigadier General Amir Avivi, who later explained on Israeli radio that the American official accused Israel of systematically sexually abusing Palestinian women.[785]

At first, Israel did win the perception war, and was able to strike Gaza with impunity while the rest of the world defended Israel's actions or did nothing to stop it. However, as the bombing and slaughter dragged on, transforming from a revenge strike against Hamas into a long-term razing of Gaza to the ground – a full-on genocide in every sense of the word – the majority of the world (except the USG), and especially the younger generation, became increasing incensed and vocal in opposition to the Cult's Zionistic militarism and mass murder.

The Gaza Genocide

At the beginning of the Israeli invasion of Gaza, Netanyahu gave a speech during which he appealed to the biblical Amalek and instructed Israeli troops to defeat the murderous enemy.[786] Pure religious fanaticism. The Amalek reference is from 1 Samuel 15:3 which can be translated as:

Now go and smite Amalek, and utterly destroy all that they have, and spare them not; but slay both man and woman, infant and suckling, ox and sheep, camel and ass.

This is a blatant reference to mass murder or genocide of a population, including its women, children and animals, from the Jewish Bible that was written for them (see chapter 1). Amalek was painted as the arch foe of the Jews. Having a mythical and religious enemy like this is very convenient for politicians, because any current political target, be it the Palestinians, the Lebanese, the Syrians, the Yemenis, the Iranians and so on, can be labeled as 'the seed of Amalek' without any evidence. *"You know those guys over there – standing in the way of greater Israel – well we happen to know that they're the descendants of Amalek, so you need to kill them, ok?"* Of course, all the religious fundamentalists within Israel will gobble this propaganda up like there's no tomorrow. This is one reason of many why it's such a joke that Israel paints itself as an extension of Western rational principles and liberal values, and as an example of an advanced democracy. In truth, it is propelled by extreme Jewish supremacy and religious fundamentalism.

So the bombs began to fall in earnest, and the death toll began to climb. Despite Israeli leaders pretending that they were only targeting Hamas fighters (their perennial excuse), the horrific truth

Images #112-115: Gaza, razed to the ground before our eyes to make way for Greater Israel

soon emerged that Israel was wantonly mass murdering civilians and even targeting residential neighborhoods, water supplies, mosques, schools, universities and hospitals. Andrew Cayley, a senior prosecutor of the ICC (which was later to issue arrest warrants for Israeli leaders Netanyahu and Gallant, as well as Hamas leaders Sinwar and Mohammed Deif[787]), concluded that claims that Hamas fighters were hiding in hospitals were exaggerated.[788] What, Israel exaggerating or inventing claims to justify their agenda? Surely not. Gallant, by the way, was the one to come out with this declaration, a blatant violation of human rights:[789]

I have ordered a complete siege on the Gaza strip. There will be no electricity, no food, no fuel, everything is closed. We are fighting human animals and we act accordingly.

Human animals? What a cliche. If you thought the Nazi dehumanization of the Jews was part of history and something that humanity would never repeat, then you don't know Cult-controlled Israel. IDF soldiers let the truth out when they declared that *"everyone's a terrorist"*[790] as some Israelis tried to claim that every Palestinian was supporting Hamas and so was therefore a legitimate military target. This is reinforced by Jewish American physician Mark Perlemutter who, having returned from Gaza, stated that Arab children were being deliberately targeted and killed by Israeli snipers.[791] Leaked statistics from a classified Israeli military intelligence database revealed that 83% of the murdered Palestinians were civilians.[792] This was calculated as follows: Israeli intelligence listed 8,900 named Hamas and Palestinian Islamic Jihad (PIJ) as dead or probably dead since October 7th. Gaza health authorities reported that 53,000 Palestinians had been killed by Israeli attacks during the same period, including soldiers and civilians. As a percentage, 8,900 soldiers is around 17% of those killed, and thus the remaining 44,100 (83%) must have been civilians. This former Israeli sniper,[793] part of Operation Straw Widow, admitted that his team used to enter Palestinian homes by force, corral all the members into one room, then set up their sniper rifles in the rooms of the rest of the house. During that time, if any Palestinian needed to eat, drink, get medicine, go to the bathroom, etc., they had to get authorization from their Israeli captors. This soldier woke up and realized that he was brainwashed to believe he was protecting Israel, when actually, he was being used to control Palestinians – a different thing altogether. Many people such as Arab professor Nadera Shalhoub-Kevorkian and Australian Jew and anti-Zionist Antony Loewenstein have stated that Israel tests both medicine and weapons on Palestinian children:[794]

Palestinian spaces are laboratories. The invention of products and services of state-sponsored security corporations are fueled by long-term curfews and Palestinian oppression by the Israeli army.

Certain segments of the Palestinian population have been deliberately targeted, such as journalists, since Israel desperately wants to control the narrative and hide the truth of its atrocities. Aman established something called the 'Legitimization Cell,' so-called because its mission was to legitimize the Israeli perspective (hasbara propaganda) and delegitimize the Gazan and international perspective:[795]

Intelligence personnel searched for information to provide 'legitimization' for the army's actions in Gaza, failed Hamas launches, use of human shields, exploitation of the civilian population. A primary mission ... was to find Gazan journalists who could be portrayed in the media as Hamas operatives in disguise.

Since the Gaza genocide began, Israel has killed many journalists, including Anas al-Sharif (who worked for Al Jazeera) and Dr. Hassan Douhan,[796] a veteran journalist with a PhD in media and an expert in investigative reporting in Gaza. When you combine this with Israel's ban of aerial filming over Gaza, it's obvious that Israel is desperately trying to hide its genocide. Sky News journalists on an aid drop were warned that if they recorded from above, their flight would get cancelled.[797]

You may have heard Israel level the claim against Hamas that it uses 'human shields' or hides behind Palestinian civilians. Israel trots out this excuse to justify all the civilians it murders, trying to claim that Hamas fighters were hiding behind them. Not only is this an exaggeration and a justification, but the fact is that Israel does the same. This Haaretz article reveals that almost every IDF platoon in Gaza keeps a group of Palestinian slaves nearby to use as human shields.[798] Israel also deliberately puts its missile launching sites in middle of Tel Aviv, surrounded by civilians, thus using its own people as 'human shields.' This became very obvious during the 12-Day War against Iran in June 2025. This video from June 13th 2025 shows Israeli air defense systems firing from densely populated areas in Tel Aviv to intercept Iranian missiles.[799] The human shield claim is bogus for many reasons, including the fact that we know that Israel possesses the technology to conduct targeted strikes and assassinations. When it wants to, Israel precisely targets foreign military officials, politicians and scientists, e.g. for the killing of Hezbollah leader Nasrallah on September 27th 2025, and for the killing of the Iranian Islamic Revolutionary Guard Corps (IRGC) leaders and nuclear scientists on June 12th 2025. Then, when it's convenient, Israel claims they have to indiscriminately wipe out all of Gaza to get Hamas. This kind of Cult logic is reminiscent of US imperialism throughout the second half of the 20th century, which is not surprising, since it's the same Cult driving both nations and their policies. The Cult says what it wants to say when it wants to say it to achieve a particular aspect of the agenda at that moment in time, consistency and logic be damned. This is why the US supported dictators when convenient, then betrayed and killed them when convenient (e.g. Saddam Hussein).

The surveillance and technology Israel uses for assassinations has now become even more cutting-edge with the addition of AI. Israel uses AI technology against the Palestinians to further its genocidal objectives, deploying two Palantir programs in particular called Lavender and Gospel, as first revealed by +972 Magazine and Local

Call. Their investigation was based on the testimony of six Israeli intelligence officers who had all served in the army during the current war on the Gaza strip and had personal involvement with using AI to generate assassination targets. The Lavender system was programmed to designate suspected agents of Hamas and the PIJ, while the Gospel system was programmed to generate suggestions of objects that could be military targets, such as buildings. While apologists defend these programs and claim they are merely decision-making tools, and that further assessment is needed by an intelligence officer, these six sources told +972 and Local Call that *"during the first weeks of the war, the army almost completely relied on Lavender, which clocked as many as 37,000 Palestinians as suspected militants — and their homes — for possible air strikes."*[800] Lavender has played such a central role in the Israeli military's decimation of Gaza that, according to the sources, they treated the AI outputs not as 'suggestions' but *"as if it were a human decision."* This US military website notes that *"Gospel's suggestions alone are not a sufficient basis for concluding that an object is lawfully targetable. Moreover, the system does not assess potential collateral damage for a proportionality analysis or identify viable precautions in attack."*[801] Do you think the Cult psychopaths running the IDF care about that? The Gaza genocide has shown us just how close we are already to a machine war where robots kills humans – the kind of dystopian scenario that has been warned about in books and science fiction for decades. Israel likes to use its murder as marketing. Israeli arms manufacturer Rafael, for example, uses footage of a Palestinian being targeted and killed by a Spike FireFly drone in northern Gaza as promotional material for its military products.[802][803] The Palestinians, especially those in Gaza, are the lab rats where the latest cutting-edge military tech, whether it's drones, DEW or AI, can be tested by Israel on unwitting and innocent human beings. I've said it before and I'll say it again: in a grander sense, with Cult psychopaths running the world and trying to install a New World Order, we are all Palestinians.

As the genocide has continued, it has become abundantly clear that the Zionist regime will use anything as a weapon of war, including food – the distribution of it and the lack of it. Israeli opposition politicians Yair Lapid and Avigdor Lieberman said the Gaza Humanitarian Foundation, which was for some time the organization responsible for bringing food relief to Gaza, was a Mossad front, financed through foreign shell companies to hide the source of funding.[804] This Israeli-run food aid program is a way for the Cult to make Gaza even more like a concentration camp. It's a biometric collection trap, as well as a death trap. Israeli soldiers guard the food, and when the Palestinians try to get it, the IDF soldiers have been injuring them, arresting them, kidnapping them or killing them – on top of threatening them by withholding food (making them starve) unless they cooperate with Israel (e.g. spying for Israel).[805] Being the psychopath that he is, Netanyahu naturally denied that Israel has been using starvation as a war strategy, but every one of the 15 members of the UN Security Council (except the US – surprise, surprise) agreed with the assessment made during a meeting on August 2025 that there was a famine in Gaza, that Israel was using starvation as a weapon of war, and that such a starvation strategy was prohibited under international law and constitutes a war crime.[806] The Integrated Food Phase Classification (IPC), the UN-backed international hunger monitor, released an assessment in August 2025[807] which found that 514,000 Palestinians were in famine, and that number was projected to rise to 641,000 in a little over a month.

Israeli snipers have admitted deliberately shooting starving Palestinian children as they try to get food. Haaretz reported a sniper in the Nahal Brigade who said:[808]

Every day we have the same mission: to secure the humanitarian aid in the north of the Strip ... those waiting for aid try to move forward to get a good spot in line, but there is a boundary in front of them that they can't see ... a line that if they cross, I can shoot them ... it's like a game of cat and mouse. They try to come each time from a different route, and I'm there with the sniper rifle, and the officers yell at me, 'Take them down, take them down.' I fire 50–60 bullets every day. I stopped counting ... I have no idea how many [children] I've killed ... a lot.

Netanyahu-led Israel wanted the complete obliteration of Gaza much more than the return of the hostages, which were just a tool to keep the whole thing going. This is why Israel repeatedly rejected deals with Hamas that would have secured the release of all hostages and ended the war.[809] This brings to mind what Yeshayahu Leibowitz, the Orthodox Jewish intellectual and Hebrew University professor, warned about in 1968, namely that the occupation has truly corrupted Israel.[810] There is no way to pretend you are a free and liberal democracy when you kill your neighbors and steal their land, and treat some of your citizens as second-class. The occupation is truly a corrupting force. This kind of corrupting force leads to all sorts of evil, such as this incident where, according to local sources, Israeli occupation forces stole nearly one million shekels (approximately $270,000 USD) after taking over a currency exchange shop in Ramallah.[811]

Colonel Douglas MacGregor said it best: *"We need to understand something: Gaza is not a war. It is simply mass murder with US funding."*[812]

The Genocide is Undeniable

Despite all these unspeakable crimes, there are still those who try to claim that Israel is not committing genocide. Denial is an easier psychological choice than assuming responsibility, however it's not real. This denial is taken apart by Israeli historian Lee Mordechai who explains the definition of genocide and how Israel meets at least three of the five conditions, when meeting any single one of them would be sufficient for its actions to be considered genocide:[813]

My definition of genocide builds upon my understanding of the 1948 Convention on the Prevention and Punishment of the Crime of Genocide. This Convention defined genocide as "any of the [specified] acts committed with intent to destroy, in whole or in part, a national, ethnical, racial or religious group, as such." It requires two interconnected elements:

1. The commission of one or more specific acts against a group:

a. Killing members of the group

b. Causing serious bodily or mental harm to members of the group

c. Deliberately inflicting on the group conditions of life calculated to bring about its physical destruction in whole or in part

d. Imposing measures intended to prevent births within the group e. Forcibly transferring children of the group to another group

2. The intent behind the commission of one or more of the aforementioned acts.

By this definition, Israel has committed genocide. Various Israeli officials have declared genocidal intent (point #2), while Israel has committed acts 1a, 1b and 1c. It meets the condition of 1a by killing members of the group (possibly as much as a quarter of the Gazan population – more on this shortly). It meets the condition of 1b by wounding Gazans, in addition to the collective trauma they suffer arising from the repeated attacks on their land. It meets the condition of 1c by deliberately withholding food, water and life necessities, including the deliberate policy of starvation, as declared by various Israeli officials such as former Defense Minister Gallant. Many organizations and officials have affirmed that Israel is unquestionably committing genocide, including the Independent International Commission of Inquiry on the Occupied Palestinian Territory, including East Jerusalem, and Israel (part of the Human Rights Council of the UN),[814] the International Association for Genocide Scholars (IAGS)[815] and the former Director of the New York office of the UN High Commissioner for Human Rights, Craig Mokhiber, who called it a *"text-book case of genocide ... once again we are seeing a genocide unfolding before our eyes and the organization we serve appears powerless to stop it."*[816]

The Gazan death toll since the war began has been massively undercounted. It is difficult to know the true number. In July 2024, a Lancet study[817] estimated the toll could exceed 186,000 people, much higher than the 38,000 figure used by Gaza's Ministry of Health; the study asserted the death toll was higher because the official toll didn't take into account the thousands of dead buried under rubble and all the indirect deaths due to destruction of health facilities, food distribution systems and other public infrastructure. However, the true picture is even worse than that. A report[818] by Garb Yaakov, a Professor at Ben-Gurion University of the Negev in Israel, and published on The President and Fellows of Harvard College Dataverse website, suggests that the real number was 377,000 as of June 2025. The report reached this conclusion by taking the pre-October 7th war Gazan population of approximately 2.227 million, and subtracting official IDF estimates for the population remaining in what are considered Gaza's three primary enclaves, Gaza City (1 million), Mawasi (0.5 million) and Central (0.35 million), which total 1.85 million. So starting with 2.227 million and subtracting 1.85 million leaves 377,000 people unaccounted for. This does not necessarily count all Gazans, since some may not have been located in the three enclaves, but still, it does give you an idea of the scale of death that the Cult Israeli military has perpetrated – supposedly in revenge for the death of 1,200 people (around two thirds of whom were killed by the IDF anyway under the Hannibal Directive).

Another estimate is that, as of July 2025, the death toll was a staggering 434,800. This number is arrived at by taking the Lancet's calculation that 732 people die every day in Gaza from 'direct' and 'indirect' causes. There has been continuous Israeli killing every day between October 8th 2023 and January 18th 2025, then a temporary ceasefire was implemented, and then again from March 18th until the present (despite the October 2025 'ceasefire'). The writer of this article[819] calculated that there were 594 total days of killing if you calculated up to July 21st 2025; if 732 people died daily for 594 days, the true Gazan death toll was 434,800 at that time. Now, at the time of writing in November 2025, the death toll is more like

480,000, close to half a million people. This is approaching a quarter of the entire population of Gaza!

There can be no doubt that the Cult via Israel is indeed committing genocide, just as it has in the past, such as with the Armenian Genocide of 1915-1917 that was spearheaded by the CUP (the Young Turks) whom the Cult had created and funded to overthrow the Ottoman Empire. Is it really that surprising that they would commit another genocide? What is probably more surprising is the fact that the world is mostly just looking on. Bezalel Smotrich has declared genocidal intent multiple times. As he himself said, Israel can just do what it wants, because the *"the world isn't stopping"* them.

Genocide Tourism

Although it's true that the Israeli Government doesn't represent all Israelis and doesn't really care about them, there is nonetheless a sizable number of Israelis who fully support the genocide. I ascribe this to the incessant brainwashing that goes in Israeli society, where children are brought up to hate Arabs and to literally wish for their death. The sad truth is that many Israeli Jews enjoy the suffering of Gazans – and openly profess this, such as the hosts of Israel's "Two Nice Jewish Boys" podcast who highlighted that their fellow Israeli Jews enjoyed seeing people in Gaza suffer, that it made *"their daily lives more satisfying"* to know that Palestinians were hungry and homeless.[820] Sadism on full display. Meanwhile, a survey conducted in March 2025 and published by Haaretz found that 82% of Israelis supported the expulsion of the Palestinians from the Gaza strip.[821] The survey, which in and of itself is a propaganda tool, also slipped in this question to bolster the fictional Zionist narrative of a Jewish legal claim to Palestine: *"Do you support the claim that the [Israeli army] in conquering an enemy city, should act in a manner similar to the way the Israelites did when they conquered Jericho under the leadership of Joshua, i.e. to kill all its inhabitants?"* The reference is to the biblical account of the conquest of Jericho; 47% of respondents answered in the affirmative. i24 reported that in two polls from May and August 2025, either 62 or 64% of Israelis believed that *"there are no innocent people in Gaza."*[822]

Although there are Israelis who have overcome the programming, it is completely fair to say that modern-day Israel is a deeply racist and sick state. In July 2025, Israeli Jews were actually protesting for the right – their right – to anally rape Palestinian men in Israeli detention, using electric rods to sodomize them. I kid you not. In 2024, a NYT article reported that Israel was also using sleep deprivation and electric chairs on Arab prisoners, or beating prisoners in the gut until they began vomiting blood, in places such as Sde Teiman detention camp where many died.[823] If that's not sick enough for you, then perhaps this will be: Israel's burgeoning industry of genocide tourism. What is genocide tourism, you may ask? It's where Israel sends kids on field trips to witness the Gaza genocide live as part of their educational curriculum. Naturally, all Israeli Jewish children are told during these trips that the land (Gaza) is theirs. Why waste any moment for brainwashing? Also offered are boat rides in the Mediterranean at night for Jewish families to get close to Gaza and see all the destruction. Mass murder for entertainment. Didn't the Cult-owned Roman Empire show the utility of this approach by feeding Christians to the lions in front of packed Colosseum crowds? Those guiding Israeli policy are so psychopathic that they are constantly pushing the boundaries to see just how far they can go. In September 2025, Israel bombed a school for disabled children in

South Lebanon in Aita al-Shaab.[824] When people are consumed by hate and destroyed by brainwashing, they will support anything.

Hamas = Cult, IDF = Cult

One of Israel's ploys is to adamantly berate anyone who dares compare Israel's actions to Hamas' actions by declaring that there is no moral equivalence between the two. This is their attempt to gain the upper moral ground. It's the same old perception battle of psychological warfare – the enemy conducts illegitimate terrorism, but we conduct legitimate war, plus ours is done in self-defense too. In no way do I condone the Hamas Attack, but I must ask: how is it worse than the intentional targeting of journalists in Gaza to hide the truth? How is it worse than the Israeli firebombing of Palestinian women and children in their homes, schools, refugee camps and hospitals? How is it worse than the intentional policy of starvation that Israel pursues? How is worse than genocide?

The clue to unraveling this whole saga begins with observing some basic truths and asking some key questions. Hamas played right into Israel's actions with its attack. What did it think would happen? Israel has showed time and time again that it barely needs any excuse to attack its neighbors, constantly conducting false flag operations to feign being attacked to give itself the excuse to attack. It does not take much to imagine the kind of revenge Israel would take for Hamas entering its territory and killings its citizens, yet Hamas did it anyway. Why?

The truth is that Hamas does not represent or care about the average Palestinian's needs any more than the Israeli Government cares about the average Israeli's needs. Both populations had been demonstrating against their respective leadership earlier in 2023; in

August 2023, when Israelis were demonstrating against Netanyahu's attempted judicial overhaul, Gazan Palestinians were demonstrating against Hamas,[825] but Hamas violently suppressed the protests.

If Hamas and the Israeli Government are such mortal enemies, why did they cooperate to arrange a ceasefire in order to vaccinate the Gazan kids?[826] Do you really think Israel cares about the Gazan children – the same ones it has blown to bits since October 2023 to the tune of hundreds of thousands? Why would it care if they were vaccinated when it's about to rain down bombs on them? What would happen if the average people realized that they had more in common with each other than their (Cult-appointed) leaders? What would happen if the world population woke up and realized that both the Zionist Regime and Hamas are running operations using civilians as pawns in their geopolitical power struggles?

In the next chapter, I will explore this theme more, extending out to the Islamic world and a little further, to show that the Cult controls Israel's enemies and the West's adversaries just as much as it controls Israel and the West.

Sources

---

[735] https://x.com/Kahlissee/status/1907482290638487962

[736] https://x.com/pepedownunder/status/1791038670134493470 (formerly at this url, now taken down)

[737] https://www.haaretz.com/israel-news/2025-05-19/ty-article-live/amidst-large-scale-offensive-israel-to-allow-basic-amount-of-food-to-enter-gaza-pm-says/00000196-e5dc-dc4c-aff7-e7de418e0000?liveBlogItemId=326163697#326163697

[738] https://www.nbcnews.com/politics/congress/netanyahu-address-congress-first-time-oct-7-attack-israel-rcna163260

[739] https://web.archive.org/web/20210517175055/https://www.nytimes.com/2021/05/17/opinion/letters/israel-gaza-palestinians.html

[740] https://www.wsj.com/articles/SB123275572295011847

[741] https://larouchepub.com/pr/2001/2850arafat_on_hamas.html

[742] https://www.972mag.com/netanyahu-hamas-october-7-adam-raz/

[743] https://thefreedomarticles.com/open-admissions-former-israeli-shin-bet-mossad-heads/

[744] https://x.com/RT_com/status/1955379811091878321

[745] https://www.globalresearch.ca/president-bashar-al-assad-transcript-of-inauguration-speech/5391709

[746] https://www.theguardian.com/world/2025/mar/05/israeli-security-agency-says-netanyahus-policies-paved-the-way-for-2023-hamas-attack

[747] https://www.pbs.org/newshour/world/hamas-posted-video-of-mock-attack-on-social-media-weeks-before-border-breach

[748] https://www.bbc.com/news/world-middle-east-67082047

[749] https://www.axios.com/2023/12/04/israel-stocks-short-oct-7

[750] https://www.nytimes.com/2023/11/30/world/middleeast/israel-hamas-attack-intelligence.html

[751] https://www.timesofisrael.com/2-commando-companies-said-diverted-from-gaza-border-to-west-bank-days-before-oct-7/

[752] https://thegrayzone.com/2025/04/22/nova-founder-israeli-intel/

[753] https://www.nbcnews.com/id/wbna3340725

[754] https://off-guardian.org/2025/07/25/unacknowledged-false-flags-the-october-7th-hamas-attack-part-2/

[755] https://www.gov.il/en/pages/eofekmod

[756] https://www.youtube.com/watch?v=F_IAH7PnS_E

[757] https://www.radio786.co.za/video-iof-troop-even-a-cockroach-couldnt-cross-gaza-barrier/

[758] https://x.com/xIsraelExposedx/status/1950668648701628569

[759] https://x.com/malinformedtv/status/1950687058567344499

[760] https://twitter.com/LaurenWitzkeDE/status/1713344613409313003

[761] https://chananyaweissman.com/article.php?id=593

[762] https://www.timesofisrael.com/knesset-passes-law-banning-denial-of-october-7-massacre/

[763] https://www.haaretz.com/israel-news/2025-09-02/ty-article/.premium/top-idf-commander-ignored-risks-after-visiting-nova-mere-hour-before-oct-7-hamas-massacre/00000199-09f0-d21e-a9db-1bfbe01b0000

[764] https://archive.is/3wiAZ

[765] https://x.com/TheCradleMedia/status/1726625799737123024

[766] https://www.haaretz.com/israel-news/2024-07-07/ty-article-magazine/.premium/idf-ordered-hannibal-directive-on-october-7-to-prevent-hamas-taking-soldiers-captive/00000190-89a2-d776-a3b1-fdbe45520000

[767] https://www.commondreams.org/news/israel-hannibal-directive

[768] https://archive.is/xOe1H#selection-1287.0-1287.381

[769] https://www.youtube.com/watch?v=bjGL0HFTgiU

[770] https://thegrayzone.com/2023/11/25/israels-october-7-propaganda-tank-eyewitnesses/

---

[771] https://www.tmj.news/october-7-debunked/

[772] https://www.haaretz.co.il/news/politics/2023-10-20/ty-article-magazine/.premium/0000018b-499a-dc3c-a5df-ddbaab290000

[773] https://www.youtube.com/watch?v=wQqxQXu0uQM

[774] https://thecradle.co/articles/how-israeli-forces-trapped-and-killed-ravers-at-the-nova-festival

[775] https://www.haaretz.com/israel-news/2023-11-18/ty-article/.premium/israeli-security-establishment-hamas-likely-didnt-have-prior-knowledge-of-nova-festival/0000018b-e2ee-d168-a3ef-f7fe8ca20000

[776] https://thefreedomarticles.com/is-israel-using-dews-against-gaza-palestinians/

[777] https://x.com/Etanetan23/status/1786805180609994813

[778] https://www.bitchute.com/video/PlM4bcAxPzEN

[779] https://matt1up.substack.com/p/oct-7th-fraud-composites

[780] https://www.aljazeera.com/news/2023/2/28/israel-releases-settlers-arrested-after-anti-palestinian-attacks

[781] https://www.aljazeera.com/news/2023/3/1/israel-arrests-settlers-after-anti-palestinian-pogrom

[782] https://www.bitchute.com/video/Qv3dsRaFtOq5

[783] https://www.thetimes.com/magazines/the-times-magazine/article/israel-hamas-rape-investigation-evidence-october-7-6kzphszsj

[784] https://electronicintifada.net/blogs/ali-abunimah/israel-still-cant-find-any-7-october-rape-victims-prosecutor-admits

[785] https://www.jpost.com/israel-hamas-war/article-793420

[786] https://x.com/mtracey/status/1718360354764238929

[787] https://news.un.org/en/story/2024/11/1157286

[788] https://www.theguardian.com/law/2024/dec/11/claims-of-hamas-fighters-in-gaza-hospitals-may-have-been-exaggerated-says-senior-icc-prosecutor

---

[789] https://www.youtube.com/shorts/ZbPdR3E4hCk

[790] https://www.haaretz.com/israel-news/2024-12-18/ty-article-magazine/.premium/idf-soldiers-expose-arbitrary-killings-and-rampant-lawlessness-in-gazas-netzarim-corridor/00000193-da7f-de86-a9f3-fefff2e50000

[791] https://x.com/JoeBrolly1993/status/1899142407465119951

[792] https://thecradle.co/articles/leaked-israeli-data-shows-civilians-make-up-83-percent-of-palestinians-killed-in-gaza

[793] https://x.com/abierkhatib/status/1820253312886694039

[794] https://www.palestinechronicle.com/israeli-pharmaceutical-firms-test-medicines-on-palestinian-prisoners/

[795] https://thecradle.co/articles/israels-army-formed-special-intel-unit-to-justify-killing-of-hundreds-of-gaza-journalists

[796] https://x.com/gazanotice/status/1960016078660079911

[797] https://x.com/iwasnevrhere_/status/1950003049457389968

[798] https://www.haaretz.com/opinion/2025-03-30/ty-article-opinion/.premium/in-gaza-almost-every-idf-platoon-keeps-a-human-shield-a-sub-army-of-palestinian-slaves/00000195-e627-deaf-a397-f6674e390000

[799] https://x.com/RamAbdu/status/1933635772554621377

[800] https://www.972mag.com/lavender-ai-israeli-army-gaza/

[801] https://lieber.westpoint.edu/gospel-lavender-law-armed-conflict/

[802] https://scheerpost.com/2025/07/23/israels-genocide-is-big-business-and-the-face-of-the-future/

[803] https://x.com/QudsNen/status/1944088627169878123

[804] https://www.newarab.com/news/ex-israeli-ministers-hint-mossad-behind-controversial-ghf

[805] https://thecradle.co/articles/israel-kills-over-50-aid-seekers-at-ghf-sites-in-one-week-since-launch

[806] https://thecradle.co/articles/washington-stands-alone-at-un-security-council-defending-manmade-famine-in-gaza

---

[807] https://www.ipcinfo.org/fileadmin/user_upload/ipcinfo/docs/IPC_Famine_Review_Committee_Report_Gaza_Aug2025.pdf

[808] https://www.haaretz.com/israel-news/2025-09-16/ty-article-magazine/.premium/i-saw-the-bodies-of-children-moral-injury-and-mental-strain-breaking-idf-soldiers/00000199-5277-d907-a5db-77f7e80d0000
https://x.com/Megatron_ron/status/1967900343770996857

[809] https://www.aa.com.tr/en/middle-east/israeli-channel-exposes-secret-protocols-showing-netanyahu-blocked-gaza-ceasefire-hostage-swap-deal/3650671

[810] https://www.972mag.com/netanyahu-hamas-october-7-adam-raz/

[811] https://x.com/QudsNen/status/1960367837270131078

[812] https://www.bitchute.com/video/DhocC675NmtK

[813] https://witnessing-the-gaza-war.com/appendix-1-why-genocide-18-6-24/

[814] https://www.ohchr.org/sites/default/files/documents/hrbodies/hrcouncil/sessions-regular/session60/advance-version/a-hrc-60-crp-3.pdf

[815] https://genocidescholars.org/wp-content/uploads/2025/08/IAGS-Resolution-on-Gaza-FINAL.pdf

[816] https://www.theguardian.com/world/2023/oct/31/un-official-resigns-israel-hamas-war-palestine-new-york

[817] https://www.thelancet.com/journals/lancet/article/PIIS0140-6736(24)01169-3/fulltext

[818] https://dataverse.harvard.edu/dataset.xhtml?persistentId=doi%3A10.7910%2FDVN%2FQB75LB

[819] https://stevendonziger.substack.com/p/shock-israel-has-killed-207-of-gazas

[820] https://x.com/MaxBlumenthal/status/1951024104993177945

[821] https://www.middleeasteye.net/news/majority-israelis-support-expulsion-palestinians-gaza-poll

[822] https://x.com/GUnderground_TV/status/1960359718930530570

[823] https://web.archive.org/web/20240606043728/https://www.nytimes.com/2024/06/06/world/middleeast/israel-gaza-detention-base.html

[824] https://today.lorientlejour.com/article/1477139/a-crime-against-childhood-in-aita-al-shaab-israel-destroys-a-school-for-children-with-disabilities.html

[825] https://www.nytimes.com/2023/08/07/world/middleeast/gaza-strip-protests-hamas.html

[826] https://thefreedomarticles.com/hamas-israel-agree-ceasefire-to-vax-gazan-kids/

CHAPTER 18: CULT CONTROL OF BRICS, THE CULTIVATED OPPOSITION FOR WWIII

"Iran is Israel's best friend and we do not intend to change our position in relation to Tehran, because Khomeini's regime will not last forever."

– Then Israeli Minister of Defense (and later PM) Yitzhak Rabin in 1987[827]

"Multipolarity is not a system of international relations that insists upon the legal equality of nation-states."

– Russian 'independent' think tank Katehon[828]

Just as the Cult created and controlled the Nazis (as discussed in chapter 8), so too do they control the current enemies and adversaries that are pushed into position on the international stage. The New World Order appears to be led by Israel, the US and the UK, and in many ways those countries are pushing it forward very fast, especially by way of militarily dominating weaker nations. However, the Cult progresses via the Hegelian dialectic of thesis-antithesis-synthesis, or problem-reaction-solution, so in order to take their next step geopolitically, they need one group of countries to oppose another group of countries so that two sides can fight it out. For this reason, they carefully CULT-ivate the opposition. Superficially, the sides battle in what seems to be an intense conflict, while underneath, all sides are controlled by the same force. Let's see how this is playing out right now with the BRICS group, focusing especially on three of their key members: Iran, Russia and China.

Best Frenemies Forever: Israeli-Iranian Covert Cooperation

We'll start by taking a closer look at Iran, since many people are falsely pinning their hopes on this country as the only genuine opposition to Israel in the region. But are these two really enemies … or frenemies?

Iran was targeted early on for its oil by the Cult-led British Empire. After the US became the world's superpower at the end of WWII, and Truman signed off on the creation of the CIA, it wasn't long before Iran was in the crosshairs again, this time American ones. Psychopath Allen Dulles (here he is again) oversaw Operation Ajax in 1953 to overthrow the democratically-elected Mohammad Mosaddegh who wanted to nationalize Iran's oil industry. The CIA installed a king, Shah Mohammad Reza Pahlavi, who held power for over two and a half decades. As mentioned earlier in this book, under the Shah, a new and very brutal police force was established called SAVAK. It was the CIA and the Mossad (along with the French intelligence service SDECE) which helped train SAVAK during its formative years.[829] SAVAK would go on to torture thousands of dissident Iranians during its reign of terror. Israel's strategic doctrine in the 1950s and 1960s, known as the Periphery Doctrine, consisted of Israel building alliances with non-Arab states that were hostile to pan-Arab nationalism. Israel thus joined in a Periphery Alliance with Iran and Türkiye, establishing a pact known as the Trident. This included economic cooperation, intelligence sharing and arms trading. Iran supplied Israel with oil, even after the 1967 Six-Day War when many Arab nations imposed boycotts, and Israel provided

Iran with advanced agricultural and technological assistance, helping them develop infrastructure.

The year 1979 was one of great upheaval for Iran as the Islamic Revolution deposed the Shah and brought Ayatollah Khomeini to power. Khomeini's signature rhetoric was to vehemently denounce Israel as a tool of Western imperialism and deny its legitimacy to exist as a nation. Under Khomeini, Iran severed diplomatic ties with Israel, expelled Israeli personnel and gave the Israeli embassy in Tehran to the PLO. However, despite these actions and the impressive-sounding rhetoric, Khomeini's impassioned tirades were just words, not policy. At deeper levels, the Israeli-Iranian connection continued to flourish. More than just exist, it would actually strengthen, since the very next year, the Iran-Iraq War would begin, which was to last 8 years from 1980 to 1988. During this time, Israel took Iran's side and sold them tons of weapons. In 1982, then Israeli Defense Minister Ariel Sharon announced on television that Israel would continue selling weapons to Iran, even in spite of American opposition. Iran responded to this announcement with denial and the introduction of a resolution to expel Israel from the UN – but it was all for show. The weapon trade went on. Ex-Israeli spy Ari Ben-Menashe, to whom I have referred many times in this book, details his involvement in the deals, which were linked to the Iran-Contra scandal. Israel feared Saddam Hussein and Iraq much more than they feared Iran, so for them, arming Iran was an obvious choice; Saddam was an actual threat to the Zionist State, unlike the Persians. The covert cooperation between Israel and Iran was so strong that the US worried that Israel could be supplying US-made parts or weapons to Iran.[830] In fact, in 2014, the Jewish Telegraphic Agency reported that two Israeli arms dealers were arrested for trying to sell spare parts for American F-4 Phantom jets to Iran.[831]

Despite the positioning of Iran as Israel's biggest enemy, and a thorn in America's side, the truth is far more nuanced. Did you know that in October 2001, Iran fought alongside US military against the Taliban in a war in Herat, Afghanistan? Javad Zarif, later Iran's Foreign Minister, agreed that Iran would accept the possibility of US jets accidentally flying through its air space during a US attack on Iraq.[832] This was the same Zarif who said, *"Israel has turned the Islamic Republic into a security threat, and Iran has played into this narrative, claiming, 'Yes, I am that threat.'"*[833] Zarif spoke at a Chatham House event in 2016,[834] an organization connected to the Royal Institute for International Affairs (RIIA), part of the Round Table group of NWO think tanks. Is this something you would expect from a nation that was genuinely opposed to the NWO? Former Iranian President Hassan Rouhani also attended and spoke in 2014 at Davos, the elite annual meeting of the World Economic Forum.[835] Iranian leaders appear to be part of the club.

Other past and current Iranian leaders have Cult connections, too. It turns out that former President Mahmoud Ahmadinejad, who made headlines for his supposed 'Holocaust Denial,' has Jewish heritage. His original family name was Sabourjian, which in Iran is officially listed as a Jewish name, meaning 'cloth weaver.' He is a crypto-Jew; is he a Sabbatean-Frankist? Current Supreme leader Ali Khamanei is a graduate of Russia's Patrice Lumumba University or 'Friendship University.'[836] According to Yuri Bezmenov, this massive university was under the direct control of the Committee for State Security (KGB) and the Central Committee, where *"future leaders of the so-called 'National Liberation Movements' [were] being educated and selected carefully."*[837] The KGB was dissolved in 1991 but was succeeded by the Foreign Intelligence Service (SVR) and what would later become the Federal Security Service (Federalnaya Sluzhba Bezopasnosti or FSB). Interestingly, another important Middle Eastern leader also attended the Friendship University – none other than Mahmoud Abbas, chairman of Fatah and the PLO, and the president of the PA.[838] So, the minds of several Arab and Muslim leaders have been shaped by Russian intelligence. To what degree are these men controlled by the Cult?

During the 1979 Islamic Revolution, the Iranian priestly class of mullahs came to power. According to Gust Avrakotos, a CIA agent featured in *Charlie Wilson's War* by George Crile, at the time of the Islamic Revolution, half of the mullahs (40,000) were on the KGB payroll, and the other half were on the Mossad payroll.[839] As mentioned earlier, the SAVAK was trained and established by American, Israeli and French intelligence; and then in 1979 the mullahs were influenced or controlled by Russian and Israeli intelligence. Israeli intelligence is the common denominator in both regimes, but regardless of that, at the very highest levels, all the world's intelligence agencies lead back to the Satanic Cult that runs the world. In the first few days of the 12-Day War, due to the Mossad infiltration of Iran, Israel was able to successfully target and assassinate numerous senior Iranian commanders and scientists. The Mossad also successfully smuggled weapons into Iran ahead of the strikes that targeted Iran's defense from within (explosive drones targeted missile launchers near Tehran). It is clear that the Mossad has deeply penetrated Iran; in an incredibly rare move, the Mossad even released video from some of its operations inside the country.[840]

Image #116: Iran's pyramidal parliament building. Note the 33 windows

Iran is home to the most Jews in the Middle East outside of Israel. Are most of these Jews genuinely anti-Zionist, or has the Iranian Jewish community become a breeding ground for the Mossad to recruit agents and sayanim? Iran's Parliament or Majlis building is a giant pyramid with 33 windows. Just as Iran opposed Saddam Hussein in the 1980s, who was a genuine threat to Zionist regional supremacy, Iran also (very strangely) welcomed the death of Libyan leader Muammar Gaddafi.[841] You would think someone like Gaddafi – clearly a victim of US/NATO imperialism who dared to speak out against Zionism and even accused Israel of being behind JFK's death (see chapter 11) – would be someone whom Iran would protect and support, all the more so because Libya was one of the countries on General Wesley Clark's list of '7 countries in 5 years' … a list that finished off with Iran. Why would Iran cheer on the murder of a nation's leader that was targeted by the US-NATO-Israeli war machine, when Iran itself is on that list and being targeted by that same war machine?

What is *really* going on with Iran?

Israel's and Iran's Performative Wars

For the first time ever, the ongoing tension between Israel and Iran erupted into a physical military conflict in 2024. Since then, the two nations have had three brief military exchanges, known by the Iranians as Operation True Promise I (April 2024), Operation True Promise II (October 2024) and Operation True Promise III (June 2025), with this last one also being known as the 12-Day War. In all three cases, there was something decidedly stage managed and performative about the interactions, leaving astute observers to wonder whether these nations were really at war, or whether they were simply playing their part according to the Cult script. In Operation True Promise I, Iran gave 72 hours notice of their planned attack to the regional countries hosting US military bases, according to Iranian Foreign Minister Hossein Amir-Abdollahian.[842] In similar fashion, for Operation True Promise II, Iran reportedly alerted Arab countries before the attacks (though this time the warning was shorter).[843] For the 12-Day War, Iran knew by March 2025 that it might be hit, so it moved its uranium, according to Iranian scientist Mahmoud Reza Aghamiri and former chief commander of the IRGC and Khamenei advisor Mohsen Rezaie.[844] Iran warned Trump before its final strike (the off ramp to finish the 12-Day War) on the US Military base at Al Udeid in Qatar on June 23rd 2025.[845] In an interview with Fox News, Trump also admitted that Iran *"called me to tell me 'we're going to hit a certain location, but we're not going to hit it. It's going to be outside of the perimeter.'"*[846] Trump was referring to Iran's strike against a US base in Iraq in retaliation for his assassination of Qassem Soleimani. The casual way Trump explained this indicates that this kind of exchange and calculation is part of normal geopolitical diplomacy. Ask yourself: would real war be conducted in this way, where one side alerts the enemy before striking?

There are a few ways to interpret this behavior. It may make the most sense to look at it on a spectrum, with real at one end and fake/performative at the other end. There are many places in between these two poles. One interpretation is that the conflict and war has been real, but Iran is trying to act ethically and to minimize casualties, especially civilian deaths. Another interpretation is that Iran is somewhere in the middle of the spectrum; it really does want to damage and destroy Israel, but doesn't want to risk open war, so it engages in controlled brinkmanship. It knows it has to strike back at Israel to save face, to pacify its domestic population and to back up its claim to be a leader, or the leader, of the Islamic world. So, to this end, it doles out anti-Zionist rhetoric, proxy warfare, public posturing, symbolic missile attacks and a controlled geopolitical spectacle, all carefully calibrated to let off some steam while maintaining pressure and not provoking an all-out war. A third interpretation is that all of the brief Israeli-Iranian military conflicts from 2024 and 2025 are essentially theater. The leaders of each nation may enjoy hurting the other, but they are actors that have to keep to the scripted events where the Cult, as usual, controls both sides. Both sides use each other as the archenemy and the external threat in order to pander to and impress their domestic audiences, bolster nationalism, unite divergent factions and deflect from internal problems. Meanwhile, both countries toe the line, follow the NWO agenda and push their populations forward step by step into a totalitarian One World Government.

Cult-Controlled Russia

We can trace the control of Russia by the Cult back to some of the key events already covered in this book: namely, the 1815 Vienna Conference (where the Tsar of Russia saw through the Rothschild plan to form a world government and rejected it) and the 1917 Russian Revolution (where the Rothschilds got revenge on the Tsar and his family, killing them and installing the murderous Bolshevik regime). This was followed up by the 1917-1922 Russian Civil War between the Reds (the Bolsheviks) and the Whites (the right-leaning officers of the Russian Empire). Since at least that time, over 100 years ago now, the Cult has controlled Russia, including during WWII and its aftermath, the Cold War. The USSR was one of the two world superpowers for all of its existence, and it did a tremendous job of pushing Communism throughout the world. Although the Cult played off the ideologies of capitalism and Communism against each other in Hegelian fashion for maximum benefit, it is crucial to know that Communism, being derived from marxism, is a Cult creation that has resulted in untold suffering for humanity. Marxism was dreamt up by the Cult who used Karl Marx to put his name on the theory and spread it. Later on, the Frankfurt School in Germany spread cultural marxism which may have been just as deadly for human freedom, as it has led to political correctness and woke ideology. Historical leaders of Communistic countries have killed millions of their own people and other people through democide, famines and wars. Although the USSR has dissolved and modern-day Russia has embraced capitalism more than before, the legacy of Communism still remains throughout the world, and still lives on in China, a country we will look at shortly.

Although a sizable portion of the Alternative Media has portrayed Russian President Vladimir Putin in a good light, and has sympathized with Russia during the Russo-Ukraine War which broke out in 2022, the truth is that Russia, like Iran, cannot offer genuine opposition to the Cult since it has itself been infiltrated. Putin, a former KGB agent, rose through the ranks to become the Director of the FSB, appointed by then-President Boris Yeltsin. Putin held this role for around one year before leaving to step into his new appointment as Russian Prime Minister. Once a spy, always a spy; you never truly leave the intelligence community. In a 2017 speech,[847] WEF founder Klaus Schwab mentioned Putin as a Young Global Leader, but Putin is not mentioned on any archived member list. Did Schwab misspeak? Perhaps, but Putin has been on very good terms with him nonetheless. Putin was also excellent friends with war criminal and mega insider Henry Kissinger, who was, as I suggested in *The International Satanic Network Exposed*, extremely high up (and potentially the highest) in the human hierarchy of the Satanic Cult. Putin himself is not above using a false flag operation to consolidate his power; he has blood on his hands from the 1999 apartment bombing in Ryazan, Russia, which he used to his advantage to change the public perception of him. His tough military response to the bombings transformed his image from an obscure nobody to a great crisis leader. The 'bad guys' to take the fall were the Chechens. This is why around the time of 9/11 Putin was hoping to form more of an alliance with George Bush Jr. and the US, so that together they could fight 'terrorism' which was the new concept

Image #117: Putin and Kissinger were old friends until Kissinger's death

being pushed on the public in both Russia and the West. Iain Davis writes:[848]

Putin had operational control of the organisation that planned and carried out the Russian apartment bombings. The highly coordinated and well-planned operation killed 317 Russian men, women and children and injured approximately 630 more in just 17 days. Putin then exploited the resultant public fear and anger to seize power. The only reason you haven't heard more about the Russian apartment bombings from the West's corporate-controlled media is that Western power brokers treat the people that they claim to rule with equal disdain. To expose Russia's pivotal false flag operation would be to expose the West's own. Russia had its 9/11 and 7/7 first.

And now we return to Chabad Lubavitch, who become very relevant to the story. Although Chabad has a presence in America, they are far from the only Jewish sect or organization with power. The situation is different in Russia; according to some rabbis, *"Judaism in Russia is run 98% by Chabad."*[849] This same rabbi describes Putin's very close relationship with the Jews, stemming from the fact he was taken in by a Jewish family as a boy. When Putin was a young child, he lived in an apartment building in St. Petersburg, and when he would come home from school, his parents were out working, so he ended up spending time with a religious Hasidic Jewish family that lived in an adjacent apartment. When there was nobody to take care of him, they would take him in, he would do his homework with them, and so he spent his days growing up in the house of Orthodox Jews. This formed Putin's character and has led to him looking very favorably upon Jewish interests within Russia, as well as upon Israel. The rabbi continued:

Image #118: Putin with his very good friend, Chief Rabbi of Russia, Berel Lazar

One of the other elements for the success of Judaism in Russia ... has been the friendship to the Jewish world of the President of Russia, which is Vladimir Putin ... Putin may not be good for Russia, but he's definitely good for the Jews of Russia.

One the key figures involved in the Jewish supervision of Putin is Rabbi Berel Lazar, who is an Orthodox, Chabad-Lubavitch Hasidic rabbi. Lazar is so well known for his friendship with Putin that he is sometimes called 'Putin's rabbi.' Lazar is one of only two Chief

Rabbis of Russia, and his connection to Chabad Lubavitch is very strong, since his parents were among the first emissaries of Rabbi Menachem Mendel Schneerson, the Jewish supremacist first introduced in chapter 2 who believed that Jewish and non-Jewish souls were completely different entities, and that non-Jews were made to serve Jews. Lazar, who also spent time in America in his youth and speaks fluent English, has said the following about Putin, Russia, Israel and the Jews:

"Putin loves Israel."[850]

"There's practically a daily briefing ... Russia to Israel, Israel to Russia ... about what's going on in Syria."[851]

"Politically, Russia and Israel are very, very strong ... they're on the phone every single day .... whatever Russia is doing today in Middle East is fully in coordination with Israel."[852]

The Russian-Jewish connection is indeed very strong and very significant. Although up to this point I have focused on how America has helped Israel, and the CIA-Mossad alliance, the truth is that Israel was built up by Russia, and maintains a very close relationship with Russia despite its relationship with US. Stalin's USSR was the first country to grant de jure recognition to Israel on May 17th 1948, just three days after the Israeli Declaration of Independence; almost two million Russian-speaking Jews live in Israel, which is a sizable percentage (close to 20%) given that Israel's total population is only about 10 million. Since the fall of the Soviet Union, hundreds of thousands of Russian Jews emigrated to Israel, and many are dual Russian-Israeli citizens. Whatever Israel's exact relationship is with the US, the CIA knows that whatever Israel gets or steals from America, it most likely gives to Russia; likewise, whatever alliance

Image #119: Putin hosts the black hat rabbis

Russia has with Iran, it also helps Israel – for example, in 2012, WikiLeaks publicized an email exchange between employees of Stratfor, the US-based global intelligence company, which showed that Israel and Russia swapped military codes for other nations' weapons systems: *"Israel gave Russia the 'data link codes' for unmanned aerial vehicles that the Jewish state sold to Georgia, and in return, Russia gave Israel the codes for Tor-M1 missile defense systems that Russia sold Iran."*[853] During the 12-Day War, Putin said that Moscow would not help Iran militarily despite the recent strategic agreement signed between them, explaining that Russia must stay neutral because *"almost two million people from the former Soviet Union and the Russian Federation reside in Israel. It is almost a Russian-speaking country today. And, undoubtedly, we always take this into account in Russia's contemporary history."*[854]

The infiltration goes both ways. Just as the Mossad infiltrates the intelligence agencies of other countries, so too do those countries attempt to infiltrate the Mossad. It seems the Russians have had past success in doing this; a 1987 article *"Soviet spies infiltrate Mossad, sources say"* details how the Russians got agents in Israel and thus got their hands on US intelligence, including that stolen by Jonathan Pollard:[855]

A Justice Department source said U.S. counterintelligence agents became aware of the Israeli-Soviet espionage pipeline when data stolen by Jonathan Jay Pollard, a U.S. Navy analyst convicted of spying for Israel, was 'traced to the Eastern bloc.' Intelligence sources said data reaching the Soviets via this route included sensitive U.S. weapons technology and strategic information about the defense forces of Turkey, Pakistan and moderate Arab countries, including Saudi Arabia. U.S. intelligence analysts said the Pollard data was traded to the Soviets in return for promises to increase emigration of Soviet Jews to Israel.

Image #120: empty dark suits – i.e. Cult agents devoid of empathy – run the world, including Eurasia

In 2017, Putin commented that 'dark suits' run the US and whatever figurehead puppet president that gets installed in the White House:[856]

You know, I've communicated with one US president, and with the second, and with the third ... presidents come and go but the politics remains the same. Do you know why that is? Because the bureaucracy has a lot of power. So a person is elected, he comes with his ideas. Then people with briefcases come to visit him – well dressed, in dark suits, kind of like mine. Except instead of a red tie it's black or navy. And then they explain what to do, and the whole rhetoric changes, you see? This happens from one administration to the next.

What he didn't say, however, is that the same goes for many countries, including Russia itself. The Cult, via the central bank, the military forces and intelligence agencies of each nation, runs the world. Unfortunately for those desperately wanting freedom and peace in the world, and an escape from the impending NWO, Russia is no different. The truth is that Russia is pushing the same technocratic agenda as the US and the West, but in some ways even harder, because as explained earlier, power is moving east, and China-Russia is the next planned center of world power for the NWO conspirators. Here are some of the recent moves Russia has made:

– Banning Virtual Private Networks (VPNs), which help internet anonymity;[857]

– Building trial 15 minute cities;[858]

– Trialling biometric terminals in 2020[859] and planning a nationwide facial recognition payment system later this year (in 2025);[860]

– Pushing the digital ruble, part of the Cult banking agenda to make everyone use programmable money, regardless of whether they call it 'CBDC' or 'stablecoin.' Russia is setting a rollout date of September 1st 2026;[861]

– Supporting UN Agenda 2030, including the World Health Organization (WHO), the Pandemic Treaty, 'sustainable development,' the manmade climate change hoax, carbon markets and a carbon tax (as revealed by the "Joint Statement of the Russian Federation and the People's Republic of China on the International Relations Entering a New Era and the Global Sustainable Development" from February 4th 2022 posted on the Kremlin website);[862]

– Pushing AI society-wide, the ultimate Cult agenda to enslave humanity as AI encompasses the entire world.[863]

Given all this evidence, if you live in the West and can recognize the Cult control over the US, UK, EU and all other Western nations, do you still think Russia is going to defeat the NWO and come to save you?

Cult-Controlled China

For the Cult, China is the model they want to export to the rest of the world. China is the rising world superpower, having already overtaken the USA in metrics such as trade and GDP by PPP (purchasing power parity). Do you think that the Cult, whose stated goal is world domination, would therefore not do everything it could to ensure its control over China? China is not only Cult-controlled but is the model for the coming technocratic, totalitarian NWO. Despite its harsh authoritarian rule, many globalist insiders have expressed their admiration for China, such as hated former Canadian PM Justin Trudeau,[864] WEF founder and transhumanist Klaus Schwab[865] and the late banker David Rockefeller, at one time head of the NWO bloodline Rockefeller family. In fact, here is what Rockefeller said in a 1973 article published in the NYT (see image #121):[866]

Whatever the price of the Chinese Revolution, it has obviously succeeded not only in producing more efficient and dedicated administration, but also in fostering high morale and community of purpose ... The social experiment in China under Chairman Mao's leadership is one of the most important and successful in human history.

If the NWO conspirators are extolling the virtues of someone, you'd better steer clear of that person. Mao Tse-Tung, as it turns out, was given funding by none other than America's Yale University, where he was encouraged to spread marxist thought.[867] Yale is a Cult stomping ground which has produced many famous spies, including James Angleton, as well as two alums which went on to become CIA Directors, George Bush Sr. and James Woolsey. History professor Robin Winks, author of the book *Cloak and Gown: Scholars in the Secret War 1939-1961*, said:[868]

From Yale's class of 1943 alone, at least 42 young men entered intelligence work, largely in the OSS, many to remain on after the war to form the core of the new CIA ... Rightly or wrongly, a historian could, in assessing the link between the university and the agency, declare in 1984 that Yale had influenced the CIA more than any other university did.

Yale is also home to the infamous Order of the Skull and Bones (also called Order 322 and The Brotherhood of Death), a secret society which has filled the American aristocracy for centuries. In the 2004 presidential race, both political leaders in the two-party system (George Bush Jr. for the Republicans and John Kerry for the Democrats) were 'Bonesmen' from this order. George Bush Sr. and Prescott Bush were also members. Initiation rituals include lying naked in a coffin and revealing all your sexual secrets, plus many other dark ceremonies and Satanic rituals using real human skulls. Of course, the information given during these rituals by new initiates could easily be used against them for blackmailing purposes later on to control them when they are in positions of power.

To return to Yale-linked Mao, the Chinese authoritarian went on to establish a highly centralized and ruthless government. His

The New York Times

PLAY THE CROSSWORD

From a China Traveler

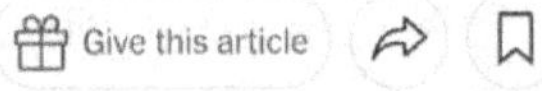

By David Rockefeller
Aug. 10, 1973

One is impressed immediately by the sense of national harmony. From the loud patriotic music at the border onward, there is very real and pervasive dedication to Chairman Mao and Maoist principles. Whatever the price of the Chinese Revolution, it has obviously succeeded not only in producing more efficient and dedicated administration, but also in fostering high morale and community of purpose.

The social experiment in China under. Chairman Mao's leadership is one of the most important and successful in human history. How extensively China opens up and how the world interprets and reacts to the social innovations and life styles she has developed is certain to have a profound impact on the future of many nations.

Image #121

Cultural Revolution instilled fear in the hearts of Chinese citizens who were forbidden at one point from owning violins or anything Western (because that was deemed capitalistic and 'bad'). Censorship was at off the charts. His Great Leap Forward caused the 1959–1961 Great Chinese Famine, making it the largest or second-largest famine in human history, and led to the death of an estimated 15 to 55 million people. China has been racing forward for a long time with population surveillance, but unlike in the West, where there are at least nominal protections for individual rights, in the Chinese collectivist Communistic system, there are none. The result is millions of cameras watching you everywhere, and even electronic billboards which display the face, name and other details of certain citizens who have broken the rules (some of them by innocent offenses such as jaywalking) in an attempt to publicly shame them.

China is racing forward on the technological front. At the time of writing, it has implanted brain chips into three different people.[869] Despite whatever flowery rhetoric the NWO controllers use, this is in preparation for the coming neural net or similar technology where people will be connected to the internet via brain chips, microchips, nano chips or some kind of electronic mesh. The AI race that the NWO manipulators are trying to sell the public worldwide is fake; what is occurring is actually vast, interconnected AI cooperation, where China and the US are helping each other in equal parts to build the AI control grid – because they are both controlled by the Cult. The US and China have co-authored over 47,000 research papers on AI.[870]

In 2009, both China[871] and Russia[872] proposed the idea of a global currency managed by the International Monetary Fund (IMF), an organization set up and run by Cult international banksters.

Another example of many is that Trump let US corporation Nvidia sell AI chips to China.[873] If the US and China were really deadly foes or even competitive adversaries, why would Trump allow this? The answer is simple. Because, at the very top, they are all on the same side. They are all working together towards a common goal – the enslavement of the rest of their populations who are not in the tiny 0.01% upper class. All the political talk about enemies and future wars is just for public consumption. There may be future wars, but they will be orchestrated Cult productions.

BRICS = Controlled Opposition

And so that brings us to BRICS, the group that has formed in opposition to the US-led West and which is rapidly expanding its membership. The original five members, from which BRICS got its name, were Brazil, Russia, India, China and South Africa. Recently, the group has added other Eurasian regional powers such as Iran and Saudi Arabia. Is BRICS genuine opposition that will save us from the US-led NWO? Not on your life. Right from the start, BRICS was a Cult creation, just like so many other things as I have shown in this book. The acronym BRICS itself was thought up at Goldman Sachs, a long-time Western financial institution with deep ties to the Cult. At first, it was just BRIC before South Africa joined.

All of the five original BRICS members have plans for programmable money, irrespective of whether they call it a CBDC or something else. Unfortunately, all of the digital money systems they are trialling have 'interoperability' baked into the formula, meaning eventual integration into the planned NWO international digital financial system. BRICS members Iran, Russia and China all participated in and fully promoted the hoax that was the COVID 'pandemic' (or better put the COVID scamdemic), following draconian and illogical WHO pandemic protocols, which meant enforcing mask wearing, digital health monitoring, lockdowns and vaccination mandates. BRICS touts its vision of a 'multipolar world order' however upon closer examination this does not appear to be a genuine alternative to a bankster-led One World Government, but rather a pushback against the exploitative domination for over a century of the US-led West. The multipolar world order doesn't resist the Cult or their globalist frameworks, but rather seems like a tamer variant of the same NWO, just with more power being given to the East and Global South rather than the West. In their own ways, BRICS member states actively conduct or promote climate control laws, internal surveillance of their own populations, censorship, digital IDs and AI governance. As stated above, the most powerful BRICS nations, Russia and China, released a statement enthusiastically supporting Agenda 2030. Iain Davis writes:[874]

The multipolar world order ends the last vestiges of national sovereignty. It is the geopolitical Great Reset: the culmination of the oligarch's longstanding plan to establish a system of global governance that affords them dominion over all. If the multipolar system proceeds, which seems likely, the 193 nations—give or take—of the world will eventually be incorporated into a few global poles.

This aligns 100% with the known modus operandi of the Cult – advance incrementally, step by step, so as to dilute resistance to the end goal. If the final goal is one centralized dictatorial world government controlling everything, then creating regional blocs or poles along the way is simply a necessary step. This plot is not about sharing power equally; that's just the selling point.

BRICS is opposition? Give me a break!

The Khazarian Cult Lusts after its Original Homeland … Ukraine

There is a deeper agenda behind the Russo-Ukraine War than merely just US imperialism or NATO expansion. The truth is that Ukraine occupies the land where the Kingdom of Khazaria used to be! That's right: Ukraine is modern-day Khazaria. This truth is borne out by the not-so-hidden Israeli-Ukrainian connection. For example, in 2022, Ukrainian President Volodymyr Zelensky (also spelt Zelenskyy) said that *"Ukraine will be like a Big Israel"* and that his *"vision for Ukraine's post-conflict future included having armed forces in 'all institutions, supermarkets, cinemas, there will be people with weapons.' In Israel, images of armed civilians, settlers and soldiers are commonplace, and the government invokes security frequently. Zelenskyy, who is Jewish, has on several occasions stressed the importance of*

Image #122: Zelensky (4th from right) with the Chabad Lubavitch black hat rabbis

Image #123: Valerii Zaluzhnyi (left), who is being groomed to be the next Ukrainian president, holds a menorah with a Temple of Solomon in the background

maintaining close ties with Israel, which he hailed as a model for Ukraine."[875] Israel has been arming Ukraine the entire time; Israeli Ambassador to Ukraine Michael Brodsky revealed that the IDF has been giving Patriot missile defense systems to Ukraine.[876] Israel has also been supplying electronic warfare systems to Ukraine so it can defend against drone attacks; since Russia has been using Iranian-made drones against Ukraine, Israel also benefits from this by seeing how their tech performs against Iranian made weapons.[877] In fact, the connection between Israel and Ukraine is so strong that in January 2025, Israeli government official Sharren Haskel proposed handing over Russian-made weapons (seized from Hezbollah in Lebanon) to Ukraine.[878] Zelensky was injected with popularity and made into a president only due to Ukrainian-born Israeli billionaire oligarch Ihor Kolomoisky, who was also funding the corrupt drug addict Hunter Biden.[879] Meanwhile, the crest of Ukraine, the symbol by which Ukraine is well known, very closely resembles the Khazarian tamga (see image #124). The tamga is defined as an abstract seal or brand used by Eurasian nomads initially as a livestock branding for a particular tribe, clan or family. There are some who even suggest that both the Ukrainian crest and the Khazarian tamga resemble the Moloch sigil with an inverted pentagram.

Another clue to the Khazarian connection behind the Russo-Ukraine War comes from former Chabad leader, Rebbe Schneerson. There is a purported record of a speech he made revealing his plans for decimating the Slavs by instigating a war between Ukraine and Russia. It is difficult to prove the authenticity of the speech, however it was published in the Vologda newspaper 'Slavyanin' in 2001 in Russia; the speech is alleged to have been given in 1994. I will reproduce parts of it below (with slight grammatical edits). Given everything we know about the Satanic Cult, the Khazars, Sabbatean-Frankism, Israel and Chabad Lubavitch, it rings true, but I will just present the information; you be the judge as to how authentic it is. There can be no doubt that the plan it describes has been happening not only in the Slavic world but all over the planet:[880]

First of all, we will divide the Slavic nations (of 300 million, half of them Russians) into the small countries with weak and severed connections. For this, we will use our old method: Divide and conquer. We will try to pit these countries against each other, and suck them into civil wars for the sake of mutual destruction. The Ukrainians would think that they are fighting against the expansionist Russia and struggling for their independence. They would think that they have finally gained their freedom, while they become fully subdued by us. The same will be thought by Russians, as though they defend their national interests to return their lands, "illegally" taken away from them, and so on. We will do all of this under the guise of different sovereignties, the struggle for their national ideals. At the same time, we will not give either party any self-determination, based on the national values and traditions. In this war of fools, the Slavic moronic herd will be weakening itself and strengthening us, the main controllers of the chaos ... Moreover, we will fully protect ourselves. In the consciousness of the Slavic fools (uninitiated), we will lay such stereotypes of thinking in which the world "anti-Semite" would become the most terrible word. The word "Jew" would be pronounced in a whisper.

We will not allow any nationalism to evolve. And we will destroy by fire and sword all those nationalist movements that seek to lead people out of our dictate, as it is done in Georgia, Armenia and Serbia. Instead, we will insure the full prosperity of our nationalism –

Crest of Ukraine **Khazarian Tamga**

Map of

New Khazaria
&
Greater Israel

"Blocking the Great Silk Road"

RUSSIA
EU
TARTARIA
NEW
KHAZARIA
Kiev
Rabbi Shneerson City
Sarkel
CRIMEA
Kerch
Istanbul
Black Sea
Atil
GHUZZ
Aral Sea
Caspian Sea
KHWARIZM
Shivat Sion
Tel-Tsion
Tel-Ha-Bustan
GREATER
Bik'at Ha-Yam
Aram-Tsova
Shaar-Kadesh
Damesek
Bagdad
Shoshan
YERUSHALAIM
IRAN
Tel Amuna
Kochau-Yair
Eitsion-Gever
Maoz-Tzur
Hereu-Gidon
ISRAEL
Goshen
Einau
Medina
Arayot
Tel-Dor
Reut
Eitam
Negba
FRICA
communitarian.ru

Images #124 & 125: will Greater Israel extend all the way to Ukraine to form a New Khazaria?

Zionism, and, more precisely: Jewish fascism, which, in its secrecy and power, is super-fascism. It is not for nothing that in 1975, the UN General Assembly adopted a resolution which defined Zionism as the most blatant "form of racism and racial discrimination", but repealed this resolution in 1992, because of our triumphant march across the planet. We have made [the] UN a weapon for our goals of seizing power over "all kingdoms and nations."

We will deprive the population of Slavs of their national elite, which is the one that determines the development of events and the progress of the country, and, ultimately, the whole course of history. To do this, we will lower their level of education – in the next five years, we will close half of their universities, and it is us who will get educated at the other half.

We will allow the Armenians there, Chechens, Gypsies and others. We will work to ensure that the governments of the Slavic countries would contain as little as possible of the indigenous peoples who will be replaced by our Jewish elite. In the mass media – radio, television, press, art, literature, theater, cinema – we will gradually push out national staff and replace them with our staff or, in extreme cases, the cosmopolitan staff. We will undertake the reform in education, and limit the teaching of subjects that strengthen and systematize the thought process in the left and the right brain hemispheres: a) Language and Literature, b) Physics and Mathematics. As for the history, there is nothing to say. We will give our own history to the cattle, and show that the entire human evolution was moving towards the recognition of the God's chosen nation of Jews to be masters over the entire world. Corrupt the youth and make them perverts – and you win the nation! This is our motto. We will deprive your community of young people, degrading it with sex, rock music, violence, alcohol, smoking, drugs, that is, we will deprive your society of the future. We will strike at the family, destroying it, we will reduce [the] birth rate.

These grandiose goals will be implemented in several stages. Already 85% of the continental shelf of the Arctic Ocean ended up in our hands, thanks to confusing agreements signed under Gorbachev and Yeltsin and that are not explained to the people (the general public is not yet aware of it) ... However, there is still a structured organization – the Orthodox clergy. We will send there the members of our Jewish clergy, who will become Russian Orthodox Priests. Talmud permits them to perform the rituals of other religions, keeping intact their Judaism deep inside.

We will bribe the rest of them. And we will destroy those who will not succumb to us. Russians no longer have any more or less organized structures, and cattle cannot unite and establish them, because Russian cattle already became drunkards and got degraded, and is incapable of structuring. In the last century, the United States purchased Alaska from Russia. In the XXI century, the US will buy the entire Siberia, including Siberian territory between the Yenisei River to the West, the Pacific Ocean in the East and the border of China, between the Arctic Ocean in the North and Mongolia and North Korea in the south. These lands are two times higher than the territory of the United States. An acre of land will be purchased for as low as $1,000, and for the entire Siberia, the US will pay $3 trillion over 20 years. Annual payments will be $200 million, half of which will be spent on the purchase of goods in the United States.

For all these activities paramount for us, we will give monarchy to [the] Slavic cattle under the guise of "democratic transition." Everyone in the herd will get a puppet president ... We will have in

Image #126: the late Rebbe Schneerson (right), leader of Chabad Lubavitch and a Jewish supremacist to his core, speaks to a young Benjamin Netanyahu (left)

our hands only the strings attached to the hands of the president. And we'll pull these strings in such a way as it is necessary to the implementation of our grandiose plan of conquering all the tribes and kingdoms, their subordination to our superior nation, chosen by God of Israel.

But money is most important. Money do[es] everything. Money [is] power. Money [is] force. Man with money has weapons, most advanced weapons, and the army of mercenaries. Money owns [the] media, which is fooling the billions of human cattle. Money bribe[s] the people we need. Money eliminate[s] those who do not submit to us. Money bomb[s] those resisting us – Iraqis, Serbs, and, in the future – Russians. Capital and taking power decide everything. We practice our skills in the accumulation of capital and the seizure of power for more than three millennia, and no one will defeat us in this. You [cattle] do not have money. You [cattle] do not have power. And you [cattle] will not ever have money and power. We will not give money and power to you! We hate you immensely! This hatred gives us strength to smile charmingly in your face. Our hatred gives us strength to win your trust and control you [cattle] under the guise of "care" about you and your children, grandchildren and your great grandchildren who would never be born.

World reserves of industrial raw materials are depleted, and by the beginning of the next millennium, "Western society" will not be able to retain its current level of consumption without replenishment from new sources – the colonial countries-donors. Therefore, our aspirations are directed at Russia now with the dual purpose: first – the elimination of the most powerful and independent empire, which occupies one-sixth of the earth. The second is the acquisition of its wealth, which constitute 60-70% of total world reserves of raw materials and 75-80% of open world's oil and gas reserves that are concentrated in Siberia and the continental shelf of the Arctic Ocean.

Finally, the speech ends with the all-important acknowledgement that the Satanic Cult that runs Israel is lusting after its true ancestral homeland – not in the Middle East, but in the Caucasus:

Looking back in history, it must be admitted that these lands are the ancient ancestral lands of the Jewish Khazaria, that is Israel, captured by Kiev's Rus (the ancient state of Russia with the capital in Kiev) in the tenth century. The Slavs are temporary guests on these lands and are subject to eviction. We will return this territory, and build the Great Khazaria – the Jewish state – on these fertile lands the same way as, 50 years ago, we created Israel, squeezing the Palestinians out. Israelis will partially relocate here, and we will drive Slavic cattle out far to the north, beyond Moscow. There will be a small Northern Territory, a reservation with a compact population — a reservation, like Indian reservations in America.

The East Will Not Resist or Offer an Alternative to the Cult-Led NWO

The Cult has been just as active in the East as in the West, bringing many countries in Eurasia under its control for over a century. The Cult conquered the Ottoman Empire in 1908, leading to the creation of modern day Türkiye in 1923. The Cult conquered Russia in 1917, leading to the creation of the USSR in 1922. Via the conquering of the Ottoman Empire, the Cult oversaw the creation of modern day Saudi Arabia in 1932 under Ibn Saud (see chapter 14 for the background to the fake Saudi Royals who are crypto-Jews). The Cult conquered China in 1949, as its pet invention of Communism (derived from marxism) found fertile ground to grow and spread. The Cult infiltrated Iran, causing revolution and chaos there in both 1953 and 1979. Some of the past and present leaders of these Eurasian nations have been trained by the Cult at its universities and think tanks. Given all this, why would we think that any of these nations, or any alliance formed by these nations, would be a genuine alternative to the NWO?

The same dystopian Cult agenda of surveillance, censorship, carbon taxes, social credit scores, smart cities and AI governance is being rolled out in Eurasia – and across the world – as it is in the West. The idea of a multipolar world sounds great in theory, but are the countries pushing this idea, chiefly Russia and China, really interested in a world of shared power including at the citizen level? If so, then why does China rule its citizens in such strict, authoritarian, technocratic style? Or is multipolarity just the means (a stepping stone to centralization) to get to the NWO with as little fuss as possible?

The BRICS alliance is another reminder that no one is going to save us but ourselves. Once enough people stop looking outside – whether to politicians, alliances or anyone else – for heroes and saviors, but rather start looking within and using their own power, we will cease to give our power away to the Satanic Cult which operates via deception. This especially goes for Donald Trump, who is 100% owned by Israel to the point where he unabashedly praises the genocide. This is what he said to thc Israeli Knesset, speaking about American weapons going to Israel to kill Gazans:[881]

Bibi would call me so many times, can you get me this weapon, that weapon ... But we'd get them here, wouldn't we, huh? ... you used them well.

Sources

[827] https://newlinesmag.com/argument/iran-and-israels-covert-pragmatic-friendship/

[828] https://katehon.com/en/1290-multipolarity-the-definition-and-the-differentiation-between-its-meanings.html

[829] https://www.cia.gov/readingroom/docs/CIA-RDP90-00552R000505290007-5.pdf

[830] https://newlinesmag.com/argument/iran-and-israels-covert-pragmatic-friendship/

[831] https://www.jta.org/2014/02/20/israel/israeli-arms-dealers-arrested-for-attempted-arms-sales-to-iran

[832] https://web.archive.org/web/20160307164140/https://www.nytimes.com/2016/03/07/world/middleeast/us-conferred-with-iran-before-iraq-invasion-book-says.html

[833] https://iranwire.com/en/politics/135094-oil-and-weapons-irans-covert-ties-with-israel-in-the-1980s/

[834] https://www.youtube.com/watch?v=oPKhi1hjvgQ

[835] https://www.weforum.org/stories/2014/01/hassan-rouhani-10-quotes-future-iran/

[836] https://www.youtube.com/watch?v=bN_oEJEp9Ro

[837] https://www.eurochicago.com/2011/07/interview-with-yuri-bezmenov/

[838] https://eng.rudn.ru/cooperation/honorary-doctors/mahmoud-abbas/

[839] Charlie Wilson's War, pg. 441

[840] https://www.youtube.com/watch?v=U_H1QL8vGRs

[841] https://www.ynetnews.com/articles/0,7340,L-4137235,00.html

[842] https://www.rferl.org/a/iran-ship-raid-hormuz/32903851.html

[843] https://www.middleeasteye.net/live-blog/live-blog-update/iran-informed-us-shortly-attack-israel-report?nid=394896&topic=Israel%2527s%2520war%2520on%2520Gaza&fid=532396

[844] https://www.dropsitenews.com/p/iran-nuclear-program-united-states-attacks-israel

[845] https://www.cbsnews.com/news/trump-iran-early-notice-qatar-attacks-us-base/

[846] https://www.youtube.com/watch?v=6cL6Sag-X_Y, 8:00 minute mark

[847] https://www.youtube.com/watch?v=AoBRnrtX9U4

[848] https://iaindavis.com/putins-false-flag/

[849] https://www.bitchute.com/video/fm7uxQ6sjYQ1

[850] Ibid.

[851] Ibid.

[852] Ibid.

[853] https://www.ynetnews.com/articles/0,7340,L-4196367,00.html

[854] https://off-guardian.org/2025/07/15/what-did-brics-just-declare/

[855] https://www.upi.com/Archives/1987/12/14/Soviet-spies-infiltrate-Mossad-sources-say/5861566456400/

[856] https://thefreedomarticles.com/dark-suits-rule-us-presidents-putin/

[857] https://thefreedomarticles.com/russia-not-anti-nwo-bans-vpns-builds-15-minute-cities/

[858] Ibid.

[859] https://privacyinternational.org/examples/3560/russia-trials-biometric-payments

[860] https://idtechwire.com/russia-plans-nationwide-facial-recognition-payment-system-in-2025/

[861] https://www.theblock.co/post/363167/russia-2026-digital-ruble-rollout-public-skeptical

[862] http://www.en.kremlin.ru/supplement/5770

[863] https://thefreedomarticles.com/russia-pushes-society-wide-artificial-intelligence/

864 https://www.youtube.com/watch?v=sLTGbtfkh_s

865 https://humanevents.com/2022/11/23/wef-founder-klaus-schwab-says-china-is-role-model-for-many-countries

866 https://www.nytimes.com/1973/08/10/archives/from-a-china-traveler.html

867 https://psypolitics.org/2020/07/05/the-political-career-of-mao-yale-and-the-reorientation-of-thought/

868 https://yaledailynews.com/blog/2002/12/06/yale-spy-story-goes-hollywood/

869 https://rumble.com/v6rwbd7-china-has-implanted-3-humans-with-brain-chips-video-209.html

870 https://seemorerocks.substack.com/p/the-ai-race-the-us-and-china-share

871 https://www.theguardian.com/business/2009/mar/24/china-reform-international-monetary-system

872 https://www.reuters.com/article/markets/currencies/kremlin-aide-imf-should-study-global-currency-idUSL7933144/

873 https://www.dailymail.co.uk/news/article-14907101/trump-america-nvidia-sells-ai-chips-china.html

874 https://iaindavis.com/multipolar-world-order-part-4/

875 https://www.aljazeera.com/news/2022/4/5/zelenskyy-says-wants-ukraine-to-become-a-big-israel

876 https://news.am/eng/news/887103.html

877 https://www.timesofisrael.com/in-first-israel-said-to-authorize-sale-of-defensive-military-equipment-to-ukraine/

878 https://thedefensepost.com/2025/01/22/israel-transfer-weapons-ukraine/

879 https://worldview.stratfor.com/situation-report/ukraine-president-zelensky-and-oligarch-kolomoisky-pandora-papers

880 https://web.archive.org/web/20160522051719/https://justice4poland.com/2016/05/17/chabad-leader-messiah-menachem-mendel-schneerson-on-his-plans-for-destroying-ukraine-and-russia-reprint/

---

[881] https://www.timesofisrael.com/full-text-of-trumps-knesset-speech-youve-won-you-cant-beat-the-world-its-time-for-peace/

CHAPTER 19: THE PLANNED 3RD TEMPLE MESSIANIC ERA = THE AI TOTALITARIAN NWO

"Israel was created as the instrument to bring about the Battle of Armageddon and the fulfillment of prophecy, a war that will be so terrible, where nuclear weapons will be used, so that American citizens and the other people of the world will ... beg for no more war ... the only way we can guarantee no more war is if we destroy the sovereignty of nations and we come together as one humanity in a One World Government."

– Patriot and conspiracy researcher Bill Cooper[882]

"In Jerusalem, the United Nations will build a shrine of the prophets to serve the federated union of all continents; this will be the seat of the Supreme Court of Mankind, to settle all controversies among the federated continents, as prophesied by Isaiah ..."

– First Israeli PM David Ben-Gurion[883]

So far, this book has traced the history of a cult that arose in ancient times in the Middle East, and has carried its deluded and psychopathic lineage all the way down to the current day. It is based on the notion of its own supremacy and of treating anyone outside itself as subhuman. This cult is responsible for some of the most heinous crimes of recorded human history, including its instigation of murderous wars, bloody revolutions, assassinations, false flag operations and genocide. Now, we are entering a period of history where this cult is clamoring for its final goal – the erection of a Third Temple in Israel (built on the "Temple Mount") and the return of the messiah marking the beginning of the messianic or golden era. This religious gobbledygook is not just nonsense but is actually code for something far more sinister.

Even some Israeli leaders can see for themselves that religious fanatics are taking over Israel. Former PM Ehud Olmert has spoken out against the Gaza genocide and the extremist Israeli ministers (like Smotrich and Ben-Gvir who are part of Netanyahu's cabinet) who push for permanent land grabs of Arab territory via settlement expansions and extreme violence against Israel's neighbors. Olmert see them as a greater threat to the country's long-term security than any external foe. *"These guys are the enemy from within,"* he said.[884] These religious fundamentalists are the ones running Israel, a fact which makes a mockery of Netanyahu's and Israel's claims to be an extension or outpost of Western rational or democratic values.

At this point, some perceptive readers may be wondering: *I thought it was the international, secular, atheistic Jews that were behind Zionism and the creation of Israel (as described by people like Winston Churchill, chapter 7). Now you're saying it's the religious Jews running Israel. What happened?* Here's one way to look at it: the Satanic Cult hiding behind and within Judaism wanted to hijack it for their own ends. To do that effectively, they needed to break Jewish adherents from traditional morality. They needed to overthrow moral rabbis and Jewish leaders, supplanting their teachings with a new doctrine of salvation through sin. They needed to destroy religion in order to create a new religion (break the old, create the new, order out of chaos). Playing around with Jewish identity by making 'Jewishness' a race and a nation served the Cult so they could increase new 'Jewish' followers, then gradually convert them to the Satanic doctrine via love of money, love of power, devotion to Israel the nation, etc. They have always sought to control the narrative, and thus put themselves in the position of power where they define what 'Jewishness' means.

What ties it all together is the use of prophecy. I think the most accurate description of prophecy, at least in the way that the Cult uses it, is the skillful manipulation of storytelling and narrative to produce a state of affairs beneficial to the storyteller. In other words, prophecy is a technique of control and manipulation. It is about inculcating a receptive state in listeners or followers so that they believe that the story being told is true or will become true. On deeper levels, prophecy uses hypnotic suggestion to give the story an aura of divinity and inevitability, so that those listening believe that IT IS WRITTEN and divinely ordained to be true or come true. Prophecy not only dilutes resistance to an agenda because of the perceived aura of inevitability, but actually uses the listener's ability to create and manifest (an ability that every single human being has just by virtue of being alive) to make itself come true in a self-fulfilling cycle. The term 'hyperstition' was coined by philosopher Nick Land in the mid-1990s[885] to describe excessive superstition. Hyperstition means the belief in a mythology, story, narrative or prophecy that hastens its physical manifestation.

The trick relies on pulling out some old holy book, written by someone, somewhere (who knows who and who knows when), and using that to justify a current acton. This trick is not particular to Judaism; it has been and still is used by many figures of all religious stripes. It's the same trick that both Sabbatai Zevi and Jacob Frank used when they proclaimed themselves messiah, and they had the added trick of being able to claim that because they were the messiah, it was therefore a period of 'messianic times,' and so 'anything goes.' That meant the inversion of normal moral laws. Prophecy gives the appearance of something divine, religious and supernatural to something that is actually just the plan of some very evil and corrupted individuals (and the dark forces controlling them).

One variation of this scam is the 'end times' hoax. This one has literally been going on for thousands of years! There has always been someone or other proclaiming that the end of the world is just around the corner. The end times hoax is aimed at both Jews and Christians to get them to unite behind the idea of the Third Temple, which I will discuss shortly. The messiah program is essentially identical to the savior program – the disempowering idea that you need some person outside of yourself to save you. Although other religions like Hinduism don't believe in a coming messiah, the hero/savior program can still be seen in the guru culture there, where some traditions insist that to truly learn 'the way,' you have to find a guru and give all your power over to him. Politicians exploit this deep psychological need by framing themselves as the hero, including deliberately standing in front of backdrops so that a seal appears as a halo over their head. The Dune science fiction book series features a secret society group known as the Bene Gesserit who deliberately plant religious stories among common people in societies or planets that they want to infiltrate in the future; then, when the time is ripe, they send one of their agents to appear as the 'hero' or 'messiah' of the story they themselves wrote, and thus they exert control over that society because they have an operative in a respected position of power. This scam works even better when employing religious and superstitious overtones, because people can be brainwashed into not questioning religious figures who they perceive as 'holy' or 'sacred.' Sound familiar?

What is the Third Temple?

For a long time now, Jewish religious extremists have been obsessed with the capturing of Jerusalem, and then within Jerusalem, the capturing of a particular piece of land which is known as Al-Aqsa Mosque or Dome of the Rock to the Muslim world, and Temple Mount to the Jewish world. This temple is to be a 'new Solomon's Temple' and a 'third' temple despite the fact that, as covered earlier in this book, there is no historical evidence that Solomon was a real man who lived in the past, nor historical evidence that the Jews had two previous temples. Remember, the Jews were given their written history around 270 BC based on the works of Plato and other Greeks. Sabbatean-Frankism continued the 12th and 13th century obsession of the Knights Templar ambition to build a 'Solomon's Temple' on the exact point of Dome of the Rock. The fundamentalists claim that the messiah can't come, the messianic era cannot begin and the Jews cannot 'return home' until this third temple is built at the exact location of Al-Aqsa Mosque. So, is this just superstitious fanaticism or is there something else behind this obsession?

To answer that, let's look at what Chabad themselves say about the purpose of the temple. On the webpage entitled "Why On Earth Do We Need a Third Temple?" it brings in, once again, Cult operative Rebbe Schneerson:[886]

In 1953, a young student at Yeshiva University asked the Rebbe, Rabbi Menachem M. Schneerson, how a 20th century world could handle the building of an ancient temple and all the social and ritual changes that come with it. The Rebbe patiently explained that the

Messianic Era is not just a change in demographics. It's a quantum leap in the way human beings perceive their world. Once that change has occurred, things that seem absurd to us today will appear perfectly reasonable.

This is a clue that the building of the third temple is not just about a physical structure but rather something that will affect the perception of humanity. Hmmm … highly intriguing. Remember, the modus operandi of the Cult is infiltration and deception involving the manipulation of perception. This is why the Cult controls the worlds' intelligence agencies so it can manipulate information. Elsewhere on the same webpage are constant references to world peace being achieved after the building of the temple. Is this the kind of peace that dictators promise, which means centralized control for them, no freedom for the people under them, and a break in the infighting between the warlords at the top? Chabad also reveals that the third temple would be a 'gateway of heaven' since it would be a threshold or interface. They don't use the word 'portal' but that is implied. There is another center not that far from Israel, on the border of Switzerland and France, called CERN (with a 666 logo), which is trying to open portals with other dimensions. Strange and mysterious rituals have been filmed at the CERN site.[887] Chabad further states:

An explanation provided by Chabad thought is that the location of the temple is a gateway, or interface, between heaven and earth. The Temple itself, with all its chambers and accoutrements, is a kind of resonance chamber, or amplifier, as well as a broadcaster of that system to the rest of the world.

So, putting this all together, we have a plan to build some kind of structure that will radically alter human perception to the point where humanity will be living in a different age. This building will generate a portal or interface between dimensions, then broadcast some kind of new frequency or technology to the entire world. This dovetails exactly with what David Icke (as well as others like Richard Willett) have been saying about the true function of this temple: as the basis for a new technological control grid for the entire Earth. What if this temple is actually the continuation of what Israel has already been doing for decades – the headquarters or cyber epicenter of planetary-wide control of information (and therefore perception)? In chapter 12, I covered how Israel already had backdoors into microchips and computers around the world. If Israel has a backdoor into everything electronic, this means total control of cyberspace and total control of information … and thus in the end total control of human perception. What if the promised golden age is nothing but a ruse? What if this prophesied 'messianic era' is nothing but another name for the New World Order, regardless of whether you call it The Great Reset, the Fourth Industrial Revolution (4IR), the singularity, the merging of man with machine or the advent of AI Governance? The hard pushing of transhumanism is really posthumanism, because it is the scheme to remove our humanity. The hard pushing of AI is the scheme to bring our thoughts, minds and perception under total control. Given the history of modern-day Israel and how the Cult runs that country, would it really be surprising that they plan to use it as the HQ and the gateway hub for the NWO? Icke writes:[888]

This background to the Smart Grid and Israel's central role in its development and control explains what appears at face value to be crazy claims by these messianic lunatics of the Sabbatian-Frankist Death Cult about installing a 'world ruler' on the throne of Jerusalem at the site of a rebuilt Solomon's Temple. Control of cyberspace in the world as it is today would give them that very control and via an AI connection to the human mind control over all human perception.

Another connecting piece of information here is that the Israel-Palestine zone sits at the intersection of three continents: Europe, Asia and Africa. Important planetary ley lines intersect at this point, which may explain the historical importance given to Jerusalem by many cultures. Its geopolitical and energetic location may make Jerusalem in general, and the Dome of the Rock in particular, a highly significant location as a command center for a control grid. Icke reminds us that the Sabbatean-Frankist Cult uses words very differently to the rest of us, including to the rest of non-Cult Jews: *"To the Death Cult, the arrival of 'Zion' is the arrival of their global control system which is being constructed all around us every day. Remember the 'Zion mainframe' in the Matrix movies?"*[889] Richard Willett writes:[890]

So it is not beyond the realms of possibility that the message "broadcast" from the Temple will be delivered to every human being, and Human 2.0, on planet earth via a combination of Neuralink and StarLink systems ... If we combine the fact that Musk wants to litter our night sky with his Thiel funded low orbit satellites with his beliefs that we must combine ourselves with technology if we are to keep up with the advances of artificial intelligence [t]hen I think it is fair to assume that part of that "keeping up with" artificial intelligence will eventually require Human 2.0 to be connected to these machines via Starlink low orbit satellites.

Coincidentally or not, another Chabad article talks about people having 'clouds' during the third temple messianic era to visit the temple:[891]

The Midrash goes on to explain that this was impossible to do during the first two Temples, but that in the era of the Third Temple we will have "clouds" that will transport us to Jerusalem and the Temple, enabling us to visit the Holy Temple on a much more frequent basis.

Given that 'the cloud' in technological jargon also means a group of remote servers that hold your data, is this a hidden way of saying that the 'cloud' (Cult-controlled computers and AI) will 'transport' you to the 'temple' (entrain your frequencies via remote and wireless mass mind control technology to put you into a state of docility and submission)? Perhaps Israel would also broadcast other things from the third temple, such as the seven Noahide Laws, which are as follows:

1. Do not worship idols or false gods
2. Do not blaspheme or curse god
3. Do not commit murder
4. Do not commit adultery or engage in sexual immorality
5. Do not steal
6. Do not eat flesh torn from a living animal
7. Establish courts of justice

At first glance these might seem like a good or reasonable set of moral rules, but a closer examination reveals some problems. The first two reinforce the idea of a jealous imposter god worried about his image. Why would a truly omnipotent and beneficent god responsible for your creation need 'worship' from you or need anything from you at all? Why would such a divine being care if you worshipped other entities or care if you cursed it? These two laws are highly suggestive of the hidden truth that the 'god' here is the chief Archon or Demiurge responsible for putting twisted ideas in people's heads, such as that there are a 'chosen people.' In some versions, the seventh law contains a clause advocating capital punishment, in stark contradiction to the third law (to not commit murder), and could easily be seized upon by authoritarians to justify centralized control. Likewise, the seventh advocates the establishment of courts, which sounds eerily similar to the Ben-Gurion quote at the start of this chapter (in turn derived from the prophet Isaiah) that revealed the plan for Jerusalem to be the seat of a World Court. So, if Jerusalem has a One World Court, is the plan for Jerusalem to also have a One World Bank and a One World Army? In other words, for Israel-controlled Jerusalem to be the home of the NWO One World Government?

Israel and its Planned Third Temple – The Intended HQ of the NWO

Right now, all roads do not lead to Rome, but rather, to Israel. The evidence suggests that Israel is being set up to become the headquarters of the NWO dictatorship. Chabad Lubavitch, which is a Cult organization through and through, offers a great window into the coming plan, and they are quite open about what it entails. Chabad directly controls or indirectly influences the world's top leaders, including Trump, Putin, Netanyahu, Zelensky and Argentinian President Javier Milei, as well as lower politicians such as RFK Jr. and Ron DeSantis, in addition to other movers and shakers such as Zionist Jared Kushner who wants to steal Gaza and develop the real estate there on blood-soaked land.

The Greater Israel project, a plot which Israeli leaders barely even try to conceal anymore, is not just a blatant land grab. It's preparing the way for the Cult to make Israel a regional power, on the way to a world power. It's preparing the way for the Cult to join up Israel with their Khazarian homeland of Ukraine. The psychopathic

Cult wants complete domination of the entire world so that there are no countries, regions or zones outside its control.

The question is: will humanity continue to allow this?

Sources

---

882 https://www.bitchute.com/video/Qg9rCmz9k519

883 https://christianobserver.net/jerusalem-will-be-the-seat-of-the-supreme-court-of-mankind-david-ben-gurion/

884 https://www.theguardian.com/world/2025/jul/13/israel-humanitarian-city-rafah-gaza-camp-ehud-olmert

885 https://www.tandfonline.com/doi/full/10.1080/14626268.2025.2503164#abstract

886 https://www.chabad.org/library/article_cdo/aid/2261/jewish/Why-On-Earth-Do-We-Need-a-Third-Temple.htm

887 https://www.bitchute.com/video/jWH4vLuEtNEL

888 The Trigger, pg. 846

889 Ibid. pg. 794

890 https://richardwillett.substack.com/p/broadcasting-from-the-temple

891 https://www.chabad.org/library/article_cdo/aid/3716004/jewish/Messiah-the-Third-Temple.htm

CHAPTER 20: FINAL WORDS

"Jewish people have fallen for the trap of accepting the perception program instilled from birth that the rest of the world hates them and so believing they must be protected by the psychopaths posing as their saviors ... They have fallen for the myth of a Chosen people when we are all the same consciousness having different brief and transitory experiences in what we call 'the world.'"

– David Icke[892]

"[The Luciferian spirit] went from ... the Templars to the Freemasons to the Sabbatean sect ... from the Sabbateans into Eastern Europe, from the Sabbateans into the Frankists into the Vatican."

– Robert Morningstar[893]

I have spent this entire book talking about the Cult that destroyed countries, started wars, killed JFK, did 9/11 and is committing genocide as I type these words. It would be fitting then, in this final chapter, to look at exactly what makes a cult a cult. What are the characteristics of a cult? Here's what I think are the salient points:

1. **Charismatic, authoritarian leaders:** cults are characterized by dictatorial leaders who demand complete obedience. If you don't follow the rules, you're ostracized, punished or killed. Given this, what do you think of the Jesuits and the fact that Ignatius Loyola demanded total obedience? What do you think of the leaders of

the Bolsheviks, Nazis and Chinese Communists? Interesting how Communistic and fascistic governments around the world both tend to have leaders like this …;

2. **Faultless leaders:** cults (or rather, those in charge of them) push the idea that the leaders can do no wrong and that all members should fully and unreservedly trust them. Given this, what do you think of the fact that official Catholic Church doctrine teaches that the Pope is infallible?;

3. **Isolation from former friends and family:** as members are brought further into the cult, they are deliberately cut off from friends and family, and thus less likely to have balanced perspectives on life and the true motivations of the cult's leaders. This is partially achieved by the cult promoting dependency on the group and promoting fear of (and punishment for) leaving the group;

4. **The individual is nothing:** cults demand members put the interests of the 'group' or the 'cause' (as defined by the charismatic, authoritarian, faultless leader) ahead of the individual. This same phenomenon can be observed whenever politicians appeal to the 'common good' while they trample individual rights. This is the essence of collectivism and collectivist systems. The cult aims to suppress individuality via powerful peer pressure. It also encourages members to fully invest their identity with the cult;

5. **The use of sophisticated programming and brainwashing techniques to heighten suggestibility:** without their informed consent, members are deliberately targeted with manipulative techniques of persuasion to make them suggestible, docile,

pliable and subservient, resulting in their severe disempowerment and a diminishment of their potential as human beings, and sometimes getting to the point where they must be psychologically 'deprogrammed' after they leave or escape;

6. **Suspension of critical judgment:** this one accompanies points #4 and #5 above. As the individual becomes less and less, the group becomes more and more, and leaders encourage members to suspend their critical thinking altogether, to fully give themselves over to the cause of the cult and to fully trust the leaders' words (commands);

7. **Information and perception management:** cult leaders insist that members only get their information and beliefs from cult-approved sources, and actively try to mold the perception of their followers to suit their own agendas; and

8. **The 'Us vs. Them' dichotomy:** cult leaders draw a sharp distinction between those inside the cult and those outside the cult, encouraging black-and-white thinking from their members;

9. **Obsession:** a cult demands obsession with its beliefs, ideology and goals, to the point where members are induced to reach the point where they will willingly kill or die for them.

The word cult comes from the Latin 'cultus' (meaning worship) which is highly appropriate for the Satanic Cult given its connection with Yahweh/Yaldabaoth and its rituals with otherworldly entities. In addition to the nine points above pertaining to cults in general, the distinguishing features of the Satanic Cult are its belief in its own supremacy and its psychopathy. The supremacy leads it to think it, and it alone, has the right to rule. Anyone outside of its group is to be controlled, dominated and enslaved. The psychopathy leads it to view anyone outside its group as 'the other' and 'subhuman' – a mere resource to be exploited, just like Nature and the planet itself.

Cults can arise within any group or movement, but especially within religions, and nationalist and political movements. It is not surprising that the Satanic Cult behind all the main world events – false flag operations, assassinations, revolutions, wars, genocides – has spawned smaller cults worldwide which resemble its mindset and modus operandi, such as the Sabbatean-Frankists, the Jesuits, the Round Table groups, the Illuminati and many more. In English we have the phrase 'cult of personality' which describes a situation where a leader rises to prominence, where the whole movement becomes about that person and where people blindly believe in that person, not the values or principles that the movement originally championed. Politicians of any stripe and color can adeptly exploit the tendency of the crowd to fall into cult-like behavior. That's why the Cult studies social engineering and mass hypnosis so closely. The political left and right are equally susceptible to it. The Trump MAGA movement has cult-like characteristics, especially when Trump said that the catch-cry 'America First' means *"whatever he says it does."*[894] This is the tyrant's favorite position to establish, because it allows them to rule on a whim, guided by their desires and agendas, or by whatever force bribes and blackmails them, divorced from independent principles and values, and divorced from the wishes of the people who put them in power.

The last point (#9) on obsession is very important to understand. What characterizes all these Israeli agents everywhere? Devotion to Israel. Putting Israel first above all else – including for dual citizens who are also US citizens, Australian citizens, French citizens, etc. What is a prerequisite for working at the Mossad? Devotion to Israel.

In the case of the Mossad, it's being willing to kill or die for Israel. When you can bring people to the point of obsession, they are easy to manipulate.

Doctor, Doctor, It's a Very Bad Case of … Projection and Possession

I have repeatedly emphasized throughout this book that the Cult accuses others of the exact things it does itself. This is the psychological phenomenon of projection. It comes from disowning and suppressing parts of ourselves, then hiding that out of sight in the shadow. This mechanism can protect us against situations that are potentially too traumatic to handle at the moment, but a problem rapidly arises when everything is shoved back into the shadow. The spiritual journey we all undertake requires us to become more conscious. The idea is to become aware of the shadow so that it can be integrated into our full being rather than denied and pushed away. The more conscious you are, the more conscious you are of your own shadow, by the very definition of the concept.

From this perspective, the Cult can be viewed as a deeply unconscious group which constantly projects all of its own hatred and fear onto others, when it is the source. All it basically knows how to do is manipulate, infiltrate and project.

Remember: everything the Zionist Regime accuses the Palestinians of, or Hamas of, or Islamic terrorists of, are things it does itself. Israel teaches its children from a young age to hate Arabs (Israeli children sing *"we will annihilate everyone in Gaza"*[895]*)*. It is therefore unsurprising that entire units of the IDF go into Gaza, declaring their intention to *"wipe out the seed of Amalek"* and that there *"are no uninvolved civilians."*[896] Israel uses its own citizens – and Palestinians – as human shields. Israel uses terrorism to achieve its political goals. Israel, not Iran, is the number one terrorist state in the world, along with the US, which are intricately connected via the Mossad-CIA nexus.

Of course, the projection is not even the deepest level at which the Cult insanity can be analyzed. Ultimately, we are talking about delusion, madness, demonic possession and an inter-dimensional nonhuman force that runs the mindset of earthly Cult agents.

How the Cult Controls the World

I have shown how the Cult arose, infiltrated, gained control and came to run the world. Broadly speaking, there are four main areas it has control over from which it gains its power:

– Control of military force (covered in chapter 10 with Israeli nukes and in chapter 13 with Israeli control over the US, the strongest military in the world)

– Control of money (covered in chapter 3)

– Control of technology (covered in chapter 12)

– Control of ideology/narrative, especially media and religion (covered in chapters 13 and 19)

The first step in combatting a problem is being aware that it exists. Now that we know the areas the Cult uses to try to dominate, the time is past due for us to find alternative systems and refuse to acquiesce with our own enslavement.

Of particularly note is ideology and narrative – perception management. The one we need to watch out for, as the Gaza genocide reaches its climax, is the third temple agenda based on manipulative prophecy. Remember, any religious prophecy can be used as a cloak to mask a real agenda, and by claiming some past prophet saw it in a dream, then writing it down in scriptural narrative in a 'holy' book, the current controllers of that religion can MAKE it happen by directing the attention of their adherents towards the event. Humans create by focusing attention (thought and emotion) on an idea, and manifesting it into existence. Thus, any group that can divert, influence and control the manifestation ability of a large number of people has tremendous power.

We are what we tell ourselves. Jewish stories that speak of Jews as the superior 'Chosen Ones,' of the glorification of genocide, of obedience to a jealous 'god' who demands only he is worshipped and of fear of enemies (like Amalek and Haman) who are constantly ready to kill Jews all shape what some Jews today have become. These stories have also influenced the establishment and development of modern-day Israel, which has become a twisted, racist and psychopathic state.

It's ONE Cult!

If there is just one message to take away, it's this: there is one group, a Satanic Cult, which is running the world. It arose thousands of years ago, at the very least. We picked up the trail in this book as it began to make its presence manifest through the Zaddikim, then continued up through the ages to the Sabbatean-Frankists before spreading around the world thanks to the financing of the Rothschilds. It manifests itself through various groups, organizations, think tanks and secret societies, especially through nations like Israel and the US, and most especially through agencies like the Mossad and the CIA, which are one unit at the very top.

It's time to end the morass of confusion. It's the Nazis! It's the Masons! It's the Mafia! It's the Jews! It's the Khazarians! It's the Jesuits! It's the Vatican! It's the Russians! It's the Communists! It's the Chinese! It's the Muslims! It's the Fascists! There is one dark force, one Cult, behind them all. All these Cult creations spring from the same source. This foundational truth explains everything. This is why, as aware people have noticed for a long time, that the Zionist extremists seem so Nazi-like. That the brutal Nazis seemed not really different to the brutal Soviets. That the 'liberal' West pushes the same Agenda 2030 dystopia as technocratic China. That BRICS supports the same social credit score and digital ID agenda as Europe. That the political left and right are exactly the same on anything that actually matters in society. That the Nazi love of eugenics, based on their deluded idea of their own supremacy, is really no different to the elevation of the 'Chosen Ones,' based on their deluded idea of their own supremacy. It's the same mentality, the same attitude and the same delusion – because it's all from the same source.

It's a Satanic Cult, not a Jewish Cult. The Cult running the world is ultimately bigger than just the Khazarians, just the Sabbatean-Frankists or just the Zionists. Sometimes there is infighting, e.g. when the Mossad plotted to kill George Bush Sr. in Madrid in 1991. However, if you dig deeper you find that the Bush bloodline via Prescott Bush helped fund the Russian Revolution and the Nazis, via George Bush Sr. helped plan the JFK assassination and invade many nations, and via George Bush Jr. helped oversee 9/11, the War on Terror and the illegal invasion of several Middle Eastern nations at Israel's behest. What loyal Cult servants. It's like the mafia that pulls together to face external threats and embark on domination despite their family infighting.

Image #127: Still think it's just a conspiracy theory? The above 'Greater Israel' military patch is worn by Israeli soldiers

It's one Cult with its megalomaniac agents who think they can do anything and get away with it. Remember what the Mossad agents who went on CBS after the Hezbollah pager attack incident said:[897]

We create a pretend world ... We write the screenplay, we're the directors, we're the producers, we're the main actors ... the world is our stage.

Will the World Stop the Cult Greater Israel Third Temple Agenda?

And so, we stand at a point in time when we can gaze backwards and clearly see the long, long list of Cult crimes that has, sadly, greatly shaped the direction of humanity. This book has attempted to show how the obsessive and Satanic Cult mindset has wrought absolute havoc with the world for millennia, all the way from the delusions of the Zaddikim, the conversion of the Khazars, the inversions of the Sabbatean-Frankists, the greed of the Rothschilds, the infiltrations of the Illuminati to the creation of toxic ideologies and movements like Communism, fascism, Zionism, Bolshevism and Nazism, not to mentioned countless assassinations, false flag operations, revolutions, wars and genocides.

We stand at a point in time when Israel is going all out for its goal of Greater Israel. The Cult is getting off on all the theft, murder and war that are necessary in achieving it – going on a rampage of killing for its vision. By continuing the settlements all over the West Bank, it aims to create irreversible facts on the ground so that no contiguous and viable State of Palestine could ever be created. Israeli soldiers trumpet the agenda loud and clear by wearing arm patches showing the map of Greater Israel.

We stand at a point in time when the Cult is going all out for its messianic golden era, which is code for its New World Order. It is going all out for a third temple centralized cyberspace headquarters, from where it plans to conduct mass mind control and perception management of the entire Earth, using low earth orbit satellites, the mobile phone network of 5G, 6G, 7G and beyond, as well as AI. This technological control grid could be far more enslaving and all-encompassing than ever before in written human history.

Up until now, the world has mostly looked on and done nothing. As deluded psychopath and Israeli Finance Minister Bezalel Smotrich boasted:[898]

The world isn't stopping us.

Will the world stop them?

What will you do?

Sources

[892] The Trigger, pg. 785

[893] https://www.youtube.com/watch?v=F55IpZuxQ1U, 61-minute mark

[894] https://www.theatlantic.com/politics/archive/2025/06/trump-interview-iran-israel/683192/

[895] https://x.com/Kahlissee/status/1939464736443089076

[896] https://x.com/AdameMedia/status/1939530067098341757

[897] https://www.cbsnews.com/news/israeli-mossad-pager-walkie-talkie-hezbollah-plot-60-minutes/

[898] https://x.com/jeremyscahill/status/1924487041963720753/photo/1

BIBLIOGRAPHY

1666 Redemption Through Sin, 2015, Robert Sepehr

Alice in Wonderland and the World Trade Center Disaster, 2002, David Icke

The Anglo American Establishment, 1981, Carroll Quigley

The Biggest Secret, 1999, David Icke

By Way of Deception, 1990, Victor Ostrovsky

Conjuring Hitler, 2005, Guido Preparata

The Creature from Jekyll Island, 1994, G. Edward Griffin

Final Judgment: The Missing Link in the JFK Assassination Conspiracy, 5th Edition, 1994, Michael Collins Piper

The Financial Origins of National Socialism or Hitler's Secret Backers, 1933, Sidney Warburg

Hitler's Jewish Soldiers: The Untold Story of Nazi Racial Laws and Men of Jewish Descent in the German Military, 2002, Dr. Bryan Mark Rigg

Illuminati – The Cult that Hijacked the World, 2011, Henry Makow

The Invention of the Jewish People, 2009, Shlomo Sand

Jewish Fundamentalism in Israel, 1999, Israel Shahak and Norton Mezvinsky

The Jews of Khazaria, 2006, Kevin Alan Brook

Kennedy's Last Stand: Eisenhower, UFOs, MJ-12 and JFK's Assassination, 2013, Michael Salla

Methodical Conclusion, 2016, Rebekah Roth

Methodical Deception, 2015, Rebekah Roth

Methodical Exposure, 2018, Rebekah Roth

Methodical Illusion, 2015, Rebekah Roth

Nobody's Girl, 2025, Virginia Roberts Giuffre and Amy Wallace

Not in His Image, 2006, John Lamb Lash

Plato and the Creation of the Hebrew Bible, 2017, Russell Gmirkin

The Predators vs. The People, 2024, Mees Baaijen

Profits of War: Inside the Secret U.S.-Israeli Arms Network, 1992, by Ari Ben-Menashe

Rise and Kill First: The Secret History of Israel's Targeted Assassinations, 2018, Rosen Bergman

The Single Global Mafia, 2024, Paul Cudenec

Solving 9/11, Christopher Bollyn, 2012

The Suppressed History of American Banking, 2016, Xaviant Haze

The Thirteenth Tribe, 1976, Arthur Koestler

The Trigger, 2019, David Icke

To Eliminate the Opiate, Volume 1, 1974, Rabbi Marvin Antelman

To Eliminate the Opiate, Volume 2, 2002, Rabbi Marvin Antelman

Tragedy and Hope 101, 2016, Joe Plummer

Wall Street and the Bolshevik Revolution, 1974, Antony Sutton

Wall Street and the Bolshevik Revolution, 1976, Antony Sutton

Where Did the Towers Go? Evidence of Directed Free-Energy Technology on 9/11, 2005, Judy Wood

Zionism – History of Jewish Heresy, 2024, David Livingstone

INDEX

C

D

N

O

P

Q

R

X

Y

Z

9/11

Made in United States
Cleveland, OH
15 December 2025